Lecture Notes in Computer Science

552

Edited by G. Goos and J. Hartmanis

Advisory Board: W. Brauer D. Gries J. Stoer

S. Prehn, W.J. Toetenel (eds.)

VDM '91
Formal Software
Development Methods

4th International Symposium of VDM Europe
Noordwijkerhout, The Netherlands
October 21-25, 1991
Proceedings

Volume 2: Tutorials

Springer-Verlag
Berlin Heidelberg New York
London Paris Tokyo
Hong Kong Barcelona
Budapest

S. Prehn   W. J. Toetenel (Eds.)

VDM '91
Formal Software
Development Methods

4th International Symposium of VDM Europe
Noordwijkerhout, The Netherlands
October 21-25, 1991
Proceedings

Volume 2: Tutorials

Springer-Verlag
Berlin Heidelberg New York
London Paris Tokyo
Hong Kong Barcelona
Budapest

Series Editors

Gerhard Goos
GMD Forschungsstelle
Universität Karlsruhe
Vincenz-Priessnitz-Straße 1
W-7500 Karlsruhe, FRG

Juris Hartmanis
Department of Computer Science
Cornell University
Upson Hall
Ithaca, NY 14853, USA

Volume Editors

Søren Prehn
Computer Resources International A/S
Bregnerødvej 144, P. O. Box 173, DK-3460 Birkerød, Denmark

Hans Toetenel
Delft University of Technology, Faculty of Technical Mathematics and Informatics
P. O. Box 356, 2600 AJ Delft, The Netherlands

CR Subject Classification (1991): D.2

ISBN 3-540-54868-8 Springer-Verlag Berlin Heidelberg New York
ISBN 0-387-54868-8 Springer-Verlag New York Berlin Heidelberg

© Springer-Verlag Berlin Heidelberg 1991
Printed in Germany

Typesetting: Camera ready by author
Printing and binding: Druckhaus Beltz, Hemsbach/Bergstr.
45/3140-543210 - Printed on acid-free paper

Preface

The proceedings of the fourth VDM Symposium, VDM '91, are published in two volumes, of which this is the second. Previous VDM symposia were held in March 1987 (in Brussels, Belgium), in September 1988 (in Dublin, Ireland) and in April 1990 (in Kiel, Germany). Proceedings from the previous symposia were also published by Springer-Verlag in the Lecture Notes in Computer Science series, as volumes 252, 328 and 428, respectively.

All Vienna Development Method symposia have been organised by VDM Europe. VDM Europe was formed in 1985 as an advisory board sponsored by the Commission of the European Communities. The VDM Europe working group consisted of researchers, software engineers and programmers, all interested in promoting the industrial usage of formal methods for software development. The group met three to four times a year to present, discuss and disseminate recent results, problems and experiences. VDM Europe focused on the industrial usage of model-oriented formal methods, in particular VDM and closely related methods such as MetaSoft and RAISE, and supported the efforts to standardise the VDM notation, first within BSI, and later within ISO.

While the two first VDM symposia were mainly dedicated to research and practise of VDM, the third symposium - VDM and Z - presented a broader view. This, the fourth VDM symposium, goes even further. In tutorials and in papers, a larger number of methods for formal software development are presented.
Parallel to this development, it has been decided to reshape VDM Europe into Formal Methods Europe (FME). FME will primarily be oriented towards technology transfer to ensure that industry is continuously aware of available formal methods, their documentation and their support tools.
The proceedings of this symposium clearly reflect this trend.

The *Tutorials* volume includes four introductory tutorials (on *LARCH, Refinement Calculus, VDM,* and *RAISE*) and four advanced tutorials (on *ABEL, PROSPECTRA, The B Method,* and *The Stack*). While there are certainly other methods available which are or could be used fruitfully in industry, we believe that the tutorials of VDM '91 present a comprehensive account of the current state of the art.

The *Conference* volume has four parts: contributions of invited speakers, papers, project reports and tools demonstration abstracts. The three invited talks cover three different aspects of formal software development. The 31 *papers* cover both theory and practice. However, as compared with earlier VDM symposia, the emphasis is more on *development*: methods and calculi for development, verification and verification tools support, experiences from doing developments, and the associated theoretical problems with respect to semantics and logic. The 7 *project reports* present (shorter) accounts of experiences from specific projects. The 14 *tools demonstration* abstracts highlight the capabilities of formal methods support tools, all of which are demonstrated during the symposium.
We trust that you will find the material available in these proceedings useful.

Delft   Søren Prehn
August 1991   Hans Toetenel

Acknowledgements

Many people have contributed to the planning, organisation and success of VDM '91.

Executive Programme Committee

Patrick Behm	Søren Prehn (chair)
Andrzej Blikle	Hans Toetenel
Hans Langmaack	Jim Woodcock
Peter Lucas	

Organisation Commitee

Nico Plat	Hans Toetenel (chair)
Kees Pronk	Hans Tonino

Local Organiser

Lodewijk Bos

Invited Speakers

Michael Jackson
Robin Milner
John Guttag

Panelists

Wlad Turski
Martyn Thomas

In addition, the invaluable contributions of the following should be acknowledged: Dines Bjørner for advice, inspiration and persistence; Horst Hüncke, Karel de Vriendt and Alejandro Moya, CEC, for their continued support to VDM Europe and Formal Methods Europe; Nico Plat for the organisation of the Tools Demonstration, and Toos Brussee, Coby Bouwer and Trudy Stoute at the secretariat of the Faculty of Technical Mathematics and Informatics of the Delft University of Technology; Hans Wössner and Alfred Hofmann of Springer-Verlag for their continued interest in VDM publications.

Referees

The submitted papers - whether accepted or rejected - were refereed by the following external referees. This symposium would not have been possible without their voluntary and dedicated work.

Mark A. Ardis
Marek Bednarczyki
Dines Bjørner
Dominique Bolignano
Andrej Borzyszkowski
Heinz Brix
Hans Bruun
Peter Michael Bruun
Karl-Heinz Buth
Neil Butler
Christine Choppy
Bent Dandanell Holdt-Jørgensen
Tim Denvir
Jeremy Dick
Martin Fränzle
David Garlan
Chris George
Susan Gerhardt
Anthony Hall
Bo Stig Hansen
Michael Reichardt Hansen
Anne Haxthausen
Kees van Hee
Wolfgang Henhapl
Friedrich von Henke
Götz Hofmann
Bernard Hohlfeld
Ronald Huijsman
Cliff B. Jones
Ulrik Jörring
Jan van Katwijk
Steve King
Dirk Kinnaes

Beata Konikowska
Ryszard Kubiak
Yves Ledru
Jacek Leszczylowski
Peter Lupton
Hans Henrik Løvengreen
Lynn Marshall
Fernando Mejia
Kees Middelburg
Dave Neilson
Mogens Nielsen
Stephen O'Brien
Wieslaw Pawlowski
Jan Storbank Pedersen
Brian Ritchie
Gunter Schmidt
Uwe Schmidt
Pierre-Yves Schobbens
Chris Sennet
Stefan Sokolowski
Marian Srebrny
Werner Struckmann
Andrej Tarlecki
Karel de Vlaminck
Reinhard Völler
Jozef Winkowski
Chris van Westrhenen
William Wood
John Wordsworth
Raymond Zavodnik
Job Zwiers

Contents of Volume 2

Preface v

Contents ix

A Tutorial on Larch and LCL, A Larch/C Interface Language 1
John V. Guttag, James J. Horning

A Tutorial on the Refinement Calculus 79
J.C.P. Woodcock

Tutorial Lecture Notes on the Irish School of the VDM .141
Micheál Mac an Airchinnigh

The RAISE Specification Language: A Tutorial 238
Chris George

Formal Development with ABEL 320
Ole-Johan Dahl, Olaf Owe

The PROSPECTRA Methodology and System: Uniform Transformational (Meta-)
Development 363
Bernd Krieg-Brückner, Einar W. Karlsen, Junbo Liu, Owen Traynor

The B Method for Large Software. Specification, Design and Coding (Abstract) 398
J.R. Abrial

Mathematical Methods for Digital Systems Development .406
Don I. Good, William D. Young

Contents of Volume 1

Preface v

Table of contents ix

Invited Speakers

Description Is Our Business 1
  Michael Jackson

Concurrent Processes as Objects 9
  Robin Milner

The Larch Approach to Specification 10
  John V. Guttag

Papers

Formal Specification in Metamorphic Programming 11
  David A. Penny, Richard C. Holt, Michael W. Godfrey

Formalizing Design Spaces: Implicit Invocation Mechanisms 31
  David Garlan, David Notkin

On Type Checking in VDM and Related Consistency Issues 45
  Flemming Damm, Bo Stig Hansen, Hans Bruun

Combining Transformation and Posit-and-Prove in a VDM Development 63
  T. Clement

A Case for Structured Analysis/Formal Design 81
  Nico Plat, Jan van Katwijk, Kees Pronk

A Model-oriented Method for Algebraic Specifications Using COLD-1 as Notation 106
  Reinder J. Bril

A Mechanical Formalization of Several Fairness Notions 125
  David M. Goldschlag

Specification and Stepwise Development of Communicating Systems 149
  Stephan Rössig, Michael Schenke

Writing Operational Semantics in Z: A Structural Approach 164
  Marc Benveniste

EZ: A System for Automatic Prototyping of Z Specifications 189
  Veronika Doma, Robin Nicholl

Z and High Level Petri Nets 204
  K.M. van Hee, L.J. Somers, M. Voorhoeve

An Approach to the Static Semantics of VDM-SL 220
  Hans Bruun, Bo Stig Hansen, Flemming Damm

Behavioural Extension for CSP 254
  Michael J. Butler

Cpo's do not form a Cpo, and yet Recursion Works 268
  Marek A. Bednarczyk, Andrzej M. Borzyszkowski

LPF and MPLω-A Logical Comparison of VDM SL and COLD-K 279
  C.A. Middelburg, G.R. Renardel de Lavalette

Tactical Tools for Distributing VDM Specifications 309
  Thierry Cattel

An Attempt to Reason About Shared-State Concurrency in the Style of VDM 324
  Ketil Stølen

Reasoning About VDM Specifications 343
  Morten Elvang-Gøransson

Formal Specification of a Proof Tool 356
  R.D. Arthan

Reasoning About VDM Developments Using The VDM Support Tool in Mural 371
  J.C. Bicarregui, B. Ritchie

EVES: An Overview 389
  Dan Craigen, Sentot Kromodimoeljo, Irwin Meisels, Bill Pase, Mark Saaltink

Deriving Transitivity of VDM-Reification in DEVA 406
  Matthias Weber

Upgrading the Pre-and Postcondition Technique 428
  H.B.M. Jonkers

The Formal Development of a Secure Transaction Mechanism 457
  Paul Smith, Richard Keighley

Formal Development of a Serial Copy Management System 477
  Gerard R. Renardel de Lavalette

Specification and Refinement in an Integrated Database Application Environment 496
Klaus-Dieter Schewe, Joachim W. Schmidt, Ingrid Wetzel

Techniques for Partial Specification and Specification of Switching Systems 511
Pamela Zave, Michael Jackson

Specification of the MAA Standard in VDM .526
G.I. Parkin, G.O'Neill

Unintrusive Ways to Integrate Formal Specifications in Practice 545
Jeannette M. Wing, Amy Moormann Zaremski

Reports

An Overview of HP-SL 571
Stephen Bear

CICS Project Report:
Experiences and Results from the Use of Z in IBM .588
Iain Houston, Steve King

A Debugger for A Meta-IV-like Meta-language 597
D. Kinnaes, K. De Vlaminck

An Executable Subset of Meta-IV with Loose Specification 604
Peter Gorm Larsen, Paul Bøgh Lassen

Using VDM within an Object-Oriented Framework 619
Lynn S. Marshall, Linda Simon

The Integrated Software Development and Verification System Ates 629
A. Puccetti

Using RAISE - First Impressions from the LaCoS Applications 645
D.L. Chalmers, B. Dandanell, J. Gørtz, J.S. Pedersen, E. Zierau

A Specification of a Complex Programming Language Statement 658
P. McParland, P. Kilpatrick

Tools description

The PROSPECTRA System 668
Berthold Hoffmann , Bernd Krieg-Brückner

The Visual Presentation of VDM Specifications 670
Jeremy Dick, Jérôme Loubersac

mural and SpecBox 673
  Richard Moore, Peter Froome

The VDM Domain Compiler: A VDM Class Library Generator 675
  Uwe Schmidt, Hans-Martin Hörcher

The Delft VDM-SL Front End 677
  Nico Plat, Kees Pronk, Marcel Verhoef

Prototyping with Temporal VDM: A Status Report 681
  H. Heping, H. Zedan

The ExSpect tool 683
  K.M. van Hee, L.J. Somers, M. Voorhoeve

Cadiz - Computer Aided Design in Z 685
  David Jordan

The HP-ST Toolset 687
  Chris Dollin

The RAISE Toolset 689
  The CRI RAISE Tools Group

The IBM Z Tool 691
  Iain Houston

The VDM-SL Editor and Consistency Checker 693
  Flemming M. Damm, Hans Bruun, Bo Stig Hansen

B-Tool 695
  Matthew Lee, Ib. H. Sørensen

A VDM Subset Compiler 697
  Christoph Blaue

Index of Authors 699

A Tutorial on Larch and LCL, A Larch/C Interface Language

John V. Guttag*and James J. Horning[†]

1 Introduction

The Larch family of languages is used to specify program interfaces in a two-tiered definitional style. Each Larch specification has components written in two languages: one that is designed for a specific programming language and another that is independent of any programming language. The former are the *Larch interface languages*, and the latter is the *Larch Shared Language (LSL)*.

This tutorial material on Larch has three parts. Part 1, this part, is a short overview of the Larch approach to specification.

Part 2 contains material excerpted from a report describing version 2.3 of LSL. It introduces all the features of the language and briefly discusses how they are intended to be used.

Part 3 contains material aimed primarily at the C programmer who wishes to begin to integrate formal specifications into the program development cycle. It presents a specification language targeted specifically at C and discuss how it can be used to support a style of C programming in which abstraction plays a vital role.

*Address: MIT LCS, 545 Technology Square, Cambridge, MA, USA. Support for this work was provided by the Advanced Research Projects Agency of the Department of Defense, monitored by the Office of Naval Research under contract N00014-89-J-1988, and by the National Science Foundation under grant CCR-8910848.

[†]Address: DEC SRC, 130 Lytton Ave, Palo Alto, CA, USA

Larch, and especially LSL, has benefited from our study of other specification languages. However, since this is intended strictly as a tutorial for those who might wish to use Larch, we do not discuss these influences here. Instead we give a short Larch bibliography and refer the reader to discussions contained in those papers.

The material presented here is excerpted from two reports on Larch: *Report on the Larch Shared Language: Version 2.3*, by John V. Guttag, James J. Horning, and Andrés Modet, and *Introduction to LCL, A Larch/C Interface Language*, by John V. Guttag and James J. Horning. These reports can be obtained by writing to Reports Distribution, Digital Equipment Corporation Systems Research Center, 130 Lytton Avenue, Palo Alto, CA 94301-1044, USA, or by sending e-mail to src-report@src.dec.com.

2 A Short Overiew of Larch

The most vexing problems in building systems concern overall system organization and the integration of components. Modularity is the key to controlling them, and specifications are essential for achieving program modularity. Abstraction boundaries make it possible to understand programs one component at a time. However, an abstraction is intangible. Without a precise description, there is no way to know what it really is, and it is easy to confuse an abstraction with one of its implementations.

Specifications can be written in natural languages, in semi-formal notations (with a restricted syntax but no formal semantics), or in truly formal notations. The potential advantages of formal specifications are that they have unambiguous meanings and are subject to manipulation by programs. The latter advantage can be fully realized only by using tools that support constructing and reasoning about them. The Larch Project is developing languages, tools, and techniques to aid in the productive application of formal specifications to software design, implementation, integration, and maintenance.

A Larch *interface specification* describes the interface that a program component provides to *clients* (programs that use it). Each interface specification is written in a programming-language-dependent *Larch interface language*. It relies on definitions from an *auxiliary specification*, written in a programming-language-independent specification language, the *Larch Shared*

Language (LSL).

The Larch family of specification languages support:

- *Specification reuse.* Many language-independent abstractions are useful in a wide variety of specifications, for example, integers, lists, sets, queues, arrays, relations, mappings, and orders. Larch encourages the accumulation of open-ended collections of reusable specification components in LSL handbooks.

- *Abstraction.* Larch supports a style of program design in which data and functional abstractions play a prominent role.

- *Development tools.* The Larch languages are designed for use with tools that support the construction and checking of specifications, implementations, and clients.

Many informal specifications have a structure similar to Larch's. They rely on auxiliary specifications, but leave them implicit. They describe an interface in terms of concepts—such as sets, lists, or files—with which readers are assumed to be familiar. But they don't define them. Readers may misunderstand such specifications unless their intuitive understanding precisely matches the specifier's. And there's no way to be sure that such intuitions match. LSL specifications solve this problem by mathematically defining the terms that appear in interface specifications. LSL is presented in accompanying material.

An interface specification provides information that is needed both to write client programs and to write acceptable implementations. A critical part of a component's interface is its communication with its environment. Communication mechanisms differ from one programming language to another, sometimes in subtle ways. It is easier to be precise about communication when the specification language reflects the programming language. Such specifications are generally shorter than those written in any "universal" interface language. They are also clearer to programmers who implement interfaces and to programmers who use them.

Each Larch interface language deals with what can be observed about the behavior of program components written in a particular programming language. It provides a way to write assertions about program states. It incorporates notations that are specific to its programming language for constructs such as side effects, exception handling, concurrency, and iterators. Its simplicity or complexity depends largely on the simplicity or complexity of its programming language.

Each Larch interface language has a mechanism for specifying abstract data types. If its programming language doesn't provide direct support for them (as C does not), the mechanism is designed to be compatible with the general style of the programming language.

LCL is a Larch interface language designed to specify program components written in, or called from, the standard C programming language. For comparison, LM3, a Larch interface language for Modula-3 is described in [Jones 91].

Larch encourages a separation of concerns, with mathematical abstractions in the LSL tier, and programming pragmatics in the interface tier. We encourage specifiers to keep the difficult parts in the LSL tier, for several reasons:

- LSL abstractions are more likely to be reusable than interface specifications.

- LSL has a simpler underlying semantics than most programming languages (and hence than most interface languages), so that specifiers are less likely to make mistakes.

- It is easier to make and check claims about semantic properties of LSL specifications than about semantic properties of interface specifications.

3 Acknowledgments

The Larch Shared Language has evolved over many years. We have freely borrowed the best ideas we could find in other specification languages, and have received helpful criticism and suggestions from too many people to enumerate here. Martin Abadi, Steve Garland, Bill McKeeman, Andrés Modet, Jim Saxe, and Jeannette Wing have made important contributions to the recent evolution of the language.

Bill McKeeman provided the impetus for the design of LCL by insistently reminding us that Larch should be applied to "a language that real programmers take seriously." He also helped us recruit Joe Wild and Gary

Feldman, whose interest, intellectual involvement, and hard work made LCL and the LCL Checker real. Jeannette Wing designed the first Larch interface language (for CLU); Kevin Jones designed one for Modula-3 concurrent with the design of LCL; Steve Garland implemented early versions of the LSL and LCL Checkers. All three participated in the design of the LCL language. Daniel Jackson, Mark Reinhold and Mark Vandevoorde all helped to debug the language. Mike Burrows reviewed an early version of the LCL report and contributed many substantive (and useful) comments and suggestions. Finally, we are grateful to Bob Taylor, Sam Fuller, and Becky Will for believing in and supporting the development of LCL.

4 An Abbreviated Larch Bibliography

[Garland, Guttag, and Horning 90] S.J. Garland, J.V. Guttag, and J.J. Horning, "Debugging Larch Shared Language Specifications," *IEEE TSE* Vol. 16, No. 9, September 1990, pp. 1044-1057; also available as Digital Equipment Corporation Systems Research Center Report 60, 1990.

[Guttag, Horning, and Wing 85] J.V. Guttag, J.J. Horning and J.M. Wing, "The Larch Family of Specification Languages," *IEEE Software*, September 1985, pp. 24-36.

[Guttag et al. 90] John V. Guttag, James J. Horning, and Andrés Modet, *Report on the Larch Shared Language: Version 2.3*, Digital Equipment Corporation, Systems Research Center Research Report 58, April 14, 1990.

[Guttag and Horning 91] John V. Guttag and James J. Horning *Introduction to LCL, A Larch/C Interface Language*, Digital Equipment Corporation, Systems Research Center Research Report 74, July 24, 1990.

[Jones 91] Kevin D. Jones, *LM3: A Larch Interface Language for Modula-3. A Definition and Introduction. Version 1.0*, Digital Equipment Corporation, Systems Research Center Research Report 72, June 10, 1991.

[Wing 90] Jeannette M. Wing, "Using Larch to Specify Avalon/C++ Objects," *IEEE TSE*, Vol. 16, No. 9, September 1990, pp. 1076-1088.

Part 2:
An Introduction to the
Larch Shared Language

1 Simple Algebraic Specifications

LSL's basic unit of specification is a *trait*. A trait may describe an abstract
data type or may encapsulate a property shared by several data types.
Consider the following specification of tables that store values in indexed
places:

```
Table: trait
  introduces
      new: → Tab
      add: Tab, Ind, Val → Tab
      __∈__: Ind, Tab → Bool
      lookup: Tab, Ind → Val
      isEmpty: Tab → Bool
      size: Tab → Card
  asserts ∀ i, i': Ind, val: Val, t: Tab
      lookup(add(t, i, val), i') == if i = i' then val else lookup(t, i')
      ¬(i ∈ new)
      i ∈ add(t, i', val) == i = i' ∨ i ∈ t
      size(new) == 0
      size(add(t, i, val)) == if i ∈ t then size(t) else size(t) + 1
      isEmpty(t) == size(t) = 0
```

This is similar to a conventional algebraic specification, as it would be written
by many others. The part of the specification following **introduces** declares
a list of *operators* (function identifiers), each with its *signature* (the *sorts* of
its domain and range). Every operator used in a trait must be declared; the
signatures are used to sort-check *terms* (expressions) in much the same way
as function calls are type-checked in programming languages. The remainder
of this specification constrains the operators by means of equations.

An equation consists of two terms of the same sort, separated by ==.

Equations of the form *term* == true can be abbreviated by simply writing
the term; thus the second equation in the trait above is an abbreviation for
$\neg(i \in \text{new})$ == true.

The characters "__" in an operator declaration indicate that the operator will
be used in mixfix expressions. For example, $\in$ is declared as a binary infix
operator. Infix, prefix, postfix, and distributed operators are integral parts
of many familiar notations, and their use can contribute substantially to the
readability of specifications. LSL's grammar for mixfix terms is intended
to ensure that legal terms parse as readers expect—even without studying
the grammar. Writers of specifications should study the grammar—although
fully parenthesized terms are always acceptable.[1]

The name of a trait is independent of the names that appear within it. In
particular, we do not use sort identifiers to name units of specification. A
trait need not correspond to an abstract data type, and often does not.

Each trait defines a *theory* (a set of formulas without free variables) in typed
first-order logic with equality. Each theory contains the trait's assertions, the
conventional axioms of first-order logic, everything that follows from them,
and nothing else. This interpretation guarantees that the formulas in the
theory follow only from the presence of assertions in the trait—never from
their absence. This is in contrast to algebraic specification languages based
on initial or final algebras. Our interpretation is essential to ensure that all
theorems proved about an incomplete specification remain valid when it is
completed.

LSL requires that each trait be *consistent:* it must not define a theory
containing the equation true == false. Consistency is often difficult to
prove, and is undecidable in general. But inconsistencies are often easy to

---

[1] LSL has a very simple precedence scheme for operators: postfix operators
consisting of a period followed by an identifier bind most tightly. Other user-
defined operators and the built-in Boolean negation operator ($\neg$) bind more
tightly than the built-in in equational operators (= and $\neq$), which bind more
tightly than the built-in Boolean connectives ($\wedge$, $\vee$, and $\Rightarrow$), which bind more
tightly than ==. For example, the term $x + w.a.b = y \vee z$ is equivalent
to $((x + ((w.a).b)) = y) \vee z$. LSL allows unparenthesised infix terms with
multiple operators at the same precedence level only if they are the same;
it associates such terms from left to right. Thus $x \wedge y \wedge z$ is equivalent to
$(x \wedge y) \wedge z$, but $x \vee y \wedge z$ isn't allowed.

detect, and can be a useful indication that there is something wrong with a trait.

2 Getting Richer Theories

Equational theories are useful, but a stronger theory is often needed, for example, when specifying an abstract data type. The constructs **generated by** and **partitioned by** provide two ways of strengthening equational specifications.

A **generated by** clause asserts that all values of a sort can be generated by a given list of operators, thus providing a "generator induction" schema for the sort. For example, the natural numbers are generated by 0 and successor, and the integers are generated by 0, successor, and predecessor.

The axiom "Tab **generated by** new, add", if added to Table, could be used to prove theorems by induction over new and add, such as

$$\forall\, t\text{: Tab} \left(\text{isEmpty}(t) \vee \exists\, i\text{: Ind} \left(i \in t \right) \right)$$

A **partitioned by** clause asserts that all distinct values of a sort can be distinguished by a given list of operators. Terms that are not distinguishable using any of the partitioning operators of their sort are equal. For example, sets are partitioned by $\in$, because sets that contain the same elements are equal.

The axiom "Tab **partitioned by** $\in$, lookup", if added to Table, could be used to derive theorems that do not follow from the equations alone, such as

$$\forall\, t\text{: Tab},\, i,\, i'\text{: Ind},\, v\text{: Val}$$
$$\left(\text{add}(\text{add}(t,\, i,\, v),\, i',\, v) = \text{add}(\text{add}(t,\, i',\, v),\, i,\, v) \right)$$

3 Combining Traits

Table contains a number of totally unconstrained operators (e.g., $+$). Such traits are not very useful. Additional assertions dealing with these operators could be added to Table. However, for modularity, it is often better to include a separate trait by reference. This makes it easier to reuse pieces of other specifications and handbooks. We might add to trait Table:

  includes Cardinal

The theory associated with the including trait is the theory associated with the union of all of the **introduces** and **asserts** clauses of the trait body and the included traits.

It is often convenient to combine several traits dealing with different aspects of the same operator. This is common when specifying something that is not easily thought of as an abstract data type. Consider, for example, the following specifications of properties of relations:

> Reflexive: **trait**
>   **introduces** $\_ \diamond \_$: T, T → Bool
>   **asserts** ∀ t: T
> $t \diamond t$

> Symmetric: **trait**
>   **introduces** $\_ \diamond \_$: T, T → Bool
>   **asserts** ∀ t, t': T
> $t \diamond t' == t' \diamond t$

> Transitive: **trait**
>   **introduces** $\_ \diamond \_$: T, T → Bool
>   **asserts** ∀ t, t', t'': T
> $(t \diamond t' \wedge t' \diamond t'') \Rightarrow t \diamond t''$

> Equivalence1: **trait**
>   **includes** Reflexive, Symmetric, Transitive

The trait Equivalence1 has the same associated theory as the following less structured trait:

> Equivalence2: **trait**
>   **introduces** $\_ \diamond \_$: T, T → Bool
>   **asserts** ∀ t, t', t'': T
> $t \diamond t$
> $t \diamond t' == t' \diamond t$
> $(t \diamond t' \wedge t' \diamond t'') \Rightarrow t \diamond t''$

4 Renaming

Equivalence1 relies heavily on the use of the same operator symbol, $\diamond$, and the same sort identifier, T, in three included traits. In the absence of such happy coincidences, renaming can be used to make names coincide, to keep them from coinciding, or simply to replace them with more suitable names, for example,

Equivalence: **trait**
   includes (Reflexive, Symmetric, Transitive) ($\equiv$ **for** $\diamond$)
The phrase Tr(name1 **for** name2) stands for the trait Tr with every occurrence of name2 (which must be either a sort or operator name) replaced by name1. If name2 is a sort identifier, this renaming may change the signatures associated with some of the operators in **Tr**.

If Table were augmented by the **generated by, partitioned by,** and **includes** clauses of the two previous sections, the specification

SparseArray: **trait**
   includes Integer,
     Table(Arr **for** Tab, defined **for** $\in$, assign **for** add,
       _[_] **for** lookup, Int **for** Ind)

would be equivalent to

SparseArray: **trait**
   includes Integer, Cardinal
   introduces
     new: $\to$ Arr
     assign: Arr, Int, Val $\to$ Arr
     defined: Int, Arr $\to$ Bool
     _[_]: Arr, Int $\to$ Val
     isEmpty: Arr $\to$ Bool
     size: Arr $\to$ Card
   asserts
     Arr **generated by** new, assign
     Arr **partitioned by** defined, _[_]
     $\forall$ i, i': Int, val: Val, t: Arr
       assign(t, i, val)[i'] == **if** $i = i'$ **then** val **else** $t[i']$
       $\neg$defined(i, new)
       defined(i, assign(t, i', val)) == $i = i'$ $\vee$ defined(i, t)
       size(new) == 0
       size(assign(t, i, val)) ==
         if defined(i, t) **then** size(t) **else** size(t) $+ 1$
       isEmpty(t) == size(t) $= 0$

Note that the infix operator symbol _$\in$_ was replaced by the operator defined, and that the operator lookup was replaced by the mixfix operator symbol _[_]. Renamings preserve the order of operands.

Any sort or operator in a trait can be renamed when that trait is referenced in another trait. Some, however, are more likely to be renamed than others. It is often convenient to single these out so that they can be renamed positionally. For example, if the header for the `SparseArray` trait had been "`SparseArray(Val)`: **trait**", the phrases "**includes** `SparseArray(Int)`" and "**includes** `SparseArray(Int for Val)`" would be equivalent.

5 Stating Intended Consequences

It is not possible to prove the "correctness" of a specification, because there is no absolute standard against which to judge correctness. But specifications can contain errors, and specifiers need help in locating them. Since LSL specifications cannot generally be executed, they cannot be tested in the way that programs are commonly tested. LSL sacrifices executability in favor of brevity, clarity, and flexibility, and provides other ways to check specifications.

This section briefly describes ways in which specifications can be augmented with redundant information to be checked during validation. A separate paper discusses the use of LP, the Larch Prover [Garland, Guttag, and Horning 1990] to assist in specification debugging.

Checkable properties of LSL specifications fall into three categories: *consistency*, *theory containment*, and *completeness*. As discussed earlier, the requirement of consistency makes any trait whose theory contains `true == false` illegal.

Claims about theory containment are made using **implies**. Consider the claim that `SparseArray` guarantees that an array with a defined element isn't empty. To indicate that this claim should be checked, we could add to `SparseArray`

> **implies** $\forall$ *a:* Arr, *i:* Int $\mathrm{defined}(i, a) \Rightarrow \neg\mathrm{isEmpty}(a)$

The theory claimed to be implied can be specified using the full power of the language, including equations, **generated by** and **partitioned by** clauses, and references to other traits. In addition to assisting in error detection, implications help readers confirm their understanding, and can simplify reasoning about higher-level traits.

The initial design of LSL incorporated a built-in requirement of completeness. However, we quickly concluded that this was better left to the specifier's discretion. It is useful to check certain aspects of completeness long before a specification is finished, yet most finished specifications (intentionally) don't fully define all their operators. Claims about how complete a specification is are made using **converts**. Adding the claim "**implies converts isEmpty**" to `Table` says that the trait's axioms fully define `isEmpty`. This means that, if the interpretations of all the other operators are fixed, there is a unique interpretation of `isEmpty` satisfying the axioms.

Now consider adding the stronger claim "**implies converts isEmpty, lookup**" to `Table`. The meaning of terms of the form `lookup(new, i)` is not defined by the trait, so it isn't possible to verify this claim. The incompleteness could be resolved by adding another axiom to the trait, for example, "`lookup(new, i) == errorVal`". However, the specifier of `Table` should not be concerned with whether `Val` has an `errorVal` operator, and should not be required to introduce irrelevant constraints on `lookup`. Extra axioms give readers more details to assimilate. They may preclude useful specializations of a general specification. And sometimes there is no reasonable axiom that would make an operator convertible (consider division by 0).

LSL provides an **exempting** clause that lists terms that need not be defined. The claim "**implies converts isEmpty, lookup exempting** $\forall$ *i:* Ind `lookup(new, i)`)" means that, if interpretations of the other operators and of all terms matching `lookup(new, i)` are fixed, there are unique interpretations of `isEmpty` and `lookup` that satisfy the trait's axioms. This is provable from the specification.

6 Recording Assumptions

It is useful to construct general specifications that can be specialized in a variety of ways. Consider, for example,

Bag(E): **trait**
  introduces
    { }: → B
    insert, delete: E, B → B
    __∈__: E, B → Bool
  asserts
    B **generated by** { }, insert
    B **partitioned by** delete, ∈
    ∀ b: B, e, e': E
      ¬(e ∈ { })
      e ∈ insert(e', b) == $e = e'$ ∨ e ∈ b
      delete(e, { }) == { }
      delete(e', insert(e, b)) ==
        if $e = e'$ **then** b **else** insert(e, delete(e', b))

We might specialize this to IntegerBag by renaming E to Int and including it in a trait in which operators dealing with Int are specified, for example,

IntegerBag: **trait**
  includes Integer, Bag(Int)

The interactions between Integer and Bag are very limited. Nothing in Bag makes any assumptions about the meaning of the operators, such as 0, +, and <, that are defined in Integer. Consider, however, extending Bag to Bag1 by adding an operator rangeCount,

Bag1(E): **trait**
  includes Bag, Cardinal
  introduces
    rangeCount: E, E, B → Card
    __<__: E, E → Bool
  asserts ∀ e, e', e'': E, b: B
    rangeCount(e, e', { }) == 0
    rangeCount(e, e', insert(e'', b)) ==
        rangeCount(e, e', b) + (**if** $e < e''$ ∧ $e'' < e'$ **then** 1 **else** 0)

As written, Bag1 makes no assumptions about the properties of the < operator. Suppose, however, that we wish to require that, in any specialization of this trait, < provides an ordering on the values of sort E. We can add such a requirement with an *assumption*:

Bag2(E): trait
    assumes TotalOrder(E)
    includes Bag, Cardinal
    introduces rangeCount: E, E, B → Card
    asserts ∀ e, e', e'': E, b: B
      rangeCount(e, e', { }) == 0
      rangeCount(e, e', insert(e'', b)) ==
           rangeCount(e, e', b) + (**if** $e < e''$ ∧ $e'' < e'$ **then** 1 **else** 0)
    implies ∀ e, e', e'': E, b: B
      $e' \leq e''$ ⇒ rangeCount(e, e', b) $\leq$ rangeCount(e, e'', b)

The theory associated with Bag2 is the same as if TotalOrder(E) had been included rather than assumed; Bag2 inherits all the declarations and axioms of TotalOrder. Therefore, the assumption can be used to derive various properties of Bag2, including the implication that rangeCount is monotonic in its second argument.

The difference between **assumes** and **includes** appears when Bag2 is used in another trait. Whenever a trait with assumptions is included or assumed, its assumptions must be *discharged*. For example, in

IntegerBag2: trait
    includes Integer, Bag2(Int)

the assumption to be discharged is that the (renamed) theory associated with TotalOrder is a subset of the theory associated with Integer. When a trait includes a trait with assumptions, it is often possible to determine that these assumptions are discharged by noticing that the same traits are assumed or included in the including trait. For example, Integer itself might directly include TotalOrder.

7 Built-In Operators and Overloading

In our examples, we have freely used various Boolean operators. We have also used some heavily overloaded and apparently unconstrained operators: if__then__else__, =, and ≠. Although these operators are definable within LSL, they are built into the language. This allows them to have appropriate syntactic precedence. More importantly, it guarantees that they have consistent meanings in all LSL specifications, so readers can rely on their intuitions about them. For example, the built-in definition of = guarantees that for any terms t1 and t2, t1 = t2 == **true** if and only if t1 == t2.

In addition to the built-in overloaded operators, LSL provides for user-defined overloadings. Each operator must be declared in an **introduces** clause and consists of an identifier (e.g., empty) or operator symbol (e.g., __<__) and a signature. The signatures of most occurrences of overloaded operators are deducible from context. Consider, for example,

```
OrderedString(E, Str): trait
  assumes TotalOrder(E)
  introduces
    empty: → Str
    insert: E, Str → Str
    __<__: Str, Str → Bool
  asserts
    Str generated by empty, insert
    ∀ e, e': E, s, s': Str
      empty < insert(e, s)
      ¬(s < empty)
      insert(e, s) < insert(e', s') == e < e' ∨ (e = e' ∧ s < s')
  implies TotalOrder(Str)
```

The operator symbol < is used in the last equation to denote two different operators, one relating terms of sort Str and the other, terms of sort E, but their contexts determine unambiguously which is which. LSL provides notations for disambiguating an overloaded operator if context does not suffice. Any subterm of a term can be qualified by its sort. For example, "a:S = b" explicitly indicates that a is of sort S. Since the two operands of = must have the same sort, this qualification also implicitly defines the signatures of = and b. Outside of terms, overloaded operators can be disambiguated by directly affixing their signatures.

8 Enumerations, Tuples, and Unions

Enumerations, tuples, and unions provide compact, readable representations for common kinds of theories. They are just syntactic shorthands for things that could be written in LSL without them.

The enumeration shorthand defines a finite set of distinct constants and an operator that enumerates them. For example,

Temp **enumeration of** cold, warm, hot

is equivalent to including a trait whose body is:

introduces

    cold, warm, hot: $\rightarrow$ Temp

    succ: Temp $\rightarrow$ Temp

asserts

    Temp **generated by** cold, warm, hot

    equations

        cold $\neq$ warm

        cold $\neq$ hot

        warm $\neq$ hot

        succ(cold) == warm

        succ(warm) == hot

The tuple shorthand is used to introduce fixed-length tuples. For example,

    C **tuple of** hd: E, tl: S

is equivalent to including a trait whose body is:

introduces

    [__, __]: E, S $\rightarrow$ C

    __.hd: C $\rightarrow$ E

    __.tl: C $\rightarrow$ S

    set_hd: C, E $\rightarrow$ C

    set_tl: C, S $\rightarrow$ C

asserts

    C **generated by** [__, __]

    C **partitioned by** .hd, .tl

    $\forall$ e, e': E, s, s': S

        $[e, s]$.hd == e

        $[e, s]$.tl == s

        set_hd($[e, s], e'$) == $[e', s]$

        set_tl($[e, s], s'$) == $[e, s']$

Each field name (e.g., hd) is incorporated in two distinct operators (e.g., __.hd:C$\rightarrow$E and set_hd:C,E$\rightarrow$C).

The union shorthand corresponds to the tagged unions found in many programming languages. For example,

    S **union of** atom: A, cell: C

is equivalent to including a trait whose body is:

S_tag enumeration of atom, cell
introduces
    atom: A → S
    cell: C → S
    __.atom: S → A
    __.cell: S → C
    tag: S → S_tag
asserts
    S generated by atom, cell
    S partitioned by .atom, .cell, tag
    ∀ a: A, c: C
      atom(a).atom == a
      cell(c).cell == c
      tag(atom(a)) == atom
      tag(cell(c)) == cell

Each field name (e.g., atom) is incorporated in three distinct operators (e.g., atom:→S_tag, atom:A→S, and __.atom:S→A).

9 Characters and symbols

LSL was designed for use with an open-ended collection of programming languages, support tools, and input/output facilities, each of which may have its own lexical conventions and capabilities. To avoid conflicts, LSL assigns fixed meanings to only a small number of characters. To conform to local conventions and to exploit locally available capabilities, LSL's character and token classes are open-ended, and can be tailored for particular uses by *initialization files*, as discussed in Appendix II.

Contiguous sequences of identifier characters (alphanumerics and underscore) and contiguous sequences of operator characters (asterisk, plus, minus, period, slash, less-than, equal, greater-than) form single tokens. Whitespace characters are insignificant except for separating tokens. Each of the remaining characters constitutes a separate token.

There are several semantically equivalent forms of LSL. Any of these forms can be mechanically translated into any other without losing information.

- *Presentation forms* are used in environments with rich sets of characters (e.g., ∀, ∧, ∨, ∈), including this report.
- *Interchange form* is an encoding of LSL using a subset of the ASCII

character set. Characters outside this subset are represented by *extended characters*—sequences of characters from the subset, set off by a backslash (or another designated character). Interchange form is the "lowest common denominator" for LSL. Each Larch tool must be able to parse it, and to generate it on demand.

- *Interactive forms* are used by Larch editors, browsers, checkers, etc., for input and output. Many will not be limited to character strings for input and output, and some may impose additional constraints and equivalences (e.g., case folding, operator precedence).

10 Further Examples

We have now covered all the facilities of the Larch Shared Language. The next series of examples illustrates their coordinated use.

The trait Container abstracts the common properties of data structures that contain elements, such as sets, bags, queues, stacks, and strings. Container is useful both as a starting point for specifications of many different data structures and as an assumption when defining generic operators over such data structures.

The **generated by** clause in Container asserts that each value of sort C can be constructed from new by repeated applications of insert. This assertion is carried along when Container is included in or assumed by other traits, even if they introduce additional operators with range C. Theorems proved by induction over new and insert will be valid in the theories associated with all such traits.

```
Container(E, C): trait
   introduces
      new: → C
      insert: E, C → C
   asserts C generated by new, insert
```

The trait LinearContainer includes Container. It constrains new and insert, inherited from Container, as well as the additional operators it introduces. The **partitioned by** clause indicates that next, rest, and isEmpty form a complete set of observers for sort C: for any terms t1 and t2 of sort C, if the equalities next(t1) == next(t2), rest(t1) == rest(t2), and isEmpty(t1) == isEmpty(t2) all hold, then t1 == t2. The axioms for next and rest are intentionally very weak (defining their meaning only for single-element containers) so that LinearContainer can be specialized to define stacks, queues, priority queues, and strings. The **converts** clause adds checkable redundancy to the specification by claiming that this trait fully defines isEmpty.

    LinearContainer(E, C): **trait**
      includes Container
      introduces
        isEmpty: C → Bool
        next: C → E
        rest: C → C
      asserts
        C **partitioned by** next, rest, isEmpty
        ∀ c: C, e: E
          isEmpty(new)
          ¬isEmpty(insert(e, c))
          next(insert(e, new)) == e
          rest(insert(e, new)) == new
      implies converts isEmpty

PriorityQueue specializes LinearContainer by adding another operator, ∈, and by further constraining next, rest, and insert. The first implication states a fact that can be proved using the induction rule inherited from Container. It may be helpful in reasoning about PriorityQueue and may help readers solidify their understanding of the trait. The second implication states that the trait defines next and rest (except when applied to new), isEmpty, and ∈. The axioms that convert isEmpty are inherited from LinearContainer.

```
PriorityQueue(E, Q): trait
   assumes TotalOrder(E)
   includes LinearContainer(Q for C)
   introduces __∈__: E, Q: → Bool
   asserts ∀ e, e': E, q: Q
      next(insert(e, q)) ==
         if q = new then e else if next(q) < e then next(q) else e
      rest(insert(e, q)) ==
         if q = new then new
            else if next(q) < e then insert(e, rest(q)) else q ¬(e ∈ new)
      e ∈ insert(e', q) == e = e' ∨ e ∈ q
   implies
         ∀ q: Q, e: E
         e ∈ q ⇒ ¬(e < next(q))
      converts next, rest, isEmpty, ∈
         exempting next(new), rest(new)
```

Unlike the preceding traits in this section, PriorityQueue specifies an abstract data type constructor. In such a trait there is a distinguished sort, sometimes called the "type of interest" or "data sort". An abstract data type's operators can be categorized as generators, observers, and extensions (sometimes in more than one way). A set of generators produces all the values of the distinguished sort. The extensions are the remaining operators whose range is the distinguished sort. The observers are the operators whose domain includes the distinguished sort and whose range is some other sort. An abstract data type specification usually converts the observers and extensions. The distinguished sort is usually partitioned by at least one subset of the observers and extensions. For example, in PriorityQueue, Q is the distinguished sort, new and insert form a generator set, rest is an extension, next, isEmpty, and ∈ are the observers, and next, rest, and isEmpty form a partitioning set.

A good heuristic for generating enough equations to adequately define an abstract data type is to write an equation defining the result of applying each observer or extension to each generator. For PriorityQueue, this rule suggests writing equations for rest(new), next(new), isEmpty(new), $e ∈$ new, rest(insert(e, q)), next(insert(e, q)), isEmpty(insert(e, q)), and $e ∈$ insert(e', q). PriorityQueue contains explicit equations for four of the eight, and inherits equations for two more from LinearContainer. The remaining two terms, next(new) and rest(new), are explicitly exempted.

The next two traits, PairwiseExtension and PairwiseSum, specify generic operators that can be used with various kinds of ordered containers.

Given a binary operator on elements, o, PairwiseExtension defines a new binary operator on containers, $\odot$. The result of applying $\odot$ to a pair of containers is a container whose elements are the results of applying o to corresponding pairs of their elements. The assumption of LinearContainer ensures that the notion of "corresponding pair" is well-defined; to understand why Container would not suffice, imagine defining $\odot$ consistently for a Bag. The **exempting** clause indicates that, although the result of applying $\odot$ to containers of unequal size is not specified, this is not an oversight. Since o is totally unconstrained in this trait, there aren't yet many interesting implications to state.

PairwiseExtension(E, C): **trait**
  assumes LinearContainer
  introduces
    __o__: E, E $\rightarrow$ E
    __$\odot$__: C, C $\rightarrow$ C
  asserts $\forall$ e, e': E, c, c': C
    new $\odot$ new == new
    insert(e, c) $\odot$ insert(e', c') == insert(e o e', $c \odot c'$)
  implies converts $\odot$
    exempting $\forall$ e: E, c: C
      new $\odot$ insert(e, c),
      insert(e, c) $\odot$ new

Now we specialize PairwiseExtension by binding o to an operator, +, whose definition is to be taken from the trait Cardinal.

PairwiseSum(C): **trait**
  assumes LinearContainer(Card for E)
  includes Cardinal,
    PairwiseExtension(Card for E, + for o, $\oplus$ for $\odot$)
  implies (Associative, Commutative) ($\oplus$ for o, C for T)

The validity of the implication that $\oplus$ is associative and commutative stems from the replacement of o by +, whose axioms in a suitable trait Cardinal would imply its associativity and commutativity. The implication could then be proved by induction over new and insert.

11 Significant Decisions in the Design of LSL

Our basic assumption was that specifications will be constructed and checked incrementally. This led us to a design that ensures that adding axioms to a trait never invalidates theorems. The need to maintain this monotonicity property led us to construe the equations of a trait as denoting a first-order theory. Neither the initial algebra nor the final algebra interpretation of a set of equations has this property.

Many traits correspond to complete abstract data types, but many others do not. So we included independent constructs to identify complete sets of constructors (**generated by**) and complete partitioning sets (**partitioned by**). Separating them provides useful flexibility.

The freedom to rename any of a trait's operators or sorts is also useful. In effect, all names appearing in a trait are formal parameters. An early version of LSL had only explicit lambda abstraction. We soon discovered that it was hard to get a trait's formal parameter list "right." If we kept it short, we often wished to substitute for a name that hadn't been included. If we used a longer list, we frequently didn't need to rename most of the potential parameters, and supplied the same names for the actuals as the formals. This experience led us to abolish explicit parameter lists in LSL 1.1; all renaming was of the form "id1 **for** id2." But the restriction to explicit renaming also proved cumbersome. In the current design, the specifier can choose to rename either positionally or explicitly.

Specifiers shouldn't start from scratch each time; LSL specifications are reusable. Handbooks of LSL specifications—some specialized for particular application domains—play an important role in specification development. (The examples used in this report are, for expository purposes, atypically complete.) We chose not to build into LSL many constructs that can easily be supplied by handbook traits.

Reading specifications is an important activity. People read syntactic objects (traits), rather than semantic objects (theories). So we chose to define the mechanisms for combining LSL specifications syntactically. However, for each of our combining operations on traits, there is a corresponding operation on theories such that the theory associated with any combination of traits is the same as the combination of their associated theories.

There is a tension in the design of the syntax for terms. On one hand, we want to allow specifiers as much notational flexibility as we can. On the other, it is important that both people and tools be able to parse terms in interface language specifications without reference to operator declarations (which are off in LSL traits). Our grammar for terms is fairly flexible, but—because there is no way to specify the precedence of user-defined operators—requires more parentheses than we would like.

Operator names in LSL include full signatures, unlike many programming languages, where overloaded operators are qualified by a single type or by a module name. This decision resulted from our desire to make heavy use of overloading in interface specifications. Contextual disambiguation means that it is not usually necessary to clutter up terms with explicit sorts.

We made a conscious attempt to reduce the number of characters reserved by LSL, to avoid conflicts with programming language usages (which will be reflected in interface languages), to avoid conflicts with notations from mathematics and application domains (which will be reflected in handbooks), and to avoid problems with different character sets in different environments. There isn't any real choice about commas, colons, and parentheses; fortunately, their uses in mathematics and most programming languages are compatible. We reserved these four characters and then used them throughout, in preference to other characters, such as semicolons and brackets. We took almost exactly the opposite approach for keywords, which appear in traits, but not in interface specifications. We deliberately chose distinctive keywords and reserved them.

LSL's constructs for introducing checkable redundancy into specifications were chosen to expose classes of errors that we expect to be common. These facilities help specifiers increase the chance that a specification with an unintended meaning will be detectably illegal, in much the same way that type systems increase the chance that an erroneous program will be detectably illegal. In contrast to our emphasis on syntactic mechanisms for combining traits, we included a number of semantic constraints on their legality. This means that a theorem prover is needed to fully check traits. The constructs for checking have other costs: LSL would be considerably smaller without them, and it takes about as long to learn the part of the language involved with checking as it does to learn the part required to generate theories.

The Larch approach frequently leads to traits in which many things are left unconstrained, so traits are not required to completely define all operators. Instead, **converts** clauses allow the specifier to include checkable claims about completeness, which can reflect the trait's intended uses in interface specifications. Exactly what it means to completely define an operator was a delicate design issue for LSL. The meaning of a **converts** clause is that, given any fixed interpretations for the other operators and the exempted terms, the interpretations of the converted operators that satisfy the trait's axioms are unique.

LSL 1.1 contained two additional constructs, **imports** and **constrains**, that were used to claim that one theory was a conservative extension of another. We found that these constructs were difficult to explain, to use effectively, and to check, so we have dropped them from the language.

In many respects, LSL is distinguished from other specification languages as much by what it doesn't include as by what it does.

LSL provides no construct for hiding operators. The hiding constructs of other specification languages allow the introduction of auxiliary operators that don't have to be implemented. These operators are not completely hidden, since they must be read to understand the specification, and they are likely to appear in reasoning based on the specification. The two-tiered structure of Larch specifications means that none of the operators appearing in an LSL trait have to be implemented; they are all auxiliary functions to be used in writing interface specifications. We could say that the entire LSL tier is "hidden."

LSL does not provide constructs for specifying partial functions or error algebras. There is no mechanism other than sort checking for restricting the domain of operators. Terms such as lookup(new, i) are allowed, and no special error elements are built into the language to represent the values of such terms. As discussed in the next piece of this tutorial preconditions and errors are handled in Larch interface languages.

Similarly, nondeterminism is left to the interface languages. It is frequently useful to write incomplete specifications that allow different interpretations of equality (and have non-isomorphic models). Thus, for many traits there are terms that are neither provably equal nor provably unequal. However, it is always the case in LSL that for every term t, t == t. The mathematical basis of algebra, and of LSL, depends on the validity of freely substituting equals for equals. This would be destroyed by the introduction of "nondeterministic functions."

We chose not to include higher-order entities in LSL. Traits are simple textual objects. Their associated theories are first-order theories. We sidestepped the subtle semantic problems associated with parameterized theories, theory parameters, and the like. **Includes** and **assumes** clauses, together with renamings, make possible much of the reuse for which higher-order theories are advocated.

Appendix 1. Lexical Structure

LSL was designed for use with an open-ended collection of programming languages, support tools, and input/output facilities, each of which may have its own lexical conventions and capabilities. To avoid conflicts, LSL assigns fixed meanings to only a small number of characters. To conform to local conventions and to exploit locally available capabilities, LSL's character and token classes are open-ended, and can be tailored by *initialization files*.

There are several semantically equivalent forms of LSL. Any of these forms can be mechanically translated into any other without losing information. *Interchange form* is an encoding of LSL using a subset of the ASCII character set. Characters outside this subset are represented by extended characters. Interchange form is the "lowest common denominator" for LSL. *Presentation forms* are used in environments with rich sets of characters, including this report. *Interactive forms* are used by Larch editors, browsers, checkers, etc., for input and output.

Contiguous sequences of identifier characters and contiguous sequences of operator characters form single tokens. Whitespace characters are insignificant except for separating tokens. Each of the remaining characters constitutes a separate token.

Character classification: Each character (or extended character) is classified as one of *idChar*, *opChar*, *whiteChar*, *extensionChar*, or *singleChar*. *whiteChar* contains blank, tab, and end-of-line. The required members of the other character classes are

idChar	ABCDEFGHIJKLMNOPQRSTUVWXYZ
idChar	abcdefghijklmnopqrstuvwxyz
idChar	0123456789
idChar	_
opChar	* + − . / < = >
extensionChar	\
singleChar	, : ( )

Unassigned characters can be assigned to any character class by a line in the initialization file like those above: the name of a class followed by characters to be assigned to it (possibly separated by *whiteChars*). Assigned characters cannot be reassigned. Characters that have not been explicitly assigned are classified as *singleChars*.

Extended characters start with an *extensionChar*. If the character following the *extensionChar* is an *idChar*, a comma, a colon, or a parenthesis, the extended character includes all following contiguous *idChars*; otherwise it extends only through the next character (which must be a visible character). The entire extended character is classified as though it were a character; if it has not been assigned, it is classified as a *singleChar*. Unlike other character classes, assignment of a new *extensionChar* returns the previous *extensionChar* to unassigned status. Extended characters—even those classified as *idChars*—are not included in other extended characters.

The special class *endCommentChar* initially contains end-of-line. Any real character may be assigned to this class, but extended characters cannot. It is the only character class that is not disjoint from each of the others.

Token formation: Contiguous sequences of *idChars* and contiguous sequences of *opChars* form single tokens. *whiteChars* are insignificant except for separating tokens. Each *singleChar* constitutes a separate token.

Token translation: A token may be defined as a *synonym* for another token by including a line in the initialization file of the form

       synonym *oldToken newToken*

All occurrences of *newToken* are translated to *oldToken*.

Token classification: The initial members of the token classes are

quantifierSym	\forall
logicalOp	\and \or \implies
eqOp	\eq \neq
equationSym	\equals
eqSepSym	\eqsep
selectSym	\select
openSym	\(
sepSym	\,
closeSym	\)
simpleId	\:
mapSym	\arrow
markerSym	\marker
commentSym	\comment

Unassigned tokens can be assigned to any token class by a line in the initialization file like those above: the name of a class followed by tokens to be assigned to it. Assigned tokens cannot be reassigned. Any tokens in a trait that have not been explicitly assigned are classified according to the following rules:

- If the token is a sequence of *idChars* that occurs as a terminal symbol of the grammar (a *keyword*), then that symbol.
- If the token is any other sequence of *idChars*, then *simpleId*.
- If the token is a *singleChar* that occurs as a terminal symbol of the grammar (comma, colon, or parenthesis), then that symbol.
- If the token is a sequence of *opChars*, then *simpleOp*.
- If the token is an extended character starting with an opening parenthesis, such as "\(large", then *openSym*.
- If the token is an extended character starting with a comma, then *sepSym*.
- If the token is an extended character starting with a closing parenthesis, then *closeSym*.
- If the token is an extended character starting with a colon, then *simpleId*.
- Otherwise, *simpleOp*.

If the token is classified as a *commentSym*, then it and all following characters up through the first occurrence of an *endCommentChar* are discarded, like *whiteChars*.

Initialization: The initialization file is processed before any traits. The extensions on each line are effective on all subsequent lines.

Part 3:
Introduction to LCL,
A Larch/C Interface Language

1 LCL preliminaries

This tutorial describes most of LCL (version 1.0) and gives an informal description of its semantics. It discusses some LCL tools, but it is not a user's guide for any of them.

LCL is not a C dialect or preprocessor. Programs specified and developed with LCL are C programs, accepted by ordinary C compilers. The use of LCL will tend to encourage some styles of development, but it does not change the programming language.

Before presenting any interface specifications, we discuss the intended relation between LCL specifications and C programs, the structure of LCL function specifications, and the relation of names appearing in LCL specifications to values in C states.

1.1 LCL specifications and C implementations

C is a general and flexible language that is used in many different ways. A common style for organizing programs is to construct them as a set of program units, often called *modules*. A module consists of an *interface* and an *implementation*. The interface is a collection of types, functions, variables, and constants for use in other modules, called its *clients*.

A C module M is typically represented by three files:

- M.c contains most of its implementation, including function definitions and private data declarations.

- M.h contains a description of its interface, plus parts of its implementation. Comments provide an informal specification of the module for the guidance of client programmers. Type declarations, function prototypes, constant definitions, declarations of external variables, and macro definitions provide all the information about M that is needed to compile its clients.

- M.o contains its compiled form. Such files are linked together to create executable files.

C modules specified using LCL have two additional files:

- M.lcl contains its LCL interface specification, a formal description of the types, functions, variables, and constants provided for clients, together with comments providing informal documentation. It replaces M.h as documentation for client programmers. The extra information it provides will also be exploited by a planned *LCLint* tool to perform more extensive checking than an ordinary C lint.

- M.lh is a header file derived automatically from M.lcl to be included in M.h. Mechanical generation of .lh-files file saves the user from having to repeat information in the .h-file. This reduces the bulk of the implementation and avoids an opportunity for error. The implementation portion of M.h must still be provided by the implementor.

M.lcl may also refer to another kind of file:

- .lsl-files contain auxiliary specifications in the form of LSL *traits*. A trait precisely defines operators used in .lcl-files.

Traits are the principal reusable units in Larch specifications. An interface specification (.lcl-file) may refer to more than one trait and a trait may be referred to by more than one interface. Commonly useful traits are collected into handbooks.

1.2 Function specifications

A C function may communicate with its callers by returning a result, by accessing objects accessible to the caller, or by modifying such objects. The specification of each function in an interface can be studied, understood, and used without reference to the specifications of other functions. A specification consists of a function prototype followed by a body of the form:

requires $reqP$;
modifies $modList$;
ensures $ensP$;

A specification places constraints on both clients and implementations of the function. The *requires clause* states restrictions on the arguments with which the client is allowed to call it. The *modifies* and *ensures clauses* place constraints on its behavior when it is called properly. They relate two states, the state when the function is called, which we call *pre*, and the state when it terminates, which we call *post*. A requires clause refers only to values in *pre*. An ensures clause may also refer to values in *post*, including the value returned by the function, written as *result*.[1]

A modifies clause says what a function is allowed to change. It says that the function must not change the value of any objects visible to the caller except for a specified list. Any other object must have the same value in *pre* and *post*. If there is no modifies clause, then nothing may be changed. Of course, it would be an error to include a const parameter in a modifies clause.

For each call, it is the responsibility of the client to make the requires clause true in the pre state. Having done that, the client may presume that: the function will terminate, the ensures clause will be true on termination, and changes will be limited to the objects indicated in the modifies clause. The client need not be concerned with how this happens.

The implementor of a function is entitled to presume that the requires clause holds on entry, and is not responsible for the function's behavior if it does not. Since a function's behavior is totally unconstrained unless its requires clause is satisfied, it is good style to use the weakest feasible requires clause. An omitted requires is equivalent to the weakest possible requirement,

---

[1]Part of the post state is the point to which control will be transferred. For most invocations, this is the return address of the pre state; constructs like exit, abort, and longjump can be specified as modifications of the pseudo-variable *control*.

requires true.

In summary, a specification as a whole is a predicate on the pre and post states, interpreted as

$reqP(\text{pre})$ =>

$(terminates \wedge modP(\text{pre}, \text{post}) \wedge ensP(\text{pre}, \text{post}))$

where => stands for logical implication, and $\wedge$ stands for conjunction (logical and).

1.3   States and names

Simplifying slightly, *states* are mappings from *locs* (locations) to *objects*. Each variable identifier names a loc. The major kinds of objects are:

- *basic values.* These are mathematical abstractions, like the integer 3 and the letter A. Such values are independent of the state of any computation. LSL is used to give meaning to basic values.

- *locs.* These store objects; for example, intLocs store objects of type int. The *value stored in a loc* in a state is the object to which the state maps the loc.

- *structs.* These are collections of locs, each denoted by a member name. For example, given the variable declaration
  struct {int first; char second;} s;
  s.first denotes an intLoc and s.second a charLoc.

- *unions.* These are similar to structs, except that their locs overlap.

- *arrays.* These are bounded vectors of adjacent locs, indexed from 0. If a is an array, maxIndex(a) is its upper bound.[2]

- *pointers.* These are references to collections of one or more adjacent locs, each denoted by an offset from a base address. They can be thought of as triples consisting of a loc and two bounding indexes. For example, given the code

---

[2]C does not make the values of maxIndex and minIndex available at runtime, but they are useful for specifying and reasoning about programs.

```
int a[100];
int *p;
p = &(a[1]);
```

*p denotes an intLoc in the region allocated to a, and minIndex(p) and maxIndex(p) denote the maximum number of intLocs before and after *p, respectively (1 and 98). These locs are accessible using arithmetic on p.

The following LCL primitives are available for accessing the pre and post states:

- ^can be applied to locs, arrays and structs. It is used to extract their values from the pre state. It cannot be applied directly to unions, but can be applied to the loc yielded by applying a field selector to a union.

  - When applied to a loc, it yields the value stored in that loc in the pre state).

  - When applied to an array, it yields a vector of the same length containing the values stored in the array's locs in the pre state.

  - When applied to a struct, it yields a tuple containing the values stored in the struct's locs in the pre state.

- ' is like ^, but extracts values from the post state.

- * is used, as in C, to dereference a pointer,[3] producing its loc with offset 0.

- ->, as in C, is a syntactic shorthand to dereference a pointer to a struct and then select one of its members. For example, a->b is equivalent to (*a).b .

- [i] is used, as in C, to index into an array, producing a loc.

- [] is applied to a pointer to cast it into an array. For example, p[] is an array whose first loc is *p and whose upper bound is maxIndex(p), and p[]^ is a vector.

---

[3]It is also used to dereference an abstract ref, as described in Section 2.6.

LCL is strongly typed. Each identifier's type defines the kind of objects to which it can map in any state. Similarly, each LSL value has a unique *sort*. To connect the two languages, there is a mapping from C types (and LCL abstract types) to LSL sorts. Each built-in type of C, each type built from C type constructors (e.g., int *), and each abstract type defined in LCL is *based on* an LSL sort. LCL specifications are written using types and values. The properties of these values are defined in LSL, using operators on the sorts on which those types are based.

A standard LSL trait defines operators of the sorts upon which C builtin types and type constructors are based. Users familiar with C will already know what these operators mean.

Consider the specification fragment:

```
void f(int i, int a[], const int *p) {
  requires i >= 0 /\ i <= maxIndex(a);
  modifies a;
  ensures a[i]' = (*p)^ + 1;
  }
```

Since ints are passed by value in C, i denotes not an intLoc but an int value.[4] The expression a[i] denotes the *i*th loc of the array a. Applying ' to this loc yields the int it stores in the post state. Applying * to the pointer p yields an intLoc. Applying ^ yields its int value in the pre state. The other operators are defined by the standard trait for int.

2   A guided tour through a specification

To illustrate the use of most of LCL's features, we present and discuss a small specification. This example is only superficially realistic; it was structured to use language constructs in the order we want to discuss them. It is not really a typical specification, or an especially wonderful program design. As you study this tutorial, you will probably find it instructive to consider alternative designs and how they would be specified.

The example in this section uses various conventions for names, formatting, comments, etc. These are not mandated by LCL; specifications should

---

[4]Within the implementation of f, a loc will be associated with the formal, but since that loc does not exist in the environment of the caller of f, it is not relevant to the specification.

be written using the conventions of the organization for which they are intended. Because the example is being used to document LCL features, rather than a real interface, the density of comments embedded within the formal text is low, and most of the comments are in the accompanying prose.

This example has been machine-checked (just as the prose has been mechanically spell-checked). The .lcl- and .lsl-files have been checked by the LCL and LSL Checkers, respectively. The .lh-files were automatically generated by the LCL Checker. The .lh-, .h-, and .c-files were compiled by gcc (this took somewhat longer than all the Larch checking). Finally, the compiled code was exercised by a test driver. Although we tried to be very careful at each stage of development, each of the mechanical checks caught some errors that we had not. Based on this experience, we expect that when LCLint is available, it will find a few more errors (just as we expect that careful readers will find a few typos in the prose). These will probably be errors that would manifest themselves only in very unusual circumstances, and would therefore be difficult to root out by testing.

2.1   Gender

The interface specified in Figure 1, gender, exports a type, a constant, and two functions to its clients.

The first line defines an *exposed type*, also named gender, using a C typedef. Clients of this interface are being told exactly how gender is represented as a C type. They may deal with gender values in any way allowed by standard C. However, LCL's type checking is stricter than standard C's. LCL uses name equality for type checking, and LCLint will warn programmers about type violations that C lint will not catch.[5]

The theory of C's types and type constructors is built into LCL. C's enum types are axiomatized using LSL's *enumeration of* shorthands, and struct types using *tuple of* shorthands.

The *constant declaration* gives a symbolic name for an important property of the interface: the size of the longest string gender_sprint is allowed to return. LCL interface constants may be implemented either by macro definitions or by C const variables.

---

[5]But, in deference to long tradition, LCLint will use structural type checking on calls to standard library functions.

```
/* Exports one type, a function to convert genders to        */
/* strings and a function to (trivially) initialize the module. */

typedef enum {MALE, FEMALE, gender_ANY} gender;

constant int gender_maxPrintSize = lenStr("unknown gender");

uses sprint(gender, char[]);

int gender_sprint(char s[], gender g) {
   requires maxIndex(s) >= gender_maxPrintSize;
   modifies s;
   ensures isSprint(s', g)
           /\ result = lenStr(s')
           /\ result <= gender_maxPrintSize;
   }
void gender_initMod(void) { ensures true; }
```

Figure 1: gender.lcl

A *uses* clause invokes and auxiliary specification—an LSL trait that defines operators used in the LCL specification. Users familiar with the operators involved may not need to examine such traits closely, but most users are expected to read them. The uses clause here incorporates an LSL specification that gives the meaning of operators such as isSprint and lenStr. It also says the sort T of sprint.lsl is to be replaced by the sort gender (on which the type gender is based) and the sort String by whatever sort the type char[] is based on (its name isn't important).

The function gender_sprint is typical of a kind found in many interfaces. It converts gender values into a string form suitable for printing, and returns the length of that string. Its specification begins with its *function prototype*. LCL prototypes are more restricted than C's. For example, LCL requires that each of the formal parameters be named, although names are optional in C. This guarantees that the specification can refer to any parameter by name. Since all functions in an interface are exported, the keyword extern will be added automatically when gender.lh is generated.

LCL distinguishes between pointers and arrays in prototypes. In a C prototype, char *s and char s[] are essentially equivalent. In an LCL prototype, however, char *s allows access to all of the characters from *(s - minIndex(s)) to *(s + maxIndex(s)), while char s[] allows access only to the characters from s[0] to s[maxIndex(s)].

The body of the specification consists of three clauses. The requires clause says that the array s must be big enough to hold the longest string that will ever be returned. The modifies clause says that only the contents of the array s can be changed. The ensures clause constrains the new value of s and the function's result.[6]

Arrays are passed by reference in C, so the formal s refers to the array, rather than its contents. The term s' denotes the vector of characters contained by the locs in s upon return from gender_sprint. Since parameters of enumeration types are passed by value, g denotes a value of type gender. The meanings of isSprint and lenStr are given in Figures 2 and 3, which are discussed below.

This specification does not say what string will be generated for each gender value—only that it will have certain properties. We might want such freedom, for example, in a module that will have different implementations for different countries or languages. This specification doesn't even require an implementation to be *deterministic*; for example, it doesn't require gender_sprint(s, MALE) to always put the same chars in s, or to always return the same int value. Although our implementation of gender doesn't take advantage of this freedom, later interfaces will have implementations that do.

The trait sprint.lsl was written for specifying functions that convert values to strings. It includes the library trait string, which specifies the operators nullTerminated and lenStr. Note that string trait, like C, defines the value of lenStr only when it is applied to a null-terminated string.

The trait in Figure 3 is intentionally weak. It doesn't say much about the meanings of its operators. This allows considerable flexibility in implementing the interface functions.[7] The first two assertions guarantee that different T values will have different string forms, without specifying

---

[6]A good rule of thumb is that each object in the modifies clause should appear in primed form at least once in the ensures clause.

[7]It is hard to write a specification that leaves the implementation so much flexibility, but still imposes the necessary constraints. sprint is the most subtle trait in this tutorial.

% Define the relation between C's vectors of chars and
% C's conventions for null-terminated character strings.

```
string: trait
includes integer
introduces
    null: -> char
    empty: -> String
    append: String, char -> String
    len: String -> int
    nullTerminated: String -> bool
    throughNull: String -> String
    sameStr: String, String -> bool
    lenStr: String -> int
    % and many other operators not used here ...

asserts
    String generated by empty, append
    forall s, s1, s2: String, c: char
        len(empty) == 0;
        len(append(s, c)) == len(s) + 1;

        not(nullTerminated(empty));
        nullTerminated(append(s, c)) ==
                        c = null \/ nullTerminated(s);

        nullTerminated(s) =>
            throughNull(append(s, c)) = throughNull(s);
        not(nullTerminated(s)) =>
            throughNull(append(s, null)) = append(s, null);

        sameStr(s1, s2) == throughNull(s1) = throughNull(s2);

        lenStr(s) == len(throughNull(s)) - 1
        % and many other axioms not needed here ...
```

Figure 2: string.lsl fragment

```
% Defines minimum requirements for an unparse function that
% converts from a T to a String without losing information.

sprint(T, String): trait

includes string

introduces
    parse: String -> T
    unparse: T -> String
    isSprint: String, T -> bool

asserts
    T partitioned by unparse
    forall t: T, s: String
        parse(unparse(t)) == t;
        isSprint(s, t) == parse(s) = t /\ nullTerminated(s)
```

Figure 3: sprint.lsl

what those forms are. The second equation gives two important properties of acceptable string forms. We could repeat these properties in the interface specification of each such function, but it is better to get them right once, and then reuse the trait.

In this example, we include an initMod function as part of every interface. Later we will discuss the way in which we use these functions. The function gender_initMod is required by its specification to have no visible effect, since it modifies nothing and returns no value. The absence of a requires clause (equivalent to *requires true*) says that it must always terminate.

From gender.lcl the LCL Checker generates the file gender.lh, Figure 4. This is used in the implementation of gender.h, Figure 5, and hence, gender.c, Figure 6.

By convention, we start our .h-files with a #if that makes sure that including them more than once into the same module will not cause a problem. Both gender.c and all clients of gender will include gender.hIn turn, gender.h includes gender.lh, which provides prototypes. The implementation

```
typedef enum {MALE, FEMALE, gender_ANY} gender;

extern int gender_sprint(char s[], gender g);
extern void gender_initMod(void);
```

Figure 4: gender.lh

```
#if !defined(gender_h_expanded)
#define gender_h_expanded
#define gender_maxPrintSize (sizeof("unknown gender"))

#include "gender.lh"

#define gender_initMod()
#endif
```

Figure 5: gender.h

```
#include <string.h>
#include "gender.h"

int gender_sprint (char s[], gender g) {
    static char *resultstr[] ={"male", "female", "unknown gender"};

    s[0] = '\0';
    (void) strncat(s, resultstr[g], gender_maxPrintSize-1);

    return strlen(s);
}
```

Figure 6: gender.c

of the function gender_initMod is also in gender.h.

2.2 Employee

The employee interface, Figure 7, directly exports to its clients two constants, three exposed types, and three functions.

The *imports* clause says that the specification of the employee interface depends on the specification of the gender interface; it gives employee and its clients access to the type gender and the function gender_sprint. It also makes the trait associated with the gender interface available for use in the specification of the employee interface. Such specification dependencies should not be confused with implementation dependencies, where one module is used within the implementation of another; clients should not be concerned with what modules the implementation uses.

The constant clause equates the C constant maxEmployeeName and the LSL constant MaxEmployeeName. Looking in employeeName.lsl, Figure 8, we see that the implementation has a great deal of freedom in implementing this constant; any int greater than zero is allowed.

The exposed types in this interface are conventional. We will later ensure that (in any database) each Social Security Number (ssNum) identifies a unique employee, so we can use it as a key into the database. Cf. Figure 17 and the discussion on page 2.4.

Like gender.lcl, employee.lcl uses the sprint trait. This means that employee incorporates sprint.lsl twice, with different renamings: directly with employee for T, and indirectly with gender for T. It also uses employeeName, which was written specifically for use in employee.lcl, and needs no renamings.

In addition to employee_sprint and employee_initMod functions, this interface exports the function employee_setName. This function returns a value of type bool, the one builtin type of LCL that is missing from C. When LCL specifications are checked, bool is treated as a distinct type. If the type identifier bool appears in an LCL specification, the Checker places #include "bool.h" in the corresponding .lh-file. A typical bool.h is shown in Figure 9.

The requires clause in employee_setName says that it should be called only with null-terminated strings. The implementation is entitled to rely on this. Indeed, it often must. It is not generally possible to determine at

```
imports gender;

constant int maxEmployeeName = MaxEmployeeName;
constant int employee_maxPrintSize =
            maxEmployeeName + gender_maxPrintSize + 30;

typedef enum {MGR, NONMGR, job_ANY} job;
typedef char employeeName[maxEmployeeName];
typedef struct {int ssNum;
                employeeName name;
                int salary;
                gender gen;
                job j;} employee;

uses employeeName, sprint(employee, char[]);

bool employee_setName(employee *e, employeeName na) {
   requires nullTerminated(na^);
   modifies e->name;
   ensures result = lenStr(na^) < maxEmployeeName
           /\ (if result
                then sameStr(e->name', na^)
                     /\ nullTerminated(e->name')
                else unchanged(e->name));
   }
int employee_sprint(char s[], employee e) {
   requires maxIndex(s) >= employee_maxPrintSize;
   modifies s;
   ensures isSprint(s', e)
           /\ result = lenStr(s')
           /\ result <= employee_maxPrintSize;
   }
void employee_initMod(void) {
   ensures true;
   }
```

Figure 7: employee.lcl

runtime the maxIndex of an array. Yet without a guarantee that a string is null-terminated, it is not safe to search for its terminating null. The search might run past the end of the allocated storage and generate references to nonexistent memory. Completely defensive programming just isn't possible in C.

The modifies clause says that employee_setName may change the name field, e->name, of its first argument, but nothing else. This is a finer-grained constraint on modification than is possible using only C's const qualifier. Unlike requires and ensures clauses, a modifies clause constrains everything it doesn't mention.

The ensures clause says that employee_setName will have one of two outcomes. It will either:

- Make the name field of its first argument the same as its second argument (when both are interpreted as strings), make the new value

```
employeeName: trait

includes string(employeeName for String), integer

introduces MaxEmployeeName: -> int

asserts equations
    MaxEmployeeName > 0
```

Figure 8: employeeName.lsl

```
#if !defined(bool_h_expanded)
#define bool_h_expanded
#define FALSE 0
#define TRUE (!FALSE)
typedef int bool;
#define bool_initMod()
#endif
```

Figure 9: bool.h

```
#include "bool.h"
#include "gender.h"

typedef enum {MGR, NONMGR, job_ANY} job;
typedef char employeeName[maxEmployeeName];
typedef struct {int ssNum;
                employeeName name;
                int salary;
                gender gen;
                job j;} employee;

extern bool employee_setName(employee *e, char na[]);

extern int employee_sprint(char s[], employee e);

extern void employee_initMod(void);
```

Figure 10: employee.lh

of the name field be null-terminated, and return TRUE, or

- Change nothing and return FALSE.

Furthermore, the first outcome will occur exactly when the new name fits, (i.e., lenStr(na^) < maxEmployeeName). The use of *result* in several subterms of an ensures clause is a frequent idiom. Since the predicate in the ensures clause is just a logical formula, it makes no semantic difference whether the equation for *result* is written first or last. We are free to choose an order that helps the exposition or emphasizes some particular aspect of the specification.

A number of design decisions are recorded in employee.lcl. It says which functions must be implemented, and for each function it indicates both the conditions that must hold at the point of call and the conditions that must hold upon return. This constitutes a contract between the implementation and the clients of employee that establishes a "logical firewall," allowing their programmers to proceed independently of each other, relying only on the interface specification.

The file employee.lh, Figure 10, is automatically constructed from employee.lcl. In addition to the appropriate typedefs and function prototypes,

```
#if !defined(employee_h_expanded)
#define employee_h_expanded

#define maxEmployeeName 20
#define employee_maxPrintSize (maxEmployeeName + gender_maxPrintSize + 30)
#include "employee.lh"

#define employee_initMod()\
            do {bool_initMod(); gender_initMod();} while (0)
#endif
```

Figure 11: employee.h

it #includes the .h-files of the explicitly imported interface gender and the implicitly imported interface bool.

The file employee.h, Figure 11, defines the constant maxEmployeeName using a macro. Because of a restriction imposed by C, this definition must precede the inclusion of employee.lh, since the constant is used in the typedef of employee_name contained in employee.lh. The #define cannot be automatically generated because the LCL processor has no way of knowing what value the constant is to have; the specification leaves that decision to the implementation.

The file employee.h also implements employee_initMod. Our convention is for each module to initialize any modules it explicitly imports. Thus employee_initMod calls gender_initMod. Since the specification of this function guarantees that it modifies nothing, calling it multiple times cannot have effects visible to clients.

In general, M.h contains, in order:

- A test of whether M_h_expanded is defined in the current context. This makes sure, for example, that a client of employee can safely include both employee.h and gender.h without getting an error caused by a second occurrence of the type definition for gender.

- A definition of M_h_expanded.

- Definitions of all constants declared in M.lcl, either as macros or as C const variables.

```
#include <string.h>
#include "employee.h"

bool employee_setName(employee *e, employeeName na) {
    int i;

    for (i = 0; na[i] != '\0'; i++)
        if (i == maxEmployeeName) return FALSE;
    strcpy(e->name, na);
    return TRUE;
}
int employee_sprint(char s[], employee e) {
    char gstring[gender_maxPrintSize];
    static char *jobs[] = {"manager", "non-manager", "unknown job"};

    gender_sprint(gstring, e.gen);

    (void) sprintf(s, "%d,      %s,      %s,      %s,         $%d",
                      e.ssNum, e.name, gstring, jobs[e.j], e.salary);
    return strlen(s);
}
```

Figure 12: employee.c

- Concrete representations (typedefs) for any abstract types declared in M.lcl. Abstract data types are discussed in the next section.

- An include of M.lh.

- Macros, if any, for inline implementations of functions with prototypes in M.lh.

The implementation of employee_setName in employee.c, Figure 12, relies on the requires clause in its specification. It may crash if na^ isn't null-terminated.

2.3 Empset

The interface empset.lcl, Figure 13, exports a set of functions and an *abstract data type*. Types specified in LCL can be either exposed or abstract.

```
/* empset is a set of employees          */
/* set.lsl can be found in an LSL handbook */

imports employee;
abstract type empset;
uses set(employee for Elem, empset for Set),
     sprint(empset, char□);

void empset_init(empset *s) {
   modifies *s;
   ensures (*s)' = { };
   }
void empset_final(empset *s) {
   modifies *s;
   ensures trashed(*s);
   }
void empset_clear(empset *s) {
   modifies *s;
   ensures (*s)' = { };
   }
bool empset_insert(empset *s, employee e) {
   modifies *s;
   ensures result = not(e \in (*s)^) /\ (*s)' = insert(e, (*s)^);
   }
void empset_insertUnique(empset *s, employee e) {
   requires not(e \in (*s)^);
   modifies *s;
   ensures (*s)' = insert(e, (*s)^);
   }
bool empset_delete(empset *s, employee e) {
   modifies *s;
   ensures result = e \in (*s)^ /\ (*s)' = delete(e, (*s)^);
   }
empset *empset_union(empset *s1, empset *s2) {
   ensures (*result)' = (*s1)^ \union (*s2)^ /\ fresh(*result);
   }
```

Figure 13: empset.lcl, part 1

```
empset *empset_disjointUnion(empset *s1, empset *s2) {
   requires (*s1)^ \intersect (*s2)^ = { };
   ensures (*result)' = (*s1)^ \union (*s2)^ /\ fresh(*result);
   }
void empset_intersect(empset *s1, empset *s2) {
   modifies *s1;
   ensures (*s1)' = (*s1)^ \intersect (*s2)^;
   }
int empset_size(empset *s) {
   ensures result = size((*s)^);
   }
bool empset_member(employee e, empset *s) {
   ensures result = e \in (*s)^;
   }
bool empset_subset(empset *s1, empset *s2) {
   ensures result = (*s1)^ \subset (*s2)^;
   }
employee empset_choose(empset *s) {
   requires (*s)^ != { };
   ensures result \in (*s)^;
   }
int empset_sprint(char s[], empset *es) {
   requires maxIndex(s) >= (size((*es)^) * employee_maxPrintSize);
   modifies s;
   ensures isSprint(s', (*es)^)
           /\ result = lenStr(s')
           /\ result <= (size((*es)^) * employee_maxPrintSize);
   }
void empset_initMod(void) {
   ensures true;
   }
```

Figure 13: empset.lcl, part 2

As we have seen, exposed types are specified using C typedefs. Abstract types are specified by specifying a collection of functions that create, examine, and manipulate their values, leaving their representation as a "secret" of the implementation.

Although C provides no direct support for abstract types, there is a style of C programming in which they play a prominent role. The programmer relies on conventions to ensure that the implementation of an abstract type can be changed without affecting the correctness of clients. The key restriction is that clients never directly access the representation of an abstract value. All access is through the functions provided in its interface.

To ensure that client programs are independent of the way abstract types are represented, several restrictions on their use are necessary. Values of abstract types must not be assigned with = or compared with ==.[8] Without these restrictions, the choice of representations would be severely limited; for example, if comparison using == were allowed, structs could not be used at the top-level of a representation. More importantly, these operators would likely have surprising semantics in client programs. Consider, for example, two empsets, *s1* and *s2*. Suppose each empset was implemented by a pointer to some data structure, with NIL representing the empty set. The expression *s1* == *s2* would return true whenever two empty sets were compared, but otherwise would return false whenever two distinct objects were compared, even if they had the same values as sets. The statement *s1* = *s2* would make *s1* and *s2* point into the same data structure; modifications to either set would then change both.

For the same reasons that assignment of abstract types is not allowed, using values of abstract types as parameters or as results is forbidden. References are passed and returned, instead. For example, empset_union takes and returns values of type empset *, rather than empset.

Type checking for abstract types (like that for exposed types) in both the LCL Checker and LCLint is based on type names, not on their representations. However there are two differences in the way LCLint will check the use of abstract types. First, for exposed types, calls to functions from the standard C library will be checked using the representation of the type. For abstract types, names will be used for all type checking. Second, within the implementation of the module exporting an abstract type, the

---

[8]Ref abstract types, discussed below, are an exception to this rule.

type's representation will be used. This allows the implementation to access the internal structure that is hidden from clients.

The first two functions, empset_init and empset_final are typical of functions found in interfaces exporting abstract types. Since an abstract type cannot be assigned outside its implementation, its variables must be initialized by calling a function in its interface. By convention, an object of an abstract type T is initialized by the T_init function before any other use. LCLint will check for this in the same way it checks for uninitialized variables of exposed types. Once it has been initialized, no reference to it should be passed to T_init again.

A client of empset should call empset_final when it knows that an empset object will never be referenced again. The clause *ensures trashed(*s)* says that upon return from empset_final nothing can be assumed about the storage pointed to by s in the pre state. References to that loc could even cause the client program to crash. A good implementation of empset_final will free storage that is no longer needed, although this specification does not require it to. Since a client has no information about how an empset is represented, it cannot directly free one. For example, if empset is implemented as a pointer to a data structure, the call free(&s1) would free only the pointer, not the data structure.

The third function in the interface, empset_clear, appears to have the same specification as empset_init. However, empset_clear is provided for reinitializing an existing empset, rather than initializing a new one, and LCLint will treat it differently, because it is not the mandatory initialization function. As we will see later, empset_init and empset_clear implemented very differently.

The functions empset_insert and empset_insertUnique both add an employee to an empset. The chief difference is that empset_insertUnique requires that the employee to be added is not already present. This makes it possible to implement the function more efficiently. However, if the requirement is violated, the behavior of empset_insertUnique is totally unconstrained by the specification. The implementation we give later does not check the requirement. If it is violated the implementation returns without complaint, but it breaks a representation invariant—thus leading to unpredictable behavior on subsequent uses of the empset.

The functions empset_union and empset_disjointUnion both return the union of two empsets. Once again, the requires clause makes it possible to implement one more efficiently than the other. Notice that even though *s1 and *s2 are not modified, the specifications refer to (*s1)^ and (*s2)^. The ^ is needed because *s1 and *s2 refer to locs containing empsets. These must be evaluated in some state to get an empset. Here *s1 and *s2 contain the same value in the pre and post states. We use ^ rather than ' for objects that are guaranteed to have the same values in both states.

Both functions are required (by *fresh(*result)*) to return sets that are not aliased to any objects visible in the pre state. Thus the sets that they return can be modified without affecting the values of other sets. One way of implementing this is to allocate new storage.

The requires clause of empset_choose is necessary to guarantee that the ensures clause is satisfiable. If (*s)^ is empty, it is not possible to return an employee that is a member of it. Should (*s)^ contain more than one element, the specification is silent as to which member empset_choose returns. The implementation we present later gains efficiency by being abstractly non-deterministic: A single empset value may have many different representations (depending on the order in which its elements were inserted), and the value returned by empset_choose is determined by the representation value passed in.

Although the remaining functions are a necessary part of this interface, they don't illustrate any new LCL features. Its implementation is given in an appendix to the report from which this material is excerpted.

The specifications presented to this point have been in the ASCII form in which they can be entered for checking by the tools. One of the planned tools is a prettyprinter that will take this raw form, and convert it to a more readable form using the capabilities of a modern formatting system and a laser printer or bitmapped display device. Figure 14 shows sample of what its output will look like. The analogous tool for LSL is already in use.

```
/* empset is a set of employees */
/* set.lsl can be found in an LSL handbook */

imports employee;
abstract type empset;
uses set(employee for Elem, empset for Set),
    sprint(empset, char[]);

void empset_init(empset *s) {
    modifies *s;
    ensures (*s)' = {};
    }
void empset_final(empset *s) {
    modifies *s;
    ensures trashed(*s);
    }
void empset_clear(empset *s) {
    modifies *s;
    ensures (*s)' = {};
    }
bool empset_insert(empset *s, employee e) {
    modifies *s;
    ensures result = ¬(e ∈ (*s)^) ∧ (*s)' = insert(e, (*s)^);
    }
void empset_insertUnique(empset *s, employee e) {
    requires ¬(e ∈ (*s)^);
    modifies *s;
    ensures (*s)' = insert(e, (*s)^);
    }
bool empset_delete(empset *s, employee e) {
    modifies *s;
    ensures result = e ∈ (*s)^ ∧ (*s)' = delete(e, (*s)^);
    }
empset *empset_union(empset *s1, empset *s2) {
    ensures (*result)' = (*s1)^ ∪ (*s2)^ ∧ fresh(*result);
    }
```

Figure 14: empset.lcl fragment, prettyprinted

2.4 DBase

Up to now we have presented modules by first giving an interface specification, then its auxiliary LSL specification, and finally, its implementation. This works well when the reader has good *a priori* intuition about the meaning of the abstractions used in the interface specification. When such intuition cannot be relied upon, it is often better to present the auxiliary specification first, as we do here.

The definitions in trait dbase, Figure 16 use operators defined by the traits associated with gender and employee. But LSL specifications are programming-language-independent, and hence aren't allowed to reference LCL specifications. We could copy the operator definitions into dbase.lsl, but this would be another opportunity for unchecked discrepancies between parts of the specification. Instead, dbase.lsl, Figure 16, documents them as assumptions. Figure 15, dbaseAssumptions, indicates what must be supplied by any environment in which trait dbase is used. These assumptions are discharged in dbase.lcl by the imports of gender and employee; someday the LCL Checker will make sure that all assumptions are discharged.

Figure 16 introduces operators to create, manipulate, and query dbase

```
dbaseAssumptions: trait

includes integer,
        set(employee for Elem, empset for Set)

gender enumeration of MALE, FEMALE, gender_ANY

job enumeration of MGR, NONMGR, job_ANY

employee tuple of ssNum: int,
                  name: employeeName,
                  salary: int,
                  gen: gender,
                  j: job
```

Figure 15: dbaseAssumptions.lsl

values and then provides axioms giving their meanings. Once these operators are understood, it is straightforward to understand the specifications of the functions exported by dbase.lcl, Figure 17 (just as an understanding of the conventional operators on finite sets is the basis for understanding the specifications of the functions in empset.lcl).

The dbase module encapsulates a database and a set of functions to query and manipulate it. It exports two exposed types, dbase_q and dbase_status, and a number of functions. It also contains our first use of global variables. LCL uses the same scope rules as C. However, LCL extends the function prototype by including a list of the *global* variables referenced by the function. For example, hire is allowed to reference d, but not initNeeded. LCLint will check that each global variable accessed by the function body appears in this list.

As it happens, dbase has only *private* variables, defined for use only in the specification itself. Client code can refer to the functions specified

```
dbase: trait

assumes dbaseAssumptions

dbase_q tuple of g:gender, j: job, l: int, h: int
dbase_status enumeration of dbase_OK, salERR, genderERR,
                            jobERR, duplERR
introduces
   new: -> dbase
   hire: dbase, employee -> dbase
   fire, promote: dbase, int -> dbase
   setSal: dbase, int, int -> dbase
   find: dbase, int -> employee
   employed: dbase, int -> bool
   numEmployees: dbase -> int
   match: gender, gender -> bool
   match: job, job -> bool
   query: dbase, dbase_q -> empset
```

Figure 16: dbase.lsl, part 1

```
asserts
   dbase generated by new, hire
   dbase partitioned by query
   forall e: employee, k: int, g, gq: gender, j, jq: job,
          q: dbase_q, sal: int, d: dbase
     fire(new, k) == new;
     fire(hire(d, e), k) ==
        if e.ssNum = k then fire(d, k) else hire(fire(d, k), e);
     promote(new, k) == new;
     promote(hire(d, e), k) ==
        if e.ssNum = k
        then hire(promote(d, k), set_j(e, MGR))
        else hire(promote(d, k), e);
     setSal(new, k, sal) == new;
     setSal(hire(d, e), k, sal) ==
        if e.ssNum = k
        then hire(setSal(d, k, sal), set_salary(e, sal))
        else hire(setSal(d, k, sal), e);
     find(hire(d, e), k) == if e.ssNum = k then e else find(d, k);
     employed(new, k) == false;
     employed(hire(d, e), k) ==
        if e.ssNum = k then true else employed(d, k);
     numEmployees(new) == 0;
     numEmployees(hire(d, e)) == numEmployees(d)
          + (if employed(d, e.ssNum) then 0 else 1);
     match(gq, g) == gq = gender_ANY \/ g = gq;
     match(jq, j) == jq = job_ANY \/ j = jq;
     query(new, q) == { };
     query(hire(d, e), q) ==
        if match(q.g, e.gen) /\ match(q.j, e.j)
          /\ q.l <= e.salary /\ e.salary <= q.h
        then insert(e, query(d, q)) else query(d, q)
```

Figure 16: dbase.lsl, part 2

```
imports employee, gender, empset;

typedef struct{gender g; job j; int l; int h;} dbase_q;
typedef enum {dbase_OK, salERR, genderERR, jobERR,
              duplERR} dbase_status;
private abstract type dbase;
private dbase d;
private bool initNeeded = true;

uses dbase, sprint(dbase, char[]);

dbase_status hire(employee e) dbase d; {
   modifies d;
   ensures
     (if result = dbase_OK then d' = hire(d^, e) else unchanged(d))
     /\ result = (if e.gen = gender_ANY then genderERR
                  else if e.j = job_ANY then jobERR
                  else if e.salary < 0 then salERR
                  else if employed(d^, e.ssNum) then duplERR
                  else dbase_OK);
   }
void uncheckedHire(employee e) dbase d; {
   requires e.gen != gender_ANY /\ e.j != job_ANY
            /\ e.salary > 0 /\ not(employed(d^, e.ssNum));
   modifies d;
   ensures d' = hire(d^, e);
   }
bool fire(int ssNum) dbase d; {
   modifies d;
   ensures result = employed(d^, ssNum)
                    /\ (if result then d' = fire(d^, ssNum)
                        else unchanged(d));
   }
```

Figure 17: dbase.lcl, part 1

```
int query(dbase_q q, empset *s) dbase d; {
   modifies *s;
   ensures (*s)' = (*s)^ \union query(d^, q)
          /\ result = size((*s)' - (*s)^);
   }
bool promote(int ssNum) dbase d; {
   modifies d;
   ensures result = (employed(d^, ssNum)
          /\ find(d^, ssNum).j = NONMGR)
          /\ (if result then d' = promote(d^, ssNum)
              else unchanged(d));
   }
bool setSalary(int ssNum, int sal) dbase d; {
   modifies d;
   ensures result = employed(d^, ssNum)
          /\ (if result then d' = setSal(d^, ssNum, sal)
              else unchanged(d));
   }
int dbase_sprint(char s[]) dbase d; {
   requires
      maxIndex(s) >= (numEmployees(d^) * employee_maxPrintSize);
   modifies s;
   ensures isSprint(s', d^)
          /\ result = lenStr(s')
          /\ result <= (numEmployees(d^) * employee_maxPrintSize);
   }
void dbase_initMod(void) dbase d; bool initNeeded; {
   modifies d, initNeeded;
   ensures if initNeeded^
          then d' = new /\ not(initNeeded') else unchanged(all);
   }
```

Figure 17: dbase.lcl, part 2

in dbase.lcl, but cannot refer to private types and variables. Furthermore, since they are not exported, the private types and variables need not be implemented. The type dbase is defined only to declare the private variable d. Neither the type dbase nor the variable d appears in our implementation.

Notice that there is no dbase_init function for the private type dbase. Any necessary initialization of the private variable d can be done in dbase_initMod, which has access to the private variables.

The variable initNeeded is used to ensure that dbase_initMod is idempotent. This guarantees that multiple clients can use the data base, and can each call dbase_initMod, to ensure that the data base is initialized, without worrying about interfering with one another.

The function hire is closely related to the operator hire of dbase.lsl. The difference is that it does some error checking and returns a result indicating the outcome of this checking.

The function uncheckedHire is even more similar to the LSL operator, since it does no error checking. Of course, if it is called when its requires clause does not hold, it is likely to do something unfortunate that may not be detected for quite some time, for example, when the employee is fired. Both functions modify the private variable d. Since d is a global variable rather than a formal parameter, it can be accessed directly; there is no need to pass in a pointer to it.

The function query is also closely related to the LSL operator query. But the operator returns an empset and the function returns an int: the number of employees added to *s as the required *side effect* of calling it. This is a common C idiom.

Now we can show that dbase preserves the property that there is at most one employee in d with any given ssNum. The function dbase_initMod ensures that d starts out empty. The only functions that are allowed to add employees to d are hire and uncheckedHire. If hire is called with an employee whose ssNum is already in d, its specification says that it must return duplERR and leave d unchanged. And uncheckedHire's requires clause forbids calling it with an employee whose ssNum is already in d— any subsequent havoc is purely the responsibility of uncheckedHire's client.

The only thing of note about dbase.lh, Figure 18, is that the private variables and private type do not appear in it.

```
#include "bool.h"
#include "gender.h"
#include "employee.h"
#include "empset.h"

typedef enum {dbase_OK,
              salERR,
              genderERR,
              jobERR,
              duplERR} dbase_status;
typedef struct{gender g; job j; int l; int h;} dbase_q;

extern dbase_status hire(employee e);
extern void uncheckedHire(employee e);
extern bool fire(int ssNum);
extern int query(dbase_q q, empset *s);
extern bool promote(int ssNum);
extern bool setSalary(int ssNum, int sal);
extern int dbase_sprint(char s[]);
extern void dbase_initMod(void);
```

Figure 18: dbase.lh

The implementation of dbase is presented in an appendix to the report from which this material is excerpted.

2.5 Driver

Before looking at the abstractions used in the implementation of dbase, we pause to take a look at some code that uses dbase. Figure 19 is part of a program we used to test our implementations of the modules specified earlier in this section.

The program begins with a series of #includes of the .h-files for the modules containing functions or types that it uses directly. It does not include any subsidiary modules that they may use. While the included .h-files are necessary to compile the driver, to understand the code one need look only at the corresponding .lcl-files. If the implementation of one of the used modules, such as empset, should change, the driver will have to be re-compiled, but the code will not have to be changed.

After declaring some variables, the driver initializes the included modules (except for stdio). LCLint will issue a warning if this initialization is not done immediately following the declarations of the function main. Since the author of main has no way of knowing what modules are used in the implementations of the included modules, the various initMod functions must themselves call the initMod functions of the modules they use. This could result in some initMod functions being called twice, which is why their specifications typically require them to be idempotent.

The driver then initializes the the variable es. Our conventions require this because empset is an abstract type. LCLint will issue a warning if a locally declared variable of an abstract type isn't initialized immediately following the module initializations.

Finally, the driver calls some of the specified functions. Effects that are fully constrained by specifications, such as the result returned by fire, are checked internally. Where the specification allows a variety of acceptable effects, output is printed so it can be checked by hand or by a test harness (against previous runs).

```
#include <stdio.h>
#include "bool.h"
#include "gender.h"
#include "employee.h"
#include "empset.h"
#include "dbase.h"

int main(int argc, char *argv[]) {

    employee e;
    empset es;
    empset *emptr;
    char na[10000];
    int i, j;
    dbase_status stat;
    dbase_q q;

/* Initialize the LCL-specified modules that were included */
    bool_initMod();
    gender_initMod();
    employee_initMod();
    empset_initMod();
    dbase_initMod();

/* Initialize all of the variables of abstract types */
    empset_init(&es);
```

Figure 19: drive.c fragment, part 1

```
/* Perform tests */
    for (i = 0; i < 20; i++) {
        e.ssNum = i;
        e.salary = 1000 * i;
        if (i < 10) e.gen = MALE; else e.gen = FEMALE;
        if (i < 15) e.j = NONMGR; else e.j = MGR;
        (void) sprintf(na, "J. Doe %d", i);
        employee_setName(&e, na);
        if ( (i/2)*2 == i) hire(e);
            else {uncheckedHire(e); stat = hire(e);}
        }
    if (stat == duplERR) printf("Error 1: Duplicate not found\n");

    (void) dbase_sprint(na);
    printf("Should print 20 employees:\n%s\n", na);

    dbase_initMod();  /* Should have no effect */

    if (!fire(17)) printf("Error 2: 17 not fired\n");

    q.g = FEMALE; q.j = job_ANY; q.l = 15800; q.h = 18500;
    if ((i = query(q, &es)) != 2)
        printf("Error 3: Wrong number found %d\n", i);
    (void) empset_sprint(na, &es);
    printf("Should print two employees: \n%s\n", na);

    /* ... */
}
```

Figure 19: drive.c fragment, part 2

```
imports employee;

constant int eref_maxPrintSize = employee_maxPrintSize + 27;

abstract type employee ref eref;

uses sprint(eref, char[]);

int eref_sprint(char s[], eref er) {
    requires maxIndex(s) >= eref_maxPrintSize;
    modifies s;
    ensures isSprint(s', er)
            /\  result = lenStr(s') /\ result <= eref_maxPrintSize;
    }
void eref_initMod(void) {
    ensures true;
    }
```

Figure 20: eref.lcl

2.6   Eref

Now we move down a level of abstraction, and specify some modules that
are useful in implementing the modules defined above. The next example
introduces a new kind of type constructor. The constructor *ref* is a more
abstract version of the * used in exposed types. Like all abstract types, values
of ref types can be accessed only through the functions exported from the
interface in which they are declared. Unlike other abstract types, however,
the interface implicitly exports a constant and four functions (type_alloc,
type_free, type_set, and type_get) in addition to those explicitly specified in
the .lcl-file. The functions correspond to builtin operations on C pointers.
Since their meaning is determined by LCL, they do not appear explicitly in
the .lcl-file, but they must be implemented.

Figure 20 exports a ref type, eref. Figure 21 specifies its four implicitly
exported functions, using a subset of LCL's pointer operations. The functions
eref_free, eref_set and eref_get have unconstrained behavior when they are

```
imports eref;

constant eref erefNIL = NIL;

eref eref_alloc(void) {
   ensures fresh(*result);
   }
void eref_free(eref er) {
   requires er != erefNIL;
   modifies *er;
   ensures trashed(*er);
   }
void eref_set(eref er, employee e) {
   requires er != erefNIL;
   modifies *er;
   ensures (*er)' = e;
   }
employee eref_get(eref er) {
   requires er != erefNIL;
   ensures result = (*er)^;
   }
```

Figure 21: eref.lcl's implied interface

called with erefNIL.

Unlike LCL's other abstract types, ref types can be assigned using =, passed as parameters, returned from functions, and compared using ==. Since they can be assigned, there is no need for the type initialization function that must be provided for other abstract types.

Refs can be used in much the same way as pointers: to create sharing in data structures, to assign large objects inexpensively and pass them into and out of functions, to check inexpensively whether two objects are the same, to handle data structures whose size varies dynamically, etc.

There are some operations on pointers that are not available for ref types. There is no arithmetic on ref types. Although LCL allows the use of * and -> on ref types in specifications, LCLint won't allow their use on ref types in

```
#include "bool.h"
#include "employee.h"

extern eref eref_alloc(void);
extern void eref_free(eref er);
extern void eref_set(eref er, employee e);
extern employee eref_get(eref er);
extern int eref_sprint(char s□ , eref er);
extern void eref_initMod(void);
```

Figure 22: eref.lh

client code. Instead, clients must use the functions exported by the interface.

Though ref types are more limited than pointer types, using them has some advantages:

- It provides a level of abstraction. The implementor can change the implementation, e.g., from a pointer to an index into an array, without worrying about invalidating client code.

- It allows private storage management, even if the chosen representation is a pointer. For example, a compacting storage manager can be written, since all access must be via functions in the module.

- It is more general, allowing references to data that is in another address space, on another machine, on a disk, etc.

Figure 22 contains the .lh-file generated by LCL from eref.lcl. Notice that it includes prototypes for the implicit functions.

Figures 23 and 24 contain an implementation of eref. It is not a particularly interesting implementation, but it does show that there is considerable freedom in implementing ref types. The only constraints are that the top-level representation (int here) is assignable and comparable (using ==), and that implementations of the exported functions meet their specifications. Because the implementation variable eref_Pool is used in three macro definitions, C requires it to be declared *extern* in eref.h, even though clients of eref are not supposed to reference it—or even know about its existence, since it doesn't appear in eref.lcl.

```
#if !defined(eref_h_expanded)
#define eref_h_expanded

#define eref_maxPrintSize (employee_maxPrintSize + 27)

#include "employee.h"

typedef int eref;

/* Private type defs used in macros.  */
typedef enum {used, avail} eref_status;
typedef struct {employee * conts;
                eref_status * status;
                int size;
                int index;} eref_ERP;

extern eref_ERP eref_Pool;

#include "eref.lh"

#define erefNIL (-1)
#define eref_free(er)  (eref_Pool.status[er] = avail)
#define eref_set(er, e) (eref_Pool.conts[er] = e)
#define eref_get(er) (eref_Pool.conts[er])
#endif
```

Figure 23: eref.h

```c
#include <stdio.h>
#include "eref.h"

eref_ERP eref_Pool;      /* private */
static bool needsInit = TRUE;  /* private */

eref eref_alloc(void) {
  int i, res;
  int * tmp;

  for (i=0;
       (eref_Pool.status[i] == used) && (i < eref_Pool.size);
       i++);
  res = i;
  eref_Pool.status[res] = used;
  if (res == eref_Pool.size - 1) {
    eref_Pool.conts =
     (employee *) realloc(eref_Pool.conts,
                          2*eref_Pool.size*sizeof(employee));
    eref_Pool.status =
     (eref_status *) realloc(eref_Pool.status,
                          2*eref_Pool.size*sizeof(eref_status));
    eref_Pool.size = 2*eref_Pool.size;
    for (i = res+1; i < eref_Pool.size; i++)
        eref_Pool.status[i] = avail;
  }
  return (eref) res;
}
int eref_sprint(char s[], eref er) {
  int len;
  (void) sprintf(s, "eref: %d. Employee: ", (int) er);
  len = strlen(s);
  return len + employee_sprint(&(s[len]), eref_get(er));
}
```

Figure 24: eref.c, part 1

```
void eref_initMod(void) {
  int i;
  const int size = 2;

 /* So that initMod will be idempotent */
  if (needsInit == FALSE) return;
  needsInit = FALSE;

  bool_initMod();
  employee_initMod();
  eref_Pool.conts = (employee *) malloc(size*sizeof(employee));
  eref_Pool.status =
            (eref_status *) malloc(size*sizeof(eref_status));
  eref_Pool.size = size;
  eref_Pool.index = 0;
  for (i = 0; i < size; i++) eref_Pool.status[i] = avail;
}
```

Figure 24: eref.c, part 2

2.7 Erc

Figure 27 specifies functions operating on an abstract type, erc (for employee ref collection), that contains erefs. An erc is basically a bag with a pair of functions that make it possible to iterate over its elements. It is used in the implementation of empset and dbase.

The iteration functions add some complexity to the specification. This shows up most notably in erc.lsl, Figure 25. The partitioned by clause indicates that erc values can be viewed as pairs of bags; the relevant portions

```
erc: trait
  includes bag(eref, erefBag)

  introduces
    { }: -> erc
    add, yield, delete: eref, erc -> erc
    val, wereYielded, toYield: erc -> erefBag
    __ \in __: eref, erc -> Bool

  asserts
    erc generated by { }, add, yield
    erc partitioned by val, wereYielded
    forall ic: erc, e, e1: eref
      val({ }) == { };
      val(add(e, ic)) == insert(e, val(ic));
      val(yield(e, ic)) == val(ic);
      val(delete(e, ic)) == delete(e, val(ic));

      wereYielded({ }) == { };
      wereYielded(add(e, ic)) == wereYielded(ic);
      wereYielded(yield(e, ic)) == insert(e, wereYielded(ic));
      wereYielded(delete(e, ic)) == delete(e, wereYielded(ic));

      toYield(ic) == val(ic) - wereYielded(ic);

      e \in ic == e \in val(ic)
```

Figure 25: erc.lsl

```
bag(Elem, Bag): trait
  introduces
    { }: -> Bag
    insert, delete: Elem, Bag -> Bag
    __ \in __: Elem, Bag -> Bool
    {__}: Elem -> Bag
    __ \union __, __ - __: Bag, Bag -> Bag
    % ...

  asserts
    Bag generated by { }, insert
    Bag partitioned by \in, delete
    forall e, e1: Elem, b, b1: Bag
      {e} == insert(e, { });
      delete(e, { }) == { };
      delete(e, insert(e1, b)) ==
              if e = e1 then b else insert(e1, delete(e, b));
      not(e \in { });
      e \in insert(e1, b) == e = e1 \/ e \in b;
      b \union { } == b;
      b \union insert(e, b1) == insert(e, b) \union b1;
      b - { } == b;
      b - insert(e, b1) == delete(e, b - b1)
      % ...
```

Figure 26: bag.lsl fragment

of bag.lsl are given in Figure 26. The operator val maps an erc to the bag of erefs that have been inserted (and not deleted). The operator wereYielded maps an erc to the bag of values that have been marked as yielded (by the yield operator). The derived operator toYield maps an erc to the bag of values that remain to be yielded. These operators are used in the specification of the functions erc_iterStart and erc_yield.

```
imports eref;

abstract type erc;

uses erc, sprint(erc, char[]);

void erc_init(erc *c) {
   modifies *c;
   ensures (*c)' = { };
   }
void erc_clear(erc *c) {
   modifies *c;
   ensures (*c)' = { };
   }
void erc_insert(erc *c, eref er) {
   modifies *c;
   ensures (*c)' = add(er, (*c)^);
   }
bool erc_delete(erc *c, eref er) {
   modifies *c;
   ensures result = er \in (*c)^
          /\ (*c)' = delete(er, (*c)^);
   }
bool erc_member(eref er, erc *c) {
   ensures result = er \in (*c)^;
}
```

Figure 27: erc.lcl, part 1

```
eref erc_iterStart(erc *c) {
   modifies *c;
   ensures if val((*c)^) = { }
              then result = erefNIL /\ unchanged(*c)
              else result \in val((*c)^)
                  /\ val((*c)') = val((*c)^)
                  /\ wereYielded((*c)') = {result};
   }
eref erc_yield(erc *c) {
   modifies *c;
   ensures if toYield((*c)^) = { }
              then result = erefNIL /\ unchanged(*c)
              else result \in toYield((*c)^)
                  /\ (*c)'= yield(result, (*c)^);
   }
void erc_join(erc *c1, erc *c2) {
    modifies *c1;
    ensures val((*c1)') = val((*c1)^) \union val((*c2)^)
           /\ wereYielded((*c1)') = { };
    }
int erc_sprint(char s[], erc *c) {
    requires maxIndex(s) >= (size(val((*c)^)) * eref_maxPrintSize);
    modifies s;
    ensures isSprint(s', (*c)^)
           /\ result = lenStr(s')
           /\ result <= (size(val((*c)^)) * eref_maxPrintSize);
    }
void erc_initMod(void) {
   ensures true;
   }
void erc_final(erc *c) {
   modifies *c;
   ensures trashed(*c);
   }
```

Figure 27: erc.lcl, part 2

Typically, client code that uses these functions will be of the form,

```
eref er;
erc s;
. . .
for(er = erc_iterStart(s);
    er != erefNIL;
    er = erc_yield(s)) {
        Body of loop that does something with each er from s.
    }
```

If the body of the loop were guaranteed not to change the erc being iterated over, both the specification and the implementation of erc could be considerably simplified. However, such a restriction is not usually reasonable. Allowing for modifications within the body of the loop raises several questions about the semantics of the functions, among them,

- If an element is inserted in the erc within the body of the loop will it be yielded?

- If, within the body of the loop, an element gets deleted before it has been yielded does it get yielded?

- If, within the body of the loop, an element gets yielded, deleted and then reinserted, does it get yielded again?

The answers, according to this specification, are Yes, No, and Yes, respectively.

Again, the implementation is not presented here, but does appear in the report from which this material is excerpted.

2.8   Ereftab

Ereftab, Figures 28 and 29, is the last module in our example. It is used to create a one-to-one mapping from employees to erefs. It makes it unnecessary to store multiple copies of the same employee record within the implementation of empset.

The intended use of ereftab_insert is to put an employee in the table only after a lookup has failed to find an eref for that employee. The requires clause of ereftab_insert formalizes this property, and allows the implementation not to duplicate a test that has just been made by the client.

The implementation of ereftab is unremarkable, and is not presented.

```
imports employee, eref;

abstract type ereftab;

uses ereftab, sprint(ereftab, char[]);

void ereftab_init(ereftab *t) {
   modifies *t;
   ensures (*t)' = empty;
   }
eref ereftab_insert(ereftab *t, employee e) {
   requires getERef((*t)^, e) = erefNIL;
   modifies *t;
   ensures (*t)' = add((*t)^, e, result) /\ fresh(*result);
   }
bool ereftab_delete(ereftab *t, eref er) {
   modifies *t, *er;
   ensures result = in((*t)^, er)
       /\ (if result
            then (*t)' = delete((*t)^, er) /\ trashed(*er)
            else unchanged(*t, *er));
   }
```

Figure 28: ereftab.lcl, part 1

```
eref ereftab_lookup(employee e, ereftab *t) {
    ensures result = getERef((*t)^, e);
    }
int ereftab_sprint(char s[], ereftab *t) {
    requires maxIndex(s) >= (size((*t)^) * eref_maxPrintSize);
    modifies s;
    ensures isSprint(s', (*t)^)
            /\ result = lenStr(s')
            /\ result <= (size((*t)^) * eref_maxPrintSize);
    }
void ereftab_final(ereftab *t) {
    modifies *t, reach((*t)^);
    ensures trashed(*t)
            /\ \forall e:employee
                ((getERef((*t)^, e) != erefNIL)
                => trashed(*getERef((*t)^, e)));
    }
void ereftab_initMod(void) {
    ensures true;
    }
```

Figure 28: ereftab.lcl, part 2

```
ereftab: trait

includes integer

introduces
   empty: -> ereftab
   add: ereftab, employee, eref -> ereftab
   delete: ereftab, eref -> ereftab
   getERef: ereftab, employee -> eref
   erefNIL: -> eref
   in: ereftab, eref -> bool
   size: ereftab -> int

asserts
   ereftab generated by empty, add
   ereftab partitioned by getERef

   forall e, e1: employee, er, er1: eref, t: ereftab
     delete(empty, er) == empty;
     delete(add(t, e, er), er1) ==
        if er = er1 then t else add(delete(t, er1), e, er);

     in(empty, er) == false;
     in(add(t, e, er), er1) == er = er1 \/ in(t, er);

     getERef(empty, e1) == erefNIL;
     getERef(add(t, e, er), e1) ==
        if e = e1 then er else getERef(t, e1);

     size(empty) == 0;
     size(add(t, e, er)) == 1 + (if in(t, er) then 0 else 1)
```

Figure 29: ereftab.lsl

```
typedef struct _elem{eref val; struct _elem *next;} ercElem;
typedef ercElem * ercSet;
typedef struct {ercSet vals; ercSet nextY; ercSet prevY;} erc;
```

Figure 30: erc's representation

2.9   Notes on the implementations

Here we take opportunity to make some comments about the relationship of these specifications to the implementations presented in the report from which this material is excerpted.

In writing specifications, the emphasis is entirely on ease of understanding. Code should be reasonably easy to understand, but efficiency must also be considered. Consider, for example, the representation for ercs, Figure 30. Though the specification is written as if an erc consists of a pair of bags, the implementation uses a single linked list and three pointers into it. The pointer val points to the head of the list, prevY to the most recently yielded element, and nextY to the element to be yielded next. Within erc.c, erc is treated as an exposed type, that is, erc values are treated as structs. LCLint will allow this exposure within the implementation of an interface, even though it will generate an error message if client code attempts to treat an erc as a struct.

The implementation of empset uses an erc to represent an empset, Figure 31. It also uses a non-exported module-level variable, known, of type ereftab, declared in empset.c. Known is used to avoid allocating space for the same employee multiple times. The first time an employee is inserted into any empset it is also inserted into known and a newly allocated eref is inserted into the erc. On subsequent inserts of the same employee into any empset, the old eref is reused. This auxiliary data structure is shared by the implementation of all objects of type empset, but this sharing is not visible to clients.

The implementation of dbase is considerably longer than that of the other modules specified here. It is also somewhat different in structure. Unlike empset.h and erc.h, dbase.h contains no typedef (though it does inherit typedefs, of exposed type, from dbase.lh). This is because dbase.lcl exports no abstract types and the implementation of dbase doesn't use any macros

```
typedef erc empset;    /* This is in empset.h  */

ereftab known; /* This is in empset.c */
```

Figure 31: empset's representation

```
#define firstERC mMGRS
#define lastERC fNON
#define numERCS (lastERC - firstERC + 1)

typedef enum {mMGRS, fMGRS, mNON, fNON} employeeKinds;

erc db[numERCS];

/* Invariant: The data base is partitioned by
   val(db[mMGRS]), val(db[mNON]), val(db[fMGRS]), val(db[fNON]) */

bool initDone = FALSE;
```

Figure 32: dbase.c fragment

that depend on locally defined types. Information pertinent to compiling only the implementation itself is restricted to dbase.c, Figure 32.

The private variables d and initNeeded from dbase.lcl are implemented by the variables db and initDone, in dbase.c. We chose different names for the variables in the implementation to emphasize that there is no necessary correspondence between module-level variables appearing in the implementation and private variables appearing in the specification. It is purely accidental that both of our private specification variables correspond to single implementation variables; one of our earlier implementations of the interface used four distinct ercs to represent d.

The correctness of the implementations of the functions in dbase.c depends upon the maintenance of a representation invariant. That this holds can be shown by an inductive argument:

- It is established by dbase_initMod,

- For each function specified in dbase.lcl, if the invariant and the requires clause hold on entry, the invariant will hold upon termination. In discharging this step of the proof, it is necessary to examine even those functions whose specification does not allow them to modify d, since they might still modify the representation of d.

The implementation of dbase includes several functions that do not appear in dbase.lcl and therefore are not accessible to clients. It would be acceptable for these functions to break the invariant temporarily (though, in fact, they don't).

3 Summary

We have tried to present enough information to allow the C programmer to begin to use LCL. Our example specifications demonstrate most features of the language. Our example implementations illustrate a style of C programming in which specifications are used to establish firewalls between modules.

People writing client programs need look only at the specifications to discover what they need to know about the functional behavior of the modules that they use. This saves them the trouble of examining the code (which, even given our rather simplistic implementations, is considerably longer than the specifications). Furthermore, it increases the likelihood of client programs continuing to work despite changes to the implementations of of modules that they are built on.

LCL 1.0 is not sufficiently expressive to to specify all reasonable modules that one might implement in C. For example, there is no provision made for function parameters and no treatment of concurrency. We expect to address both of these in a future version.

Despite these omissions, we feel that LCL 1.0 is ready for practical use. Many modules of most programs can be well-specified using LCL. The LSL and LCL checkers, though still under development, have proved extremely useful in early trials. The development of LCLint is underway, and we believe that such a tool, combined with careful specifications, can uncover a large number of typical errors.

A Tutorial on the Refinement Calculus

J.C.P. Woodcock

Oxford University Computing Laboratory

Programming Research Group

The following three papers, "The Refinement Calculus", "An Introduction to Refinement in Z", and "Two Refinement Case Studies", constitute a tutorial on the use of Morgan's refinement calculus.

The first paper introduces the calculus and illustrates its basic laws with two small case studies. It is important to see how such a calculus might be used as part of a development process, and the second paper describes one possible development process for the Z notation. Part of this process involves the use of the refinement calculus for producing code from concrete mathematical descriptions. The third paper gives slightly longer examples of developments. In both case studies, the data refinement and the operation decomposition are performed using calculational techniques.

The Refinement Calculus

J.C.P. Woodcock
Oxford University Computing Laboratory
Programming Research Group

Abstract

In this paper we introduce the refinement calculus,[1] and describe a number of basic Laws governing its use. We describe the guarded command language and how its constructs may be introduced during the development of code from specifications. Each Law of the calculus is illustrated with an example of its use; at the end of the Section, most of these Laws are demonstrated with a suitable case study.

1   The Specification Statement

The refinement calculus contains a language of guarded commands and *specification statements*. The anatomy of a specification statement is

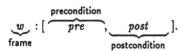

The frame is a—possibly empty—list of variables, and the precondition and postcondition are each a predicate on a single state: the before-state and the after-state, respectively. The specification statement describes a task for an implementor: a program is required that terminates whenever *pre* is true, and when it does so, it produces a correct result, satisfying *post*. The specification statement is pronounced in something like the following manner:

> By changing only the variables *w*, and by assuming that the state satisfies *pre*, change it so that it satisfies *post*.

At the specification level, it is important to remember that if we don't mention the fate of a variable in an operation, then anything might happen to its value. An operation is a relation, and we constrain its behaviour further by adding a stonger predicate. In a sequential programming language such as Pascal, if a program statement doesn't mention a variable (in an assignment for example), then it doesn't change. In the refinement calculus, we see a half-way house: if a variable is not in the frame, then, as in a programming language, it cannot be changed, no matter what we say in the postcondition; if it is mentioned in the frame, then it may be changed, and we can constrain its after-value by adding a stonger predicate.

---

[1]For a more detailed exposition of the calculus, see (Morgan, 1990). However, the reader should be aware of many minor notational differences between that text and this. These have arisen because of our integration of the calculus with the notations of Z.

In a specification statement, the precondition and postcondition are separated, but note that the postcondition is not a predicate on a pair of states, as is the case in a Z schema or a VDM operation.

Example 1 *The operation that finds the root in the interval $[a, b]$ of a continuous function f, providing that it has one, is*

$$Bisect \; \hat{=} \; m : [f(a) \times f(b) \leq 0 \wedge a \leq b, |f(m)| < 0.1 \wedge a \leq m \leq b].$$

2 Extremities

Certain specification statements have particular names. The specification statement "$w : [false, true]$" is called **abort**. It is never guaranteed to terminate (it has precondition *false*); if it does terminate, it might produce any result (postcondition *true*).

The specification statement "$w : [true, true]$" is called **choose** w. It is always guaranteed to terminate, but it might produce any result.

The specification statement "$: [true, true]$" is called **skip**. It is always guaranteed to terminate, without changing anything (its frame is empty).

The specification statement "$w : [true, false]$" is called **magic**. It is always guaranteed to terminate, and when it does so, it establishes the impossible (a state satisfying *false*).

3 Some Simple Laws

A program in the refinement calculus may consist of a single specification statement, or it may consist entirely of code in the guarded command language, or it may consist of a mixture of specification statements and code. An example of the latter is

$$x, y : [x = X \wedge y = Y, x = X - Y \wedge y = X]; \; x := y - x.$$

The task of developing code in the refinement calculus usually starts with a single specification statement, goes through several intermediate stages of mixed programs, and ends up with code in the guarded command language, free from specification statements. If a program contains no specification statements, then we call it *code*. In this Section, we give some Laws for refining programs.

One way of improving a specification is to do more than was required. Thus, if *post'* is a stronger predicate than *post*, then any client who was satisfied with $w : [pre, post]$ must also be satisfied with $w : [pre, post']$.[2] This corresponds to the removal of non-determinism.

Law 1 (strengthen postcondition "sp") If *post'* $\Rightarrow$ *post* then

$$w : [pre, post] \sqsubseteq w : [pre, post'].$$

---

[2]Remember that in this example, and in what follows, *post'* is just another mathematical variable.

Example 2 *Since $x < 0.01 \Rightarrow x < 0.1$, we have that*

$$m : [f(a) \times f(b) \le 0 \wedge a \le b, |f(m)| < 0.1 \wedge a \le m \le b]$$
$$\sqsubseteq \text{``sp''} \quad m : [f(a) \times f(b) \le 0 \wedge a \le b, |f(m)| < 0.01 \wedge a \le m \le b].$$

This refinement step has improved the accuracy of the result computed by this specifcation statement.

Another simple way of improving a specification is to make it apply to more situations than was asked for. Thus, if *pre'* is a weaker predicate than *pre*, then any client who was satisfied with $w : [pre, post]$ must also be satisfied with $w : [pre', post]$, since it works at least as often. This corresponds to the widening of preconditions.

Law 2 (weaken precondition "wp") If $pre \Rightarrow pre'$ then

$$w : [pre, post] \sqsubseteq w : [pre', post].$$

Example 3 *Since*

$$f(a) \times f(b) \le 0 \wedge a \le b \Rightarrow f(a) \times f(b) \le 0,$$

we have that

$$m : [f(a) \times f(b) \le 0 \wedge a \le b, |f(m)| < 0.01 \wedge a \le m \le b]$$
$$\sqsubseteq \text{``wp''} \quad m : [f(a) \times f(b) \le 0, |f(m)| < 0.01 \wedge a \le m \le b].$$

This refinement step means that we now require an implementation to produce a correct result even when a and b don't describe an interval. It seems that we have given up too much: if $b < a$, then the postcondition is not going to be satisfiable.

Definition 1 (feasibility) $w : [pre, post]$ is feasible iff

$$pre \Rightarrow \exists w : T \bullet post.$$

Recalling our definition of the precondition of an operation defined using a schema, we can see that feasibility is a check that the predicate that we claim is the precondition, *pre*, is at least as strong as the real precondition. If a specification is infeasible, then we cannot refine it to code; all code is feasible. Thus, an infeasible specification cannot lead to incorrect code, since it cannot lead to any code at all. For this reason, we are not *obliged* to perform feasibility checks during our development; however, there is always the opportunity of doing so.

Example 4 *Since*

$$\neg(f(a) \times f(b) \le 0 \Rightarrow \exists m \bullet |f(m)| < 0.01 \wedge a \le m \le b)$$

the specification

$$m : [f(a) \times f(b) \le 0, |f(m)| < 0.01 \wedge a \le m \le b]$$

is infeasible.

Law 3 (assignment "assI") If $pre \Rightarrow post[E/w]$ then[3]

$$w, x : [pre, post] \sqsubseteq w := E.$$

Example 5 *Since* $x = X - Y \wedge y = Y \Rightarrow (x = X - Y \wedge y = X)[(x + y)/y]$, *we have*

$$x, y : [x = X - Y \wedge y = Y, x = X - Y \wedge y = X]$$
$$\sqsubseteq \text{"assI"} \quad y := x + y.$$

Since $x = X \wedge y = Y \Rightarrow (x = X - Y \wedge y = Y)[(x - y)/x]$, *we have*

$$x, y : [x = X \wedge y = Y, x = X - Y \wedge y = Y]$$
$$\sqsubseteq \text{"assI"} \quad x := x - y.$$

Since $x = X - Y \wedge y = X \Rightarrow (x = Y \wedge y = X)[(y - x)/x]$, *we have*

$$x, y : [x = X - Y \wedge y = X, x = Y \wedge y = X]$$
$$\sqsubseteq \text{"assI"} \quad x := y - x.$$

In the refinement calculus, we introduce program variables using a declaration that is rather like an axiomatic definition: we name the variables, say what sets they range over, and add an invariant.

Law 4 (introduce local block "varI") If w and x are disjoint, then

$$
\begin{aligned}
&w : [pre, post] \sqsubseteq \\
&\quad \| [\ var\ x : T \mid inv \bullet \\
&\qquad\quad w, x : [pre, post] \\
&\quad] \| .
\end{aligned}
$$

Example 6

Bisect

$= \text{"by definition"}$

$\quad m : [f(a) \times f(b) \le 0 \wedge a \le b, \mid f(m) \mid < 0.1 \wedge a \le m \le b]$

$\sqsubseteq \text{"varI"}$

$\quad \| [\ var\ x, y \bullet$

$\qquad x, y, m : [f(a) \times f(b) \le 0 \wedge a \le b, \mid f(m) \mid < 0.1 \wedge a \le m \le b]$

$\quad] \| .$

---

[3]In (Morgan, 1990), the notation for substitution $P[t/x]$ (P with term t consistently substituted for free occurrences of the variable x) is not used; instead, a notation for *replacement* is used, $P[x \backslash t]$ (P with free occurrences of the variable x replaced by term t). Replacement is more suggestive of the refinement rule for assignment; substitution is a standard notation.

We usually abbreviate this as

> *Bisect*
>
> $\sqsubseteq$ var x, y •
>
> $x, y, m : [f(a) \times f(b) \le 0 \wedge a \le b, | f(m) | < 0.1 \wedge a \le m \le b].$

The presence of invariants means that we must tighten up our notion of feasibility.

Definition 2 (feasibility) $w : [pre, post]$ is feasible iff

$$pre \wedge inv \Rightarrow \exists w : T \bullet inv \wedge post.$$

Law 5 (skip command "skipI") If $pre \Rightarrow post$ then

$$w : [pre, post] \sqsubseteq \text{skip}.$$

Example 7 *Since $x = 5 \wedge y = x^3 \Rightarrow x = 5$, we have that*

> $x, y : [x = 5 \wedge y = x^3, x = 5]$
>
> $\sqsubseteq$ skip.

Law 6 (sequential composition "semI") For any predicate *mid*

> $w : [pre, post]$
>
> $\sqsubseteq w : [pre, mid]; \ w : [mid, post].$

Example 8 *Suppose that we want to swap two variables, and, perversely, we don't want to use a local variable to store the intermediate value. The development of the code is as follows:*

> $x, y : [x = X \wedge y = Y, x = Y \wedge y = X]$
>
> $\sqsubseteq$ "semI"
>
> > $x, y : [x = X \wedge y = Y, x = X - Y \wedge y = X];$ [◁]
> >
> > $x, y : [x = X - Y \wedge y = X, x = Y \wedge y = X]$ [†]
>
> $\sqsubseteq$ "semI"
>
> > $x, y : [x = X \wedge y = Y, x = X - Y \wedge y = Y];$ [◁]
> >
> > $x, y : [x = X - Y \wedge y = Y, x = X - Y \wedge y = X]$ [†]
>
> $\sqsubseteq$ "assI" $x := x - y$
>
> ‡ $\sqsubseteq$ "assI" $y := x + y$
>
> † $\sqsubseteq$ "assI" $x := y - x.$

Note the use of marginal markers. We shall be using a convention that the left-hand ($\triangleleft$) always points to the next part of the program to be refined. Other marginal markers, such as the obelisk and double obelisk used here, refer to parts of the program whose development proceeds at a later point. Thus, we end up with a flattened tree as the record of the development. It is not difficult to see how the tree may be walked in order to extract the code from the development. If we do this, we obtain

$$x, y : [x = X \wedge y = Y, x = Y \wedge y = X]$$
$$\sqsubseteq$$

$$x := x - y;$$
$$y := x + y;$$
$$x := y - x.$$

It is easier to see the final code once it has been retrieved from the development; however, it becomes more difficult to see how it was obtained once the development record has been thrown away. 📖

Very often, we require combinations of some of the previous basic Laws. The following is a good example of this.

Law 7 (following assignment "fassI") For any term E

$$w, x : [pre, post]$$
$$\sqsubseteq w : [pre, post[E/x]]; \ x := E.$$

This is an easy Law to apply. First we decide upon the assignment that we would like to perform, then we calculate the new specification statement. 📖

4 Conditional Statements

In the guarded command language, the conditional statement has the form

if $G_1 \rightarrow com_1$
□ $G_2 \rightarrow com_2$
$\vdots$
□ $G_n \rightarrow com_n$
fi.

Each of the branches $G_i \rightarrow com_i$ is called a guarded command, with G_i the guard, and com_i the command. When the conditional is activated the guards $G_1, G_2, \ldots, G_n$ are evaluated, and one of the commands whose guard is true is executed. If no guard is true, then the program aborts. A more compact notation for the conditional uses a generalised notation

if □ $i \bullet G_i \rightarrow com_i$ fi.

Law 8 (conditional "ifI") If $pre \Rightarrow \bigvee i \bullet G_i$ then

$$w : [pre, post]$$
$$\sqsubseteq \text{if } \square \ i \bullet G_i \rightarrow w : [G_i \wedge pre, post] \text{ fi}.$$

Whenever the specification is required to terminate, the conditional must not abort; thus the pre-condition must establish that at least one guard is true. Whichever branch is taken must implement the specification, but we can strengthen the precondition with the guard in the knowledge that it must be true for that branch to have been taken.

Example 9 *Given two variables x and y, we require a program that will ensure that $x \leq y$, by preserving their values, or swapping them if necessary:*

$$x, y : [x = X \wedge y = Y, (X \leq Y \Rightarrow x = X \wedge y = Y) \wedge (Y \leq X \Rightarrow x = Y \wedge y = X)]$$
$$\sqsubseteq \text{ "iff"}$$
$$\quad \text{if } x \leq y \rightarrow x, y : [x \leq y \wedge x = X \wedge y = Y,$$
$$\quad\quad (X \leq Y \Rightarrow x = X \wedge y = Y) \wedge (Y \leq X \Rightarrow x = Y \wedge y = X)] \quad\quad [\triangleleft]$$
$$\quad \square \; y \leq x \rightarrow x, y : [y \leq x \wedge x = X \wedge y = Y,$$
$$\quad\quad (X \leq Y \Rightarrow x = X \wedge y = Y) \wedge (Y \leq X \Rightarrow x = Y \wedge y = X)] \quad\quad [\triangleright]$$
$$\quad \text{fi}$$
$$\sqsubseteq \text{skip}$$
$$\dagger \sqsubseteq \text{ "assI"} \quad x, y := y, x.$$

Notice that the disjunction of the guards is true, thus validating the introduction of the conditional. The program is

$$\text{if } x \leq y \rightarrow \text{skip}$$
$$\square \; y \leq x \rightarrow x, y := y, x$$
$$\text{fi}.$$

5 Logical Constants

The capital letters that have appeared in our programs in this paper are called *logical constants*, and they are not code. They are in fact an extremely helpful logical device. Since they are not code, they must be eliminated in order to reach the final program in a development. The proper declaration of a logical constant is

$$\|[\text{con } X : T \bullet prog]\| \, .$$

This introduces a logical constant named X, which ranges over T. Its scope is delimited by the local block brackets. We can think of con X as choosing a value for X which makes subsequent preconditions *true*, if possible. This is a kind of *angelic non-determinism*, and may be contrasted with var x, which is *demonic*. Logical constants should not be confused with the sort of constants that one might find in a real programming language. For example, one might wish to declare a constant whose value is the maximum integer on some machine. This is done in the guarded command language by introducing a variable, and constraining it to be constant:

$$
\begin{aligned}
&[\![\\
&\quad \mathbf{var}\ maxint : \mathsf{N}\ |\ maxint = 32768\ \bullet \\
&\quad\ \vdots \\
&]\!]\ .
\end{aligned}
$$

Example 10 *We want to specify a program that must strictly increase a variable x twice:*

$$[\![\ \mathbf{con}\ X \bullet x : [x = X, x > X]\ ]\!];\ [\![\ \mathbf{con}\ X \bullet x : [x = X, x > X]\ ]\!]$$

We must be careful of the scope of our logical constants.

Logical constants may be used to give names to things that must exist. A simple example of this is the way in which they may be used to fix the before value of a variable. That is what is being done in the block

$$[\![\ \mathbf{con}\ X \bullet x : [x = X, x > X]\ ]\!]\ .$$

The logical constant X takes a value that makes subsequent preconditions true, if possible. Within the scope of X, there is only one precondition $x = X$, and so X takes on this value: namely, the value of x before the specification statement. This kind of thing happens so frequently that we introduce an abbreviation.

Abbreviation 1 (initial variables) Zero-subscripted variables in the postcondition of a specification statement refer to the before-values of those variables:

$$
\begin{aligned}
&w : [pre, post] \triangleq \\
&\quad [\![\ \mathbf{con}\ X : T\ \bullet \\
&\quad\qquad w : [pre \wedge x = X, post[X/x_0]] \\
&\quad]\!]\ .
\end{aligned}
$$

The fact that we can use zero-subscripted variables does not change our view that a postcondition is a predicate on a just a single state, since these variables are explained using logical constants.

Example 11

$$
\begin{aligned}
&x : [true, x > x_0] \\
&=\ \text{``by definition''} \\
&\quad [\![\ \mathbf{con}\ X : T \bullet x : [x = X, (x > x_0)[X/x_0]]\ ]\!] \\
&=[\![\ \mathbf{con}\ X : T \bullet x : [x = X, x > X]\ ]\!]\ .
\end{aligned}
$$

$$
\begin{aligned}
&x : [true, x > x_0];\ x : [true, x > x_0] \\
&=\ \text{``by definition''} \\
&\quad [\![\ \mathbf{con}\ X : T \bullet x : [x = X, x > X]\ ]\!];\ [\![\ \mathbf{con}\ X : T \bullet x : [x = X, x > X]\ ]\!]\ .
\end{aligned}
$$

88

More generally, we can introduce a logical constant in much the same way as we would introduce an existential quantifier.

Law 9 (introduce logical constant "conI") If $pre \Rightarrow (\exists\, C : T \bullet pre')$, and C is a fresh name, then

$$w : [pre, post]$$
$$\sqsubseteq [\![\, con\ C : T \bullet w : [pre', post]\,]\!]\,.$$

Getting rid of logical constants is important, since they are not code. If a logical constant is no longer mentioned in a program, then we can eliminate it (again, in much the same way as removing an existential quantifier).

Law 10 (eliminate logical constant "conE") If C occurs nowhere in $prog$, then

$$[\![\, con\ C : T \bullet prog\,]\!] \sqsubseteq prog.$$

If we use initial variables, then we must be careful with the application of certain Laws. The assignment introduction Law must be changed in order to cope with the fact that the precondition and postcondition use different names for the same values.

Law 11 (assignment introduction§ "assI§") If $pre \wedge w = w_0 \Rightarrow post[E/w]$ then

$$w, x : [pre, post] \sqsubseteq w := E$$

Example 12 *Since*

$$x = x_0$$
$$\Leftrightarrow x + 1 = x_0 + 1$$
$$\Leftrightarrow (x = x_0 + 1)[x + 1/x],$$

we have

$$x : [true, x = x_0 + 1] \sqsubseteq x := x + 1.$$

If a zero-subscripted variable is used in a postcondition P, then it refers to the value of the variable before that specification statement. If we break the statement in two using semI, then the zero-subscripted variable in P now refers to the value of the variable *at the mid-point*. The Law is updated to avoid this mistake.

Law 12 (sequential composition introduction§ "semI§") For fresh constants X,

$$w, x : [pre, post]$$
$$\sqsubseteq$$
$$\quad |[\ con\ X\ \bullet$$
$$\qquad x : [pre, mid];$$
$$\qquad w, x : [mid[X/x_0], post[X/x_0]]$$
$$\quad]|\ .$$

The predicate *mid* must not contain initial variables other than x_0.

Example 13

$$x : [true, x = x_0 + 2]$$
$$\sqsubseteq \text{"semI§"}\quad con\ X\ \bullet$$
$$\quad x : [true, x = x_0 + 1];$$
$$\quad x : [x = X + 1, x = X + 2].$$

Law 13 (following assignment "fassI§") For any expression E,

$$w, x : [pre, post]$$
$$\sqsubseteq$$
$$\quad w, x : [pre, post[E/x]]$$
$$\quad x := E$$

Law 14 (leading assignment "lassI§") For any expression E,

$$w, x : [pre[E/x], post[E_0/x_0]]$$
$$\sqsubseteq$$
$$\quad x := E;$$
$$\quad w, x : [pre, post]$$

Finally in this Section, we give a Law for contracting the frame in a specification statement: if we drop the name of a variable from the frame, then it cannot change; thus, we can drop the zero-subscript on any of its occurrences in the postcondition.

Law 15 (contract frame "contF")

$$w, x : [pre, post] \sqsubseteq w : [pre, post[x/x_0]].$$

6 Iteration

In the guarded command language, the loop construct is rather similar in form to the conditional:

do $G_1 \rightarrow com_1$
□ $G_2 \rightarrow com_2$
  ⋮
□ $G_n \rightarrow com_n$
od,

with the generalised notation

do □ $i \bullet G_i \rightarrow com_i$ od.

When the loop is activated the guards $G_1, G_2, \ldots, G_n$ are evaluated, and one of the commands whose guard is true is executed. This is done repeatedly until no guard is true, when the loop terminates. We give a simplified form of the introduction rule, which is applicable to developing a loop with a single branch.

Law 16 (loop introduction 1 "doI1")

$w : [inv, inv \wedge \neg G]$
$\sqsubseteq$ do $G \rightarrow w : [inv \wedge G, inv \wedge 0 \leq V < V_0]$ od.

The task of the developer is to discover an invariant inv, a guard G, and a variant V.

The more general form of the Law involves many branches.

Law 17 (loop introduction "doI")

$w : [inv, inv \wedge \neg(\bigvee i \bullet G_i)]$
$\sqsubseteq$ do □ $i \bullet G_i \rightarrow w : [inv \wedge G_i, inv \wedge 0 \leq V < V_0]$ od.

7 Case Study: The Reset Operation

Consider part of a simple storage manager in an operating system which contains an allocation map b. The map b is represented by a total function from resources, which are called blocks, and are numbered contiguously from 1 to n, to either the name of the user owning the block, or to the special value vacant if no user owns it

$b : (1..n) \rightarrow V.$

User names are drawn from the set U, and the disjoint union type V is defined as

$V ::= \text{vacant} \mid user \langle\!\langle U \rangle\!\rangle.$

The reset operation has the task of assigning the value vacant to every resource in the allocation map. Its specification is given by

$$Reset \triangleq b : [true, \operatorname{ran} b = \{vacant\}].$$

Our first step in developing the code for this rather simple operation is to use an obvious transformation of the postcondition:

$$Reset = b : [true, \forall j : 1..n \bullet b\ j = vacant].$$

The motivation for this is that we intend to implement the operation using a loop, and the universal quantifier points to the way that the loop might be developed. One strategy for loop development is to take such a quantified expression, and replace a constant by a variable. The following shorthand helps us in doing this:

$$freed(i, b) \triangleq \forall j : 1..i \bullet b\ j = vacant.$$

The development of the code follows in rather a detailed manner. The refinement calculus should be used with a light touch, rather than in this heavy-handed manner; however, we go into greater detail so that the reader may follow this, the first case study.

$b : [true, freed(n, b)]$

$\sqsubseteq$ var $j \mid 1 \leq j \leq n+1 \bullet$ [4]

    $j, b : [true, freed(n, b)]$

$\sqsubseteq$ "semI"[5]

    $j, b : [true, freed(j-1, b)];$ [◁]

    $j, b : [freed(j-1, b), freed(n, b)]$ [1]

$\sqsubseteq$ "assI $(freed(j-1, b) \wedge 1 \leq j \leq n+1)[1/j]$"[6]

    $j := 1$

$[1] \sqsubseteq$ "sp $freed(j-1, b) \wedge j = n+1 \Rightarrow freed(n, b)$"[7]

    $j, b : [freed(j-1, b), freed(j-1, b) \wedge j = n+1]$

$\sqsubseteq$ "doI1"[8]

    do $j \neq n+1 \rightarrow$

        $j, b : [j \neq n+1 \wedge freed(j-1, b),$

                $0 \leq n-j+1 < n-j_0+1 \wedge freed(j-1, b)]$

    od

---

[4]The variable j will be used as a loop counter; thus it will range from the smallest element in the domain of b to just after the highest.

[5]We introduce the semicolon in order to choose the loop invariant. At the beginning of the loop, and after each iteration, we will have freed all the blocks up, but not including j. The specification statement before the semicolon must establish the invariant, and the after must be developed into the loop.

[6]If we set j to 1, then we have freed no blocks.

[7]We need to put the invariant into the postcondition before we can apply the loop introduction rule.

[8]We must choose a variant. $n - j + 1$ will do: when we enter the loop with $j = 1$, we have n more iterations to perform.

⊑ "fassI"[9]

$\quad j, b : [j \neq n+1 \wedge freed(j-1,b), j \neq n+1 \wedge freed(j,b)];$ $\qquad$ [◁]

$\quad j := j+1$

⊑ "assI $j \neq n+1 \wedge freed(j-1,b)$

$\qquad \Rightarrow (j \neq n+1 \wedge freed(j,b))[(b \oplus \{j \mapsto \mathsf{vacant}\})/b]$"[10]

$\quad b := b \oplus \{j \mapsto \mathsf{vacant}\}.$

We included the proof obligations as part of the annotations of the refinement steps; here is a summary of those obligations (the trivial arithmetic ones have been discarded):

$freed(0,b)$

$freed(j-1,b) \wedge j = n+1 \Rightarrow freed(n,b)$

$j \neq n+1 \wedge freed(j-1,b) \Rightarrow j \neq n+1 \wedge freed(j, b \oplus \{j \mapsto \mathsf{vacant}\}).$

Obviously, the second predicate follows from Leibnitz's Law; the first and third are simple properties of *freed*.

Summarising our development, we have that

Reset

⊑

$\quad [\![\mathbf{var}\ j \mid 1 \leq j \leq n+1 \bullet$

$\qquad j := 1;$

$\qquad \mathbf{do}\ j \neq n+1 \rightarrow$

$\qquad\qquad b := update(b,j,\mathsf{vacant});$

$\qquad\qquad j := j+1$

$\qquad \mathbf{od}$

$\quad]\!] .$

This might be translated into Pascal as

procedure *Reset*;

$\quad$ for $j := 1$ to n do $b[j] := \mathsf{vacant}.$

8 Case Study: Translating Numbers

We would like to develop an algorithm that converts numbers from a base β to the base 10. For an $n+1$ digit number, a solution that requires more than n multiplications is not acceptable.

The key to this development is to recall Horner's rule about evaluating polynomials:

$$\textstyle\sum_{i=1}^{n} a_i \times z^{i-1} = H_{1,n}$$

---

[9] In the implementation of the body of the loop, we shall need to increment j. Since we started j with the value 1, the assignment to j must be done at the end of the loop.

[10] The only thing left to do is to free the next element of b, that is, the jth element.

where

$$H_{n,n} = a_n$$
$$H_{i,n} = a_i + x \times H_{i+1,n} \qquad \text{for } i < n$$

Now, suppose that we have a number in base β with digits $a_n a_{n-1} \ldots a_2 a_1$, then our algorithm must satisfy the specification

$$d : [true, d = \textstyle\sum_{i=1}^{n} a_i \times \beta^{i-1}].$$

Now, if we substitute β for x in the definitions of H, we obtain

$$G_{n,n} = a_n$$
$$G_{i,n} = a_i + \beta \times G_{i+1,n} \qquad \text{for } i < n$$

and our specification can be rewritten as

$$d : [true, d = G_{1,n}].$$

The strategy for calculating the code for this algorithm is quite clear: we can develop a loop which varies the first index of G. It is easy enough to establish $G_{n,n}$, and we want to end up with $G_{1,n}$, so the loop counter is decreasing, and the invariant will involve $d = G_{j,n}$, for loop counter j.

$$d : [true, d = G_{1,n}]$$

$\sqsubseteq$ **var** $j : 1 .. n$ •

$\qquad d, j : [true, d = G_{1,n}]$

$\sqsubseteq$ "semI"

$\qquad d, j : [true, d = G_{j,n}];$ $\qquad\qquad\qquad\qquad\qquad\qquad\qquad$ [◁]

$\qquad d, j : [d = G_{j,n}, d = G_{1,n}]$ $\qquad\qquad\qquad\qquad\qquad\qquad\qquad$ [†]

$\sqsubseteq$ "assI"

$\qquad d, j := a_n, n$

$† \sqsubseteq$ "sp"

$\qquad d, j : [d = G_{j,n}, d = G_{1,n} \wedge j = 1]$

$\sqsubseteq$ "sp"

$\qquad d, j : [d = G_{j,n}, d = G_{j,n} \wedge j = 1]$

$\sqsubseteq$ "doI"

$\qquad$ **do** $j \neq 1 \rightarrow$

$\qquad\qquad d, j : [j \neq 1 \wedge d = G_{j,n}, 0 \leq j < j_0 \wedge d = G_{j,n}]$

$\qquad$ **od**

$= d, j : [(j \geq 0 \wedge d = G_{j+1,n})[j-1/j], (0 \leq j \leq j_0 \wedge d = G_{j,n})[j_0 - 1/j_0]]$

$\sqsubseteq$ "lassI"

$\qquad j := j - 1;$

$\qquad d, j : [j \geq 0 \wedge d = G_{j+1,n}, 0 \leq j \leq j_0 \wedge d = G_{j,n}]$

$\sqsubseteq$ "doI,conF"

$\qquad d := a_j + x \times d$

Thus, we have derived the following program:

```
|[ var j : 1 .. n •
      d, j := a_n, n;
      do j ≠ 1 →
            j := j − 1;
            d := a_j + x × d
      od
]| .
```

9 Reference

1. C. Morgan, *Programming from Specifications*, Prentice Hall International (1990).

10 Exercises

The first nine exercises are taken from Morgan (1990).

1. Which of the following can be justified by "wp" and "sp"?

    (a) $x : [true, x \geq 0] \sqsubseteq x : [true, x = 0]$.

    (b) $x : [x \geq 0, true] \sqsubseteq x : [x = 0, true]$.

    (c) $x : [x \geq 0, x = 0] \sqsubseteq x : [x = 0, x \geq 0]$.

    (d) $x : [x = 0, x \geq 0] \sqsubseteq x : [x \geq 0, x = 0]$.

    (e) $y : [x > 0, x > y \geq 0] \sqsubseteq y : [true, x > y \geq 0]$.

    (f) $y : [true, x > y \geq 0] \sqsubseteq y : [true, y = 0]$.

    (g) $y : [x > 0, x > y \geq 0] \sqsubseteq y : [true, y = 0]$.

2. Show that anything refines **abort** and that **magic** refines anything.

3. Develop code from the specification

    ```
    |[con X, Y •
          x, y : [x = X ∧ y = Y, x = Y ∧ y = X]
    ]|
    ```

    that uses a local variable to the swap the values.

4. Derive the Following Assignment Law fassI.

5. Write a specification statement that finds a square root y of x if x is non-negative, and sets y to 0 if x is negative. Prove that your answer is feasible.

6. Revise your answer to the last question so that when x is negative initially, the statement still terminates, but without choosing any particular value for y. Prove that your answer is feasible.

7. What is

    $: [false, false]$?

8. An infeasible specification cannot be refined by any code; show that all code is feasible.

9. Prove that

$$\|[\text{con } X \bullet z : [z = X, z = X^4]]\| \sqsubseteq z := z^2; \ z := z^2.$$

10. Develop some code that will sum the elements of an array; that is, it will implement the following specification statement:

$$s : [true, s = \sum_{i=1}^{n} a[i]],$$

for an n-element array a of numbers.

11. Suppose that we have an unordered array of values; develop some code to check whether or not an element x is present in the array.

12. Suppose that the array in the last question is in ascending order; develop some code to check whether or not x is present.

13. Given an integer $r \geq 0$, develop an algorithm that will find the number of non-negative integers i and j such that $i \leq j$ and $i^2 + j^2 = r$.

An Introduction to Refinement in Z

J.C.P. Woodcock
Oxford University Computing Laboratory
Programming Research Group

Abstract

We describe how specifications written in the Z notation may be refined to code. The process
uses a data refinement technique based on schemas, and an operation refinement technique based
on the refinement calculus.

We describe the process of refinement from Z specifications into code as the movement between
ive levels, as depicted in Figure 1. We start from an abstract specification written in Z. By the
process of data refinement, we produce a concrete design. The concrete design may be translated
into the refinement calculus to produce an abstract algorithm. By the process of operation refinement,
we produce a program written in the guarded command language. Finally, the guarded command
program may be translated into the chosen programming language. Two of these processes are
called refinement, and two are translations. There are four notations that will be used: mathematics
and schemas, the refinement calculus, the guarded command language, and the target programming
language, each addressing different aspects of the development process. In this Section, we describe
something about the whole process by giving three examples of program developments. In later
sections, we consider each of the stages in program development in detail.

1 Data Refinement in Z

A specification contains an abstract model of data and the operations upon it; a design contains a
concrete model of data with design decisions, and the concrete operations. The process of producing
a design from a formal specification consists mainly of recording, explaining, and justifying these
decisions. The motivation for refining a specification is two-fold:

- *Implementation:* the design is nearer to the level of the programming language;

- *Efficiency:* the space/time trade-off.

Consider the following two examples of the specification of a system that controls the turnstiles
at the entrances to a football ground.

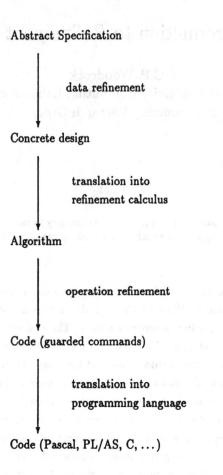

Figure 1: Stages in Program Development

1.1 Specification of a Football Ground Entry System I

Requirements We require a system that will monitor the access to a football ground. The system should keep track of the people who are inside the ground, and forbid entry by more than a specified number of people at any time.

Let P be the set of all football supporters:

$$[P],$$

and let *maxentry* be the maximum number of people that may enter the ground at any time:

$$\vert\ maxentry : \mathbb{N}.$$

The state of our system is given by

```
┌─IB ──────────────────────────────────
│ s : P P
├───────────────────────────────────────
│ #s ≤ maxentry
└───────────────────────────────────────
```

Initially, there is no one in the ground:

$$Init \triangleq [IB' \mid s' = \varnothing]$$

A person who is not already inside the ground may enter it, providing there is enough room:

$$\Delta IB \triangleq IB \wedge IB'$$

```
┌─Enter ───────────────────────────────
│ ΔIB
│ p? : P
├───────────────────────────────────────
│ #s < maxentry
│ p? ∉ s
│ s' = s ∪ {p?}
└───────────────────────────────────────
```

A person who is in the ground may leave it:

```
┌─Leave ───────────────────────────────
│ ΔIB
│ p? : P
├───────────────────────────────────────
│ p? ∈ s
│ s' = s \ {p?}
└───────────────────────────────────────
```

1.2 Specification of a Football Ground Entry System II

Let P be the set of all football supporters:

$$[P],$$

and let *maxentry* be the maximum number of people that may enter the ground at any time:

$$\mid maxentry : \mathbb{N}.$$

The state of our system is given by an injective sequence no longer than *maxentry*:

```
┌─ CIB ─────────────────────────────────
│ l : seq P
├───────────────────────────────────────
│ #l ≤ maxentry
│ l ∈ N ⤖ P
└───────────────────────────────────────
```

The length of l really does calculate the number of people inside the ground, since l contains no duplicates (it is injective). Initially, there is no one in the ground:

$$CInit \cong [CIB' \mid l' = \langle\rangle]$$

A person who is not already inside the ground may enter it, providing there is enough room:

$$\Delta CIB \cong CIB \wedge CIB'$$

```
┌─ CEnter ──────────────────────────────
│ ΔCIB
│ p? : P
├───────────────────────────────────────
│ #l < maxentry
│ p? ∉ ran l
│ l' = l ⌢ ⟨p?⟩
└───────────────────────────────────────
```

A person who is in the ground may leave it:[1]

```
┌─ CLeave ──────────────────────────────
│ ΔCIB
│ p? : P
├───────────────────────────────────────
│ p? ∈ ran l
│ l' = l ↾ (P \ {p?})
└───────────────────────────────────────
```

---

[1] Recall that ↾ is the filter operation on sequences. The sequence $t \upharpoonright S$ is obtained by removing all those elements of t not in S, and preserving the order of the remaining elements.

1.3 Comparison

Now although both of these specifications describe the same system, the first seems more abstract: it doesn't have the added detail of using a sequence to record the people in the ground. The use of this sequence certainly makes the second specification a bit more awkward: we have to say that it contains no duplicates, for example. The second specification also makes certain design decisions: new people are always appended to the *end* of the sequence.

We regard the first description as the abstract specification of the system, and the second as perhaps the first step on the way to producing a design. We have it in mind to implement the set of persons' names using an array, in which of course the elements are ordered. We take a design decision to order the names according to their arrival. This design decision should be recorded, so that what we are doing is clear; we record it using a *retrieve relation:*[2]

$$\begin{array}{|l}\hline \text{\textit{Retrieve}} \\ \hline IB \\ CIB \\ \hline s = \operatorname{ran} l \\ \hline \end{array}$$

Retrieve describes the relationship between the abstract specification and the concrete design, and thus is a formal record of the design step. It will help us to show that the second specification is a correct implementation of the first. Just documenting the retrieve relation is an important and valuable thing to do; however, we can go further, and prove the design correct, and we give proof methods to do this.

2 An Example Program Development

Requirements Produce a program that finds the average of some numbers.[3]

Specification We presume that the program should find the arithmetic mean of some natural numbers. We shall describe a simple interface in which there are two operations: the first *Enters* a number into the program, and the second calculates the *Mean* of the numbers so far entered. We shall model the state of the program using a sequence of natural numbers:

$$\begin{array}{|l}\hline \text{\textit{S}} \\ \hline s : \operatorname{seq} \mathsf{N} \\ \hline \end{array}$$

Initially, the sequence of numbers is empty:

$$InitS \triangleq [S' \mid s' = \langle\rangle]$$

---

[2]A retrieve relation is so-called because it allows us to retrieve the abstraction from amongst the implementation details. Another popular term is *abstraction relation*, or *abstraction invariant*.

[3]This example was due originally to Carroll Morgan, and was used as an example of a natural situation in which the retrieve relation is not functional from concrete to abstract states.

Operation	Precondition
InitS	true
Enter	true
Mean	$s \neq \langle\rangle$

Figure 2: Specification of the Mean Machine

Now, each number must be entered into the sequence:

$$\begin{array}{|l}
\hline
\text{\_\_Enter\_\_} \\
\Delta S \\
n? : \mathbb{N} \\
\hline
s' = s \,\hat{}\, \langle n? \rangle \\
\hline
\end{array}$$

The arithmetic mean of a series is its sum divided by its length:

$$\begin{array}{|l}
\hline
\text{\_\_Mean\_\_} \\
\Xi S \\
m! : \Re \\
\hline
s \neq \langle\rangle \\
m! = \dfrac{\sum_{i=1}^{\#s}(s\ i)}{\#s} \\
\hline
\end{array}$$

This result makes sense only if the length of the sequence is strictly positive. We summarise the interface in Figure 2.

Design Clearly, it is not necessary to keep the entire sequence of numbers that has been input into our program, there is a much more efficient way of computing the mean. We can calculate the mean from just two quantities: the sum of the numbers so far, and the size of the sample. In the specification, we were not interested in efficiency, but in finding a good way of saying what had to be done: the definition of arithmetic mean is usually given in terms of a series of numbers. However, the mean is best computed using a different description.

The state in our design contains the sum of the sample so far, and its size:

$$\begin{array}{|l}
\hline
\text{\_\_D\_\_} \\
sum : \mathbb{N} \\
size : \mathbb{N} \\
\hline
\end{array}$$

Initially, the sample is empty:

$$InitD \triangleq [D' \mid sum' = 0 \wedge size' = 0]$$

When we enter a number, we add it to the running total, and increase the sample size:

Operation	Precondition
InitD	*true*
EnterD	*true*
MeanD	$size \neq 0$

Figure 3: Design of the Mean Machine

EnterD
ΔD
$n? : \mathbb{N}$

$sum' = sum + n?$
$size' = size + 1$

The mean is computed by dividing the sum of the sample by its size:

MeanD
ΞD
$m! : \Re$

$size \neq 0$
$m! = \frac{sum}{size}$

We summarise the interface in Figure 3.

Retrieve Relation   The relationship between specification and design should be obvious:

Retrieve
S
D

$sum = \sum_{i=1}^{\#s}(s\ i)$
$size = \#s$

The correctness of our design should also be quite obvious: if we take *EnterD* and *MeanD*, and replace *sum* and *size* by the expressions that *Retrieve* gives us for them in terms of *s*, then we obtain the abstract descriptions of these operations.

Implementation I   As we have already seen in our use of schemas, the practice of having a single predicate characterising an operation is very convenient from the point of view of specification combinators. As we shall see later, the practice of having a pair of predicates is very convenient from the point of view of program combinators. We now translate our design into the refinement calculus using a mixture of program code and *specification statements in which pre and postconditions are* *separated:*[4]

> var *sum*, *size* : N •
>
> ...
>
> procedure *enter* (val *n*? : N);
>
>   *sum*, *size* : $[true, sum = sum_0 + n? \wedge size = size_0 + 1]$;
>
> procedure *mean* (res *m*! : $\Re$);
>
>   *m*! : $[size \neq 0, m! = \frac{sum}{size}]$.

The body of the procedure *enter* consists of a specification that says that the global variables *sum* must be increased by the value of the input parameter *n*?, and *size* must be incremented; no other variables may be changed. The body of the procedure *mean* consists of a specification that says that the output parameter *m*! must have the final value $\frac{sum}{size}$; the implementor may assume that *size* is not 0 (this probably makes life simpler); and no other variables may be changed.

Implementation II Next, we fill in some more detail, refining the specification statements into code in the guarded command language. The result is a program free of specification statements:

> var *sum*, *size* : N •
>
> ...
>
> procedure *enter* (val *n*? : N);
>
> |[
>
>   *sum* := *sum* + *n*?;
>
>   *size* := *size* + 1
>
>   ]|;
>
> procedure *mean* (res *m*! : $\Re$);
>
>   *m*! := *sum*/*size*.

---

[4]The notation *w* : [*pre*, *post*] specifies a program that may assume that the state satisfies the predicate *pre*, and must leave the state satisfying *post* changing only the variables in *w*. Notice that we decorate the before-variables, rather than the after-variables.

Final Code Finally, we translate from the guarded command language into our chosen target language:

```
program meanmachine (input, output);
    var n, sum, size : N;  m : ℜ;
    procedure enter (val n? : N);
        begin
            sum := sum + n?;
            size := size + 1
        end;
    procedure mean (res m! : ℜ);
        m! := sum/size;
    begin
        sum := 0;
        size := 0;
        while not eof do
            begin
                read(n);
                enter(n)
            end;
        mean(m);
        write(m)
    end.
```

Notice that we have added some more detail about that which was left informal throughout the development: we have now shown how to use the interface. The style that we used in specifying this program is very popular: it is to give a description of the components that can be used to solve a problem. Our program actually computes

$$\alpha, \omega : [\alpha \neq \langle\rangle, \omega = \left\langle \frac{\sum_{i=1}^{\#\alpha}(\alpha\ i)}{\#\alpha} \right\rangle],$$

where α is the input stream and ω is the output stream. It might have been more satisfactory to start from a specification such as this.

3 Another Example

Requirements Write a program that finds the maximum of some numbers.

Specification Define S, $InitS$ and $Enter$ as before. The maximum of a sequence of numbers is any member of the sequence that is at least as large as all the others:

$$
\begin{array}{|l}
\hline
\_Max\_\rule{0pt}{0pt}\hrulefill \\
\Delta S \\
max! : \mathbb{N} \\
\hline
s \neq \langle\rangle \\
s' = s \\
max! \in \operatorname{ran} s \\
\forall n : \operatorname{ran} s \bullet n \leq max! \\
\hline
\end{array}
$$

Design   It is more efficient to keep the current maximum of a series of numbers; initially, this figure is 0:

$$D_1 \cong [h : \mathbb{N}]$$

$$InitD_1 \cong [D_1' \mid h' = 0]$$

Each time we consider the next element of the series, we reconsider the current maximum:

$$
\begin{array}{|l}
\hline
\_EnterD_1\_\rule{0pt}{0pt}\hrulefill \\
\Delta D_1 \\
n? : \mathbb{N} \\
\hline
n? \geq h \Rightarrow h' = n? \\
h \geq n? \Rightarrow h' = h \\
\hline
\end{array}
$$

Calculating the maximum is simple—it is the current maximum:

$$
\begin{array}{|l}
\hline
\_MaxD_1\_\rule{0pt}{0pt}\hrulefill \\
\Delta D_1 \\
max! : \mathbb{N} \\
\hline
h' = h \\
max! = h \\
\hline
\end{array}
$$

Final Code   The program that implements this design is as follows:

```
program maxmachine (input, output);
    var n, h : N;
    procedure enter (val n? : N);
        if n? > h then h := n?;
    procedure max (res max! : N);
        max! := h;
    begin
        h := 0;
        while not eof do
            begin
                read(n);
                enter(n)
            end;
        max(n);
        write(n)
    end.
```

4   Concepts of Data Refinement

Writing formal specifications is a worthwhile activity in its own right: the advantages to be gained in getting a good understanding of a system and a simple description are manifold. However, we seem to go through three stages: first we might find how pleasing it is to specify systems using mathematics; next we start to use the power of mathematics to prove things about our descriptions; finally, we remember what we were trying to do in the first place, namely, to develop programs! The next part of this paper describes one way of progressing from specification through design and into code.

5   The Notion of Refinement

Refinement is all about improving programs: a refinement T of a specification S is somehow better. This improvement may be in terms of efficiency, robustness, accuracy, or whatever. We shall write

$$S \sqsubseteq T$$

to denote the fact that S is refined by T.

In Z there is a particular notion of refinement that we use to show that a sequential program P is a refinement of a specification S; that is, that $S \sqsubseteq P$. Typically, we shall find a number of designs $D_1, \ldots, D_n$ such that

$$S \sqsubseteq D_1 \sqsubseteq \ldots D_n \sqsubseteq P.$$

However, it is worth noting that there is nothing God-given about the notion of refinement that we shall use: other notions are appropriate in other situations. For example, in CSP (Hoare, 1985), there is *trace* refinement, where process P is refined by process Q whenever the set of traces of Q are contained within the set of traces of P. A trace is the sequence of events in which a process has participated up to some moment; the set of traces of a process contains every possible trace for the process. Thus, trace refinement ensures that Q cannot have a trace of its behaviour which would not be permitted by P. This notion of refinement is suitable for describing how certain properties of a system must be preserved during design and implementation, in particular, *safety properties*: the system must not do anything bad.

There are other properties of processes that are not preserved by trace refinement: in particular, nondeterministic behaviour, and freedom from deadlock and livelock. Different notions of refinement are needed to capture these properties. Yet another notion of refinement is needed to preserve non-functional system properties, such as *security*.

Returning to Z, operations are rather like relations between states. The next Section considers a notion of refinement of relations that is a simplified view of refinement of operations.

5.1 Refining Relations

Suppose that we choose to define a notion of refinement between relations $\sqsubseteq_{\mathcal{R}}$ as follows: $R \sqsubseteq_{\mathcal{R}} S$ whenever

- the domain of S is at least as big as that of R; and

- within the domain of R, S respects R.

Formally, we have that

$$
\begin{array}{l}
\rule{6cm}{0.4pt}\;[X, Y]\rule{6cm}{0.4pt} \\
\quad \_ \sqsubseteq_{\mathcal{R}} \_ : (X \leftrightarrow Y) \leftrightarrow (X \leftrightarrow Y) \\
\rule{12cm}{0.4pt} \\
\quad \forall \, desired, proposed : (X \leftrightarrow Y) \bullet \\
\qquad desired \sqsubseteq_{\mathcal{R}} proposed \Leftrightarrow \\
\qquad\quad (\mathrm{dom}\ desired) \subseteq (\mathrm{dom}\ proposed) \\
\qquad\quad ((\mathrm{dom}\ desired) \lhd proposed) \subseteq desired
\end{array}
$$

Thus, when we take a relation R and refine it to a relation S, we can do two things: enlarge the domain of R; and remove nondeterminism from R.

Example 1 Suppose that we have

$$R \, \hat{=} \, \{1 \mapsto 1, 1 \mapsto 2, 2 \mapsto 2, 2 \mapsto 3\}$$
$$S \, \hat{=} \, \{1 \mapsto 1, 2 \mapsto 2, 2 \mapsto 3, 3 \mapsto 3\}$$

Then we have that $R \sqsubseteq_{\mathcal{R}} S$, since the domain of R has been increased

$$(\mathrm{dom}\ R) = \{1, 2\} \subseteq \{1, 2, 3\} = (\mathrm{dom}\ S)$$

and we have removed one of the pairs $(1 \mapsto 2)$

$$
\begin{aligned}
(\mathrm{dom}\ R) &\lhd S \\
&= \{1, 2\} \lhd S \\
&= \{1, 2\} \lhd \{1 \mapsto 1, 2 \mapsto 2, 2 \mapsto 3, 3 \mapsto 3\} \\
&= \{1 \mapsto 1, 2 \mapsto 2, 2 \mapsto 3\} \\
&\subseteq \{1 \mapsto 1, 1 \mapsto 2, 2 \mapsto 2, 2 \mapsto 3\} \\
&= R
\end{aligned}
$$

Example 2 Suppose that we have

$$R \, \hat{=} \, \{1 \mapsto 1, 1 \mapsto 2, 2 \mapsto 2, 2 \mapsto 3\}$$
$$S \, \hat{=} \, \{1 \mapsto 1, 3 \mapsto 3\}$$

Then we have that $\neg (R \sqsubseteq_{\mathcal{R}} S)$, since

$$(\mathrm{dom}\ R) = \{1, 2, 3\} \nsubseteq \{1, 3\} = (\mathrm{dom}\ S)$$

Thus, we can remove pairs to reduce nondeterminism, but we cannot remove pairs to make the domain smaller.

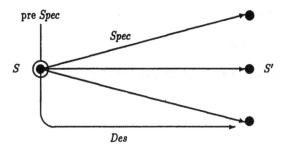

Figure 4: Operation Refinement

5.2 Refining Operations

The refinement relation which we have just discussed is very similar to the one which we shall use. Suppose that *Spec* and *Des* are schemas which describe operations on a state S—that is, they obey our conventions about dashed and undashed variables—but have no input or output. We shall say that *Spec* $\sqsubseteq_S$ *Des*, whenever

1. $\forall S \bullet$ pre *Spec* $\Rightarrow$ pre *Des*

2. $\forall S, S' \bullet$ pre *Spec* $\land$ *Des* $\Rightarrow$ *Spec*

This definition is rather similar to relation refinement, except that it is interpreted in the language of schemas: the first condition may be described as *weakening the precondition*, and the second as *strengthening the postcondition*.

Example 3 Define the state S as

$$S \cong [x : \mathsf{N}]$$
$$\Delta S \cong S \land S'$$

The following operation decreases the value of X

```
__Decrease_____
  ΔS
  _____
  x ≠ 0
  x' < x
_____
```

Obviously, the precondition for *Decrease* is

$$\text{pre } Decrease \Leftrightarrow [x : \mathsf{N} \mid x \neq 0]$$

Suppose that we propose an implementation of *Decrease* which simply decrements X by 1

```
__Decrement_____
  ΔS
  _____
  x ≠ 0
  x' = x - 1
_____
```

Again, the precondition is simple

pre $Decrement \Leftrightarrow [x : \mathsf{N} \mid x \neq 0]$

It is not difficult to check that we have a refinement, since the first condition is trivially satisfied, and we have that

$$x \neq 0 \wedge x' = x - 1 \Rightarrow x \neq 0 \wedge x' < x$$

Thus,

$Decrease \sqsubseteq_S Decrement$

Example 4 Using the state from the last example, suppose that we have the operation

```
_Spec_____
ΔS
_____
0 ≤ x ≤ 2
x' ≤ x + 1
```

and that we are offered the implementation

```
_Program₁_____
ΔS
_____
x' = 0
```

We have the following preconditions

pre $Spec \Leftrightarrow [S \mid 0 \leq x \leq 2]$
pre $Program_1 \Leftrightarrow S$

Thus,

$\forall S \bullet$ pre $Spec \Rightarrow$ pre $Program_1$

That the result has been strengthened rest on the fact that 0 is a least element

$\forall n : \mathsf{N} \bullet 0 \leq n$

Thus,

pre $Spec \wedge Program_1$
$\quad \Leftrightarrow [S \mid 0 \leq x \leq 2] \wedge [\Delta S \mid x' = 0]$
$\quad \Leftrightarrow [\Delta S \mid 0 \leq x \leq 2 \wedge x' = 0]$
$\quad \Rightarrow [\Delta S \mid 0 \leq x \leq 2 \wedge x' \leq x + 1]$
$\quad \Leftrightarrow Spec$

5.3 Data Refinement

When we construct an abstract specification, we choose mathematical data types that may be easily understood; when we write a program, we choose programming language data types that may be executed efficiently. These two activities are in tension, and we must use some idea of refinement to bridge the gap. Just as we discussed above, we must document the precise relationship between the abstract structures in the specification, and the concrete structures in the implementation.

Consider the following system states

$$S_1 \cong [x_1 : \mathbb{P}\,\mathbb{N} \mid \#x_1 \leq n]$$
$$S_2 \cong [x_2 : seq[\mathbb{N}] \mid \#x_2 \leq n \land x_2 \in \mathbb{N} \rightarrowtail \mathbb{N}]$$
$$S_3 \cong [x_3 : Array[\mathbb{N}]; \ p : (1 \mathinner{\ldotp\ldotp} n) \mid ((1 \mathinner{\ldotp\ldotp} p) \lhd x_3) \in \mathbb{N} \rightarrowtail \mathbb{N}]$$

where

$$Array[X] \cong (1 \mathinner{\ldotp\ldotp} n) \to X$$

We can consider these three states to be modelling the same thing: a collection of n distinct numbers. In S_1, we find the most abstract model: a set with cardinality not greater than n. In S_2 there is a less abstract model: a sequence of numbers, without repetition (the sequence is *injective*) bounded in length by n. Finally, in S_3 we find the most concrete model: an array with fixed length n, and no repeated elements, and a counter which indicates how much of the array is in use. This is at the level of a programming language data structure, but notice that we have given a mathematical definition of what an array is: a total function from a set of indices to some set. Thus, when we move from S_1 to S_2, we introduce an order on the numbers in the state; when we move from S_2 to S_3, we introduce the idea of a fixed length data structure. We can think of S_1 as a specification, S_2 as a design, and S_3 as an implementation, and we can document the precise relationships between them. We call these the *retrieve relations:* they allow us to retrieve an abstract description from a more concrete one.[5]

To retrieve the abstract description given by S_1 from the concrete description given by S_2, we need to throw away the detail about the order of the elements in the sequence. We document the retrieve relation using a schema

```
┌─ Retr₁ ─────────────────────────────────
│ S₁
│ S₂
├─────────────────────────────────────────
│ x₁ = ran x₂
```

To retrieve the abstract description given by S_2 from the concrete description given by S_3, we need to throw away the detail about the unused elements in the array

```
┌─ Retr₂ ─────────────────────────────────
│ S₂
│ S₃
├─────────────────────────────────────────
│ x₂ = (1 .. p) ◁ x₃
```

It is only by being precise about the refinement by showing the retrieve relation that we can say how the array and counter model the collection of n distinct numbers.

The retrieve relation between S_3 and S_1 must first throw away the unused elements, and then throw away the order. This is simply the composition of the two retrieve relations that we have documented

$$(Retr_1 \land Retr_2) \setminus S_2$$
$$\Leftrightarrow [S_1; \ S_3 \mid x_1 = \mathrm{ran}((1 \mathinner{\ldotp\ldotp} p) \lhd x_3)]$$

---

[5]An alternative name for the retrieve relation is *the abstraction relation.*

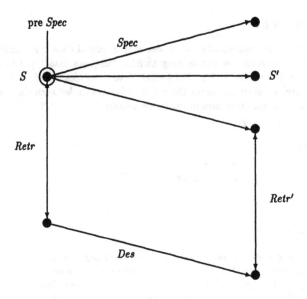

Figure 5: Data Refinement

5.4 The Proof Opportunities in Refinement

We have spoken in generalities about refinement; now is the time to explain precisely what we shall mean by a refinement, by saying what proof opportunites are generated by a development step. Suppose that we have an abstract state *AS*, an abstract initial state *InitAS*, an abstract operation *AOp*, a concrete state *CS*, a concrete initial state *InitCS*, and a concrete operation *COp*. Furthermore, suppose that there is a retrieve relation between them *Retr*.

Initial States   Each possible initial concrete state must represent a possible initial abstract state

$$InitCS \vdash \exists AS' \bullet InitAS \land Retr'$$

Applicability   The concrete operation must terminate whenever the abstract operation is guaranteed so to do

$$\text{pre } AOp \land Retr \vdash \text{pre } COp$$

Correctness   Finally, we must make sure that the concrete operation is correct: if *AOp* is guaranteed to terminate, then the state after *COp* must represent a possible abstract state in which *AOp* could terminate

$$\text{pre } AOp \land Retr \land COp \vdash \exists AS' \bullet AOp \land Retr'$$

5.5 Functional Refinement

As is pointed out in the *Z Reference Manual*, a simpler set of conditions can be used if the retrieve relation is functional from concrete to abstract: that is, that each concrete state represents exactly one abstract state. For this to be so, we must prove that

$$CS \vdash \exists_1 AS \bullet Retr$$

Two of the three conditions are now simplified, since we have factored out the proof that *Retr* is functional.

(Functional) Initial States

$$InitCS \land Retr' \vdash InitAS$$

(Functional) Correctness

$$\text{pre } AOp \land Retr \land COp \land Retr' \vdash AOp$$

A sufficient condition for proving that a retrieve relation is a total function, is to show that there is an equation defining each abstract component's value in terms of concrete components and total functions. This is a commonly found retrieve relation.

XXXXX

6 From Schemas to Specification Statements

We describe some precise rules due to King for translating from the notations of the schema calculus into those of the refinement calculus. We give a translation rule that bridges the gap, and four derived rules that help to make the transition smoother.

7 The Translation Rule

Recall the route that we have chosen for developing code from Z specifications:

1. abstract specification using schemas;

2. data refinement using schemas;

3. translation into the refinement calculus;

4. algorithm refinement using the refinement calculus;

5. translation into the target programming language.

In this section we address the problem of how to formalise the translation at stage (3).[6]

First, the change must be made between the conventions for distinguishing before and after-variables. Suppose that *Op* is a schema obeying the schema calculus convention, then $[Op]$ denotes the schema *Op* with the convention changed to that of the refinement calculus.

Rule 1 (change conventions "chconv") If *Op* is an operation on a state containing the variables v, then

$$[Op] \cong Op[v_0, v/v, v'].$$

Next we consider the translation from schemas to specification statements.

Rule 2 (transformation to refinement calculus "trc") Suppose we have a schema describing an operation with inputs i and outputs o on the state S, containing variables v:

$$
\begin{array}{|l}
\hline
\,S \\\hline
v : T \\\hline
inv \\
\hline
\end{array}
$$

---

[6]The connection that we present between Z and the refinement calculus was first worked out by (King, 1990).

$$
\begin{array}{|l}
\hline
\_Op_____ \\
\Delta S \\
i : I \\
o : O \\
\hline
pred \\
\hline
\end{array}
$$

The description of the state translates into the following declaration:

var $v : T \mid inv.$

The operation translates into the following specification statement:

$v, o: [\text{pre } Op \;, \; [Op]].$

Notice that the schemas are used as predicates in this specification statement. ▱

Example 5 The operation *Enrol0* is translated as follows. First, recall its definition:

$$
\begin{array}{|l}
\hline
\_Enrol0_____ \\
\Delta Class \\
s? : Student \\
\hline
s? \notin (n \cup y) \\
n' = n \cup \{s?\} \\
y' = y \\
\hline
\end{array}
$$

Its translation into the decoration conventions of the refinement calculus is:

$$
\begin{array}{|l}
\hline
\_[Enrol0]_____ \\
[\Delta Class] \\
s? : Student \\
\hline
s \notin n_0 \cup y_0 \\
n = n_0 \cup \{s\} \\
y = y_0 \\
\hline
\end{array}
$$

The translation into the refinement calculus gives us the specification statement

$n, y: [\text{pre } Enrol0 \;, \; [Enrol0]]$

$= $ "by the previous calculation of pre *Enrol0*"

$$
n, y: \left[\left(\begin{array}{c} s \notin (n \cup y) \\ \#(n \cup y) < max \end{array} \right) , \; [Enrol0] \right]
$$

$= $ "by definition"

$$
n, y: \left[\left(\begin{array}{c} s \notin (n \cup y) \\ \#(n \cup y) < max \end{array} \right) , \; \left(\begin{array}{c} s \notin n_0 \cup y_0 \\ n = n_0 \cup \{s\} \\ y = y_0 \end{array} \right) \right]
$$

$= $ "sp in both directions"

$$
n, y: \left[\left(\begin{array}{c} s \notin (n \cup y) \\ \#(n \cup y) < max \end{array} \right) , \; \left(\begin{array}{c} n = n_0 \cup \{s\} \\ y = y_0 \end{array} \right) \right]
$$

$= $ "expF"

$$
n: \left[\left(\begin{array}{c} s \notin (n \cup y) \\ \#(n \cup y) < max \end{array} \right) , \; n = n_0 \cup \{s\} \right]
$$

▱

3 Some Derived Rules

In this Section, we describe some derived rules that have been found to be useful in moving from descriptions in the schema calculus to programs in the refinement calculus.

The simplest rule deals with an operation defined using disjunction.

Rule 3 (Conditional Introduction "ifT1") Suppose we have

$$Op \triangleq Op_1 \vee Op_2.$$

If the preconditions of Op_1 and Op_2 can be expressed in our target programming language. We can translate Op to a conditional:

    if pre $Op_1 \rightarrow Op_1^*$
    □ pre $Op_2 \rightarrow Op_2^*$
    fi

where Op_i^* are the specification statements which result from the use of the translation rule.

The transformation in ifT1 required that the preconditions of Op_1 and Op_2 could be simply expressed in the target programming language. The next Law describes a more complicated situation.

Rule 4 (Conditional Introduction "ifT2") Suppose we have

$$Op \triangleq Op_1 \vee Op_2$$

and the precondition of Op_1 is a complex expression. Then we can translate this to

    var b : *Boolean*
    $b: [true , b \Leftrightarrow$ pre $Op_1]$;
    if $b \rightarrow Op_1^*$
    □ pre $Op_2 \rightarrow Op_2^*$
    fi

where b is some fresh variable, and Op_1^* and Op_2^* are as above. Clearly, if pre $Op_2 = \neg$pre Op_1, then we can simplify the second guard to $\neg b$.

The most general version of the conditional rule allows us to evaluate any expression before the conditional, and to store the result in a fresh variable.

Rule 5 (Conditional Introduction "ifT3") With Op as above, the refinement calculus version becomes

    var r : T
    $r: [true , \phi]$;
    if $\psi_1 \rightarrow w: [\phi \wedge \psi_1 , [Op_1]]$
    □ $\psi_2 \rightarrow w: [\phi \wedge \psi_2 , [Op_2]]$
    fi

where ϕ, ψ_1 and ψ_2 are any predicates, which satisfy the side conditions

1. $\phi \wedge ($pre $Op_1 \vee$ pre $Op_2) \Rightarrow (\psi_1 \vee \psi_2)$

2. $\phi \wedge ($pre $Op_1 \vee$ pre $Op_2) \Rightarrow (\psi_i \Rightarrow [$pre $Op_i])$ for $i = 1, 2$

Notice that if pre $Op_1 = \neg$pre Op_2, the antecedents above simplify to ϕ, leaving

1'. $\phi \Rightarrow (\psi_1 \vee \psi_2)$

2'. $\phi \Rightarrow (\psi_i \Rightarrow$ pre $Op_i)$

The final way in which we can use the structure of the Z specification to help us with the structure of the refinement calculus program is when we notice that the operation is described as the conjunction of two other operations which act on disjoint parts of the state.

Rule 6 (Sequential Composition "semT") Suppose we have

$$Op \cong Op_1 \wedge Op_2$$

where Op_1 and Op_2 take the forms

$$Op_1 \cong [\Delta S \mid s_1' = s_1 \wedge P_1(s_2, s_2')]$$
$$Op_2 \cong [\Delta S \mid s_2' = s_2 \wedge P_2(s_1, s_1')]$$

where s_1 and s_2 are disjoint (vectors of) state variables, and P_1 and P_2 are predicates showing how part of the state is altered. Then we have two possibilities: we can either update first s_1 and then s_2, or *vice versa*. So Op becomes either

$$s_1 : [\text{pre } Op_2 \,, \; [P_2]] \,;$$
$$s_2 : [\text{pre } Op_1 \,, \; [P_1]]$$

or

$$s_2 : [\text{pre } Op_1 \,, \; [P_1]] \,;$$
$$s_1 : [\text{pre } Op_2 \,, \; [P_2]]$$

9 References

1. C.A.R. Hoare, *Communicating Sequential Processes*, Prentice Hall International (1985).

2. S. King, "Z and the Refinement Calculus", Technical Monograph PRG-79, Oxford University Computing Laboratory, Programming Research Group, February 1990.

10 Exercises

1. Write down the retrieve relation for the *mazmachine* design.

2. In Section 2, we presumed that the program should find the arithmetic mean of some natural numbers; perhaps the client wanted something else as well. Consider the following variations:

   (a) the program should find the arithmetic mean of some integers;

   (b) the program should find the mode of some natural numbers;

   (c) the program should find the median of some natural numbers.

   For each variation, produce a new specification and design, and document their retrieve relations.

3. Show that $\sqsubseteq_R$ and $\sqsubseteq_S$ are partial orders. [To prove that relation refinement is a *partial order*, show that it is reflexive ($S \sqsubseteq_R S$), antisymmetric ($S \sqsubseteq_R T \wedge T \sqsubseteq_R S \Rightarrow S = T$), and transitive ($S \sqsubseteq_R T \wedge T \sqsubseteq_R U \Rightarrow S \sqsubseteq_R U$).

4. Define the relations

   $$bitless \cong \{1 \mapsto 0, 2 \mapsto 1, 2 \mapsto 0, 3 \mapsto 2, 3 \mapsto 1\}$$
   $$alwayszero \cong \{1, 2, 3, 4\} \times \{0\}$$

   Is $bitless \sqsubseteq_R alwayszero$?

5. Given the relation

$$\{0 \mapsto 0, 0 \mapsto 1, 2 \mapsto 1, 2 \mapsto 2, 3 \mapsto 3\}$$

Which of the following relations are refinements?

(a) $\{0 \mapsto 0\}$

(b) $\{0 \mapsto 0, 0 \mapsto 1, 0 \mapsto 2, 2 \mapsto 2\}$

(c) $\{0 \mapsto 0, 2 \mapsto 2, 3 \mapsto 3\}$

(d) $\{0 \mapsto 0, 0 \mapsto 1, 0 \mapsto 3, 2 \mapsto 1, 3 \mapsto 3\}$

(e) $\{0 \mapsto 1, 2 \mapsto 3, 2 \mapsto 2\}$

(f) $\{0 \mapsto 1, 2 \mapsto 1, 1 \mapsto 2, 3 \mapsto 3\}$

(g) $\{0 \mapsto 0, 1 \mapsto 0, 1 \mapsto 1, 1 \mapsto 2, 1 \mapsto 3, 2 \mapsto 2, 3 \mapsto 3\}$

6. Define two further possible implementations of the *Spec* of Example 4

```
┌─ Program₂ ─────────────────────────────────────────────────────────
│ ΔS
├──────────────
│ x′ = 0 ∨ x′ = 1
└────────────────────────────────────────────────────────────────────
```

```
┌─ Program₃ ─────────────────────────────────────────────────────────
│ ΔS
├──────────────
│ x′ = 0 ∨ x′ = 3
└────────────────────────────────────────────────────────────────────
```

Which of the following hold?

(a) *Spec* $\sqsubseteq_S$ *Program₂*

(b) *Spec* $\sqsubseteq_S$ *Program₃*

(c) *Program₁* $\sqsubseteq_S$ *Program₂*

(d) *Program₁* $\sqsubseteq_S$ *Program₃*

(e) *Program₂* $\sqsubseteq_S$ *Program₁*

(f) *Program₂* $\sqsubseteq_S$ *Program₃*

(g) *Program₃* $\sqsubseteq_S$ *Program₁*

(h) *Program₃* $\sqsubseteq_S$ *Program₂*

7. We say that m divides n whenever n is an exact multiple of m:

```
│ _divides_ : N ↔ N
├──────────────────
│ ∀ m, n : N •
│     m divides n ⇔ ∃ k : N • k × m = n.
```

Define the following two relations:

```
│ R, S : N ↔ N
├──────────────────
│ ∀ x, y : N •
│     (x, y) ∈ R ⇔ (2 divides x ∧ y = 2) ∨ (3 divides x ∧ y = 3)
│     (x, y) ∈ S ⇔ (3 divides x ∧ y = 3) ∨ (¬(3 divides x) ∧ y = 2).
```

Is $R \sqsubseteq_R S$?

8. Which of the following relations refine the relation R of the previous question, and why?

$$S_1, S_2, S_3 : \mathsf{N} \leftrightarrow \mathsf{N}$$

$$\forall x : \mathsf{N}; \; y : \mathsf{Z} \bullet$$
$$(x, y) \in S_1 \Leftrightarrow (3 \; divides \; x \wedge y \in \{3, -3\}) \vee (\neg(3 \; divides \; x) \wedge y \in \{2, -2\})$$
$$(x, y) \in S_2 \Leftrightarrow (2 \; divides \; x \wedge y = 2) \vee (\neg(2 \; divides \; x) \wedge y = 3)$$
$$(x, y) \in S_3 \Leftrightarrow (6 \; divides \; x \wedge y = 3) \vee (\neg(6 \; divides \; x) \wedge y = 2)$$

9. Suppose that

$$A \sqsubseteq_{\mathcal{R}} C$$
$$B \sqsubseteq_{\mathcal{R}} D$$
$$\mathrm{ran}\, A \subseteq \mathrm{dom}\, B;$$

prove that

$$A \,;\, B \sqsubseteq_{\mathcal{R}} C \,;\, D.$$

10. We would like to write part of a program that finds out whether a given number is present in a collection of numbers stored in the state. Specify the state S_1 which contains a bag of numbers, and the operation $Find_1$ on this state which takes a number as input, and returns an output with the value *yes* providing the input is in the bag (its behaviour is unspecified otherwise). $Find_1$ should have no side-effects, and *yes* is drawn from the free data type

$$Reply ::= yes \mid no.$$

11. Now make a design step that represents the bag as a sequence: specify the state S_2 which contains a seq of numbers, and the operation $Find_2$ on this state which takes a number as input, and returns an output with the value *yes* exactly when the input is in the sequence.

12. Write down the retrieve relation between S_1 and S_2, and prove that $Find_2$ correctly implements $Find_1$.

13. Now strengthen the specification to S_3 and $Find_3$ by handling the case when the input is not in the bag, but keeping the data representation unchanged.

14. Prove that $Find_3$ correctly implements $Find_2$.

15. Construct S_4 and $Find_4$ by changing the representation of the collection of numbers in the state so that they are maintained in increasing order.

16. Prove that $Find_4$ correctly implements $Find_3$.

17. Finally, write some code that implements $Find_4$.

18. Of course, if you have correctly answered the previous questions, then your code should implement $Find_1$; deduce that this is true by proving that the data refinement ordering is partial.

Two Refinement Case Studies

J.C.P. Woodcock
Oxford University Computing Laboratory
Programming Research Group

Abstract

We present two case studies in refinement: the Class Manager and the Save Area.

1 Case Study: The Class Manager

We present a calculation of some code that refines the Class Manager specification. First we propose a concrete state, and document the retrieve relation. Using this we calculate the concrete *Enrol* operation, using a straightforward strategy to simplify it. Next, we translate into the refinement calculus, and calculate the guarded command code. The inventiveness in the development lies in the description of the concrete state; all else is supposed to be calculation.

1.1 The Concrete State

Recall the abstract state of the Class Manager:

$$\begin{array}{|l}
\hline
\mathit{Class} \underline{\hspace{8cm}} \\
n, y : \mathbf{P}\ \mathit{Student} \\
\hline
y \cap n = \varnothing \\
\#(y \cup n) \leq \mathit{clmax} \\
\hline
\end{array}$$

We shall use an array to store the names of students, and whether they have passed their examination. We introduce a free data type to record the latter:

$$\mathit{Pass} ::= \mathit{yes} \mid \mathit{no}.$$

Our concrete class contains a fixed length array, and a high-water mark that indicates how much of the array is currently in use:

$$\begin{array}{|l}
\hline
\mathit{CClass} \underline{\hspace{8cm}} \\
ar : 1\mathinner{\ldotp\ldotp}\mathit{clmax} \rightarrow \mathit{Student} \times \mathit{Pass} \\
num : 0\mathinner{\ldotp\ldotp}\mathit{clmax} \\
\hline
(((1\mathinner{\ldotp\ldotp}num) \lhd ar)\,\mathbin{;} \mathit{first}) \in \mathbf{N} \rightarrowtail \mathit{Student} \\
\hline
\end{array}$$

Of course, the high-water mark makes it very simple to determine whether the class is full or not. The invariant requires that there are no duplicate names in the active part of the array (that is, in the array below the high-water mark). For each student s who is enrolled and recorded as having passed the examination, there is an element (s, yes) in the active part of the array, and similarly, or each student s who is enrolled and recorded as not having passed the examination, there is an element (s, no) in the active part of the array. This is formalised in our retrieve relation:

$$
\begin{array}{|l}
\hline
\_Retr_____ \\
Class \\
CClass \\
\hline
y = \mathrm{ran}(((1 \mathinner{.\,.} num) \lhd ar \rhd (Student \times \{yes\})) \mathbin{;} first) \\
n = \mathrm{ran}(((1 \mathinner{.\,.} num) \lhd ar \rhd (Student \times \{yes\})) \mathbin{;} first) \\
\hline
\end{array}
$$

It should not be difficult to see that $Retr$ is a total surjective function from concrete to abstract states.

1.2 The Enrol Operation

Recall the definition of the $Enrol$ operation; the successful part was defined as

$$
\begin{array}{|l}
\hline
\_Enrol0_____ \\
\Delta\, Class \\
s? : Student \\
\hline
s? \notin (n \cup y) \\
n' = n \cup \{s?\} \\
y' = y \\
\hline
\end{array}
$$

Using the retrieve function, we calculate the concrete version of this part of the operation to be:

$$
\begin{array}{|l}
\hline
\_CEnrol0_____ \\
\Delta\, CClass \\
s? : Student \\
\hline
s? \notin \mathrm{ran}(((1 \mathinner{.\,.} num) \lhd ar \rhd (Student \times \{yes\})) \mathbin{;} first) \\
\qquad \cup \mathrm{ran}(((1 \mathinner{.\,.} num) \lhd ar \rhd (Student \times \{yes\})) \mathbin{;} first) \\
\mathrm{ran}(((1 \mathinner{.\,.} num') \lhd ar' \rhd (Student \times \{yes\})) \mathbin{;} first) \\
\qquad = \mathrm{ran}(((1 \mathinner{.\,.} num) \lhd ar \rhd (Student \times \{yes\})) \mathbin{;} first) \cup \{s?\} \\
\mathrm{ran}(((1 \mathinner{.\,.} num') \lhd ar' \rhd (Student \times \{yes\})) \mathbin{;} first) \\
\qquad = \mathrm{ran}(((1 \mathinner{.\,.} num) \lhd ar \rhd (Student \times \{yes\})) \mathbin{;} first) \\
\hline
\end{array}
$$

We take each of the three predicates in turn and try to simplify them. The first simply describes the partitioning of the array by the $Pass$ values:

$$s? \notin \mathrm{ran}(((1 \mathinner{.\,.} num) \lhd ar \rhd (Student \times \{yes\})) \mathbin{;} first)$$

$$\cup \operatorname{ran}(((1 \mathinner{\ldotp\ldotp} num) \lhd ar \rhd (Student \times \{yes\})) \mathbin{;} first)$$

$\Leftrightarrow$ "by a property of functions"

$$s? \notin \operatorname{ran}((1 \mathinner{\ldotp\ldotp} num) \lhd (ar \mathbin{;} first))$$

Next we take the second predicate and try to simplify it. The strategy is to transform the right-hand side into something resembling the left-hand side. To do this, we must drive the singleton set $\{s?\}$ as far as possible inside the expression involving ar. Having done this, we hope to be able to determine some suitable values for the concrete components.

$$\operatorname{ran}(((1 \mathinner{\ldotp\ldotp} num) \lhd ar \rhd (Student \times \{yes\})) \mathbin{;} first) \cup \{s?\}$$

$=$ " by a property of ran, for some $x \in 1 \mathinner{\ldotp\ldotp} clmax$"

$$\operatorname{ran}(((1 \mathinner{\ldotp\ldotp} num) \lhd ar \rhd (Student \times \{yes\})) \mathbin{;} first) \cup \operatorname{ran}\{x \mapsto s?\}$$

$=$ "since ran is disjunctive"

$$\operatorname{ran}((((1 \mathinner{\ldotp\ldotp} num) \lhd ar \rhd (Student \times \{yes\})) \mathbin{;} first) \cup \{x \mapsto s?\})$$

$=$ "by a property of composition"

$$\operatorname{ran}((((1 \mathinner{\ldotp\ldotp} num) \lhd ar \rhd (Student \times \{yes\})) \mathbin{;} first) \cup (\{x \mapsto (s?, y)\} \mathbin{;} first))$$

$=$ "since composition is disjunctive"

$$\operatorname{ran}((((1 \mathinner{\ldotp\ldotp} num) \lhd ar \rhd (Student \times \{yes\})) \cup \{x \mapsto (s?, y)\}) \mathbin{;} first)$$

$=$ "by a property of $\rhd$, providing $y \neq yes$"

$$\operatorname{ran}((((1 \mathinner{\ldotp\ldotp} num) \lhd ar \rhd (Student \times \{yes\}))$$
$$\cup(\{x \mapsto (s?, y)\} \rhd (Student \times \{yes\}))) \mathbin{;} first)$$

$=$ "since $\rhd$ is disjunctive"

$$\operatorname{ran}((((1 \mathinner{\ldotp\ldotp} num) \lhd ar) \cup \{x \mapsto (s?, y)\}) \rhd (Student \times \{yes\})) \mathbin{;} first)$$

$=$ "the union is functional only if we have $x \notin 1 \mathinner{\ldotp\ldotp} n$; by a property of overriding"

$$\operatorname{ran}((((1 \mathinner{\ldotp\ldotp} num) \cup \{x\}) \lhd (ar \oplus \{x \mapsto (s?, y)\}) \rhd (Student \times \{yes\})) \mathbin{;} first).$$

Thus, we have that if $y = no$ and $x \notin 1 \mathinner{\ldotp\ldotp} num$,

$$\operatorname{ran}(((1 \mathinner{\ldotp\ldotp} num') \lhd ar' \rhd (Student \times \{yes\})) \mathbin{;} first)$$
$$= \operatorname{ran}((((1 \mathinner{\ldotp\ldotp} num) \cup \{x\}) \lhd (ar \oplus \{x \mapsto (s?, no)\}) \rhd (Student \times \{yes\})) \mathbin{;} first)$$

This equality holds if

$$1 \mathinner{\ldotp\ldotp} num' = (1 \mathinner{\ldotp\ldotp} num) \cup \{x\} \wedge ar' = ar \oplus \{x \mapsto (s?, no)\}$$

We get a solution for num' only if we take $x = num + 1$. So we have calculated that we must have

$$num' = num + 1 \land ar' = ar \oplus \{num' \mapsto (s?, no)\}.$$

It remains for us to check that these values also satisfy the third predicate:

$\mathrm{ran}(((1 \mathinner{\ldotp\ldotp} num') \lhd ar' \rhd (Student \times \{yes\})) \fatsemi first)$

= "substituting $num + 1$ and $ar \oplus \{num' \mapsto (s?, no)\}$ for num' and ar'''"
  $\mathrm{ran}(((1 \mathinner{\ldotp\ldotp} num + 1) \lhd (ar \oplus \{num + 1 \mapsto (s?, no)\})$
  $\rhd(Student \times \{yes\})) \fatsemi first)$

= "by a property of overriding"
  $\mathrm{ran}(((((1 \mathinner{\ldotp\ldotp} num) \lhd ar) \cup \{num + 1 \mapsto (s?, no)\})$
  $\rhd(Student \times \{yes\})) \fatsemi first)$

= "since $\rhd$ is disjunctive"
  $\mathrm{ran}((((1 \mathinner{\ldotp\ldotp} num) \lhd ar \rhd (Student \times \{yes\}))$
  $\cup(\{num + 1 \mapsto (s?, no)\} \rhd (Student \times \{yes\}))) \fatsemi first)$

= "by a property of $\rhd$"
  $\mathrm{ran}(((1 \mathinner{\ldotp\ldotp} num) \lhd ar \rhd (Student \times \{yes\})) \fatsemi first).$

Summarising our calculations, we have the following description of the concrete $Enrol0$ operation:

$$\boxed{\begin{array}{l} CEnrol0 \\ \hline \Delta CClass \\ s? : Student \\ \hline s? \notin \mathrm{ran}((1 \mathinner{\ldotp\ldotp} num) \lhd (ar \fatsemi first)) \\ num' = num + 1 \\ ar' = ar \oplus \{num' \mapsto (s?, no)\} \end{array}}$$

We now calculate its precondition. The abstract precondition was

$$\boxed{\begin{array}{l} \text{pre } Enrol0 \\ \hline Class \\ s? : Student \\ \hline s? \notin (n \cup y) \\ \#(n \cup y) < clmax \end{array}}$$

and the concrete version of this is

$$
\begin{array}{|l}
\hline
\text{pre } CEnrol0 \\\\
\hline
CClass \\\\
s? : Student \\\\
\hline
s? \notin \mathrm{ran}((1 \mathinner{.\,.} num) \lhd (ar \mathbin{\fatsemi} first)) \\\\
\#(\mathrm{ran}((1 \mathinner{.\,.} num) \lhd (ar \mathbin{\fatsemi} first))) < clmax \\\\
\hline
\end{array}
$$

The second predicate simplifies easily:

$$\#(\mathrm{ran}((1 \mathinner{.\,.} num) \lhd (ar \mathbin{\fatsemi} first))) < clmax$$

$\Leftrightarrow$ "since $(1 \mathinner{.\,.} num) \lhd (ar \mathbin{\fatsemi} first)$ is injective by the state invariant on $CClass$"

$$\#(\mathrm{dom}((1 \mathinner{.\,.} num) \lhd (ar \mathbin{\fatsemi} first))) < clmax$$

$\Leftrightarrow$ "by a property of $\lhd$"

$$\#((1 \mathinner{.\,.} num) \cap \mathrm{dom}(ar \mathbin{\fatsemi} first)) < clmax$$

$\Leftrightarrow$ "since $first$ is total"

$$\#((1 \mathinner{.\,.} num) \cap \mathrm{dom}\, ar) < clmax$$

$\Leftrightarrow$ "by the declaration of ar"

$$\#((1 \mathinner{.\,.} num) \cap (1 \mathinner{.\,.} clmax)) < clmax$$

$\Leftrightarrow$ "since $num < clmax$"

$$\#(1 \mathinner{.\,.} num) < clmax$$

$\Leftrightarrow$ "by a property of $\#$"

$$num < clmax$$

In summary:

$$
\begin{array}{|l}
\hline
\text{pre } CEnrol0 \\\\
\hline
CClass \\\\
s? : Student \\\\
\hline
s? \notin \mathrm{ran}((1 \mathinner{.\,.} num) \lhd (ar \mathbin{\fatsemi} first)) \\\\
num < clmax \\\\
\hline
\end{array}
$$

There were two error cases for the operation: the class might be full or the student might already be enroled. We form the concrete versions of these two parts of the operations. The first situation is described by

$$
\begin{array}{|l}
\hline
\_Full_____ \\
\Xi\,Class \\
resp! : Response \\
\hline
\#(n \cup y) = clmax \\
resp! = full \\
\hline
\end{array}
$$

The concrete counterpart is

$$
\begin{array}{|l}
\hline
\_CFull_____ \\
\Xi\,CClass \\
resp! : Response \\
\hline
num = clmax \\
resp! = full \\
\hline
\end{array}
$$

The second situation is described by

$$
\begin{array}{|l}
\hline
\_Found_____ \\
\Xi\,Class \\
s? : Student \\
resp! : Response \\
\hline
s? \in (n \cup y) \\
resp! = found \\
\hline
\end{array}
$$

The concrete counterpart is

$$
\begin{array}{|l}
\hline
\_CFound_____ \\
\Xi\,CClass \\
s? : Student \\
resp! : Response \\
\hline
s? \in \mathrm{ran}((1 .. num) \lhd (ar \,\fatsemi\, first)) \\
resp! = found \\
\hline
\end{array}
$$

As we can see from Figure 1, the concrete preconditions overlap in the same way that the abstract ones did, and thus refinement by parts is appropriate.

$$CEnrol \;\widehat{=}\; (CEnrol0 \land Success) \lor CFull \lor CFound.$$

1.3 Refinement to Code

The concrete enrol operation translates into the following specification statement:

$$CE == CClass, resp! : [true, [(CEnrol0 \land Success) \lor CFull \lor CFound]].$$

Operation	Precondition
CEnrol0	$s? \notin \mathrm{ran}((1 .. num) \lhd (ar \, \mathbf{;} \, first))$ $num < clmax$
CFull	$num = clmax$
CFound	$s? \in \mathrm{ran}((1 .. num) \lhd (ar \, \mathbf{;} \, first))$

Figure 1: Preconditions for the Concrete Class Manager

The development into code is straightforward. First, we make use of the ease with which we can determine whether the class is full or not. Next, we search for the student name in the array, to see whether the student is already enroled. Finally, we enrol the student if appropriate.

CE

$\sqsubseteq$ "ifT1"

    if $num = clmax \rightarrow$

        $resp! : [num = clmax, num = clmax \wedge resp! = full]$ $\lhd$

    $\square \; num < clmax \rightarrow$

        $CClass, resp! : [num < clmax, |(CEnrol0 \wedge Success) \vee CFound|](1)$

    fi

$\sqsubseteq$ "assI"

    $resp! := full$

We shall implement (1) using one of our special rules for introducing a conditional. By looking at the preconditions of *CEnrol0* and *CFound*, it is clear that we need to search for the name $s?$ in the array. Define a schema which expresses the fact that a student's name is not in our array up to some point w:

```
┌─ NotInPrefix ──────────────────────────────
│ CClass
│ s? : Student
│ w : 1 .. num + 1
├─────────────────────────────────────────────
│ s? ∉ ran((1 .. w − 1) ◁ (ar ; first))
└─────────────────────────────────────────────
```

When we have searched for a name in the array, we shall require that we haven't missed it (*NotInPrefix*), and that w either points outside the active part of the array, or it points to where $s?$ is stored in the array:

```
┌─ Search ───────────────────────────────────
│ NotInPrefix
├─────────────────────────────────────────────
│ w ≤ num ⇒ (ar ; first) w = s?
└─────────────────────────────────────────────
```

(1) $\sqsubseteq$ "ifT3" var $w : 1 .. clmax$ •

$\qquad$ $w : [num < clmax, Search]$; $\qquad\qquad\qquad\qquad\qquad\qquad\qquad$ $\lhd$

$\qquad$ if $w \in 1 .. num \rightarrow$

$$CClass, resp! : \left[\begin{pmatrix} num < clmax \\ Search \\ w \in 1 .. num \end{pmatrix}, [CFound] \right] \qquad (2)$$

$\qquad$ $\square$ $w = num + 1 \rightarrow$

$$CClass, resp! : \left[\begin{pmatrix} num < clmax \\ Search \\ w = num + 1 \end{pmatrix}, [(CEnrol0 \wedge Success)] \right] \qquad (3)$$

$\qquad$ fi

$\sqsubseteq$ "wp, definition of $Search$"

$\qquad$ $w : [true, NotInPrefix \wedge (w \leq num \Rightarrow (ar\,;\,first)w = s?)]$

$\sqsubseteq$ "semI"

$\qquad$ $w : [true, NotInPrefix]$;

$\qquad$ $w : [NotInPrefix, NotInPrefix \wedge (w \leq num \Rightarrow (ar\,;\,first)\ w = s?)]$ $\qquad$ (4)

$\sqsubseteq$ "assI"

$\qquad$ $w := 1$

(4) $\sqsubseteq$ "doI"

$\qquad$ do $w \leq num \wedge (ar\,;\,first)\ w \neq s? \rightarrow$

$$w : \left[\begin{pmatrix} w \leq num \\ (ar\,;\,first)w \neq s? \\ NotInPrefix \end{pmatrix}, \begin{pmatrix} 0 \leq num - w + 1 < num - w_0 + 1 \\ NotInPrefix \end{pmatrix} \right]$$

$\qquad$ od

$\sqsubseteq$ "assI"

$\qquad$ $w := w + 1$

(2) $\sqsubseteq$ "wp, definition of $CFound$"

$$resp! : \left[\begin{pmatrix} num < clmax \\ Search \\ w \in 1 .. num \end{pmatrix}, \begin{pmatrix} s? \in \mathrm{ran}((1 .. num) \lhd (ar\,;\,first)) \\ resp! = found \end{pmatrix} \right]$$

$\sqsubseteq$ "assI"

$resp! := found$

(3) $\sqsubseteq$ "wp, definitions of $CEnrol0$ and $Success$"

$$CClass, resp! : \left[\begin{pmatrix} num < clmax \\ Search \\ w = num + 1 \end{pmatrix}, \begin{pmatrix} num = num_0 + 1 \\ ar = ar_0 \oplus \{num \mapsto (s?, no)\} \\ resp! = ok \end{pmatrix} \right]$$

$\sqsubseteq$ "assI"

$\quad num, ar, resp! := num + 1, ar \oplus \{num + 1 \mapsto (s?, no)\}, ok$

ollecting the code, we have developed the following program:

```
|[
    if num = clmax → resp! := full
    □ num < clmax →
        |[ var w : 1 .. clmax •
            w := 1;
            do w ≤ num ∧ (ar ; first) w ≠ s? → w := w + 1 od;
            if w ∈ 1 .. num → resp! := found
            □ w = num + 1 →
                num, ar, resp! := num + 1, ar ⊕ {num + 1 ↦ (s?, no)}, ok
            fi
        ]|
    fi
]|
```

his translates into the Pascal code

```
const clmax = 35;
type Student = array [1 .. 16] of char;
     Pass = (yes, no);
     Record =
         record
             name : Student;
             status : Pass
         end;
var ar : array [1 .. clmax] of Record;
    num : 0 .. clmax;
```

procedure *enrol* (*s?* : *Student*; **var** *resp!* : *Response*);
    var $w : 1 .. clmax$;
    if $num = clmax$ **then**
        $resp! := full$
    else
        begin
            $w := 1$;
            while $w \leq num \wedge ar[w].name \neq s?$ **do**
                $w := w + 1$;
            if $w \leq num$ **then**
                $resp! := found$
            else
                begin
                    $num := num + 1$;
                    $ar[w].name := s?$;
                    $ar[w].status := no$;
                    $resp! := ok$
                end
        end;

2 Case Study: The Save Area

We present the specification and development of a Save Area.[1]

A Save Area is a module in an operating system with two operations, *Save* and *Restore*, by means of which records may be stored and retrieved in a last-in, first-out manner. Such a module may be useful in a check-pointing scheme, for instance, where the current state of a record structure is saved. At a later time, the system can be restored to this state. It should be noted that there will not always be sufficient room to store a new record.

The specification is nondeterministic, allowing us to delay taking a particular design decision too early. The design proceeds in two steps: first, an architectural decision is taken that introduces a two-level memory; second, the representation of the data structure used in main memory is decided. The design is produced using calculation. A new state is proposed, and its relation to the old state is documented. Next, the new operations are calculated from the old ones' definitions and the relation between them. The lowest level of design provides the starting point for the calculation of the code using the refinement calculus.

2.1 Specification

Our specification will leave abstract the details of the records being manipulated; let

[R]

---

[1]This specification was used as part of Ib Holm Sørensen's lectures on data refinement. His treatment of the development used an informal technique based on schemas. A similar development has been used by John Wordsworth.

be the set of all records. An operation returns a status report drawn from the set

$$St ::= ok \mid full \mid empty.$$

The state of our abstract description of the Save Area contains only a sequence of records, order being important:

```
┌─ S ────────────────────────────────────────────────────
│ sa : seq R
└────────────────────────────────────────────────────────
```

Initially, no records have been stored:

```
┌─ InitS ────────────────────────────────────────────────
│ S'
├────────────────────────────────────────────────────────
│ sa' = ⟨⟩
└────────────────────────────────────────────────────────
```

We shall use the sequence in the state as a stack, with its head as the right-most element. Thus, when a record is stored, it is appended to the sequence:

```
┌─ Save0 ────────────────────────────────────────────────
│ ΔS
│ r? : R
│ st! : St
├────────────────────────────────────────────────────────
│ sa' = sa ⌢ ⟨r?⟩
│ st! = ok
└────────────────────────────────────────────────────────
```

Although it is easy to see that $Save0$ is total, sometimes the $Save$ operation does not work. As was pointed out in the requirements, there is not always enough room to store the new record. We don't have enough state information to be able to explain the circumstances under which $Save$) will fail. We could remedy this by adding a new component that describes the amount of store left. We could update this value every time we modify sa. We could still remain abstract about the nature of records, by loosely specifying a function $size : R \rightarrow N$ that determines how much space we need to store a record. However, that doesn't capture the essence of the problem that we are faced with here. The amount of free space left in the system is influenced by many other factors than simply the size of the records and the number of them that we have stored. We still do not have enough information to update the amount of free space: we need to model the rest of the system in some way. Pursuing this path leads only to something not very abstract and not very modular. Better is to admit that we do not know the circumstances—at this level of abstraction—that determine the amount of free space, and therefore the success or failure of the $Save$ operation. This leads us to a nondeterministic specification, rather than a loose specification.

The error case is described by the operation

$$
\begin{array}{|l}
\_SaveFullErr _____ \\
\Xi S \\
st! : St \\
\hline
st! = full \\
\end{array}
$$

Our complete description of *Save* is the nondeterministic operation

$$Save \triangleq Save0 \lor SaveFullErr.$$

The *Restore* operation is specified in two parts. We can restore a record whenever there is at least one record in *sa*:

$$
\begin{array}{|l}
\_Restore0 _____ \\
\Delta S \\
r! : R \\
st! : St \\
\hline
sa \neq \langle\rangle \\
sa = sa' \frown \langle r!\rangle \\
st! = ok \\
\end{array}
$$

However, if *sa* is empty, then we must return an error message:

$$
\begin{array}{|l}
\_RestoreEmptyErr _____ \\
\Xi S \\
st! : St \\
\hline
sa = \langle\rangle \\
st! = empty \\
\end{array}
$$

Restore is the wholly deterministic operation formed by the disjunction of the two parts that we have specified:

$$Restore \triangleq Restore0 \lor RestoreEmptyErr.$$

The preconditions for the operations in the interface to the Save Area are collected in Figure 2.

2.2 Design

Our first design decision is an architectural one: we shall introduce a two-level memory. We expect that very large amounts of data will be saved, and we shall quickly exhaust the main memory available to our program. Besides our expensive, fast main memory we have cheap, high volume, slow access backing stores. Our design is based on the following idea. Since the amount of main memory that we can use is bounded in size, we shall represent our use of it with a bounded sequence. Once we exhaust the available main memory, we shall copy it onto backing store. When we exhaust the supply of records being restored, we shall copy one main memory's worth from backing store.

Operation	Precondition
Save0	*true*
SaveFullErr	*true*
Save	*true*
Restore0	$sa \neq \langle\rangle$
RestoreEmptyErr	$sa = \langle\rangle$
Restore	*true*

Figure 2: Preconditions for the Save Area

Let n be the number of records that we can save in main memory (it makes sense that we can store at least one):

$$\frac{n : \mathbf{N}}{n \geq 1.}$$

A bounded sequence is one whose length does not exceed n; a full sequence is one whose length is n:

$$
\begin{array}{|l}
\hline
[X] \\
\hline
bseq : \mathbf{P}(\operatorname{seq} X) \\
fseq : \mathbf{P}(\operatorname{seq} X) \\
\hline
bseq = \{\, s : \operatorname{seq} X \mid \#s \leq n \,\} \\
fseq = \{\, s : \operatorname{seq} X \mid \#s = n \,\}. \\
\hline
\end{array}
$$

Our state consists of main and secondary memory. Main memory is a bounded sequence of records, and secondary memory is a list of full sequences:

$$
\begin{array}{|l}
\hline
D \\
\hline
mm : bseq[R] \\
sm : \operatorname{seq}(fseq[R]) \\
\hline
\end{array}
$$

We can extract the abstract Save Area by ordering all the records in the concrete state; we need to flatten the list of full records, and take care that we reproduce the abstract order. This is documented in our first retrieve relation:

$$
\begin{array}{|l}
\hline
Retr \\
\hline
S \\
D \\
\hline
sa = (\frown / sm) \frown mm \\
\hline
\end{array}
$$

Notice that *Retr* is a total surjective function from concrete to abstract states: every concrete state represents some abstract state; every abstract state can be represented this way; each concrete state represent exactly one abstract state. Suppose that n is 3, and there are seventeen records in the abstract state:

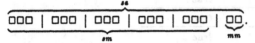

Clearly, there is exactly one way to break sa up into sm and mm: sm contains fifteen records split into five blocks of three; mm contains the odd two records; order is preserved throughout. Similarly, there is exactly one way to put the contents of sm and mm together to make sa, whilst preserving order. However, there are two concrete realisations for an abstract state which has a multiple of n records, and so the retrieve function is not injective.

The new initialisation is described by the following schema, derived from $InitS$ under $Retr'$:

$$
\begin{array}{|l}
\hline
D' \\
\hline
(\frown/\, sm') \frown mm' = \langle\rangle \\
\hline
\end{array}
$$

There is an unique solution to this equation:

$$(\frown/\, sm') \frown mm' = \langle\rangle$$

$\Leftrightarrow$ "by a property of catenation"

$$(\frown/\, sm' = \langle\rangle) \wedge (mm' = \langle\rangle)$$

$\Leftrightarrow$ "by a property of distributed catenation"

$$(sm' = \langle\rangle) \wedge (mm' = \langle\rangle).$$

Thus, the initialisation of the two-level system is given by

$$
\begin{array}{|l}
\hline
\;InitD \\
\hline
D' \\
\hline
mm' = \langle\rangle \\
sm' = \langle\rangle \\
\hline
\end{array}
$$

The concrete version of $Save0$ is given by substitution into the abstract version:

$$
\begin{array}{|l}
\hline
\Delta D \\
r? : R \\
st! : St \\
\hline
(\frown/\, sm') \frown mm' = (\frown/\, sm) \frown mm \frown \langle r? \rangle \\
st! = ok \\
\hline
\end{array}
$$

There are two obvious solutions to the equation defining the concrete state change:

$$\frown/\, sm' = (\frown/\, sm) \frown mm$$
$$mm' = \langle r? \rangle$$

and

$$\frown/\,sm' = \frown/\,sm$$
$$mm' = mm \frown \langle r?\rangle.$$

In the first case, we have

$$\frown/\,sm' = (\frown/\,sm)\frown mm$$

    ⇔ "by a property of distributed catenation"
$$\frown/\,sm' = \frown/(sm \frown \langle mm\rangle)$$

    ⇐ "since $\frown/$ is a function"
$$sm' = sm \frown \langle mm\rangle$$

But this solution must maintain the state invariant, and so sm' must be a sequence of full sequences; thus

$$sm \frown \langle mm\rangle \in \text{seq}(fseq[R])$$

    ⇔ "property of sequences"
$$sm \in \text{seq}(fseq[R]) \wedge mm \in fseq[R]$$

    ⇔ "by the invariant on D"
$$mm \in fseq[R]$$

    ⇔ "by the definition of $fseq$"
$$mm \in \text{seq}\,R \wedge \#mm = n$$

    ⇔ "by the invariant on D"
$$\#mm = n.$$

Also, mm' must satisfy its state invariant, so

$$\langle r?\rangle \in bseq[R]$$

    ⇔ "by the definition of $bseq$"
$$\langle r?\rangle \in \text{seq}\,R \wedge \#\langle r?\rangle \le n$$

    ⇔ "by a property of sequences"
$$r? \in R \wedge \#\langle r?\rangle \le n$$

$\Leftrightarrow$ "by the declaration of $r?$"

$\#\langle r?\rangle \leq n$

$\Leftrightarrow$ "by a property of sequences"

$1 \leq n$

$\Leftrightarrow$ "by the definition of n"

true

In the second case, we have

$mm \frown \langle r?\rangle \in bseq[R]$

$\Leftrightarrow$ "by the definition of $bseq$"

$mm \frown \langle r?\rangle \in seq\, R \wedge \#(mm \frown \langle r?\rangle) \leq n$

$\Leftrightarrow$ "by a property of sequences"

$mm \in seq\, R \wedge \langle r?\rangle \in seq\, R \wedge \#(mm \frown \langle r?\rangle) \leq n$

$\Leftrightarrow$ "by the state invariant on D"

$\langle r?\rangle \in seq\, R \wedge \#(mm \frown \langle r?\rangle) \leq n$

$\Leftrightarrow$ "by a property of sequences"

$r? \in R \wedge \#(mm \frown \langle r?\rangle) \leq n$

$\Leftrightarrow$ "by the declaration of $r?$"

$\#(mm \frown \langle r?\rangle) \leq n$

$\Leftrightarrow$ "by a property of $\#$"

$(\#mm) + \#\langle r?\rangle \leq n$

$\Leftrightarrow$ "by a property of $\#$"

$(\#mm) + 1 \leq n$

$\Leftrightarrow$ "by a property of numbers"

$\#mm < n$

Thus, the successful part of our concrete save operation is given by

$$\begin{array}{|l}
\hline \text{\_\_CSave0\_\_} \\
\Delta D \\
r? : R \\
st! : St \\
\hline
((\#mm = n \wedge mm' = \langle r? \rangle \wedge sm' = sm \frown \langle mm \rangle) \ \vee \\
(\#mm < n \wedge mm' = mm \frown \langle r? \rangle \wedge sm' = sm)) \\
st! = ok \\
\hline
\end{array}$$

The error case is trivially calculated:

$$\begin{array}{|l}
\hline \text{\_\_CSaveFullErr\_\_} \\
\Xi D \\
st! : St \\
\hline
st! = full \\
\hline
\end{array}$$

This gives our full description of the new interface:

$$CSave \triangleq CSave0 \vee CSaveFullErr.$$

2.3 Further Design

Now we address how the data held in main memory is to be implemented. A bounded sequence may be represented by a fixed-length array with a counter recording how long the sequence is. A fixed-length array is modelled by a total function from the indices to the target type:

$$\begin{array}{|l}
\hline \text{\_\_}[X]\text{\_\_} \\
Array : \mathbf{P}(\mathbf{N} \nrightarrow X) \\
\hline
Array = (1 \mathinner{\ldotp\ldotp} n) \rightarrow X. \\
\hline
\end{array}$$

Our new design contains an array, a counter, and the representation of the secondary memory unchanged:

$$\begin{array}{|l}
\hline \text{\_\_}D1\text{\_\_} \\
ma : Array[R] \\
p : 0 \mathinner{\ldotp\ldotp} n \\
sm : \text{seq}(fseq[R]) \\
\hline
\end{array}$$

The bounded sequence may be reconstructed from the array, by throwing away the waste above the counter:

$$\begin{array}{|l}
\hline \text{\_\_}Retr1\text{\_\_} \\
D \\
D1 \\
\hline
mm = (1 \mathinner{\ldotp\ldotp} p) \lhd ma \\
\hline
\end{array}$$

Notice that this is a total surjective function from concrete to abstract. Every fixed-length array, trimmed of its waste, represents a sequence. Every bounded sequence can be padded out with arbitrary values to make the fixed-length array. Once the waste has been trimmed, the array denotes an unique bounded sequence.

We proceed with the calculation of the latest version of the $Save0$ operation:

$$
\begin{array}{|l}
\Delta D \\
r? : R \\
st! : St \\
\hline
(\#((1 .. p) \lhd ma) = n \land \\
\quad (1 .. p') \lhd ma' = \langle r? \rangle \land \\
\quad sm' = sm \frown ((1 .. p) \lhd ma)) \ \lor \\
(\#((1 .. p) \lhd ma) < n \land \\
\quad (1 .. p') \lhd ma' = ((1 .. p) \lhd ma) \frown \langle r? \rangle \land \\
\quad sm' = sm) \\
st! = ok
\end{array}
$$

The term $\#((1 .. p) \lhd ma)$ occurs twice; it is simply p:

$\#((1 .. p) \lhd ma)$

$=$ "by a property of functions"

$\quad \#(\mathrm{dom}((1 .. p) \lhd ma))$

$=$ "by a property of dom"

$\quad \#((1 .. p) \cap \mathrm{dom}\, ma)$

$=$ "by the definition of ma"

$\quad \#((1 .. p) \cap (1 .. n))$

$=$ "by a property of $\cap$ and $..$"

$\quad \#(1 .. min\{p, n\})$

$=$ "since $p \in 0 .. n$"

$\quad \#(1 .. p)$

$=$ "by a property of $\#$"

$\quad p.$

This makes the operation look a little better:

$$
\begin{array}{|l}
\hline
\Delta D \\
r? : R \\
st! : St \\
\hline
((p = n \land \\
\quad (1 .. p') \lhd ma' = \langle r? \rangle \land \\
\quad sm' = sm \frown ((1 .. p) \lhd ma)) \lor \\
(p < n \land \\
\quad (1 .. p') \lhd ma' = ((1 .. p) \lhd ma) \frown \langle r? \rangle \land \\
\quad sm' = sm)) \\
st! = ok \\
\hline
\end{array}
$$

Our operation has become a disjunction; we proceed by analysing the two cases. In case $p = n$, we have

$$(1 .. p') \lhd ma' = \langle r? \rangle$$

So $(1 .. p') \lhd ma'$ is a singleton sequence; thus, p' must take the value 1, and ma' may take any value, so long as its first element is $r?$. sm' must take the value

$$sm \frown ((1 .. n) \lhd ma)$$

which, since dom ma is by definition $1 .. n$, is simply

$$sm \frown \langle ma \rangle$$

In case $p < n$, we have

$$(1 .. p') \lhd ma' = ((1 .. p) \lhd ma) \frown \langle r? \rangle$$

Now, if this equality holds, then the length of the sequence on both sides must be equal. Thus

$$\#((1 .. p') \lhd ma') = \#(((1 .. p) \lhd ma) \frown \langle r? \rangle)$$

$\Leftrightarrow$ "by a property of $\#$"
$$\#((1 .. p') \lhd ma') = \#((1 .. p) \lhd ma) + 1$$

$\Leftrightarrow$ "by the previous result"
$$p' = p + 1.$$

We can use this result in our next calculation:

$$(1 .. p') \lhd ma' = ((1 .. p) \lhd ma) \frown \langle r? \rangle$$

$\Leftrightarrow$ "since $p' = p + 1$"

$$(1 \mathbin{..} (p+1)) \lhd ma' = ((1 \mathbin{..} p) \lhd ma) \mathbin{\frown} \langle r? \rangle$$

$\Leftrightarrow$ "by a property of $\frown$"
$$(1 \mathbin{..} (p+1)) \lhd ma' = ((1 \mathbin{..} p) \lhd ma) \oplus \{ \#((1 \mathbin{..} p) \lhd ma) + 1 \mapsto r? \}$$

$\Leftrightarrow$ "by the previous result"
$$(1 \mathbin{..} (p+1)) \lhd ma' = ((1 \mathbin{..} p) \lhd ma) \oplus \{ p + 1 \mapsto r? \}$$

$\Leftrightarrow$ "by a property of $\oplus$"
$$(1 \mathbin{..} (p+1)) \lhd ma' = (1 \mathbin{..} (p+1)) \lhd (ma \oplus \{ p + 1 \mapsto r? \}).$$

Now, there are many solutions for ma', but an obvious one is

$$ma' = ma \oplus \{ p + 1 \mapsto r? \}.$$

To summarise, our new operation has been simplified to

```
┌─ CCSave0 ──────────────────────────────────────────────
│ ΔD1
│ r? : R
│ st! : St
├────────────────────────────────────────────────────────
│ ((p = n ∧
│      p' = 1 ∧
│      ma' 1 = r? ∧
│      sm' = sm ⌢ ⟨ma⟩) ∨
│  (p < n ∧
│      p' = p + 1 ∧
│      ma' = ma ⊕ {p + 1 ↦ r?} ∧
│      sm' = sm))
│ st! = ok
└────────────────────────────────────────────────────────
```

The error case is trivially disposed of:

```
┌─ CCSaveFullErr ────────────────────────────────────────
│ ΞD1
│ st! : St
├────────────────────────────────────────────────────────
│ st! = full
└────────────────────────────────────────────────────────
```

Our new design has led us to this definition of the *Save* operation:

$$CCSave \mathrel{\hat{=}} CCSave0 \lor CCSaveFullErr.$$

2.4 Refinement to Code

We can now proceed to code; however, we shall continue to leave abstract the interface with the secondary memory. First, define *save* to be the refinement calculus translation of *CCSave*:

$$save == D1, st!: [true , \lfloor CCSave \rfloor] .$$

Let us break up our *CCSave0* operation into its two component disjunctions:

```
┌─ CCUpdateSM ─────────────────────────────────
│ ΔD1
│ r? : R
│ st! : St
├──────────────────────────────────────────────
│ p = n
│ p' = 1
│ ma' 1 = r?
│ sm' = sm ⌢ ⟨ma⟩)
│ st! = ok
└──────────────────────────────────────────────
```

```
┌─ CCUpdateMM ─────────────────────────────────
│ ΔD1
│ r? : R
│ st! : St
├──────────────────────────────────────────────
│ p < n
│ p' = p + 1
│ ma' = ma ⊕ {p + 1 ↦ r?}
│ sm' = sm
│ st! = ok
└──────────────────────────────────────────────
```

We refine *save* as follows:

$save$

$\sqsubseteq$ "by definition"

$$D1, st!: \begin{bmatrix} true , & \begin{array}{c} \lfloor CCUpdateMM \rfloor \\ \vee \\ \lfloor CCUpdateSM \vee CCSaveFullErr \rfloor \end{array} \end{bmatrix}$$

$\sqsubseteq$ "iff"

$\quad$ if $p < n \rightarrow$

$\qquad D1, st!: [p < n , \lfloor CCUpdateMM \rfloor]$ $\qquad\qquad$ ◁

$\square\ p = n \rightarrow$

$\qquad D1, st!: [p = n\ ,\ [CCUpdateSM \vee CCSaveFullErr]] \qquad (1)$

fi

$\sqsubseteq$ "by definition"

$$p, ma, st!: \left[p < n\ ,\ \begin{pmatrix} p = p_0 + 1 \\ ma = ma_0 \oplus \{p_0 + 1 \mapsto r?\} \\ st! = ok \end{pmatrix} \right]$$

$\sqsubseteq$ "assI"

$$p, ma, st! := p + 1, ma \oplus \{p + 1 \mapsto r?\}, ok$$

$(1) \sqsubseteq$ "by definition"

$$p, ma, sm, st!: \left[p = n\ ,\ \begin{pmatrix} p = 1 \\ ma\ 1 = r? \\ sm = sm_0 \ ^\frown \langle ma_0 \rangle \\ st! = ok \end{pmatrix} \vee \begin{pmatrix} p = p_0 \\ ma = ma_0 \\ sm = sm_0 \\ st! = full \end{pmatrix} \right]$$

$\sqsubseteq$ "semI§" con $X \bullet$

$$st!, sm: \left[true\ ,\ \begin{pmatrix} st! = ok \\ sm = sm_0 \ ^\frown \langle ma \rangle \end{pmatrix} \vee \begin{pmatrix} st! = full \\ sm = sm_0 \end{pmatrix} \right] ; \qquad (2)$$

$$p, ma: \left[\begin{pmatrix} st! = ok \\ sm = X \ ^\frown \langle ma \rangle \end{pmatrix} \atop \begin{matrix} \vee \\ \begin{pmatrix} st! = full \\ sm = X \end{pmatrix} \end{matrix}\ ,\ \begin{pmatrix} p = 1 \\ ma\ 1 = r? \\ sm = X \ ^\frown \langle ma_0 \rangle \\ st! = ok \end{pmatrix} \atop \begin{matrix} \vee \\ \begin{pmatrix} p = p_0 \\ ma = ma_0 \\ sm = X \\ st! = full \end{pmatrix} \end{matrix} \right] \qquad \triangleleft$$

$\sqsubseteq$ "ifI"

$\quad$ if $st! = ok \rightarrow$

$$p, ma: \left[\begin{pmatrix} st! = ok \\ sm = X \ ^\frown \langle ma \rangle \end{pmatrix} ,\ \begin{pmatrix} p = 1 \\ ma\ 1 = r? \\ sm = X \ ^\frown \langle ma_0 \rangle \\ st! = ok \end{pmatrix} \right] \qquad \triangleleft$$

$\quad \square\ st! = full \rightarrow$

$$p, ma: \left[\begin{pmatrix} st! = full \\ sm = X \end{pmatrix} , \begin{pmatrix} p = p_0 \\ ma = ma_0 \\ sm = X \\ st! = full \end{pmatrix} \right] \tag{3}$$

fi

$\sqsubseteq$ "assI"

$\quad p, ma := 1, ma \oplus \{1 \mapsto r?\}$

$(3) \sqsubseteq$ "skipI"

$\quad$ **skip**

The code produced by this refinement is:

if $p < n \rightarrow$

$\quad p, ma, st! := p + 1, ma \oplus \{p + 1 \mapsto r?\}, ok$

$\square\ p = n \rightarrow$

$\quad st!, sm: \left[true , \begin{pmatrix} st! = ok \\ sm = sm_0 \frown \langle ma \rangle \end{pmatrix} \vee \begin{pmatrix} st! = full \\ sm = sm_0 \end{pmatrix} \right] ;$

$\quad$ **if** $st! = ok \rightarrow$

$\qquad p, ma := 1, ma \oplus \{1 \mapsto r?\}$

$\quad \square\ st! = full \rightarrow$

$\qquad$ **skip**

$\quad$ **fi**

fi.

Tutorial Lecture Notes
on the
Irish School of the *VDM*

Mícheál Mac an Airchinnigh
Department of Computer Science
Trinity College, Dublin, Ireland

1   Introduction

"Partial differential equations became and remain the heart of mathematics"
[19] p.671.

In the Irish School of the *VDM* we take the view that a formal (development) method is essentially **constructive applied mathematics**. *Ergo*, the starting point of all work must be the problem domain. Given a problem to solve, we first build a model. Such model-building is the counterpart to the formulation of the partial differential equation. Not surprisingly, just as there are well-known partial differential equations that have been adapted to problem domains other than those for which they were originally designed, so we find that the same is true of the *VDM* domain models. Having constructed the model, we then ask pertinent questions about it—said questions being at the very heart of all requirements capture. We have postulated the existence of the model before putting the questions. In practice, in real applications, the model frequently emerges as a result of such questions. Moreover, there will usually be multiple models, each of which represents a particular view. Answers to said questions may lead to *closed form solutions*—'simple' expressions—or to *constructive solutions*, the counterpart of the iterative methods for solving partial-differential equations—recursive algorithms—and sometimes both forms of solution may co-exist. Examples will be given in subsequent sections.

This being a tutorial on the Irish School of the *VDM*, one is obliged to provide, on the one hand, an in-depth detailed *introduction* to the method and notation and, on the other, to exhibit the breadth of its scope. The method is not merely a matter of knowledge and the application of technical skills but also embraces a particular philosophy of computing, a point of considerable importance that underpins the very concept of 'school'. Said philosophy is sketched out in a doctoral thesis [22].

For the purposes of exposition *we will consider* the Irish School of the *VDM* to be a formal development method for the specification, design and implementation of systems which consists of five parts:

1. a terse abstract mathematical notation;

2. a style of use and development;

3. the discovery of theorems and their proof;

4. semantics;

5. a standard collection of models.

Each of these aspects is briefly elaborated upon in this introductory section and developed more fully in the context of a suite of problems in subsequent sections.

The phrase '*we will consider*', used above, is intended to be understood in the same spirit as Hilbert's famous '*Wir denken uns*'—let us suppose—in the context of Euclidean Geometry. That is to say, the Irish School of the *VDM* may be considered to be a branch of constructive mathematics that is of interest in its own right. Thus, just as practical scientific problems led to the formulation of partial differential equations the solution of which, in turn, "created the need for mathematical developments in the theory of functions, the calculus of variations, series expansions, ordinary differential equations, algebra, and differential geometry"[19] p.671, so the application of the Irish School of the *VDM* is opening up a whole new branch of constructive mathematics. In other words, there is a perspective of the School that has **overtly** nothing whatsoever to do with the specification, design and implementation of systems.

1.1 Notation

"φανερὸν οὖν ὅτι καὶ τὰς λύσεις τῶν μύθων ἐξ αὐτοῦ δεῖ τοῦ μύθου συμβαίνειν, καὶ μὴ ὥσπερ ἐν τῇ Μηδείᾳ ἀπὸ μηχανῆς καὶ ἐν τῇ Ἰλιάδι τὰ περὶ τὸν ἀπόπλουν" ΑΡΙΣ-ΤΟΤΕΛΟΥΣ ΠΕΡΙ ΠΟΙΗΤΙΚΗΣ **1454b** [18].

Notation is a vehicle for communication, but only for those for whom it is intelligible. A facility in the use of notation is similar to that of any language, whether natural—such as that of the above Greek passage—or artificial—such as a programming language. Such facility comes with experience and practice and binds one to a particular world of culture and ideas. It is to be expected, therefore that the neophyte to the Irish School of the *VDM*, even one well-versed in the notation of other Schools, will experience a certain culture-shock. It is not so much that the material *per se* differs radically from that of other Schools; rather, it is a matter of notation and learning how to interpret expressions written in same.

Verbosity and complexity of expression in formal specification hinders the discovery of theorems and the carrying out of proofs. To be blunt, such specifications are ugly—offend the æsthetic sense. The traditional style of use of the *VDM* contradicts some of the most basic notational principles of mathematics, a *VDM* style which leans toward the 'meaningfullness' of syntax. For example, in specifying an unbounded stack of integers, say, it is 'normal' to give a domain equation such as

$$STACK = INT^* \qquad (1)$$

or, in the English School, to write **seq of** *INT* on the right hand side. But the names *STACK* and *INT* are pure conveniences for the clients. Using the standard mathematical symbol for integers, $\mathbf{Z}$, the model is nothing more than $\mathbf{Z}^*$, a model which has many more interpretations than that of 'stack'. In Mathematics, variable names are always single letters, whether Roman or Greek. On the contrary, it is customary in the *VDM* to use (multiletter) abreviations of 'meaningful' names, e.g., $stk \in STACK$ to denote a stack. In the Irish School, verbose specifications are used for 'public consumption'; all the real work is done in the abstract.

1.1.1 On the Abuse of Notation

Abuse of notation is a fundamental part of mathematical culture. It is a deliberate abandoning of the strictly precise and formal denotation of mathematical entities. Such abuse is naturally abhorrent to the strict formal methodists—especially those who insist that the notation be processable by computing machinery. The Irish School of the *VDM* tries to strike a balance between the liberalism of mathematics and the conservatism of formal methods. Specifically, it is formal in the sense that nothing is left implicit. However, the liberal mathematical approach which opens the door to the potential of *fruitful ambiguity* is equally supported. The term 'ambiguity' denotes an expression that has more than one meaning. To describe an expression as fruitfully ambiguous is to assert that whereas within a given context the meaning is completely determined, nevertheless, one often has the opportunity to see another meaning that enriches the interpretation. As a consequence, specifications in the Irish School of the *VDM* are, in general, not amenable to direct processing; on the other hand they are 'sufficiently' complete to permit transformation into a form that *is* processable. Consequently, were one to be **strict** in the interpretation of the word 'formal' as understood in the twentieth century, then the method of the Irish School is not 'formal'.

1.1.2 A Sampling of Notation in the Irish School

Much of the material in subsequent sections is organised to introduce the notation and method of the Irish School. Nevertheless, it is proper to give a little of the flavour at this stage.

The basic structures of (power)set, sequence and map are considered to result from the application of functors $\mathcal{P}(-)$, $(-)^*$, and $(- \underset{m}{\rightarrow} -)$, respectively, applied to sets/domains. The '$-$' is simply an argument placeholder, which is sometimes omitted.

1. Let A denote some set/domain. Then the powerset functor $\mathcal{P}$ constructs $\mathcal{P}A$:

$$\mathcal{P}: A \mapsto \mathcal{P}A \tag{2}$$

Consequently, given a function $f: A \mapsto B$, then there is a corresponding $\mathcal{P}f$ induced by the functor $\mathcal{P}$ such that

$$\mathcal{P}f: \mathcal{P}A \mapsto \mathcal{P}B \tag{3}$$

The null element of $\mathcal{P}A$ is denoted $\emptyset$, the standard symbol in mathematics. For all (total) functions f, $\mathcal{P}f(\emptyset) = \emptyset$.

2. For some set/domain A the star functor $*$ constructs the set/domain of sequences:

$$*: A \mapsto A^* \tag{4}$$

and, given a function $f: A \mapsto B$, then we have

$$f^*: A^* \mapsto B^* \tag{5}$$

For the null element, the chosen symbol is Λ, and $f^*(\Lambda) = \Lambda$.

3. Let A and C denote some sets/domains, then the set/domain of maps (i.e., partial functions) is contructed

$$\underset{m}{\rightarrow} : A \times C \mapsto A \underset{m}{\rightarrow} C \tag{6}$$

Given functions $f: A \mapsto B$ and $g: C \mapsto D$, then

$$f \underset{m}{\rightarrow} g: A \underset{m}{\rightarrow} C \mapsto B \underset{m}{\rightarrow} D \tag{7}$$

For the null map θ, we have $(f \underset{m}{\rightarrow} g)(\theta) = \theta$.

Thus the basic structures are all built in a uniform way and the very mechanism by which this is accomplished induces corresponding functional iterators for said structures. A comparison with other Schools is invited.

The notion of currying is also fundamental. Consider the operation of deletion of a map μ with respect to a set S, denoted $S \blacktriangleleft \mu$. We feel free to write this expression in curried form as $\blacktriangleleft [S] \mu$ or $\blacktriangleleft_S \mu$. The same notation is then employed for deletion of all elements of a sequence with respect to a set and for classical set difference. The significance of the notation comes into full play when used in combination with other operators. For instance, let $\mu \in X \underset{m}{\rightarrow} \mathcal{P}Y$. Suppose that we are required to construct the derived map μ' such that every element in the range of μ is deleted with respect to the set S. If $\mathcal{I}$ denotes the identity function then the solution is immediately given by

$$\mu' = (\mathcal{I} \underset{m}{\rightarrow} \blacktriangleleft_S)\mu \tag{8}$$

In passing, it is worth noting that all deletion operators may be classified as endomorphisms of particular monoids [22], an aside that points to the foundations of the Irish School. Thus, apart from such notational convenience, currying is of considerable theoretical importance in the entire School [22].

Lest one might still be curious about the reason for the specific Greek passage chosen to head this subsection, a few remarks will elucidate. It is an excerpt from Aristotle's work on Greek theatre and the passage itself points to an undesirable element thereof—the **deus ex machina**—a phrase that is current in philosophy and mathematics to denote the employment of a 'surprise resolution' of a particular problem, a solution that could not be foreseen within the context of previous development. Not only does the passage serve the purpose of highlighting the nature of notation, but has proven fruitful in the analysis and specification of requirements. Indeed, the whole discourse provides an opportunity to give fresh insight into the process of system specification and development. Details are given in [22]. The Irish School of the *VDM* is more than a matter of technical skills.

1.2 Development

In the *VDM*, in general, much of the method consists in the construction of a sequence of models $MODEL_i$, $i \in \mathbb{N}$, such that for each pair $MODEL_j$ and $MODEL_{j+1}$, $MODEL_{j+1}$ is said to be a reification or refinement of $MODEL_j$ and that, consequently, the latter is more abstract than the former. The relationship between the two is formally characterised by a retrieve function $\Re_{j+1,j}$:

$$MODEL_j$$
$$\Big\uparrow \Re_{j+1,j} \tag{9}$$
$$MODEL_{j+1}$$

Such a view is entirely consistent with the (programming language) notion of a separate 'implementation' (module) corresponding to an abstract data type 'specification' (module). Consider a *curried* operation Op_j which gives the transformation $Op_j \colon MODEL_j \mapsto MODEL'_j$, then for a comparable reified operation Op_{j+1}, we have

$$
\begin{array}{ccc}
MODEL_j & \xrightarrow{\ Op_j\ } & MODEL'_j \\
\Big\uparrow \Re_{j+1,j} & & \Big\uparrow \Re'_{j+1,j} \\
MODEL_{j+1} & \xrightarrow{\ Op_{j+1}\ } & MODEL'_{j+1}
\end{array}
\tag{10}
$$

and, to prove that $MODEL_{j+1}$ correctly implements $MODEL_j$ **with respect to** Op_{j+1} and Op_j, one is obliged to demonstrate commutativity of the diagram, i.e., that:

$$Op_j \circ \Re_{j+1,j} = \Re'_{j+1,j} \circ Op_{j+1} \tag{11}$$

Moreover such proofs **must** be carried out for **each** defined operation. **N.B.** The priming of the right hand side is intended to indicate the full generality of the scheme. In 'state-to-state' transformations $MODEL'_j = MODEL_j$; in evaluation transformations, it is frequently the case that $MODEL'_{j+1} = MODEL'_j$.

1.2.1 Elaboration versus Reification

Conceptually, reification may be considered to be a 'downward' development in the sense that the reified model is, in some sense, more concrete, i.e., nearer to the implementation, than the abstract model.

However, there is also, in the Irish School, the distinct notion of a 'sideways' or 'collateral' development which is termed an elaboration.

A simple example, taken from [22], will illustrate the distinction. Consider a spelling-checker dictionary, which is completely and adequately modelled by

$$\delta_0 \in DICT_0 = \mathcal{P}W \tag{12}$$

To check the spelling of a given word w, is simply a matter of looking it up in the dictionary δ_0:

$$Lkp_0[w]\delta_0 \overset{\triangle}{=} \chi[w]\delta_0 \tag{13}$$

A standard reification is to implement sets via sequences, subject to the usual invariant: 'no duplicates' and equivalence classes based on canonical ordering. The corresponding model is

$$\delta_1 \in DICT_1 = W^* \tag{14}$$

and the lookup function specified by

$$Lkp_1[w]\delta_1 \triangleq \chi[w]\delta_1 \tag{15}$$

The two models are related by the retrieve function

$$DICT_0 = \mathcal{P}W$$
$$\uparrow \mathfrak{R}_{10} = elems \tag{16}$$
$$DICT_1 = W^*$$

Technically, this expression for the retrieve function is an abuse of notation. Strictly, we ought to write, for all $\delta_1 \in DICT_1$, then $\mathfrak{R}_{10}(\delta_1) = \delta_0 \in DICT_0$. At the domain equation level, it is more formal to write $\mathcal{P}\mathfrak{R}_{10}(DICT_1) = DICT_0$.

An alternative path of development is to *extend the concept* of the spelling checker dictionary to one which, for each word, contains a corresponding set of definitions:

$$\delta_2 \in DICT_2 = W \underset{m}{\rightarrow} \mathcal{P}DEF \tag{17}$$

As well as using this dictionary to check the spelling of a word:

$$Lkp_2[w]\delta_2 \triangleq \chi[w]\delta_2 \tag{18}$$

there is, in addition, a second lookup operation for which there is **no counterpart** in the original abstract model—to look up the definition of a word

$$Lkp'_2[w]\delta_2 \triangleq \delta_2(w) \tag{19}$$

subject to the obvious pre-condition. Of course, such an operation returns a (possibly empty) set of definitions.

This elaboration conceptually *covers* the spelling checker dictionary, in the sense that for any operation that we might wish to perform on $\delta_0 \in DICT_0$ there is an exact counterpart for a $\delta_2 \in DICT_2$. But the reverse is not true. Such coverings, which are of considerable importance in automata theory, and known by that name [10], are also subject to proof via retrieve functions. Thus, we may write, with the usual abuse of notation,

$$DICT_0 = \mathcal{P}W \xleftarrow{\mathfrak{R}_{20} = dom} DICT_2 = W \underset{m}{\rightarrow} \mathcal{P}DEF \tag{20}$$

Naturally, such elaborated models are also the meat for reification.

1.2.2 Classes of Models

In real specifications of complex systems, one does not have a single model as a starting point but rather a class of inter-related models, each of which is formulated from a different perspective. One might artificially bind together such a collection of models into something called the 'state', a binding which does violence to the whole notion of reification and elaboration. For it is clear that different views, formulated by different models, might call for totally disjoint, though inter-related, developments, the inter-relationships being dictated by those of the actual system.

1.3 Theorems and Proof

> "When toy-examples [in the *VDM*] are scaled-up to real examples, formal proofs are either discarded (and the method no longer acceptable as formal), or they become a serious bottleneck in development" [25] p.3.

In considering the degree of truth of the above quotation, one must examine some of the terms used. First, in the view of the Irish School there is no such thing as a "toy-example". There are minimal (abstract) models. As to whether formal proofs are discarded, we would tend to agree, but not in the context of the Irish School. If "formal proofs become a serious bottleneck in development", then it is probable that there is not enough reuse of specifications, theorems and proofs, or, indeed, the very nature, and purpose, of doing proof is misunderstood.

There is a misconception that the *primary* purpose of proof is to verify correctness of something—such a misconception arising very likely from the phrase 'proving programs correct'. In the Irish School, one views a proof as an opportunity to uncover a misunderstanding in the problem being solved—to debug the requirements, in other words.

With respect to the paucity of reuse in specifications, this is undoubtedly due to the fact that much formal specification is conducted in a manner similar to programming—reinvention of wheels—a problem aggravated by the domain-specificity of the specification and, consequently, the actual use of 'meaningful' names!

1.3.1 Proof in the Irish School

> "Leibnitz is reported to have stated that 'any such method [*methodus inveniendi*, to invent solutions of mathematical problems] which proceeds from the assumption of a solution is never a *methodus demonstrandi*, a method of proof'". [12] p.74.

Unlike all other Schools of the *VDM* (and most formal methods) which rely on predicate logic, to a greater or lesser extent, to carry through formal proofs, the Irish School uses classical mathematical methods. Mathematicians rarely, if ever, use logic in proving. It is a fundamental principle/belief of the Irish School that such should be the case with the application of formal methods in real software engineering. In any case, there being much work done using logic and not enough using mathematics, logical proof *per se* is absolutely prohibited!

Technically, in the Irish School, the universal quantifier, ∀, is implicitly understood, since it does not cause a problem. On the other hand, the existential quantifier, ∃, could not possibly be accepted unless there is a constructive demonstration of said existence. Whereas one is permitted the freedom to think in terms of the (unique) existence of something—the School does not enforce some sort of mental censorship—an expression of same without (constructive) domonstration is considered valueless.

A word on the notion of constructive proof within constructive applied mathematics is necessary. There are at least three variants of constructive mathematics 'opposed' to classical mathematics: "Bishop's constructive mathematics, the recursive constructive mathematics of the Russian School, and Brouwer's intuitionistic mathematics" [7]. Without wishing to state to which of these, if any, the Irish School is, or could be, affiliated, it is simply to be noted that the problems addressed by the Irish School are different and peculiar to computing—the constructive mathematics is **applied** mathematics. The Irish School does not seek to *reconstitute mathematics constructively*. A constructive proof in the Irish School is the analogue of the 'straight-edge and compass' proof in Euclidean Geometry, which is "the method of proving existence that Aristotle and Euclid adopted" [19] p.52. This philosophy of constructive proof was very strongly reinforced by Eilenberg's foundational work on *Automata, Languages and Machines*—"All the arguments and proofs are constructive. A statement asserting that something exists is of no interest unless it is accompanied by an algorithm (i.e., an explicit or effective procedure) for producing this 'something'" [9] p.xiii.

1.3.2   The Operator Calculus

Impressed by the effectiveness of the (differential and integral) calculus to solve real world problems, there naturally followed the realisation that a similar sort of calculus was needed in formal methods. A calculus allows one to use a standard set of techniques to solve different, though related, problems effectively and without continual recourse to foundational matters. In other words, by the application of operators, technical problem solving skills become habitual and the thinking more profitably employed in understanding and formulating the problem to be solved.

Therefore, a secondary purpose in doing proofs is to reinforce said skills. That is to say, in formal methods facts are uncovered—lemmas and theorems. The proving of such facts, and the employment of same in proving other facts, reinforces them directly. Such a system is termed *mnemotechnic* by Pólya [5] p.218, the foremost writer on mathematical pedagogy and problem solving. To do specifications without proof is worse than useless, for it misleads the specifier into thinking that the problem to be solved is the correct one.

1.3.3   Relativity and Refutation

When one 'reads' (published) mathematics and formal specifications, one is at first astounded by the apparent technical complexity of the theorems and their proofs and hopefully one is automatically prompted to wonder how anyone could ever have been so clever to have discovered them in the first place. Such published work is, of course, only the final stage in a very lengthy process and the latter is rarely, if ever, described or documented. Indeed, it is just that process which is the most significant for any real learning and scientific advancement. On the other hand, a description of the process by which any major theorem and its proof (or domain equation and related algorithms) are discovered/developed would take up an inordinate amount of space relative to the theorem and its proof. For pragmatic reasons, therefore, it does not seem likely that the current style in scientific publishing is going to change for the foreseeable future.

In spite of the existence of such a pragmatic barrier, a notable attempt at highlighting the issue was made by Imre Lakatos in a collection of essays that were subsequently published under the title *Proofs and Refutations: The Logic of Mathematical Discovery* [20]. This little work, which captured much of the spirit of the Irish School with respect to methodological issues in the formal specification and development of systems, was adopted wholeheartedly.

In the specific domain of formal methods, the basic message is that truth is relative. In the very act of formulating a theorem, the language used may be imprecise. There may be hidden assumptions, which subsequently must be exposed as lemmas. In establishing a proof, one must also give equal weight to the refutation. Therefore, the search for and deployment of counterexamples is crucial to success. Indeed, it is in the very act of proving that the lemmas are uncovered.

Consequently, whereas the formulation of the problem in terms of models and operations is a key first step, the furnishing of theorems, proofs **and** refutations is an equally important counterbalance. It was the determination to provide such proofs for published specifications in a Lakatosian spirit that led to the particular distinguishing characteristics of the Irish School of the *VDM*—characteristics that proved vital in the real application of formal methods to industrial system specification. Said Lakatosian spirit is exemplified throughout the remainder of this tutorial.

1.4   Semantics

> "It should be noted that a study of the mathematical foundations is by no means an essential preliminary to using [the *VDM*], any more than a study of the foundations of arithmetic is essential for everyday calculations" [26] p.43.

It appears to be a firmly established tradition that every formal specification language, used to provide the formal semantics of other systems (and languages), must itself be provided with a *formal* semantics. This, of course, might be deemed to be necessary where the overriding concern is the construction of computer based tools to process the specifications. But the chief concern was "to provide some guarantee that every grammatical construct in the notation [of the *VDM*] means something in the mathematical framework on which the notation is based [...]" [27] p.49. In the case of the *VDM*, one of the earliest efforts was to ground such semantics on Dana Scott's domain theory [26, 27], with particular attention being paid to the issue of recursive domain equations. More recently, with the emergence of an international standard for the *VDM* specification language, undertaken within the auspices of the British Standards Institute, a domain theory 'less complex' than that of Scott's, has been constructed [29].

It is precisely by virtue of the fact that expressions in the notation of the *VDM* standard may be interpreted as grammatical expressions of a formal language, that any sort of formal denotational semantics is at all possible. An immediate corollary follows. The *VDM* standard specification language, *qua* language, is inherently inflexible, a result that contradicts the spirit of the 'founding fathers':

> "We wish, as we have done in the past, and as we intend to continue doing in the future, to further develop the notation [of the *VDM* specification language] and to express notions in ways for which no mechanical interpreter system can ever be provided" [3] p.33.

Since the Irish School of the *VDM* adheres strictly to the founding fathers' spirit, then any idea of relying on a formal denotational semantics to give meaning to specifications **must** be abandoned. The ultimate question, therefore, had to be addressed. Upon what could the meaning of specifications written in the notation of the Irish School be based? The answer was immediate and inevitable—recourse must be had to 'ordinary classical traditional' mathematics. A *foundation* for such a semantics, within classical algebra, was begun with a seminal paper, presented at the first international *VDM* Symposium, 1987 [21], the notation of which leaves much to be desired, and 'culminated' with a doctoral thesis in 1990 [22]. Since, the notation is 'open-ended', there is always the obligation to say what it means.

Even an abbreviated account of the foundations of the Irish School would occupy an inordinate amount of space. Rather than attempt an inadequate account, oblique references to the foundations are made in the context of examples. We restrict ourselves to the remark that *classical* algebra provides the basis—monoids and their morphisms. Full details are contained in [22].

1.5 Standard Models and their 'Solutions'

> "The first real success with partial differential equations came in renewed attacks on the vibrating-string problem, typified by the violin string [...]

$$\frac{\partial^2 y(t, x)}{\partial t^2} = a^2 \frac{\partial^2 y(t, x)}{\partial x^2} \tag{21}$$

> [...] Thus what is now called the wave equation in one spatial dimension appears for the first time" [19] p.504.

There are two apparent extremes in the spectrum of the 'specification' of algorithms. At one end, we have the traditional use of data structures and (pseudo)code, characterised by details, engineering optimisations, and verbosity. The other extreme is the abstract notation of mathematics where many of the details are 'left to the reader'. The Irish School of the *VDM* purports to be a golden mean between these extremes.

In applied mathematics, the use of the standard models expressed as partial differential equations was undoubtedly a major factor in scientific progress. It is the ultimate paragon of 'reuse' as desired by computer scientists. In the litterature, the impression is given that reuse is a textual or syntactic matter, in the sense of 'copying'—that existing 'specifications' might be reused without (or at least with little) modification. The reality is that reuse is only possible at the conceptual level and expressed in terms of standard models. To reuse is to redo within a standard framework.

Glancing at the contents of the *Collected Algorithms of the ACM*, one is forced to ask: "What is the likelihood that a science of the *Archeology of Algorithms* will emerge in the twenty-first century as a respectable discipline?" The answer must be a definitive one, with probability 1. Many algorithms are simply computer programs, written in defunct or almost defunct programming languages and targeted for computing machinery that will inevitably become obsolete. Indeed, it is also very likely that the great algorithms of the past will have to be reconstructed from whatever descriptive text accompanies the program text rather than from a reverse-engineering of the code itself.

One of the *major* goals of the Irish School is to lay the foundations for such reconstruction now by attempting to identify standard models and to express the great algorithms in a form that is both rigorous, complete, and machine/code independent. A brief introduction on the notion of standard *VDM* models now follows. A model consists of a domain equation, invariants and operators. Since a comprehensive treatment is given in [22], emphasis is placed solely on the domain equation in this section.

1.5.1 The $\mathcal{P}X$ Model

Let X denote any set of elements. Then $\mathcal{P}X$ denotes the power set of X. For example, if $X = \{a, b, c\}$, then

$$\mathcal{P}X = \{\emptyset, \{a\}, \{b\}, \{c\}, \{a, b\}, \{a, c\}, \{b, c\}, X\} \tag{22}$$

Whereas a is an element of X, $\{a\}$ is an element of $\mathcal{P}X$. As an aside, it is worth noting that $\mathcal{P}X$, furnished with appropriate operators, is the basis of topology.

Although of considerable importance in the *VDM*, $\mathcal{P}X$ is rarely used to model key entities of a system. Rather, in practice, it is found to be employed in a secondary rôle, as the key constituent *part* of some other model. Nevertheless, it is, of itself, the standard model for answering 'existence' questions:

1. Let W denote the domain of words. Then the standard model for a spelling checker dictionary, given earlier, is
$$DICT = \mathcal{P}W \tag{23}$$

    The relevant 'existence' question is: is the word w spelt correctly? In the model, this must be interpreted to mean: does the word w exist in a spelling checker dictionary $\delta \in DICT$?

2. Let $\mathbf{N}$ denote the set of natural numbers. Then $\mathcal{P}\mathbf{N}$ denoes sets of sets of natural numbers. We do not distinguish notationally between finite sets, potentially infinite sets (of whatever order), or existentially infinite sets. In practice, we construct what we require. In other words, we refuse to be drawn into a philosophical debate on the notions of infinity or continuity and prefer to demonstrate. But it *is* clear that if X is finite, then $\mathcal{P}X$ is finite. For example, consider the question: is there an element in $\mathcal{P}\mathbf{N}$ which consists solely of prime numbers and which is infinite? In classical

mathematics, the answer is affirmative—the set of prime numers is infinite [13] p.401. In the Irish School, the relevant question is: can one construct the set of prime numbers? Again the answer is in the affirmative. There is a non-terminating algorithm that does the job—the sieve of Eratosthenes [14] p.105.

1.5.2 The X^* Model

The sequence is fundamental and *essential* to computing. Every program/algorithm in a programming language, *qua* language, is a sequence or reducible to a sequence. For otherwise, the Church-Turing Thesis would be violated.

Let X denote any set of elements. The X^* denotes the set of sequences of elements taken from X. For example, if $X = \{a, b, c\}$, then

$$X^* = \{\Lambda, \langle a \rangle, \langle b \rangle, \{c\}, \tag{24}$$
$$\langle a, b \rangle, \langle b, a \rangle, \langle a, c \rangle, \langle c, a \rangle, \langle b, c \rangle, \langle c, b \rangle, \tag{25}$$
$$\langle a, a \rangle, \langle a, a, a \rangle, \langle a, a, a, a \rangle, \dots, \tag{26}$$
$$\dots\} \tag{27}$$

Note, that following the usual convention in the theory of formal languages, we are prepared to write a sequence such as $\langle a, b, a, c \rangle$ in the form $abac$, and vice-versa.

A comparison with the $\mathcal{P}X$ domain shows that X^* is a much more complex domain. If X is finite then X^* is **not finite**. Like the $\mathcal{P}X$ model, the domain of sequences rarely plays a primary rôle in the specification of entities of a system. But, again, there are entities for which it is perfectly suited:

1. This is the standard model for (unbounded) stacks and queues.

2. Let I denote the domain of single word instructions and $\mathbf{Z}$ denote the domain of integers. Assume that $I \cap \mathbf{Z} = \emptyset$. Define $W = I \cup \mathbf{Z}$. Then, if we are prepared to use a sequence indexing scheme of origin 0, the standard model of sequential computer memory is simply
$$W^* = (I \cup \mathbf{Z})^* \tag{28}$$

3. We have already noted that X^* is a standard model for the implementation of sets as sequences. Thus the spelling checker dictionary might be 'implemented' by

$$DICT' = W^* \tag{29}$$

subject to the appropriate invariant.

4. Let C denote the domain of characters. Then we might consider a word to be adequately modelled by
$$WORD = C^* \tag{30}$$

5. Elements of a vector space of dimension n over some field, denoted X^n, are sequences of length n in X^*. Thus, vectors, matrices, tensors may all be modelled by X^*.

The $\mathcal{P}X$ model is more abstract than X^*, being given by the retrieve function

$$\mathcal{P}X \xleftarrow{\quad \mathfrak{R} = elems \quad} X^* \tag{31}$$

Comment: Since neither the notion of duplicates nor that of the ordering of elements is in the conceptual universe of sets, then this retrieve function is, in some sense, universal, though **not unique!** For example, there is a dual retrieve function that takes sequences to sets such that the resulting set is the complemented model of the original sequence

$$\mathcal{P}X \xleftarrow{\quad \mathfrak{R}' = \triangleleft [\, elems -]X \quad} X^* \tag{32}$$

Thus the sequence $\sigma \in X^*$ retrieves to the set of elements in X and not in σ, denoted by $\triangleleft [\, elems\, \sigma]X$. For example, if $X = \{a, b, c\}$ and $\sigma = \langle a, b, a \rangle$, then

$$\triangleleft [\, elems\, \sigma]X = \triangleleft [\{a, b\}]\{a, b, c\} = \{c\} \tag{33}$$

Although one might have difficulty finding a suitable real application for such a retrieve function, its existence is of theoretical interest.

1.5.3 The $X \underset{m}{\rightarrow} Y$ Model

This model holds pride of place in the *VDM* in exactly the same way that the concept of function occupies in classical mathematics. Specifically, it denotes the domain of all partial functions from X to Y, a domain which includes the set of all total functions from X to Y, denoted Y^X. Thus we have

$$Y^X \subset X \underset{m}{\rightarrow} Y \tag{34}$$

Again we take $X = \{a, b, c\}$. Let $Y = \{0, 1\}$. Then

$$X \underset{m}{\rightarrow} Y \;=\; \{\theta, \tag{35}$$

$$[a \mapsto 0], [a \mapsto 1], [b \mapsto 0], [b \mapsto 1], \ldots, \tag{36}$$

$$[[a \mapsto 0], [b \mapsto 0]], [[a \mapsto 0], [b \mapsto 1]], \ldots \tag{37}$$

$$[[a \mapsto 0], [b \mapsto 0], [c \mapsto 0]], \ldots \tag{38}$$

$$\ldots\} \tag{39}$$

If X and Y are finite, then $X \underset{m}{\rightarrow} Y$ is finite and consequently the latter is no more complex than $\mathcal{P}X$. Note that Y^X contains exactly those elements μ for which $dom\,\mu = X$. In the example, we have

$$Y^X \;=\; \{[[a \mapsto 0], [b \mapsto 0], [c \mapsto 0]], \tag{40}$$

$$[[a \mapsto 0], [b \mapsto 1], [c \mapsto 0]], \tag{41}$$

$$\ldots\} \tag{42}$$

The $X \underset{m}{\rightarrow} Y$ model is *the* standard model *par excellence* for formal specifications.

1. The models $\mathcal{P}X$ are isomorphic to 2^X, where it is customary to take $2 = \{0, 1\}$ or $2 = \{false, true\}$. Thus

$$\mathcal{P}X \cong 2^X \subset X \xrightarrow{\;}_{m} 2 \tag{43}$$

2. The models X^* may always be regarded as specific instances of $\mathbf{N}_1 \xrightarrow{\;}_{m} X$ where the indexing origin is assumed to be 1.

   This is the theoretical basis for the introduction of *slices* in the Irish School [22]. A slice is used as the mechanism be which one transforms abstract index-free sequence oriented specifications into indexed array oriented implementations in programming languages.

There is a universal natural retrieve function from maps to sets:

$$\mathcal{P}X \xleftarrow{\;\;\Re = dom\;\;} X \xrightarrow{\;}_{m} Y \tag{44}$$

The tutorial abounds with applications of the basic $X \xrightarrow{\;}_{m} Y$ model. However, it is instructive to illustrate, in the abstract, what forms such models might take.

1.5.4   The $X \xrightarrow{\;}_{m} \mathcal{P}Y$ Model

Contrary to the customary practice in $\mathcal{Z}$, where relations and bags have a distinguishing notation, such is not the case in the *VDM*. Relations, $X \xrightarrow{\;}_{m} \mathcal{P}Y$, and bags, $X \xrightarrow{\;}_{m} \mathbf{N}_1$, are merely instances of the $X \xrightarrow{\;}_{m} Y$ model. Details and rationale are given in [22]. Whereas the Irish School of the *VDM* is forcefully insistent on the expressiveness of appropriate abstract notation, it also employs the counterbalancing principle of Ockham's Razor to avoid excessiveness of distinct notation.

There are many occasions when it is helpful to consider $X \xrightarrow{\;}_{m} \mathcal{P}Y$ as the standard model of (binary) relations. We may, however, choose to use the domain of ordered pairs $\mathcal{P}(X \times Y)$ as an alternative model. Most importantly, in the Irish School, the model $X \xrightarrow{\;}_{m} \mathcal{P}Y$ is frequently employed without any recourse whatsoever to the name 'relation'.

1. Let V denote the domain of vertices (also called nodes). Then the standard model of a simple graph is

$$V \xrightarrow{\;}_{m} \mathcal{P}V \tag{45}$$

   Different classes of simple graph are then determined by appropriate invariants or domain constraints. This model is an adequate abstraction for *both* the adjacency matrix and the incidence list structures recommended in the implementation of graph algorithms—details are given later.

2. For every $\mu \in X \underset{m}{\rightarrow} Y$ model there is a corresponding inverse image model $\mu^{-1} \in$ $(X \underset{m}{\rightarrow} Y)^{-1} = Y \underset{m}{\rightarrow} \mathcal{P}X$. Thus the mathematical concepts of inverse function and inverse image are unified quite naturally within the VDM. A model together with its inverse image model both belong to the same class of models from which a development may be said to be generated.

3. Let V denote the domain of variables and Σ denote the domain of terminals, subject to the constraint that $V \cap \Sigma = \emptyset$. Define $S = V \cup \Sigma$ to be the set of variables and terminals. Then $S^* = (V \cup \Sigma)^*$ denotes the domain of sentential forms. Consequently, the domain of context-free grammars (i.e., productions), named by $\mathcal{CFG}$, is given by the standard model

$$\mathcal{CFG} = X \underset{m}{\rightarrow} Y \tag{46}$$

$$= X \underset{m}{\rightarrow} \mathcal{P}Z \tag{47}$$

$$= X \underset{m}{\rightarrow} \mathcal{P}(S^*) \tag{48}$$

$$= V \underset{m}{\rightarrow} \mathcal{P}((V \cup \Sigma)^*) \tag{49}$$

$$\tag{50}$$

Distinguishing between the different classes of context-free grammar is then a matter of specifying appropriate invariants or constraints.

1.5.5 The $X \underset{m}{\rightarrow} (Y \underset{m}{\rightarrow} Z)$ Model

It has already been stated that curried functions/algorithms are of crucial significance in the Irish School. For example, the usual addition of natural numbers may be expressed as the curried function $plus \colon \mathbf{N} \longrightarrow \mathbf{N} \longrightarrow \mathbf{N}$ where

$$plus[x]y \overset{\triangle}{=} y + x \tag{51}$$

We might wish to write this in map notation as $[x \mapsto [y \mapsto y + x]] \in plus$ where $plus$ is considered to be

$$plus = [0 \mapsto [0 \mapsto 0 + 0, 1 \mapsto 1 + 0, 2 \mapsto 2 + 0, \ldots], \tag{52}$$
$$1 \mapsto [0 \mapsto 0 + 1, 1 \mapsto 1 + 1, 2 \mapsto 2 + 1, \ldots], \tag{53}$$
$$\ldots] \tag{54}$$

In other words, we may wish to view $plus$ as an element of $\mathbf{N}_1 \underset{m}{\rightarrow} (\mathbf{N}_1 \underset{m}{\rightarrow} \mathbf{N}_1)$. By inspection, we note that $plus(0)$ and $plus(1)$ are the identity and successor functions, respectively. But the domain $\mathbf{N}_1 \underset{m}{\rightarrow} (\mathbf{N}_1 \underset{m}{\rightarrow} \mathbf{N}_1)$ allows for other possibilities, viz.

$$\mu = [2 \mapsto [0 \mapsto 0, 1 \mapsto 1, 2 \mapsto 2, \ldots], \tag{55}$$
$$3 \mapsto [0 \mapsto 1, 1 \mapsto 2, 2 \mapsto 3, \ldots], \tag{56}$$
$$\ldots] \tag{57}$$

where we have chosen to index the same 'internal' partial functions on natural numbers, $(N \underset{m}{\rightarrow} N)$, with the prime numbers. The point of this little demonstration, apart from exemplifying the nature of the standard model, is to point to an as yet unexplored world wherein the functions of mathematics may be placed in a *VDM* setting!

1. Let X denote the domain of parts and N_1 denote the domain of strictly positive natural mumbers. Then a bill of material is given by the standard model

$$X \underset{m}{\rightarrow} (X \underset{m}{\rightarrow} N_1) \tag{58}$$

2. Let X, Y and H denote the domain of real numbers. Then a height map of a terrain may be represented by the equation

$$X \underset{m}{\rightarrow} (Y \underset{m}{\rightarrow} H) \tag{59}$$

3. Let Q denote the domain of states and Σ denote an input alphabet, i.e., a set of tokens. Then a standard model for a finite state machine (as transition diagram) is

$$\Sigma \underset{m}{\rightarrow} (Q \underset{m}{\rightarrow} Q) \tag{60}$$

Automata theory may also be developed within the *VDM*.

If necessary, we may be prepared to 'forget' the Z domain:

$$X \underset{m}{\rightarrow} \mathcal{P}Y \xleftarrow{\quad \Re = (\mathcal{I} \underset{m}{\rightarrow} dom) \quad} X \underset{m}{\rightarrow} (Y \underset{m}{\rightarrow} Z) \tag{61}$$

This is especially important in graph theory where Z denotes 'weights' or 'costs' associated with edges and we wish to focus exclusively on the connectivity aspect. For a bill of material, we have

$$X \underset{m}{\rightarrow} \mathcal{P}X \xleftarrow{\quad \Re = (\mathcal{I} \underset{m}{\rightarrow} dom) \quad} X \underset{m}{\rightarrow} (X \underset{m}{\rightarrow} N_1) \tag{62}$$

We have suggested that the standard models of the *VDM* play a rôle similar to the partial differential equations in mathematics. The analogy is even stronger. Corresponding to initial and boundary conditions of the latter, we have domain invariants and constraints. Finally, solutions to partial differential equations—closed form and iterative—have almost exact analogous counterparts in the *VDM*. There is one distinct difference between the two. Whereas, existence theorems play an important rôle in partial differential equations, in the Irish School, the counterpart must be constructive!

1.6 Resumé

For those unfamiliar with model-oriented specification methods such as the *VDM* or $\mathcal{Z}$, much of the material of this chapter will have probably passed them by. Thus, it should be revisited frequently in the course of perusing the rest of the material in subsequent chapters. For those who *are* familiar with such methods, but are unfamiliar with the Irish School, much the same advice will still hold.

Experience comes with practice. Though it is not just a simple matter of the acquisition of technical skills and familiarity with the notation. The Irish School knows no bounds in its applications. Whatever is computable is a valid object of its attention. Unfortunately, space does not permit inclusion of applications within formal language theory and automata theory, nor within computer graphics, nor within numerical methods, all of which addresses the formulation of algorithms in the style of the Irish School. The chosen material to be presented covers much of the classical application within the domain of system specification. An exception is made for some material on graph algorithms which arise out of a practical consideration.

The material in the remainder of the tutorial is structured as follows. Section 2 leads with a detailed presentation of a temperature chart, which may be supposed to be a constituent part of a larger weather system. It is **not** a 'toy system'. Rather, it is the basis for the elaboration and development of a real system. Given such a basic model, the scene is then set for considering developments and proofs—the material of Section 3. But the Irish School of the *VDM* does not restrict itself to system specification and development. In Section 4 we demonstrate its applicability to the reconstruction and analysis of algorithms—a subject of interest in its own right. The final concluding section is an invitation to explore/further the work of the Irish School of the *VDM*.

2 The Model as Universe of Discourse

A basic pedagogical principle is to start with the known and to develop the unknown. In formal methods deployment in industry, there are usually two parties: the formal methodists, for whom the formal method is the known, and the problem domain experts, for whom the problem domain is known. Neither party is, at first, knowledgeable in the other's domain. With application, each does acquire knowledge/expertise in the other domain, with the measure of acquisition being in favour of the formal methodists. For this reason, it is imperative that for the purposes of real technology transfer that some domain experts be trained in the formal methods and thus become 'model owners' of the problem in question.

In this section we wish to consider all those models which, in the abstract, have the form

$$\mu \in MODEL = X \xrightarrow{m} Y \tag{63}$$

where X and Y are considered to be 'simple', i.e., atomic domains. Without loss of generality, we shall focus on a specific instance, a temperature chart—a problem domain familiar to everyone—which is considered to be a mapping from cities to temperatures:

$$\mu \in TMP\_CHRT = CTY \xrightarrow[m]{} TMP \qquad (64)$$

The domain of cities is finite and consists of a set of names:

$$c \in CTY = \text{DUBLIN} \mid \text{CHICAGO} \mid \text{LONDON} \mid \ldots \mid \text{NEW YORK} \mid \text{PARIS} \mid \text{TOKYO} \qquad (65)$$

The domain of temperatures is taken to be the set of integers:

$$t \in TMP = \mathbf{Z} \qquad (66)$$

Note that we do not make any reference to a particular temperature scale, such as Celsius, Fahrenheit, etc. Nor do we bother to eliminate 'outlandish' temperatures such as -1456723. Technically, we mean that there is a non-trivial invariant on the domain of the form

1    $inv\text{-}TMP\_CHRT: TMP\_CHRT \longrightarrow \mathbf{B}$
.1 $inv\text{-}TMP\_CHRT(\mu) \triangleq \ldots$

and we do not wish to consider it in any detail for the moment.

2.1   Asking Questions

With a view to requirements modelling, the purpose of a model is to ask questions and demonstrate that answers can be given entirely in terms of the model. If such answers can not be found then the model is inadequate. Generally, we seek obvious closed form solutions before considering recursive algorithmic solutions. In practice, in seeking a closed form solution, one works with typical abstract examples. Thus for a temperature chart the typical example must be of the form

$$\mu = [c_1 \mapsto t_1, \ldots, c_k \mapsto t_j, \ldots, c_n \mapsto t_m] \qquad (67)$$

where the number of cities n is usually greater than the number of recorded temperatures m. In other words, one normally expects to find at least two cities with the same recorded temperature. The atypical or special case is an empty temperature chart θ.

In this section, certain obvious questions are asked and their solutions given. The purpose of the question/answer material presented here is primarily intended to introduce the notation and method. But in real applications, they are the primary means for modelling requirements. There is a certain amount of repetition which is deliberately introduced to enforce the message.

QUESTION 2.1 *What is the set of cities the temperatures of which are recorded in a temperature chart μ?*

$$dom\,\mu \tag{68}$$

Comment: Consider the typical temperature chart

$$\mu = [c_1 \mapsto t_1, \ldots, c_k \mapsto t_j, \ldots, c_n \mapsto t_m] \tag{69}$$

then the set of cities is

$$dom\,\mu = \{c_1, \ldots, c_k, \ldots, c_n\} \tag{70}$$

QUESTION 2.2 *How many cities have temperatures recorded in a temperature chart μ?*

$$card \circ dom\,\mu \tag{71}$$

or, equivalently as

$$|\,dom\,\mu| \tag{72}$$

Comment: Consider the typical temperature chart

$$\mu = [c_1 \mapsto t_1, \ldots, c_k \mapsto t_j, \ldots, c_n \mapsto t_m] \tag{73}$$

then we have immediately

$$dom\,\mu \;=\; \{c_1, \ldots, c_k, \ldots, c_n\} \tag{74}$$
$$|\,dom\,\mu| \;=\; |\{c_1, \ldots, c_k, \ldots, c_n\}| \tag{75}$$
$$=\; n \tag{76}$$

The more abstract notation, $|-|$, which is conventional in mathematics, is preferred in general. There are cases when the functional/operator form is much better.

QUESTION 2.3 *Which temperatures are recorded in a temperature chart μ?*

$$rng\,\mu \tag{77}$$

Comment: Consider the typical temperature chart

$$\mu = [c_1 \mapsto t_1, \ldots, c_k \mapsto t_j, \ldots, c_n \mapsto t_m] \tag{78}$$

then we have immediately

$$rng\,\mu = \{t_1, \ldots, t_j, \ldots, t_m\} \tag{79}$$

QUESTION 2.4 *How many temperatures are recorded?*

$$\text{card} \circ \text{rng}\,\mu = |\,\text{rng}\,\mu\,| \tag{80}$$

Comment: Consider the typical temperature chart

$$\mu = [c_1 \mapsto t_1, \ldots, c_k \mapsto t_j, \ldots, c_n \mapsto t_m] \tag{81}$$

then we have immediately

$$
\begin{aligned}
\text{rng}\,\mu &= \{t_1, \ldots, t_j, \ldots, t_m\} & (82)\\
|\,\text{rng}\,\mu\,| &= |\{t_1, \ldots, t_j, \ldots, t_m\}| & (83)\\
&= m & (84)
\end{aligned}
$$

Having considered typical examples of a temperature chart and computed the values $|\,\text{dom}\,\mu\,|$ and $|\,\text{rng}\,\mu\,|$, then the following lemma for temperature charts follows:

LEMMA 2.1 *For all temperature charts μ, $|\,\text{dom}\,\mu\,| \geq |\,\text{rng}\,\mu\,|$, with strict equality if and only if μ is a 1-1 map.*

It is **never** the case that $|\,\text{dom}\,\mu\,| < |\,\text{rng}\,\mu\,|$. The lemma is universal over all maps. Therefore, it always true that

LEMMA 2.2 *For all maps $\mu \in MODEL = X \xrightarrow{m} Y$, $|\,\text{dom}\,\mu\,| \geq |\,\text{rng}\,\mu\,|$, with strict equality if and only if μ is a 1-1 map.*

Comment: Since we have a universal lemma on maps $\mu \in X \xrightarrow{m} Y$, we are in a position to develop proofs in the *VDM* as a mnemotechnic system, that is to say, for every operation to be introduced, we may verify that the lemma holds.

Now that the use of the typical example has been thoroughly demonstrated, albeit in simple solutions, one may be more brief.

QUESTION 2.5 *Is the city c recorded in a temperature chart μ?*

$$c \in \text{dom}\,\mu \tag{85}$$

Comment: This is the usual notation of the other Schools. In the Irish School, the set membership operator '$\in$' is used exclusively for non-deterministic choice of an element e from a non-empty set S in expressions such as

$$\text{let } e \in S \text{ in } \ldots \tag{86}$$

For testing whether or not an element e belongs to a set S, the characteristic function notation is preferred:

$$\chi_\mu(c), \text{ or } \chi[c]\mu \tag{87}$$

Comment: Strictly, one ought to write either $\chi[c]\,\text{dom}\,\mu$ or $\chi[(c, -)]\mu$, where '$-$' denotes an arbitrary argument. But, since there is no ambiguity, 'overloading' of an operator or function is strongly emphasised. Thus, membership tests for sets S, sequences σ, and (domain of) maps μ, are denoted by $\chi[e]S$, $\chi[e]\sigma$, and $\chi[e]\mu$, respectively.

QUESTION 2.6 *Which cities have temperature t?*

Before presenting the specification it is pedagogically useful to pause and invite one to do a simple exercise: Write a program to compute this result in one's own favourite programming language.

In the *VDM* the solution is given by

$$\mu^{-1}(t) \tag{88}$$

The expression $\mu^{-1}(t)$ is read as the inverse image of t under μ. Formally, we define

$$\mu^{-1}(t) \triangleq \{c \mid \chi[\![c]\!]\mu \wedge \mu(c) = t\} \tag{89}$$

There are three particular cases that are distinguished. In the case that there is no city c in the temperature chart μ that has the temperature t, i.e., $\neg\chi[\![t]\!] \, rng \, \mu$, then we have the empty set:

$$\mu^{-1}(t) = \emptyset \tag{90}$$

In the case that there is only one city c_j in the temperature chart μ which has the temperature t_j, i.e., $\exists! c_j(\chi[\![c_j]\!]\mu \wedge \mu(c_j) = t_j)$, then we have:

$$\mu^{-1}(t_j) = \{c_j\} \tag{91}$$

Finally, in the case that there are at least two distinct cities c_{k1} and c_{kn} in the temperature chart μ which have the same temperature t_k, i.e., $\exists c_{k1}, c_{kn}(c_{k1} \neq c_{kn} \wedge \mu(c_{k1}) = \mu(c_{kn}) = t_k)$, we have:

$$\mu^{-1}(t_k) = \{c_{k1}, c_{k2}, \dots, c_{kn}\} \tag{92}$$

We have defined the inverse image of a single temperature t under μ. Let us now generalise the definition to a set of temperatures $T = \{t_1, t_2, \dots, t_k\}$. First let us iterate over the set T with μ^{-1} to give:

$$\mathcal{P}\mu^{-1}T \;=\; \{\mu^{-1}(t_1), \mu^{-1}(t_2), \dots, \mu^{-1}(t_k)\} \tag{93}$$
$$=\; \{S_1, S_2, \dots, S_j\} \tag{94}$$

Then the set of cities S which is the inverse image of T under μ^{-1} may be obtained by

$$S = S_1 \cup S_2 \cup \dots \cup S_j \tag{95}$$

In the *VDM* this is given succinctly as the reduction

$$S \;=\; {}^\cup\!/\{S_1, S_2, \dots, S_j\} \tag{96}$$
$$=\; {}^\cup\!/ \circ \mathcal{P}\mu^{-1}T \tag{97}$$

In the particular case that $T = rng \, \mu$ we have

$${}^\cup\!/ \circ \mathcal{P}\mu^{-1} \circ rng \, \mu = dom \, \mu \tag{98}$$

and by an abuse of notation we are prepared to write, though rarely,

$$\mu^{-1} \circ rng \, \mu \triangleq {}^\cup\!/ \circ \mathcal{P}\mu^{-1} \circ rng \, \mu = dom \, \mu \tag{99}$$

Upon consideration of several concrete examples we note that the iteration of the inverse image operator μ^{-1} over the range of a temperature chart μ always gives a partition of the domain of μ. This is a simple theorem on temperature charts.

THEOREM 2.1 *The expression $\mathcal{P}\mu^{-1} \circ rng\, \mu$ denotes a partition of $dom\, \mu$.*

Not surprisingly, the theorem is universal to all maps $\mu \in MODEL = X \underset{m}{\longrightarrow} Y$.

THEOREM 2.2 *Let μ denote a map in $MODEL = X \underset{m}{\longrightarrow} Y$. Then $\mathcal{P}\mu^{-1} \circ rng\, \mu$ is a partition of $dom\, \mu$.*

For an exact formal specification of the meaning of partition, see [22]. Thus far the solutions to the questions have been closed form solutions. Let us now consider a typical question for which the solution is *customarily* expressed as a recursive algorithm. A closed form solution also exists and will be presented later.

QUESTION 2.7 *Which cities have the minimum temperature?*

In this case we present the solution as a sequence of recursive functions in order to demonstrate that *development* in the Irish School of the *VDM* is a much broader notion than the concept of refinement and reification as commonly understood in the other Schools. First we give a straightforward naïve solution:

2   *Min*: $TMP\_CHRT \longrightarrow \mathcal{P}CTY$
.1 $Min(\mu) \triangleq$
.2 $\mu = \theta$
.3 $\rightarrow \emptyset$
.4 $\rightarrow$ let $(c,t) \in \mu$ in
.5 $Min[\{c\} \triangleleft \mu](\mu, \{c\})$

Annotations:

(2.4) An entry in the map $\mu = [\dots, c \mapsto t, \dots]$ may always be considered to be an ordered pair (c, t).

(2.5) Having picked an arbitrary (c, t) pair, we consider t to be the **initial** minimum temperature and consequently record c as the corresponding city. Experienced programmers would immediately observe that one ought to record the current minimum temperature t. We then proceed to iterate over the structure to obtain the fixed point solution. Since we do not record the current minimum temperature then we are obliged to refer to the μ to obtain that value and, consequently, it is passed as a 'read-only' structure. This is a regular feature of specifications in the Irish School.

The $Min[\dots]$ is the tail-recursive function

3   *Min*: $TMP\_CHRT \longrightarrow (TMP\_CHRT \times \mathcal{P}CTY) \longrightarrow \mathcal{P}CTY$
.1 $Min[\theta](\overline{\mu}, S) \triangleq S$
.2 $Min[[c \mapsto t] \cup \mu](\overline{\mu}, S) \triangleq$
.3   let $\overline{c} \in S$ in
.4   let $\overline{t} = \overline{\mu}(\overline{c})$ in

.5 $t < \bar{t} \rightarrow Min[\![\mu]\!](\bar{\mu}, \{c\})$
.6 $t = \bar{t} \rightarrow Min[\![\mu]\!](\bar{\mu}, S \cup \{c\})$
.7 $t > \bar{t} \rightarrow Min[\![\mu]\!](\bar{\mu}, S)$

Annotations:

(3.1) The read-only structure is denoted $\bar{\mu}$.

(3.4) Given a city $\bar{c} \in S$ that has the current minimum temperature we look up its value $\bar{t}$. There are then three possible cases to consider ...

Looking at the signature of the tail-recursive function, we might wish to obtain a more *symmetrical* form that has the merit of emphasising the 'read-only' nature of the temperature chart $\bar{\mu}$:

4     $Min: TMP\_CHRT \longrightarrow (TMP\_CHRT \times \mathcal{P}CTY) \longrightarrow (TMP\_CHRT \times \mathcal{P}CTY)$
.1 $Min[\![\theta]\!](\bar{\mu}, S) \triangleq (\bar{\mu}, S)$
.2 $Min[\![[c \mapsto t] \cup \mu]\!](\bar{\mu}, S) \triangleq$
.3   let $\bar{c} \in S$ in
.4   let $\bar{t} = \bar{\mu}(\bar{c})$ in
.5 $t < \bar{t} \rightarrow Min[\![\mu]\!](\bar{\mu}, \{c\})$
.6 $t = \bar{t} \rightarrow Min[\![\mu]\!](\bar{\mu}, S \cup \{c\})$
.7 $t > \bar{t} \rightarrow Min[\![\mu]\!](\bar{\mu}, S)$

in which case we also need to modify the 'top level' function:

5     $Min: TMP\_CHRT \longrightarrow \mathcal{P}CTY$
.1 $Min(\mu) \triangleq$
.2 $\mu = \theta$
.3 $\rightarrow \emptyset$
.4 $\rightarrow$ let $(c, t) \in \mu$ in
.5 $\pi_2 \circ Min[\![\{c\} \triangleleft \mu]\!](\mu, \{c\})$

Annotations:

(5.5) The projection operator π_2 selects the second component of the ordered pair to give the result.

'Case' constructs, which include 'if–then–else' constructs, such as the above do not give a concise specification. Therefore, one seeks to 'eliminate' them in a natural way. To illustrate this point, let us introduce the *ad hoc* operator $\diamond$ and define

$$t_j \diamond t_k \triangleq \begin{cases} 1, & \text{if } t_j < t_k \\ 2, & \text{if } t_j = t_k \\ 3, & \text{if } t_j > t_k \end{cases} \tag{100}$$

Then $\pi_{t \diamond \bar{t}}$ denotes a projection function which depends on t and $\bar{t}$. Using this notation we may rewrite the body of the tail-recursive function *Min* in the form

6   let $\bar{c} \in S$ in
.1 let $\bar{t} = \bar{\mu}(\bar{c})$ in
.2 $\pi_{t\bar{o}\bar{t}}\big(Min[\mu](\bar{\mu}, \{c\}), Min[\mu](\bar{\mu}, S \cup \{c\}), Min[\mu](\bar{\mu}, S)\big)$

Factoring out the $Min[\mu]$ gives

7   let $\bar{c} \in S$ in
.1 let $\bar{t} = \bar{\mu}(\bar{c})$ in
.2 $Min[\mu] \circ \pi_{t\bar{o}\bar{t}}\big((\bar{\mu}, \{c\}), (\bar{\mu}, S \cup \{c\}), (\bar{\mu}, S)\big)$

It is also 'obvious' that we may move the projection operator inside the parentheses to give

8   let $\bar{c} \in S$ in
.1 let $\bar{t} = \bar{\mu}(\bar{c})$ in
.2 $Min[\mu]\big(\bar{\mu}, \pi_{t\bar{o}\bar{t}}(\{c\}, S \cup \{c\}, S)\big)$

The tail-recursive function now has the form

9    $Min: TMP\_CHRT \longrightarrow (TMP\_CHRT \times \mathcal{P}CTY) \longrightarrow (TMP\_CHRT \times \mathcal{P}CTY)$
.1 $Min[\theta](\bar{\mu}, S) \triangleq (\bar{\mu}, S)$
.2 $Min[[c \mapsto t] \cup \mu](\bar{\mu}, S) \triangleq$
.3   let $\bar{c} \in S$ in
.4   let $\bar{t} = \bar{\mu}(\bar{c})$ in
.5 $Min[\mu]\big(\bar{\mu}, \pi_{t\bar{o}\bar{t}}(\{c\}, S \cup \{c\}, S)\big)$

The next stage in the transformation is the elimination of the 'let' constructs. They are used solely for the purpose of obtaining the current minimum temperature value $\bar{t}$. If we record this value at each stage then we do not need to include the 'read-only' structure $\bar{\mu}$ and consequently we have

10    $Min: TMP\_CHRT \longrightarrow (\mathcal{P}CTY \times TMP) \longrightarrow (\mathcal{P}CTY \times TMP)$
.1 $Min[\theta](S, \bar{t}) \triangleq (S, \bar{t})$
.2 $Min[[c \mapsto t] \cup \mu](S, \bar{t}) \triangleq$
.3 $Min[\mu]\big(\pi_{t\bar{o}\bar{t}}(\{c\}, S \cup \{c\}, S), \pi_{t\bar{o}\bar{t}}(t, \bar{t}, \bar{t})\big)$

and the top-level function now takes the form

11    $Min: TMP\_CHRT \longrightarrow \mathcal{P}CTY$
.1 $Min(\mu) \triangleq$
.2 $\mu = \theta$
.3 $\rightarrow \emptyset$
.4 $\rightarrow$ let $(c,t) \in \mu$ in
.5 $\pi_1 \circ Min[\{c\} \triangleleft \mu](\{c\}, t)$

where $Min[\{c\} \triangleleft \mu](\{c\}, t)$ returns the pair (S_{min}, t_{min}). The projection function π_1 was used to select the set of cities S_{min} which has minimum temperature t_{min}. But, of course, it is clear that there is a certain amount of redundancy in the result. Specifically, given t_{min} then the corresponding set of cities is specified by $\mu^{-1}(t_{min})$. In other words, the last line of the above specification may also have been written as $\mu^{-1} \circ \pi_2 \circ Min[\{c\} \triangleleft \mu](\{c\}, t)$. We might then wish to eliminate all reference to the actual set of cities in the tail-recursive form.

But we do not jump to the conclusion that having found a solution to the question in hand then we may proceed to rush ahead to look at other questions. Even our original solution was subjected to a variety of transformations. The 'final' solution suggested that we need only compute the minimum temperature and then specify the required result using the inverse image operator. (*Which solution would one choose as the basis for an implementation?*) The specification of the set of cities which have the minimum temperature may be formulated in an entirely different way:

12    $Min: TMP\_CHRT \longrightarrow \mathcal{P}CTY$
.1 $Min(\mu) \triangleq$
.2 $\mu = \theta$
.3 $\rightarrow \emptyset$
.4 $\rightarrow$ let $t_{min} = {^\downarrow}/ \circ rng\ \mu$ in
.5 $\mu^{-1}(t_{min})$

where ${^\downarrow}/$ denotes the reduction of a non-empty set with respect to the min operator $\downarrow$. Elimination of the 'let' construct gives the simpler form:

13    $Min: TMP\_CHRT \longrightarrow \mathcal{P}CTY$
.1 $Min(\theta) \triangleq \emptyset$
.2 $Min(\mu) \triangleq \mu^{-1} \circ {^\downarrow}/ \circ rng\ \mu$

An obvious question may be posed. What is the relationship between the two forms of the minimum function? Can one be transformed into the other?

Quite clearly, the specification of the set of cities which have the maximum temperature is the dual of the above and, thus, we need not consider it in any detail. However, it is frequently the case that one wishes to compute both a minimum and a maximum at the same time, the effort to do so being approximately equal to the computation of any one of them. Let us introduce a maxmin operator $\updownarrow$ where

$$a \updownarrow b \triangleq \begin{cases} (a,b), & \text{if } a \geq b \\ (b,a), & \text{otherwise.} \end{cases}$$

One then considers the problem of rewriting the specification of the set of cities which have a minimum temperature in terms of this new operator—an exercise.

Having illustrated the basic approach in developing specifications via constructions of solutions to problems posed as questions with respect to some model, we now demonstrate how said questions and solutions may be reformulated in a 'traditional and conventional' VDM style which has its origins in the construction of denotational semantics.

2.2 Denotational Semantics

Let us now take a different point of view with respect to a temperature chart—that of an entity which is to be manipulated by a human operator (or program module). We might begin by assuming that there is some definite set of operations to be performed such as

1. create an initially empty temperature chart;

2. enter a new (city, temperature) pair to an existing temperature chart;

3. update the temperature of a given city in an existing temperature chart;

3. delete a (city, temperature) pair from an existing temperature chart;

4. look up the temperature of a city in a temperature chart;

5. asking whether the temperature of a given city is recorded in a temperature chart.

For convenience, a concrete syntactic form for each operation is presented, a form which recalls the style of the Ada programing language. Then an abstract syntactic form for each operation follows. Finally, the semantic function for each operation is specified.

2.2.1 The Create Operation

We wish to specify the creation of an initially empty temperature chart. An Ada-like syntactic signature might have the form

14   **func** create() **return** *TMP_CHRT*

In the *VDM* we use a syntactic domain such as

$$Crea_0 :: \{nil\} \tag{101}$$

where the argument of the create command is empty, here denoted by *nil*. Given such a command we then express its meaning with respect to the universe of discourse—the semantic domains. The name of the semantic function might be given traditionally by

Int-Crea$_0$, where the prefix *Int-* abbreviates 'interpretation', a word which recalls the concept of an 'interpreter' in compiler theory, for indeed that is precisely what is being constructed in the abstract. The notion of state to state transformation is embraced by such a prefix.

But, the create command is clearly a constant function, returning a value, and by another rule, we ought to write *Eval-Crea$_0$* as the name of the semantic function, where *Eval-* is intended to denote evaluation. We clearly have a conflict, one that may be resolved by adding a third rule: if the end result of a function is the domain in question, then use the *Int-* prefix. Consequently, we write:

15    $Int\text{-}Crea_0: Crea_0 \longrightarrow TMP\_CHRT$

.1 $Int\text{-}Crea_0[mk\text{-}Crea_0(nil)] \triangleq \theta$

Annotations:

(15.1) The argument of the semantic function *Int-Crea$_0$*, is an element of the syntactic domain *Crea$_0$*. Such an element is a parse tree, the root of which is traditionally denoted by the tag or label constructed by prefixing the name of the syntactic domain with a make constructor, denoted *mk-*. Such parse trees are the *exact* equivalent to parse trees in PROLOG where the tag is a PROLOG functor.

Note that there is a lot of 'heavy machinery' to express the simple fact that the result of the create command is a null structure: θ. One might be tempted to do away with all the verbosity *ab initio*; but this would be pedagogically wrong—there is a bridge between the world of (programming) languages and the (pure abstract) notation of mathematics and this bridge is the *VDM*. Once this fundamental reality is grasped, then we may indeed joyfully forsake the verbosity.

2.2.2   The Enter Operation

The next operation to be considered is the entering of a new (city, temperature) pair to an existing temperature chart. Again we first present a typical programming language syntactic signature for comparison ultimately with the formal semantics of the operation:

16   **proc** enter(c: *CTY*, t: *TMP*, **in out** μ: *TMP_CHRT*)

The key words **in out** are basically synonymous with the 'var' of Pascal. In the abstract, the enter command is given by the syntactic domain:

$$Ent_0 :: CTY \times TMP \tag{102}$$

which basically denotes a space of tagged ordered pairs (c, t). Formally, such an element is denoted $mk\text{-}Ent_0(c, t)$. With experience, abbreviated non-tagged forms, such as (c, t), are encouraged, where there is little possibility of ambiguity. The meaning of the enter command is given by

17      $Int\text{-}Ent_0\colon Ent_0 \longrightarrow TMP\_CHRT \longrightarrow TMP\_CHRT$

.1 $Int\text{-}Ent_0[mk\text{-}Ent_0(c,t)]\mu \triangleq \mu \cup [c \mapsto t]$

Annotations:

(17.1) Of course, in the *VDM*, the expression $\mu \cup [c \mapsto t]$ is only well-defined under very explicit constraints, namely that c **must not occur** in the domain of μ. Such a constraint may be given by an explicit pre-condition.

In the Irish School of the *VDM* such membership constraints are preferably given in terms of a characteristic function. The pre-condition may, therefore, be expressed in the form:

18      $pre\text{-}Ent_0\colon Ent_0 \longrightarrow TMP\_CHRT \longrightarrow \mathbf{B}$

.1 $pre\text{-}Ent_0[mk\text{-}Ent_0(c,t)]\mu \triangleq \neg\chi[c]\mu$

We take the view that pre-conditions are to be understood as basic lemmas for proofs. On the other hand, we feel quite free to introduce a 'do not care' symbol, $\perp$, as a placeholder to signal that should the pre-condition be violated then, in reality, some action must be taken in an implementation. The specification then takes the form:

19      $Int\text{-}Ent_0\colon Ent_0 \longrightarrow TMP\_CHRT \longrightarrow TMP\_CHRT$

.1 $Int\text{-}Ent_0[mk\text{-}Ent_0(c,t)]\mu \triangleq$

.2 $\neg\chi[c]\mu$

.3 $\to \mu \cup [c \mapsto t]$

.4 $\to \perp$

and we **insist** that $\perp$ **must not necessarily** be interpreted as an error or exception!

2.2.3   The Update Operation

Given the existence of a non-empty temperature chart, and the fact that in reality temperatures change with time, there **must** be an operation to update the temperature of a given city in an existing temperature chart. Such an update operation might have the syntactic signature of the form

20   **proc** $update(c\colon CTY, t\colon TMP, \mathbf{in\ out}\ \mu\colon TMP\_CHRT)$

The corresponding syntactic domain is evidently

$$Upd_0 :: CTY \times TMP \tag{103}$$

In comparing this domain with that of the enter command, it is quite obvious that the two are isomorphic. Hence an untagged form (c, t) might belong to either domain. For precisely such cases, in order to 'disambiguate' *formally* such expressions, the originators of the *VDM* introduced the tagged notation, $mk\text{-}Upd_0(c,t)$. There is, however, no real ambiguity, since the expressions always occur in very precisely defined contexts. The semantics of the update operation are specified by

21    $Int\text{-}Upd_0\colon Upd_0 \longrightarrow TMP\_CHRT \longrightarrow TMP\_CHRT$

.1 $Int\text{-}Upd_0[mk\text{-}Upd_0(c,t)]\mu \stackrel{\triangle}{=} \mu + [c \mapsto t]$

Anotations:

(21.1) The expression $\mu + [c \mapsto t]$ is intended to denote the 'override' or *overwrite* of
the existing value of the temperature of c in the chart μ by the 'new' temperature t. However, the formal definition of the override operator, $+$, is such that
it also covers that of the extend operator, $\cup$, used in the specification of the semantics of the enter operation. That is to say, if c is not in the domain of μ,
then $\mu + [c \mapsto t] = \mu \cup [c \mapsto t]$. In general, the operator is not commutative and
consequently, some Schools—viz., the English School— prefer to use the symbol $\dagger$,
rather than $+$, to denote the operator, a choice which has considerable merit. There
are theoretical advantages in permitting the override operator to cover the extend
operator—$(TMP\_CHRT, +, \theta)$ is a monoid. But there is also a danger in practice
in *relying* on it to do so. In general, in *practical specifications* it is better to restrict the use of the operator to those cases where the concept of strict updating
of existing values is involved. Historically, the override operator was introduced to
give meaning to the assignment statement of programming languages, a purpose for
which it is ideally suited.

To enforce the semantics of strict updating, and thus to eliminate the possibility of *covering* the extend operation, it is essential to provide the appropriate pre-condition:

22    $pre\text{-}Upd_0\colon Upd_0 \longrightarrow TMP\_CHRT \longrightarrow \mathbf{B}$

.1 $pre\text{-}Upd_0[mk\text{-}Upd_0(c,t)]\mu \stackrel{\triangle}{=} \chi[\![c]\!]\mu$

2.2.4   The Delete Operation

It is customary in specifications to allow for the possibility of diminishing a structure by
removing existing elements. Such deletion is the formal inverse of the enter operation. One
might wonder whether it is practical in the case of the temperature chart. We could always
argue that were a particular city's temperature sensor to be destroyed through natural
disaster or otherwise, then we must *de facto* delete it. Or perhaps, a city administration
is obliged to pay for the benefit of having its temperature recorded in the temperature
chart and then defaults on its payments. Common (financial) sense suggests that it
be eliminated. Whether such arguments are persuasive or not, we define the operation
to delete a (city, temperature) pair from an existing temperature chart. To a program
module such a facility might be offered in the syntactic form of

23   **proc** delete($c\colon CTY$, **in out** $\mu\colon TMP\_CHRT$)

for which the *VDM* provides the corresponding syntactic domain

$$Del_0 :: CTY \tag{104}$$

and the semantics

24     $Int\text{-}Del_0: Del_0 \longrightarrow TMP\_CHRT \longrightarrow TMP\_CHRT$

.1 $Int\text{-}Del_0[\![mk\text{-}Del_0(c)]\!]\mu \triangleq \{c\} \blacktriangleleft \mu$

Annotations:

(24.1)   In traditional classical mathematics, and in the Danish School, such an operation is usually expressed as $\mu \setminus \{c\}$. The form $\{c\} \blacktriangleleft \mu$ is preferred by the English School and the $\mathcal{Z}$ practitioners. Not only does it signify very natural desirable mathematical properties [22], but also is more convenient in practical proofs. For these reasons, it is also the choice of the Irish School.

One will note that there is no pre-condition given. This is purely a matter of taste. The operation is completely defined whether or not c occurs in the domain of the temperature chart μ. But, from a practical point of view, it may be a requirement that if such be not the case then an error message must be given. Then, we would be obliged to include an appropriate pre-condition.

2.2.5   The Lookup Operation

Of all the possible operations on a temperature chart, *the* most important one, from a conceptual point of view, is to be able to look up the temperature of a city in a temperature chart; for, otherwise, of what possible use could such a chart be? The Ada-like syntactic signature is

25   **func** look_up($c: CTY$, **in** $\mu: TMP\_CHRT$) **return** TMP

and we note that this is the first operation to return a result that is not a temperature chart. The look up operations are elements of the syntactic domain

$$Lkp_0 :: CTY \tag{105}$$

and the semantics are rather obvious

26     $Eval\text{-}Lkp_0: Lkp_0 \longrightarrow TMP\_CHRT \longrightarrow TMP$

.1 $Eval\text{-}Lkp_0[\![mk\text{-}Lkp_0(c)]\!]\mu \triangleq \mu(c)$

Annotations:

26.0)   Since we are *evaluating*, then the appropriate prefix to the command is *Eval-*.

Again a pre-condition has been deliberately omitted, inviting one to reason on the absolute necessity thereof and to construct same. On the other hand, we prefer to provide an operation that we might employ before invoking commands such as a look up command— a request to determine whether or not a given city is recorded in a temperature chart, or more precisely, whether the temperature of a given city ..., etc.

2.2.6   The Is-recorded Operation

In examining the pre-conditions of all the commands which we have considered so far, it is clear that they turn upon the truth or falsity of the statement whether or not a city is in the domain of a temperature chart, denoted by the expression $\chi[c]\mu$. We may wish to introduce an explicit command to verbalise such an expression—asking whether the temperature of a given city is recorded in a temperature chart. From a programming language point of view we might expect a syntactic form such as

27   **func** is_recorded(c: CTY, **in** μ: TMP_CHRT) **return B**

The syntactic domain, which is isomorphic to that of both the delete command and the look up command, is

$$Rec_0 :: CTY \tag{106}$$

The semantics is simply:

28   $Eval\text{–}Rec_0$: $Rec_0 \longrightarrow TMP\_CHRT \longrightarrow \mathbf{B}$
.1 $Eval\text{–}Rec_0[mk\text{–}Rec_0(c)]\mu \triangleq \chi[c]\mu$

Referring back to the questions that we posed earlier, it is clear that there are many other possible commands that we may wish to introduce. The principle is simple—every question, alternatively, answer or expression, invites a corresponding potential command. Sufficient material has been provided such that one may now do this in a well-structured and coherent manner. It is also quite apparent that the conventional denotational semantics style of specification is largely a matter of the *heavy syntactic sugaring* of very simple *VDM* expressions.

Having covered some of the basic aspects of the notation and method of the Irish School, within the context of a practical case study, there are many possible directions that we might take. Before choosing one, we briefly digress to ilustrate some notational variants of the semantic functions that bring to mind the syntactic forms of programming languages.

2.3   Abbreviated Forms

The semantic functions for each of the operations are now presented in a more terse style. In place of a semantic function name such as $Int\text{–}Ent_0$, the name of the operation is used: Ent_0; in place of the name of a syntactic domain such as Ent_0, the actual structure is used: $CTY \times TMP$. With these conventions, the specification of the semantic functions appear less verbose. For the record, the specifications now have the form:

29   $Crea_0$: $\{nil\} \longrightarrow TMP\_CHRT$
.1 $Crea_0[nil] \triangleq \theta$

30 $Ent_0 \colon CTY \times TMP \longrightarrow TMP\_CHRT \longrightarrow TMP\_CHRT$
.1 $Ent_0[\![c, t]\!]\mu \triangleq \mu \cup [c \mapsto t]$

31 $pre\text{-}Ent_0 \colon CTY \times TMP \longrightarrow TMP\_CHRT \longrightarrow \mathbf{B}$
.1 $pre\text{-}Ent_0[\![c, t]\!]\mu \triangleq \neg\chi[\![c]\!]\mu$

32 $Upd_0 \colon CTY \times TMP \longrightarrow TMP\_CHRT \longrightarrow TMP\_CHRT$
.1 $Int\text{-}Upd_0[\![c, t]\!]\mu \triangleq \mu + [c \mapsto t]$

33 $pre\text{-}Upd_0 \colon CTY \times TMP \longrightarrow TMP\_CHRT \longrightarrow \mathbf{B}$
.1 $pre\text{-}Upd_0[\![c, t]\!]\mu \triangleq \chi[\![c]\!]\mu$

34 $Del_0 \colon CTY \longrightarrow TMP\_CHRT \longrightarrow TMP\_CHRT$
.1 $Del_0[\![c]\!]\mu \triangleq \{c\} \blacktriangleleft \mu$

35 $Lkp_0 \colon CTY \longrightarrow TMP\_CHRT \longrightarrow TMP$
.1 $Lkp_0[\![c]\!]\mu \triangleq \mu(c)$

36 $Rec_0 \colon CTY \longrightarrow TMP\_CHRT \longrightarrow \mathbf{B}$
.1 $Rec_0[\![c]\!]\mu \triangleq \chi[\![c]\!]\mu$

One more notational remark is probably in order. Consider the enter command above. There are many occasions where we prefer to use a structure definition in place of its name in the signature. The name is, after all, only a convenience! But, of course, such a step is a total rupture with the conventions of programming languages, and for that reason alone it is often desirable. For example, instead of TMP_CHRT we would write $CTY \underset{m}{\rightarrow} TMP$. The semantics of the enter command would then take the form

37 $Ent_0 \colon CTY \times TMP \longrightarrow (CTY \underset{m}{\rightarrow} TMP) \longrightarrow (CTY \underset{m}{\rightarrow} TMP)$

.1 $Ent_0[\![c, t]\!]\mu \triangleq \mu \cup [c \mapsto t]$

Finally, with a view to *real reuse*, we abstract almost completely from the real problem domain of temperature charts and write:

38 $Ent_0 \colon X \times Y \longrightarrow (X \underset{m}{\rightarrow} Y) \longrightarrow (X \underset{m}{\rightarrow} Y)$

.1 $Ent_0[\![\; x, y]\!]\mu \triangleq \mu \cup [x \mapsto y]$

which is just a verbalising of the basic expression $\mu \cup [x \mapsto y]$. The use of 'almost' is needed to cover the retained use of the name Ent_0.

2.4   Temperature Chart System

Let us now extend the universe of discourse of temperature charts by introducing the notion of a collection of named temperature charts. We might now suppose that a temperature chart is particular to a given country, for example. The collection of such named temperature charts will be called a temperature chart system and modelled as follows:

$$\varsigma \in TMPCHRT\_SYS = TCn \xrightarrow{m} TMP\_CHRT \tag{107}$$

where TCn denotes the domain of country names, say:

$$i \in TCn = \text{IRELAND} \mid \text{FRANCE} \mid \ldots \mid \text{JAPAN} \tag{108}$$

In the abstract, we are effectively studying the model

$$\mu \in MODEL = K \xrightarrow{m} (X \xrightarrow{m} Y) \tag{109}$$

which may be interpreted as a refinement or development of $X \xrightarrow{m} Y$. Alternatively, we may view *this* model as the original and the previous one as a convenient abstraction for the purpose of analysis and proofs. In other words, in practical applications, it is not necessarily true that one starts or should start with the most abstract model!

2.5   Asking Questions

Let us now ask a set of questions similar to those posed above in the case of the simple temperature chart. As before, we will use a typical example in formulating solutions

$$\varsigma = [i_1 \mapsto \mu_1, \ldots, i \mapsto \mu, \ldots i_n \mapsto \mu_m] \tag{110}$$

where the temperature charts have the form

$$\begin{aligned}
\mu_1 &= [\ldots] \\
\ldots &= \ldots \\
\mu &= [c_1 \mapsto t_1, \ldots, c_k \mapsto t_j, \ldots, c_{n'} \mapsto t_{m'}] \\
\ldots &= \ldots \\
\mu_m &= [\ldots]
\end{aligned} \tag{111}$$

QUESTION **2.8** *What is the set of cities the temperatures of which are recorded in the temperature chart identified by i in the system ς?*

$$dom(\varsigma(i)) \tag{112}$$

Comment: Note the assumption that there is an existing identifier i in the system. Therefore, we have the more rigorous response

$$\chi[\![i]\!]\varsigma \rightarrow dom(\varsigma(i)), \bot \tag{113}$$

Alternatively we may say that $\chi[\![i]\!]\varsigma$ is a pre-condition.

QUESTION 2.9 *What is the set of cities the temperatures of which are recorded in the temperature chart system ς?*

$$^\cup\!/ \circ \mathcal{P} \, dom \circ rng \, \varsigma \tag{114}$$

Comment: We build up such a solution in the following manner. Given

$$\varsigma = [i_1 \mapsto \mu_1, \ldots, i_k \mapsto \mu_j, \ldots i_n \mapsto \mu_m] \tag{115}$$

We extract the set of temperature charts

$$
\begin{aligned}
rng \, \varsigma \quad &= \quad rng[i_1 \mapsto \mu_1, \ldots, i \mapsto \mu, \ldots i_n \mapsto \mu_m] \tag{116}\\
&= \quad \{\mu_1, \ldots, \mu, \ldots, \mu_m\} \tag{117}
\end{aligned}
$$

Iterating over this set with a domain operator $\mathcal{P} \, dom$ gives the sets of cities in each temperature chart:

$$
\begin{aligned}
\mathcal{P} \, dom \circ rng \, \varsigma \quad &= \quad \mathcal{P} \, dom \, \{\mu_1, \ldots, \mu, \ldots, \mu_m\} \tag{118}\\
&= \quad \{dom \, \mu_1, \ldots, dom \, \mu, \ldots, dom \, \mu_m\} \tag{119}\\
&= \quad \{\{c_{11}, \ldots, \}, \ldots, \{c_1, \ldots\}, \ldots, \{c_{m1}, \ldots\}\} \tag{120}
\end{aligned}
$$

The final result is then obtained by applying reduction with respect to set union: $^\cup\!/$.

QUESTION 2.10 *Which temperatures are recorded in the temperature chart identified by i in the system ς?*

$$rng(\varsigma(i)) \tag{121}$$

QUESTION 2.11 *Which temperatures are recorded in the temperature chart system ς?*

$$^\cup\!/ \circ \mathcal{P} \, rng \circ rng \, \varsigma \tag{122}$$

QUESTION 2.12 *Is the city c recorded in the temperature chart identified by i in the system ς?*

$$\chi[c]\varsigma(i) \tag{123}$$

QUESTION 2.13 *Is the city c recorded in the temperature chart system ς?*

$$\chi[c](^\cup\!/ \circ \mathcal{P} \, dom \circ rng \, \varsigma) \tag{124}$$

Alternatively, we may define the solution by

$$^\vee\!/ \circ \mathcal{P}(\chi[c]) \circ rng \, \varsigma \tag{125}$$

where $^\vee\!/$ denotes reduction with respect to 'logical or' and, consequently,

$$\chi[c](^\cup\!/ \circ \mathcal{P} \, dom \circ rng \, \varsigma) = {}^\vee\!/ \circ \mathcal{P}(\chi[c]) \circ rng \, \varsigma \tag{126}$$

Comment: Again we propose to show the development of the solution. Clearly, we have

$$
\begin{aligned}
\mathcal{P}(\chi[c]) \circ rng \, \varsigma \quad &= \quad \mathcal{P}(\chi[c]) \circ rng[i_1 \mapsto \mu_1, \ldots, i \mapsto \mu, \ldots i_n \mapsto \mu_m] \tag{127}\\
&= \quad \mathcal{P}(\chi[c])\{\mu_1, \ldots, \mu, \ldots, \mu_m\} \tag{128}\\
&= \quad \{\chi[c]\mu_1, \ldots, \chi[c]\mu, \ldots, \chi[c]\mu_m\} \tag{129}
\end{aligned}
$$

resulting in one of three possibilities, in the non-trivial case: $\{false\}$, $\{true\}$, or $\{false, true\}$. **N.B.** The possibility of the same city c occurring in two distinct temperature charts is **not** ruled out!

QUESTION 2.14 *Which cities have temperature t in the temperature chart identified by i in the system ς?*

$$\left(\varsigma(i)\right)^{-1}(t) \tag{130}$$

QUESTION 2.15 *Which cities have temperature t?*

$$\cup/\left((\mathcal{P}(-^{-1}) \circ rng\,\varsigma)(t)\right) \tag{131}$$

Comment: The strange looking expression $\mathcal{P}(-^{-1})$ needs an explanation, one which is properly given in the context of a computation. Given a system ς, we may extract the set of temperature charts:

$$rng\,\varsigma = \{\mu_1, \ldots, \mu, \ldots, \mu_m\} \tag{132}$$

If one computes the inverse image of t with respect to each chart, then we have the set of sets of cities:

$$\{\mu_1^{-1}(t), \ldots, \mu^{-1}(t), \ldots, \mu_m^{-1}(t)\} \tag{133}$$

which, by an abuse of notation, we may write in the form

$$\{\mu_1^{-1}, \ldots, \mu^{-1}, \ldots, \mu_m^{-1}\}(t) \tag{134}$$

The set of function operators might now be written as

$$\{(-^{-1})\mu_1, \ldots, (-^{-1})\mu, \ldots, (-^{-1})\mu_m\} = \mathcal{P}(-^{-1})\{\mu_1, \ldots, \mu, \ldots, \mu_m\} \tag{135}$$

which leads to the proposed solution. Whereas, the solution has a certain elegance, the 'abuse of notation' does impell us to seek a justification for its use. Specifically, we need to demonstrate that such a result may also be computed effectively by a recursive algorithm. Clearly, the computation of inverse images may be accomplished effectively by an algorithm similar to that which computed the set of cities having a minimum temperature in a temperature chart—one of the reasons for going into details in its presentation. The question of using a set of function operators applied to a temperature t is all that really needs to be addressed. Upon reflection, it should be obvious that, interpreting each μ^{-1} as an algorithm, the expression

$$\{\mu_1^{-1}, \ldots, \mu^{-1}, \ldots, \mu_m^{-1}\}(t) \tag{136}$$

suggests an iteration, one governed by the indexing mechanism of the temperature charts in the system.

In fact, whilst considering such expressions involving inverse images, the Irish School of the *VDM* is currently developing a theory of inverse image maps.

QUESTION 2.16 *Which cities have the minimum temperature in the temperature chart identified by i in the system ς?*

$$(\varsigma = \theta \vee \varsigma(i) = \theta) \rightarrow \emptyset, \left(\varsigma(i)\right)^{-1}(\downarrow/ \circ rng\,\varsigma(i)) \tag{137}$$

Comment: In this solution, we take care to show that questions involving a minimum/maximum require that one operate on non-empty structures.

QUESTION **2.17** *Which cities have the minimum temperature in the system ς?*

$$(\varsigma = \theta) \quad \lor \quad (rng(\{\theta\} \triangleleft \varsigma) = \theta) \tag{138}$$

$$\rightarrow \quad \emptyset, \tag{139}$$

$$\rightarrow \quad {}^{\cup}/\Big(\mathcal{P}(--^{-1}) \circ rng(\{\theta\} \triangleleft \varsigma)$$
$$({}^{\downarrow}/ \circ \mathcal{P}({}^{\downarrow}/) \circ \mathcal{P}\, rng \circ rng(\{\theta\} \triangleleft \varsigma)\Big) \tag{140}$$

Comment: Such solutions might be considered 'difficult to understand', a complaint that was/is frequently heard of APL 'one-liners'. Such remarks show a complete misunderstanding of the purpose of such expressions. They are not intended to be read at all! All expressions, whether in the *VDM* or in mathematics, are an invitation to reconstruct the solution.

First we observe, that if we ignore the special case of empty-structures, then the solution has the form

$$ {}^{\cup}/\Big(\mathcal{P}(--^{-1}) \circ rng\, \varsigma({}^{\downarrow}/ \circ \mathcal{P}({}^{\downarrow}/) \circ \mathcal{P}\, rng \circ rng\, \varsigma)\Big) \tag{141}$$

We should be able to see at a glance that $\mathcal{P}\, rng \circ rng\, \varsigma$ gives a set of temperatures for each chart in the system:

$$\mathcal{P}\, rng \circ rng\, \varsigma = \{\{t_{11}, \ldots\}, \ldots, \{t_1, \ldots\}, \ldots, \{t_{m1}, \ldots\}\} \tag{142}$$

Then the 'global' minimum t_{min} is the minimum of the set of local minima:

$$
\begin{aligned}
t_{min} &= {}^{\downarrow}/ \circ \mathcal{P}({}^{\downarrow}/) \circ \mathcal{P}\, rng \circ rng\, \varsigma & (143)\\
&= {}^{\downarrow}/ \circ \mathcal{P}({}^{\downarrow}/)\{\{t_{11}, \ldots\}, \ldots, \{t_1, \ldots\}, \ldots, \{t_{m1}, \ldots\}\} & (144)\\
&= {}^{\downarrow}/\{{}^{\downarrow}/\{t_{11}, \ldots\}, \ldots, {}^{\downarrow}/\{t_1, \ldots\}, \ldots, {}^{\downarrow}/\{t_{m1}, \ldots\}\} & (145)\\
&= {}^{\downarrow}/\{t_{1,min}, \ldots, t_{j,min}, \ldots, t_{m,min}\} & (146)
\end{aligned}
$$

and the expressed solution is really of the form

$$ {}^{\cup}/\Big(\mathcal{P}(--^{-1}) \circ rng\, \varsigma(t_{min})\Big) \tag{147}$$

a form which we have met before. Two further observations are in order. First, it is clear that the expression $\mathcal{P}({}^{\downarrow}/) \circ \mathcal{P}\, rng$ may also be written as $\mathcal{P}({}^{\downarrow}/ \circ rng)$. Secondly, we may prefer to take the union of all the sets of temperatures before taking a minimum, giving the result in the form

$$ {}^{\cup}/\Big(\mathcal{P}(--^{-1}) \circ rng\, \varsigma({}^{\downarrow}/ \circ {}^{\cup}/ \circ \mathcal{P}\, rng \circ rng\, \varsigma)\Big) \tag{148}$$

Although this latter specification is exactly equivalent to the first solution given, it is clear that the first one forms a basis for an efficient implementation.

As in the case of the simple temperature chart, we now give a traditional denotational semantics representation for some operations on the temperature chart system.

2.6 Denotational Semantics

For the extended model we also propose an incomplete set of operations. Instead of specifying syntactic domains, the semantic functions are given directly in the terse style.

2.6.1 The Create Command

The create operation has the effect of introducing a new empty temperature chart into the system, an operation which is the exact couterpart of that for the model of the simple temperature chart. It is taken for granted that one would be able to specify a corresponding create operation to give an empty temperature chart system.

$$39 \quad Crea: TCn \longrightarrow TMPCHRT\_SYS \longrightarrow TMPCHRT\_SYS$$
$$.1 \quad Crea[i]\varsigma \triangleq \varsigma \cup [i \mapsto \theta]$$

The sole restriction on the operation is to ensure that a new name i is introduced for the new chart:

$$40 \quad pre\text{-}Crea: TCn \longrightarrow TMPCHRT\_SYS \longrightarrow \mathbf{B}$$
$$.1 \quad pre\text{-}Crea[i]\varsigma \triangleq \neg\chi[i]\varsigma$$

2.6.2 The Erase Command

The erase command is the formal inverse of the above create command. However, as will be elaborated upon below in the context of the put command, if $(i_a, \mu) \in \varsigma$, then $\{i_a\} \blacktriangleleft \varsigma$ may actually still contain a pair (i_b, μ), where $i_a \neq i_b$, i.e., the temperature chart μ has **not** been erased!

$$41 \quad Eras: TCn \longrightarrow TMPCHRT\_SYS \longrightarrow TMPCHRT\_SYS$$
$$.1 \quad Eras[i]\varsigma \triangleq \{i\} \blacktriangleleft \varsigma$$

subject to the pre-condition:

$$42 \quad pre\text{-}Eras: TCn \longrightarrow TMPCHRT\_SYS \longrightarrow \mathbf{B}$$
$$.1 \quad pre\text{-}Eras[i]\varsigma \triangleq \chi[i]\varsigma$$

2.6.3 The Put Command

This operation is used both to enter a new (city, temperature) pair to an existing temperature chart *and* to update an existing temperature for a given city in a temperature chart.

$$43 \quad Put: TCn \times CTY \times TMP \longrightarrow TMPCHRT\_SYS \longrightarrow TMPCHRT\_SYS$$
$$.1 \quad Put[i, c, t]\varsigma \triangleq$$
$$.2 \qquad \chi[c]\varsigma(i)$$

$$.3 \qquad \rightarrow \varsigma + [i \mapsto \varsigma(i) + [c \mapsto t]]$$
$$.4 \qquad \rightarrow \varsigma + [i \mapsto \varsigma(i) \cup [c \mapsto t]]$$

Annotations:

(43.3) update existing city temperature.

(43.4) enter new (city, temperature) pair.

The following pre-condition is deliberately minimal in order to illustrate some important points, which will be developed later.

44 $\quad$ pre-*Put*: $TCn \times CTY \times TMP \longrightarrow TMPCHRT\_SYS \longrightarrow \mathbf{B}$

.1 $\quad$ pre-*Put*$[i, c, t]\varsigma \triangleq \chi[i]\varsigma$

Comment: It is possible, through a combination of create and put commands to build up a temperature chart system such that there are two distinct names i_a and i_b with $\varsigma(i_a) = \varsigma(i_b) = \mu$. In other words, our model permits the possibility of aliases.

2.6.4 The Get Command

If we have put information into the system then we must be able to retrieve it. The get command serves that purpose.

45 $\quad$ *Get*: $TCn \times CTY \longrightarrow TMPCHRT\_SYS \longrightarrow TMP$

.1 $\quad$ *Get*$[i, c]\varsigma \triangleq (\varsigma(i))(c)$

subject to the pre-condition:

46 $\quad$ pre-*Get*: $TCn \times CTY \longrightarrow TMPCHRT\_SYS \longrightarrow \mathbf{B}$

.1 $\quad$ pre-*Get*$[i, c]\varsigma \triangleq \chi[i]\varsigma \wedge \chi[c]\varsigma(i)$

2.6.5 The Delete Command

This is the *formal* inverse of the *second* part of the put command. It is used to delete a city from a temperature chart.

47 $\quad$ *Del*: $TCn \times CTY \longrightarrow TMPCHRT\_SYS \longrightarrow TMPCHRT\_SYS$

.1 $\quad$ *Del*$[i, c]\varsigma \triangleq \varsigma + [i \mapsto \{c\} \blacktriangleleft \varsigma(i)]$

which has the same pre-condition as the get command:

48 $\quad$ pre-*Del*: $TCn \times CTY \longrightarrow TMPCHRT\_SYS \longrightarrow \mathbf{B}$

.1 $\quad$ pre-*Del*$[i, c]\varsigma \triangleq \chi[i]\varsigma \wedge \chi[c]\varsigma(i)$

This concludes the first part of the tutorial. We have looked at a simple model and a putative refinement. Operations on the models were derived as solutions to certain, admittedly well-posed, questions. Both closed form expressions and an algorithmic recursive/iterative form were exhibited. For completeness, we exhibited the relationship between these forms and the conventional denotational semantics forms. It ought to be absolutely clear which form is preferred in the Irish School.

Although simple lemmas were discovered, no proofs were given. It is now necessary to ask what relationship the two models bear to one another with respect to the operations presented. In other words, the very existence of two related models invites the construction of proofs. Again it is necessary to reiterate that 'mere correctness' is **not** the goal. On the contrary, we expect to 'debug' the models by carring out proofs. Such debugging will lead to the uncovering of hidden lemmas, which always prove to be considerable importance in real requirements modelling.

We may indeed take the view that *TMPCHRT_SYS* is a development of *TMP_CHRT* and decide to verify that the operations on the former correspond to operations on the latter. Since *TMPCHRT_SYS* is a specific development step which fits into a standard paradign—partitioning—we will discuss these matters under the heading 'Design and Proof', the subject of the next section.

3 Standard Development Steps

What is design?

Such a question is of the same nature as: *What is (the meaning of) life?*, one that does not really have an answer. It is better experienced than described. In the world of design, wherein 'software design' seems to be an exception, drawing plays a major rôle. Indeed, the French for 'design' is *dessein* which also means 'drawing' or 'sketch'. It might be argued that flowcharts, bubble diagrams, booch diagrams, etc., are the software design counterparts of the drawing or sketch, but not very convincingly, we feel.

In the Irish School, drawing/sketching plays a major rôle in the development of specifications, though the opposite impression would be obtained from the presentation of the textual material in this tutorial. Each and every question/solution has its corresponding diagram which helps to illustrate the meaning, and the form of such diagrams are more like what one finds in mathematics rather than in software engineering. In practice they are constructed on a blackboard/whiteboard and on quadrille paper. The sketch has meaning in the interactive dialogue of development and loses much of same once finished/fixed. Inclusion of such sketches in formal documents is laborious and space-consuming. One form of diagram, which is of critical importance in presenting developments, is the commuting diagram, many examples of which are presented in this section.

Design involves both *form* and *function* and whereas much attention is paid to the latter in software engineering, there seems to be very little appreciation of the former *as understood in other domains*, to wit the essential aspect of æsthetics, frequently expressed via geometry/shape. Indeed, form in software engineering often reduces to a matter of debate on syntactic forms. It is not clear whether there can ever be a notion of geometry/shape in software engineering—an open challenge! In the Irish School, æstetics of form is also largely a matter of syntax or notation, but one which clearly emphasises the symbiosis of form and function in design.

To construct effective proofs, the Irish School abandoned formal predicate logic and returned to the mainstream of mathematics. Proofs are intended to enlighten the prover, to be carried out as a dialogue that others might concur. In short proving is a social activity. Hence, there is little enthusiasm for 'proofs by machine'—the theorem-provers. Whilst being an interesting application of computing technology, and one which is of high academic merit, we feel that proving is essentially a human activity. We are not opposed to computer-aided proving tools *per se*. But we do insist that a human **must** be able to check the proof and there **must** be another group of humans who are prepared to agree that the proof is valid—even should it be invalid! The (in)famous case of the VIPER chip is noteworthy in this respect [23].

To be formal and yet to abandon formal logic implied the need for a replacement. In the Irish School this led to the construction of an operator calculus. Proofs in the Irish style abound in the remainder of the tutorial.

There has been a sufficient number of developments conducted in the *VDM* (and in other formal methods) for us to hypothesise that the time is ripe to set down a foundation for standard development steps. A beginning was made and recorded in [22] in the context of models of a dictionary and it was obvious that an enormous amount of labour was required to develop the ideas. By working in the context of standard *abstract* models, and studying standard development steps with accompanying proofs, it became clear that a real mathematics for software engineering could be constructed, a mathematics that bore much resemblance to the usual mathematics employed in 'ordinary' engineering. To emphasise this point, four types of development are introduced for the temperature chart models, and proofs are given for the enter operation. The steps have been named for convenience:

1. partitioning or subdividing

2. splitting

3. parameterising

4. joining

Each is presented in a separate subsection.

3.1 Partitioning or Subdividing

It was remarked upon earlier that the construction of *TMPCHRT_SYS* might be regarded as the result of partitioning the original *TMP_CHRT* by country, an extremely reasonable interpretation in practice. But should the original chart have been intended for a single country, then we might wish to partition it according to a country's traditional regions: county, or *departement*, etc. Since, the very notions of 'temperature', 'city', etc., are solely for practical convenience in a specific problem domain, we might just as well consider the problem in the abstract. Therefore, given any model of the form $X \underset{m}{\rightharpoonup} Y$, and the partitioned model $K \underset{m}{\rightharpoonup} X \underset{m}{\rightharpoonup} Y$, where K is the partitioning domain, then we immediately have

$$\mu \in M_0 = X \underset{m}{\rightharpoonup} Y$$

$$\left| \Re_{10}(\varsigma) = {}^{\cup}/ \circ rng(\varsigma) \right. \tag{149}$$

$$\varsigma \in M_1 = K \underset{m}{\rightharpoonup} (X \underset{m}{\rightharpoonup} Y)$$

where ${}^{\cup}/ \circ rng$ is the customary operator for retrieving an original from a partitioned domain. To test the hypothesis that it is so, we will examine the enter command for both models:

$$Ent_0[c, t]\mu \stackrel{\Delta}{=} \mu \cup [c \mapsto t] \tag{150}$$

$$\begin{array}{ccc}
TMP\_CHRT & \xrightarrow{\quad Ent_0[c,t] \quad} & TMP\_CHRT \\[4pt]
\Big\uparrow {}^{\cup}/ \circ rng & & \Big\uparrow {}^{\cup}/ \circ rng \\[4pt]
TMPCHRT\_SYS & \xrightarrow{\quad Ent_1[i,c,t] \quad} & TMPCHRT\_SYS
\end{array} \tag{151}$$

$$Ent_1[i, c, t]\varsigma \stackrel{\Delta}{=} \varsigma + [i \mapsto \varsigma(i) \cup [c \mapsto t]] \tag{152}$$

and to establish that Ent_1 is the formal counterpart of Ent_0 we must try to prove that the diagram commutes:

$$Ent_0[c, t] \circ ({}^{\cup}/ \circ rng) = ({}^{\cup}/ \circ rng) \circ Ent_1[i, c, t] \tag{153}$$

Considering the right hand side—which is usually tackled first in all Int– type commands— we attempt the following proof using the operational calculus

49   $({}^{\cup}/ \circ rng) \circ Ent_1[i, c, t]\varsigma$
  .1 $= ({}^{\cup}/ \circ rng)(\varsigma + [i \mapsto \varsigma(i) \cup [c \mapsto t]])$
  .2 $= ({}^{\cup}/ \circ rng)\big((dom\,[i \mapsto \varsigma(i) \cup [c \mapsto t]]) \blacktriangleleft \varsigma) \cup [i \mapsto \varsigma(i) \cup [c \mapsto t]]\big)$
  .3 $= ({}^{\cup}/ \circ rng)\big((\{i\} \blacktriangleleft \varsigma) \cup [i \mapsto \varsigma(i) \cup [c \mapsto t]]\big)$
  .4 $= {}^{\cup}/\big(rng(\{i\} \blacktriangleleft \varsigma) \cup rng\,[i \mapsto \varsigma(i) \cup [c \mapsto t]]\big)$
  .5 $= {}^{\cup}/ \circ rng(\{i\} \blacktriangleleft \varsigma) \cup {}^{\cup}/ \circ rng\,[i \mapsto \varsigma(i) \cup [c \mapsto t]]$
  .6 $= {}^{\cup}/ \circ rng(\{i\} \blacktriangleleft \varsigma) \cup {}^{\cup}/\{\varsigma(i) \cup [c \mapsto t]\}$
  .7 $= {}^{\cup}/ \circ rng(\{i\} \blacktriangleleft \varsigma) \cup (\varsigma(i) \cup [c \mapsto t])$
  .8 $= ({}^{\cup}/ \circ rng(\{i\} \blacktriangleleft \varsigma) \cup \varsigma(i)) \cup [c \mapsto t]$
  .9 $= {}^{\cup}/ \circ rng\,\varsigma \cup [c \mapsto t]$
  .10 $= Ent_0[c, t]({}^{\cup}/ \circ rng\,\varsigma)$
  .11 $= Ent_0[c, t] \circ ({}^{\cup}/ \circ rng)\varsigma$

Annotations:

49.2) We use the formal definition of the map override operator

$$\mu_j + \mu_k = (dom\,\mu_k \mathbin{\lhd} \mu_j) \cup \mu_k \tag{154}$$

49.4) The range operator distributes over map extend

$$rng(\mu_j \cup \mu_k) = rng(\mu_j) \cup rng(\mu_k) \tag{155}$$

49.5) Reduction with respect to map extend is a law of sets of disjoint maps

$$^{\cup}/(S_j \cup S_k) = {}^{\cup}/S_j \cup {}^{\cup}/S_k \tag{156}$$

Comment: In an earlier commentary on the proof the word 'homomorphism' was used in place of the word 'law', a use which was challenged by a former student, Fred Cummins, on the grounds that sets of disjoint maps are not defined with respect to the extend operator—violation of closure. For example, let D denote the domain of disjoint maps

$$D = \{[x \mapsto a], [y \mapsto b]\} \tag{157}$$

Define $S_j = \{[x \mapsto a]\}$ and $S_k = \{[y \mapsto b]\}$. Then it is obviously true that

$$
\begin{aligned}
^{\cup}/(S_j \cup S_k) &= {}^{\cup}/(D) & (158)\\
&= {}^{\cup}/S_j \cup {}^{\cup}/S_k & (159)\\
&= [x \mapsto a] \cup [y \mapsto b] & (160)\\
&= [x \mapsto a, y \mapsto b] \notin D & (161)
\end{aligned}
$$

Indeed, for any *a priori* domain of disjoint maps D, and any non-empty set S of such maps, $^{\cup}/S \notin D$, since for any element $\mu \in S$ then $dom\,\mu \cap dom\,{}^{\cup}/S = dom\,\mu$. Consequently, we are forced to refer to the above property simply as a law—**not as a homomorphism.**

It would appear that we have established the required result. However, we must be suspicious of the proof in a Lakatosian sense—try to refute it with a counter-example. The arguments used in establishing (49.2) and (49.4) are unassailable. Let us, therefore, focus on the validity of the application of the $^{\cup}/$ law. The result is invalid if and only if there is an element $\overline{\mu}$, in $rng(\{i\} \mathbin{\lhd} \varsigma)$ for which $\overline{\mu}$ and $\varsigma(i) \cup [c \mapsto t]$ are not disjoint. On the basis of the precondition for Ent_1 we are assured that this can only be the case if $\overline{\mu} = \mu \in rng(\{i\} \mathbin{\lhd} \varsigma)$ and such a situation arises if and only if $|\varsigma^{-1}(\mu)| > 1$. In other words, ς is a surjective map, i.e., there exists a j, $j \neq i$, such that $\varsigma(j) = \varsigma(i)$. Consequently, the temperature chart system

$$\varsigma_0 = [i \mapsto \mu, j \mapsto \mu] \tag{162}$$

is a specific counter-example. What should now be done—reject the proof? We have arrived at a point where we must decide upon an invariant for *TMPCHRT_SYS*. Either we must permit aliasing or outlaw it! Specifically, the choices are:

(a) We can 'save' the situation by adding a new precondition to Ent_1:

$$|\varsigma^{-1} \circ \varsigma(i)| = 1 \qquad (163)$$

But then our proof will only work for just those special cases.

(b) We could further insist that we do not permit aliasing in the temperature chart system, i.e., that $\forall \varsigma \in TMPCHRT\_SYS = TCn \underset{m}{\rightarrow} TMP\_CHRT$, ς is injective.

This may be accomplished by the invariant

$$|\,dom\,\varsigma| = |\,rng\,\varsigma| \qquad (164)$$

Now the proof is sound as it stands.

But what if we *do* wish to permit aliasing? Let i be a temperature chart identifier in the system ς. Let $\mu = \varsigma(i)$ denote the temperature chart identified by i. The set of aliases, which includes i is denoted by $\varsigma^{-1} \circ \varsigma(i)$. We may now give two possible interpretations for the enter operation.

(1) In this interpretation, which we shall call the *aliasing interpretation*, all aliases must identify the same temperature chart. If we add a new city, temperature pair, (c, t), to $\mu = \varsigma(i) \neq \theta$, then we must ensure that every name in $\varsigma^{-1} \circ \varsigma(i)$ identifies $\mu \cup [c \mapsto t]$. Then we must modify our specification of Ent_1:

> 50 $Ent_1 : TCn \times CTY \times TMP \longrightarrow TMPCHRT\_SYS \longrightarrow TMPCHRT\_SYS$
> .1 $Ent_1[i, c, t]\varsigma \triangleq$
> .2 $\chi[i]\varsigma \wedge \neg\chi[c]\varsigma \rightarrow (\varsigma +^{\cup}\!/ \circ \mathcal{P}(\jmath[\varsigma(i) \cup [c \mapsto t]])\varsigma^{-1} \circ \varsigma(i), \varsigma)$

where $\jmath : TMP\_CHRT \longrightarrow (TCn \longrightarrow TMPCHRT\_SYS)$, denotes the injection function defined by

$$\jmath : \mu \mapsto (i \mapsto [i \mapsto \mu]) \qquad (165)$$

Therefore, $\jmath[\mu]i = [i \mapsto \mu]$. It is a useful exercise to take a concrete example such as $\varsigma = [\ldots, i \mapsto \mu, \ldots, i_j \mapsto \mu, \ldots]$ and work through the details of the enter command to verify the intended result.

(2) There is also a reasonable interpretation for which the original specification of Ent_1 is valid—if at some stage two different names identify the same temperature chart, say i and a, and then after the enter operation $Ent_1[i, c, t]$, a will identify the old temperature chart. This is a reasonable way to capture the notion of versions. In this interpretation, the *version interpretation*, the proof given above fails and we must find another proof. In this tutorial the proof for the aliasing interpretation is given next. That for the version interpretation is left as an exercise.

3.1.1 Aliasing Interpretation

From the above discussion we may simply state that we are required to prove that the following diagram commutes.

$$Ent_0[c,t]\mu \triangleq \mu \cup [c \mapsto t] \tag{166}$$

$$
\begin{array}{ccc}
TMP\_CHRT & \xrightarrow{\quad Ent_0[c,t] \quad} & TMP\_CHRT \\[4pt]
\Big\uparrow {}^{\cup}\!/\circ rng & & \Big\uparrow {}^{\cup}\!/\circ rng \\[4pt]
TMPCHRT\_SYS & \xrightarrow{\quad Ent_1[i,c,t] \quad} & TMPCHRT\_SYS
\end{array}
$$

$$Ent_1[i,c,t]\varsigma \triangleq \varsigma + {}^{\cup}\!/\circ \mathcal{P}(\jmath[\varsigma(i) \cup [c \mapsto t]])\varsigma^{-1} \circ \varsigma(i) \tag{167}$$

First, we consider the right hand side

51   $({}^{\cup}\!/\circ rng) \circ Ent_1[i,c,t]\varsigma$

.1 $= {}^{\cup}\!/\circ rng \left(\varsigma + {}^{\cup}\!/\circ \mathcal{P}(\jmath[\varsigma(i) \cup [c \mapsto t]])\varsigma^{-1} \circ \varsigma(i)\right)$

.2 $= {}^{\cup}\!/\circ rng \left((dom({}^{\cup}\!/\circ \mathcal{P}(\jmath[\varsigma(i) \cup [c \mapsto t]])\varsigma^{-1} \circ \varsigma(i)) \blacktriangleleft \varsigma)\right.$

.3 $\left. \cup {}^{\cup}\!/\circ \mathcal{P}(\jmath[\varsigma(i) \cup [c \mapsto t]])\varsigma^{-1} \circ \varsigma(i)\right)$

.4 $= {}^{\cup}\!/\circ rng \left((\varsigma^{-1} \circ \varsigma(i) \blacktriangleleft \varsigma) \cup {}^{\cup}\!/\circ \mathcal{P}(\jmath[\varsigma(i) \cup [c \mapsto t]])\varsigma^{-1} \circ \varsigma(i)\right)$

.5 $= {}^{\cup}\!/\left(rng(\varsigma^{-1} \circ \varsigma(i) \blacktriangleleft \varsigma) \cup rng \circ {}^{\cup}\!/\circ \mathcal{P}(\jmath[\varsigma(i) \cup [c \mapsto t]])\varsigma^{-1} \circ \varsigma(i)\right)$

.6 $= \left({}^{\cup}\!/\circ rng(\varsigma^{-1} \circ \varsigma(i) \blacktriangleleft \varsigma)\right)$

.7 $\cup \left({}^{\cup}\!/\circ rng \circ {}^{\cup}\!/\circ \mathcal{P}(\jmath[\varsigma(i) \cup [c \mapsto t]])\varsigma^{-1} \circ \varsigma(i)\right)$

.8 $= \left({}^{\cup}\!/\circ rng(\varsigma^{-1} \circ \varsigma(i) \blacktriangleleft \varsigma)\right) \cup \left(\varsigma(i) \cup [c \mapsto t]\right)$

.9 $= \left({}^{\cup}\!/\circ rng(\varsigma^{-1} \circ \varsigma(i) \blacktriangleleft \varsigma) \cup \varsigma\right) \cup [c \mapsto t]$

.10 $= {}^{\cup}\!/\circ rng\,\varsigma \cup [c \mapsto t]$

.11 $= Ent_0[c,t]({}^{\cup}\!/\circ rng\,\varsigma)$

.12 $= (Ent_0[c,t] \circ {}^{\cup}\!/\circ rng)\varsigma$

      quod erat demonstrandum

Annotations:

51.4) Justification given by the lemma:

    LEMMA 3.1 $dom \circ {}^{\cup}\!/\circ \mathcal{P}(\jmath[\mu])S = {}^{\cup}\!/\circ \mathcal{P}(dom \circ \jmath[\mu])S = S$

51.8) Justification given by the lemma:

    LEMMA 3.2 $rng \circ {}^{\cup}\!/\circ \mathcal{P}(\jmath[\mu])S = {}^{\cup}\!/\circ \mathcal{P}(rng \circ \jmath[\mu])S = \{\mu\}$

In carrying out the proof, two lemmas had to be used. Although it would appear that they have been pulled out of the air, they are in fact almost trivial consequences of the definition of the injection function $\jmath$. To demonstrate their validity one might proceed as follows. Let $S = \{a_1, a_2, \ldots, a_n\}$ be some set of elements in one domain and μ be the single element in another (possibly same) domain. Then

$$\mathcal{P}(\jmath[\mu])S = \{[a_1 \mapsto \mu], [a_2 \mapsto \mu], \ldots, [a_n \mapsto \mu]\} \tag{168}$$

constructs a set of disjoint maps. Application of reduction with respect to map extend gives the map

$$^\cup\!/ \circ \mathcal{P}(\jmath[\mu])S = [a_1 \mapsto \mu, a_2 \mapsto \mu, \ldots, a_n \mapsto \mu] \tag{169}$$

and taking the domain and range gives the first part of the two lemmas:

$$\operatorname{dom} \circ {}^\cup\!/ \circ \mathcal{P}(\jmath[\mu])S \;=\; \{a_1, a_2, \ldots, a_n\} = S \tag{170}$$

$$\operatorname{rng} \circ {}^\cup\!/ \circ \mathcal{P}(\jmath[\mu])S \;=\; \{\mu\} \tag{171}$$

On the other hand, starting with the expression

$$\mathcal{P}(\jmath[\mu])S = \{[a_1 \mapsto \mu], [a_2 \mapsto \mu], \ldots, [a_n \mapsto \mu]\} \tag{172}$$

and applying the domain and range operators gives

$$\mathcal{P}\operatorname{dom} \circ \mathcal{P}(\jmath[\mu])S \;=\; \mathcal{P}(\operatorname{dom} \circ \jmath[\mu])S \tag{173}$$

$$=\; \{\{a_1\}, \{a_2\}, \ldots, \{a_n\}\} \tag{174}$$

$$\mathcal{P}\operatorname{rng} \circ \mathcal{P}(\jmath[\mu])S \;=\; \mathcal{P}(\operatorname{rng} \circ \jmath[\mu])S \tag{175}$$

$$=\; \{\{\mu\}\} \tag{176}$$

Application of reduction with respect to set union gives the second part of the two lemmas, establishing the results.

$$^\cup\!/ \circ \mathcal{P}\operatorname{dom} \circ \mathcal{P}(\jmath[\mu])S \;=\; {}^\cup\!/ \circ \mathcal{P}(\operatorname{dom} \circ \jmath[\mu])S \tag{177}$$

$$=\; \{a_1, a_2, \ldots, a_n\} = S \tag{178}$$

$$^\cup\!/ \circ \mathcal{P}\operatorname{rng} \circ \mathcal{P}(\jmath[\mu])S \;=\; {}^\cup\!/ \circ \mathcal{P}(\operatorname{rng} \circ \jmath[\mu])S \tag{179}$$

$$=\; \{\mu\} \tag{180}$$

The real point worthy of note is not so much a demonstration of the proof, but rather that we have presented a detailed analysis of, and obtained universal properties of, **all** aliasing models of the form

$$K \xrightarrow[m]{} (X \xrightarrow[m]{} Y) \tag{181}$$

and the proof of the enter command is universally valid for such models.

Aside: Those familiar with the file system case study [4], will recognise that the basic model used there:

$$FS = Fn \xrightarrow[m]{} (Pn \xrightarrow[m]{} PG) \tag{182}$$

may be interpreted as a partitioning of the 'more abstract' model $Pn \xrightarrow[m]{} PG$. Hence, we have also addressed the aliasing problem of the file system.

3.2 Splitting

Given any model of the form $X \underset{m}{\rightarrow} Y$, we may wish to split it into two connected models $X \underset{m}{\rightarrow} S$ and $S \underset{m}{\rightarrow} Y$ by inserting a splitting domain S between X and Y. The relationship between the new model and the original is given by

$$\mu \in M_0 = X \underset{m}{\rightarrow} Y$$

$$\left| \mathfrak{R}_{10}(\mu_l, \mu_r) = \mu_r \circ \mu_l \right. \tag{183}$$

$$(\mu_l, \mu_r) \in M_1 = (X \underset{m}{\rightarrow} S) \times (S \underset{m}{\rightarrow} Y)$$

where there is a canonical invariant for the new model

$$inv\text{-}M_1(\mu_l, \mu_r) \overset{\triangle}{=} rng\, \mu_l = dom\, \mu_r \tag{184}$$

which asserts that the two maps μ_l and μ_r are composable. Some properties of such composable maps are given in [22].

Historically, the recognition of the importance of this splitting development arose from the specific case of the specification of the semantics of programming languages, taught to final year undergraduate students at Trinity College, Dublin, and based on the material of Jones' work [16]. Specifically, given a model of a computer store

$$STORE_0 = Id \underset{m}{\rightarrow} VAL \tag{185}$$

and its reification

$$ENV_1 = Id \underset{m}{\rightarrow} LOC \tag{186}$$

$$STORE_1 = LOC \underset{m}{\rightarrow} VAL \tag{187}$$

we were interested in verifying that the semantics of language constructs with respect to the latter corresponded with the semantics of the same constructs in $STORE_0$.

Turning to the problem of the temperature chart, it is natural to introduce the domain of temperature sensors S, such that the original model is split into the pair $CTY \underset{m}{\rightarrow} S$ and $S \underset{m}{\rightarrow} TMP$. Thus, in the new model each city is mapped to a sensor and each sensor is mapped to a temperature. One might argue that it is more realistic to suppose that a city would have more than one sensor for recording temperatures. We are prepared to agree, if necessary, and assert that our S domain is to be interpreted as a set of virtual sensors which give the mean temperature for a city. Modelling such real sensors would then be another development step.

Let us look at a typical example in the new system

$$\varsigma = (\mu_l, \mu_r) \tag{188}$$

where

$$\mu_l = [c_1 \mapsto s_1, \ldots, c_j \mapsto s_j, \ldots, c_n \mapsto s_n] \tag{189}$$

$$\mu_r = [s_1 \mapsto t_1, \ldots, s_k \mapsto t_k, \ldots, s_n \mapsto t_m] \tag{190}$$

where μ_l must be a 1–1 map, i.e., every city has a unique sensor, and of course, $rng\,\mu_l = dom\,\mu_r$. If we compose the two maps then we have

$$\mu_r \circ \mu_l = [c_1 \mapsto t_1, \ldots, c_j \mapsto t_j, \ldots, c_n \mapsto t_m] \tag{191}$$

Let us now consider the semantics of the enter command for the two models:

$$Ent_0[c, t]\mu \overset{\triangle}{=} \mu \cup [c \mapsto t] \tag{192}$$

$$
\begin{array}{ccc}
TMP\_CHRT & \xrightarrow{\;Ent_0[c,\,t]\;} & TMP\_CHRT \\[2pt]
\Big\uparrow {\scriptstyle -\,\circ\,-} & & \Big\uparrow {\scriptstyle -\,\circ\,-} \\[2pt]
TMPCHRT\_SYS & \xrightarrow{\;Ent_1[c,\,t]\;} & TMPCHRT\_SYS
\end{array}
\tag{193}
$$

$$Ent_1[c, t](\mu_l, \mu_r) \overset{\triangle}{=} \text{let } s \in (rng\,\mu_l \not\twoheadleftarrow S) \text{ in } (\mu_l \cup [c \mapsto s], \mu_r \cup [s \mapsto t]) \tag{194}$$

where, for convenience, we write $(\mu_l, \mu_r) = \varsigma$. A brief notational remark is in order. Formally, the splitting gives the model

$$\varsigma \in TMPCHRT\_SYS = (CTY \underset{m}{\rightharpoonup} S) \times (S \underset{m}{\rightharpoonup} \times TMP) \tag{195}$$

Rather than use $\pi_1\varsigma$ and $\pi_2\varsigma$ to denote the left and right maps, we have chosen to introduce a separate ordered pair notation, for convenience. Note also that in defining the Ent_1 command, we have introduced a new sensor s automatically! We do have an objection to this on æsthetic grounds. The problem is that the name of the sensor domain, occuring in the expression 'let $s \in (rng\,\mu_l \not\twoheadleftarrow S)$ in ...', does not appear in the signature. We generally abhor the use of domain names in such a fashion, though we continue to do so for the present. The problem is easily resolved by explicitly introducing the new sensor as an argument to the enter command.

Let us now prove that the Ent_1 command 'implements' the Ent_0 command, i.e., that

$$Ent_0[c, t] \circ (-\circ-) = (-\circ-) \circ Ent_1[c, t] \tag{196}$$

Since we know intuitively that it does, then in constructing the proof we shall be more interested in uncovering hidden lemmas, i.e., exploring the properties of the new system. Proceeding *formally*, the right hand side gives

52    $(- \circ -) \circ Ent_1[c, t](\mu_l, \mu_r)$

.1 $= (- \circ -)(\mu_l \cup [c \mapsto s], \mu_r \cup [s \mapsto t])$

.2 $= (\mu_r \cup [s \mapsto t]) \circ (\mu_l \cup [c \mapsto s])$

.3 $= (\mu_r \circ \mu_l) \cup ([s \mapsto t] \circ [c \mapsto s])$

.4 $= (\mu_r \circ \mu_l) \cup [c \mapsto t]$

.5 $= \big((- \circ -)(\mu_l, \mu_r)\big) \cup [c \mapsto t]$

.6 $= Ent_0[c, t]\big((- \circ -)(\mu_l, \mu_r)\big)$

.7 $= Ent_0[c, t] \circ (- \circ -)(\mu_l, \mu_r)$

.8   **Q.E.D.**

Annotations:

52.3) The passage from (52.2) to this line is absolutely necessary to carry through the proof using the operator calculus. Examples and diagrams suggest the absolute validity of the following corresponding general lemma on composable maps [22]:

LEMMA 3.3 *Let (f_j, g_j) and (f_k, g_k) be pairs of composable maps such that $dom\ f_j \cap dom\ f_k = \emptyset$ and $dom\ g_j \cap dom\ g_k = \emptyset$. Then*

$$(f_j \cup f_k) \circ (g_j \cup g_k) = (g_j \circ f_j) \cup (g_k \circ f_k) \tag{197}$$

Indeed, it is so obviously true that we do not feel any need to prove the lemma 'from first principles'. However, as an exercise in foundations, it is a simple challenge.

If we consider other operations on these models, which we already know reduce to simple basic expressions such as $\mu + [c \mapsto t]$ and $\{c\} \blacktriangleleft \mu$, then proofs such as the above will lead to corresponding key lemmas on composable maps with respect to map override and map removal, respectively. However, the corresponding lemmas are slightly more complex than the above, the complexity being due to the deletion operator in both cases and the possibility of 'aliasing'. Formulation of the lemmas is left as a challenge; proofs of same is an even greater one.

Such lemmas and proofs which arise in the study of commuting diagrams between pairs of models are at the heart of the development of the operational calculus itself, and constitute a major portion of the mathematical theory behind the Irish School. Historically, in order to prove that one model 'implements' another, in a general way, the need for such an operational calculus arose. The very act of applying the calculus led to the uncovering of the lemmas. Another essential related aspect of this development was the elimination of verbose notations and the recognition of the rôle that curried functions had to play.

One might be concerned that such a large amount of 'theoretical' work would hinder/impede a real development. The opposite is, in fact, the case. The results we obtain are universal—ultimate reuse. New theoretical work is only necessary for models which have not yet already been studied, i.e., fall outside the 'standard set'.

3.3 Parameterising

Lest it should be supposed that such development steps as we have been discussing are breaking new ground, we now propose the adoption of a classical technique from mathematics and apply it to the *VDM*.

Consider the equation of a unit circle with centre $(0,0)$.

$$x^2 + y^2 = 1 \tag{198}$$

It is not possible to express this in the form $y = f(x)$, where f is a single-valued function of x. The classical solution to this problem is to introduce a pair of functions $(f(u), g(u)) = (x, y)$ where u denotes a parameter. For the circle we may write

$$(x,y) = (\cos\theta, \sin\theta), \qquad 0 \le \theta < 2\pi \tag{199}$$

It is natural to extend this idea of parameterisation to the domain $X \underset{m}{\rightarrow} Y$. Specifically, let us choose a totally ordered set P. Then, a map μ, is said to be parameterised with respect to the pair of maps $\mu_x \in P \underset{m}{\rightarrow} X$ and $\mu_y \in P \underset{m}{\rightarrow} Y$, if and only if μ_x is bijective, i.e., $|\operatorname{dom}\mu_x| = |\operatorname{rng}\mu_x|$, they satisy the invariant

$$\operatorname{dom}\mu_x = \operatorname{dom}\mu_y \tag{200}$$

and the retrieve function

$$\mu \in M_0 = X \underset{m}{\rightarrow} Y$$

$$\left\uparrow \Re_{10}(\mu_x, \mu_y) = \mu_y \circ \mu_x^{-1} \right. \tag{201}$$

$$(\mu_x, \mu_y) \in M_1 = (P \underset{m}{\rightarrow} X) \times (P \underset{m}{\rightarrow} Y)$$

Consideration of a simple example, such as the temperature chart, shows quite clearly the idea. Just to be different, we choose a concrete example. Given

$$\mu = [c_1 \mapsto t_1, c_2 \mapsto t_1, c_3 \mapsto t_2] \tag{202}$$

We note, in particular, that c_1 and c_2 both have the same temperature t_1. Let us introduce the parameterisation based on natural numbers $P = \mathbf{N}$ to give

$$\mu_c = [0 \mapsto c_1, 1 \mapsto c_2, 2 \mapsto c_3] \tag{203}$$
$$\mu_t = [0 \mapsto t_1, 1 \mapsto t_1, 2 \mapsto t_2] \tag{204}$$

Now consider the question: what is the temperature of c_2? Since μ_c is bijective by construction, then we obtain the index $\mu_c^{-1}(c_2)$ and look up the result

$$\mu_t(\mu_c^{-1}(c_2)) \tag{205}$$

One is invited to draw comparisons between this model and the use of arrays and inverted files in computing. One has already compared it to the splitting model and noted both the similarities and differences. In addition, one is also invited to ponder on why it was suggested that the P domain be a totally ordered set. What advantage does it give? What other possibilities are there? Other lines of enquiry concern the study of parameterisation in mathematics and an investigation on its import for formal specifications.

Whilst such questions are of considerable importance in the Irish School, we will mundanely continue on with a definition of an enter command for the new model and a corresponding proof of the commutativity of the usual diagram. Abstractly, we may consider the development as an exercise in inverse image manipulation—an exercise which of itself justifies the work.

$$Ent_0[c, t]\mu \triangleq \mu \cup [c \mapsto t] \tag{206}$$

$$
\begin{array}{ccc}
TMP\_CHRT_0 & \xrightarrow{\quad Ent_0[c, t] \quad} & TMP\_CHRT_0 \\[1ex]
\Big\uparrow \Re_{10} & & \Big\uparrow \Re_{10} \\[1ex]
TMP\_CHRT_1 & \xrightarrow{\quad Ent_1[c, t] \quad} & TMP\_CHRT_1
\end{array}
\tag{207}
$$

$$Ent_1[c, t](\mu_c, \mu_t) \triangleq (\mu_c \cup [p \mapsto c], \mu_t \cup [p \mapsto t]) \tag{208}$$

where $p \in (dom\,\mu_x \triangleleft P)$. Again the similarity with the splitting model is noted. Formally we are required to prove that

$$Ent_0[c, t] \circ \Re_{10} = \Re_{10} \circ Ent_1[c, t] \tag{209}$$

In the case of the splitting model we used a pair (μ_l, μ_r) in the proof. In this case, we demonstrate the use of projection operators. The right hand side gives

$$
\begin{aligned}
53 \quad & \Re_{10} \circ Ent_1[c, t]\mu_p \\
.1 \quad & = \left((\pi_2 \circ -) \circ (\pi_1 \circ -)^{-1}\right) \circ Ent_1[c, t]\mu_p \\
.2 \quad & = \left((\pi_2 \circ -) \circ (\pi_1 \circ -)^{-1}\right)\left((\pi_1\mu_p \cup [p \mapsto c]), (\pi_2\mu_p \cup [p \mapsto t])\right) \\
.3 \quad & = (\pi_2 \circ \left((\pi_1\mu_p \cup [p \mapsto c]), (\pi_2\mu_p \cup [p \mapsto t])\right)) \\
.4 \quad & \qquad \circ (\pi_1 \circ \left((\pi_1\mu_p \cup [p \mapsto c]), (\pi_2\mu_p \cup [p \mapsto t])\right))^{-1} \\
.5 \quad & = (\pi_2\mu_p \cup [p \mapsto t]) \circ (\pi_1\mu_p \cup [p \mapsto c])^{-1} \\
.6 \quad & = (\pi_2\mu_p \cup [p \mapsto t]) \circ ((\pi_1\mu_p)^{-1} \cup [p \mapsto c]^{-1}) \\
.7 \quad & = \left((\pi_2\mu_p) \circ ((\pi_1\mu_p)^{-1})\right) \cup \left([p \mapsto t] \circ [p \mapsto c]^{-1}\right) \\
.8 \quad & = \Re_{10}(\mu_p) \cup [c \mapsto t] \\
.9 \quad & = Ent_0[c, t]\Re_{10}(\mu_p)
\end{aligned}
$$

Annotations

(53.1) For a given $\mu_p = (\mu_c, \mu_t)$, the retrieve function $\Re_{10}$ gives $\mu_t \circ \mu_c^{-1}$. We may write this in the form

$$\Re_{10}(\mu_c, \mu_t) = \mu_t \circ \mu_c^{-1} \tag{210}$$

Since $\pi_1\mu_p = \mu_c$ and $\pi_2\mu_p = \mu_t$, then we have immediately

$$\Re_{10}(\pi_1\mu_p, \pi_2\mu_p) = \pi_2\mu_p \circ (\pi_1\mu_p)^{-1} \tag{211}$$

With a little abuse of notation, we are prepared to factor out the μ_p to give

$$\Re_{10}((\pi_1-, \pi_2-)\mu_p) = ((\pi_2-) \circ (\pi_1-)^{-1})\mu_p \tag{212}$$

Addition of a few composition operators for clarity gives the intended form.

(53.6) To get this result, there must be a lemma on inverse maps which has the specific form

$$(\mu_c \cup [p \mapsto c])^{-1} = (\mu_c)^{-1} \cup ([p \mapsto c])^{-1} \tag{213}$$

Since, by construction, μ_c is bijective, then the result is indeed true and can be generalised in the usual way for bijective maps. One is invited to consider the case for surjective maps as an exercise.

(53.7) This result has already been established by a lemma for the splitting case.

To conclude this development step and to illustrate other possibilities, those familiar with the notion of parameterisation and/or some basic principles in optimisation, will wish to *join* the parameterised domains to give the model

$$P \xrightarrow[m]{} X \times Y \tag{214}$$

and, with appropriate subscript adjustment, to insert it *between* the previous two as follows

$$\begin{array}{ccc}
\mu_0 & \xrightarrow{\;Ent_0[\![c,t]\!]\;} & \mu \cup [c \mapsto t] \\
\Big\uparrow {\scriptstyle \Re_{10}} & & \Big\uparrow {\scriptstyle \Re_{10}} \\
\mu_1 & \xrightarrow{\;Ent_1[\![c,t]\!]\;} & \mu_1 \cup [p \mapsto (c,t)] \\
\Big\uparrow {\scriptstyle \Re_{21}} & & \Big\uparrow {\scriptstyle \Re_{21}} \\
(\mu_c, \mu_t) & \xrightarrow{\;Ent_2[\![c,t]\!]\;} & (\mu_c \cup [p \mapsto c], \mu_t \cup [p \mapsto t])
\end{array} \tag{215}$$

The implied exercise should be clear.

3.4 Joining

We concluded the previous subsection by introducing, as an exercise, the development step of *joining*, whereby a model is 'simplified' or compacted. Probably the most well-known example of such a development step in the litterature occurs in the *file system* case study [1]. Given the model, in a slightly modified form

$$FS_1 \ :: \ CTLG_1 \times DIRS_1 \times PGS_1 \tag{216}$$
$$CTLG_1 \ = \ Fn \xrightarrow{m} Dn \tag{217}$$
$$DIRS_1 \ = \ Dn \xrightarrow{m} DIR_1 \tag{218}$$
$$PGS_1 \ = \ Pa \xrightarrow{m} PG \tag{219}$$
$$DIR_1 \ = \ Pn \xrightarrow{m} Pa \tag{220}$$

Then by joining the Dn and Pa domains to give a single domain of addresses Adr, where $Adr = Dn \cup Pa$, we get the (intermediate) result

$$FS_1 \ :: \ CTLG_1 \times DIRS_1 \times PGS_1 \tag{221}$$
$$CTLG_1 \ = \ Fn \xrightarrow{m} Adr \tag{222}$$
$$DIRS_1 \ = \ Adr \xrightarrow{m} DIR_1 \tag{223}$$
$$PGS_1 \ = \ Adr \xrightarrow{m} PG \tag{224}$$
$$DIR_1 \ = \ Pn \xrightarrow{m} Adr \tag{225}$$

This may be compacted further by joining the domains $DIRS_1$ and PGS_1 to give a single domain of disks

$$DSK_2 = (Adr \xrightarrow{m} DIR_1) \cup (Adr \xrightarrow{m} PG) = Adr \xrightarrow{m} (DIR_1 \cup PG) \tag{226}$$

Using appropriate subscripting, the resulting joined model is

$$FS_2 \ :: \ CTLG_2 \times DSK_2 \tag{227}$$
$$CTLG_2 \ = \ Fn \xrightarrow{m} Adr \tag{228}$$
$$DSK_2 \ = \ Adr \xrightarrow{m} (DIR_2 \cup PG) \tag{229}$$
$$DIR_2 \ = \ Pn \xrightarrow{m} Adr \tag{230}$$

Consider the case of the suggested exercise above where we joined the parameterised temperature chart and inserted it *between* the two given models. Let us now, instead, consider the join as a development step subsequent to the parameterisation and write it in the form

$$Ent_2[c,t](\mu_c,\mu_t) \triangleq (\mu_c \cup [p \mapsto c], \mu_t \cup [p \mapsto t]) \tag{231}$$

$$
\begin{array}{ccc}
TMP\_CHRT_2 & \xrightarrow{\ Ent_0[c,t]\ } & TMP\_CHRT_2 \\[2pt]
\Big\uparrow \Re_{12} & & \Big\uparrow \Re_{12} \\[2pt]
TMP\_CHRT_1 & \xrightarrow{\ Ent_1[c,t]\ } & TMP\_CHRT_1
\end{array}
\tag{232}
$$

$$Ent_1[c, t]\mu_1 \stackrel{\triangle}{=} \mu_1 \cup [p \mapsto (c, t)] \tag{233}$$

where the retrieve function $\Re_{12}$ is a *splitting*, given by

$$\Re_{12}(\mu_1) \stackrel{\triangle}{=} ((I \underset{m}{\rightarrow} \pi_1)\mu_1, (I \underset{m}{\rightarrow} \pi_2)\mu_1) \tag{234}$$

Proof of the commutativity of the diagram requires that we show that

$$Ent_2[c, t] \circ \Re_{21} = \Re_{21} \circ Ent_1[c, t] \tag{235}$$

Starting with the right hand side and applying the operator calculus gives

54   $\Re_{21} \circ Ent_1[c, t]\mu_1$

.1 $= \Re_{21}(\mu_1 \cup [p \mapsto (c, t)])$

.2 $= \left((I \underset{m}{\rightarrow} \pi_1)(\mu_1 \cup [p \mapsto (c, t)]), (I \underset{m}{\rightarrow} \pi_2)(\mu_1 \cup [p \mapsto (c, t)])\right)$

.3 $= \left((I \underset{m}{\rightarrow} \pi_1)\mu_1 \cup (I \underset{m}{\rightarrow} \pi_1)[p \mapsto (c, t)],\right.$

.4 $\left.(I \underset{m}{\rightarrow} \pi_2)\mu_1 \cup (I \underset{m}{\rightarrow} \pi_2)[p \mapsto (c, t)]\right)$

.5 $= \left((I \underset{m}{\rightarrow} \pi_1)\mu_1 \cup [p \mapsto c],\right.$

.6 $\left.(I \underset{m}{\rightarrow} \pi_2)\mu_1 \cup [p \mapsto t]\right)$

.7 $= Ent_2[c, t]\left((I \underset{m}{\rightarrow} \pi_1)\mu_1, (I \underset{m}{\rightarrow} \pi_2)\mu_1\right)$

.8 $= Ent_2[c, t] \circ \Re_{21}(\mu_1)$

.9   **Q.E.D.**

Formulation of the corresponding lemma that permits the proof to be carried through is left as an exercise.

Focusing exclusively on *map-based* models, a few simple and obvious standard development paradigms have been presented. When one adds in the full range of modelling artifacts of the *VDM* an enormous range of development paradigms is added. Unfortunately, there are not very many published examples of such developments with corresponding rationale and intepretation and such examples that do exist have not been adequately generalised. It goes without saying that the accompanying *complete* proofs are rarely given. Even in this section, the proofs have been indicative only, in so far that a single operation—the enter command—was presented. For balance one is referred to the complete detailled proof of the splitting step of the file system, given in [22].

An attempt has been made to *name* the development steps: partitioning, splitting, etc., in the hope that the names would convey some idea of the concepts involved and to try to suggest connections with other areas of computer science, especially in the domain of programming. For example, partitioning is intended to suggest the notions of file systems, hashing, etc. That is to say, we wish to use the *VDM* material to link into specific implementation technologies and, also importantly, to suggest that the latter might be abstracted by certain *VDM* paradigms.

At times it is difficult to distinguish between computing domains and mathematical domains. For example, automata theory, algorithm theory and graph theory are all addressed by both computer scientists and mathematicians, each group having its own particular viewpoint, notation and concerns. In fact, said concerns are a matter of the problems/questions that each find interesting and, frequently the intersection problem set is not very large. Since the Irish School of the *VDM* takes the view that its method and notation strikes a happy mean between that of the mathematicians, which leaves much to the imagination, and that of the computer scientists, which is often too implementation oriented, much effort is devoted to 're-presenting' classical work with a view to capturing its constructive essence. The next section presents some material on this aspect of the School.

4 Opening Remarks

The bill of material is a 'standard' example of a recursive domain definition in the *VDM* [15, 2], which has even migrated to $\mathcal{Z}$ [8]. Of all the operations that one might wish to perform on a bill of material, the parts-explosion algorithm is distinguished. The example proved to be an interesting test case for the Irish School and was thoroughly discussed in [22].

In interpreting the domain equation of a bill of material, i.e., examining the models that it specifies, one notes there are two distinct interpretations at the conceptual level:

(1) bill of material '*as finished product*';

(2) bill of material '*in the making*'.

An awareness of this distinction at the conceptual level is important when manipulating the corresponding structures. In addition, the concept of 'bill of material in the making' may also be interpreted as multiple bills of material 'as product'. This is a direct consequence of the recursive nature of the definition.

Hithertofore, in the tutorial, we have *de-emphasised* the rôle that the invariant plays in formal specifications. In this chapter, we begin to address that imbalance. In the Irish School, the invariant is used to analyse the problem domain in question. Proofs that operations on a model preserve the invariant, are an opportunity to learn more about the model and those operations. To be able to perform such proofs, especially using the operator calculus, the form of the invariant is important. That is to say, the invariant is unique. But the expressions that it might take are manifold. In the case of the bill of material a new result is presented. Specifically, the invariant for the domain of bill of material is given in terms of what is called an annihilator function, 'discovered' on 11th February 1991. The material is not intended to be complete. Rather than work out all possible details here, certain key problems to be solved are presented, some of which are stated in the form of hypotheses.

4.1 Model 0

Following [2], we denote the *domain* of bills of material by the equation

$$\gamma_1 \in BOM_1 = X \underset{m}{\rightharpoonup} (X \underset{m}{\rightharpoonup} N_1) \tag{236}$$

subject to an invariant which we have still to specify

$$inv\text{--}BOM_1(\gamma_1) \triangleq \ldots \tag{237}$$

An actual bill of material *as product* may be presented in a variety of forms, one of which is the *indented* bill of material. For example, consider a hypothetical snow shovel, the assembly of which may be denoted by the following [30]:

1605 snow shovel

```
        13122 top handle assembly (1)
            457 top handle (1)
            082 nail (2)
            11495 bracket assembly (1)
                129 top handle bracket (1)
                1118 top handle coupling (1)

        048 scoop shaft connector (1)
        118 shaft (1)
        082 nail (2)
        14127 rivet (4)
        314 scoop assembly (1)
            2142 scoop (1)
            019 blade (1)
            14127 rivet (6)
```

For convenience, in analysing the nature (i.e., properties or characteristics) of a bill of material it is customary to "forget" the number of constituent parts and to focus exclusively on the *form* of the structure of a bill of material. Such "forgetting" recalls the concept of the **forgetful functor** in Category Theory. Technically, we work in the more abstract domain

$$\gamma_0 \in BOM_0 = X \underset{m}{\rightharpoonup} \mathcal{P}X \tag{238}$$

which is, of course, also subject to an invariant

$$inv\text{--}BOM_0(\gamma_0) \triangleq \ldots \tag{239}$$

Formally, the 'forgetful function', which is usually known as a *retrieve* function in the VDM, a name which is more appropriate when dealing with concepts of refinement and reification in a development step, is given by

$$\mathcal{R}_{10}(\gamma_1) \triangleq (\mathcal{I} \underset{m}{\rightharpoonup} dom)\gamma_1 \tag{240}$$

Aside: The emphasis on the name of 'forgetful function' rather than *retrieve* function for this problem domain is of significant conceptual import (especially in the context of the real application of the Irish School of the *VDM* to real industrial problem solving/modelling). We wish to insist that the *starting point* for the modelling of a bill of material is the domain equation for BOM_1 and **not** that for BOM_0. In other words, there is no question of starting with the latter and proceeding to the former via a reification. Rather, we introduce BOM_0 solely for the purpose of analysing the problem to be solved.

Remarks: We will now proceed to examine, in detail, the nature of the BOM_0 domain. First, it is now appropriate to make a few observations on the form of expressions (i.e., notation) used:

(a) We use the **convention** that a basic part x is recorded in a bom γ_0 as an element of the form $[x \mapsto \emptyset]$. The use of this convention is critical in what follows.

(b) The equation is written abstractly on the right hand side in order to suggest that bills of material are just one of the classes of entities modelled by $X \xrightarrow{m} \mathcal{P}X$. Such a class is distinguished, characterised by an invariant, to be discussed below.

(c) We use γ_0 instead of β_0 to recall that a bill of material is a (directed acyclic) graph. In addition, the symbol β is usually associated, in the Irish School, with elements in the domain of bags.

(d) The set of basic parts is denoted by $\gamma_0^{-1}(\emptyset)$. Even this may prove too cumbersome in some proofs and we feel free to introduce the abbreviated form $\gamma_\emptyset^{-1}$.

(e) Consequently, $\gamma_0^{-1}(\emptyset) \triangleleft \gamma_0$ denotes an element of the domain $x \xrightarrow{m} \mathcal{P}'X$, where $\mathcal{P}'X$ denotes $\{\emptyset\} \triangleleft \mathcal{P}X$.

Upon introducing a domain equation it is of paramount importance to get a feel for the sort of (abstract) models that one is dealing with. In other words, one must construct a few typical examples. Such constructions have, of course, a particular psychological value. They are, however, of crucial importance in determining the invariant, the subject of which we now take up.

4.1.1 The Invariant

Note that we speak of **the** invariant, rather than **an** invariant. The purpose of the invariant is to characterise the class of elements in $X \xrightarrow{m} \mathcal{P}X$ which represent/model a bill of material *using the convention* on the representation of basic parts given earlier.

Consider the form of the invariant taken from [2] which has been rewritten somewhat in the style of the Irish School of the *VDM*, an important first stage in all our development work when using/reusing the specifications developed by those of other Schools:

55    $inv\text{-}BOM_0\text{:}\, (X \underset{m}{\rightharpoonup} \mathcal{P}X) \longrightarrow \mathbf{B}$

.1 $inv\text{-}BOM_0(\gamma_0) \triangleq$

.2 $(\forall S \in rng\, \gamma_0)(S \subseteq dom\, \gamma_0)$

.3 $\wedge\, (\forall x \in dom\, \gamma_0)(x \notin Parts(x, \gamma_0))$

Annotations:

(55.0) Note that the structure $X \underset{m}{\rightharpoonup} \mathcal{P}X$ rather than the name BOM_0 is used in the signature.

(55.2) "all recorded"—all constituent parts of an assembly are recorded. In the notation of the Irish School this part of the invariant could be expressed in the equivalent form

$$^{\cup}\!/ \circ rng\, \gamma_0 \subseteq dom\, \gamma_0 \tag{241}$$

where the reduction with respect to set union, $^{\cup}\!/ \circ rng\, \gamma_0$, is the equivalent of the usual mathematical form '$\bigcup rng\, \gamma_0$' employed by the English School. However, the second part of the invariant expressly prohibits the possibility of $^{\cup}\!/ \circ rng\, \gamma_0 = dom\, \gamma_0$ and, consequently, it is more precise to state this part of the invariant as

$$^{\cup}\!/ \circ rng\, \gamma_0 \subset dom\, \gamma_0 \tag{242}$$

(55.3) "none recursively"—there are no cycles.

The *Parts* operation is specified by

56    $Parts\text{:}\, X \times (X \underset{m}{\rightharpoonup} \mathcal{P}X) \longrightarrow \mathcal{P}X$

.1 $Parts(x, \gamma_0) \triangleq$

.2   let $S = \{x' \mid\ \ x' \in dom\, \gamma_0\text{:}\, x' \in \gamma_0(x)$

.3 $\vee\, (\exists x'' \in S, x' \in \gamma_0(x''))\}$

.4   in S

Annotations:

(56.3) Note the occurrence of S within the body of the let clause. Consequently, we conclude that the specification is given by a recursive let clause. The result of the *Parts* operation is a *minimal fixed point* solution of said clause. Whereas such a specification is elegant, we have three serious objections:

(i) It is difficult to apply the specification in the sense of explaining its meaning with respect to an example. In other words, it is not truly *apodeictic*, in the sense of Kant [17]. (Such philosophical references are an important part of the School's culture!) How can we be sure that it is correct? Its very form does not appeal directly to intuition.

(ii) It is difficult to see where it comes from in the first place and, consequently, difficult to teach the underlying technique to others.

(iii) Most important of all, it is impossible to use in conjunction with the operator calculus for conducting proofs.

It is always useful to have a stock of elementary examples of elements in $X \underset{m}{\rightharpoonup} \mathcal{P}X$ which are **not** bills of material:

$$\mu_0 = [x \mapsto \{x\}] \tag{243}$$
$$\mu_1 = [x_j \mapsto \{x_k\}, x_k \mapsto \{x_j\}] \tag{244}$$
$$\mu_2 = [x_j \mapsto \{x_k\}] \tag{245}$$

Such elements are often used as counter-examples to test specifications.

Further remarks:

(243) the singleton cyclic graph: direct recursion violates the "none recursively" part of the invariant given below;

(244) the doublet cyclic graph: mutual recursion violates the "none recursively" part of the invariant;

(245) violates the "all recorded" part of the invariant.

One uses such counter-examples to test the appropriateness of the above form of the invariant.

Such was the feeling of dissatisfaction with this form of the invariant that an alternative form was sought. Given the nature of the *Parts* algorithm used, it seemed that the parts-explosion algorithm might be adapted to provide a better constructive form.

4.1.2 Parts Explosion

Historically, the specification given here, to compute all the consituent parts of a given part x in a bill of material γ_0, was derived from the parts explosion algorithm presented below in the context of the model BOM_1. The intention in so doing was to find another form of the invariant that was more intuitive, that was constructive, and that could be used in operator calculus style proofs.

57    $\mathcal{E} : X \times (X \underset{m}{\rightharpoonup} \mathcal{P}X) \longrightarrow \mathcal{P}X$

  .1 $\mathcal{E}(x, \gamma_0) \stackrel{\Delta}{=} \pi_2 \circ \mathcal{E}[\gamma_0(x)](\gamma_0, \emptyset)$

Annotations:

1 (a)) **If γ_0 is a bill of material** and $x \in dom\,\gamma_0$, then $\mathcal{E}$ is terminating and well-defined.

(57.1 (b)) Since $\mathcal{E}[\gamma_0(x)](\gamma_0, \emptyset)$ returns a pair (γ_0, T), then to select the required result T, the projection operator π_2 is required.

The body of the algorithm is binary recursive:

58    $\mathcal{E} \colon \mathcal{P}X \longrightarrow (X \underset{m}{\rightharpoonup} \mathcal{P}X) \times \mathcal{P}X \longrightarrow (X \underset{m}{\rightharpoonup} \mathcal{P}X) \times \mathcal{P}X$

.1 $\mathcal{E}[\emptyset](\gamma_0, T) \triangleq (\gamma_0, T)$

.2 $\mathcal{E}[\{x\} \uplus S](\gamma_0, T) \triangleq \mathcal{E}[S] \circ \mathcal{E}[\gamma_0(x)](\gamma_0, T \cup \{x\})$

Annotations:

(58.2) The form $\{x\} \uplus S$ is used to denote a non-empty set which contains an arbitrary element x. The expression $\mathcal{E}[S]$ suggests breadth traversal; $\mathcal{E}[\gamma_0(x)]$ suggests depth traversal.

Let us 'test' the specifcation with the counter-example $\mu_0 = [x \mapsto \{x\}]$:

59    $\mathcal{E}(x, \mu_0)$
.1 $= \pi_2 \circ \mathcal{E}[\mu_0(x)](\mu_0, \emptyset)$
.2 $= \pi_2 \circ \mathcal{E}[\{x\}](\mu_0, \emptyset)$
.3 $= \pi_2 \circ \mathcal{E}[\emptyset] \circ \mathcal{E}[\mu_0(x)](\mu_0, \{x\})$
.4 $= \pi_2 \circ \mathcal{E}[\mu_0(x)](\mu_0, \{x\})$

and the algorithm is clearly non-terminating. Therefore, it can not be used as is to specify the invariant—we run into a circularity argument. To break the circularity, it is necessary to generalise the algorithm by marking the paths traversed, a standard result from graph theory. In order to motivate or discover the result, it is worth noting that we may rewrite the above parts explosion by recording the parts found, in a simple bag—a non-trivial observation:

60    $\mathcal{E} \colon X \times (X \underset{m}{\rightharpoonup} \mathcal{P}X) \longrightarrow \mathcal{P}X$

.1 $\mathcal{E}(x, \gamma_0) \triangleq \mathrm{dom} \circ \pi_2 \circ \mathcal{E}[\gamma_0(x)](\gamma_0, \theta)$

61    $\mathcal{E} \colon \mathcal{P}X \longrightarrow (X \underset{m}{\rightharpoonup} \mathcal{P}X) \times (X \underset{m}{\rightharpoonup} \mathbf{N_1}) \longrightarrow (X \underset{m}{\rightharpoonup} \mathcal{P}X) \times (X \underset{m}{\rightharpoonup} \mathbf{N_1})$

.1 $\mathcal{E}[\emptyset](\gamma_0, \beta) \triangleq (\gamma_0, \beta)$

.2 $\mathcal{E}[\{x\} \uplus S](\gamma_0, \beta) \triangleq \mathcal{E}[S] \circ \mathcal{E}[\gamma_0(x)](\gamma_0, \beta \oplus [x \mapsto 1])$

Note how the bag is actually used to count occurrences. Instead of counting we wish to use a mechanism for marking. It is now easy to produce the result we seek. First we give the appropriate modification—a marking algorithm:

62 $\quad \mathcal{E}: X \times (X \underset{m}{\rightharpoonup} \mathcal{P}X) \longrightarrow (X \underset{m}{\rightharpoonup} \mathcal{P}X) \times (X \underset{m}{\rightharpoonup} \mathbf{N})$

.1 $\quad \mathcal{E}(x, \gamma_0) \triangleq$
.2 $\qquad$ let $\mu = [x_j \mapsto 0 \mid x_j \in dom\,\gamma_0]$ in
.3 $\qquad \mathcal{E}[\gamma_0(x)](\gamma_0, \mu + [x \mapsto 1])$

Annotations:

62.0) The form $X \underset{m}{\rightharpoonup} \mathbf{N}$ is used in the signature rather than forms such as $X \underset{m}{\rightharpoonup} \{0,1\}$ or $X \underset{m}{\rightharpoonup} \{\text{UNVISITED}, \text{VISITED}\}$ to suggest the conceptual link between a bag and a marking and, at the same time, to highlight the difference—there is no 0 in a bag.

62.2) All parts or nodes are initially marked as UNVISITED.

62.3) The initial part x is marked as VISITED.

The recursive part is

63 $\quad \mathcal{E}: \mathcal{P}X \longrightarrow (X \underset{m}{\rightharpoonup} \mathcal{P}X) \times (X \underset{m}{\rightharpoonup} \mathbf{N}) \longrightarrow (X \underset{m}{\rightharpoonup} \mathcal{P}X) \times (X \underset{m}{\rightharpoonup} \mathbf{N})$

.1 $\quad \mathcal{E}[\emptyset](\gamma_0, \mu) \triangleq (\gamma_0, \mu)$
.2 $\quad \mathcal{E}[\{x\} \uplus S](\gamma_0, \mu) \triangleq$
.3 $\qquad \mu(x) = 0$
.4 $\qquad \rightarrow \mathcal{E}[S] \circ \mathcal{E}[\gamma_0(x)](\gamma_0, \mu + [x \mapsto 1])$
.5 $\qquad \rightarrow \mathcal{E}[S](\gamma_0, \mu)$

Annotations:

63.4) If x has not already been visited, $\mu(x) = 0$, then mark it as visited $\mu + [x \mapsto 1]$ and continue exploring across, $\mathcal{E}[S]$, and down, $\mathcal{E}[\gamma_0(x)]$, ...

63.5) ... otherwise to avoid cycling we may only explore across. Effectively, the presence of a cycle implies that 'down' becomes 'return'.

Then, if $(\gamma_0, \mu) = \mathcal{E}(x, \gamma_0)$, the set of marked 'nodes', i.e, nodes reachable from x, is given by $\mu^{-1}(1)$. Finally, we observe, that we might have achieved the same goal by reverting to the use of a set rather than a map. Further detailed remarks on this development are contained in [22]. The only final observation that is worth making, is that, whereas we have introduced another useful result on reachability, we still have not found a satisfactory form for the invariant, satisfactory in the sense that proofs are facilitated.

4.1.3 The Annihilator

It is difficult to put in words the sequence of thought patterns that led to the discovery of this function. Certainly, manipulation of the forms $\gamma_0^{-1}(\emptyset)$ and $\gamma_0^{-1}(\emptyset) \triangleleft \gamma_0$ led to its emergence. There was perhaps a vague uneasiness about the usefulness of the parts explosion algorithm given above as a form of the invariant for operator calculus style proofs. However, the specific 'trigger' still stands out. The fact that the original parts explosion algorithm could be non-terminating led to the inescapable conclusion that another form, which was definitively always terminating, might exist. Given an element γ_0 in $X \underset{m}{\rightarrow} \mathcal{P}X$. If γ_0 was a bill of material, then $\gamma_0^{-1}(\emptyset) = \gamma_{\emptyset}^{-1}$ was always defined and

available. Consequently, elimination of these basic parts should result in a reduced bill of material, to which we might apply the same procedure. Continuing in this fashion, one might be said to annihilate the bill of material. Formally, the definition of the annihilator function is

$$64 \quad \mathcal{A}\colon (X \underset{m}{\rightarrow} \mathcal{P}X) \longrightarrow (X \underset{m}{\rightarrow} \mathcal{P}X)$$

.1 $\quad \mathcal{A}(\theta) \triangleq \theta$

.2 $\quad \mathcal{A}(\gamma_0) \triangleq$

.3 $\qquad \gamma_{\emptyset}^{-1} = \emptyset$

.4 $\qquad \rightarrow \gamma_0$

.5 $\qquad \rightarrow \mathcal{A}\big((\mathcal{I} \underset{m}{\rightarrow} \triangleleft [\gamma_{\emptyset}^{-1}]) \circ \triangleleft [\gamma_{\emptyset}^{-1}] \gamma_0\big)$

Annotations

(64.0) $\mathcal{A}$ is tail-recursive.

(64.1) This line is redundant and is only included for clarity.

(64.3) Termination is guaranteed.

(64.5) The expression $\triangleleft [\gamma_{\emptyset}^{-1}] \gamma_0$ denotes the removal of the set of basic parts $\gamma_0^{-1}(\emptyset)$ from the bom γ_0. Then all reference to such basic parts is eliminated by applying the functor $(\mathcal{I} \underset{m}{\rightarrow} \triangleleft [\gamma_{\emptyset}^{-1}])$, where $\triangleleft$ is our convention for set difference.

A further word on the notation is necessary. The original annihilator function was not expressed in the given form. It was only as a result of attempting proofs, one of which is given below, that an appropriate expressive form was developed. Such a process—**attempting proofs**—is one of the key driving forces behind the 'derivation' of the notation of the Irish School. The construction of the annihilator function $\mathcal{A}$ is a *proof* of the theorem

THEOREM 4.1 *If $\gamma_0 \in BOM_0 = X \underset{m}{\rightarrow} \mathcal{P}X$ is a bill of material, then $\mathcal{A}(\gamma_0) = \theta$.*

Consequently, we may use this result to define the class of bills of material

DEFINITION 4.1 *An element γ_0 of the domain $X \underset{m}{\rightharpoonup} \mathcal{P}X$ is a bill of material iff* $\mathcal{A}(\gamma_0) = \theta$.

Moreover the result is valid whether we consider γ_0 to be a bill of material as product or a bill of material in the making! This result may be formally incorporated into the model, it being, in fact, another form of the invariant:

$$\textit{inv--BOM}_0(\gamma_0) \triangleq (\mathcal{A}(\gamma_0) = \theta) \qquad (246)$$

We are now inspired to proceed along many directions, which are described here as hypotheses to be verified or rejected.

HYPOTHESIS 4.1 *There exists a 'join' operation, denoted by $\oplus$, on bills of material γ_j, γ_k in $X \underset{m}{\rightharpoonup} \mathcal{P}X$, such that $\gamma_j \oplus \gamma_k \in X \underset{m}{\rightharpoonup} \mathcal{P}X$ is a bill of material. This operation is associative and commutative. The structure $(BOM_0, \oplus, \theta)$ is a commutative monoid.*

The reason that the hypothesis is considered plausible is based on two observations.

(a) A bill of material may be composed of several disjoint assemblies. For example, each of the following are valid forms

$$
\begin{aligned}
\gamma_0 \;=\;& [x_1 \mapsto \emptyset, x_2 \mapsto \emptyset, \ldots, x_n \mapsto \emptyset] & (247) \\
=\;& [x_1 \mapsto \emptyset] \oplus [x_2 \mapsto \emptyset] \oplus \ldots \oplus [x_n \mapsto \emptyset] & (248) \\
\gamma_a \;=\;& [x_j \mapsto \{x_{j1}, x_{j2}\}, x_{j1} \mapsto \emptyset, x_{j2} \mapsto \emptyset, & (249) \\
& \quad x_k \mapsto \{x_{k1}, x_{k2}\}, x_{k1} \mapsto \emptyset, x_{k2} \mapsto \emptyset] & (250) \\
=\;& [x_j \mapsto \{x_{j1}, x_{j2}\}, x_{j1} \mapsto \emptyset, x_{j2} \mapsto \emptyset] & (251) \\
& \quad \oplus [x_k \mapsto \{x_{k1}, x_{k2}\}, x_{k1} \mapsto \emptyset, x_{k2} \mapsto \emptyset] & (252) \\
\gamma_b \;=\;& [x_j \mapsto \{x_1, x_2\}, x_1 \mapsto \emptyset, x_2 \mapsto \emptyset] & (253) \\
& \quad \oplus [x_k \mapsto \{x_1, x_2\}, x_1 \mapsto \emptyset, x_2 \mapsto \emptyset] & (254) \\
=\;& [x_j \mapsto \{x_1, x_2\}, x_k \mapsto \{x_1, x_2\}, x_1 \mapsto \emptyset, x_2 \mapsto \emptyset] & (255)
\end{aligned}
$$

The last example suggests more very interesting issues to be resolved, issues which address the consistency of distinct but related bills of material.

(b) The Ent_0 operation is used to add new basic parts to an existing bill of material or to join two already existing subassemblies to form a new assembly. Could not this be the basis for the definition of the $\oplus$ operation? The rationale for such a suggestion is that, for example, the operation Ent_0 on the dictionary model $DICT_0 = \mathcal{P}WORD$ generalises naturally to the set union operator and may be interpreted as the merge or join of two dictionaries [22].

Now, one familiar with the problem domain will realise that, should such a join operation exist, which has the desired properties, then we have effectively characterised a subdomain of the bills of material. For example, we do not propose that the bills of material

$[x_1 \mapsto \{x_2\}, x_2 \mapsto \emptyset]$ and $[x_1 \mapsto \{x_3\}, x_3 \mapsto \emptyset]$ can be joined. They both belong to the domain $X \underset{m}{\rightharpoonup} \mathcal{P}X$, satisfy the invariant, and yet are mutually inconsistent.

Consider the domain $X \underset{m}{\rightharpoonup} \mathcal{P}X$. We know that for all $\gamma \in X \underset{m}{\rightharpoonup} \mathcal{P}X$, $\mathcal{A}(\gamma) = \theta$ if and only if γ is a bill of material. In all other cases $\mathcal{A}(\gamma) = \gamma' \neq \theta$. Another hypothesis that may have merit is the following.

HYPOTHESIS 4.2 *There exists an operation $\oplus$ on $X \underset{m}{\rightharpoonup} \mathcal{P}X$ such that $\mathcal{A}$ is an endomorphism of $(X \underset{m}{\rightharpoonup} \mathcal{P}X, \oplus, \theta)$, i.e., that:*

$$\mathcal{A}(\gamma_j \oplus \gamma_k) = \mathcal{A}(\gamma_j) \oplus \mathcal{A}(\gamma_k) \tag{256}$$
$$\mathcal{A}(\theta) = \theta \tag{257}$$

The purpose in formulating such an hypothesis is to examine the nature of the annihilator. Before turning to consider further operations on a bill of material, one more aspect of the annihilator will be presented. Define a pair of functions $f \colon X \underset{m}{\rightharpoonup} \mathcal{P}X \longrightarrow X \underset{m}{\rightharpoonup} \mathcal{P}'X$ and $g \colon X \underset{m}{\rightharpoonup} \mathcal{P}'X \longrightarrow X \underset{m}{\rightharpoonup} \mathcal{P}X$ such that

$$f \colon \gamma \mapsto \blacktriangleleft [\gamma_\theta^{-1}] \gamma \tag{258}$$
$$g \colon \gamma \mapsto (\mathcal{I} \underset{m}{\rightharpoonup} \blacktriangleleft [\gamma_\theta^{-1}]) \gamma \tag{259}$$

Note that the definitions of both f and g depend on γ_θ^{-1}. Effectively, the function f removes all occurrences of $x \mapsto \emptyset$ from the map γ. If γ is a bill of material, then $f(\gamma)$ may *still* be interpreted as a bill of material, where our convention on the representation of basic parts is omitted. In particular, the set of basic parts may be recovered from $f(\gamma)$. They are given by the expression $\gamma_\theta^{-1} = \mathrm{dom} \circ f(\gamma) \blacktriangleleft (^\cup/ \circ \mathrm{rng} \circ f(\gamma))$.

Then let $h = g \circ f$. If γ is a bill of material then there exists a natural number $n \in \mathbf{N}$ such that $h^n = \mathcal{A}$. In other words the annihilator is simply the iterated application of a function, which is to be expected since $\mathcal{A}$ is tail-recursive. Of particular note is the consequence that the domain of bills of materials is given by the (minimal) fixed point solution of a recursive function, a remark that brings us back to the point of departure.

4.1.4 Operations on BOM_0

Since we have a model, certain operations on the model are immediately suggested. We may consider such operations as the syntactic sugaring of closed form expressions, a point emphasised with respect to the temperature chart model given above. The actual operations presented here are taken from [2]. We shall be chiefly concerned with demonstrating that the operations, and their appropriate pre-conditions, satisfy the invariant.

4.1.5 The Create Command

The create command is used to give us a new empty bill of material.

65    $Crea_0 \longrightarrow (X \underset{m}{\rightharpoonup} \mathcal{P}X)$

.1 $Crea_0 \triangleq \theta$

The pre-condition is trivial.

66    $pre\text{–}Crea_0 \longrightarrow \mathbf{B}$

.1 $pre\text{–}Crea_0 \triangleq true$

Required to demonstrate that the create command satisfies the invariant, i.e., that

$$\mathcal{A}(Crea_0) = \mathcal{A}(\theta) = \theta \tag{260}$$

Proof: by definition!

4.1.6 The Enter Command

In [2] the enter command is used to build a bill of material 'from the ground up'. That is to say, given a collection of subassemblies, we form a new assembly by introducing a new part name and recording the subassembly names as immediate constituent parts. The operation is very easy to describe in diagrams and is easy to grasp in practice. To ensure that we have described it correctly in words, we need a formal specification:

67    $Ent_0 \colon X \times \mathcal{P}X \longrightarrow (X \underset{m}{\rightharpoonup} \mathcal{P}X) \longrightarrow (X \underset{m}{\rightharpoonup} \mathcal{P}X)$

.1 $Ent_0[x, S]\gamma_0 \triangleq \gamma_0 \cup [x \mapsto S]$

Annotations:

- The part name x of the new assembly must not occur already in the domain of γ_0. This fact must form part of the precondition: $\neg\chi[x]\gamma_0$.

- The set $S = \{x_1, x_2, \ldots, x_j, \ldots, x_n\}$ contains the names of existing subassemblies. Thus each x_j must already occur in the domain of the bill of material γ_0. Thus the expression $S \subset dom\,\gamma_0$ must form part of the pre-condition.

  Remark: If we write it in the form

  $$\chi[x_1]\gamma_0 \wedge \chi[x_2]\gamma_0 \wedge \ldots \chi[x_j]\gamma_0 \wedge \ldots \wedge \chi[x_n]\gamma_0 \tag{261}$$

  find an alternative expression using reduction.

- Recall that the $\cup$ operator is defined if and only if $dom\,\gamma_0 \cap dom\,[x \mapsto S] = \emptyset$, i.e., if and only if $\neg\chi[x]\gamma_0$, which is part of the pre-condition.

The pre-condition has the form:

68    $pre\text{-}Ent_0: X \times PX \longrightarrow (X \underset{m}{\rightharpoonup} PX) \longrightarrow \mathbf{B}$

.1 $pre\text{-}Ent_0[\![x, S]\!]\gamma_0 \triangleq \neg\chi[\![x]\!]\gamma_0 \wedge S \subset dom\,\gamma_0 \wedge \ldots$

where we indicate our uncertainty as to whether or not we have uncovered all the pre-conditions. In other words we are being conservative.

Required to demonstrate that

$$\mathcal{A}(Ent_0[\![x, S]\!]\gamma_0) = \mathcal{A}(\gamma_0 \cup [x \mapsto S]) = \theta \tag{262}$$

Proof: ...

We will present the details of the proof later.

4.1.7   The Remove Command

A remove command is the formal inverse of the enter command. It is used to disassemble a bill of material and, hence, works from the top down. To disassemble a bill of material we must supply the name of an assembly. The formal specification is

69    $Rem_0: X \longrightarrow (X \underset{m}{\rightharpoonup} PX) \longrightarrow (X \underset{m}{\rightharpoonup} PX)$

.1 $Rem_0[\![x]\!]\gamma_0 \triangleq \{x\} \blacktriangleleft \gamma_0$

Annotations:

- Technically the operation $\blacktriangleleft [\![\{x\}]\!]$ is valid whether or not x occurs in the domain of γ_0. If we wish to insist that x be the name of an assembly, then we must *at least* have the pre-condition $\chi[\![x]\!]\gamma_0$. The phrase *at least* is significant. Consider the example $\gamma_0 = [x \mapsto \{y\}, y \mapsto \emptyset]$. Then $\blacktriangleleft [\![\{x\}]\!]\gamma_0 = [y \mapsto \emptyset]$, which is a bill of material. But $\blacktriangleleft [\![\{y\}]\!]\gamma_0 = [x \mapsto \{y\}]$ is **not** a bill of material under our standard interpretation—one can not change the rules of the game in the middle of play. Thus $\chi[\![x]\!]\gamma_0$ is necessary but not sufficient! We **must** specify that x is the name of an assembly. This is given by the expression $\chi[\![x]\!](^\cup\!/ \circ rng\,\gamma_0 \blacktriangleleft dom\,\gamma_0)$. Why could we not just write $\{x\} = {}^\cup\!/ \circ rng\,\gamma_0 \blacktriangleleft dom\,\gamma_0$?

The pre-condition for the remove command is, therefore

70    $pre\text{-}Rem_0: X \longrightarrow (X \underset{m}{\rightharpoonup} PX) \longrightarrow \mathbf{B}$

.1 $pre\text{-}Rem_0[\![x]\!]\gamma_0 \triangleq \chi[\![x]\!]\gamma_0 \wedge \chi[\![x]\!](^\cup\!/ \circ rng\,\gamma_0 \blacktriangleleft dom\,\gamma_0) \wedge \ldots$

and the redundancy is to be noted, i.e., $\chi[\![x]\!](^\cup\!/ \circ rng\,\gamma_0 \blacktriangleleft dom\,\gamma_0) \Rightarrow \chi[\![x]\!]\gamma_0$.

Remark: In [2], the pre-condition is given, *and here we use our notation*, as

$$\chi[\![x]\!]\gamma_0 \wedge \mathcal{A}(\{x\} \blacktriangleleft \gamma_0) = \theta \tag{263}$$

This use of an invariant as part of the pre-condition is not acceptable in the Irish School! Technically, $\mathcal{A}(\{x\} \twoheadleftarrow \gamma_0)$ *is* the post-condition. Moreover, it is clearly inadequate since we wish to *prove* that the remove operation satisfies the invariant, i.e., that $\mathcal{A}(\{x\} \twoheadleftarrow \gamma_0) = \theta$.

Required to demonstrate that

$$\mathcal{A}(Rem_0[\![x]\!]\gamma_0) = \mathcal{A}(\{x\} \twoheadleftarrow \gamma_0) = \theta \tag{264}$$

Proof: ...

The details are left as an exercise.

4.1.8   The Add Command

Having studied the enter command, it becomes clear that it can not be used to modify an existing subassembly. In particular, we note that if $\gamma_0 = [x \mapsto \emptyset]$ we can not use the enter command to produce $[x \mapsto \{y\}, y \mapsto \emptyset]$. On the other hand, *starting* with $\gamma_0 = [y \mapsto \emptyset]$, then $Ent_0[\![x, \{y\}]\!]\gamma_0 = [x \mapsto \{y\}, y \mapsto \emptyset]$. The need for an update command may be deduced formally by noting that we have not yet considered an expression of the form '$\gamma_0 + \ldots$'. To modify or update an existing bill of material we use what Bjørner calls the add command. Formally, it is given by

71    $Add_0 \colon X \times X \longrightarrow (X \underset{m}{\rightharpoonup} \mathcal{P}X) \longrightarrow (X \underset{m}{\rightharpoonup} \mathcal{P}X)$

.1 $Add_0[\![x, x']\!]\gamma_0 \triangleq \gamma_0 + [x \mapsto \gamma_0(x) \cup \{x'\}]$

Annotations:

- To ensure that this update command does not *cover* the enter command, we shall require that the name of the assembly being updated, x, occurs in the domain of the bill of material γ_0. Thus $\chi[\![x]\!]\gamma_0$ is part of the pre-condition.

- What about x'? It must not be a new part name for, otherwise, the invariant will be violated immediately. Therefore, $\chi[\![x']\!]\gamma_0$ is part of the pre-condition.

  Remark: However, one may wish to take a more liberal view on this issue—permit the temporary invalidation of the invariant—with the expectation that the next operation to be performed will restore it. In such a scenario, we lift the issue of invariant satisfaction to a higher level operation which covers such intermediate operations.

- Since $\chi[\![x]\!]\gamma_0$, then let $S = \gamma_0(x)$. We may not wish to permit $\chi[\![x']\!]S$, for otherwise the add operation is redundant! Of course, there is no real harm in permitting it! Therefore, we will make $\neg\chi[\![x']\!]\gamma_0(x)$ part of the pre-condition.

- Suppose that $\gamma_0(x) = \emptyset$. Conceptually, a basic part would be transformed into an assembly. Formally it might be permitted. But then, the enter command should be invoked. Therefore, $\gamma_0(x) \neq \emptyset$ is also part of the pre-condition.

Such remarks on the meaning of the add command may be formally recorded as

72    $pre\text{-}Add_0: X \times X \longrightarrow (X \underset{m}{\rightharpoonup} \mathcal{P}X) \longrightarrow \mathbf{B}$

.1 $pre\text{-}Add_0[x, x']\gamma_0 \overset{\triangle}{=} \chi[x]\gamma_0 \wedge \chi[x']\gamma_0 \wedge (\neg\chi[x']\gamma_0(x)) \wedge (\gamma_0(x) \neq \emptyset) \wedge \ldots$

It is, of course, our sincere hope that the ellipsis is not necessary, i.e., that we have covered everything.

Required to demonstrate that

$$\mathcal{A}(Add_0[x, x']\gamma_0) = \mathcal{A}(\gamma_0 + [x \mapsto \gamma_0(x) \cup \{x'\}]) = \theta \tag{265}$$

Proof: ...

The details are left as an exercise.

4.1.9   The Erase Command

As in the case of the remove command which was the formal inverse of the enter command, then we will also need a command to undo the effect of the add command. Let us call this an erase command. The formal specification is

73    $Eras_0: X \times X \longrightarrow (X \underset{m}{\rightharpoonup} \mathcal{P}X) \longrightarrow (X \underset{m}{\rightharpoonup} \mathcal{P}X)$

.1 $Eras_0[x, x']\gamma_0 \overset{\triangle}{=} \gamma_0 + [x \mapsto \{x'\} \blacktriangleleft \gamma_0(x)]$

The specification of the pre-condition is left as an exercise:

74    $pre\text{-}Eras_0: X \times X \longrightarrow (X \underset{m}{\rightharpoonup} \mathcal{P}X) \longrightarrow \mathbf{B}$

.1 $pre\text{-}Eras_0[x, x']\gamma_0 \overset{\triangle}{=} \ldots$

Required to demonstrate that

$$\mathcal{A}(Eras_0[x, x']\gamma_0) = \mathcal{A}(\gamma_0 + [x \mapsto \{x'\} \blacktriangleleft \gamma_0(x)]) = \theta \tag{266}$$

Proof: ...

The details are left as an exercise.

4.2   Proof that Ent_0 preserves the invariant

This section illustrates the degree of detail involved in carrying out proofs for even the simplest of domains. It is important to note that we already have every expectation that the enter operation does indeed conserve the invariant. What we especially seek to demonstrate is the critical rôle that the pre-condition plays in establishing the result.

Given that $\mathcal{A}(\gamma) = \theta$. Required to prove that $\mathcal{A}(Ent_0[x, S]\gamma) = \theta$. The proof is given in considerable detail in order to demonstrate clearly the formal rigour of the method of the Irish School and to exhibit the necessary sort of arguments based on classical algebra. First we observe that

75    $\mathcal{A}(Ent_0[x,S]\gamma)$

.1 $= \mathcal{A}(\gamma \cup [x \mapsto S])$

.2 $= \mathcal{A}((\mathcal{I} \underset{m}{\rightrightarrows} \blacktriangleleft [\bar{\gamma}_0^{-1}]) \circ \blacktriangleleft [\bar{\gamma}_0^{-1}]\bar{\gamma})$

where $\bar{\gamma}$ is used to denote $\gamma \cup [x \mapsto S]$, for convenience. Quite clearly, we have completed the proof if we can now demonstrate that

$$\mathcal{A}((\mathcal{I} \underset{m}{\rightrightarrows} \blacktriangleleft [\bar{\gamma}_0^{-1}]) \circ \blacktriangleleft [\bar{\gamma}_0^{-1}]\bar{\gamma}) = \theta \tag{267}$$

For simplicity we will consider the expression $(\mathcal{I} \underset{m}{\rightrightarrows} \blacktriangleleft [\bar{\gamma}_0^{-1}]) \circ \blacktriangleleft [\bar{\gamma}_0^{-1}]\bar{\gamma}$. There are two cases to consider:

Case $S = \emptyset$:

76    $(\mathcal{I} \underset{m}{\rightrightarrows} \blacktriangleleft [\bar{\gamma}_0^{-1}]) \circ \blacktriangleleft [\bar{\gamma}_0^{-1}]\bar{\gamma}$

.1 $= (\mathcal{I} \underset{m}{\rightrightarrows} \blacktriangleleft [\bar{\gamma}_0^{-1}]) \circ \blacktriangleleft [\bar{\gamma}_0^{-1}](\gamma \cup [x \mapsto S])$

.2 $= (\mathcal{I} \underset{m}{\rightrightarrows} \blacktriangleleft [\bar{\gamma}_0^{-1}])(\blacktriangleleft [\bar{\gamma}_0^{-1}]\gamma \cup \blacktriangleleft [\bar{\gamma}_0^{-1}][x \mapsto S])$

.3 $= (\mathcal{I} \underset{m}{\rightrightarrows} \blacktriangleleft [\bar{\gamma}_0^{-1}])(\blacktriangleleft [\bar{\gamma}_0^{-1}]\gamma \cup \blacktriangleleft [\gamma_0^{-1} \cup \{x\}][x \mapsto S])$

.4 $= (\mathcal{I} \underset{m}{\rightrightarrows} \blacktriangleleft [\bar{\gamma}_0^{-1}])(\blacktriangleleft [\bar{\gamma}_0^{-1}]\gamma \cup \blacktriangleleft [\gamma_0^{-1}] \circ \blacktriangleleft [\{x\}][x \mapsto S])$

.5 $= (\mathcal{I} \underset{m}{\rightrightarrows} \blacktriangleleft [\bar{\gamma}_0^{-1}])(\blacktriangleleft [\bar{\gamma}_0^{-1}]\gamma \cup \blacktriangleleft [\gamma_0^{-1}]\theta)$

.6 $= (\mathcal{I} \underset{m}{\rightrightarrows} \blacktriangleleft [\bar{\gamma}_0^{-1}])(\blacktriangleleft [\bar{\gamma}_0^{-1}]\gamma \cup \theta)$

.7 $= (\mathcal{I} \underset{m}{\rightrightarrows} \blacktriangleleft [\bar{\gamma}_0^{-1}]) \circ \blacktriangleleft [\bar{\gamma}_0^{-1}]\gamma$

.8 $= (\mathcal{I} \underset{m}{\rightrightarrows} \blacktriangleleft [\bar{\gamma}_0^{-1}]) \circ \blacktriangleleft [\gamma_0^{-1} \cup \{x\}]\gamma$

.9 $= (\mathcal{I} \underset{m}{\rightrightarrows} \blacktriangleleft [\bar{\gamma}_0^{-1}]) \circ \blacktriangleleft [\gamma_0^{-1}] \circ \blacktriangleleft [\{x\}]\gamma$

.10 $= (\mathcal{I} \underset{m}{\rightrightarrows} \blacktriangleleft [\bar{\gamma}_0^{-1}]) \circ \blacktriangleleft [\gamma_0^{-1}]\gamma$

.11 $= (\mathcal{I} \underset{m}{\rightrightarrows} \blacktriangleleft [\gamma_0^{-1} \cup \{x\}]) \circ \blacktriangleleft [\gamma_0^{-1}]\gamma$

.12 $= (\mathcal{I} \underset{m}{\rightrightarrows} \blacktriangleleft [\gamma_0^{-1}]) \circ (\mathcal{I} \underset{m}{\rightrightarrows} \blacktriangleleft [\{x\}]) \circ \blacktriangleleft [\gamma_0^{-1}]\gamma$

.13 $= (\mathcal{I} \underset{m}{\rightrightarrows} \blacktriangleleft [\gamma_0^{-1}]) \circ \blacktriangleleft [\gamma_0^{-1}] \circ (\mathcal{I} \underset{m}{\rightrightarrows} \blacktriangleleft [\{x\}])\gamma$

.14 $= (\mathcal{I} \underset{m}{\rightrightarrows} \blacktriangleleft [\gamma_0^{-1}]) \circ \blacktriangleleft [\gamma_0^{-1}]\gamma$

and since $\mathcal{A}((\mathcal{I} \underset{m}{\rightrightarrows} \blacktriangleleft [\gamma_0^{-1}]) \circ \blacktriangleleft [\gamma_0^{-1}]\gamma) = \theta$ then we have established the required result for the case $S = \emptyset$.

Annotations:

(76.2) Removal with respect to a set, $\triangleleft [\bar{\gamma}_{\emptyset}^{-1}]$, is an endomorphism of the monoid

$$(({X} \xrightarrow[m]{} \mathcal{P}Y), +, \theta) \tag{268}$$

(76.3) Since $S = \emptyset$, then x is a basic part and $\bar{\gamma}_{\emptyset}^{-1} = (\gamma \cup [x \mapsto S])^{-1}(\emptyset) = \gamma_{\emptyset}^{-1} \cup \{x\}$. We might wish to be more precise and write $\bar{\gamma}_{\emptyset}^{-1} = \gamma_{\emptyset}^{-1} \uplus \{x\}$, since by the pre-condition, $\neg \chi [x] \gamma$.

(76.4) By the composition law of the removal endomorphisms.

(76.10) Since $\neg \chi [x] \gamma$.

(76.12) By the composition law of the removal endomorphisms which is conserved by the composition law of map iterators.

(76.14) The final stage is an especially significant step in the proof. We argue that, for $S = \emptyset$,

$$({I} \xrightarrow[m]{} \triangleleft [\{x\}]) \gamma = \gamma \tag{269}$$

This can be true if and only if $\neg \chi [x]^{\cup} / \circ$ rng γ. Now, one might reason that, since $\neg \chi [x] \gamma$, then $\neg \chi [x]^{\cup} / \circ$ rng γ. For otherwise the invariant would be violated. But we *seek* to establish the invariant with respect to the annihilator $\mathcal{A}$. Clearly, we have stumbled across a hidden lemma. We could always save the situation, of course, by adding an extra pre-condition to the enter operation:

$$\neg \chi [x] \gamma \Rightarrow \neg \chi [x]^{\cup} / \circ \text{rng } \gamma \tag{270}$$

But, it seems more interesting to state the result as a lemma.

LEMMA 4.1 *If there is some element x in the merged range of the structure $\gamma \in X \xrightarrow[m]{} \mathcal{P}X$ which is not in the domain of γ, then γ does not represent a bill of material:*

$$\neg \chi [x] \gamma \wedge \chi [x]^{\cup} / \circ \text{rng } \gamma \Rightarrow \mathcal{A}(\gamma) \neq \theta \tag{271}$$

We now turn to the second part of the proof:

Case $S \neq \emptyset$:

77 $\quad ({I} \xrightarrow[m]{} \triangleleft [\bar{\gamma}_{\emptyset}^{-1}]) \circ \triangleleft [\bar{\gamma}_{\emptyset}^{-1}] \bar{\gamma}$

.1 $\quad = ({I} \xrightarrow[m]{} \triangleleft [\bar{\gamma}_{\emptyset}^{-1}]) \circ \triangleleft [\bar{\gamma}_{\emptyset}^{-1}](\gamma \cup [x \mapsto S])$

.2 $\quad = ({I} \xrightarrow[m]{} \triangleleft [\bar{\gamma}_{\emptyset}^{-1}])(\triangleleft [\bar{\gamma}_{\emptyset}^{-1}] \gamma \cup \triangleleft [\bar{\gamma}_{\emptyset}^{-1}][x \mapsto S])$

.3 $\quad = ({I} \xrightarrow[m]{} \triangleleft [\bar{\gamma}_{\emptyset}^{-1}])(\triangleleft [\bar{\gamma}_{\emptyset}^{-1}] \gamma \cup \triangleleft [\gamma_{\emptyset}^{-1}][x \mapsto S])$

$$.4 \qquad = (\mathcal{I} \underset{m}{\to} \blacktriangleleft [\bar{\gamma}_{\emptyset}^{-1}])(\blacktriangleleft [\bar{\gamma}_{\emptyset}^{-1}]\gamma \cup [x \mapsto S])$$

$$.5 \qquad = (\mathcal{I} \underset{m}{\to} \blacktriangleleft [\bar{\gamma}_{\emptyset}^{-1}])(\blacktriangleleft [\gamma_{\emptyset}^{-1}]\gamma \cup [x \mapsto S])$$

$$.6 \qquad = (\mathcal{I} \underset{m}{\to} \blacktriangleleft [\bar{\gamma}_{\emptyset}^{-1}])(\blacktriangleleft [\gamma_{\emptyset}^{-1}]\gamma) \cup (\mathcal{I} \underset{m}{\to} \blacktriangleleft [\bar{\gamma}_{\emptyset}^{-1}])[x \mapsto S]$$

$$.7 \qquad = (\mathcal{I} \underset{m}{\to} \blacktriangleleft [\gamma_{\emptyset}^{-1}])(\blacktriangleleft [\gamma_{\emptyset}^{-1}]\gamma) \cup (\mathcal{I} \underset{m}{\to} \blacktriangleleft [\gamma_{\emptyset}^{-1}])[x \mapsto S]$$

$$.8 \qquad = (\mathcal{I} \underset{m}{\to} \blacktriangleleft [\gamma_{\emptyset}^{-1}])(\blacktriangleleft [\gamma_{\emptyset}^{-1}]\gamma) \cup [x \mapsto \blacktriangleleft [\gamma_{\emptyset}^{-1}]S]$$

and at this stage we pause. Another interesting hidden lemma has been uncovered.

Annotations:

77.3) Since $S \neq \emptyset$, then x can not be a basic part and, therefore, $\bar{\gamma}_{\emptyset}^{-1} = \gamma_{\emptyset}^{-1}$.

77.4) Follows directly as a consequence from the fact that x is not a basic part.

77.6) The map iterator $(\mathcal{I} \underset{m}{\to} \blacktriangleleft [\bar{\gamma}_{\emptyset}^{-1}])$ is an endomorphism of $((X \underset{m}{\to} PY), +, \theta)$.

We have every reason to be optimistic that the enter operation conserves the invariant for the case $S \neq \emptyset$, i.e, that

$$\mathcal{A}(\gamma) = \theta \wedge \gamma \neq \theta \Rightarrow \mathcal{A}((\mathcal{I} \underset{m}{\to} \blacktriangleleft [\bar{\gamma}_{\emptyset}^{-1}]) \circ \blacktriangleleft [\bar{\gamma}_{\emptyset}^{-1}]\bar{\gamma}) = \theta \qquad (272)$$

However, assuming that the enter operation does indeed conserve the invariant, then in carrying out the proof we have effectively reached a result which may be demonstrated to give

$$
\begin{aligned}
\mathcal{A}(\bar{\gamma}) &= \mathcal{A}(\gamma \cup [x \mapsto S]) & (273) \\
&= \mathcal{A}((\mathcal{I} \underset{m}{\to} \blacktriangleleft [\bar{\gamma}_{\emptyset}^{-1}]) \circ \blacktriangleleft [\bar{\gamma}_{\emptyset}^{-1}]\bar{\gamma}) & (274) \\
&= \mathcal{A}((\mathcal{I} \underset{m}{\to} \blacktriangleleft [\gamma_{\emptyset}^{-1}])(\blacktriangleleft [\gamma_{\emptyset}^{-1}]\gamma) \cup (\mathcal{I} \underset{m}{\to} \blacktriangleleft [\gamma_{\emptyset}^{-1}])[x \mapsto S]) & (275) \\
&= \mathcal{A}((\mathcal{I} \underset{m}{\to} \blacktriangleleft [\gamma_{\emptyset}^{-1}])(\blacktriangleleft [\gamma_{\emptyset}^{-1}]\gamma) \cup [x \mapsto \blacktriangleleft [\gamma_{\emptyset}^{-1}]S]) & (276) \\
&\neq \mathcal{A}((\mathcal{I} \underset{m}{\to} \blacktriangleleft [\gamma_{\emptyset}^{-1}])(\blacktriangleleft [\gamma_{\emptyset}^{-1}]\gamma)) \cup \mathcal{A}((\mathcal{I} \underset{m}{\to} \blacktriangleleft [\gamma_{\emptyset}^{-1}])[x \mapsto S]) & (277)
\end{aligned}
$$

and consequently, it is not true in general that, for disjoint maps $\mu_1, \mu_2 \in X \underset{m}{\to} PY$

$$\mathcal{A}(\mu_1 \cup \mu_2) \neq \mathcal{A}(\mu_1) \cup \mathcal{A}(\mu_2) \qquad (278)$$

To establish this result, it is sufficient to present a counterexample. Let γ be a bill of material which consists of exactly one basic part, $\gamma = [x_1 \mapsto \emptyset]$. Then

$$Ent_0[x_2, \{x_1\}]\gamma = [x_1 \mapsto \emptyset] \cup [x_2 \mapsto \{x_1\}] = [x_2 \mapsto \{x_1\}, x_1 \mapsto \emptyset] \qquad (279)$$

It is quite obvious that

$$\mathcal{A}([x_1 \mapsto \emptyset] \cup [x_2 \mapsto \{x_1\}]) = \mathcal{A}([x_2 \mapsto \{x_1\}, x_1 \mapsto \emptyset]) \qquad (280)$$
$$= \theta \qquad (281)$$
$$\mathcal{A}([x_1 \mapsto \emptyset]) \cup \mathcal{A}([x_2 \mapsto \{x_1\}]) = \theta \cup [x_2 \mapsto \{x_1\}] \qquad (282)$$
$$= [x_2 \mapsto \{x_1\}] \qquad (283)$$

On the other hand, it is indeed the case that

$$\mathcal{A}(\gamma \cup [x \mapsto S]) = \mathcal{A}(\gamma) \cup \mathcal{A}([x \mapsto S]) \qquad (284)$$

in precisely those cases where S consists of basic parts only. To continue with our proof, we are faced with demonstrating that

$$\mathcal{A}((\mathcal{I} \underset{m}{\rightharpoonup} \blacktriangleleft [\gamma_{\theta}^{-1}])(\blacktriangleleft [\gamma_{\theta}^{-1}]\gamma) \cup [x \mapsto \blacktriangleleft [\gamma_{\theta}^{-1}]S]) = \theta \qquad (285)$$

There are two cases to consider. If $S \neq \emptyset$ consists only of basic parts then

$$(\mathcal{I} \underset{m}{\rightharpoonup} \blacktriangleleft [\gamma_{\theta}^{-1}])[x \mapsto S] = [x \mapsto \blacktriangleleft [\gamma_{\theta}^{-1}]S] = \emptyset \qquad (286)$$

and the problem is reduced to the case for the enter operation with $S = \emptyset$, which we have already proved. Therefore, the interesting case is for $\blacktriangleleft [\gamma_{\theta}^{-1}]S \neq \emptyset$. By construction $\blacktriangleleft [\gamma_{\theta}^{-1}]S$ must consist of a set of non-basic parts. Therefore, $\blacktriangleleft [\gamma_{\theta}^{-1}]S \subseteq dom\,\gamma$ which is guaranteed by that portion of the pre-condition which asserts that $S \subseteq dom\,\gamma$ and the result is established.

We have succeeded in proving that the enter operation does indeed conserve the invariant expressed in terms of the annihilator $\mathcal{A}$. In carrying out the proof using the operator calculus it is clear to what extent the calculus is able to do most, *but not all*, of the work. The proof still relies on conventional mathematical reasoning and argument.

4.2.1 The Purpose of Proof

To the 'outsider' the most likely reaction to the foregoing proof and others of the same ilk is one of horror/terror/fright. There is absolutely no point in reading it or simply admiring it. One must redo it, reconstruct it if you will. Cryptic remarks such as "removal with respect to a set, $\blacktriangleleft [\bar{\gamma}_{\theta}^{-1}]$, is an endomorphism of the monoid $((X \underset{m}{\rightharpoonup} PY), +, \theta)$", used to justify a derivation, will seem enigmatic to all but those who have the necessary technical background [22]. There just has been no room to elaborate upon such technical matters in the tutorial.

Recall that the purpose of a proof is to assist in the analysis of the problem domain. From that of the enter command, it is absolutely clear that, although the specification looks trivial—effectively $\gamma_0 \cup [x \mapsto S]$—the command itself is complex, the complexity being bound up with the nature of the set S. The proof suggests that we may subdivide the enter command into two distinct subcommands: $Ent_0[x, \emptyset]$ to enter basic parts and $Ent_1[x, S]$, $S \neq \emptyset$, to join subassemblies. But even the latter command may be subdivided. In general, S will consist of non-basic parts S_a and basic parts S_b. We may wish to introduce $Ent_{11}[x, S_a]$ and $Ent_{12}[x, S_b]$. Then each of these commands may be proved to satisy the invariant separately—the complexity of the proof being reduced accordingly. However, one further question must be posed. Are the three subcommands $Ent_0[x, \emptyset]$, $Ent_{11}[x, S_a]$, and $Ent_{12}[x, S_b]$ sufficient to cover the original enter command?

It is possible to construct an example such that the answer to the above question is negative. However, the three commands in conjunction with the add command *is* sufficient. We now focus on the add command used to update a bill of material. It is clear that a sequence of add commands

$$Add_0[x, x_n] \circ \ldots \circ Add_0[x, x_j] \circ \ldots \circ Add_0[x, x_1]\gamma_0 \qquad (287)$$

may be generalised to a single $Add_0[x, S]$, where $S = \{x_1, \ldots, x_j, \ldots, x_n\}$. Thus if we have $S = S_a \cup S_b$, then

$$Add_0[x, S_b] \circ Ent_{11}[x, S_a] = Add_0[x, S_a] \circ Ent_{12}[x, S_b] = Ent_0[x, S] \qquad (288)$$

For the sake of technical elegance, we find that we are forced to consider a composition of commands in a particular order so that satisfaction of the invariant is always guaranteed. This result suggests that, in practice, from the point of view of real users we have the choice of (i) forcing an order on the construction process, an order determined by the notion of invariant satisfaction, or (ii) allowing the user the freedom to build the bill of material in a natural way and without any worry about invariant conservation until completion. From an ergonomics point of view, the second choice is dictated.

Thus, even though we pride ourselves in the formulation of specifications and proofs of conservation of invariants and delight in the technicalities of the mathematics thus generated, we must not lose sight of the 'real requirements', whatever they might be. That is not to say that one should not do all of the above technical work. Indeed, it is often the case that such technical work leads to an exposure of the real requirements with the *added benefit* of a rigorous understanding of the problem domain.

The real problem to be addressed in this chapter is a study of the bill of material domain given by

$$BOM_1 = X \underset{m}{\rightarrow} (X \underset{m}{\rightarrow} N_1) \qquad (289)$$

We have spent sufficient time working on an abstraction of that domain, primarily with a view to elaborating on the nature and rôle of the invariant. Let us return to the real problem.

4.3   Model 1

The domain of bills of material is modelled by the equation

$$\gamma_1 \in BOM_1 = X \underset{m}{\rightarrow} (X \underset{m}{\rightarrow} N_1) \qquad (290)$$

where the invariant may be given in the form:

$$inv\text{-}BOM_1(\gamma_1) \;=\; inv\text{-}BOM_0(\Re_{10}(\gamma_1)) \wedge \ldots \qquad (291)$$

$$=\; inv\text{-}BOM_0((\mathcal{I} \underset{m}{\rightarrow} dom)\gamma_1) \wedge \ldots \qquad (292)$$

$$=\; \mathcal{A}((\mathcal{I} \underset{m}{\rightarrow} dom)\gamma_1) \wedge \ldots \qquad (293)$$

We have studied it under the retrieve function

$$\mathfrak{R}_{10} = (\mathcal{I} \underset{m}{\rightharpoonup} dom) \tag{294}$$

where we 'forget' the numerical information. It is important to note that two distinct bills of material γ_1 and γ_1' in $X \underset{m}{\rightharpoonup} (X \underset{m}{\rightharpoonup} N_1)$ map to the same γ_0 in $X \underset{m}{\rightharpoonup} \mathcal{P}X$. For example, if $\gamma_1 = [x_1 \mapsto [x_2 \mapsto m], x_2 \mapsto \theta]$, $\gamma_1' = [x_1 \mapsto [x_2 \mapsto n], x_2 \mapsto \theta]$, $m, n \in N_1$, $m \neq n$, then

$$(\mathcal{I} \underset{m}{\rightharpoonup} dom)\gamma_1 = (\mathcal{I} \underset{m}{\rightharpoonup} dom)\gamma_1' = [x_1 \mapsto \{x_2\}, x_2 \mapsto \emptyset] \tag{295}$$

Thus, in general, we may distinguish those operations on a bill of material which specifically address the interest in the numerical information from all other operations. The numerical information is modelled by a bag domain $X \underset{m}{\rightharpoonup} N_1$, the properties of which are presented in [22]. Suffice it to say that a bag may be considered to be an abstract formal model of a purse of money. Let β denote such a purse and suppose that we wish to add n coins of type x. Then $\beta \oplus [x \mapsto n]$ denotes the result. Such coins may be added, one at at time, giving the equivalent result $\beta \oplus n \otimes [x \mapsto 1]$. Basically, the properties of the $\oplus$ and $\otimes$ operators are inherited from addition and multiplication of natural numbers. This is the *interpretation* of bag as a counter mechanism, for which a use may be found in many areas of computer science. There is another *interpretation* of bag as a multi-set—a set with multiple elements—for which there are inherited operations such as union and intersection. It is the former interpretation which proves most useful in the bill of materials problem. The principal operation on a bill of material which addresses the numerical information is the parts-explosion algorithm, discussed next.

4.3.1 Parts-Explosion

The form of the parts-explosion algorithm .given here was derived from that of [2] and originally presented in [22]. The process/method by which such a derivation was carried out is recorded only in manuscript form. Since we have already discussed it in detail in its *abstract* form, only a few brief remarks will be added here.

78    $\mathcal{E}: X \longrightarrow (X \underset{m}{\rightharpoonup} (X \underset{m}{\rightharpoonup} N_1)) \longrightarrow (X \underset{m}{\rightharpoonup} N_1)$

.1 $\mathcal{E}[x]\gamma \triangleq \pi_2 \circ \mathcal{E}_1[\gamma(x)](\gamma, \theta)$

where

79    $\mathcal{E}: N_1 \longrightarrow (X \underset{m}{\rightharpoonup} N_1) \longrightarrow (X \underset{m}{\rightharpoonup} (X \underset{m}{\rightharpoonup} N_1)) \times (X \underset{m}{\rightharpoonup} N_1)$

$\longrightarrow (X \underset{m}{\rightharpoonup} (X \underset{m}{\rightharpoonup} N_1)) \times (X \underset{m}{\rightharpoonup} N_1)$

.1 $\mathcal{E}_n[\theta](\gamma, \beta) \triangleq (\gamma, \beta)$

.2 $\mathcal{E}_n[[x \mapsto m] \cup \mu](\gamma, \beta) \triangleq$
    $\gamma(x) = \theta$

$$.4 \qquad \to \mathcal{E}_n[\![\mu]\!](\gamma, \beta \oplus n \otimes [x \mapsto m])$$
$$.5 \qquad \to \mathcal{E}_n[\![\mu]\!] \circ \mathcal{E}_{mn}[\![\gamma(x)]\!](\gamma, \beta)$$

Annotations:

79.4) If we meet a basic part, x, then the accumulated number of its occurrences, n, is added into the bag of basic parts. It is also worth observing that this expression may be written in terms of the bag singleton $\beta_x = [x \mapsto 1]$ in the form

$$\mathcal{E}_n[\![\mu]\!](\gamma, \beta \oplus mn \otimes \beta_x) \tag{296}$$

If we are prepared to generalise the latter in order that it produces a bag of *all* of the parts of which x is composed then we obtain:

$$80 \quad \mathcal{E}: X \longrightarrow (X \underset{m}{\rightrightarrows} (X \underset{m}{\rightrightarrows} \mathbf{N_1})) \longrightarrow (X \underset{m}{\rightrightarrows} \mathbf{N_1})$$

$$.1 \quad \mathcal{E}[\![x]\!]\gamma \triangleq \gamma^{-1}(\theta) \lhd \left(\pi_2 \circ \mathcal{E}_1[\![\gamma(x)]\!](\gamma, \theta)\right)$$

Annotations:

- The expression $\gamma^{-1}(\theta)$ denotes the set of basic parts in this model. We use it to restrict the result. Thus, if $\mathcal{E}_1[\![\gamma(x)]\!](\gamma, \theta) = (\gamma, \tau)$, then $\pi_2(\gamma, \tau)$ gives the bag of all parts τ and $\gamma^{-1}(\theta) \lhd \tau$ denotes the bag of basic parts as required.

The main body of the algorithm is

$$81 \quad \mathcal{E}: \mathbf{N_1} \longrightarrow (X \underset{m}{\rightrightarrows} \mathbf{N_1}) \longrightarrow (X \underset{m}{\rightrightarrows} (X \underset{m}{\rightrightarrows} \mathbf{N_1})) \times (X \underset{m}{\rightrightarrows} \mathbf{N_1})$$
$$\longrightarrow (X \underset{m}{\rightrightarrows} (X \underset{m}{\rightrightarrows} \mathbf{N_1})) \times (X \underset{m}{\rightrightarrows} \mathbf{N_1})$$

$$.1 \quad \mathcal{E}_n[\![\theta]\!](\gamma, \beta) \triangleq (\gamma, \beta)$$
$$.2 \quad \mathcal{E}_n[\![[x \mapsto m] \cup \mu]\!](\gamma, \beta) \triangleq$$
$$.3 \qquad \mathcal{E}_n[\![\mu]\!] \circ \mathcal{E}_{mn}[\![\gamma(x)]\!](\gamma, \beta \oplus n \otimes [x \mapsto m])$$

Annotations:

81.3) Using the notation for a bag singleton $\beta_x = [x \mapsto 1]$, we may write this expression in the form

$$\mathcal{E}_n[\![\mu]\!] \circ \mathcal{E}_{mn}[\![\gamma(x)]\!](\gamma, \beta \oplus mn \otimes \beta_x) \tag{297}$$

This is the most compact form of the algorithm to date and it is very difficult to see how it might be reduced further. It gives the essence of the parts-explosion algorithm.

4.3.2 Operations on BOM_1

Strictly speaking one ought to give the full specification of all the operations on $\gamma \in BOM_1$ and verify that they faithfully 'implement' those given earlier for the more abstract model. Here we confine ourselves to the enter command, $Ent_1[x, \beta]$, and, rather than demonstrating that

$$Ent_0[x, S] \circ \Re_{10} = \Re_{10} \circ Ent_1[x, \beta] \tag{298}$$

where $dom\, \beta = S$, we will show its relationship to the parts-explosion algorithm.

4.3.3 The Enter Command

Let $\beta = [x_1 \mapsto m_1, \ldots, x_k \mapsto m_k]$ be a bag of parts such that x and $S = dom\, \beta = \{x_1, \ldots, x_k\}$ satisfy the pre-condition of the enter command with respect to $\gamma_0 = (\mathcal{I} \underset{m}{\rightharpoonup} dom$

Then, we may define the enter command with respect to γ_1 as follows:

82    $Ent_1 \colon X \times (X \underset{m}{\rightharpoonup} \mathbf{N}_1) \longrightarrow (X \underset{m}{\rightharpoonup} (X \underset{m}{\rightharpoonup} \mathbf{N}_1)) \longrightarrow (X \underset{m}{\rightharpoonup} (X \underset{m}{\rightharpoonup} \mathbf{N}_1))$

.1 $Ent_1[x, \beta]\gamma_1 \overset{\Delta}{=} \gamma_1 \cup [x \mapsto \beta]$

subject to the pre-condition

83    $pre\text{-}Ent_1 \colon X \times (X \underset{m}{\rightharpoonup} \mathbf{N}_1) \longrightarrow (X \underset{m}{\rightharpoonup} (X \underset{m}{\rightharpoonup} \mathbf{N}_1)) \longrightarrow \mathbf{B}$

.1 $pre\text{-}Ent_1[x, \beta]\gamma_1 \overset{\Delta}{=} pre\text{-}Ent_0[x, dom\, \beta](\mathcal{I} \underset{m}{\rightharpoonup} dom)\gamma_1 \wedge \ldots$

To test our understanding of the meaning of the enter operation we may examine its relationship with the parts-explosion algorithm. If indeed the pre-condition is met then the parts-explosion of the new bill of material is just the sum of all the bags of each subassembly x_k of the original bill of material multiplied by the m_k **and in addition** the multiples of the basic parts occuring in β. In other words we have the theorem:

THEOREM 4.2

$$\mathcal{E}[x] \circ Ent_1[x, \beta]\gamma = \sum_{i=1}^{k} m_i \otimes \beta_i \tag{299}$$

where, for definiteness we assume $\beta \neq \theta$,

$$b_i = \begin{cases} \beta_{x_i}, & \text{if } x_i \text{ is a basic part } \textbf{not} \text{ in another subassembly} \\ \beta_{x_i} \oplus \mathcal{E}[x_j]\gamma, & \text{if } x_i \text{ is a basic part } \textbf{in} \text{ another subassembly } x_j, i \neq j \\ \mathcal{E}[x_i]\gamma, & \text{otherwise} \end{cases} \tag{300}$$

and β_{x_i} denotes the singleton bag $[x_i \mapsto 1]$.

Comment: The formulation of this theorem proved difficult and only resulted *after* the proof was carried out for an earlier inadequate forumulation. The complicating factor is, of course, due to the enter command itself. If x_i is a basic part which does not occur elsewhere in a subassembly named in β, then the contribution to the overall result is simply $[x_i \mapsto m_i] = m_i \otimes \beta_{x_i}$. If, on the other hand, x_i is a basic part which is being joined to a subassembly x_j named in β of which it is already already a constituent part, then the result of $m_j \otimes \mathcal{E}[x_j]\gamma$ must be augmented by $m_i \otimes \beta_{x_i}$. Otherwise, if x_i is not a basic part, then the result is straightforward. The earlier formulation, referred to above, was simply

$$\mathcal{E}[x] \circ Ent_1[x, \beta]\gamma = \sum_{i=1}^{k} m_i \otimes \mathcal{E}[x_i]\gamma \tag{301}$$

In other words, it is the basic parts which are the complicating factor.

Proof: To prove the theorem we may proceed as follows. Let $\bar{\gamma} = Ent_1[x, \beta]\gamma = \gamma \cup [x \mapsto \beta]$. Then

$$\bar{\gamma}^{-1}(\theta) = (\gamma \cup [x \mapsto \beta])^{-1}(\theta) = \gamma^{-1}(\theta) \tag{302}$$

By definition of the part-explosion algorithm we have

84   $\mathcal{E}[x] \circ Ent_1[x, \beta]\gamma$
.1 $= \mathcal{E}[x]\bar{\gamma}$
.2 $= \bar{\gamma}^{-1}(\theta) \triangleleft \pi_2 \mathcal{E}_1[\bar{\gamma}(x)](\bar{\gamma}, \theta)$
.3 $= \gamma^{-1}(\theta) \triangleleft \pi_2 \mathcal{E}_1[\beta](\bar{\gamma}, \theta)$

Let us now focus on the expression $\mathcal{E}_1[\beta](\bar{\gamma}, \theta)$. By definition

85   $\mathcal{E}_n[\beta](\bar{\gamma}, \tau)$
.1 $= \mathcal{E}_n[[x_j \mapsto m_j] \cup \beta'](\bar{\gamma}, \tau)$
.2 $= \mathcal{E}_n[\beta'] \circ \mathcal{E}_{m_j n}[\bar{\gamma}(x_j)](\bar{\gamma}, \tau \oplus n \otimes [x_j \mapsto m_j])$

In the case of the initial computation, of course, $n = 1$ and $\tau = \theta$. Using the bag singleton notation, we will now concentrate on the expression

$$\mathcal{E}_{m_j n}[\bar{\gamma}(x_j)](\bar{\gamma}, \tau \oplus m_j n \otimes \beta_{x_j}) \tag{303}$$

But this is just the invocation of the main body of another parts-explosion algorithm $\mathcal{E}[x_j]\bar{\gamma}$, with initial bag $\tau \oplus m_j n \otimes \beta_{x_j}$ and a multiplier $m_j n$. If, in fact, x_j is a basic part not occuring in another named assembly, then by definition $\mathcal{E}_{m_j n}[\bar{\gamma}(x_j)]$ returns its arguments $(\bar{\gamma}, \tau \oplus m_j n \otimes \beta_{x_j})$ and the overall contribution is $m_j \otimes \beta_{x_j}$, recalling that $n = 1$ and $\tau = \theta$.

For notational convenience, let us define a form of the parts-explosion algorithm, $\mathcal{E}'$, that does not extract the basic parts:

$$\mathcal{E}'[x]\gamma \triangleq \mathcal{E}_1[\gamma(x)](\gamma, \theta) \tag{304}$$

Then its relation to the parts-explosion algorithm is simply

$$\mathcal{E}[x]\gamma = \gamma^{-1}(\theta) \triangleleft \pi_2 \mathcal{E}'[x]\gamma \tag{305}$$

Now for any starting bag σ, the computation of $\mathcal{E}_1[\gamma(x)](\gamma, \sigma)$ gives $\sigma \oplus \pi_2 \mathcal{E}'[\![x]\!]\gamma$. Introducing a multiplier m, we also immediately have

$$\mathcal{E}_m[\gamma(x)](\gamma, \sigma) = \sigma \oplus m \otimes \pi_2 \mathcal{E}'[\![x]\!]\gamma \tag{306}$$

Therefore, the expression $\mathcal{E}_{m_j n}[\bar{\gamma}(x_j)](\bar{\gamma}, \tau \oplus m_j n \otimes \beta_{x_j})$ may be written in the form

$$\tau \oplus (m_j n \otimes \beta_{x_j}) \oplus (m_j n \otimes \pi_2 \mathcal{E}'[\![x_j]\!]\bar{\gamma}) = \tau \oplus m_j n \otimes (\beta_{x_j} \oplus \pi_2 \mathcal{E}'[\![x_j]\!]\bar{\gamma}) \tag{307}$$

But $\bar{\gamma}(x_j) = (\gamma \cup [x \mapsto ([x_j \mapsto m_j] \cup \beta')])(x_j) = \gamma(x_j)$. Hence

$$\mathcal{E}_1[\beta](\bar{\gamma}, \theta) = \mathcal{E}_1[\beta'](\bar{\gamma}, \tau \oplus m_j n \otimes (\beta_{x_j} \oplus \pi_2 \mathcal{E}'[\![x_j]\!]\gamma)) \tag{308}$$

and by deduction, the computation of $\mathcal{E}_1[\![\beta]\!](\bar{\gamma}, \theta)$ gives

$$(\bar{\gamma}, \oplus m_1 \otimes (\beta_{x_1} \oplus \pi_2 \mathcal{E}'[\![x_1]\!]\gamma) \oplus \ldots \oplus m_j \otimes (\beta_{x_j} \oplus \pi_2 \mathcal{E}'[\![x_j]\!]\gamma) \oplus \ldots) \tag{309}$$

where we have supplied the initial conditions $n = 1$ and $\tau = \theta$. Therefore, the expression $\gamma^{-1}(\theta) \triangleleft \pi_2 \mathcal{E}_1[\![\beta]\!](\bar{\gamma}, \theta)$ may be written in the form

$$\gamma^{-1}(\theta) \triangleleft (m_j \otimes (\beta_{x_1} \oplus \pi_2 \mathcal{E}'[\![x_1]\!]\gamma) \oplus \ldots \oplus m_j \otimes (\beta_{x_j} \oplus \pi_2 \mathcal{E}'[\![x_j]\!]\gamma) \oplus \ldots) \tag{310}$$

Since restriction of a map with respect to a set is an endomorphism of bags, $S \triangleleft (\beta_j \oplus \beta_k) = (S \triangleleft \beta_j) \oplus (S \triangleleft \beta_k)$ [22], then the above reduces to

$$\ldots m_j \otimes (\gamma^{-1}(\theta) \triangleleft \beta_{x_j} \oplus \gamma^{-1}(\theta) \triangleleft \pi_2 \mathcal{E}'[\![x_j]\!]\gamma \ldots \tag{311}$$

But if x_j is not a basic part then, $\gamma^{-1}(\theta) \triangleleft \beta_{x_j} = \theta$. If, on the other hand, x_j is a basic part then $\gamma^{-1}(\theta) \triangleleft \beta_{x_j} = \beta_{x_j}$. Finally, by definition, $\gamma^{-1}(\theta) \triangleleft \pi_2 \mathcal{E}'[\![x_j]\!]\gamma = \mathcal{E}[\![x_j]\!]\gamma$ and the theorem follows.

4.4 Graph Theory in the *VDM*

In studying the bill of material problem and being aware that it was a concrete instance of a directed acyclic graph, it was natural to consider to what extent application of the Irish School of the *VDM* might affect the presentation of the subject of graph theory. In particular, the simple elegant form of the parts-explosion algorithm which might be configured either as a depth-first search or breadth-first search, by a transposition of recursive calls, prompted the question whether or not traditional graph-theoretical litterature was equally enlightening. If it were then most of the material in the remainder of this section could have been omitted. Let us begin by quoting a typical definition:

> "A *graph* $G(V, E)$ is a structure which consists of a set of *vertices* $V = \{v_1, v_2, \ldots\}$ and a set of *edges* $E = \{e_1, e_2\}$; each edge is *incident* to the elements of an unordered pair of vertices $\{u, v\}$ which are not necessarily distinct" [11].

Because of the 'problem' of the multiple occurrences of undirected edges, it is advisable to supply a definitional invariant:

"Graphs and digraphs which have no parallel edges are called *simple*" [11].

The term 'problem' used in connection with the representation of multiple edges or parallel edges of a graph is deliberately provocative, challenging one to find an adequate abstract model to represent them and concurrently to philosophise on the manner in which it could be said that such multiple occurrences *might be distinguished*.

Now the elegance of the presentation on the bill of material was undoutedly due to the abstract domain model

$$X \xrightarrow{m} \mathcal{P}X \tag{312}$$

which is the standard *VDM* model for relations. Perhaps, then we should examine what is traditionally taken to be the concrete representation for graphs in computer science.

4.5 Data Structures

It is customary in the literature, e.g. [28, 6, 11, 24], to cite two principle types of data structure for the (computer) representation of (simple) graphs:

1. the adjacency matrix;

2. the incidence list.

The latter structure is preferred, on the basis of efficiency, where the adjacency matrix is sparse, and it is now customary to present graph algorithms for the incidence list only. In the specification of graph algorithms, *our* first concern is adequateness and clarity of expression rather than issues of efficiency. In particular, we seek domain equations that exhibit the natural structure of the graph and that enjoy certain æsthetic mathematical properties. It will be argued that the appropriate domain equation is just an abstraction of the incidence list. Indeed, we shall see that distinctions between adjacency matrix and incidence list are only indicative of the wide range of choices of models at the abstract level of specification. First, let us consider the adjacency matrix. We shall show how one might start from a rather obvious model and develop alternative models, one of which is a rather nice abstraction of the incidence list.

4.5.1 The Adjacency matrix

Consider the simple graph and its accompanying adjacency matrix shown in Figure 1. It is quite obvious how the adjaceny matrix is formed: the u, v entry contains a 1 if there is an edge from u to v and a 0, otherwise. In the *VDM* we may wish to use the map construct to represent such a matrix:

$$\begin{aligned}
(v_1, v_1) &\mapsto 0, \quad (v_1, v_2) \mapsto 1, \quad (v_1, v_3) \mapsto 1, \quad \ldots \\
(v_2, v_1) &\mapsto 1, \quad (v_2, v_2) \mapsto 0, \quad (v_2, v_3) \mapsto 1, \quad \ldots \\
(v_3, v_1) &\mapsto 1, \quad (v_3, v_2) \mapsto 1, \quad (v_3, v_3) \mapsto 0, \quad \ldots \\
&\ldots
\end{aligned} \tag{313}$$

Such a map, μ_0, is an element of the domain equation

$$\mu_0 \in ADJ\_MATRIX_0 = V^2 \xrightarrow{m} \{0, 1\} \tag{314}$$

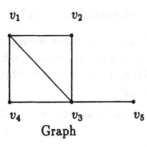

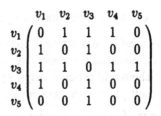

	v_1	v_2	v_3	v_4	v_5
v_1	0	1	1	1	0
v_2	1	0	1	0	0
v_3	1	1	0	1	1
v_4	1	0	1	0	0
v_5	0	0	1	0	0

Graph   Adjacency matrix

Figure 1: A conventional matrix representation

If we agree that $V = \{v_1, v_2, v_3, v_5, v_5\}$, then μ_0 is, in fact always a function. It is important to note, moreover, that there is no notion of inherent ordering in the chosen model.

We may prefer instead the isomorphic model

$$\mu_1 \in ADJ\_MATRIX_1 = V \xrightarrow[m]{} (V \xrightarrow[m]{} \{0,1\}) \qquad (315)$$

which may be interpreted as specifying the domain of adjacency matrices in row order (or, if one prefers in column order). The above example, in the row order interpretation, would then read

$$\begin{aligned}
v_1 &\mapsto [v_1 \mapsto 0, v_2 \mapsto 1, v_3 \mapsto 1, \ldots] \\
v_2 &\mapsto [v_1 \mapsto 1, v_2 \mapsto 0, v_3 \mapsto 1, \ldots] \\
v_3 &\mapsto [v_1 \mapsto 1, v_2 \mapsto 1, v_3 \mapsto 0, \ldots]
\end{aligned} \qquad (316)$$

$$\cdots$$

Referring again to the first model, μ_0, we may wish to record, just those entries which are non-zero. This leads to the domain equation

$$\mu_2 \in ADJ\_MATRIX_2 = V^2 \xrightarrow[m]{} \{1\} \qquad (317)$$

But, such a model is isomorphic to the domain of ordered-pairs model

$$\mu_3 \in ADJ\_MATRIX_3 = \mathcal{P}(V^2) \qquad (318)$$

which is one model that might be chosen for (binary) relations. Similarly, the row order model might be modified to give

$$\mu_4 \in ADJ\_MATRIX_4 = V \xrightarrow[m]{} (V \xrightarrow[m]{} \{1\}) \qquad (319)$$

and this in turn is, of course, isomorphic to

$$\mu_5 \in ADJ\_MATRIX_5 = V \xrightarrow[m]{} \mathcal{P}V \qquad (320)$$

which is the classic standard domain equation—the usual *VDM* model of (binary) relations—which we recall being the domain of the bill of material structure! It is also, of course, *the* abstract model of the incidence list, abstract in the sense that order is omitted. We shall deal with this point later. Before proceeding to discuss further derivative models, we illustrate the representation of the sample graph as μ_5:

$$
\begin{aligned}
v_1 &\mapsto \{v_2, v_3, v_4\}, \\
v_2 &\mapsto \{v_1, v_3\}, \\
v_3 &\mapsto \{v_1, v_2, v_4, v_5\}, \\
v_4 &\mapsto \{v_1, v_3\}, \\
v_5 &\mapsto \{v_3\}
\end{aligned}
\tag{321}
$$

Rather than use the very specific $\{1\}$ in ADJ_MATRIX_2 and ADJ_MATRIX_4, we might prefer to generalise to $\mathbf{N}_1$, giving us the models

$$
\mu_6 \in ADJ\_MATRIX_6 = V^2 \underset{m}{\rightharpoonup} \mathbf{N}_1
\tag{322}
$$

and

$$
\mu_7 \in ADJ\_MATRIX_7 = V \underset{m}{\rightharpoonup} (V \underset{m}{\rightharpoonup} \mathbf{N}_1)
\tag{323}
$$

In these models we *do* have the possibility of recording the *number* of occurrences of multiple edges, but no way of distinguishing between them. Once again, we have obtained the canonical model of the bill of material! With a little manipulation we have obtained a total of 8 different models starting with an obvious model of the adjacency matrix and *none* of the models used the notion of order! Before addressing this point, it would be useful to present the first 6 models together and to show explicitly the inter-relationships:

$$
\begin{array}{ccc}
\mathcal{P}(V^2) & \longleftrightarrow & V \underset{m}{\rightharpoonup} \mathcal{P}V \\[2mm]
\Big\uparrow dom & & \Big\uparrow (\mathcal{I} \underset{m}{\rightharpoonup} dom) \\[2mm]
V^2 \underset{m}{\rightharpoonup} \{1\} & \longleftrightarrow & V \underset{m}{\rightharpoonup} (V \underset{m}{\rightharpoonup} \{1\}) \\[2mm]
\Big\uparrow \mathcal{F} & & \Big\uparrow (\mathcal{I} \underset{m}{\rightharpoonup} \mathcal{F}) \\[2mm]
V^2 \underset{m}{\rightharpoonup} \{0,1\} & \longleftrightarrow & V \underset{m}{\rightharpoonup} (V \underset{m}{\rightharpoonup} \{0,1\})
\end{array}
$$

where $\mathcal{F}$ is an auxillary function used to 'forget' the zero values.

4.5.2 The Incidence list

Whereas the concept of 'matrix' originates within mathematics, the incidence list is a computing *invention*. Therefore, being of 'mechanical' origin, one finds that authors frequently need to 'explain' it:

> "For each of the vertices, the edges incident to it are listed. This *incidence list* may simply be an array or may be a linked list. We may need a table which tells us the location of the list for each vertex and a table which tells us for each edge its two endpoints (or start-vertex and end-vertex, in case of a digraph)" [11].

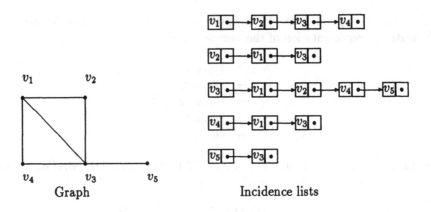

Figure 2: A conventional incidence list representation

Consider the running example. The incidence lists for each vertex are shown in Figure 2. The diagram suggests a 'pointer-based' implementation. From the point of view of the *VDM* specification, we may again choose the map as the basic model and specify the totality of incidence lists as the mapping from vertices to sequences of vertices, thus, deciding immediately to include the notion of order:

$$\sigma_0 \in INC\_LIST_0 = V \underset{m}{\rightarrow} V^\star \tag{324}$$

In this model the example is represented by

$$
\begin{aligned}
v_1 &\mapsto \langle v_1, v_2, v_3, v_4 \rangle \\
v_2 &\mapsto \langle v_1, v_3 \rangle \\
v_3 &\mapsto \langle v_1, v_2, v_4, v_5 \rangle \\
v_4 &\mapsto \langle v_1, v_3 \rangle \\
v_5 &\mapsto \langle v_3 \rangle
\end{aligned}
\tag{325}
$$

But, of course, such a representation may be interpreted as the reification, subject to an invariant, of the usual abstract domain equation

$$\sigma_1 \in INC\_LIST_0 = V \underset{m}{\rightarrow} \mathcal{P}V \tag{326}$$

which we have already obtained as *ADJ_MATRIX*$_5$ above. Since, it is an adequate abstraction of both the adjacency matrix and the incidence list—where we hypothesise that order is not an essential feature—we choose to 'canonise' this model and write

$$\gamma \in GRPH = V \underset{m}{\rightarrow} \mathcal{P}V \tag{327}$$

4.5.3 Depth-First Search

Having decided upon a model for the study of graph theory, we may now proceed to ask questions and obtain either closed-form solutions and/or algorithms. What better way to begin the study than by looking at the depth-first search algorithm.

4.5.4 Nishizeki & Chiba Version

Consider the following 'specification' of a depth-first search 'algorithm' given in [24] p.30:

> "A depth-first search of an undirected graph $G = (V, E)$ partitions E into two
> sets T and B, where T comprises a spanning forest of G. The edge (x, y) is
> placed into T if vertex y was visited for the first time immediately following a
> visit to x. The edges in T are called *tree edges*. The remaining edges, called
> *back edges*, are placed into B".

The algorithm which is given below, is practically a verbatim copy of a similar algorithm
in [6] p.177.

```
86   procedure DEPTH-FIRST-SEARCH:
 .1  begin
 .2     T := ∅;
 .3     for all v in V do mark v "new";
 .4     while there exists a vertex v in V marked "new" do
 .5          SEARCH(v)
 .6  end.


87   procedure SEARCH(v):
 .1  begin
 .2     mark v "old";
 .3     for each vertex w in Adj(v) do
 .4         if w is marked "new" then
 .5             begin
 .6                 add (v, w) to T;
 .7                 SEARCH(v)
 .8             end
 .9  end;
```

Annotations:

87.7) This is a typographical error; the correct form should read 'SEARCH(w)'.

To the undiscerning, the above algorithm looks impressive if only by virtue of its apparent simplicity, a simplicity suggested by its brevity of form. This is **not** an acceptable specification according to the principles of the Irish School of the *VDM* for the following reasons:

1. It is imperative, though recursive and iterative—hence already an 'optimised' form for a particular architecture;

2. The algorithm is to produce a partition (T, B). Yet B is not explicitly constructed; in [6] we are assured that "all edges in E not placed in T are considered to be in B". But what is this to mean in a formal sense?

3. The phrase *while* there exists ... is **not** an objectionable 'there exists' predication *per se*.

The transformation of the above 'algorithm' into a form acceptable to the Irish School is now presented. The principal technique by which this is accomplished turns on the equivalence of tail-recursive functions and while loops, the theory of which is elaborated upon in [22]. In particular, it is to be noted that the transformation is done in *development stages* in much the same way as models are elaborated or reified, a process which has already been exhibited in the discussion of the algorithm to compute the set of cities which have the minimum temperature in a temperature chart, given earlier.

4.5.5 Nishizeki & Chiba Algorithm in the *VDM*—Version 1

An acceptable specification that is an *almost* an exact **equivalent** (proof?) to the above, constructed line for line, is the following:

88    $DFS: (V \underset{m}{\rightarrow} \mathcal{P}V) \longrightarrow (V \underset{m}{\rightarrow} \mathcal{P}'V)$

.1 $DFS(\gamma) \triangleq$
.2   let $\mu = [v \mapsto \text{"new"} \mid v \in dom\,\gamma]$ in
.3   let $\tau = \theta$ in
.4 $\pi_3 \circ \mathcal{S}[\![dom\,\gamma]\!](\gamma, \mu, \tau)$

Annotations:

(88.0) Note that, to be faithful to the Nishizeki and Chiba algorithm, the domain of the spanning forest must be given by $V \underset{m}{\rightarrow} \mathcal{P}'V$, where $\mathcal{P}'V \triangleq \{\emptyset\} \triangleleft\!\!\!- \mathcal{P}V$, and not by $V \underset{m}{\rightarrow} \mathcal{P}V$. There are technical reasons why $V \underset{m}{\rightarrow} \mathcal{P}'V$ is chosen to be the formal equivalent of the domain of relations $\mathcal{P}(V^2)$ in the Irish School of the *VDM*. Note in particular that it is the analogue of the bag domain $X \underset{m}{\rightarrow} \mathbb{N}_1$, where the 0 is expressly prohibited [22]. For the sake of æsthetics and in order that the definition of spanning forest be compatible with that of bills of material, this will be remedied in the next version.

(88.3) The spanning forest $\tau \in V \underset{m}{\rightarrow} \mathcal{P}'V$ is a map and not a set and is initialised as such.

(88.4) We assume that the result of the computation is the spanning forest itself and consequently the third component of the parameter list is returned.

The above $\mathcal{S}$ is specified by

89    $\mathcal{S}: \mathcal{P}V \longrightarrow (V \underset{m}{\rightarrow} \mathcal{P}V) \times (V \underset{m}{\rightarrow} \{\text{"old"} \mid \text{"new"}\}) \times (V \underset{m}{\rightarrow} \mathcal{P}'V)$

$\longrightarrow (V \underset{m}{\rightarrow} \mathcal{P}V) \times (V \underset{m}{\rightarrow} \{\text{"old"} \mid \text{"new"}\}) \times (V \underset{m}{\rightarrow} \mathcal{P}'V)$

.1 $S[\emptyset](\gamma, \mu, \tau) \triangleq (\gamma, \mu, \tau)$
.2 $S[\{v\} \uplus R](\gamma, \mu, \tau) \triangleq$
.3 $\quad \mu(v) = \text{"new"}$
.4 $\quad\quad \to S[R] \circ S[v](\gamma, \mu, \tau)$
.5 $\quad\quad \to S[R](\gamma, \mu, \tau)$

Annotation:

(89.0) The S function is the formal tail-recursive equivalent of the '*while* there exists a vertex v in V marked "new" *do* ...'.

The $S[v]$ is specified by

90 $\quad S: V \longrightarrow (V \underset{m}{\rightharpoonup} \mathcal{P}V) \times (V \underset{m}{\rightharpoonup} \{\text{"old"} \mid \text{"new"}\}) \times (V \underset{m}{\rightharpoonup} \mathcal{P}'V)$

$\quad\quad\quad \longrightarrow (V \underset{m}{\rightharpoonup} \mathcal{P}V) \times (V \underset{m}{\rightharpoonup} \{\text{"old"} \mid \text{"new"}\}) \times (V \underset{m}{\rightharpoonup} \mathcal{P}'V)$

.1 $S[v](\gamma, \mu, \tau) \triangleq$
.2 $\quad$ let $\mu' = \mu + [v \mapsto \text{"old"}]$ in
.3 $\quad\quad S_v[\gamma(v)](\gamma, \mu', \tau)$

Annotations:

(90.3) The phrase '*for* each vertex w in Adj(v) *do* ...' is also translated into a tail-recursive function S_v. Since the ancestor v is required for further construction it is supplied conveniently as a subscript. Note that $\gamma(v)$ is the equivalent of Adj(v).

Finally, the S_v is specified by

91 $\quad S: V \longrightarrow \mathcal{P}V \longrightarrow (V \underset{m}{\rightharpoonup} \mathcal{P}V \times V \underset{m}{\rightharpoonup} \{\text{"old"} \mid \text{"new"}\} \times V \underset{m}{\rightharpoonup} \mathcal{P}'V)$

$\quad\quad\quad \longrightarrow (V \underset{m}{\rightharpoonup} \mathcal{P}V \times V \underset{m}{\rightharpoonup} \{\text{"old"} \mid \text{"new"}\} \times V \underset{m}{\rightharpoonup} \mathcal{P}'V)$

.1 $S_v[\emptyset](\gamma, \mu, \tau) \triangleq (\gamma, \mu, \tau)$
.2 $S_v[\{w\} \uplus R](\gamma, \mu, \tau) \triangleq$
.3 $\quad \mu(w) = \text{"new"}$
.4 $\quad\quad \to S_v[R] \circ S[w](\gamma, \mu, \tau \oplus [v \mapsto \{w\}])$
.5 $\quad\quad \to S_v[R](\gamma, \mu, \tau)$

Annotations:

(91.4) The expression $\tau \oplus [v \mapsto \{w\}]$ is used in analogy to the $\oplus$ operation for bags. It is formally defined by

$$\tau \oplus [v \mapsto \{w\}] \triangleq \chi[v]\tau \to \tau + [v \mapsto \tau(v) \cup \{w\}], \tau \cup [v \mapsto \{w\}] \tag{328}$$

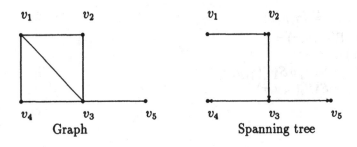

Figure 3: An illustration of the result of the *DFS* algorithm

Overall remarks:

1. The imperative algorithm has been transformed into a composition of recursive algorithms.

2. Rather than use different names, the different search algorithms have all been denoted by the root name S. Each is distinguished by its arguments and there is no ambiguity. Such overloading is a common feature of the Irish School.

3. Although it is stated that the algorithm "partitions E into two sets T and B", it is quite obvious that the given algorithm does nothing of the sort. The question we must ask is what exactly is the nature of B and more importantly how is it to be constructed? Indeed, we are led to two possibilities:

   (i) B can be constructed *a posteriori* directly from both γ and T;

   (ii) B can be constructed concurrently with T by the *DFS* algorithm itself.

Before proceeding to examine the issues raised, it is worthwhile to look at an example. Consider the graph given in Fig. 3. The *DFS* algorithm constructs the spanning forest shown in the same diagram. Since the graph is connected, then, of course, the spanning forest is a single spanning tree. However, when we consider the corresponding expressions, we see what is in reality computed. The formal expressions for the graph and the spanning tree are

$$\gamma = [\qquad\qquad\qquad\qquad \tau = [$$
$$v_1 \mapsto \{v_2, v_3, v_4\}, \qquad\qquad v_1 \mapsto \{v_2\},$$
$$v_2 \mapsto \{v_1, v_3\}, \qquad\qquad v_2 \mapsto \{v_3\},$$
$$v_3 \mapsto \{v_1, v_2, v_4, v_5\}, \qquad\qquad v_3 \mapsto \{v_4, v_5\}$$
$$v_4 \mapsto \{v_1, v_3\}, \qquad\qquad]$$
$$v_5 \mapsto \{v_3\}$$
$$]$$

Remark: It is to be noted that the models for both undirected graph and directed graph are of identical form, that is to say both belong to $V \xrightarrow{m} \mathcal{P}'V$. But in the case of the

directed graph we impose the *conceptual constraint* that an entry such as '$v_3 \mapsto \{v_4, v_5\}$' is to be interpreted to mean that (v_3, v_4) and (v_3, v_5) are directed edges. There is no such interpretation to be given to the graph model. Entries just indicate edges. An additional observation is in order. The spanning tree—as directed graph—does **not** contain entries of the form '$v \mapsto \emptyset$'. Since the preferred model of directed graphs in the Irish School is $V \xrightarrow{m} \mathcal{P}V$, where basic parts or sink nodes are explicity recorded, then we may wish to

'post-process' the result by adding in the 'missing' information. For details, see [22]. Here it suffices to note that the missing information is obtainable from $dom\,\tau \vartriangleleft {}^{\cup}\!/\circ rng\,\tau$. The missing structure of back edges, B, denoted here by β, is clearly

$$\beta = [$$
$$v_3 \mapsto \{v_1\},$$
$$v_4 \mapsto \{v_1\}$$
$$]$$

The issue of the *a posteriori* computation of β from γ and τ is, at the time of writing, unresolved.

4.5.6 Nishizeki & Chiba Algorithm in the *VDM*—Version 2

Since the original algorithm deals with a *forest* rather than a single connected graph and we will wish to compare it with other versions of depth-first search (and indeed with breadth-first search algorithms), the first stage is to restrict the algorithm to a connected graph. At the same time, we will eliminate the recursive function $S[v]$, the sole purpose of which, it will be noted, is to mark a visited node. The resulting simplified algorithm is, therefore:

92 $\quad DFS\!:(V \xrightarrow{m} \mathcal{P}V) \longrightarrow (V \xrightarrow{m} \mathcal{P}'V)$

.1 $\quad DFS(\gamma) \triangleq$
.2 $\qquad$ let $\mu = [v \mapsto \text{``new''} \mid v \in dom\,\gamma]$ in
.3 $\qquad$ let $\tau = \theta$ in
.4 $\qquad$ let $v \in dom\,\gamma$ in
.5 $\qquad \pi_3 \circ S_v[\gamma(v)](\gamma, \mu + [v \mapsto \text{``old''}], \tau)$

Annotations:

92.4) We pick an arbitrary node v.

92.5) Since we start at some arbitrary node v, then we must immediately mark it as visited $\mu + [v \mapsto \text{``old''}]$.

Now the principal part of the algorithm is a simple search routine S_v. Note that the subscript v may be interpreted to denote the ancestor node:

93    $\mathcal{S}: V \longrightarrow PV \longrightarrow (V \xrightarrow[m]{} PV) \times (V \xrightarrow[m]{} \{\text{"old"} \mid \text{"new"}\}) \times (V \xrightarrow[m]{} \mathcal{P}'V)$

$\longrightarrow (V \xrightarrow[m]{} PV) \times (V \xrightarrow[m]{} \{\text{"old"} \mid \text{"new"}\}) \times (V \xrightarrow[m]{} \mathcal{P}'V)$

.1 $\mathcal{S}_v[\![\emptyset]\!](\gamma, \mu, \tau) \triangleq (\gamma, \mu, \tau)$

.2 $\mathcal{S}_v[\![\{w\} \uplus R]\!](\gamma, \mu, \tau) \triangleq$

.3 $\mu(w) = \text{"new"}$

.4 $\to \mathcal{S}_v[\![R]\!] \circ \mathcal{S}_w[\![\gamma(w)]\!](\gamma, \mu + [w \mapsto \text{"old"}], \tau \oplus [v \mapsto \{w\}])$

.5 $\to \mathcal{S}_v[\![R]\!](\gamma, \mu, \tau)$

The similarity of the above with the bill of material parts-explosion algorithm is striking! Indeed, were we to interpret the spanning tree structure as the counterpart of the table of basic parts, an analogy which is obviously fully justified, then it is clear that the only real extra information is the node marking structure μ. But, such a remark triggers the observation that at (93.4), we may write

$$\mathcal{S}_w[\![\gamma(w)]\!] \circ \mathcal{S}_v[\![R]\!](\gamma, \mu + [w \mapsto \text{"old"}], \tau \oplus [v \mapsto \{w\}]) \tag{329}$$

giving us the breadth-first search algorithm!

4.5.7   Nishizeki & Chiba Algorithm in the VDM—Version 3

Now we are ready to consider the construction of the set of back edges B, here denoted by β. The appropriate modification to the top-level function is obvious:

94    $DFS: (V \xrightarrow[m]{} PV) \longrightarrow (V \xrightarrow[m]{} \mathcal{P}'V)^2$

.1 $DFS(\gamma) \triangleq$

.2   let $\mu = [v \mapsto \text{"new"} \mid v \in dom\,\gamma]$ in

.3   let $\tau = \theta, \beta = \theta$ in

.4   let $v \in dom\,\gamma$ in

.5   let $(\gamma, \mu', \tau', \beta') = \mathcal{S}_v[\![\gamma(v)]\!](\gamma, \mu + [v \mapsto \text{"old"}], \tau, \beta)$ in

.6 (τ', β')

In the construction of the set of back edges, it is clear that this must occur when the successor $w \in \gamma(v)$ of v is already marked as old **and** said successor is not the immediate ancestor of v. But how shall this latter fact be determined? The solution is simply given by checking the spanning tree structure being built, i.e., w is an immediate ancestor of v if and only if $w \in \tau(v)$. The corresponding modification is, therefore

95    $\mathcal{S}: V \longrightarrow PV \longrightarrow (V \xrightarrow[m]{} PV) \times (V \xrightarrow[m]{} \{\text{"old"} \mid \text{"new"}\}) \times (V \xrightarrow[m]{} \mathcal{P}'V)^2$

$\longrightarrow (V \xrightarrow[m]{} PV) \times (V \xrightarrow[m]{} \{\text{"old"} \mid \text{"new"}\}) \times (V \xrightarrow[m]{} \mathcal{P}'V)^2$

.1 $\mathcal{S}_v[\![\emptyset]\!](\gamma, \mu, \tau, \beta) \triangleq (\gamma, \mu, \tau, \beta)$

.2 $\mathcal{S}_v[\![\{w\} \uplus R]\!](\gamma, \mu, \tau, \beta) \triangleq$

.3 $\mu(w) = \text{"new"}$

.4
$$\rightarrow S_v[\![R]\!] \circ S_w[\![\gamma(w)]\!](\gamma, \mu + [w \mapsto \text{``old''}], \tau \oplus [v \mapsto \{w\}], \beta)$$

.5
$$\rightarrow \chi[w]\tau(v)\big(S_v[\![R]\!](\gamma, \mu, \tau, \beta), S_v[\![R]\!](\gamma, \mu, \tau, \beta \oplus [v \mapsto \{w\}])\big)$$

In keeping with the spirit of the Irish School of the *VDM* we may wish to rewrite the latter expression (95.5) as

$$S_v[\![R]\!] \circ \chi[w]\tau(v)\big((\gamma, \mu, \tau, \beta), (\gamma, \mu, \tau, \beta \oplus [v \mapsto \{w\}])\big) \tag{330}$$

or indeed as

$$S_v[\![R]\!]\big(\gamma, \mu, \tau, \chi[w]\tau(v)(\beta, \beta \oplus [v \mapsto \{w\}])\big) \tag{331}$$

where we feel free to write $\chi[x]\!]S \rightarrow E_1, E_2$ as $\chi[x]\!]S(E_1, E_2)$ by invoking the 'abuse of notation' principle.

4.5.8 Nishizeki & Chiba Algorithm in the *VDM*—Version 4

Ever keeping in mind the importance of simplicity and æsthetics whilst striving for an *adequate* abstraction, we note that the marking structure μ is simply a model of a characteristic function and, consequently, it may be replaced by a set. However, it *is* important to note that the marking structure *is* the model for the real implementation strategy of using a bit in the node to determine whether it has been visited or not! Thus, instead of starting out with an initialised structure such as

$$\text{let } \mu = [v \mapsto \text{``new''} \mid v \in dom\,\gamma] \text{ in} \ldots \tag{332}$$

we might as well use

$$\text{let } \mu = \emptyset \text{ in} \ldots \tag{333}$$

Moreover, we may feel free to be utterly ruthless and eliminate the 'let' constructs, giving

96    $DFS\!: (V \xrightarrow[m]{} \mathcal{P}V) \longrightarrow (V \xrightarrow[m]{} \mathcal{P}'V)^2$

.1 $DFS(\theta) \triangleq (\theta, \theta)$

.2 $DFS([v \mapsto R] \cup \gamma) \triangleq$

.3 $(\pi_3 - \bowtie \pi_4 -)S_v[\![R]\!]([v \mapsto R] \cup \gamma, \{v\}, \theta, \theta)$

Annotations:

96.3) The expression $(\pi_3 - \bowtie \pi_4 -)$ denotes the formation, $\bowtie$, of an ordered pair consisting of the third, π_3, and fourth, π_4, elements of the returned quadruple.

97    $S\!: V \longrightarrow \mathcal{P}V \longrightarrow (V \xrightarrow[m]{} \mathcal{P}V) \times \mathcal{P}V \times (V \xrightarrow[m]{} \mathcal{P}'V)^2$

$$\longrightarrow (V \xrightarrow[m]{} \mathcal{P}V) \times \mathcal{P}V \times (V \xrightarrow[m]{} \mathcal{P}'V)^2$$

.1 $S_v[\![\emptyset]\!](\gamma, \mu, \tau, \beta) \triangleq (\gamma, \mu, \tau, \beta)$

.2 $S_v[\![\{w\} \uplus R]\!](\gamma, \mu, \tau, \beta) \triangleq$

$$.3 \quad \neg\chi[w]\mu$$
$$.4 \quad \rightarrow \mathcal{S}_v[R] \circ \mathcal{S}_w[\gamma(w)](\gamma, \mu \cup \{w\}, \tau \oplus [v \mapsto \{w\}], \beta)$$
$$.5 \quad \rightarrow \mathcal{S}_v[R]\big(\gamma, \mu, \tau, \neg\chi[w]\tau(v)(\beta \oplus [v \mapsto \{w\}], \beta)\big)$$

We may now compare our result with the original. Although it appears to be very cryptic, it at least has the merit of being complete and rigorous, even to the extent of giving the signatures involved. However, we note that neither the original nor the *VDM* versions have been 'proved correct'. To do this, it is necessary to examine properties of graphs which remain invariant with respect to the algorithm.

However, we have shown something of the nature of the work in algorithm refinement carried out in the Irish School, in this case within the context of the reverse-engineering of published algorithms.

In studying the litterature on depth-first search, it was a little suprising to discover that there is no such thing as *the* depth-first search 'algorithm'. There *is* the notion of depth-first search **technique** which gives rise to various algorithms designed for specific problem-solving activities. Naturally, the question arises whether or not in all such algorithms there is a common kernel form. Consequently, it was felt to be imperative to pick a second representative sample for analysis, and what better source than Tarjan.

4.5.9 Tarjan Version

"Backtracking, or depth-first search, is a technique which has been widely used for finding solutions to problems in combinatorial theory and artificial intelligence [...] but whose properties have not been widely analyzed. [...] There are many ways of searching a graph, depending upon the way in which edges to search are selected. Consider the following choice rule: when selecting an edge to traverse, always choose an edge emanating from the vertex most recently reached which still has unexplored edges. A search which uses this rule is called a *depth-first search*. Thus a depth-first search is very easy to program either iteratively of recursively, provided we have a suitable computer representation of a graph" [28].

In presenting his version of the depth-first search algorithm, one which, according to Even [11], is similar to that of Trémaux, Tarjan uses the notions of vertex numbering and the father of a vertex. The algorithm takes a single connected graph as argument. Note also that, in contrast to the Nishizeki & Chiba version above, the set of back-edges, p, as well as the spanning tree, P, is explicitly constructed during the course of the algorithm.

```
BEGIN
    INTEGER i;
    PROCEDURE DFS(v,u);
        COMMENT vertex u is the father of vertex v
                in the spanning tree being constructed;
    BEGIN
        NUMBER(v) := i := i + 1;
```

```
        FOR w in the adjacency list of v DO
            BEGIN
                IF w is not yet numbered THEN
                    BEGIN
                        construct arc v → w in P;
                        DFS(w,v);
                    END
                ELSE IF NUMBER(w) < NUMBER(v) and w ≠ u
                    THEN construct arc v- → w in p;
            END;
        END;
        i := 0;
        DFS(s,0);
    END;
```

4.5.10 Tarjan Algorithm in the *VDM*—Version 1

As before, we give a line-by-line translation of Tarjan's algorithms into the *VDM*. The top-level recursive function is

$$98 \quad DFS\colon (V \xrightarrow{m} \mathcal{P}V) \longrightarrow (V \xrightarrow{m} \mathcal{P}'V)^2$$

$.1 \quad DFS(\gamma) \triangleq$
$.2 \qquad \text{let } \mu = \theta, \tau = \theta, \beta = \theta \text{ in}$
$.3 \qquad \text{let } i = 0, s \in dom\,\gamma, v_\perp \in (dom\,\gamma \blacktriangleleft V) \text{ in}$
$.4 \qquad \text{let } (\gamma, \mu', \tau', \beta') = \mathcal{S}_i[s, v_\perp](\gamma, \mu, \tau, \beta) \text{ in}$
$.5 \qquad (\tau', \beta')$

Annotations

98.3) Tarjan used 0 as the initial 'father' of the start vertex s to initialise the algorithm, thereby de facto assuming that vertex labels are natural numbers. Here we choose to be more abstract, and choose some $v_\perp$ which is **not** a vertex of the graph, in question.

The recursive function $\mathcal{S}_i$ is specified by

$$99 \quad \mathcal{S}\colon \mathbf{N}_1 \longrightarrow V \times V \longrightarrow (V \xrightarrow{m} \mathcal{P}V) \times (V \xrightarrow{m} \mathbf{N}_1) \times (V \xrightarrow{m} \mathcal{P}V)^2$$

$$\longrightarrow (V \xrightarrow{m} \mathcal{P}V) \times (V \xrightarrow{m} \mathbf{N}_1) \times (V \xrightarrow{m} \mathcal{P}V)^2$$

$.1\ \mathcal{S}_i[v, u](\gamma, \mu, \tau, \beta) \triangleq \mathcal{S}_{i+1}[\gamma(v), v, u](\gamma, \mu \cup [v \mapsto i+1], \tau, \beta)$

annotations:

99.1) Clearly, the sole purpose of the function is simply an initialisation of certain parameters.

The essential part of the search is given by

100 $\quad S: \mathbf{N}_1 \longrightarrow \mathcal{P}V \times V \times V \longrightarrow (V \underset{m}{\rightarrow} \mathcal{P}V) \times (V \underset{m}{\rightarrow} \mathbf{N}_1) \times (V \underset{m}{\rightarrow} \mathcal{P}V)^2$

$$\longrightarrow (V \underset{m}{\rightarrow} \mathcal{P}V) \times (V \underset{m}{\rightarrow} \mathbf{N}_1) \times (V \underset{m}{\rightarrow} \mathcal{P}V)^2$$

.1 $\quad S_i[\emptyset, v, u](\gamma, \mu, \tau, \beta) \triangleq (\gamma, \mu, \tau, \beta)$

.2 $\quad S_i[\{w\} \uplus R, v, u](\gamma, \mu, \tau, \beta) \triangleq$

.3 $\qquad \neg \chi[w]\mu$

.4 $\qquad \rightarrow S_i[R, v, u] \circ S_i[w, v](\gamma, \mu, \tau \oplus [v \mapsto \{w\}], \beta)$

.5 $\qquad \rightarrow \mu(w) < \mu(v) \wedge w \neq u$

.6 $\qquad \rightarrow S_i[R, v, u](\gamma, \mu, \tau, \beta \oplus [v \mapsto \{w\}])$

.7 $\qquad \rightarrow S_i[R, v, u](\gamma, \mu, \tau, \beta)$

4.5.11 Tarjan Algorithm in the *VDM*—Version 2

Upon elimination of the recursive function $S_i[v, u]$, the sole purpose of which is the initialisation of parameters, and the elimination of some 'let' constructs, we obtain the form

101 $\quad DFS: (V \underset{m}{\rightarrow} \mathcal{P}V) \longrightarrow (V \underset{m}{\rightarrow} \mathcal{P}'V)^2$

.1 $\quad DFS(\gamma) \triangleq$

.2 $\qquad s \in dom\,\gamma, v_\perp \in (dom\,\gamma \blacktriangleleft V)$ in

.3 $\qquad$ let $(\gamma, \mu, \tau, \beta) = S_1[\gamma(s), s, v_\perp](\gamma, [s \mapsto 1], \theta, \theta)$ in

.4 $\qquad (\tau, \beta)$

102 $\quad S: \mathbf{N}_1 \longrightarrow \mathcal{P}V \times V \times V \longrightarrow (V \underset{m}{\rightarrow} \mathcal{P}V) \times (V \underset{m}{\rightarrow} \mathbf{N}_1) \times (V \underset{m}{\rightarrow} \mathcal{P}V)^2$

$$\longrightarrow (V \underset{m}{\rightarrow} \mathcal{P}V) \times (V \underset{m}{\rightarrow} \mathbf{N}_1) \times (V \underset{m}{\rightarrow} \mathcal{P}V)^2$$

.1 $\quad S_i[\emptyset, v, u](\gamma, \mu, \tau, \beta) \triangleq (\gamma, \mu, \tau, \beta)$

.2 $\quad S_i[\{w\} \uplus R, v, u](\gamma, \mu, \tau, \beta) \triangleq$

.3 $\qquad \neg \chi[w]\mu$

.4 $\qquad \rightarrow S_i[R, v, u] \circ S_{i+1}[\gamma(w), w, v](\gamma, \mu \cup [w \mapsto i+1],$

$\qquad\qquad\qquad\qquad \tau \oplus [v \mapsto \{w\}], \beta)$

.5 $\qquad \rightarrow \mu(w) < \mu(v) \wedge w \neq u$

.6 $\qquad \rightarrow S_i[R, v, u](\gamma, \mu, \tau, \beta \oplus [v \mapsto \{w\}])$

.7 $\qquad \rightarrow S_i[R, v, u](\gamma, \mu, \tau, \beta)$

4.5.12 Tarjan Algorithm in the *VDM*—Version 3

Finally, we wish to bring the specification into as close as possible a correspondence with version 4 of the Nishizeki & Chiba algorithm. For this purpose, the recursive call $S_i[R, v, u]$ will be written in the form $S_{u,v}^i[R]$ where the counter i suggests iteration and the subscript u, v suggests the transition from the father u to the child v. The final version of the algorithm is, therefore

103   $DFS: (V \underset{m}{\rightarrow} \mathcal{P}V) \longrightarrow (V \underset{m}{\rightarrow} \mathcal{P}'V)^2$

.1 $DFS(\theta) \triangleq (\theta, \theta)$

.2 $DFS([v \mapsto R] \cup \gamma) \triangleq$

.3   let $v_\perp \in (dom([v \mapsto R] \cup \gamma) \blacktriangleleft V)$ in

.4 $(\pi_3 - \bowtie \pi_4 -)\mathcal{S}^1_{v_\perp, v}[R]([v \mapsto R] \cup \gamma, [v \mapsto 1], \theta, \theta)$

104   $\mathcal{S}: \mathbf{N}_1 \longrightarrow \mathcal{P}V \times V \times V \longrightarrow (V \underset{m}{\rightarrow} \mathcal{P}V) \times (V \underset{m}{\rightarrow} \mathbf{N}_1) \times (V \underset{m}{\rightarrow} \mathcal{P}V)^2$

              $\longrightarrow (V \underset{m}{\rightarrow} \mathcal{P}V) \times (V \underset{m}{\rightarrow} \mathbf{N}_1) \times (V \underset{m}{\rightarrow} \mathcal{P}V)^2$

.1 $\mathcal{S}^i_{u,v}[\![\emptyset]\!](\gamma, \mu, \tau, \beta) \triangleq (\gamma, \mu, \tau, \beta)$

.2 $\mathcal{S}^i_{u,v}[\![\{w\} \uplus R]\!](\gamma, \mu, \tau, \beta) \triangleq$

.3 $\neg \chi[w]\mu$

.4 $\rightarrow \mathcal{S}^i_{u,v}[R] \circ \mathcal{S}^{i+1}_{v,w}[\gamma(w)](\gamma, \mu \cup [w \mapsto i+1],$

              $\tau \oplus [v \mapsto \{w\}], \beta)$

.5 $\rightarrow \mathcal{S}^i_{u,v}[R]\big(\gamma, \mu, \tau,$

              $(\mu(w) < \mu(v) \wedge w \neq u \rightarrow \beta \oplus [v \mapsto \{w\}], \beta)\big)$

Remark: It will be noted that the criterion for the construction of back edges given by Tarjan appears to be more elaborate than that for the construction of same in the Nishizeki & Chiba algorithm. An immediate question arises: are they equivalent in some sense?

The work on the *re-presentation* of graph theory is still in an embryonic state. Although we have canonised the model $V \underset{m}{\rightarrow} \mathcal{P}V$ and will continue to present solutions for it, there may very well be other models which will prove better in some sense. In the case of the depth-first search algorithms studied, while it is pleasing to have derived abstract recursive forms which exhibit structural similarity, we believe that they can be massaged further. The end-goal is typified by the work done on the parts-explosion algorithm for the bill of material.

We do not always feel *obliged* to explain how such abstract algorithms may be reified into implementations with respect to either time or space efficiency. The culture of the Irish School automatically incorporates the sense of implementation issues with respect both to models and algorithms [22]. For a trivial example, the use of subscripts and superscripts is a suggestive expressive notational form; such marks are readily transformed into additional arguments of the functions concerned. We have also demonstrated, though without explanation, how easy it is to transform imperative algorithms into tail-recursive algorithms—a transformation technique that comes with experience. As a final remark to conclude this particular section, we note our concern that, as is evident from the *Collected Algorithms of the ACM*, there is a great danger that within 100 years, the discipline of the archeology of algorithms and programs (whereby one uncovers/rediscovers famous algorithms) will become a highly respected one—there is already enough material for its establishment today. In one sense, the industry's concern with reverse-engineering is leading in that direction. Reuse of models and abstract models is the essence of reuse, not reuse of programs, which is a facile issue of copying, much like the ancient manuscripts were copied by scribes before the age of printing. In short, reuse is about ideas and mathematics.

5 The Beginning

It is reported that in judging whether a book is good or not, critics often confine themselves to the first page of a manuscript. In writing this tutorial, that fact was borne in mind. For that reason, the opening quotation on the centrality of partial differential equations in mathematics is intended to convey the 'subtle' message that there is *no royal road to formal methods*, to paraphrase a famous quotation.

Aristotle's emphasis on the primacy of 'plot' in Greek drama is mirrored by another publishing convention—a good beginning, a good middle, and a good ending—with the unstated assumption that the three parts ought to be related.

Human nature being what it is, it is common to find a reader who having started at the beginning and when the going gets tough, then turns to see the ending and from that to judge whether the time would be well spent perusing the middle. In this case the ending is entitled 'The Beginning' to signify that the **Book** of the Irish School is just being written, the term 'book' being used in a *Meta–IV*ical sense.

5.1 What is the Irish School of the *VDM*?

The name was coined in 1990 to distinguish the notation, the style of use and development, and the *mathematical philosophy* underpinning the *VDM* as taught by the author in final year undergraduate degree courses at Trinity College Dublin and as employed in industrial contracts in the US, from other 'forms' of the *VDM* used elsewhere. The other forms were categorised under the names 'Danish School', 'English School' and 'Polish School'. However, one ought not to infer that the names refer to national regions. The Danish School (named after Dines Bjørner) is, in fact, the form of *VDM* used widely in parts of western Europe—Denmark, the Netherlands, Germany—and which has also penetrated the US via the Software Engineering Institute. The English School is named after Cliff Jones, but is not confined to the UK. The Polish School is named after Andrezj Blickle. The Irish School is an offshoot of the Danish School and has borrowed from the other Schools.

To appreciate the distinction between the Schools, one must be familiar with the work of each. Unfortunately, such categorisation tends to give the impression of denomination-alism, schism, etc. If one were to try to pin down the *essential* distinction between the Schools, then the Irish School would unhesitatingly answer that it is distinguished by its philosophy [22]. This tutorial has been designed to give a brief account of the Irish School and in a sense to define it. Consequently, a certain degree of prerequisite familiarity with the *VDM* has been taken for granted in presenting the tutorial material.

5.2 Applied Constructive Mathematics

The School abhors the name 'formal method' because the word 'formal' has acquired connotations in this century with which it would prefer **not** to be associated—formal logic, formal language, formal proof, etc. It would prefer to call itself *the Irish School of (Applied) Constructive Mathematics*, thus forsaking even the VDM tag. But from a pragmatic perspective, 'formal method' currently sells well in (some parts of) industry.

With reference to the middle part of the tutorial, and in particular to the 'simple' temperature chart system, it is evident why Oliveira should assert that "[formal proofs] become a serious bottleneck in development" [25]. The reason is simple. We formal methodists are on the threshold of establishing a branch of mathematics peculiar to computing and at a stage comparable to the beginnings of Geometry. Results are being obtained but not many are prepared to devote the time and effort to analyse them, i.e., establish the theorems and carry out the detailled proofs. There is absolutely no reason to believe that we might proceed at a speed that exceeds the pace of development of comparable results in mathematics. But that is not a reason to give up, nor can it be used as an excuse to forego the deployment of formal methods in industry.

5.3 Specification versus Proof

In industrial application of the Irish School of the VDM most of the effort is focused on the construction of the models—on the specification. The reason is simple—in most cases there are no pre-existing models to which one may refer. We are breaking new ground. However, when we speak of models, we are, of course, referring to the standard models—the counterparts of the partial differential equations.

But we have also discovered that in real applications, specification without proof is fraught with danger. Indeed, it was the single-minded determination to carry out proofs that forced the development of much of the notation (viz., the operator calculus) and style of use of the Irish School of the VDM. Formal logic plays no part here.

At present we may confidently speak about theories such as 'the Theory of Temperature Chart Systems', 'the Theory of Bills of Material', etc., (meaning the standard models which abstract the entities referred to), in much the same way as one might speak about 'the Theory of the Wave Equation'. We are still far removed from anything like a 'Theory of Partial Differential Equations'. However, there is now enough material (within the VDM) to write definitive books on each subject.

5.4 Whither now?

When one considers the complexity of systems in use and in the course of being developed and how few are the formal methodists in number, one is tempted to despair. To achieve some sort of perspective and balance in the midst of developmental chaos, the Irish School has but one motto—"*The results must still be 'true' in 100 years*". The history of Geometry teaches that we ought not to look too far ahead. Finally we note that there is a direct relationship between the ability of the 'students' of the Irish School and the number of errors that they can identify and correct in the technical work of the 'masters'. For, to be able to identify errors, there must be understanding. Even so shall this tutorial be measured.

References

[1] Dines Bjørner. Stepwise transformation of software architectures. In Dines Bjørner and Cliff B. Jones, editors, *Formal Specification & Software Development*, chapter 11, pages 353–77. Prentice/Hall International, Englewood Cliffs, New Jersey, 1982.

[2] Dines Bjørner. *Software Architectures and Programming Systems Design, Vol. II. Basic Abstraction Principles.* Department of Computer Science, Technical University of Denmark, Lyngby, Denmark, September 1988. The material constituted the Lecture Notes of Dines Bjørner for the CEC sponsored VDM'88 Symposium Tutorial, Trinity College, Dublin, Ireland. It is a draft of a publication to appear.

[3] Dines Bjørner and Cliff B. Jones, editors. *The Vienna Development Method: The Meta-Language, Lecture Notes in Computer Science 61.* Springer-Verlag, Berlin, 1978.

[4] Dines Bjørner and Cliff B. Jones, editors. *Formal Specification and Software Development.* Prentice/Hall International, Englewood Cliffs, New Jersey, 1982.

[5] G. Pólya. *How to Solve It, A New Aspect of Mathematical Method.* Princeton University Press, second edition, 1957.

[6] Alfred V. Aho, John E. Hopcroft, and Jeffrey D. Ullman. *The Design and Analysis of Computer Algorithms.* Addison-Wesley Publishing Company, Reading, Massachusetts, 1974.

[7] Douglas Bridges and Osvald Demuth. On the Lebesgue Measurability of Continuous Functions in Constructive Analysis. *BULLETIN (New Series) of the American Mathematical Society*, 24(2):259–76, April 1991.

[8] Antoni Diller. *Z: An Introduction to Formal Methods.* John Wiley & Sons, Chichester, England, 1990.

[9] Samuel Eilenberg. *Automata, Languages, and Machines, Volume A.* Academic Press, New York, 1974.

[10] Samuel Eilenberg. *Automata, Languages, and Machines, Volume B.* Academic Press, New York, 1976.

[11] Shimon Even. *Graph Algorithms.* Computer Science Press, Inc., 9125 Fall River Lane, Potomac, Maryland, 1979.

[12] Heinrich W. Guggenheimer. *Differential Geometry.* Constable and Company, Ltd., London, 1963. The 1977 Dover edition is cited.

[13] Sir Thomas Heath. *A History of Greek Mathematics, Volume I: From Thales to Euclid.* Clarendon Press, Oxford, 1921. The Dover Publications 1981 reprint is cited.

[14] Sir Thomas Heath. *A History of Greek Mathematics, Volume II: From Aristarchus to Diophantus.* Clarendon Press, Oxford, 1921. The Dover Publications 1981 reprint is cited.

[15] Cliff B. Jones. *Software Development: A Rigorous Approach.* Prentice-Hall International, London, 1980.

[16] Cliff B. Jones. Modelling concepts of programming languages. In Dines Bjørner and Cliff B. Jones, editors, *Formal Specification & Software Development*, chapter 4, pages 85–123. Prentice/Hall International, Englewood Cliffs, New Jersey, 1982.

[17] Immanuel Kant. *Critique of Pure Reason.* Macmillan Education, Ltd., London, 1781, 1787. Translated from the German by Norman Kemp Smith, 1921.

[18] Rudolfus Kassel, editor. *ARISTOTELIS DE ARTE POETICA LIBER.* Oxford University Press, Oxford, 1965.

[19] Morris Kline. *Mathematical Thought from Ancient to Modern Times.* Oxford University Press, Oxford, 1972.

[20] Imre Lakatos. *Proofs and Refutations: The Logic of Mathematical Discovery.* Cambridge University Press, 1976. Edited by John Worrall and Elie Zahar.

[21] Mícheál Mac an Airchinnigh. Mathematical Structures and their Morphisms in *Meta–IV*. In D. Bjørner, C. B. Jones, M. Mac an Airchinnigh, and E. J. Neuhold, editors, *VDM'87, VDM—A Formal Method at Work, Lecture Notes in Computer Science* **252**, pages 287–320. Springer-Verlag, Berlin, 1987.

[22] Mícheál Mac an Airchinnigh. *Conceptual Models and Computing.* Department of Computer Science, Trinity College, Dublin, Ireland, 1990.

[23] Robert Matthews. The Chip with a sting in its tale. *New Scientist*, (1777):20–1, 13 July 1991.

[24] T. Nishizeki and N. Chiba. *Planar Graphs: Theory and Algorithms.* North-Holland, Amsterdam, 1988.

[25] J. N. Oliveira. A Reification Calculus for Model-Oriented Software Specification. *Formal Aspects of Computing*, 2(1):1–23, 1990.

[26] Joseph E. Stoy. Foundations of Denotational Semantics. In Dines Bjørner, editor, *Abstract Software Specifications, Lecture Notes in Computer Science* **86**, pages 43–99. Springer-Verlag, Berlin, 1980.

[27] Joseph E. Stoy. Mathematical Foundations. In Dines Bjørner and Cliff B. Jones, editors, *Formal Specification and Software Development*, pages 47–81. Prentice/Hall International, Englewood Cliffs, New Jersey, 1982.

[28] Robert Tarjan. Depth-first search and linear graph algorithms. *SIAM Journal on Computing*, 1(2):146–160, June 1972.

[29] Andrzej Tarlecki and Morten Wieth. A Naive Domain Universe for *VDM*. In D. Bjørner, C. A. R. Hoare, and H. Langmaack, editors, *VDM '90, VDM and Z — Formal Methods in Software Development, Lecture Notes in Computer Science* **428**, pages 552–79. Springer-Verlag, Berlin, 1990.

[30] Thomas E. Vollmann, William L. Berry, and D. Clay Whybark. *Manufacturing Planning and Control Systems*. Richard D. Irwin, Ltd., Homewood, Illinois, 1984.

The RAISE Specification Language
A Tutorial

Chris George

CRI A/S*

1 The RAISE background

RAISE — Rigorous Approach to Industrial Software Engineering — was an ESPRIT project running from 1985 to 1990 and consuming about 120 person years of effort. Dansk Datamatik Center (taken over by Computer Resources International in 1988) were the main contractor. STC Technology (now BNR Europe) were the second partner producing the RAISE technology. Nordisk Brown Boveri (now SYPRO) and part of ICL (now owned by Fujitsu) were involved mainly as industrial trialists. The aim of RAISE was to produce a method for the rigorous development of software, based on a wide spectrum specification language, with accompanying tools and technology transfer material.

The main inspiration at the start of the RAISE project was VDM, which was seen as having two major deficiencies. It lacked modularity and it could not deal with concurrency.

There was also what was then seen as a completely different approach, the algebraic. This differed from the model based approach of VDM and Z both in terms of how things were specified but also in how the specification language was given a semantics. It was not at all clear how the two could be combined. Doing so was a major achievement of the RAISE Specification Language — RSL.

The modularity in RSL is largely inspired by the algebraic languages (CLEAR, ASL, etc.). Concurrency is based on process algebras — close to CSP and CCS, but with the interlock operator.

And, of course, it was high time there were some decent tools!

RSL is a 'wide spectrum' language. This means that it has features allowing its use for very abstract, initial specifications and also for more concrete developments of initial specifications that can be easily (or even automatically) translated into a programming language.

We originally wanted a wide spectrum language so that we stayed within one language, and hence within one semantic framework at all development levels. In fact it turns out

---

*Bregnerødvej 144, DK-3460 Birkerød, Denmark. e-mail: cwg@csd.cri.dk

that the ability to mix styles at the same development level, and even within the same module, is very useful.

This tutorial introduces RSL in four parts — applicative, imperative, concurrent, and modular. It is necessarily incomplete — a comprehensive tutorial on RSL can be found in [Rlg91], which also provides a reference section giving the syntax and describing informally the well-formedness rules and semantics. There is then a section on the RAISE method and finally a brief description of the RAISE tools.

An overview of RAISE can be found in [ErP91].

2 Applicative specifications

2.1 Basic concepts

We first introduce some basic concepts, mainly through an example RSL specification of a database for registering voters at an election. The following specification allows people to register as voters and for it to be checked whether a person is registered:

DATABASE =
  class
    type
      Person,
      Database = Person-**set**
    value
      empty : Database,
      register : Person × Database → Database,
      check : Person × Database → **Bool**
    axiom
      empty ≡ {},
      ∀ p : Person, db : Database • register(p,db) ≡ {p} ∪ db,
      ∀ p : Person, db : Database • check(p,db) ≡ p ∈ db
  end

2.1.1 Modules

A simple module definition has the form:

  id =
    class
      declarations
    end

where a declaration may begin with a keyword (**type, value, axiom**) indicating the kind of declaration to come, followed by one or more definitions of that kind. So *DATABASE* defines the types *Person* and *Database*, the values *empty* (a constant), *register* (a function) and *check* (a function) and three axioms.

2.1.2 Type declarations

A type is a set of logically related values together with a number of predefined value literals (representing values), and predefined value operators (representing function values) for generating and manipulating these values.

An example of a built-in (i.e. predefined) type is **Nat**. It contains all the natural numbers represented by the literals: 0,1,2,.... Among the predefined operators which can be applied to natural numbers is the addition operator +, so value expressions like '5 + 7' of type **Nat** can be written.

In addition to the built-in types, one is allowed to define one's own types. In our example specification there are two such definitions, for *Person* and for *Database*.

Person is defined merely by presenting it as a new type identifier, which defines *Person* as an abstract type. This is a type with no predefined operators for generating and manipulating its values, except for = and ≠. Such a type is also called a 'sort'.

Every type has an 'equal' operator = and a 'not equal' operator ≠, which are applicable to values of the type.

The fact that *Person* is defined as an abstract type reflects the requirements, where no information is given about how people are identified in terms of their name and the like. We abstract from such details.

The definition for the type *Database* equates it to the type expression *Person*-**set**. This is an abbreviation definition where the name *Database* is specified to be an abbreviation for the type *Person*-**set**.

We could have chosen another representation for the database, but modelling it as a set seems natural since the order of registration is irrelevant and no person may be registered more than once.

2.1.3 Value declarations

In our example specification there are three value definitions. Each of them gives the name of a value and its type.

The first value definition defines the constant value *empty* of the type *Database*. This value simply represents the empty database.

The actual value that the identifier *empty* represents is not described in the value definition, but instead in one of the axioms. Likewise for the other value identifiers.

The second value definition defines the function *register* that adds a person to the database. Suppose the "current" database is *db* and that we want to register the person *Hamid*, then *register(Hamid, db)* represents the database after having made the registration.

The type of *register* is represented by the type expression
Person × *Database* → *Database*.

This type expression is built up by applying two type operators (like the -**set** operator used for defining *Database*) × and →. The first binds more tightly, so in this type expression the type operator × (Cartesian product) is applied to the pair *Person* and *Database*, and the type operator → (function space) is applied to the pair consisting of the resulting Cartesian product and *Database*.

The third value definition defines the function *check*, that when applied to a person and a database, returns a Boolean value within the built-in type **Bool**. This type contains two values represented by the literals **true** and **false**. The function is supposed to return **true** if and only if the person is registered in the database.

Until now we have only explained how values are defined by giving their name and type. In the next section, we shall see how the actual values that value names represent can be characterized by axioms.

To summarize, in the simple case which we consider here, a module provides zero or more named types together with zero or more named values.

2.1.4 Axiom declarations

Axioms express properties of value names. In our example there are three axioms. The first axiom defines the name *empty* to represent the empty set (of people).

Note the use of the symbol ≡ (equivalence) instead of = (equality). These two operators have almost the same meaning in applicative contexts, but their meanings are fundamentally different in state-based and concurrency-based contexts (see section 3.1.6 and section 4.1.9). For reasons of consistency the ≡ symbol will normally be used as the "outermost comparing operator" in axioms.

The second axiom in our example expresses that the function *register* adds a person *p* to a database *db* by making the set union of the database, which is a set, and the singleton set containing the person.

The axiom is a quantified expression reading as follows: for all people *p* and for all databases *db*, *register* applied to the pair *(p,db)* must be equivalent to $\{p\} \cup db$.

The third axiom defines the function *check*. A person is registered if that person belongs to the set representing the database.

The collection of axioms is complete in the sense that for each value identifier the axioms state exactly what value within its type each identifier represents. Thus, for example, *empty* is defined to represent nothing but the empty set. Likewise, the function *register* represents the one and only function that adds its first argument to its second argument.

Axioms do, however, not need to be complete. The ultimate extreme is the situation where there are no axioms at all. In that case the value identifier may represent any value within its type.

An example of an incomplete axiom is the following. Suppose that we want to re-specify the function *check* in such a way that it returns **true** for any person *p* and database *db* if *p* is in the database and, possibly, some additional condition is satisfied. This can be expressed with the following axiom:

axiom
  ∀ p : Person, db : Database • check(p,db) ⇒ p ∈ db

The axiom says that for every person *p* and for all databases *db*, if the predicate *check(p,db)* holds, then $p \in db$.

This axiom is incomplete since several *check* functions within
Person × Database → **Bool** satisfy it. One such function is the one originally specified by the axiom:

axiom
   ∀ p : Person, db : Database • check(p,db) ≡ p ∈ db

Another function is one that satisfies the following axiom:

axiom
   ∀ p : Person, db : Database • check(p,db) ≡ p ∈ db ∧ old_enough(p)

Here the function *old_enough* is supposed to return **true** if a person is old enough to vote, according to some rule.

An identifier that is not completely specified through the axioms is said to be under-specified.

Axioms may be named for documentation purposes and for reference in proofs. The axioms defining *empty*, *register* and *check* can for example be written as follows, where axiom names bracketed with [and] precede the axioms:

axiom
   [empty_axiom]
      empty ≡ {},
   [register_axiom]
      ∀ p : Person, db : Database • register(p,db) ≡ {p} ∪ db,
   [check_axiom]
      ∀ p : Person, db : Database • check(p,db) ≡ p ∈ db

2.1.5 Combining value and axiom declarations

RSL provides shorthands for combining value and axiom declarations when the axioms have particular forms. We could, for example, have defined the constant *empty* as follows:

value
   empty : Database = {}

This is an explicit definition. We can also give implicit definitions, such as

value
   empty : Database • empty ⊆ {}

It turns out that the condition here is strong enough to define *empty* uniquely, but of course this is not generally the case.

2.2 Built-in types

Three kinds of types have been presented: built-in types, like **Nat**, abstract types (sorts), like *Person*, and compound types, like *Database*, which was defined as containing sets of *Persons*.

In this section all the built-in types provided by RSL are introduced. These are represented by the type literals: **Bool** (Booleans), **Int** (integers), **Nat** (natural numbers), **Real** (real numbers), **Char** (characters), **Text** (texts) and **Unit** (the singleton type).

For each built-in type, the value literals and the operators associated with that type are described. Note that every type has an 'equal' operator = and a 'not equal' operator ≠. These two operators will not be described further.

2.2.1 Booleans

The Boolean type literal **Bool** represents the type containing the two truth values **true** and **false**.

If expressions If expressions choose between the evaluation of two alternatives, the choice depending on a Boolean expression. For example:

if x > y **then** x − y **else** y − x **end**

The two expressions **then** and **else** must have the same type which is also the type of the whole if expression.

Often one may want to nest if expressions, and a shorthand syntax allows us to write:

if x < 0 **then** x − 1
elsif x > 0 **then** x + 1
else 0
end

Connectives No operators other than = and ≠ are defined on **Bool**. Instead, a number of connectives are defined, which together with their Boolean argument expressions are short for certain if expressions. The only prefix connective is ~, which is negation. The infix connectives are ∧ (and), ∨ (or) and ⇒ (implies). These are defined by the following equivalences:

~e ≡ **if** e **then false else true end**
e ∧ e′ ≡ **if** e **then** e′ **else false end**
e ∨ e′ ≡ **if** e **then true else** e′ **end**
e ⇒ e′ ≡ **if** e **then** e′ **else true end**

This gives a 'conditional logic' for RSL that agrees with classical logic for defined values but also allows possibly undefined values to cause no ill effects when used sensibly. Consider for example the following expression where x and *epsilon* are real numbers:

$(x \neq 0.0) \land (1.0/x < \text{epsilon})$

and suppose that $x=0.0$. The evaluation of the constituent expression $1.0/x$ is under-specified since 'real division' has the pre-condition that the second argument must be different from zero (0.0). (It is under-specified in RSL because we have no idea what a program language might do with it. It might raise an exception. Its behaviour might be quite arbitrary. It might even not terminate.) Fortunately, with the interpretation of $\land$ in terms of an if expression, this constituent expression will never be evaluated when $x=0.0$.

The meanings of the Boolean infix connectives (and in particular their meanings when applied to RSL's non-terminating value **chaos**) are summarized in the following truth tables. The left column in each table indicates the left argument of the connective whilst the top row indicates the right argument.

$\land$	true	false	chaos
true	true	false	chaos
false	false	false	false
chaos	chaos	chaos	chaos

$\lor$	true	false	chaos
true	true	true	true
false	true	false	chaos
chaos	chaos	chaos	chaos

$\Rightarrow$	true	false	chaos
true	true	false	chaos
false	true	true	true
chaos	chaos	chaos	chaos

Quantifiers   The following expression is an example of a quantified expression:

$\forall x : \textbf{Nat} \cdot (x = 0) \lor (x > 0)$

and it reads: "for all natural numbers x, either x is equal to 0 or x is greater than 0".

The quantifier $\forall$ binds the identifier x, and the x immediately following $\forall$ is called a binding. The $x : \textbf{Nat}$ is called a typing.

We say that x is "bound" within the quantified expression. On the other hand, x is "free" within the expression $(x = 0) \lor (x > 0)$

A quantifier is one of $\forall$, $\exists$ and $\exists!$, read as 'for all', 'there exists' and 'there exists exactly one'.

Axiom quantifications Sometimes several axioms within an axiom declaration are quantified over a common set of value names as is the case in our election *DATABASE* module. One may instead make an 'axiom quantification' as follows:

>**axiom forall** p : Person, db : Database •
>   empty ≡ {},
>   register(p,db) ≡ {p} ∪ db,
>   check(p,db) ≡ p ∈ db

2.2.2 Integers

The integer type literal **Int** represents the type containing the negative as well as non-negative whole numbers.

Operators The signatures of the operators for integers are

>abs : Int → Int
>\> : Int × Int → **Bool**
>< : Int × Int → **Bool**
>≥ : Int × Int → **Bool**
>≤ : Int × Int → **Bool**
>\+ : Int × Int → **Int**
>− : Int × Int → **Int**
>∗ : Int × Int → **Int**
>/ : Int × Int $\xrightarrow{\sim}$ **Int**
>\ : Int × Int $\xrightarrow{\sim}$ **Int**
>↑ : Int × Int $\xrightarrow{\sim}$ **Int**

There is one prefix operator **abs** for taking the 'absolute value' of an integer; the others are all binary infix operators.

The relational operators $>, \geq, <, \leq$ and the arithmetic operators $+, -, *$ and are all standard from mathematics.

/ is 'integer division' so that, for example, $5/2 = 2$. \ is 'integer remainder' so that, for example, $5\backslash 3 = 2$. These are both partial — they are under-specified if the second argument is zero. ↑ is exponentiation. It is partial — it is under-specified if the second argument is negative or if both arguments are zero.

2.2.3 Natural numbers

The natural number type literal **Nat** is a subtype of the integer type (i.e. all **Nats** are **Ints**). Consequently, all the integer operators are defined for natural numbers.

2.2.4 Real numbers

The real number type literal **Real** represents the type containing the (mathematical) real numbers, like *0.0* and *3.14*. Note that real number literals must be written with a decimal point.

Conversion operators The integer type is not considered a subtype of the real number type, in contrast to the natural number type which is a subtype of the integer type. One set of operators is thus defined for the integers (section 2.2.2) and another set of operators is defined for the reals (see below). There is for example both an 'integer addition' operator and a 'real addition' operator.

Since the two worlds are separated and since there will typically be a need in calculations to switch from one world to the other, two conversion operators **int** (real to integer) and **real** (integer to real) are defined. The **int** operator returns the nearest integer towards zero.

Other operators The other operators for reals have types as follows:

abs : **Real** $\rightarrow$ **Real**
$>$: **Real** $\times$ **Real** $\rightarrow$ **Bool**
$<$: **Real** $\times$ **Real** $\rightarrow$ **Bool**
$\geq$: **Real** $\times$ **Real** $\rightarrow$ **Bool**
$\leq$: **Real** $\times$ **Real** $\rightarrow$ **Bool**
$+$: **Real** $\times$ **Real** $\rightarrow$ **Real**
$-$: **Real** $\times$ **Real** $\rightarrow$ **Real**
$*$: **Real** $\times$ **Real** $\rightarrow$ **Real**
$/$: **Real** $\times$ **Real** $\overset{\sim}{\rightarrow}$ **Real**
$\uparrow$: **Real** $\times$ **Real** $\overset{\sim}{\rightarrow}$ **Real**

Note that the 'real division' performs the traditional arithmetic division without truncation.

The real exponentiation operator is partial in that its result is under-specified if the first argument is zero and the second argument is not positive, or if the first argument is negative and the second argument is not a whole number.

2.2.5 Characters

The character type literal **Char** represents the type containing the characters 'A','B',...,'a','b',.... Note that a character begins and ends with '.

2.2.6 Texts

The text type literal **Text** represents the type containing strings of characters. A text begins and ends with ", such as "this is a text".

2.2.7 The unit type

The unit type literal **Unit** represents the type containing the single value '()'. It might appear strange to have a type with only one value. It is, however, quite useful when dealing with imperative and concurrent specifications, as we shall see later.

2.3 Products

A product is an ordered finite collection of values of possibly different types, such as (1,true,"John"), which has type **Int** × **Bool** × **Text**. This type contains all triples whose first element is an integer, second is a Boolean and third is a text.

2.4 Bindings and typings

In this section we develop further the concepts of binding and typing. The concepts were briefly introduced in connection with quantified Boolean expressions (section 2.2.1) and they will be used extensively later. As an example, consider the quantified expression:

$$\forall\, x : \textbf{Nat} \cdot (x = 0) \lor (x > 0)$$

The $x : $ **Nat** following $\forall$ is a typing consisting of the binding x and the type expression **Nat**.

2.4.1 Bindings

A binding is a structure of identifiers, possibly grouped by parentheses, like x, (x), (x,y). The purpose of bindings is to give names to values, extended to giving names to sub-components of product values. That is, a value can be matched against a binding, resulting in a collection of definitions.

The matching of values against bindings takes place for example in a let expression, such as:

$$\text{let } (x,y) = v \text{ in } x + 1 \text{ end}$$

The value v is matched against the binding (x,y) before the expression $x+1$ is evaluated. If v is the value $(1,(\textbf{true},\textbf{false}))$ then the let expression would evaluate to 2.

Let expressions will be explained in more detail in section 2.12.

The value $(1,(\textbf{true},\textbf{false}))$ can be matched against any of the bindings x, (x,y) and $(x,(y,z))$.

2.4.2 Single typings

Examples of single typings are:

$$x : \textbf{Int} \times (\textbf{Bool} \times \textbf{Bool})$$
$$(x,y) : \textbf{Int} \times (\textbf{Bool} \times \textbf{Bool})$$
$$(x,(y,z)) : \textbf{Int} \times (\textbf{Bool} \times \textbf{Bool})$$

In each case a binding is given a type, associating identifiers with types in the obvious way. In the second single typing above, x is associated with **Int** while y is associated with **Bool** × **Bool**. A single typing is thus a way of defining identifiers together with their types.

2.4.3 Multiple typings

A multiple typing is a shorthand for associating the same type with more than one binding. For example, the following two typings (the first multiple, the second single) are equivalent:

y,z : **Bool**
(y,z) : **Bool** × **Bool**

2.4.4 Typing lists

It is often convenient to associate several identifiers with various types at the same time. Typing lists are lists of single and multiple typings that are equivalent to single typings. For example, the typing list

x : **Int**, y,z : **Bool**

is equivalent to (but easier to write and read than):

(x, (y, z)) : **Int** × (**Bool** × **Bool**)

2.5 Functions

A function is essentially a mapping from values of one type to values of another type. A function, say f, that maps values of a type T_1 to values of a type T_2 is total if for every value in T_1, f returns a value in T_2. A function is partial, if there exist values within T_1 for which f might not return values in T_2. The type of a total function is written $T_1 \rightarrow T_2$ and the type of a partial function is written $T_1 \overset{\sim}{\rightarrow} T_2$.

The properties of functions may be defined in a variety of styles, with abstract property oriented styles at one end of the spectrum, and concrete algorithm oriented styles at the other.

2.5.1 Definitions by axioms

For the purpose of illustration we choose one example which we specify in several ways in order to show different possibilities. The function has the signature (name and type):

value fraction : **Real** → **Real**

and is supposed to return *1.0/x* for any real number argument $x \neq 0.0$, and to return *0.0* for the argument *x=0.0*. A first solution is:

axiom
    $\forall$ x : **Real** • fraction(x) ≡ **if** x = 0.0 **then** 0.0 **else** 1.0/x **end**

Alternatively one could define the function through two axioms, one for the zero case and one for the non-zero case:

axiom
 fraction(0.0) $\equiv$ 0.0,
 $\forall$ x : **Real** • x $\neq$ 0.0 $\Rightarrow$ (fraction(x) $\equiv$ 1.0/x)

2.5.2 Explicit function definitions

A shorter way of writing the function signature and single axiom is called an explicit function definition:

value
 fraction : **Real** $\rightarrow$ **Real**
 fraction(x) $\equiv$ **if** x = 0.0 **then** 0.0 **else** 1.0/x **end**

Suppose that we make the *fraction* function partial at zero. That is, we do not specify how the function behaves for the argument *x=0.0*. This can be done as follows:

value
 partial_fraction : **Real** $\xrightarrow{\sim}$ **Real**
 partial_fraction(x) $\equiv$ 1.0/x
 pre x $\neq$ 0.0

This is an explicit function definition with a pre-condition following the keyword **pre**. Note that the pre-condition does not say that the function must be undefined when the pre-condition is false; it only says that we may not use its definition to deduce any properties of the function when it is false. It might return some particular value; it might not terminate. Hence partial functions are potentially partial rather than necessarily so (which means that they may be implemented by total functions).

2.5.3 Function expressions

Another possibility is to use a function expression (or lambda abstraction):

value fraction : **Real** $\rightarrow$ **Real**
axiom
 fraction $\equiv$ λ x : **Real** • **if** x = 0.0 **then** 0.0 **else** 1.0/x **end**

2.5.4 Higher order functions

Since function types are just like other types, a function can in particular take a function as parameter and return a function as result. Consider for example the definition:

value
    twice : (Int $\overset{\sim}{\rightarrow}$ Int) $\rightarrow$ Int $\overset{\sim}{\rightarrow}$ Int
    twice(f) $\equiv \lambda$ i : Int • f(f(i))

Function arrows associate to the right, so the type of *twice* could instead have been written:

    twice : (Int $\overset{\sim}{\rightarrow}$ Int) $\rightarrow$ (Int $\overset{\sim}{\rightarrow}$ Int)

The function *twice* when applied to a function f returns a function (represented by the function expression) that when applied to an integer i applies f twice.
    Some examples of *twice* applications are:

    twice(λ i : Int • i + 1) = λ i : Int • i + 2
    twice(λ i : Int • i + 1)(1) = 3

Note that *twice* can be applied to only one argument (as in the first expression) when it will return a function.
    We do not need to use a function expression to define *twice*. We can also write an axiom like:

axiom
    $\forall$ f : Int $\overset{\sim}{\rightarrow}$ Int, i : Int • twice(f)(i) $\equiv$ f(f(i))

In yet another way of defining *twice* we could use the built-in operator $\circ$ for function composition. For arbitrary types T_1, T_2 and T_3 this has the type:

    $\circ$: $(T_2 \overset{\sim}{\rightarrow} T_3) \times (T_1 \overset{\sim}{\rightarrow} T_2) \rightarrow T_1 \overset{\sim}{\rightarrow} T_3$

2.5.5 Implicit definition of functions

The function definitions given so far have all been algorithmic in the sense that they suggest a strategy for constructing an answer. Function definitions can also be more predicative in the sense of just saying what properties the result must have, based on the arguments.
    Consider the following specification of the square-root function:

value
    square_root : **Real** $\overset{\sim}{\rightarrow}$ **Real**
    square_root(x) **as** s
        post s * s = x $\wedge$ s $\geq$ 0.0
        pre x $\geq$ 0.0

The function *square_root* is only necessarily defined for non-negative real numbers as expressed by **Real** and the pre-condition following **pre**.

When applied to a non-negative real x it returns a value, call it s, that satisfies the post-condition following **post**.

Note that if we had omitted the condition that the result s be non-negative, *square_root* would have been under-specified. Functions defined by post conditions are often under-specified, just like implicit value definitions. Part of the art of specification is never saying more than you need to, to allow room for the developer to make appropriate decisions later. Premature decisions are likely to be less than optimal.

2.5.6 Algebraic definition of functions

RSL also allows for a more "algebraic" style of function definition. Consider the specification of integer lists. A list is an ordered sequence of elements. One can construct a new list by adding an element to an old list. The added element is referred to as the head of the new list while the old list contained in the new list is referred to as the tail.

```
LIST =
  class
    type List
    value
      empty : List,
      add : Int × List → List,
      head : List ⇢ Int,
      tail : List ⇢ List
    axiom forall i : Int, l : List •
      [head_add]
        head(add(i,l)) ≡ i,
      [tail_add]
        tail(add(i,l)) ≡ l
  end
```

The *List* type is given as an abstract type since we do not explicitly say how lists are represented.

If the *empty* constant were not there, we would not be able to write any list expressions. For example, the list of numbers from 1 to 3 is expressed as
add(1,add(2,add(3,empty))).

The *head* and *tail* functions are partial in that they are not necessarily defined for the empty list. This is reflected in the axioms where nothing is said about *head(empty)* and *tail(empty)*.

The *head_add* axiom says that adding an element i to a list and then taking the head gives the element i.

The *tail_add* axiom says that adding an element to a list l and then taking the tail gives the original list l.

So we have as a consequence of these axioms:

head(add(1,add(2,add(3,empty)))) $\equiv$ 1
tail(add(1,add(2,add(3,empty)))) $\equiv$ add(2,add(3,empty))

2.5.7 Example: A Database

Consider the specification of a database. The database associates unique keys with data. That is, a key is associated with at most one data element in the database. The database should provide the following functions:

- *insert* which associates a key with a data element in the database. If the key already is associated with a data element the new association overrides the old.

- *remove* which removes an association between a key and a data element.

- *defined* which checks whether a key is associated with a data element.

- *lookup* which returns the data element associated with a particular key.

The specification of this can be given in terms of algebraic function definitions.

DATABASE =
  class
    type
      Database,
      Key, Data
    value
      empty : Database,
      insert : Key $\times$ Data $\times$ Database $\to$ Database,
      remove : Key $\times$ Database $\to$ Database,
      defined : Key $\times$ Database $\to$ **Bool**,
      lookup : Key $\times$ Database $\overset{\sim}{\to}$ Data
    axiom forall k, k_1 : Key, d : Data, db : Database •
      [remove_empty]
        remove(k,empty) $\equiv$ empty,
      [remove_insert]
        remove(k,insert(k_1,d,db)) $\equiv$
          if $k = k_1$ **then** remove(k,db) **else** insert(k_1,d,remove(k,db)) **end**,
      [defined_empty]
        defined(k,empty) $\equiv$ **false**,
      [defined_insert]
        defined(k,insert(k_1,d,db)) $\equiv$ $k = k_1$ $\vee$ defined(k,db),
      [lookup_insert]
        lookup(k,insert(k_1,d,db)) $\equiv$ **if** $k = k_1$ **then** d **else** lookup(k,db) **end**
        pre $k = k_1$ $\vee$ defined(k,db)
  end

The *Database* type is given as an abstract type since we do not want to say anything about how databases are represented. Likewise, nothing is said about keys and data.

The *lookup* function is partial and is under-specified when applied to a key and a database not associating that key with a data element. There is only one axiom for *lookup*, namely *lookup_insert*, and that only applies when its pre-condition is satisfied. There is no axiom *lookup_empty* and hence the value of *lookup(k,empty)* is under-specified.

The *remove_insert* axiom is the most elaborate of the axioms. The right hand side is an if expression with two branches.

- If the key k to be removed equals the inserted key k_1, then the association of k with d is removed and the *remove* function is applied recursively to the rest. This recursive call may seem strange since one could argue that a key is at most associated with one data element and therefore only needs to be removed once. A simpler axiom would be:

  remove(k,insert(k_1,d,db)) $\equiv$ **if** k = k_1 **then** db **else** ... **end**

  This is, however, wrong. We have quantified *db* over *Database* and therefore *db* can be any database, especially one associating k with some data element.

- If the key k to be removed does not equal the inserted key k_1, then k must be removed from the remaining database. The succeeding association of k_1 with d is necessary to keep that association.

The database example illustrates a useful technique for "inventing" axioms. The technique can be characterized as follows.

1. Identify the constructors by which any database can be constructed. These are the constant *empty* and the function *insert*. Any database can thus be represented by an expression of the form:

   insert(k_1,d_1,insert(k_2,d_2,... insert(k_n,d_n,empty)...))

2. Define the remaining functions "by case" over the constructors using new identifiers as parameters. In the above axioms, *remove*, *defined* and *lookup* are defined over the two constructor expressions:

   empty
   insert(k_1, d, db)

We thus get "for free" all the left hand sides of the axioms that we need. That is:

```
remove(k,empty)
remove(k,insert(k₁,d,db))
defined(k,empty)
defined(k,insert(k₁,d,db))
lookup(k,empty)
lookup(k,insert(k₁,d,db))
```

Note, however, that we choose to make *lookup* partial; we do not include an axiom with left hand side *lookup(k,empty)* and the axiom *lookup_insert* has a precondition — it only applies to defined keys.

The list axioms (section 2.5.6) have the same form. The technique is useful in many applications, but there are of course applications where one must be more inventive when writing axioms.

2.6 Sets

A set is an unordered collection of distinct values of the same type, such as the integer set $\{1,3,5\}$.

2.6.1 Set type expressions

Both finite set types (like **Int-set**) and possibly infinite set types (like **Int-infset**) can be expressed in RSL.

In general, for any type T, T-**set** is a subtype of T-**infset**. So all the sets belonging to **Nat-set** belong to **Nat-infset** as well.

2.6.2 Set value expressions

A set may be written by explicitly enumerating its members, as in $\{\}$, $\{1,3,5\}$ or $\{1,3,5,3\}$ (where the last two represent the same set).

A set can be defined implicitly by giving a predicate which defines the members. An example of such a comprehended set expression is:

$$\{2*n \mid n : \mathbf{Nat} \cdot n \leq 3\} = \{0,2,4,6\}$$

The comprehended set expression reads: "the set of values $2*n$ where n is a natural number such that n is less than or equal to 3".

A ranged set expression represents a set of integers in a range from a lower bound to an upper bound:

$$\{3 .. 7\} = \{3,4,5,6,7\}$$
$$\{3 .. 3\} = \{3\}$$
$$\{3 .. 2\} = \{\}$$

2.6.3 Infix operators

Basic operators on sets are the 'test for membership' and its negated version. Let T be an arbitrary type, then the signatures of these two operators are:

$\in$: T × T-infset → **Bool**
$\notin$: T × T-infset → **Bool**
Examples:
  $1 \in \{2,1\}$ = **true**
  $3 \notin \{2,1\}$ = **true**

A new set can be composed from two other sets by taking their 'union', 'intersection' or 'difference':

$\cup$: T-infset × T-infset → T-infset
$\cap$: T-infset × T-infset → T-infset
$\setminus$: T-infset × T-infset → T-infset
Examples:
  $\{1,2\} \cup \{2,3\} = \{1,2,3\}$
  $\{1,2\} \cap \{2,3\} = \{2\}$
  $\{1,2\} \setminus \{2,3\} = \{1\}$

There are four operators for comparing sets, namely 'subset', 'proper subset', 'superset' and 'proper superset':

$\subseteq$: T-infset × T-infset → **Bool**
$\subset$: T-infset × T-infset → **Bool**
$\supseteq$: T-infset × T-infset → **Bool**
$\supset$: T-infset × T-infset → **Bool**
Examples:
  $\{1,2\} \subseteq \{1,2\}$ = **true**
  $\{1,2\} \subset \{1,2\}$ = **false**
  $\{1,2\} \supseteq \{1,2\}$ = **true**
  $\{1,2\} \supset \{1,2\}$ = **false**

2.6.4 Prefix operators

The 'cardinality' operator returns the size of a finite set, that is, the number of elements contained in the set:

card : T-set → **Nat**
Example:
  card $\{1,3\}$ = 2

The application of **card** to an infinite set gives **chaos**. Note that since the result is **chaos** and not just under-specified, one can always test whether some set s is infinite by writing **card** $s \equiv$ **chaos**.

2.6.5 Example: A Resource Manager

Consider the specification of a resource manager. A number of resources are to be shared between a number of users. A resource manager controls the resources by maintaining a pool (a set) of free resources.

When a user wants a resource, the resource manager *obtains* an arbitrary one from the pool. When the user no longer needs the resource, the manager *releases* it by sending it back to the pool.

RESOURCE_MANAGER =
   class
      type
         Resource,
         Pool = Resource-**set**
      value
         initial : Pool,
         obtain : Pool $\xrightarrow{\sim}$ Pool × Resource,
         release : Resource × Pool $\xrightarrow{\sim}$ Pool
      axiom forall r : Resource, p : Pool •
         obtain(p) **as** (p_1,r_1) **post** $r_1 \in p \land p_1 = p \backslash \{r_1\}$
         pre $p \neq \{\}$,
         release(r,p) $\equiv p \cup \{r\}$
         pre $r \in$ initial$\backslash$p
   end

The *Resource* type is defined as an abstract type since we don't consider here what resources are and how they are identified.

A *Pool* is defined as a set of resources. The *initial* pool is under-specified (as there is no axiom for *initial*).

The definition of *obtain* reads as follows. When applied to a pool p that is non-empty, a pair (p_1,r_1) is returned. The resource r_1 must be a member of the old pool p. The new pool p_1 is equal to the old p except for r_1, which has been removed. Note that it is under-specified which resource is obtained from a pool containing more than one resource.

The *release* function just returns a resource to the pool. The resource must, however, not be free already.

Different styles have been used for defining *obtain* and *release*. An implicit style has been used to define *obtain* since there is no "algorithmic" strategy for selecting a member from a set. We only say that the returned resource must belong to the argument pool.

An explicit style has been used for defining *release* since RSL provides the union operator $\cup$ which represents the intended behaviour.

2.6.6 Example: A Database

Consider a set version of the database algebraically specified in section 2.5.7.

```
SET_DATABASE =
   class
      type
         Record = Key × Data,
         Database = Record-set,
         Key, Data
      value
         is_wf_Database : Database → Bool,
         empty : Database,
         insert : Key × Data × Database ⥲ Database,
         remove : Key × Database ⥲ Database,
         defined : Key × Database ⥲ Bool,
         lookup : Key × Database ⥲ Data
      axiom forall k : Key, d : Data, db : Database •
         is_wf_Database(db) ≡
            (∀ k : Key, d₁,d₂ : Data •
               ((k,d₁) ∈ db ∧ (k,d₂) ∈ db) ⇒ d₁ = d₂),
         empty ≡ {},
         insert(k,d,db) ≡ remove(k,db) ∪ {(k,d)}
         pre is_wf_Database(db),
         remove(k,db) ≡ db \ {(k,d) | d : Data}
         pre is_wf_Database(db),
         defined(k,db) ≡ (∃ d : Data • (k,d) ∈ db)
         pre is_wf_Database(db),
         lookup(k,db) as d post (k,d) ∈ db
         pre is_wf_Database(db) ∧ defined(k,db)
   end
```

A database is modelled as a set of records, where a record consists of a key and a data element.

Not all databases are "well-formed". We are not interested in those holding more than one record with the same key. The function *is_wf_Database* defines when a database is well-formed. Note that this function is used in the pre-conditions of axioms for the other functions; it is clearly true of the possible results of those functions that return a value of type *Database*. It expresses an intended property of databases which we want the other functions to respect, and which they may rely on. Section 2.9 describes how a type can be defined as a subtype of another type, where the subtype is restricted to only contain the "well-formed" values.

The *empty* database is represented by the empty set.

In order to *insert* a record into the database, one must first remove any existing record with the same key. This is necessary in order to keep the database well-formed.

To *remove* a key corresponds to removing all records containing that key – note that there will be at most one such record.

A key is *defined* if the database contains a record containing that key.

Finally, to *lookup* a key corresponds to finding a data element such that a record containing the key and that data element is in the database.

The set database actually implements the database from section 2.5.7. We do not give a detailed definition of the implementation relation here, but just outline a strategy for proving the implementation.

SET_DATABASE implements *DATABASE* because:

1. *SET_DATABASE* defines all the types that *DATABASE* defines, the only change being that some sorts (*Database*) have been replaced by concrete definitions (*Database* = *Record*-**set**).

2. *SET_DATABASE* defines (with the same signatures) all the constants and functions that are defined by *DATABASE*.

3. All the axioms of *DATABASE* are true in *SET_DATABASE*. As an example consider the *DATABASE* axiom *defined_empty* (ignoring quantification):

   ⌊defined(k,empty) ≡ **false**⌋
unfold empty
   ⌊defined(k,{}) ≡ **false**⌋
unfold defined
   ⌊(∃ d : Data • (k,d) ∈ {}) ≡ **false**⌋
isin_empty
   ⌊(∃ d : Data • **false**) ≡ **false**⌋
exists_introduction
   ⌊**false** ≡ **false**⌋
is_reflexivity
   ⌊**qed**⌋

So the *DATABASE* axiom *defined_empty* is true in *SET_DATABASE*.

2.7 Lists

A list is an ordered sequence of values of the same type, possibly including duplicates, such as the integer list ⟨1,3,3,1,5⟩.

2.7.1 List type expressions

Both finite list types (like **Int***) and possibly infinite list types (like **Int**$^\omega$) can be expressed in RSL.

In general, for any type T, T^* is a subtype of T^ω. So all the lists belonging to **Nat*** belong to **Nat**$^\omega$ as well.

2.7.2 List value expressions

A list may be written by explicitly enumerating its elements, as in $\langle\rangle$, $\langle 1,1,2\rangle$ or $\langle 1,2,1\rangle$ (where the last two represent different lists)

A ranged list expression represents a list of integers in a range from a lower bound to an upper bound:

$$\langle 3 .. 7\rangle = \langle 3,4,5,6,7\rangle$$
$$\langle 3 .. 3\rangle = \langle 3\rangle$$
$$\langle 3 .. 2\rangle = \langle\rangle$$

A new list can be generated from an old list by applying a function to each member of the old list. An example of such a comprehended list expression is:

$$\langle 2*n \mid n \text{ in } \langle 0 .. 3\rangle \bullet n \neq 2\rangle = \langle 0,2,6\rangle$$

The comprehended list expression reads: "the list of values $2*n$ where n ranges over the list $\langle 0..3\rangle$ provided n is not equal to 2". Note that the ordering of the old list is preserved in the new list.

2.7.3 List indexing

A particular element of a list may be extracted by indexing, where the index must be a natural number between one and the length of the list. For example, $\langle 0,2,4\rangle(3) = 4$.

2.7.4 Infix operators

The 'concatenation' operator concatenates two lists:

$$\hat{\ } : T^* \times T^\omega \to T^\omega$$
Example:
$$\langle 2,3\rangle\hat{\ }\langle 1,3\rangle = \langle 2,3,1,3\rangle$$

Note that the first argument to the concatenation operator must be a finite list (one cannot append anything to the end of an infinite list since it has no end).

2.7.5 Prefix operators

Prefix operators on lists are 'head', 'tail', 'length', 'indices' and 'elements':

$$\textbf{hd} : T^\omega \xrightarrow{\sim} T$$
$$\textbf{tl} : T^\omega \xrightarrow{\sim} T^\omega$$
$$\textbf{len} : T^* \to \textbf{Nat}$$
$$\textbf{inds} : T^\omega \to \textbf{Nat-infset}$$
$$\textbf{elems} : T^\omega \to \textbf{T-infset}$$
Examples:
$$\textbf{hd } \langle 1,2,1\rangle = 1$$

tl $\langle 1,2,1 \rangle = \langle 2,1 \rangle$
len $\langle 1,2,1 \rangle = 3$
inds $\langle 1,2,1 \rangle = \{1,2,3\}$
elems $\langle 1,2,1 \rangle = \{1,2\}$

The head and tail operators are only defined for non-empty list arguments.

The 'length' operator returns the length a finite list. The application of **len** to an infinite list gives **chaos**. Note that since the result is **chaos** and not just under-specified, one can always test whether some list l is infinite by writing **len** $l \equiv$ **chaos**.

2.7.6 Texts are character lists

The type **Text** is really short for **Char***. That is, one can apply all the list operators to text values. Some examples are:

$''\text{abc}'' = \langle 'a','b','c' \rangle$
$'''' = \langle \rangle$
hd $''\text{abc}'' = 'a'$
$''\text{abc}'' \,^\frown\, ''\text{de}'' \,^\frown\, \langle 'f' \rangle = ''\text{abcdef}''$

2.7.7 Example: A Database

Consider a list version of the database from section 2.5.7. The database will now be a list of records, corresponding to the traditional notion of a "sequential file".

To illustrate how a specification can be implementation oriented, we shall in addition require the database to be sorted on keys. For that purpose we must assume a function *less_than* defined on pairs of keys.

The sortedness property can now be utilized when searching for a record with a particular key k: the search is terminated as soon as a key greater than or equal to k is found. If the key found is greater than k, the search has failed. This algorithm saves time (on average) if the key is not contained in the database.

We also make the function *lookup* total (for 'well-formed' databases) by returning an error value when looking up a key not in the database. We therefore define such an error value, named *not_found*.

The types *Key* and *Data* together with the function *less_than* and the constant *not_found* are now defined in a separate module. The decomposition into sub-modules reduces the size, and thereby increases the readability, of each module.

```
KEY_AND_DATA =
    class
        type Key, Data
        value
            not_found : Data,
            less_than : Key × Key → Bool
        axiom forall k,k₁,k₂,k₃ : Key •
```

[anti_reflexive]
~less_than(k,k),
[transitive]
less_than(k_1,k_2) ∧ less_than(k_2,k_3) ⇒ less_than(k_1,k_3),
[total_order]
less_than(k_1,k_2) ∨ less_than(k_2,k_1) ∨ k_1 = k_2
end

The error element *not_found* is under-specified — we do not care about the particular value at this point.

The function *less_than* is supposed to define a strong ordering on keys. If the keys were integers, the ordering could be <. The function is specified through a number of axioms. The reader should check that these axioms actually hold for <.

To specify records, we make an abstraction, "hiding" the fact that they are pairs of keys and data. For that purpose we define functions for generating new records (*new_record*), and for decomposing records (*key_of* and *data_of*).

A new module which is an extension of *KEY_AND_DATA* defines these functions.

RECORD =
  extend KEY_AND_DATA **with**
  class
    type Record = Key × Data
    value
      new_record : Key × Data → Record,
      key_of : Record → Key,
      data_of : Record → Data
    axiom forall k : Key, d : Data •
      new_record(k,d) ≡ (k,d),
      key_of(k,d) ≡ k,
      data_of(k,d) ≡ d
  end

The definition of *new_record* may look strange since it is the identity function, taking a pair and returning a pair. We are, however, able not to bother any more with how records are represented. From now on records are only created and decomposed by these three functions.

It is now time to define the database as a sorted list of records.

LIST_DATABASE =
  extend RECORD **with**
  class
    type Database = Record*
    value
      is_wf_Database : Database → **Bool**,
      empty : Database,

insert : Key × Data × Database $\overset{\sim}{\to}$ Database,
remove : Key × Database $\overset{\sim}{\to}$ Database,
defined : Key × Database $\overset{\sim}{\to}$ **Bool**,
lookup : Key × Database $\overset{\sim}{\to}$ Data

axiom forall k : Key, d : Data, db : Database •
  is_wf_Database(db) ≡
    (∀ r_1,r_2 : Record, db_left,db_right : Database •
      db = db_left ⁀ ⟨r_1,r_2⟩ ⁀ db_right ⇒
        less_than(key_of(r_1),key_of(r_2))),
  empty ≡ ⟨⟩,
  insert(k,d,db) **as** db_1
  post
    elems db_1 = (**elems** remove(k,db)) ∪ {new_record(k,d)} ∧
    is_wf_Database(db_1)
  pre is_wf_Database(db),
  remove(k,db) ≡ ⟨r | r **in** db • key_of(r) ≠ k⟩
  pre is_wf_Database(db),
  defined(k,db) ≡
    if db = ⟨⟩ ∨ less_than(k,key_of(**hd** db)) **then false**
    else key_of(**hd** db) = k ∨ defined(k,**tl** db)
    end
  pre is_wf_Database(db),
  lookup(k,db) ≡
    if db = ⟨⟩ ∨ less_than(k,key_of(**hd** db)) **then** not_found
    elsif key_of(**hd** db) = k **then** data_of(**hd** db)
    else lookup(k,**tl** db)
    end
  pre is_wf_Database(db)
end

A database is well-formed, according to *is_wf_Database*, if for any two successive records, the key of the "left" record is less than the key of the "right" record. Note that this well-formedness condition also prevents duplicate keys, i.e. two records having the same key. This is actually a consequence of the *anti_reflexive* axiom in the module *KEY_AND_DATA*.

The function *insert* is defined implicitly by saying that the result of an insertion must contain the correct set of records and that these in addition must be sorted, without duplicates (according to *is_wf_Database*). Although we are trying to be implementation oriented, the implicit style has been used in the definition of *insert*, since our particular aim at this point is to optimize the function *lookup*.

The function *remove* is defined by a list comprehension expression that removes all the records having the specified key. Note that the result will be well-formed if the database argument is.

The functions *defined* and *lookup* are defined by nearly the same prescription. They search the database sequentially for a key until either the end is reached or a greater key is found or the key is found. This algorithm depends on the database argument being well-formed, so well-formedness is needed in their pre-conditions.

Note in *defined* that due to the conditional interpretation of ∨, the function *defined* will not be applied recursively if the key is found.

In the case of *lookup*, note how the error value *not_found* is returned on failure to find the specified key.

An interesting point to note here is that *LIST_DATABASE* formally implements *DATABASE* from section 2.5.7.

Achieving this implementation relation has been our aim, but at the cost of introducing a problem: the constant *not_found* is a value of type *Data* just like any other value of *Data*. It is therefore possible to insert it into the database by *insert*. This is not the intention and users of *LIST_DATABASE* should not do this. (We could, for example, make sure that calls of *insert* do not have *not_found* as an argument.)

We could have made the function *insert* partial with the pre-condition that the inserted data element should be different from *not_found*. This would, however, destroy the implementation relation: one cannot implement a total function with a partial function and still obtain implementation.

The list database specification above is rather implementation oriented. We could have chosen to give a more abstract specification, still in terms of lists, but without the "sorting". That is to say, one can also use lists for high-level specifications.

2.8   Maps

A map is a table-like structure, very similar to a function, that maps values of one type into values of another type, such as the map from integers to Booleans
$[3 \mapsto \textbf{true}, 5 \mapsto \textbf{false}]$.

Maps are similar to functions in that a map can be applied to a domain value to return the associated range value. The difference between functions and maps lies primarily in the kinds of operators which may be applied. Maps can be viewed as finite or infinite sets of domain/range pairs which may be merged, restricted, augmented, reduced, overridden etc. Functions, on the other hand, may only be composed and applied to arguments: in particular we do not normally expect to change dynamically the set of domain values for which they are defined, or to change the results of applying them to particular domain values.

2.8.1   Map type expressions

The type of maps from T_1 to T_2 is $T_1 \xrightarrow{m} T_2$. A particular map value within this type will have a particular (possibly infinite) set of possible T_1 values as its domain and a (possibly infinite) set of T_2 values as its range.

2.8.2   Map value expressions

A map may be written by explicitly enumerating its associations, as in $[\,]$,
$[3 \mapsto \textbf{true}, 5 \mapsto \textbf{false}]$ or $[5 \mapsto \textbf{false}, 3 \mapsto \textbf{true}]$ (where the last two represent the same map).

A map can be defined implicitly by giving a predicate which defines the associations. An example of such a comprehended map expression is:

$$[n \mapsto 2*n \mid n : \mathbf{Nat} \cdot n \leq 2] = [0 \mapsto 0, 1 \mapsto 2, 2 \mapsto 4]$$

The comprehended map expression reads: "the map from n to $2*n$ where n is a natural number such that n is less than or equal to 2".

It is also possible to create a non-deterministic map. Consider for example:

$$[x \mapsto y \mid x,y : \mathbf{Nat} \cdot \{x,y\} \subseteq \{1,2\}]$$

This map maps 1 to 1 as well as to 2, and similarly for 2. Such maps should be avoided in specifications and we shall generally ignore their existence. It is, however, possible to create them. See section 2.14 for a discussion about non-determinism.

2.8.3 Application of a map

A map can be applied to a value if the value belongs to the domain of the map. For example, $[3 \mapsto \mathbf{true}, 5 \mapsto \mathbf{false}](3)$ evaluates to **true**.

2.8.4 Prefix operators

Prefix operators on maps are the 'domain' and 'range' operators:

$\mathbf{dom} : (T_1 \overset{m}{\to} T_2) \to T_1\text{-}\mathbf{infset}$
$\mathbf{rng} : (T_1 \overset{m}{\to} T_2) \to T_2\text{-}\mathbf{infset}$
Examples:
$\mathbf{dom} [3 \mapsto \mathbf{true}, 5 \mapsto \mathbf{false}] = \{3,5\}$
$\mathbf{rng} [3 \mapsto \mathbf{true}, 5 \mapsto \mathbf{false}] = \{\mathbf{true}, \mathbf{false}\}$

2.8.5 Infix operators

Infix operators on maps are 'override', 'union', 'restrict with', 'restrict to' and 'compose'.

$\dagger : (T_1 \overset{m}{\to} T_2) \times (T_1 \overset{m}{\to} T_2) \to (T_1 \overset{m}{\to} T_2)$
$\cup : (T_1 \overset{m}{\to} T_2) \times (T_1 \overset{m}{\to} T_2) \overset{\sim}{\to} (T_1 \overset{m}{\to} T_2)$
$\backslash : (T_1 \overset{m}{\to} T_2) \times T_1\text{-}\mathbf{infset} \to (T_1 \overset{m}{\to} T_2)$
$/ : (T_1 \overset{m}{\to} T_2) \times T_1\text{-}\mathbf{infset} \to (T_1 \overset{m}{\to} T_2)$
$\circ : (T_2 \overset{m}{\to} T_3) \times (T_1 \overset{m}{\to} T_2) \to (T_1 \overset{m}{\to} T_3)$
Examples:
$[3 \mapsto \mathbf{true}, 5 \mapsto \mathbf{false}] \dagger [5 \mapsto \mathbf{true}] = [3 \mapsto \mathbf{true}, 5 \mapsto \mathbf{true}]$
$[3 \mapsto \mathbf{true}] \cup [5 \mapsto \mathbf{false}] = [3 \mapsto \mathbf{true}, 5 \mapsto \mathbf{false}]$
$[3 \mapsto \mathbf{true}, 5 \mapsto \mathbf{false}] \backslash \{3\} = [5 \mapsto \mathbf{false}]$
$[3 \mapsto \mathbf{true}, 5 \mapsto \mathbf{false}] / \{3\} = [3 \mapsto \mathbf{true}]$
$[3 \mapsto \mathbf{true}, 5 \mapsto \mathbf{false}] \circ ["Klaus" \mapsto 3, "Kim" \mapsto 7] = ["Klaus" \mapsto \mathbf{true}]$

The override operator gives precedence to its second argument. The union operator is typically used when one wants to indicate that the two arguments are known to have disjoint domains. Restricting with a set removes the set from the domain; restricting by a set reduces the domain to its intersection with that set. Map composition composes two maps — its effect on application is to apply the second map and then the first. Associations for which no match exists are just removed.

2.8.6   Example: A Database

Consider a map version of the database from section 2.5.7. The map data type is very well suited for modelling the database since the database manipulations correspond closely to map operators.

MAP_DATABASE =
  class
    type
      Database = Key $\overrightarrow{m}$ Data,
      Key, Data
    value
      empty : Database,
      insert : Key × Data × Database → Database,
      remove : Key × Database → Database,
      defined : Key × Database → **Bool**,
      lookup : Key × Database $\xrightarrow{\sim}$ Data
    axiom forall k : Key, d : Data, db : Database •
      empty ≡ [ ],
      insert(k,d,db) ≡ db † [k ↦ d],
      remove(k,db) ≡ db \ {k},   •
      defined(k,db) ≡ k ∈ **dom** db,
      lookup(k,db) ≡ db(k)
      pre defined(k,db)
  end

The *Database* is a mapping from keys to data.

The *empty* database is the empty mapping.

To *insert* an association between a key and a data element corresponds to overriding the original database with the new association. Any old association between the key and some data element is overridden.

To *remove* a key corresponds to removing it from the domain.

To check whether a key is *defined* corresponds to finding out whether it belongs to the domain.

To *lookup* a key corresponds to applying the map to the key.

2.9 Subtypes

A type T_1 is a subtype of another type T_2, if all the values contained in T_1 are also contained in T_2. The type T_2 may contain values that are not in T_1. As an example, the type **Nat** of natural numbers is a subtype of **Int** of integers.

2.9.1 Subtype expressions

A type can be constrained by a predicate, resulting in a subtype (subset) of the original type. An example is $\{|\ t : \textbf{Text} \cdot \textbf{len}\ t > 0\ |\}$ which is the subtype of **Text** containing non-empty texts.

2.9.2 Maximal types

We would like to have our specifications automatically type checked. That is, expressions must have the "expected" types according to a set of rules. Since the type concept of RSL involves general predicates used to construct subtypes, type checking must be simplified in order to make it automatic. Proving relations between RSL predicates cannot in general be made automatic.

The concept of maximal type is the basis of this simplification. The idea is to simply ignore the predicates. All types are turned into maximal types (by ignoring subtype predicates) before type checking takes place.

A type is maximal if it is not a subtype of any type other than itself. The maximal type of a type T is the largest type of which T is a subtype. We now define the maximal types for the different kinds of types introduced up to this point.

The built-in types **Bool**, **Int**, **Real**, **Char** and **Unit** have themselves as maximal types.

The maximal type of **Nat** is **Int**. **Nat** contains those integers that are greater than or equal to zero. We can in fact write **Nat** as $\{|\ n : \textbf{Int} \cdot n \geq 0\ |\}$.

Types defined as sorts are maximal by definition.

The maximal type of a composite type consisting of the application of a type operator to a sequence of argument types is obtained by applying a maximal version of the type operator to the maximal types of the argument types. As an example, the maximal type of the type **Nat*** is **Int**$^\omega$.

For the complete description of composite types we assume that for any type T, T^M is the corresponding maximal type. Note that ^{M} is not a type operator in RSL, but a meta-notation. Then we can list the following rules:

$$(T_1 \times \ldots \times T_n)^M = T_1{}^M \times \ldots \times T_n{}^M$$
$$(\text{T-set})^M = T^M\text{-infset}$$
$$(\text{T-infset})^M = T^M\text{-infset}$$
$$(T^*)^M = T^{M\omega}$$
$$(T^\omega)^M = T^{M\omega}$$
$$(T_1 \underset{m}{\rightarrow} T_2)^M = T_1{}^M \underset{m}{\rightarrow} T_2{}^M$$
$$(T_1 \overset{\sim}{\rightarrow} T_2)^M = T_1{}^M \overset{\sim}{\rightarrow} T_2{}^M$$
$$(T_1 \rightarrow T_2)^M = T_1{}^M \overset{\sim}{\rightarrow} T_2{}^M$$

2.9.3 Example: A Bounded Queue

Consider a bounded version of a queue. Elements can be put into the queue and elements can be removed from the queue, in a "first in — first out" manner. The queue is bounded in that there is a maximum size, *max*, which is a natural number greater than zero, such that no queue can have more than *max* elements.

The boundedness is expressed via a subtype expression. In addition, subtypes are defined for extensible queues (with a size less than *max*) and for reducible queues (different from *empty*). The last two subtypes illustrate how partial functions can be replaced by total functions, using subtypes.

```
QUEUE =
  class
    type
      Element,
      Queue = {| q : Element* • len q ≤ max |},
      Extensible_Queue = {| q : Queue • len q < max |},
      Reducible_Queue = {| q : Queue • q ≠ empty |}
    value
      max : Nat,
      empty : Extensible_Queue,
      put : Element × Extensible_Queue → Reducible_Queue,
      get : Reducible_Queue → Extensible_Queue × Element
    axiom forall e : Element, eq : Extensible_Queue, rq : Reducible_Queue •
      max > 0,
      empty ≡ ⟨⟩,
      put(e,eq) ≡ eq ^ ⟨e⟩,
      get(rq) ≡ (tl rq,hd rq)
  end
```

2.10 Variant definitions

Using a variant definition, one can conveniently define a sort together with a number of functions and constants over that sort. That is, a variant definition is generally short for a sort definition, some value definitions and some axioms.

Among the defined values are constructors for generating values of the sort, destructors for decomposing values of the sort, and finally reconstructors for modifying values of the sort.

The axioms define the properties of the constructors, destructors and reconstructors. An important axiom is the induction axiom which states that the sort is generated by the constructors: any value within the sort is the result of a finite number of constructor applications.

2.10.1 Constructors

Consider the following example of a variant type definition:

type Set == empty | add(Elem,Set)

The type *Set*, which is recursively defined, contains two kinds of values:

1. the value *empty*. *empty* is a constant constructor.

2. values of the form *add(e,s)* where *e : Elem* and *s : Set*. *add* is a record constructor. The term 'record' stems from the fact that such constructors may be used to
   generate records, where a record is a collection of named fields.

The variant type definition is short for a sort definition, two value definitions and two
axioms. It is short for:

type Set
value
    empty : Set,
    add : Elem × Set → Set
axiom
    [disjoint]
        ∀ e : Elem, s : Set • empty ≠ add(e,s),
    [induction]
        ∀ p : Set → **Bool** •
            (p(empty) ∧ (∀ e : Elem, s : Set • p(s) ⇒ p(add(e,s)))) ⇒
                (∀ s : Set • p(s))

The *disjoint* axiom says that the *add* constructor is a function generating values different
from *empty*. The variants of variant type definitions are always disjoint.

The induction axiom says: "for all predicates *p*, if *p* holds for *empty* and *p* holding
for a set *s* implies *p* holding for *add(e,s)* for any element *e*, then *p* holds for all sets".

Observe that the truth of this induction axiom makes inductive proofs over the type
Set possible. If one can prove a property about *empty*, and one can prove the property
for any *add* extension of a *Set* satisfying the property, then one has proven that property
for all values within *Set*.

The *disjoint* axiom says that *empty* differs from *add(e,s)* for any element *e* and set *s*.
In fact, nothing is said about *add* beyond the disjointness from *empty* and the generat-
edness of *Set* by *empty* and *add*. In particular, there are no axioms stating that different
applications of *add* return different sets in *Set*. Given two different elements e_1 and e_2,
the following property is thus not necessarily a consequence — although we might like it
to be:

add(e_1,empty) ≠ add(e_2,empty)

To obtain this, we can define an observer function, *is_in*, that tests whether a particular element is in a set:

> **value** is_in : Elem × Set → **Bool**
> **axiom forall** e, e_1 : Elem, s : Set •
>   is_in(e,empty) ≡ **false**
>   is_in(e,add(e_1,s)) ≡ $e = e_1$ ∨ is_in(e,s)

This function will now distinguish the two sets above. That is, for $e_1 \neq e_2$:

> is_in(e_1,add(e_1,empty)) = **true**
> is_in(e_1,add(e_2,empty)) = **false**

and as a consequence of this we get the desired property:

> add(e_1,empty) $\neq$ add(e_2,empty)

The definition of the function *is_in* thus implies that those sets are distinguishable which we want to be distinguishable. The definition of the function *is_in* in general implies that sets show the expected behaviour in this respect: one can decide whether a particular element has been added or not.

Normally we think of a set as an unordered collection of distinct elements. The two important words here being 'unordered' and 'distinct'. None of the above axioms, however, prevent sets from being ordered or containing duplicates. To obtain this we could add the following axioms:

> **axiom forall** e, e_1, e_2 : Elem, s : Set •
>   [unordered]
>   add(e_1,add(e_2,s)) ≡ add(e_2,add(e_1,s)),
>   [no_duplicates]
>   add(e,add(e,s)) ≡ add(e,s)

In practice, though, it is not a good idea to add such axioms. It is the other functions, like *is_in*, that determine the need (or not) to distinguish set values, and by not specifying these axioms we allow for implementations that do or do not impose ordering, and do or do not allow duplication.

2.10.2 Destructors

Recall that constructors are functions for generating values of a variant type. Destructors are functions for extracting components from values of a variant type. Consider the following variant definition:

> **type** List == empty | add(head : Elem, tail : List)

The difference between this definition and the previous *Set* definition is, besides the new name *List* instead of *Set*, the existence of the destructors *head* and *tail*.

Like *Set*, the type *List* contains two kinds of values:

1. the value *empty*

2. values of the form *add(e,l)* where *e* : *Elem* and *l* : *List*.

The definition is short for a sort definition, four value definitions and four axioms. Ignoring the destructors, we get a sort definition, two value definitions and two axioms exactly as for *Set*:

type List
value
    empty : List,
    add : Elem × List → List,
axiom
    [disjoint]
       ∀ e : Elem, l : List • empty ≠ add(e,l),
    [induction]
       ∀ p : List → **Bool** •
          (p(empty) ∧ (∀ e : Elem, l : List • p(l) ⇒ p(add(e,l)))) ⇒
           (∀ l : List • p(l))

Beyond these definitions, the destructors give rise to the following ones:

value
    head : List $\overset{\sim}{\to}$ Elem,
    tail : List $\overset{\sim}{\to}$ List
axiom forall e : Elem, l : List •
    [head_add]
       head(add(e,l)) ≡ e,
    [tail_add]
       tail(add(e,l)) ≡ l

The destructors are partial in that their behaviour is under-specified for the *empty* list.

The destructors can be used to decompose *List* values generated by the *add* constructor. As an example consider the following definition of a function that replaces the head of a list:

value replace_head : Elem × List $\overset{\sim}{\to}$ List
axiom forall e : Elem, l : List •
    replace_head(e,l) ≡ add(e,tail(l))
    pre l ≠ empty

The destructor *tail* has here been used to remove the old head element before adding the new one.

2.10.3 Reconstructors

The function *replace_head* defined in the previous section can be defined in a slightly more convenient way as a reconstructor. Below we repeat the definition of *List* with the addition of the reconstructor:

> **type** List == empty | add(head : Elem ↔ replace_head, tail : List)

The occurrence of the reconstructor is short for the following definitions, to be added to the previous ones:

> **value** replace_head : Elem × List $\overset{\sim}{\to}$ List
> **axiom forall** e : Elem, l : List •
>   [head_replace_head]
>   head(replace_head(e,l)) ≡ e,
>   [tail_replace_head]
>   tail(replace_head(e,l)) ≡ tail(l)

The two axioms relate the reconstructor *replace_head* to the destructors *head* and *tail*. The *head_replace_head* axiom says that the *head* destructor recovers the new head. The *tail_replace_head* axiom says that the tail is unaffected.

2.10.4 Wildcard constructors

We have mentioned that a variant definition is short for a number of definitions including an induction axiom. The induction axiom restricts the variant type to containing only values generated by the constructors mentioned in the variant definition.

Sometimes one, however, wants to be loose about what the constructors are. As an example suppose we are specifying an interpreter for some command language. We might have decided that we want an *insert* comand to add *Data* and an *retrieve* comand to retrieve *Data* according to a *Key* value, but we want to leave open the possibility of adding more commands. Then we might start with the variant type definitions

type
   Command == insert(Key, Data) | retrieve(Key) | _,
   Output == data_output(Data) | _

We have used the 'wildcard constructor' _ in both the *Command* type and the *Output* type. The first allows us to implement *Command* with the two commands given plus, possibly, some more. The second allows us to implement *Output* with the one given (intended for use with *retrieve*) plus possibly some more. We might have new *Output* values for new commands; we may need to add some error values for inapplicable commands.

Formally, the inclusion of a wildard constructor means that no induction axiom is generated. This allows an implementation to add more variants.

It is not only the number of constructors which can be left open in a variant definition. It is also the components of a single constructor. Consider the following example:

type Record == _(name : **Text**, age : **Nat**, address : **Text**)

This is equivalent to the following declarations:

type Record
value
   name : Record → **Text**,
   age : Record → **Nat**,
   address : Record → **Text**

so all we have really said is that there are functions like *name* for extracting information from *Record* values. We are free to implement by adding more such functions (tantamount to 'adding more fields') or even to construct *Records* in some other way. We might, for example, add a personal identification number from which we could calculate age rather than store it. All we have to do in an implementation is provide an *age* function.

2.10.5 Example: Ordered Trees

Consider the specification of ordered binary trees of elements. A binary tree is either empty, or composed of an element and two subtrees: a left tree and a right tree.
    The ordering means that any of the elements in the left tree are less than the top element, which again is less than any of the elements in the right tree. A function *less_than* represents the ordering on elements.

ORDERED_TREE =
  class
    type
      Elem,
      Tree == empty | node(left : Tree, elem : Elem, right : Tree),
      Ordered_Tree = {| t : Tree • is_ordered(t) |}
    value
      is_ordered : Tree → **Bool**,
      extract_elems : Tree → Elem-**set**,
      less_than : Elem × Elem → **Bool**
    axiom forall e : Elem, t_1, t_2 : Tree •
      [is_ordered_empty]
         is_ordered(empty) ≡ **true**,
      [is_ordered_node]
         is_ordered(node(t_1,e,t_2)) ≡
               (∀ e_1 : Elem • e_1 ∈ extract_elems(t_1) ⇒ less_than(e_1,e)) ∧
               (∀ e_2 : Elem • e_2 ∈ extract_elems(t_2) ⇒ less_than(e,e_2)) ∧
            is_ordered(t_1) ∧
            is_ordered(t_2),
      [extract_elems_empty]
         extract_elems(empty) ≡ {},

[extract_elems_node]
    extract_elems(node(t_1,e,t_2)) $\equiv$ extract_elems(t_1) $\cup$ {e} $\cup$ extract_elems(t_2)

end

The type *Tree* is the type of binary trees, including the un-ordered ones. The type *Ordered_Tree* of ordered trees is defined as a subtype of *Tree*. Note that this two-step approach is generally necessary when defining subtypes of variant types.

The *is_ordered* examines whether a tree is ordered; The *extract_elems* returns all the elements contained in a tree.

When the goal is execution-time efficiency of membership test, ordered trees are well-suited for modelling large sets of elements. The execution time used for testing whether an element belongs to an ordered tree can be kept relatively low since subtrees can be ignored if they only contain elements smaller than or bigger than the element in question.

Note that we allow ourselves to talk about execution-time efficiency, although RSL is not a programming language. RSL is, however, a wide spectrum specification language supporting algorithm design. Since algorithmic RSL specifications typically will be translated into programs in some programming language, we shall feel free to consider efficiency already at the RSL level. Observe, though, that there is no formal necessity to do so.

Consider an extension of the *ORDERED_TREE* module with set-like functions for adding an element to a tree, *add*, and for testing whether an element belongs to a tree, *is_in*.

SET_FUNCTIONS =
   extend ORDERED_TREE with
   class
     value
       add : Elem $\times$ Ordered_Tree $\rightarrow$ Ordered_Tree,
       is_in : Elem $\times$ Ordered_Tree $\rightarrow$ **Bool**
     axiom forall e,e_0 : Elem, t_1,t_2 : Ordered_Tree •
     [add_empty]
       add(e,empty) $\equiv$ node(empty,e,empty),
     [add_node]
       add(e,node(t_1,e_0,t_2)) $\equiv$
          if e = e_0 **then** node(t_1,e_0,t_2)
          elsif less_than(e,e_0) **then** node(add(e,t_1),e_0,t_2)
          else node(t_1,e_0,add(e,t_2))
          end,
     [is_in_empty]
       is_in(e,empty) $\equiv$ **false**,
     [is_in_node]
       is_in(e,node(t_1,e_0,t_2)) $\equiv$
          if e = e_0 **then true**
          elsif less_than(e,e_0) **then** is_in(e,t_1)
          else is_in(e,t_2)

end

end

The definition of the function *is_in* utilises the fact that trees are ordered. That is, a subtree is ignored in the search of an element if all the elements in that subtree are either less than or greater than the element being sought. This improves execution-time efficiency of a search.

The efficiency of *is_in* could further be improved, if trees were always balanced. A tree is balanced, if its two subtrees have depths that at most differ by a chosen fixed maximum. The *add* function should then make sure that the resulting tree is balanced (resulting in a loss of efficiency of element addition).

Choosing the maximum to be one (*1*) we can obtain balanced trees as follows.

BALANCED_SET_FUNCTIONS =
   extend SET_FUNCTIONS with
   class
      type Balanced_Tree = {| t : Ordered_Tree • is_balanced(t) |}
      value
         is_balanced : Tree → **Bool**,
         depth : Tree → **Nat**,
         add_balanced : Elem × Balanced_Tree → Balanced_Tree
      axiom forall e : Elem, t_1, t_2 : Ordered_Tree, t : Balanced_Tree •
        [is_balanced_empty]
           is_balanced(empty) ≡ **true**,
        [is_balanced_node]
           is_balanced(node(t_1,e,t_2)) ≡
               abs(depth(t_1) − depth(t_2)) ≤ 1 ∧
               is_balanced(t_1) ∧
               is_balanced(t_2),
        [depth_empty]
           depth(empty) ≡ 0,
        [depth_node]
           depth(node(t_1,e,t_2)) ≡
               1 + **if** depth(t_1) > depth(t_2) **then** depth(t_1) **else** depth(t_2) **end**,
        [add_balanced_elem]
           add_balanced(e,t) **as** rt
           post extract_elems(rt) = extract_elems(t) ∪ {e}
   end

The function *is_balanced* examines whether a tree is balanced; the function *depth* calculates the depth of a tree, which is the length of the longest path in the tree. They are defined for *Tree* rather than *Ordered_Tree* to make them more general as their definitions do not depend on trees being ordered.

The function *add_balanced* adds an element to a tree. Note that since the type *Balanced_Tree* only includes balanced trees (that are also ordered by definition), the resulting tree must be both ordered and balanced due to the result type of *add_balanced*.

The post-condition style used for specifying *add_balanced* is an appropriate initial specification of that function, since a specification of a concrete insertion algorithm is rather more complicated.

We do not have to re-specify the function *is_in* since the one coming from *SET_FUNCTIONS* is still sufficient.

2.10.6 Example: A Database

Consider a version of the map database from section 2.8.6. In that example, the database manipulations *empty*, *insert*, *remove* and *lookup* were modelled as functions, one function for each. This style has in fact been applied in all examples until now.

An alternative is to only define a single function, say *evaluate*, which among its arguments takes an input command, being either an empty command, an insert command, a remove command or a lookup command.

The *evaluate* function further takes a database as argument. As result it returns a possibly changed database and an output.

The type *Input* is defined as a variant type, the variants being the different kinds of input commands. Likewise, *Output* is defined from the different kinds of outputs.

```
VARIANT_DATABASE =
  class
    type
      Database = Key ⇱ Data,
      Key, Data,
      Input ==
        mk_empty |
        mk_insert(Key, Data) |
        mk_remove(Key) |
        mk_lookup(Key),
      Output == lookup_failed | lookup_succeeded(Data) | change_done
    value
      evaluate : Input × Database → Database × Output
    axiom forall k : Key, d : Data, db : Database •
      evaluate(mk_empty,db) ≡ ([ ], change_done),
      evaluate(mk_insert(k,d),db) ≡ (db † [k ↦ d], change_done),
      evaluate(mk_remove(k),db) ≡ (db\{k}, change_done),
      evaluate(mk_lookup(k),db) ≡
        if k ∈ dom db then (db, lookup_succeeded(db(k)))
        else (db, lookup_failed)
        end
  end
```

The type *Output* contains three variants of values. Values of the form *lookup_failed* and *lookup_succeeded(d)*, where *d : Data*, are results of evaluating a *mk_lookup(k)* command, where *k : Key*. The result *lookup_failed* is returned if the key *k* is not in the domain of the database.

The *Output* value *change_done* is the result of evaluating any of the commands *mk_empty*, *mk_insert(k,d)* and *mk_remove(k)*, where *k : Key* and *d : Data*. Note that this result is not likely to be used for anything. In these cases it is only the changed database that is of interest.

2.10.7 Example: A File Directory

A number of examples have been given of recursive variant definitions (*Set*, *List* and *Tree*). Variant definitions can also define mutually recursive types. That is, several types that are recursively defined in terms of each other.

Consider the specification of a hierarchical file directory. Such a directory is a mapping from identifiers to entries. An entry is either a file or a directory.

FILE_DIRECTORY =
  class
    type
      Id, File,
      Directory = Id $\overrightarrow{m}$ Entry,
      Entry == mk_file(sel_file : File) | mk_dir(sel_dir : Directory)
  end

2.11 Case expressions

The case expression allows for the selection of one of several alternative expressions, depending on the value of some expression. For example,

type Colour == black | white | _
value
  invert : Colour → Colour,
  is_inversion Colour × Colour → **Bool**,
  invert_list : Colour* → Colour*
axiom forall c, c' : colour •
  invert(c) ≡
    case c **of**
      black → white,
      white → black,
      _ → c
    end,
  is_inversion(p) ≡
    case (p) **of**
      (=black, =white) → **true**,
      (=white, =black) → **true**,
      (c, c') → **false**
    end,
  invert_list(l) ≡

```
case l of
    ⟨⟩ → ⟨⟩,
    ⟨h⟩^t → ⟨invert(h)⟩^invert_list(t)
end
```

In each case expression there is a list of 'patterns' to which the value of the expression following **case** is matched. If the match succeeds the expression to the right of the arrow is evaluated, and this is the result of the case expression. Otherwise the next pattern is tried. (If all fail the result is under-specified.)

Patterns may be literals (like *1* or **true**), constants (like *black*), product patterns (like *(=black, =white)* or *(c, c′)*), list patterns (like *⟨⟩* or *⟨h⟩^t*), record patterns (which we shall see an example of below), or the wildard pattern _.

Values match literals or constants if they are equal to them; product, list and record patterns if they have the same structure and the components match; wildcards always.

With product, list and record patterns, identifiers in inner positions (like *c* or *h* in the examples) are bound to the appropriate components of the value if the match succeeds, the scope of such bindings being the expression to the right of the arrow. In such inner positions we need to distinguish these new identifiers and constants. The equality symbol is used to indicate a constant. So *(=black, =white)* matches only one pair of colours, while *(c, c′)* matches any pair, binding *c* to the first and *c′* to the second. (Since we don't use *c* or *c′* on the right of the arrow we could have written _ instead of *(c, c′)*.)

2.11.1 Record patterns

Record patterns are used to decompose values of variant types. Their use is illustrated in the next example.

2.11.2 Example: Ordered Trees

Consider a version of the ordered tree specification from section 2.10.5. The functions *is_ordered* and *extract_elems* were defined by two axioms each, an axiom for each kind of argument. These two functions could instead be defined in terms of case expressions. For example, for *extract_elems*:

```
value extract_elems : Tree → Elem-set
axiom forall t : Tree •
    extract_elems(t) ≡
        case t of
            empty → {},
            node(t₁,e,t₂) → extract_elems(t₁) ∪ {e} ∪ extract_elems(t₂)
        end
```

Here *empty* is a constant pattern, while *node(t₁,e,t₂)* is a record pattern. It matches any tree constructed by *node*, binding t_1 to the left subtree, *e* to the *Elem* value at the node and t_2 to the right subtree. Such cases are a natural means of writing functions over variant types. Note that the disjointness axiom for variant types means that a value of the variant type can only match one pattern in such a case expression.

2.12 Let expressions

By a let expression one can define local names for (components of) particular values. There are two kinds of let expressions, explicit and implicit.

2.12.1 Explicit let expressions

Consider the following definition of a function that replaces the head of a non-empty list by its square:

> **value** square_head : Int* $\overset{\sim}{\to}$ Int*
> **axiom forall** l : Int* •
>   square_head(l) $\equiv$ **let** h = **hd** l **in** ⟨h∗h⟩ ⌢ **tl** l **end**
>   **pre** l $\neq$ ⟨⟩

The body of the function *square_head* contains a let expression. The expression **hd** *l* is evaluated to an integer which is then bound to the value name *h*. The expression between **in** and **end** is then evaluated within the scope of this binding.

A binding (like *h*) following **let** is the simplest form of explicit let expression. Record and list patterns can also be used. For example, the body of *square_head* could have been written in either of the forms:

> **let** (h,t) = (**hd** l,**tl** l) **in** ⟨h∗h⟩ ⌢ t **end**
> **let** ⟨h⟩ ⌢ t = l **in** ⟨h∗h⟩ ⌢ t **end**

2.12.2 Implicit let expressions

Another kind of let expression is the implicit let expression. Consider the following definition of a function that sums the elements in a set of integers:

> **value** sum : Int-set $\to$ Int
> **axiom forall** s : Int-set •
>   sum(s) $\equiv$
>   **if** s = {} **then** 0
>   **else**
>   **let** i : Int • i $\in$ s **in** i + sum(s\{i}) **end**
>   **end**

An implicit let expression like this is typically non-deterministic. Each time it is evaluated it selects an arbitrary element *i* from *s*. Here it is well used in that we know from the properties of + that the result of *sum* will be deterministic. See section 2.14 for more discussion on non-determinism.

2.13 Union and short record definitions

Union and short record definitions are shorthands for particular forms of variant types.

2.13.1 Example: A Database

The database from section 2.10.6 can be rewritten using unions and short records:

UNION_DATABASE =
  class
    type
      Database = Key $\overrightarrow{m}$ Data,
      Key, Data,
      Input = Empty | Insert | Remove | Lookup,
      Empty == mk_empty,
      Insert :: sel_key : Key sel_data : Data,
      Remove :: sel_key : Key,
      Lookup :: sel_key : Key,
      Output = Lookup_Output | Change_Output,
      Lookup_Output = Lookup_Failed | Lookup_Succeeded,
      Lookup_Failed == lookup_failed,
      Lookup_Succeeded :: sel_data : Data,
      Change_Output == change_done
    value
      evaluate : Input $\times$ Database $\to$ Database $\times$ Output
    axiom forall input : Input, db : Database $\bullet$
      evaluate(input,db) $\equiv$
        case input **of**
          mk_empty $\to$ ([ ], change_done),
          mk_Insert(k,d) $\to$ (db $\dagger$ [k $\mapsto$ d], change_done),
          mk_Remove(k) $\to$ (db\\{k}, change_done),
          mk_Lookup(k) $\to$
            if k $\in$ **dom** db **then** (db, mk_Lookup_Succeeded(db(k)))
            else (db, lookup_failed)
            end
        end
  end

The definition of *Input* is a union definition. It is short for the variant type definition

type
  Input ==
    Input_from_Empty(Input_to_Empty : Empty) |
    Input_from_Insert(Input_to_Insert : Insert) |
    Input_from_Remove(Input_to_Remove : Remove) |
    Input_from_Lookup(Input_to_Lookup : Lookup)

The definition of *Insert* is a short record definition. It is short for the variant type definition

type Insert == mk_Insert(sel_key : Key, sel_data : Data)

Note that the patterns in the case expression look wrong because they appear to match components of *Input* and not *Input* itself. Similarly, the *Output* values on the right seem to be in components of *Output* rather than *Output* itself. One would expect, according to the equivalent variant type definitions for the union definitions, to have to write for the first case branch

Input_from_Empty(mk_empty) →
([ ],Output_from_Lookup_Output(Lookup_Output_from_Change_Output(change_done)))

However, in patterns one is allowed to leave out the implicit union type constructors from a record pattern when the inner pattern is a constant or record pattern. We say the pattern *mk_empty* of type *Empty* is 'coerced' to the pattern *Input_from_Empty(mk_empty)* of type *Input* when matched against a value of that type. Expressions may be coerced similarly. The value *change_done* of type *Change_Done* is coerced (twice) to a value of type *Output*.

This is to illustrate that union definitions can generally be used as an alternative to variant definitions (such as were used in the first version of this example in section 2.10.6). Union definitions are of particular use when we want to describe the types in a hierarchical fashion rather than in a single variant.

2.14 Under-specification and non-determinism

These two terms are often regarded as synonymous in specifications. In RSL they are different. For example consider the value definition.

value x : **Nat**

The identifier x is under-specified (asuming there are no axioms uniquely determining its value). Every occurrence of x, however, evaluates to the same value. For instance, the expression x − x always evaluates to *0*.

The value expression

let x : **Nat** • x < 3 **in** x **end**

on the other hand is non-deterministic. (It is actually equivalent to the non-deterministic choice *0* ⌐⌐ *1* ⌐⌐ *2*.) Two occurrences of this expression may evaluate to different values. Thus, in this case, the expression

(**let** x : **Nat** • x < 3 **in** x **end**) − (**let** x : **Nat** • x < 3 **in** x **end**)

does not evaluate to *0*, but to:

−2 ⌐⌐ −1 ⌐⌐ 0 ⌐⌐ 1 ⌐⌐ 2

See section 4.1.7 for a description of the internal choice combinator ⌐⌐.

Total functions (whose signatures use →) are always deterministic (as well as terminating). Partial functions (whose signatures use ⇢) may be non-deterministic (as well as possibly non-terminating).

2.15 Overloading and user-defined operators

RSL allows for the overloading of value identifiers and operators. An identifier or operator is overloaded at a certain point, if there are several definitions of that identifier or operator visible at that point, but with different maximal types. Some of the predefined operators are already overloaded. As an example, consider the 'less than or equal' operator $\leq$. There is an **Int** $\leq$ and a **Real** $\leq$:

> $\leq$: **Int** $\times$ **Int** $\rightarrow$ **Bool**
> $\leq$: **Real** $\times$ **Real** $\rightarrow$ **Bool**

User-defined value names may be overloaded (provided the definitions have different maximal types), and new definitions of the built-in infix and prefix operators may be given (provided they have different maximal types from the built-in ones). So we could define

type
    Set == empty | add(Elem, Set),
    List == empty | add(Elem, List)
value
    elems : List $\rightarrow$ Set,
    ^ : List $\times$ List $\rightarrow$ List
axiom
    $\forall$ l, l' : List •
      elems l $\equiv$
        case l **of**
          empty $\rightarrow$ empty,
          add(e, t) $\rightarrow$ add(e, **elems** t)
        end,
      l ^ l' $\equiv$
        case l **of**
          empty $\rightarrow$ l',
          add(e, t) $\rightarrow$ add(e, t ^ l')
        end

which overloads *empty*, *add*, **elems** and ^. Note that the abstract types *Set* and *List* are (by definition) both maximal and different.

3 Imperative specifications

3.1 Basic concepts

RSL allows declaration of variables as known from programming languages like Ada and Pascal. A variable is a container capable of holding values of a particular type. The contents of a variable can be changed by assigning a new value to the variable. A variable can thus change contents within its lifetime.

The following module defines a variable *counter* and a function *increase* that increases the counter by one for each call. The function additionally returns the value of the counter after the change.

COUNTER =
  class
    variable counter : **Nat** := 0
    value increase : **Unit** → **write** counter **Nat**
    axiom increase() ≡ counter := counter + 1 ; counter
  end

The following sections explain the individual declarations of the module.

3.1.1 Variable declarations

A variable declaration consists of the keyword **variable** followed by one or more definitions, each of which introduces a name for a variable, its type and (optionally) an initial value. If there is no intialisation the initial value is some arbitrary value within the specified type.

We shall commonly refer collectively to the declared variables as the 'state'.

3.1.2 Functions with variable access

The function *increase* from the example has the type:

  Unit → **write** counter **Nat**

That is, it is a function that when applied to a value of type **Unit** returns a value of type **Nat**. As a side-effect it may write to the variable *counter*. A function with variable access, like *increase*, is also called an operation.

The example illustrates a typical use of the type **Unit**: as parameter type for operations that only depend on the state and not on any additional parameters. The parameter type of an operation can of course be any type. We see later examples of operations with result type **Unit**, where the only interesting effect of the operations is the way they change the state.

The function has **write** access to the variable *counter*; it is also possible to specify read access (by writing, for example, **read** *counter*), or even combinations of write access to some variables and read to others. Write access implies read access (as shown by the axiom for *increase*).

3.1.3 Assignment expressions

Our example contains one assignment expression, namely *counter := counter + 1*.

There is an important point to note here: assignment is an expression. In RSL there is no distinction between expressions and statements as often seen in traditional programming languages such as Ada and Pascal. In RSL there are only expressions.

Since assignment is an expression, it must in addition to its side-effect also return a value of a certain type. The value returned by an assignment expression is the value () of type **Unit**.

3.1.4 Sequencing expressions

Two expressions (provided the first is **Unit** valued) can be combined with the sequencing combinator giving a new composite expression, as in

counter := counter + 1 ; counter

The type of a sequencing expression is the type of the second constituent expression.

3.1.5 Quantification over states

How do we interpret axioms in the context of variables? The most natural thing is to say that an axiom is **true** if it is **true** in any possible state satisfying the variable definitions. A state satisfies a variable definition if it associates the variable with a value within the variable's type.

The 'always' combinator $\square$ performs this universal quantification over states. Thus the axiom for increase is short for

axiom $\square$ (increase() $\equiv$ counter := counter + 1 ; counter)

3.1.6 Equivalence expressions

Our example contains a single axiom: ·

axiom increase() $\equiv$ counter := counter + 1 ; counter

which contains an equivalence expression. Such equivalence expressions evaluate to **true** if and only if the two expressions, evaluated in the current state, have the same effect as well as the same result. So this axiom says that evaluating *increase()* gives the same state change and the same result as the assignment to counter followed by returning the value of counter.

The equivalence also requires equivalent effects concerning **chaos**. That is, if one of the expressions evaluates to **chaos**, the other one must also do so. Note that an equivalence expression always evaluates to either **true** or **false**, it will never be **chaos** itself.

Finally, if one of the expressions is non-deterministic, the other one must show exactly the same non-determinism in order for the equivalence to hold.

When an equivalence expression occurs as an axiom, as here, it is implicitly prefixed by $\square$, as we have seen. Hence it says that for all states satisfying the variable definitions, the effects and results of the two expressions must be the same. This implies that any occurrence of *increase()* within the scope of the variable definitions can be replaced by *counter* := *counter* + *1* ; *counter* and vice versa (assuming that the replacement does not cause any name clashes).

In later sections we shall see uses of equivalence where the left hand side is not just a single function application, but a general expression. One can thus specify operations in an algebraic style similar to that described in section 2.5 for applicative functions.

3.1.7 Conditional equivalence expressions

An equivalence may be conditional on a pre-condition.

value decrease : **Unit** → **write** counter **Nat**
axiom
    decrease() ≡ counter := counter − 1 ; counter
    pre counter > 0

The axiom is short for:

axiom counter > 0 ⇒ (decrease() ≡ counter := counter − 1 ; counter)

so the equivalence holds only for all states in which the counter is strictly positive.

3.1.8 Equivalence and equality

Equivalence differs from equality in several respects.

- An equivalence expression compares effects as well as results; equality only compares results.

- An equivalence expression does not evaluate its constituent expression, so it itself has no effects; equality evaluates its constituent expressions (left to right).

- An equivalence expression always evaluates to either **true** (if the effects and results are equivalent) or **false** (otherwise). Equality may evaluate to non-deterministic expressions or to **chaos** or to **stop** (deadlock).

For example, assuming the current value of variable x is 0:

    (x := x + 1 ; 1) ≡ (x := x + 1 ; x)   is equivalent to **true**
    (x := x + 1 ; 1) = (x := x + 1 ; x)   is equivalent to x := 2 ; **false**
    (1 ⌈⌉ 2) ≡ (1 ⌈⌉ 2)   is equivalent to **true**
    (1 ⌈⌉ 2) = (1 ⌈⌉ 2)   is equivalent to **true** ⌈⌉ **false**

Equality is intended to be close to the behaviour of the equality in programming languages.

3.1.9 Example: A Database

Consider a state-based version of the database from section 2.8.6. A variable containing the database is defined, and all operations then read from and write to this variable.

DATABASE =
  class
    type Key, Data
    variable database : Key $\overrightarrow{m}$ Data
    value
      empty : Unit → write database Unit,
      insert : Key × Data → write database Unit,
      remove : Key → write database Unit,
      defined : Key → read database Bool,
      lookup : Key $\overset{\sim}{\to}$ read database Data
    axiom forall k : Key, d : Data •
      empty() ≡ database := [ ],
      insert(k,d) ≡ database := database † [k ↦ d],
      remove(k) ≡ database := database \ {k},
      defined(k) ≡ k ∈ dom database,
      lookup(k) ≡ database(k)
        pre defined(k)
  end

There are several reasons for writing state-based specifications instead of applicative specifications. Some reasons are:

1. Programs written in traditional programming languages are typically state-based. A specification that is to be implemented in such a language may be more naturally written in a state-based style.

2. The state-based style of specification reduces the number of parameters to functions.

3. Certain problems can be said to be of a state-based nature, like the database example. One may then prefer to model them as such.

3.2 Expressions revisited

In general, all expressions are evaluated in a state. This also holds for the applicative expressions introduced earlier. So we can have if expressions, case expressions, let expressions, operator and function applications etc. in which the constituent expressions may read or write to the state.

3.2.1 Expression evaluation order

Recall from section 3.1 that the two constituent expressions of an equality expression are evaluated from left to right. The general rule is that the constituent expressions of a value infix expression are evaluated from left to right for all infix operators. The other main rules for evaluation ordering are that products are evaluated left to right and that function arguments are evaluated before application.

3.3 Repetitive expressions

A repetitive expression specifies that a certain expression is repeatedly evaluated for the purpose of its side-effect. There are three forms, all known from most traditional programming languages: 'while' expressions, 'until' expressions and 'for' expressions.

They all have result-type **Unit**.

To illustrate them we give three versions of a function to calculate the sum of the values in an integer list held in a variable *list*, placing the result in a variable *result*.

value
    while_sum : **Unit** → **write** list, result **Unit**,
    until_sum : **Unit** → **write** list, result **Unit**,
    for_sum : **Unit** → **read** list **write** result **Unit**
axiom
    while_sum() ≡
        result := 0 ;
        while list ≠ ⟨⟩ **do**
            result := result + **hd** list ;
            list := **tl** list
        end,
    until_sum() ≡
        result := 0 ;
        if list ≠ <> **then**
            do
                result := result + **hd** list ;
                list := **tl** list
            until list = ⟨⟩ **end**
        else skip end,
    for_sum() ≡
        result := 0 ;
        for i **in** list **do**
            result := result + i
        end

skip is the **Unit** valued expression with no effects, which can also be written (*)*.

3.4 Local expressions

A collection of declarations can be made local to an expression by means of a local expression. For example, we could produce an applicative version of the *for_sum* function from the previous section:

```
value for_sum : Int* → Int
axiom forall l : Int* •
   for_sum(l) ≡
      local
         variable result : Int := 0
      in
         for i in l do
            result := result + i
         end ;
         result
      end
```

Local expressions are also useful for making channels local and hence only available to certain processes, as we shall see when describing concurrency.

3.5 Algebraic definition of operations

Section 2.5 described how applicative functions can be defined abstractly in terms of algebraic equivalences. We can create similar axiomatic definitions for operations, functions that access variables.

3.5.1 Example: A Database

Consider an algebraic specification of the state-based database from section 3.1.9.

```
DATABASE =
   class
      type Key, Data
      value
         empty : Unit → write any Unit,
         insert : Key × Data → write any Unit,
         remove : Key → write any Unit,
         defined : Key → read any Bool,
         lookup : Key ⇀ read any Data
      axiom forall k,k₁ : Key, d : Data •
      [remove_empty]
         empty() ; remove(k) ≡ empty(),
      [remove_insert]
         insert(k₁,d) ; remove(k) ≡
            if k = k₁ then remove(k)
            else remove(k) ; insert(k₁,d)
            end,
      [defined_empty]
         empty() ; defined(k) ≡ empty() ; false,
      [defined_insert]
```

```
            insert(k₁,d) ; defined(k) ≡
                if k = k₁ then insert(k₁,d) ; true
                else let result = defined(k) in insert(k₁,d) ; result end
                end,
        [lookup_insert]
            insert(k₁,d) ; lookup(k) ≡
                if k = k₁ then insert(k₁,d) ; d
                else let result = lookup(k) in insert(k₁,d) ; result end
                end
                pre k = k₁ ∨ defined(k)
    end
```

The reader should compare this specification with the algebraic specification of the corresponding applicative module from section 2.5.7.

The *remove_empty* axiom says that emptying the database and then removing something from it is equivalent to emptying it.

The *remove_insert* axiom says that removing a key after inserting a key-data pair depends on whether the key to be removed is equal to the one just inserted. If it is equal, it is equivalent to removing all other occurrences of the key. If not, it is equivalent to removing all other occurrences and then inserting the most recent one. Similarly for the other axioms.

The state-based database example illustrates the constructor-technique for inventing axioms, which we also saw in section 2.5.7. The technique used in the state-based case can be characterized as follows.

1. Identify the "constructor operations" by which any database can be constructed. These are the operations *empty* and *insert*. Any database can thus be generated as the side-effect of an expression of the form:

    empty() ; insert(k₁,d₁) ; ... ; insert(kₙ,dₙ)

2. Define the remaining operations "by case" over the constructor operations, using new identifiers as parameters. In the above axioms, *remove*, *defined* and *lookup* are defined over the two constructor expressions:

    empty()
    insert(k₁,d)

We thus get "for free" all the left hand sides of the axioms we need. That is:

    empty() ; remove(k)
    insert(k₁,d) ; remove(k)
    empty() ; defined(k)
    insert(k₁,d) ; defined(k)
    empty() ; lookup(k)
    insert(k₁,d) ; lookup(k)

Note, however, that we choose to make *lookup* partial; we do not include an axiom with left hand side *empty() ; lookup(k)* and the axiom *lookup_insert* has a precondition — it only applies to defined keys.

The right hand sides of the axioms *defined_insert* and *lookup_insert* are somewhat different from the corresponding applicative ones. This is due to the requirement that the side-effect of the left hand side of an equivalence must be the same as the side-effect of the right hand side. More specifically, the call *insert(k_1,d)* (or its equivalent) must occur on the right hand side since it occurs on the left hand side and since it has side-effects. Note also the use of let expressions in the two axioms. These are necessary in order to ensure that *defined(k)* and *lookup(k)* are evaluated before *insert(k_1,d)*.

You will also notice that we have not defined any variables; we have written the accesses in the operation signatures using **any**. This means that the operations have read or write access to any variables that we decide to use when we implement the database. We have freedom to decide later how many variables we need and what types they should have.

A natural question is when to be implicit about variables (by using **any**) and when to be explicit. It is difficult to give exact rules. Very roughly, one may be implicit in the following situations.

- One is not interested (yet) in what variables there are.

- In large specifications it is sometimes necessary to add extra variables to be able to define certain operations. If these operations are called by others, the extra access(es) must be added to these other operations' types, and this can in turn require more access(es) to be added to yet other operations' types. The use of **any** can avoid this problem.

Being explicit, however, has its benefits. One can from the type of an operation see exactly what variables may be accessed and how they may be accessed. This can make state-based specifications easier to read.

3.6 Post expressions

We have just seen how operations can be defined in a very abstract way in terms of algebraic equivalences. Another way of being abstract about operations is to use post expressions. We have already seen several examples of this style in the applicative case. See for instance section 2.5.5.

Consider the following specification of a *choose* operation that returns an arbitrary element from a set contained in a variable. The returned element is at the same time removed from the set, thereby changing the contents of the variable.

```
CHOOSE =
  class
    variable set : Int-set
    value choose : Unit → write set Int
```

axiom
    choose() **as** i **post** i ∈ set` ∧ set = set`\\{i}
    pre set ≠ {}
end

The pre-condition says that the operation is only specified for states where the contents of *set* is a non-empty set.

    The post-condition is a conjunction of two Boolean expressions. The first one, $i \in set$`, says that the returned *i* must be a member of *set* as this was before the call. In general, a "hooked" variable like *set*` in a post-condition refers to the contents of that variable before calling the operation. Conversely, a normal non-hooked variable refers to the contents of the variable after having called the operation. Such a non-hooked variable occurs in the second part of the post-condition, $set = set$`\\{i}. This says that the new *set* after a call must be equal to the *set* before the call, except for the chosen element which has been removed.

    Functions defined by post conditions must be total. That is, when a developer specifies an implementation of *choose* he or she must find one that terminates with a unique value for any non-empty value in the variable *set*.

4 Concurrency-based specifications

4.1 Some basic concepts

RSL provides means for specifying concurrent systems. More precisely, combinators are provided for specifying the parallel evaluation of expressions. Moreover, communication primitives are provided so that expressions evaluating in parallel can communicate with each other through 'channels'.

    The following module defines a one place buffer, *opb*, that communicates with the surrounding world through the two channels *add* and *get*. Values of type *Elem* are input from the *add* channel and are then output to the *get* channel.

```
ONE_PLACE_BUFFER =
   class
      type Elem
      channel add, get : Elem
      value opb : Unit → in add out get Unit
      axiom opb() ≡ let v = add? in get!v end ; opb()
   end
```

The following sections explain the individual declarations of the module.

4.1.1 Channel declarations

A channel declaration gives the name and type of one or more channels following the keyword **channel**.

4.1.2 Functions with channel access

The function *opb* from the example has the type:

Unit → in add out get Unit

That is, it is a function that, when called, communicates with the surroundings through the channels *add* and *get*. More specifically, it receives values from the surroundings through the *add* channel and it sends values to the surroundings through the *get* channel. A function with channel access, like *opb*, is also called a process. Processes have **in** and **out** channel accesses just like operations have **read** and **write** accesses. (Processes may also have variable accesses.)

opb will only be called for its ability to communicate through *add* and *get*, and therefore its parameter type and result type are **Unit**. We shall later see examples of more interesting parameter and result types.

4.1.3 Communication expressions

RSL provides two communication primitives: one for the input of a value from a channel and one for the output of a value to a channel.

In our example, *add?* is an input expression. Its type is the type of the channel, in this case *Elem*. It is often, as here, used in a let expression so that the value input can be used in the sequel.

get!v is an output expression. It outputs the value *v* on the channel *get*. It is **Unit** valued.

So the process *opb* repeatedly inputs a value from the *add* channel and then outputs the same value to the *get* channel. The process calls itself recursively to obtain the repetition.

Note that input and output are just expressions. As stated earlier in connection with assignment: "there are only expressions". No special syntax category is introduced for expressing communication, just as no special syntax category is introduced for expressing assignment.

4.1.4 Composing expressions in parallel

Communication through channels is the means by which expressions evaluating in parallel interact. In fact communication can only take place when input and output expressions involving the same channel are evaluated in parallel — communication is synchronised.

As an example, supose there is a channel *c* and variable *x*, both of type **Int**. Then the expression *x:=c?* ∥ *c!5* can, if communication takes place, have the effect *x:=5*.

Parallel attempts to input from a channel and to output to the channel do, however, not necessarily lead to a communication. Whether it does depends on an internal choice. The two expressions could communicate with a third expression which is put in parallel with the two. One can for example put the expression *c!7* in parallel with the two expressions as follows:

(x:=c? ∥ c!5) ∥ c!7

and then as one possible effect obtain:

x:=7 ; c!5

That is, the rightmost expression outputs the value 7 to the channel c. The leftmost expression inputs the value and stores it in x. After the communication, the communication c!5 still remains to be performed.

Note, however, that the effect may also be:

x:=5 ; c!7

or either of these sequences may occur in the reversed order, or the effect may even be that no communication takes place at all.

The parallel combinator is commutative as well as associative.

Two expression evaluations occurring in parallel should be state-independent: if one expression has write access to a variable, the other should not have access to that variable (neither read from it, nor write to it). RSL type checking does not enforce state-independency, but it is highly recommended.

As an example of a parallel system, suppose that we want to use the one place buffer as a connection between two processes called *reader* and *writer*.

READER_WRITER =
    extend ONE_PLACE_BUFFER **with**
    class
        type Input, Output
        channel
            input : Input,
            output : Output
        value
            $transform_1$: Input $\rightarrow$ Elem,
            $transform_2$: Elem $\rightarrow$ Output,
            reader : **Unit** $\rightarrow$ **in** input **out** add **Unit**,
            writer : **Unit** $\rightarrow$ **in** get **out** output **Unit**
        axiom
            reader() $\equiv$ **let** v = input? **in** add!($transform_1$(v)) **end** ; reader(),
            writer() $\equiv$ **let** v = get? **in** output!($transform_2$(v)) **end** ; writer()
    end

The *reader* process repeatedly inputs a value v from the *input* channel and outputs the value $transform_1(v)$ to the *add* channel. The *writer* process repeatedly inputs a value v from the *get* channel and outputs the value $transform_2(v)$ to the *output* channel. The functions $transform_1$ and $transform_2$ are under-specified.

We can now put the processes *reader*, *opb* and *writer* together in parallel, calling the composed process *system*.

SYSTEM =
   extend READER_WRITER **with**
   class
      value system : **Unit** → **in** input, add, get **out** output, add, get **Unit**
      axiom system() ≡ reader() ‖ opb() ‖ writer()
   end

4.1.5   Hiding channels

We can see from its accesses that the channels *add* and *get* are part of the interface of the *system* process. This is unfortunate since these channels together with the one place buffer should really be internal. A better definition makes these channels local to system.

SYSTEM =
   class
      type Input, Output
      channel
         input : Input,
         output : Output
      value system : **Unit** → **in** input **out** output **Unit**
      axiom
         system() ≡
           local
              type Elem
              channel add, get : Elem
              value
                 opb : **Unit** → **in** add **out** get **Unit**,
                 $transform_1$: Input → Elem,
                 $transform_2$: Elem → Output,
                 reader : **Unit** → **in** input **out** add **Unit**,
                 writer : **Unit** → **in** get **out** output **Unit**
              axiom
                 opb() ≡ **let** v = add? **in** get!v **end** ; opb(),
                 reader() ≡ **let** v = input? **in** add!($transform_1$(v)) **end** ; reader(),
                 writer() ≡ **let** v = get? **in** output!($transform_2$(v)) **end** ; writer()
           in
              reader() ‖ opb() ‖ writer()
           end
   end

The types *Input* and *Output* and the channels *input* and *output* are still defined at the outermost level since all these items are part of the interface of the *system* process. The rest is locally defined since it is internal.

    It may seem tedious to be forced to define all sub-processes of a process within a local expression, especially when a system consists of many sub-processes and these perhaps themselves are composite. Section 5.4 illustrates how the module concept can be used in combination with the local expression to model a hierarchy of processes.

4.1.6 External choice

The one place buffer was always only ready to input on one channel or (following an input) output on one channel. But many processes need something more general, to be able to respond to a variety of inputs or outputs in an arbitrary order.

As an example consider a specification of a many place buffer capable of holding several elements at one time. There is no limit on the size of the buffer, except that at any one time it can contain only finitely many elements.

The many place buffer process, *mpb*, holds all buffered elements in a list. The list is a parameter to *mpb*.

MANY_PLACE_BUFFER =
  class
    type
      Elem,
      Buffer = Elem*
    channel
      empty : **Unit**,
      add, get : Elem
    value mpb : Buffer → **in** empty, add **out** get **Unit**
    axiom forall b : Buffer •
      mpb(b) ≡
        empty? ; mpb(⟨⟩)
        []
        let v = add? **in** mpb(b ⌢ ⟨v⟩) **end**
        []
        if b ≠ ⟨⟩ **then** get!(hd b) ; mpb(tl b) **else stop end**
  end

The buffer is connected with the surroundings by three channels. Values are added to the buffer via the *add* channel and leave the buffer again via the *get* channel. The *empty* channel makes it possible to empty the buffer. This is done by sending a signal (the unit value () of type **Unit**) on the *empty* channel.

The axiom for *mpb* reads as follows. Assuming the buffer b, three kinds of communications may be offered:

- A value (the unit value) may be input from the *empty* channel. Upon input, the buffer process continues with the empty list as parameter, representing the empty buffer.

- A value, v, may be input from the *add* channel. Upon input, the buffer process continues with an extended list as parameter.

- If the list b is non-empty, the process may output the head of the list to the *get* channel and then continue with the tail of the list as parameter.

The else-branch of the if expression is entered if the list b is empty. That is, the else-branch is entered if the buffer contains no elements to be output to the *get* channel. The predefined expression **stop** represents deadlock — it will have no further effects. When placed in an external choice, however, by deadlocking one choice it forces one of the others to be chosen. This is because **stop** is the unit for external choice — it has the property that for any expression *value_expr*, the following equivalence holds:

$$\text{value\_expr} \;[]\; \textbf{stop} \equiv \text{value\_expr}$$

The external choice operator is such that if another process in parallel with *mpb* offers a communication on one of the channels — say it outputs a value on the add channel — and if there are no other communications possible with other parallel expressions, then the communication on the *add* channel will be chosen. The choice is called external because it is the other process that makes the choice, not *mpb*.

The external choice combinator is commutative and associative.

4.1.7 Internal choice

In addition to the external choice combinator, RSL provides an internal choice combinator $\lceil\rceil$ that specifies an internal choice between two expressions. Expressions involving an internal choice are described as non-deterministic.

The internal choice combinator is not typically used in specifications because of its generally undesirable behaviour. If we had used it instead of external choice in defining *mpb*, then when offered an output on the *add* channel, say, *mpb* could choose internally not to communicate on that channel.

We have also seen how internal choice can arise in implicit let expressions. It is also possible to write case expressions involving record patterns that are non-deterministic. And, of course, concurrent systems typically have choices of internal behaviour that cannot be influenced externally, so parallel expressions often have equivalent forms involving internal choice.

4.1.8 Example: A Database

Consider a concurrent version of the database from section 2.8.6. A database process, *database*, is defined together with channels for communicating with it.

DATABASE =
  class
    type Key, Data
    channel
      empty : **Unit**,

```
        insert : Key × Data,
        remove, defined, lookup : Key,
        defined_res : Bool,
        lookup_res : Data
    value
        database : Unit → in empty, insert, remove, defined, lookup
                                    out defined_res, lookup_res Unit,
        not_found : Data
    axiom
        database() ≡
          local
              variable : db : Key ⇥ Data := [ ]
          in
              while true do
                  empty? ; db := [ ]
                  []
                  let (k,d) = insert? in db := db † [k ↦ d] end
                  []
                  let k = remove? in db := db\{k} end
                  []
                  let k = defined? in defined_res!(k ∈ dom db) end
                  []
                  let k = lookup? in
                      if k ∈ dom db then lookup_res!(db(k))
                      else lookup_res!not_found
                      end
                  end
              end
          end
    end
```

Note we have made the database imperative and made its state (the variable *db*) local to it. We can be sure that nothing else can access this variable.

An essential task when specifying a process is to decide what the channels are and what the protocol is for their use. The specification above illustrates for example how certain channels should be used in particular sequences: an ingoing communication on the *defined* channel is always followed by an outgoing communication on the *defined_res* channel. Likewise for the channels *lookup* and *lookup_res*.

We could improve this specification by adding som 'interface functions' that observe this protocol and also give more convenient means of access. For example:

value Defined : Key → **out** defined **in** defined_res **Bool**
axiom forall k : Key • Defined(k) ≡ defined!k ; defined_res?

Using interface functions also allows us to use **any** instead of channels, similar to its use with variable accesses, as we shall see in the example in section 4.2.1.

4.1.9   Equivalence expressions

We saw in section 3.1.6 that equivalences involving $\equiv$ compared effects as well as results returned. Having added input and output expressions we need to extend our notion of equivalence to say that expressions must also have the same possible communications to be equivalent.

4.2   Algebraic definition of processes

Processes can be defined abstractly in terms of algebraic equivalences. We have already seen how this can be done for applicative functions (section 2.5) and for operations (section 3.5).

We need first to introduce a new combinator that is more "aggressive" than the parallel combinator in forcing communication between the two expressions to happen. The interlocking combinator $\|\|$ does exactly that. An expression of the form:

$$\text{value\_expr}_1 \;\|\|\; \text{value\_expr}_2$$

is evaluated by evaluating the two constituent expressions (both having type **Unit**) interlocked in parallel: the two expressions are evaluated in parallel until the evaluation of one of them comes to an end, whereupon evaluation continues with the other (just like $\|$). However: during the parallel evaluation, any external communication is prevented. The interlocking combinator may best be explained by stating some equivalences between expressions using it.

Assume the following definitions:

value e, e_1, e_2 : T
channel c, c_1, c_2 : T
variable x : T

Then the following equivalence holds:

$$x := c? \;\|\|\; c!e \equiv x := e$$

That is: since the two expressions $x{:=}c?$ and $c!e$ can communicate, they will communicate.

The corresponding equivalence for the parallel combinator is somewhat more complicated:

$$x := c? \;\|\; c!e \equiv (x := e) \;\sqcap\; ((x := c? \;;\; c!e) \;[]\; (c!e \;;\; x := c?) \;[]\; (x := e))$$

Another example involving the external choice combinator with interlock is the following:

$$(x := c_1? \;[]\; c_2!e_2) \;\|\|\; c_1!e_1 \equiv x := e_1$$

That is: the interlocking combinator forces the external choice of the expression $x := c_1?$.

These equivalences show how the interlocking combinator leaves no possible communications outstanding. In the reverse case, where both of the interlocked expressions want to communicate, but not with each other, the result is a deadlock. This is illustrated by the following equivalence:

$$x := c_1? \,\|\hspace{-3pt}\|\, c_2!e \equiv \textbf{stop}$$

The corresponding equivalence for the parallel combinator is as follows:

$$x := c_1? \,\|\, c_2!e \equiv (x := c_1? \,;\, c_2!e) \;[]\; (c_2!e \,;\, x := c_1?)$$

That is: since the two expressions cannot communicate with each other, they can only communicate with the surroundings.

The interlocking combinator is commutative but it is not associative (by contrast with the parallel combinator). It associates to the left.

4.2.1 Example: A Database

Consider an algebraic specification of a concurrency-based database. We will be implicit about channels by not defining any. Consequently, we must define a set of interface functions.

DATABASE =
    class
        type Key, Data
        value
            empty : **Unit → in any out any Unit**,
            insert : Key × Data → **in any out any Unit**,
            remove : Key → **in any out any Unit**,
            defined : Key → **in any out any Bool**,
            lookup : Key → **in any out any Data**
        value database : **Unit $\xrightarrow{\sim}$ in any out any Unit**
        axiom forall k, k_1 : Key, d : Data, tb : **Bool** $\xrightarrow{\sim}$ Unit, td : Data $\xrightarrow{\sim}$ Unit •
        [remove_empty]
            (database() $\|\hspace{-3pt}\|$ empty()) $\|\hspace{-3pt}\|$ remove(k) $\equiv$
                database() $\|\hspace{-3pt}\|$ empty(),
        [remove_insert]
            (database() $\|\hspace{-3pt}\|$ insert(k_1,d)) $\|\hspace{-3pt}\|$ remove(k) $\equiv$
                if $k = k_1$ **then** database() $\|\hspace{-3pt}\|$ remove(k)
                else (database() $\|\hspace{-3pt}\|$ remove(k)) $\|\hspace{-3pt}\|$ insert(k_1,d)
                end,
        [defined_empty]
            (database() $\|\hspace{-3pt}\|$ empty()) $\|\hspace{-3pt}\|$ tb(defined(k)) $\equiv$
                (database() $\|\hspace{-3pt}\|$ empty()) $\|\hspace{-3pt}\|$ tb(**false**)
        [defined_insert]

$$(\text{database}() \parallel \text{insert}(k_1,d)) \parallel \text{tb}(\text{defined}(k)) \equiv$$
$$\quad \text{if } k = k_1 \text{ then } (\text{database}() \parallel \text{insert}(k_1,d)) \parallel \text{tb}(\textbf{true})$$
$$\quad \text{else } (\text{database}() \parallel \text{tb}(\text{defined}(k))) \parallel \text{insert}(k_1,d)$$
$$\quad \textbf{end},$$

[lookup_insert]

$$(\text{database}() \parallel \text{insert}(k_1,d)) \parallel \text{td}(\text{lookup}(k)) \equiv$$
$$\quad \text{if } k = k_1 \text{ then } (\text{database}() \parallel \text{insert}(k_1,d)) \parallel \text{td}(d)$$
$$\quad \text{else } (\text{database}() \parallel \text{td}(\text{lookup}(k))) \parallel \text{insert}(k_1,d)$$
$$\quad \textbf{end}$$

end

The 'test' functions tb and td are introduced because interlocked expressions must be **Unit** valued.

The concurrency-based database example illustrates the constructor technique for inventing axioms, which we have previously seen applied in the state-based case as well as in the applicative case. The technique used in the concurrency-based case with interaction processes can be characterized as follows.

1. Identify the "constructor interaction processes" by which any database can be constructed. These are the processes *empty* and *insert*. Any database can thus be generated by an expression of the form:

$$\text{database}() \parallel \text{empty}() \parallel \text{insert}(k_1,d_1) \parallel \ldots \parallel \text{insert}(k_n,d_n)$$

2. Define the remaining processes "by case" over the constructor processes, using new identifiers as parameters. In the above axioms, *remove*, *defined* and *lookup* are defined over the two constructor expressions:

   empty()
   insert(k_1,d)

We thus get all the left hand sides of the axioms we need "for free". That is:

$$(\text{database}() \parallel \text{empty}()) \parallel \text{remove}(k)$$
$$(\text{database}() \parallel \text{insert}(k_1,d)) \parallel \text{remove}(k)$$
$$(\text{database}() \parallel \text{empty}()) \parallel \text{tb}(\text{defined}(k))$$
$$(\text{database}() \parallel \text{insert}(k_1,d)) \parallel \text{tb}(\text{defined}(k))$$
$$(\text{database}() \parallel \text{empty}()) \parallel \text{td}(\text{lookup}(k))$$
$$(\text{database}() \parallel \text{insert}(k_1,d)) \parallel \text{td}(\text{lookup}(k))$$

Note, however, that we choose to underspecify the effect of *lookup* and so we do not include an axiom with left hand side *(database() $\parallel$ empty()) $\parallel$ td(lookup(k))*.

We have also used **any** in the in and out accesses. This has the following advantages.

- We have avoided deciding what channels there will be and what their types will be.

- The specification places no restrictions on what channels the processes are allowed to access. The implementation of abstract interaction processes in terms of concrete interaction processes that do explicit channel communication is sometimes referred to as event refinement. This is particularly useful in that we can decide later what protocols to use, such as allowing external choices only over inputs if the programming language we want to finally implement in enforces such a restriction. (We could design in this way from the start, but only at the cost of a less abstract and less re-usable specification.)

Being explicit, however, has its benefits. From the type of a process one can see exactly what channels may be accessed and how they may be accessed. This can make concurrency-based specifications easier to read.

5 Specification compositions

5.1 Some basic concepts

Modules are the means by which to decompose specifications into comprehensible and reusable units. A module is basically a named collection of declarations. A module M_1 can be used to define another module M_2, meaning that the declarations of M_1 are used to define M_2.

As we shall see, there are two kinds of modules: objects and schemes. All the modules shown so far in this tutorial are actually schemes. Modules are the only entities that can be defined at the outermost level of a specification. In other words, a specification is a collection of module declarations.

Before introducing objects and schemes, the concept of a basic class expression is described. Class expressions are fundamental in the definition of both objects and schemes.

5.1.1 Basic class expressions

A basic class expression is simply a collection of declarations enclosed by the keywords **class** and **end**.

We have seen many examples of basic class expressions, and we have seen examples of type, value, variable, channel and axiom declarations. As we shall see, class expressions are entities in their own right, and can therefore also be defined in declarations (of schemes).

A class expression represents a class (synonym for set) of models. Each model associates an entity (value, type, variable, channel or module) with each identifier defined within the class expression. There may be more than one model because identifiers may be under-specified.

As an example consider the following class expression:

class
   value i : **Int**
   axiom i = 1 ∨ i = 2
end

This class expression represents the finite class containing two models, corresponding to the fact that *i* is under-specified. The class can be illustrated as follows:

$$\{\, [\, i \mapsto 1 \,]\,, [\, i \mapsto 2 \,]\, \}$$

The class represented by a basic class expression is the class containing all models that satisfy the declarations. Each of the two models above satisfies the declarations. Take for example the first model *[i ↦ 1]*.

This model satisfies the declaration of *i* as it maps the identifier *i* to the integer value *1*. It also satisfies the axiom for *i*. Similarly for the second model.

In fact, this description is a simplification. In order to allow extension (adding new definitions) as implementations we define the models of a class expression to include all possible extensions. This means that the class of models of any class expression is infinite. But we can characterise the classes of models for our simple example as all containing an association of the value *i* to either *1* or *2*.

Class expressions may also have other forms, as we shall see in subsequent sections. The other forms can, however, usually be expanded into equivalent basic class expressions.

In the following we see how one can give names to models (giving objects) and class expressions (giving schemes).

5.1.2 Objects

An object is essentially a named model chosen from a class of models represented by some class expression. When we write,·for example:

object O :
   class
      value i : **Int**
      axiom i = 1 ∨ i = 2
   end

the the name *O* is bound to a model from the models of the class expression. The model is arbitrary —we do not know which one *O* is bound to. All we know is that in *O* there is an integer value *i* that satisfies the axiom.

Immediately outside the declaration of *O* we can refer to the value *i* by the name '*O.i*'. Such a reference is called a qualified identifier.

There is one exception to the arbitrariness in the choice of models for an object: if the class expressions of objects define variables or channels then these are always distinct for different objects, even if the same class expressions are used to define several objects.

Note that object definitions use class expressions. Since class expressions can themselves define objects (and, as we shall see, schemes) module definitions can be nested. They can also be defined in local expressions.

5.1.3 Schemes

An object represents a model, arbitrarily chosen from the class of models represented by some class expression. In some situations it is convenient to be able to manipulate class expressions on their own before defining objects. A prerequisite for doing this is that one can name class expressions.

A named class expression is called a scheme. An occurrence of the scheme name then represents its class expression. For instance

scheme S = **class variable** v : **Int end**
object
   O_1 : S,
   O_2 : S

declares a scheme S and two objects O_1 and O_2. We can now refer to two (distinct) variables $O_1.v$ and $O_2.v$.

5.1.4 Extension

One can in RSL build a class expression in successive steps, at each step adding declarations with the **extend** operator.

As an example, suppose we want to gradually build up the scheme *LIST_S*. In the first step we decide what the state is. That is, we define the basic scheme *LIST_STATE*.

scheme LIST_STATE =
  class
    variable list : **Int***
  end

In the second step we identify all the operations on the state, but we ignore any axioms defining properties of the operations. The addition of the operations is expressed as an extension of the *LIST_STATE* scheme.

scheme LIST_OPERATIONS =
  extend LIST_STATE **with**
  class
    value
      empty : **Unit** → **write** list **Unit**,
      is_empty : **Unit** → **read** list **Bool**,
      add : **Int** → **write** list **Unit**,
      head : **Unit** $\overset{\sim}{\to}$ **read** list **Int**,
      tail : **Unit** $\overset{\sim}{\to}$ **write** list **Unit**
  end

Such an extension can be expanded into a basic class expression by simply combining the declarations of the extended class expression with the new ones. The above one can therefore be expanded into the following scheme definition.

```
scheme LIST_OPERATIONS =
    class
        variable list : Int*
        value
            empty : Unit → write list Unit,
            is_empty : Unit → read list Bool,
            add : Int → write list Unit,
            head : Unit ⁻̃→ read list Int,
            tail : Unit ⁻̃→ write list Unit
    end
```

In the third and final step we add axioms defining properties of the operations.

```
scheme LIST_S =
    extend LIST_OPERATIONS with
    class
        axiom forall i : Int ·
            empty() ≡ list := ⟨⟩,
            is_empty() ≡ list = ⟨⟩,
            add(i) ≡ list := ⟨i⟩ ˆ list,
            head() ≡ hd list
            pre ~is_empty(),
            tail() ≡ list := tl list
            pre ~is_empty()
    end
```

This scheme definition can also be expanded into one using a single basic class expression.

5.2 Renaming and hiding

In addition to the **extend** operator there are two more operators available on class expressions, namely renaming and hiding.

5.2.1 Renaming

A class expression may be renamed giving a new class expression with old names replaced by new names. As an example, consider the following renaming of the *LIST_S* scheme making it into a stack scheme.

```
scheme STACK_S =
    use stack for list, push for add, top for head, pop for tail
    in LIST_S
```

A renaming class expression can be expanded into a basic class expression. The result of the expansion is as follows.

scheme STACK_S =
  class
    variable stack : Int*
    value
      empty : **Unit** → **write** stack **Unit**,
      is_empty : **Unit** → **read** stack **Bool**,
      push : **Int** → **write** stack **Unit**,
      top : **Unit** $\overset{\sim}{\to}$ **read** stack **Int**,
      pop : **Unit** $\overset{\sim}{\to}$ **write** stack **Unit**
    axiom forall i : **Int** •
      empty() ≡ stack := ⟨⟩,
      is_empty() ≡ stack = ⟨⟩,
      push(i) ≡ stack := ⟨i⟩ ⌢ stack,
      top() ≡ **hd** stack
      pre ~is_empty(),
      pop() ≡ stack := **tl** stack
      pre ~is_empty()
  end

5.2.2 Hiding

Identifiers defined within a class expression may be hidden so that one cannot refer to them outside the class expression.

As an example we can make the *LIST_S* scheme more abstract by hiding the variable *list*. This is a common encapsulation technique which prevents variables from being accessed except through their associated operations.

scheme ABSTRACT_LIST_S = **hide** list **in** LIST_S

Another typical use of hiding is the hiding of auxiliary functions by means of which more central functions are defined.

A hiding class expression cannot immediately be expanded into a basic class expression, since hiding is not a concept expressible in basic class expressions.

Note that hiding in RSL only restricts visibility. The names hidden are not available outside the class expression but its properties are unchanged.

5.3 Parameterized schemes

The above modules specify lists with element type **Int**. A more general solution would be to turn the element type into a parameter, thereby making it possible to specify lists with arbitrary element types.

RSL allows for such parameterization by allowing schemes to be parameterized with objects.

5.3.1 Simple parameterization and instantiation

A parameterized version of lists is the following:

scheme PARAM_LIST(E : **class type** Elem **end**) =
  class
    variable list : E.Elem*
    value
      empty : **Unit** → **write** list **Unit**,
      is_empty : **Unit** → **read** list **Bool**,
      add : E.Elem → **write** list **Unit**,
      head : **Unit** $\overset{\sim}{\to}$ **read** list E.Elem,
      tail : **Unit** $\overset{\sim}{\to}$ **write** list **Unit**
    axiom forall e : E.Elem •
      empty() ≡ list := ⟨⟩,
      is_empty() ≡ list = ⟨⟩,
      add(e) ≡ list := ⟨e⟩ ^ list,
      head() ≡ **hd** list
      pre ∼is_empty(),
      tail() ≡ list := **tl** list
      pre ∼is_empty()
  end

The *PARAM_LIST* scheme is parameterized over the list element type *Elem*. More precisely, the scheme may be instantiated with any object that at least defines a type named *Elem*. When instantiated with such an object, the result will be a class expression referring to that object.

Let us instantiate the scheme with an object. Consider for example the following object providing a type *Elem* representing the integers:

object INTEGER :
  class
    type Elem = **Int**
  end

The *PARAM_LIST* scheme can now be instantiated with *INTEGER* as follows:

object INTEGER_LIST : PARAM_LIST(INTEGER)

That is, the *INTEGER_LIST* object is defined to represent some arbitrary model within the class represented by the class expression *PARAM_LIST(INTEGER)*. This class expression can be expanded into a basic class expression by replacing all occurrences of the formal parameter name *E* within the class expression defining *PARAM_LIST* with *INTEGER*.

The *INTEGER_LIST* object can now be used to maintain a list of integers. One can for example by the following expression initialise the list to contain the single integer *1*:

INTEGER_LIST.empty() ; INTEGER_LIST.add(1)

The instantiation of the *PARAM_LIST* scheme with the *INTEGER* object is well-formed since the scheme requires an object defining a type *Elem* and since the object actually provides such a type. Section 5.3.5 will explain in more detail when instantiations of parameterized schemes are well-formed.

5.3.2 Naming of parameter requirements

The parameter requirement of the *PARAM_LIST* scheme is the class expression:

class type Elem **end**

Typically one defines such requirements as schemes and one then writes scheme names as parameter requirements. We can define a scheme in this style as follows:

scheme ELEMENT = **class type** Elem **end**

We can now define the parameterized scheme as follows:

scheme PARAM_LIST(E : ELEMENT) = **class** ... **end**

This style is somewhat more pleasant than writing a basic class expression (including keywords **class** and **end**) at the place where *ELEMENT* occurs.

5.3.3 Object fittings

There are situations where the object with which we want to instantiate a parameterized scheme provides names different to the ones required by the parameter requirement. In this case the object must be subjected to a fitting at instantiation time.

Suppose for example that we wish to define a list of database commands. We first define a database command object that provides the type of commands. The database is assumed to associate natural numbers with texts.

object COMMAND :
  class
    type
      Key = **Nat**,
      Data = **Text**,
      Command ==
        mk_empty | mk_insert(Key, Data) | mk_remove(Key) | mk_lookup(Key)
  end

Before instantiating the *PARAM_LIST* scheme with this object, we notice that the type name *Command* is different from the required type name *Elem*. We further notice that the object defines more names than required. That is, besides *Command*, the following names are defined: *Key*, *Data*, *mk_empty*, *mk_insert*, *mk_remove* and *mk_lookup*.

The extra names are not a problem since the requirement just defines a minimal name space, allowing for extra names to be defined in the actual parameter object.

The difference between the actual name (*Command*) and the required name (*Elem*) is a problem. To resolve it, we must fit the *COMMAND* object at instantiation time to provide the name *Elem* instead of *Command*. This is done below.

object COMMAND_LIST : PARAM_LIST(COMMAND{Command **for** Elem})

The fitting {*Command* **for** *Elem*} fits the names that we want to use (from *COMMAND*) to the original names (from *ELEMENT*). A fitting is in general a list of such pairs.

5.3.4 More complex parameter requirements

The parameter requirement *ELEMENT* of the *PARAM_LIST* scheme is simple in the sense that it only requires a single type. A parameter requirement may be more complex; it may, for instance, require some functions to be defined over that type. In fact, since the requirement is generally a class expression, any kind of entity can be required and axioms can be given that express required properties.

5.3.5 Actual versus formal parameters

There is a relation that must hold between an actual and a formal parameter for a scheme application to be well formed. Note that a formal scheme parameter takes the form *identifier : class_expression* and an actual parameter is an object, which has an associated class expression. The relation is that the class expression of the actual parameter must 'statically implement' the class expression of the formal parameter. (The term statically implement is chosen because static implementation is the statically decidable part of the RSL implementation relation.)

To explain the static implementation relation we first generalise the notion of 'signature'. We have already used the term for the association of a name and its type in a value definition. We can similarly have a signature for a variable or channel — they have names and types. For type definitions we can say the signature of a sort definition (which is just a new type name) is merely the name of the new type. For a type abbreviation the signature associates the name of the new type with the type it is an abbreviation for. Since variant type definitions can be expanded to sort definitions plus some value and axiom declarations, and union and short record definitions can be expanded to variant definitions, we can give signatures to all type definitions. Axiom definitions have no signatures.

For schemes and objects we create a signature by associating the name of the scheme or object with, instead of a type, the class represented by its class expression, together with the classes of parameters for parameterised schemes, and the type of the index for object arrays.

There is also a notion of 'maximal class' that directly corresponds to the notion of 'maximal type'. One can obtain the maximal class of a class expression basically by ignoring all axioms and taking the maximal versions of all types and classes mentioned, just as one can obtain the maximal type of a type expression by ignoring the predicates that define subtypes and taking the maximal versions of any types mentioned. So we have a notion of 'maximal signature' involving only maximal classes and types.

The static implementation relation is now simple to formulate: class expression A statically implements class expression B if the maximal signature of A is included in the maximal signature of B. That is B must provide (at least) all the schemes, objects, types, variables, channels and values that A does, with the same maximal classes or types.

If a fitting is applied to an actual scheme parameter, the condition is that the class expression of the object to which the fitting is applied must statically implement the class expression of the formal parameter when the fitting is applied to it as a renaming. For example, we can use

COMMAND{Command **for** Elem}

as an actual parameter when the formal was $E : ELEMENT$ if the class expression of the object COMMAND statically implements

use Command **for** Elem **in** ELEMENT

This last class expression expands to

class type Command **end**

and this is indeed statically implemented by the class expression defining COMMAND.

If there are several formal parameters then there must be the same number of actuals and formals, the first actual statically implementing the first formal and so on.

It is obviously a good idea to check that an actual parameter fully implements the formal, just as it is a good idea to check that a negative integer is not used as an actual parameter to function defined only for natural numbers, but in neither case is the specification technically ill-formed. Well-formedness is defined as abiding by the static conditions that can be checked by a type checker.

5.4 Object arrays

We have seen how one can define a model as a member of a class represented by a class expression. The model may be identified by an object identifier. If several models are wanted, each being a member of the same class, one may define just as many object identifiers.

In some situations it is useful to be allowed to define an arbitrary number of models of the same class. The concept of an object array gives exactly this possibility, each model being identified by an object identifier common to them all and some additional distinct index value. For example, suppose we want to use a semaphore to ensure that a number of processes are unable to run concurrently. We want to specify this without knowing how many such processes there will be, or indeed anything else about them. So we start with two schemes to be used as parameters:

scheme INDEX = **class type** Index **end**

scheme PROCESS = **class value** process : **Unit** $\overset{\sim}{\to}$ **in any out any Unit end**

We also perhaps already have a specification of a basic semaphore:

scheme SEMAPHORE =
  class
    value get, release, sem: **Unit** $\overset{\sim}{\to}$ **in any out any Unit**
    axiom
      (sem() $\parallel$ get()) $\parallel$ release() $\equiv$ sem(),
      (sem() $\parallel$ get()) $\parallel$ get() $\equiv$ **stop**,
      sem() $\parallel$ release() $\equiv$ **stop**
  end

A semaphore will do successive gets and releases but nothing else.
    We can now specify our system.

scheme SYSTEM(I : INDEX, P[i:I.Index] : PROCESS) =
class
  value sys : **Unit** $\overset{\sim}{\to}$ **in** { P[i].**any** | I : I.Index } **out** { P[i].**any** | I : I.Index } **Unit**
  axiom
    sys() $\equiv$
      local
        object
          S : SEMAPHORE,
          A[i:I.Index] :
            class
              value
                proc : **Unit** $\overset{\sim}{\to}$ **in** P[i].**any** S.**any out** P[i].**any** S.**any Unit**
              axiom
                proc() $\equiv$ S.get() ; P[i].process() ; S.release() ; proc()
            end
      in
        $\parallel$\{ A[i].proc() | i : I.Index } $\parallel$ S.sem()
      end
end

The second parameter to *SYSTEM* is an object array — a collection of objects (each an instance of PROCESS) with an index for selecting particular objects. There is also an object array *A* defined locally to *sys*. Each *proc* in the array *A* calls the corresponding *process* from the array P, but guarded by a *get* and *release* from the semaphore object S, and then calls itself again. *sys* then needs to run all these guarded processes in parallel. It does this by means of the comprehension expression

‖{ A[i].proc() | i : I.Index }

This expression in parallel with *S.sem* completes the definition of *sys*.

Note that object arrays also necessitate some form of comprehended accesses in the signature of *sys*; the meaning of these should be clear.

6 The RAISE method

This tutorial is primarily about the RAISE specification language, RSL. In this section we will give a brief overview of the method, focusing on formal issues. For a much fuller description see the RAISE method manual, [BrG90].

6.1 Basic concepts

The goal of the RAISE method is to use a formal method to produce software that meets its requirements, is reliable, is maintainable and reusable, by a process that is predictable.

Note that there are several software engineering concerns here. We are interested in the industrial use of formality, so we have to deal with such issues. They are, however, generally outside the scope of this tutorial, but the full RAISE method covers the software lifecycle from requirements analysis through to production of code and on to maintenance and enhancement.

The kernel of formal development is the idea of stepwise development. One starts with an initial specification that is suitably abstract. It is intended to capture what a software system must do rather than the details of how it will do it. Hence it leaves open all the design decisions that can be left open. One then goes through a number of design steps, elaborating the specification to make explicit those things that were previously implicit, until one has a specification that can be conveniently (and perhaps automatically) translated into code in some programming language. Ideally these design steps will be refinements. That is, one level of the specification will conform to the previous one in maintaining all its properties. In practice, we find that not all design steps can be refinements, though they will be close to it. The method allows one to state what the exact relationship is.

6.2 Refinement relation

The refinement, or implementation relation of RSL has been mentioned earlier when we described a part of it in section 5.3.5, namely the 'static implementation' relation. This relation, maximal signature inclusion for class expressions, is a pre-requisite for implementation. The formal definition of implementation in RSL is that a class expression A is implemented by a class expression B if all the models of B are models of A. So, refinement is the process of discarding some models (i.e. possible final implementations) in favour of others.

Since we want to allow extension — the addition of new types, values etc. — as a natural form of refinement, we define the models of a class expression to include all those of its possible extensions. So the models of any class expression form an infinite class. We need a proof theoretic characterisation of these models to help us to construct and to allow us to check possible refinements.

It turns out that the definition in terms of subclasses of models is equivalent to one in terms of theory extension. So we have that class expression A is implemented by class expression B if

- the maximal signature of A is included in the maximal signature of B (B statically implements A), and then

- the theory of A is provable in B

So to characterise implementation in this way we have to describe what the 'theory' of the various kinds of class expression and their various constituent declarations are. Loosely, the 'theory' of a class expression is all the information, expressed as axioms, we ignore in calculating its maximal signature.

Apart from hiding (which does not change the theory), all class expressions can be expanded into basic class expressions — essentially collections of declarations. So most of the definition reduces to the properties of declarations. We outline what is involved for each kind of declaration.

6.2.1 Refinement for schemes and objects

For scheme and object declarations the theory is the defining class expressions (plus any parameters for schemes, which are also expressed in terms of class expressions, and array parameters for object arrays). So checking that a new scheme or object definition implements an old one is a question of checking the relation between their class expressions. Similarly for scheme parameters, except that the relation for these is co-gradient — the class expression of the old parameter must implement the class expression of the new. For object arrays the new indices must include the old — we can make the array larger.

6.2.2 Refinement for variables and channels

The only theory for variables and channels is subtype information (if any) in their types and (for variables) any initialisation. Hence the checks are that the type of a new variable or channel must be a subtype of the type of the old variable or channel, and if an old variable had an initialisation then the new one must have an initialisation to an equivalent value.

It may seem strange to allow the reduction of the type of a variable or channel. What happens if we reduce its type while assigning or communicating values now outside that type? The answer is that we get a contradiction, which produces the empty set of models. This is a refinement, according to our definition, but a singularly useless one. So the freedom to reduce the types of variables or channels is rarely used.

6.2.3 Refinement for types

Since variant type definitions expand into sort definitions (just new type names), plus some value and axiom declarations, and union and short record definitions expand into variant definitions, there are really only two kinds of type declaration — sort and abbreviation definitions. For the first there is no theory — it just introduces a new type name. For the second the theory is that the new type name is equivalent to the type expression it is an abbreviation for. Hence the new type declaration must be an abbreviation definition for the same type.

Note that this refinement rule for types is more restrictive than that found in, for example, VDM. In RSL if we write

type Set = Elem-**set**

we cannot later refine it to

type Set = Elem*

even though there is a well known retrieve function from lists to sets. The reason for the restriction is that we want to be able to substitute refinements for the originals, as will become obvious later when we discuss separate development. Clearly we cannot just replace the first of these with the second — almost any expression involving values of the type *Set* will no longer even type check!

So instead of the first we either have to use an abstract definition for *Set*:

type Set == empty | add(Elem, Set)

or else we can use a 'representation function':

type Set
value rep : Set → Elem-**set**

rep is initially only given a signature (and is hidden). To get an implementation where sets are lists we could implement *rep* as **elems**. The techniques for data refinement are then very similar to those for VDM.

6.2.4 Refinement for values

A value declaration can always be expanded into a value declaration involving only maximal types and one or more axioms. The theory is then precisely these axioms. For example, the declarations

value
   x : **Int** = 2,
   y : **Nat** • y < 3

are equivalent to

value
   x : **Int**,
   y : **Int**
axiom
   x = 2,
   $y \geq 0 \wedge y < 3$

For functions there is a little more to do: total functions can only be refined by total functions and if there are accesses in the old then the new can only have a subset of those accesses. (Otherwise, for example, the property that a function cannot affect a variable could be lost.)

It is worth noting that as a result of the way that function definitions are expanded into axioms we obtain the refinement rules for functions that we might expect: domains may be increased, pre-conditions weakened, post-conditions strengthened.

6.2.5 Refinement for axioms

The axioms are precisely the theory. So we have to show that the old axioms hold in the new class expression.

6.3 Separate development

So far we have only addressed refinement for individual modules. But we want to be able to develop systems. Now the requirement here is that we want to be able to do separate development. This is illustrated in figure 1.

The idea being illustrated is that our system S uses another module A (in this case as a parameter). Schemes S_0 and A_0 are the initial specifications of these two modules. Now we want one team of developers to be able to develop A_0 to A_m, say and another team to develop S_0 to S_n, say, quite independently. That is, the only information the S team has about A is the intial specification A_0. This is shown by the fact that in their n'th specification S_n it is still A_0 that appears in the parameter. Then we want to be able to build a final implementation configuration, represented by the objects O_1 and O_2, with confidence that we have an implementation of S_0, our original system specification. The refinement relation of RSL guarantees precisely this.

This is of course a simplified picture. But note that it scales up with many separate developments. It also allows for changes that are not implementations to be controlled. If the A team need to do a non-implementation step then they have to negotiate the changes with the S team. Effectively the specification A_0 is a contract between the two — it says what the S team can rely on and it says what the A team guarantee to maintain.

Note finally that if all the specifications, the justifications of refinement, and some supporting documentation describing the reasons for development steps are all maintained then there is an excellent basis for maintenance and extension.

There is also the basis for reuse. If another project wants an A, or something like it, they can reuse the entire development, changing it if necessary in the same way as maintenance or enhancement of the original system changes it. Eventually there may

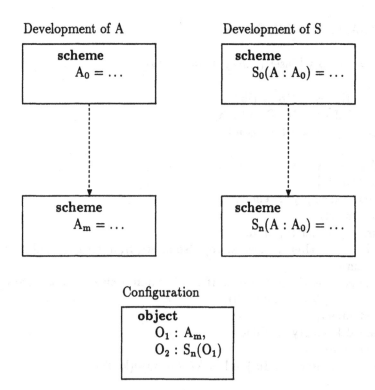

Figure 1: Separate development

be several developments starting from A_0 with different implementations with different properties like being space efficient or time efficient or being suitable for a particular programming language or operating system.

6.4   Example : A Transaction Database

We conclude with a development of a simple specification of a transactional database that processes a queue of update requests. We will use standard modules for the queue and database. The system is applicative.

We start with some schemes defining some types we will need for parameterising our components.

scheme KEY = **class type** Key **end**

scheme DATA = **class type** Data **end**

scheme ELEM = **class type** Elem **end**

We now formulate (or, in practice, find in our library) an abstract specification for an applicative database.

scheme $DATABASE_0(K : KEY, D : DATA) =$
   class
      type Db == empty | insert(K.Key, D.Data, Db)
      value
         remove : K.Key $\times$ Db $\rightarrow$ Db,
         lookup : K.Key $\times$ Db $\xrightarrow{\sim}$ D.Data,
         defined : K.Key $\times$ Db $\rightarrow$ **Bool**
      axiom
         forall k, k_1 : K.Key, d : D.Data, db : Db $\cdot$
         [remove_empty]
            remove(k, empty) $\equiv$ empty,
         [remove_insert]
            remove(k, insert(k_1, d, db)) $\equiv$
                if k = k_1 **then** remove(k, db) **else** insert(k_1, d, remove(k, db)) **end**,
         [lookup_insert]
            lookup(k, insert(k_1, d, db)) $\equiv$ **if** k = k_1 **then** d **else** lookup(k, db) **end**
            pre k = k_1 $\lor$ defined(k, db),
         [defined_empty]
            defined(k, empty) $\equiv$ **false**,
         [defined_insert]
            defined(k, insert(k_1, db)) $\equiv$ k = k_1 $\lor$ defined(k, db)
   end

We also find (or formulate) an abstract applicative queue.

scheme
$QUEUE_0(E : ELEM) =$
   class
      type Queue == empty | enq(E.Elem, Queue)
      value
         next : Queue $\xrightarrow{\sim}$ E.Elem,
         deq : Queue $\xrightarrow{\sim}$ Queue,
         is_empty : Queue $\rightarrow$ **Bool**
      axiom forall e : E.Elem, q: Queue $\cdot$
         is_empty(empty) $\equiv$ **true**,
         is_empty(enq(e, q)) $\equiv$ **false**,
         next(enq(e, q)) $\equiv$ **if** is_empty(q) **then** e **else** next(q) **end**,
         deq(enq(e, q)) $\equiv$ **if** is_empty(q) **then** empty **else** enq(e, deq(q)) **end**
   end

The initial system specification uses $DATABASE_0$ and $QUEUE_0$ to provide the *transact* function we want.

    Note the object *KD* introduced to give a suitable type *Elem* to use in instantiating $QUEUE_0$.

```
scheme SYSTEM₀(K : KEY, D : DATA) =
   class
      object
         DB : DATABASE₀(K, D),
         KD : class type Elem = K.Key × D.Data end,
         Q : QUEUE₀(KD)
      value
         transact : Q.Queue × DB.Db → DB.Db
         transact(q, db) ≡
            if Q.is_empty(q) then db
            else
               let (k, d) = Q.next(q) in
                  transact(Q.deq(q), DB.insert(k, d, db))
               end
            end
   end
```

This completes the initial specification. We now give developments of *DATABASE₀*, *QUEUE₀* and finally of *SYSTEM₀*.

For *DATABASE₁* we implement the type *Db* with the built-in map type.

```
scheme DATABASE₁(K : KEY, D : DATA) =
   class
      type Db = K.Key ⇥ D.Data
      value
         empty : Db = [ ],
         insert : K.Key × D.Data × Db → Db
         insert(k, d, db) ≡ db † [k ↦ d],
         remove : K.Key × Db → Db
         remove(k, db) ≡ db \ {k},
         lookup : K.Key × Db ⇾ D.Data
         lookup(k, db) ≡ db(k)
         pre defined(k, db),
         defined : K.Key × Db → Bool
         defined(k, db) ≡ k ∈ dom db
   end
```

For *QUEUE₁* we implement the type *Queue* with the built-in list type.

```
scheme QUEUE₁(E : ELEM) =
   class
      type Queue = E.Elem*
      value
         empty : Queue = ⟨⟩,
         enq : E.Elem × Queue → Queue
```

enq(e, q) ≡ q^⟨e⟩,
next : Queue $\xrightarrow{\sim}$ E.Elem
next(q) ≡ **hd** q
pre ~is_empty(q),
deq : Queue $\xrightarrow{\sim}$ Queue
deq(q) ≡ **tl** q
pre ~is_empty(q),
is_empty : Queue → **Bool**
is_empty(q) ≡ q = ⟨⟩

end

All we do for the final version of SYSTEM is replace $DATABASE_0$ and $QUEUE_0$ by $DATABASE_1$ and $QUEUE_1$.

scheme $SYSTEM_1(K : KEY, D : DATA) =$
  class
    object
      DB : $DATABASE_1(K, D)$,
      KD : **class type** Elem = K.Key × D.Data **end**,
      Q : $QUEUE_1(KD)$
    value
      transact : Q.Queue × DB.Db → DB.Db
      transact(q, db) ≡
        if Q.is_empty(q) **then** db
        else
          let (k, d) = Q.next(q) **in**
            transact(Q.deq(q), DB.insert(k, d, db))
          end
        end
  end

So how do we show that $SYSTEM_1$ refines $SYSTEM_0$? All we have to do is show that $DATABASE_1$ refines $DATABASE_0$ and that $QUEUE_1$ refines $QUEUE_0$.

We will sketch the justification for $DATABASE$; that for $QUEUE$ is very similar.

We first check that the new signature includes the old. This is immediate — the only change is the replacement of a sort definition for Db by an abbreviation definition.

We are left with showing that the theory of $DATABASE_1$ holds in $DATABASE_0$. This theory is recorded in the five axioms we specified plus the disjointness and induction axioms implied by the variant type definition for Db. (If we had had destructors or reconstructors in this variant type definition there would be extra axioms implied.) We have to justify these axioms in $DATABASE_1$, where of course we can use its definitions in terms of maps. We will consider *remove_insert* and (to keep the formulæ short) use case analysis, with cases $k = k_1$ and $k \neq k_1$. This us gives two (simplified) axioms

[remove_insert$_1$] $k = k_1$

$$remove(k, insert(k, d, db)) \equiv remove(k, db)$$

[remove_insert$_2$] $k \neq k_1$

$$remove(k, insert(k_1, d, db)) \equiv insert(k_1, d, remove(k, db))$$

The justification of the first is

$\llcorner remove(k, insert(k, d, db)) \equiv remove(k, db) \lrcorner$
unfold insert, remove
   $\llcorner (db \dagger [k \mapsto d]) \setminus \{k\} \equiv db \setminus \{k\} \lrcorner$
difference_override
   $\llcorner (db \setminus \{k\}) \dagger ([k \mapsto db] \setminus \{k\}) \equiv db \setminus \{k\} \lrcorner$
singleton_difference
   $\llcorner (db \setminus \{k\}) \dagger [] \equiv db \setminus \{k\} \lrcorner$
override_empty
   $\llcorner db \setminus \{k\} \equiv db \setminus \{k\} \lrcorner$
is_reflexivity
   $\llcorner \mathbf{qed} \lrcorner$

The justification of the second is very similar.

This justification has been presented in full detail. A more informal, 'rigorous' justification would, perhaps, show the unfoldings and then distribute map difference through map override. The rest is 'obvious'.

7   Tools

RAISE now has a comprehensive tool set. This includes:

- A library for storing and retrieving modules, development relations (to record refinement relations between modules, or other user-defined relations), theories (axioms that hold about modules) and hints (a space for text about other library entities). All entities, and references between entities, are version controlled.

- Entity editors for all library entities. These editors are all instantiations of the Synthesizer Generator ([ReT88]) and provide syntax directed editing and type checking.

- Tools for listing and deleting library entities and for propagating changes through versions.

- Translators for subsets of RSL to Ada and C++.

- A pretty printer for modules.

The tools are continually being enhanced and extended. In particular there is currently being developed a set of tools for generating conditions (especially those needed to show refinement) and for doing justifications (including formal proofs).

8 Acknowledgements

The RAISE method, language and tools were the result of a collective effort by the RAISE project team. In particular, most of this tutorial is based on the fuller tutorial (originally written by Klaus Havelund) in "The RAISE Specification Language" ([Rlg91]). The present author should be regarded as the editor of the tutorial in this paper.

References

[BrG90]   Brock, S., George, C., RAISE Method Manual, LACOS/CRI/DOC/3, 1990

[ErP91]   Eriksen, K. E., Prehn, S., RAISE Overview, RAISE/CRI/DOC/9, 1991

[ReT88]   Reps, T.W., Teitelbaum, T., The Synthesizer Generator, Springer Verlag, New York, 1988

[Rlg91]   The RAISE Language Group, The RAISE Specification Language, CRI/RAISE/DOC/1, 1991

Formal Development with ABEL

Ole-Johan Dahl and Olaf Owe

Department of Informatics
University of Oslo

1 Introduction

ABEL is a language together with a formal logic for use in program development. The overall goal has been to support specification and program development through semi-mechanical aids for reasoning and verification. In particular we have sought to:

- offer language constructs well suited for mechanical aids to reasoning, with some emphasis on mechanisms for constructive specification,

- encourage modularization and abstract specification of interfaces,

- facilitate reusability of modules through the use of parameters,

- offer powerful ways of putting modules together, including inheritance, restriction, inclusion, extension, as well as assumption specification and checking, and

- enable simple and manageable proof obligations, including those related to the composition of modules, in the form of first order formulas.

A major idea behind ABEL has been to allow the same language cover all stages of program development from abstract requirement specifications to efficient low level programming. Thus ABEL includes facilities for non-constructive requirements specification, constructive specification, applicative programming, and object oriented, imperative programming. (We let the term "specification" cover all of these.) We have tried to build the language around a few concepts which may be applied at all levels. Different stages may be related to each other through a concept of module simulation. If a low level module is proved to simulate an abstract one, then the latter may be used as an abstract specification of the low level module.

In the sequel we emphasize an applicative language level called TGI, which stands for *terminating generator induction*. TGI specifications give rise to convergent rewrite rules, which enable efficient manipulation of formulas and other expressions for purposes of simplification and proof. At the TGI level all proof obligations in connection with the composition of modules and module simulation are quantifier-free formulas in constructively defined functions, provided that user specified axioms are quantifier-free. ABEL includes logic for partial functions, also at the TGI level.

The ABEL language has been developed at the University of Oslo over a period of more than 15 years, mainly by the authors, and in close interaction with a regular student course on program specification and verification. The most important sources of ideas have been as follows: SIMULA 67 (classes and subclasses), the LARCH activity (generator induction), [7], and OBJ (order sorted algebras), [5].

2   The Formula Language

The syntactic core of ABEL is a strongly typed first order expression language, whose main elements are *variables*, *functions*, and *types*. As we shall see elements of all three categories may be introduced and named by the ABEL user. In the complete language we therefore distinguish between *defining* occurrences and *applied* occurrences of such named elements. A type T represents a set of *values*, V_T, of that type. The type of any variable, say x, is specified by syntactically associating the defining occurrence with a type, say T, usually by writing $x : T$. The variable is thereby restricted to range over values of type T. Similarly the defining occurrence of a function f is associated with the *profile* of the function by writing

$$f : T_1 \times T_2 \times \ldots \times T_n \longrightarrow T$$

where $n \geq 0$, and $T_1, \ldots, T_n, T$ are types. $T_1 \times T_2 \times \ldots \times T_n$ is the *domain* of the function, and T is the *codomain*. The number n is sometimes called the *arity* of the function. A *constant* is a function with arity zero. The word *signature* is our term for a set of function profiles.

The strong typing of ABEL ensures that the semantic definition of a function respects the profile in the following sense: for given argument values in the declared domain the function either has a value of the codomain type, or it has no value for these arguments. It can only be applied to arguments in the declared domain. An application of the function to given argument values is said to be *well-defined* if the function has a value for these arguments, otherwise it is said to be *ill-defined*.

ABEL uses the standard notation for function applications, $f(e_1, e_2, \ldots, e_n)$, where the parenteses are omitted if $n = 0$. In addition infix, prefix, and postfix operators consisting of special symbols and boldface script may be used, as well as other "mixfix" notations where the operator may consist of more than one symbol. In these cases the function "name" is formed by writing the symbol $\char94$ in every argument position. Examples:

$\neg\char94 : Bool \longrightarrow Bool$
$\char94 + \char94 : Int \times Int \longrightarrow Int$
$\text{if } \char94 \text{ th } \char94 \text{ el } \char94 \text{ fi} : Bool \times T \times T \longrightarrow T$

where *Bool* is the type of truth values, **f** and **t**, *Int* is the type of integers, and T is an arbitrary type. Now for instance $x + y$ and $\char94 + \char94(x, y)$ are alternative notations for an application of the addition function to the arguments x and y. The notation $x < y = z$, is shorthand for $(x < y) \wedge (y = z)$, and similar usage of other infix relational operators is allowed.

The set of Boolean, or logical, operators is standard: $\neg\char94$, $\char94 \wedge \char94$, $\char94 \vee \char94$, $\char94 \Rightarrow \char94$, $\char94 \Leftrightarrow \char94$, listed in the order of precedence. In addition $\char94 = \char94$ is an alternative equality operator for Booleans whose precedence is that of relational operators, i.e. higher than the logical ones. The ABEL syntax for quantified formulas is as follows: $\forall x : T \bullet P$, and $\exists x : T \bullet P$, where the bound variable ranges over values of the indicated type. Syntactically a quantifier

$\forall x : T\bullet$ or $\exists x : T\bullet$, is a unary (prefix) operator which binds less strongly than the other logical operators, except $\hat{}\Leftrightarrow\hat{}$.

In general a *partial order*, $\prec$, is syntactically defined for the introduced types. If $T \prec U$ holds for types T and U, then T is said to be a (proper) *subtype* of U. $T \preceq U$ means $T \prec U \vee T = U$. A subtype relationship has inclusion of the associated value sets as a semantic consequence: $T \preceq U \Rightarrow V_T \subseteq V_U$. Notice that the subtype relation is a syntactic notion; the value set inclusion is a consequence of the type definition conventions of ABEL. The reverse implication does not in general hold (however, an ABEL implementation might make it possible to establish certain subtype relations through semantic proofs).

The concept of subtypes is introduced for several purposes, one is to make strong typing of expressions more *flexible*. For example, let $Nat \prec Int$, where Nat is the type of natural numbers (non-negative integers). Then the operator $\hat{}+\hat{}$ would accept operands of either type, whereas for instance a square root function, $sqrt : Nat \longrightarrow Nat$ would require natural numbers.

At the same time typing may become *stronger*. As we shall see, it may be possible to discover "syntactic theorems" in the form of additional function profiles, like $\hat{}+\hat{} :$ $Nat \times Nat \longrightarrow Nat$. This would make it possible to identify the expression $u+v$ as being of type Nat (rather than Int) if $u, v : Nat$. Two profiles for the same function are said to be *synonymous*.

We are now in a position to define the concept of *well-formedness* of expressions and at the same time describe the typing algorithm of ABEL, somewhat simplified. The following information is assumed to be available:

1. a set of types, partially ordered by the subtype relation,

2. a set of typed variables, and

3. a signature containing function profiles, including a user provided one for each function introduced.

The signature must satisfy certain restrictions, like not containing redundant profiles. Thus, for any two synonymous profiles $f : D \longrightarrow C$ and $f : D' \longrightarrow C'$, the implication $D' \prec D \Rightarrow C' \prec C$ should hold. For type products $D = T_1 \times \ldots \times T_n$ and $D' = T_1' \times \ldots \times T_m'$ the expression $D \prec D'$ means: $m = n \wedge T_1 \preceq T_1' \wedge \ldots \wedge T_1 \preceq T_1' \wedge D \neq D'$.

- A well-formed expression of type T is either a variable of type T, or it is a function application, say $f(e_1, \ldots, e_n)$, where e_i is a well-formed expression of type T_i, $i = 1, 2, \ldots, n$, and there is a f-profile with domain part D such that $T_1 \times \ldots \times T_n \preceq D$, and T is the "smallest" codomain part of such profiles (assumed to be unique).

The signature will contain one profile if $\hat{}$ th $\hat{}$ el $\hat{}$ fi $: Bool \times T_1 \times T_2 \longrightarrow T$ for every triple of types T_1, T_2, T, not necessarily distinct, such that $T_1 \preceq T$ and $T_2 \preceq T$ and T is minimal. If there is such a type T, the two other types are said to be *related*. This implies that an if-construct can only be well-formed if the two alternatives are of related types, and if well-formed its type is the smallest common supertype. (The type conventions of ABEL ensure that the latter is unique.)

Only well-formed expressions are part of the ABEL expression language. Thereby the language, or rather a type checking device, helps the user by preventing a large class of mistakes. Notice that well-formedness is a syntactic property of expressions, entirely independent of the semantics of the occurring functions. In the sequel expressions are assumed to be well-formed.

Let an expression e be of type T. If e only contains applications of *total* functions, i.e. functions, which have values on the entire user defined domain, then e is necessarily *well-defined* for arbitrary (type correct) interpretation of its free variables, and its value must be of type T. This is true although the well-definedness of an expression in general does depend on the semantics of the functions involved.

In computer programming one frequently has to deal with partial functions, i.e. functions which do not have values on the entire domain. A suitable subtype mechanism can be of some help in this connection, since any partial function will be total on some subdomain. For instance integer division, which has no function value for the denominator 0, can be defined as a total function with the profile $\char"5E/\char"5E : Int \times Nzo \longrightarrow Int$, where Nzo is the type of non-zero integers. Thus, x/y is well-formed and well-defined for $x : Int$ and $y : Nzo$.

The last example suggests that there is a need for so called *coercion* functions for checking values of a given type for membership in a subtype. For instance x/y would give a well-defined result for $x, y : Int$, whenever $y \neq 0$. The coercion functions are expressed using a generalized mixfix format: $\char"5E \text{ as } T : U \longrightarrow T$, where the type is considered part of the function name, and $T \prec U$. The function is partial; the function value is that of the argument if the latter belongs to the subtype T, otherwise the function has no value. For e of type U the expression $e \text{ as } T$ is a well-formed expression of type T, not necessarily well-defined.

The notation $e \text{ qua } T$ can be used for changing the type from U to T without applying the coercion function. Use of this notation entails an obligation for the user to prove that the occurrence of the expression e in the given context does have a value of type T whenever well-defined. For example, the expressions $x/(y \text{ as } Nzo)$ and $x/\text{if } y \neq 0 \text{ th } y \text{ qua } Nzo \text{ el } \perp \text{ fi}$ are semantically equivalent for $x, y : Int$ and $\char"5E/\char"5E$ as above. The notation $\perp$ stands for a predefined constant with no value, pronounced "error" or "bottom". Its type is the predefined "empty" type $\emptyset$, which by definition is a proper subtype of all other types. It follows that the denominator of the second expression is of type Nzo, which makes the expression well-formed.

It is considered practical to have coercions to subtypes inserted automatically by the typing algorithm, possibly as an option controlled be the user.

3 Semantic Definitions

Having identified a set of types and the signature of a set of functions it remains to define associated semantics:

1. a set of values for each type, and

2. the semantics of the identified functions.

In the approach of abstract algebra the semantics consist of a set of equational axioms which may define both aspects of semantics indirectly through the notion of an initial (mixed) algebra. While this approach is very flexible and leads to a very abstract, i.e. implementation independent, notion of types, it may be quite demanding mathematically. For instance, difficult questions about logical consistency and ground completeness arise.

Furthermore, when semantics are based on the concept of initial algebra, the meaning of subspecifications may depend in non-obvious ways on its specification environment. ABEL therefore follows the LARCH approach in being more constructive and somewhat less abstract (to an even greater extent than LARCH itself).

3.1 Generators

In particular a so called *generator basis* (also called a constructor set) is required for each type. The generator basis, G_T, for a type T consists of a chosen subset of T-*producers*, i.e. functions with the codomain T. The generator basis G_T by definition spans the entire value set associated with the type T, in the sense that any T-value is expressible in terms of generators alone, possibly including generators of other types.

This idea can be seen as a generalization of the concept of enumeration types first introduced in PASCAL. Whereas the generator basis of an enumeration type consists of constants, a generator basis G_T in general may contain T-producers other than constants. A ground term (variable-free expression) of type T consisting exclusively of generator applications is called a *basic T-expression*. The set of basic T-expressions is called the *generator universe*, GU_T, of the type T. If T occurs in the domain of any T-generator, then GU_T is infinite. In order that GU_T be non-empty, G_T must contain at least one *relative T-constant*, i.e. a T-producer with no occurrence of T in its domain. For the moment we may assume that types are defined one by one, so that types other than T occurring in the domains of T-generators are previously defined, "underlying" types.

In ABEL one writes **genbas** $g_1, \ldots, g_n$ in order to specify the generator basis $G_T = \{g_1, \ldots, g_n\}$, where the type T is identified by context.

Examples:

1. The type *Bool* (predefined) has a generator basis consisting of the constants **f** and **t**:
   $G_{Bool} = GU_{Bool} = \{\mathbf{f}, \mathbf{t}\}$.

2. The natural generator basis for the type *Nat* of natural numbers consists of the constant 0 and a successor fucntion:

   > **func** $0 : \longrightarrow Nat$
   > **func** $S\hat{\ } : Nat \longrightarrow Nat$
   > **genbas** $0,\ S\hat{\ }$
   > giving $GU_{Nat} = \{0,\ S0,\ SS0,\ \ldots\}$.

3. The type *Int* of integers may be spanned by a generator basis consisting of 0, a successor function, and negation:

   > **func** $0 : \longrightarrow Int$
   > **func** $S\hat{\ } : Int \longrightarrow Int$
   > **func** $-\hat{\ } : Int \longrightarrow Int$
   > **genbas** $0,\ S\hat{\ },\ -\hat{\ }$
   > giving $GU_{Nat} = \{0,\ S0,\ -0,\ SS0,\ S{-}0,\ -S0,\ --0,\ SSS0,\ \ldots\}$

4. The type of finite sequences of T-values, denoted $Seq\{T\}$, may be spanned as follows, for $V_T = \{a, b, \ldots\}$:

```
func ε : ⟶ Seq{T}                          — empty sequence
func ˆ⊢ˆ : Seq{T} × T ⟶ Seq T               — append right
genbas ε, ˆ⊢ˆ
giving GU_Seq{T} = {ε, e ⊢ a, ε ⊢ b, ..., (ε ⊢ a) ⊢ a, (ε ⊢ a) ⊢ b, ..., ...}
```

5. The type of finite sets of T-values, $Set\ T$, may be spanned in a similar way:

```
func ∅ : Set{T}                            — empty set
func add : Set T × T ⟶ Set{T}              — add an element
genbas ∅, add
giving GU_Set{T} = {∅, add(∅, a), add(∅, b), ...,
                    add(add(∅, a), a), add(add(∅, a), b) ..., ...}
```

Two of these generator bases, nos. 1, 2 and 4, are such that the basic expressions are in a one-to-one relationship with the intended abstract values. Therefore these bases are said to have the *one-to-one property*. Thus, specifiying a one-to-one generator basis for a type defines the associated values to be (represented by) the corresponding basic expressions (using unique denotations for values of underlying types, if any).

For the examples 3 and 5 the abstract values must be identified with certain equivalence classes of basic expressions. For instance, the expressions 0, –0, ––0, ... , all represent the value zero, and $add(∅, a)$, $add(add(∅, a), a)$, $add(add(add(∅, a), a), a)$, ... , all represent the singleton set $\{a\}$. The need to define a corresponding equivalence relation on the generator universe represents a considerable complication of the mathematical treatment of a type, and we shall see how the one-to-one property can sometimes be obtained through the use of subtypes.

Any generator universe is partially ordered by the subterm relation, and this order is well-founded. It therefore gives rise to an induction principle, called *generator induction*. As we shall see, the principle of generator induction is useful for purposes of function definition as well as theorem proving.

3.2 Function definition

The semantics of functions (other than generators) are given by *axioms* or by explicit definitions. We may exemplify the three styles of axiomatization in ABEL through a simple example, the subtraction function for natural numbers, $ˆ-ˆ : Nat × Nat ⟶ Nat$.

3.2.1 Arbitrary first order axioms

Consider the axioms A1 : $x - 0 = x$ and A2 : $¬∃y : Nat • x - 1 < y < x$, for $x : Nat$. Are they consistent with the standard interpretation of the other occurring functions? Yes, they are, for instance by interpreting $ˆ-ˆ$ as addition or subtraction. Thus, they do not define the intended function completely. What if we add $x - 1 < x$ as a third axiom? Unfortunately the latter is inconsistent, because no natural number is less than 0. However, a slightly weaker one preserves consistency; A3 : $x ≠ 0 ⇒ x - 1 < x$. We leave it to the interested reader to discuss whether A1–3 define subtraction on natural numbers completely. (The answer is no, even if V_{Nat} is completely specified.)

The example shows that arbitrary first order axioms are not always easy to reason about (or with). This does not mean that such axioms have no place in ABEL specifications; they are indeed useful for specifying minimal requirements of functions, but not for giving complete definitions.

3.2.2 Recursive definitions

Using a successor function $S\hat{}$ for natural numbers we may provide the following recursive definition:

$$\text{def } x - y == \text{ if } x = y \text{ th } 0 \text{ el } S(x - Sy) \text{ fi}$$

The double equality sign stands for so called "strong" equality, which expresses that the two operands are equally well-defined, and equal whenever well-defined. (The standard, or "weak" equality is *strict*, i.e. has no value for ill-defined operands.) The left hand hand arguments are defining occurrences of distinct, so called *formal variables*, whose number and types are determined by the function profile and whose scope is the right hand side. The latter must contain no other free variables. The definition is said to be *constructive* if it is quantifier-free and contains only generators and constructively defined functions. If the right hand side is recursive, it should be considered well-defined only for arguments such that the recursion terminates. This is the usual "fixed point semantics", which implies that the definition is useful for bottom-up evaluation of ground terms. It is fairly easy to see that the recursion will terminate in the example definition if and only if $y \leq x$. Since evaluation of $x-y$ would not terminate for ground terms such that $x < y$, our function has no value in that case, which is reasonable in view of the required codomain *Nat*.

An advantage of explicit function definitions, compared to the use of arbitrary axioms, is that logical consistency as well as ground completeness are ensured by syntactic checks: there must be exactly one definition of every non-generator function.

3.2.3 Terminating generator induction

Definition by generator induction means using induction on an argument with respect to the syntactic structure of basic expressions (which in turn stand for abstract values). Thereby we obtain a definition of the function over the entire generator universe, which means for all values of the inductive argument. The generator induction can be expressed using a generalization of the case-construct of PASCAL for discriminating on values of enumeration types. Assume that the generator basis of *Nat* is $\{0, S\hat{}\}$. The corresponding case-construct has one alternative for either generator:

$$\text{def } x - y == \text{case } y \text{ of } 0 \to x \mid Sy' \to$$
$$\text{case } x \text{ of } 0 \to \perp \mid Sx' \to x' - y' \text{ fo fo}$$

The expression heading each alternative of a case-construct is called a *discriminator*. Notice that a discriminator corresponding to a non-constant generator has variables as arguments. These are defining occurrences of variables whose scope is the corresponding alternative expression, and serve to name the actual arguments of the leading generator application of the discriminated value. (Any variable name of the left hand side or of an outer discriminator may be reused; if so that old variable is inaccessible in the alternative.) The expression whose value is tested is called the *discriminand*. If all discriminands in the right hand side are variables, there is an alternative set of case-free defining equations, "Guttag-style" axioms, one for each innermost alternative. In our case they are:

$$x - 0 == x$$
$$0 - Sy == \perp$$
$$Sx - Sy == x - y$$

There is no restriction on depth of nested case-constructs, and the discriminand of an inner one may well be a variable introduced in an outer discriminator. This implies that the nesting of generators in the left hand sides of the case-free inductive axioms may be arbitrarily deep. If a discriminand of a case-construct is an expression other than a variable, the corresponding case-free axioms are *conditional*. (if-constructs may be treated as logical operators with respect to term rewriting, although they may be defined in terms of case expressions.)

An important advantage of generator inductive definitions is that there exist powerful syntactic checks which provide sufficient conditions for the termination of recursion. For instance, the third of the case-free axioms is recursive, but it obviously terminates since the arguments of the recursive application are subterms of those of the left hand side. The definition is therefore said to be by *terminating generator induction*, TGI. Notice that the evaluation of a variable-free application of ˆ−ˆ either terminates with a resulting value, i.e. a basic expression, or with the symbol $\perp$ which is an explicit indication that the application is ill-defined.

A definition is said to be TGI if the right hand side is quantifier-free, and all occurring functions, except generators and $\perp$, are TGI defined, and, if recursive, the recursion is "guarded" by generator induction in some textually defined sense which ensures termination. Termination checks of different complexity and strength are possible; the following one is fairly general: each recursive application must be "smaller" than the corresponding left hand side, according to the lexicographic order induced on the list of arguments by the monotonic extension of the subterm relation, for each defined function according to a fixed permutation of its arguments.

Example

The check is strong enough to permit the following inductive definition of the Ackermann function (which does not belong to the class "primitive recursive" functions):

func $Ack : Nat \times Nat \longrightarrow Nat$
def $Ack(x, y) ==$ case x of $0 \rightarrow Sy \mid Sx \rightarrow$
                case y of $0 \rightarrow Ack(x, S0) \mid Sy \rightarrow Ack(x, Ack(Sx, y))$ fo fo

which corresponds to the following set of case-free axioms:

$Ack(0, y) == Sy$
$Ack(Sx, 0) == Ack(x, S0)$
$Ack(Sx, Sy) == Ack(x, Ack(Sx, y))$

There are three recursive applications to consider: $Ack(x, S0)$, $Ack(x, Ack(Sx, y))$, and $Ack(Sx, y)$, where the last one is an argument of the second. We check the arguments from left to right: In the two first cases the left argument x is a subterm of that of the corresponding left hand side, Sx. In the third case the first argument is identical to that of the left hand side, but the second argument, y, is a subterm of the left hand one, Sy. This shows that the definition is TGI.

TGI definitions have several important advantages compared to general recursive definitions:

1. They permit a mechanical derivation of definedness predicates, see section 4.

2. They represent a *convergent set of rewrite rules*. Thus, TGI definitions are not restricted to bottom-up evaluation of ground terms, but may be used for the purpose of simplifying arbitrary expressions.

3. They are well suited for semi-mechanical proofs by generator induction, as explained in the subsection 4.4. In fact, TGI term rewriting and derived techniques are powerful proof generators for quantifier-free theorems.

3.3 Equality

For a type to have a fixed semantics, independent of its specification environment, its associated value set must be fully specified. As we have seen, however, a generator basis only determines a generator universe whose elements are not necessarily in a one-to-one correspondence with the intended abstract values.

The concept of equality on abstract values has so far been taken for granted, as it would be for any type T whose value space V_T is identified as a set of specified elements. In our approach, however, since the starting point is a generator universe, the T-values must be specified indirectly, as equivalence classes induced by defining an equivalence relation on GU_T. (If the generator basis is one-to-one these equivalence classes should be singleton sets.) Then, turning the table upside down, this equivalence relation on GU_T can be taken to be the *equality relation on T*, which can thus be defined as any other non-generator function, possibly by TGI technique.

In particular the one-to-one property of a generator basis, say $\{g_1, g_2, \ldots, g_n\}$, can be specified by defining an equality function which amounts to syntactic equality of basic T-expressions, up to equality on arguments of underlying types:

$$\textbf{def } t = t' == \textbf{case } (t, t') \textbf{ of } \overset{n}{\underset{i=1}{|}} (g_i(\bar{x}_i), g_i(\bar{x}'_i)) \rightarrow \bar{x}_i = \bar{x}'_i \mid \textbf{others } \rightarrow \textbf{f fo}$$

where nested case levels have been combined and all "off-diagonal" alternatives could be collected in a final others clause. Notice that the definition is recursive (but TGI) for those generators which are not relative constants. We may note that the TGI definition of syntactic equality of basic expressions can be constructed mechanically for any given generator basis. In ABEL one can therefore use a shorter syntax for specifying the one-to-one property:

$$\textbf{1--1 genbas } g_1, g_2, \ldots, g_n$$

In cases where a many-to-one generator basis must be used, one possibility is to define the desired equality relation explicitly.

Example 1

Consider the the type $Set\{T\}$ of finite sets of T-values, with the generator basis specified in example 5 of section 3.1. The equality may be TGI defined using the set membership and set inclusion relations as stepping stones.

$$\textbf{func } \hat{} \in \hat{} : T \times Set\{T\} \longrightarrow Bool$$
$$\textbf{def } t \in s == \textbf{case } s \textbf{ of } \emptyset \rightarrow \textbf{f} \mid add(s, t') \rightarrow t = t' \vee t \in s \textbf{ fo}$$

```
func ˆ⊆ˆ : Set{T} × Set{T} ⟶ Bool
def  s ⊆ s' == case s of ∅ → t | add(s,t) → t ∈ s' ∧ s ⊆ s' fo
def  s = s' == s ⊆ s' ∧ s' ⊆ s
```

Having defined an equality relation explicitly there is an obligation to prove that the function is in fact an equivalence relation, for instance by proving the standard axioms of reflexivity, commutativity, and transitivity for $s, s', s'' : Set\{T\}$:

$$s = s, \quad s = s' \Rightarrow s' = s, \text{ and } s = s' = s'' \Rightarrow s = s''$$

Equality must in addition be such that meaning is preserved by substitution of equals for equals in expressions. This means that the relation consisting of the equalities for all types must be a so called *congruence relation* respecting axioms of the form

$$y = y' \Rightarrow (f(\bar{x}, y, \bar{z}) == f(\bar{x}, y', \bar{z}))$$

for every function including generators and every argument position. (The strong equality is necessary for partial functions. It may be simulated using definedness predicates.) Fortunately all of these axioms are respected if all generator bases are one-to-one. But otherwise the total proof burden associated with explicit equality definition is rather formidable.

Another possibility is to define a so called *observation basis* consisting of functions with one or more arguments of the type in question. The members of an observation basis are usually "observer" functions, i.e. functions with codomains which are underlying types. The members of the observation basis are called *basic observers*. They by definition observe "all there is to see" in the abstract values of the type under definition. Thus, two basic expressions of this type are to be considered equal if and only if all possible observations on them by basic observers are (strongly) equal. An observation basis is specified by the ABEL statement **obsbas** $h_1, \ldots, h_m$, listing the chosen basic observers by name.

For example, an observation basis may be specified for $Set\{T\}$ consisting of the single function ˆ∈ˆ. This implicitly defines equality on sets as:

$$\textbf{def } s = s' == \forall t : T \bullet (t \in s) = (t \in s')$$

In general the right hand side is a conjunction of equalities, one for each argument of the type under definition in the list of basic observers. If partial functions occur, then definedness predicates are also needed in order to simulate strong equalities. Unfortunately equality definition through observation basis is only constructive if all member functions are unary; otherwise quantifiers will occur in the right hand side, as in the example.

On the other hand, an equality defined through an observation basis is necessarily an equivalence relation, and it satisfies congruence with respect to generators and basic observers. The associated proof burden is thus considerably less.

Example 2

We define a type $IMap\{X, Y\}$ of "initialized maps", which simulate total functions with domain X and codomain Y. The function values are equal to a default Y-value, identified initially, except at a finite number of X-values where the map has been updated. Two $IMap$ objects should be considered equal if and only if they have the same "function value" for all "arguments". Hence the specified observation basis.

func $init : Y \longrightarrow IMap\{X, Y\}$ — initial map
func $\hat{\ }[\hat{\ }\mapsto\hat{\ }] : IMap\{X, Y\} \times X \times Y \longrightarrow IMap\{X, Y\}$ — update map
genbas $init,\ \hat{\ }[\hat{\ }\mapsto\hat{\ }]$
func $\hat{\ }[\hat{\ }] : IMap\{X, Y\} \times X \longrightarrow Y$ — apply map
def $m[x] ==$ case m of $init(y) \rightarrow y \mid m_1[x_1 \mapsto y_1] \rightarrow$
if $x = x_1$ th y_1 el $m_1[x]$ fi fo
obsbas $\hat{\ }[\hat{\ }]$

If more than one update occurs for the same argument value, the last one takes precedence. Thus, for instance: $init(y_0)[x_1 \mapsto y_1][x_1 \mapsto y_2][x_1] = y_2$.

There is no proof obligation associated with these specifications since the only occurring function definition is for a basic observer.

It follows from the above that TGI function definitions preserve logical consistency as long as generator bases are one-to-one. There is, however, a danger of losing consistency when defining functions by generator induction over fully defined types with many-to-one bases. The reason for this may be explained by noting that generator induction in that case reveals the entire structure of the generator universe, including details which ought to be hidden inside equivalence classes. Thus, any use of such generator induction entails an obligation to prove one or more congruence axioms.

Example 3

We define a function counting the "multiplicity" of elements in finite sets by generator induction over $Set\{T\}$.

func $mpc : Set\{T\} \times T \longrightarrow Nat$
def $mpc(s, t) ==$ case s of $\emptyset \rightarrow 0 \mid add(s_1, t_1) \rightarrow$
if $t = t_1$ th $Smpc(s_1, t)$ el $mpc(s_1, t)$ fi fo

Now consistency is lost, and this becomes clear when trying to carry out the required proof of the congruence axiom $s = s' \Rightarrow mpc(s, t) = mpc(s', t)$. Counterexample: Take $add(\emptyset, a)$ for s and $add(add(\emptyset, a), a)$ for s'. They are equal sets according to the defined equality (both represent the same singleton set), but the multiplicity of a is 1 in s and 2 in s'. (The loss of consistency shows that the concept of element multiplicity has no place in connection with sets; it belongs to the type of *multisets*, also called *bags*.)

The partial lack of syntactic consistency control of TGI function definitions is a serious obstacle to the use of types with many-to-one generator bases. There are, however, ways of achieving one-to-one-ness through the use of subtypes. See sections 5.1 and 5.3.

4 Logical Foundation

A function is said to be *strict* in an argument if an error in that argument propagates. A function is said to be strict if it is strict in all arguments. A function is said to be *total* if it is well-defined for all well-defined arguments. A function is said to be *monotonic* if replacing an argument in an application with error makes the error propagate or leaves the function value unchanged. All non-monotonic operators are considered non-constructive. We say that an expression *approximates* another if they are equivalent (in all respects) whenever the former is well-defined.

We build on results from three valued logic originating from Kleene. In particular, we adapt the Kleene semantics for the logical connectives $\Rightarrow$ $\wedge$ $\vee$ and $\neg$ and the logical quantifiers. For instance, a conjunction is false if either argument is false, regardless of the well-definedness of the other argument. When one argument is true, an error in the other argument propagates, i.e. $(t \wedge \bot) == (t \wedge \bot) == \bot$ where $==$ denotes equality with respect to the three truth values t, f, and $\bot$, denoting true, false and error, respectively. The other logical connectives follow by the standard equivalences, with negation strict $(\neg\bot == \bot)$, i.e.

$$a \Rightarrow b \qquad == \neg a \vee b$$
$$a \vee b \qquad == \neg(\neg a \wedge \neg b)$$

A universal quantification may be seen as a generalized conjunction, in the standard way; and $\exists$ is equivalent to $\neg\forall\neg$. It follows that the logical connectives as well as the quantifiers are monotonic, and that they satisfy the classical distribution laws and deMorgan laws, and negations may be moved innermost in the classical way:

$$(a \vee b) \wedge c \quad == a \wedge c \vee b \wedge c$$
$$(a \wedge b) \vee c \quad == (a \vee c) \wedge (b \vee c)$$

$$\neg(a \Rightarrow b) \quad == a \wedge \neg b$$
$$\neg(a \vee b) \quad == \neg a \wedge \neg b$$
$$\neg(a \wedge b) \quad == \neg a \vee \neg b$$
$$\neg\forall x : T \bullet a \quad == \exists x : T \bullet \neg a$$
$$\neg\exists x : T \bullet a \quad == \forall x : T \bullet \neg a$$

letting x denote a variable, and a, b and c formulas. Furthermore, the following equivalences may be added for convergent rewriting when extended with capabilities for handling $\wedge$ and $\vee$ as associative, commutative operators:

$$\neg\neg a \qquad == a$$
$$a \wedge a \qquad == a$$
$$a \vee a \qquad == a$$

$$(a \vee b) \wedge a \quad == a$$
$$(a \wedge b) \vee a \quad == a$$

$$a \wedge t \qquad == a$$
$$a \wedge f \qquad == f$$
$$a \vee t \qquad == t$$
$$a \vee f \qquad == a$$

The following laws do not hold:

$$a \wedge \neg a \quad == f$$
$$a \vee \neg a \quad == t$$
$$a \Rightarrow a \quad == t \qquad\qquad\qquad (\text{only } \neg((a \Rightarrow a) == f))$$

This reflects the fact that there are three truth values.

The if- and case-constructs, both strict in the leftmost argument, satisfy the following laws:

$$\text{case } g(y) \text{ of } .. \mid g(y') \rightarrow e \mid .. \text{ fo} == e^y_{y'}$$
$$\text{case } t \text{ of } .. \mid g(y) \rightarrow e^x_t \mid .. \text{ fo} \quad == \text{case } t \text{ of } .. \mid g(y) \rightarrow e^x_{g(y)} \mid .. \text{ fo}$$
$$\text{if } a \text{ th } e \text{ el } e' \text{ fi} \quad\qquad == \text{case } a \text{ of } t \rightarrow e \mid f \rightarrow e' \text{ fo}$$

where y denotes a list of variables, and t a list of expressions, and where a^x_e denotes a with all free occurrences of x replaced by the expression e (renaming bound variables in a when needed), and a^y_t denotes simultaneous substitution.

It follows that if a th e^x_a el e'^x_a fi $==$ if a th e^x_t el e'^x_f fi

Validity

A formula a is said to be *valid* iff it is well-defined and true, i.e. $a == t$, for all possible well-defined interpretations of the free variables ("strong" interpretation). It follows that $a \wedge c$ is valid if and only if both a and c are valid, and that $a \vee c$ is valid if either a or c is valid.

In order to formalize the use of assumptions, we introduce sequents of the form $A \leadsto c$ where c, the conclusion, is a formula, and A, the assumption part, is a list of formulas. The sequent $A \leadsto c$ is said to be valid iff $A \Rightarrow c$ is valid, taking commas in the assumption part as $\wedge$'s. Thus, the sequent expresses that the conclusion must be well-defined and true unless (at least one formula in) the assumption part is well-defined and false, i.e. $\neg(A == f) \Rightarrow (c == t)$. This is called WS-logic since the assumptions have "weak" interpretation and the conclusion has "strong" interpretation.

Provability

In WS-logic, we may derive $A \leadsto \Delta c$ from $A \leadsto c$, where Δc expresses that c is well-defined, due to the strong interpretation of the conclusion. Furthermore, the classical introduction and elimination rules of natural deduction [11] are sound; in particular, we have $A, a \leadsto c$ if and only if $A \leadsto a \Rightarrow c$, we have $A \leadsto \neg c$ if and only if $A, c \leadsto f$, and we have $A, a \leadsto c$ if and only if $A, \neg c \leadsto \neg a$, which means that special rules introducing and eliminating symbols in the assumption part are not needed. The classical structural rules of sequent calculus are also sound, when the instantiation rule is restricted to well-defined substitutions, i.e. a sequent may be instantiated by replacing all occurrences of the same variable in both the assumption part and the conclusion by the same well-defined term, as formalized by the rule:

$$\frac{\begin{array}{c} A \leadsto c \\ A_e^x \leadsto \Delta e \end{array}}{A_e^x \leadsto c_e^x} \qquad \text{instantiation rule}$$

(If A and c are monotonic, it suffices that the conclusion is well-defined.)

The logical axiom $c \leadsto c$, which is trivial in classical sequent calculus, is not sound in WS-logic. Instead we have $c \leadsto c$ if and only if c is well-defined. This means that a trivial sequent requires a proof of well-definedness; thus in WS-logic nothing can be proved from meaningless assumptions, not even meaningless conclusions. This seems to be a healthy principle in computer science applications, and it fits well with proof by generator induction, see below.

By the below formalization of the well-definedness operator Δ, one may prove well-definedness requirements in a straightforward way, since $\Delta \Delta a$ is true.

Equality

Strong equality is a congruence relation satisfying the axiom $e == e$ and the rule

$$\frac{\begin{array}{c} A \leadsto e == e' \\ A \leadsto a_e^x \end{array}}{A \leadsto a_{e'}^x} \qquad \text{substitution rule}$$

Notice that with $==$ as a logical symbol, all the strong equations stated above may be taken as logical axioms.

The strict restriction of strong equality is called weak equality. The relationship between strong and weak equality may be formalized as follows by means of the well-definedness operator: $(e == e')$ is equivalent to $(\Delta e = \Delta e') \wedge (\Delta(e, e') \Rightarrow e = e')$.

4.1 Definedness

The well-definedness of the logical operators is axiomatized as follows:

$$\Delta(\bot) \qquad == f$$
$$\Delta(t) \qquad == t$$
$$\Delta(f) \qquad == t$$
$$\Delta(x) \qquad == t \qquad \text{(except when } x \text{ is a formal variable of a definition)}$$
$$\Delta(\neg a) \qquad == \Delta a$$
$$\Delta(a \wedge b) \qquad == (\Delta a \wedge (\neg a \vee \Delta b)) \vee (\Delta b \wedge (\neg b \vee \Delta a))$$
$$\Delta(a \vee b) \qquad == (\Delta a \wedge (a \vee \Delta b)) \vee (\Delta b \wedge (b \vee \Delta a))$$
$$\Delta(a \Rightarrow b) \qquad == (\Delta a \wedge (\neg a \vee \Delta b)) \vee (\Delta b \wedge (b \vee \Delta a))$$
$$\Delta(\forall x : T \cdot a) == (\forall x : T \cdot \Delta a) \vee (\exists x : T \cdot \Delta a \wedge \neg a)$$
$$\Delta(\exists x : T \cdot a) == (\forall x : T \cdot \Delta a) \vee (\exists x : T \cdot \Delta a \wedge a)$$
$$\Delta \text{if } a \text{ th } e \text{ el } e' \text{ fi} == \Delta a \wedge \text{ if } a \text{ th } \Delta e \text{ el } \Delta e' \text{ fi}$$
$$\Delta \text{case } e \text{ of } \dots \mid g_i(x_i) \rightarrow e_i \mid \dots \text{ fo} == \Delta e \wedge \text{ case } e \text{ of } \dots \mid g_i(x_i) \rightarrow \Delta e_i \mid \dots \text{ fo}$$
$$\Delta(e == e') \qquad == t$$
$$\Delta \Delta e \qquad == t$$

where $\Delta(a,b)$ denotes $(\Delta a \wedge \Delta b)$. Quantifiers range over defined values only, thus bound variables are well-defined; and so are variables introduced in a case-construct. Formal variables of a function definition, however, may not be considered always well-defined.

Notice that the equations above may be used to calculate the well-definedness of a formula such that the resulting formula is without occurrences of Δ, except for applications to formal variables and non-logical functions — the well-definedness of the latter are given below.

A formula a is well-defined if Δa is valid, and ill-defined if $(\neg \Delta a)$ is valid. It follows that $(\Delta a) \wedge a$ and $(\Delta a) \Rightarrow a$ are logically well-defined.

The left-strict versions of $\wedge, \vee, \Rightarrow$, denoted and, or, implies, respectively, are practically useful, giving more efficient execution and simpler definedness analysis. For instance,

$$\Delta(a \text{ and } b) == \Delta a \text{ and } (\neg a \text{ or } \Delta b)$$

In fact all occurrences of $\wedge$ and $\vee$ in the above right hand sides could be replaced by and and or, respectively.

4.2 Non-logical functions

For total and strict functions, such as generators and weak equality, we define

$$\Delta g(e) == \Delta e$$

letting Δ of a list be the conjunction of Δ of each list member, and letting Δ of an empty list be t. Thus, generator constants such as t, f, 0 are well-defined. In particular, for the strict restriction of Δ, denoted δ, we have $\Delta \delta e == \Delta e$. The δ-predicate may be defined constructively as follows:

$$\textbf{def} \quad \delta x == \text{case } x \text{ of others } \rightarrow t \text{ fo}$$

A constructive function definition, say

$$\mathbf{def}\quad f(y) == e$$

where y is a list of formal variables, is logically understood as the axiom schema

$$f(t) == e_t^y \qquad\qquad (f\text{-axiom})$$

for any list of terms t (of the appropriate types), well-defined or not. It follows that

$$\Delta f(t) == \Delta e_t^y \qquad\qquad (\Delta f\text{-lemma})$$

which defines the well-definedness of f if the equation has only one fix-point. For non-TGI, recursively defined functions it is possible to provide proof rules corresponding to least fix-point semantics []. If the definition is TGI, there is only one fix-point, and the well-definedness of f is implicitly defined by the Δf-lemma.

However, since the Δoperator is non-monotonic, it may not be used inside TGI definitions. For each user introduced function f, we therefore introduce a monotonic definedness predicate df with the same domain as f, and such that $df(t)$ approximates $\Delta f(t)$. ¿From a TGI-definition of f as above, we first define a temporary definedness predicate, denoted $d'f$, with domain as f but extended with one boolean argument for each argument of f:

$$\mathbf{def}\quad d'f(..,y_i,dy_i,..) == \Delta'e \qquad\qquad (d'f\text{-definition})$$

where Δ' is Δ calculated with the Δ-equations above, replacing $\Delta h(..,t_i,..)$ by $d'h(..,t_i,\Delta t_i,..)$ for each non-logical function h, and replacing occurrences of Δy_i by dy_i. It follows that the right hand side is without occurrences of Δ, and that it is monotonic and TGI if the definition of f was TGI. By induction on the nesting of functions, it follows that $\Delta f(..,t_i,..) == d'f(..,t_i,\Delta t_i,..)$.

We then define the definedness predicate of f as follows:

$$\mathbf{def}\quad df(..,y_i,..) ==\bigwedge_i \delta y_i \text{ and } d'f(..,y_i,t,..) \qquad\qquad (df\text{-definition})$$

It follows that df is total and strict, so its definedness predicate is not needed, and it is TGI if the definition of f was TGI. Furthermore, $df(t)$ is equivalent to δt and $\Delta f(t)$, and thus $df(t)$ approximates $\Delta f(t)$.

For each non-logical function f, we let df be part of the ABEL language, but not $d'f$. For total and strict f, $df(t)$ is δt. The well-definedness of a non-constructive function f may be characterized through non-logical axioms about df, or indirectly through axioms about f (because of the underlying strong interpretation). And its definedness predicate may be used to ensure well-definedness of f-applications in axioms — and also in constructive definitions of other functions if f is introduced in an assumed property.

Notice that the formula $f(x) == h(x')$ where x and x' are lists for free variables, is equivalent to $df(x) = dh(x') \wedge (df(x) \Rightarrow f(x) = h(x'))$ (since free variables range over defined values). Note that from $\leadsto df(t)$ we may derive $\leadsto \Delta f(t)$, and that from $\leadsto \delta t$ we may derive $\leadsto \Delta t$ and vice versa.

Example

¿From the above TGI-definition of the minus-function on natural numbers, we derive the following definition of its definedness predicate, $d\hat{\ } - \hat{\ }$, letting d extend the mixfix notation:

$$\text{def} \quad dx - y == (\delta x \wedge \delta y) \text{ and case } y \text{ of } 0 \to t$$
$$| \ Sy' \to t \wedge \text{case } x \text{ of } 0 \to f$$
$$| \ Sx' \to dx' - y' \text{ fo fo}$$

The right hand side simplifies to δx and δy and $y \leq x$ by inductive reasoning.

Axioms and Lemmas

A user defined axiom

$$\text{axm } a$$

is understood as a non-logical axiom

$$\rightsquigarrow a$$

taking commas in a as $\wedge$'s. Notice that this gives a strong interpretation of axioms. Free variables are implicitly universally quantified, and outermost universal quantifiers may be omitted.

A user defined lemma lma a states that $\rightsquigarrow a$ can be proved in WS-logic extended with the introduced non-logical axioms and generator induction rules. There is an obligation to prove all stated lemmas.

Example

The following lemmas may be proved about the minus-function defined above:

$$\text{lma } x, y, z : Nat \bullet$$
$$dx - y = y \leq x,$$
$$(x + y) - y = x,$$
$$y \leq x \Rightarrow x - (x - y) = y$$

The first lemma follows from the results above and the fact that free variables are well-defined (thus δy is true). The condition of the last axiom is needed to ensure well-definedness.

4.3 Rewriting

Each step in a term rewriting process consists in first instantiating a rewrite rule so that the left hand side matches a subterm of the expression being processed, and then replacing that subterm by the instantiated right hand side. Notice that strong equations, proved or given as axioms, may not be used unconditionally as rewrite rules because of the definedness premise of the instantiation rule, restricting the instantiation of free variables. However, such a strong equation may be used unconditionally if both sides are strongly equal when the free variables are taken as formal variables (which may be instantiated unconditionally).

In a Guttag axiom, say $f(x, g(y), ..) == RHS$, the variable x is a formal variable of the corresponding def-item, and may therefore be instantiated to arbitrary (type correct) expressions, well-defined or not. The variable y on the other hand corresponds to one introduced in a discriminator, which is by definition well-defined. Unfortunately, this distinction is not recognized in ordinary rewriting, and for that reason there is a subtle difference between the semantics based on unconditional rewriting with Guttag axioms and that defined for function definitions with case-constructs in the right hand side.

However, it turns out that the left hand side of a Guttag axiom approximates the right hand side, when all variables are taken as formal ones. And the Guttag style axioms form a convergent (unconditional) rewrite system. Without loss of convergence the system may be enriched with the strong equations given above for the logical operators (but not generator strictness rules). It follows that a monotonic expression approximates (in the sense of ABEL semantics) its rewrite result with this system. In particular, a well-defined, monotonic expression strongly equals the result from rewriting with Guttag axioms [3].

It is possible to generate a set of convergent rewrite rules consistent with the ABEL semantics of the case-definitions, and generator strictness, by mechanically modifying right hand sides in certain Guttag axioms (by means of a definedness operator) [8]. No such modification would be neccesary, however, in the Guttag rules for minus or plus on *Nat*.

4.4 Induction Proof

The usual rule for generator induction is sound in WS-logic:

$$\frac{.., a^x_{y_i}, .. \rightsquigarrow a^x_{g(y)}}{\rightsquigarrow \forall x : T \cdot a} \qquad \text{generator induction on } T$$

where there is one premise for each T-generator g, each premise with one assumption for each argument y_i of type T.

Example

For natural numbers (with 0 and S as generators) we get the following induction rule:

$$\frac{\rightsquigarrow a^x_0 \qquad a \rightsquigarrow a^x_{Sx}}{\rightsquigarrow \forall x : Nat \cdot a} \qquad \text{generator induction on } Nat$$

As an example, we prove the second lemma above $(x + y) - y = x$ (*) by induction on y. The first premise is rewritten to true with the rules $(x + 0) == x$ and $(x + 0) == 0$. The second premise becomes:

$$(x + y) - y = x \rightsquigarrow (x + Sy) - Sy = x \qquad (**)$$

With the rules $(x + Sy) == S(x + y)$ and $Sx - Sy == x - y$, (**) rewrites to $(*) \rightsquigarrow (*)$■ which is trivial since (*) is well-defined.

5 Modules

The module concept is essentially a mechanism for the encapsulation of specifications. A module is said to be *constructive* if the semantics of the specified functions are given by explicit definitions. In ABEL there are four different kinds of modules:

- A *type module* serves to define a type (possibly with subtypes) as well as associated functions.

- A *function module* defines a collection of functions.

- A *property module* specifies a set of minimal requirements on type parameters.

- *Class modules* are analogues of type modules for imperative, object oriented programming.

Module definitions have the following general format:

<module kind><module name> {<formal type parameters>}
    <optional clauses>   ==   <right hand side>

where < module kind> is one of **type, funcs, property**, and **class**. In the following explanations any non-exceptional statement about types is valid for classes as well.

The module name of a type module is at the same time the name of the (main) type defined by the module. For the purpose of the present review we may assume that all module (and subtype) names are distinct. The list of formal type parameters is optional. The <optional clauses> of the left hand side include syntax for the introduction of *syntactic subtypes* of the main type in a type module, see section 5.1, as well as assumption and inclusion clauses, see below.

The right hand side of a module definition is a non-empty text consisting of an optional module expression, called a *module prefix*, followed by an optional *module body* of the form:

module <list of module items> **endmodule** <optional satisfaction clause>

where the final optional clause may be used to express syntactically that the module satifies a list of properties.

A module expression consists of the module name followed by a list of actual type parameters (if any) enclosed in braces, which are type module expressions. A module expression represents an *instance* of the named module obtained by substituting the actual parameters for the occurrences of the formal ones in its right hand side. A module prefix is an instance of a module of the same kind as the one being defined. (Exception: the module prefix of a class may be a type module instance, fully constructive.) In the case of type modules the one under definition is said to be a *semantic subtype* of the module prefix. In that case the latter may contain a predicate which restricts the value space. See section 5.2 for examples of semantic subtypes.

Module items of the following kinds can, with the mentioned exceptions, occur in all kinds of modules:

- function profiles, described earlier,

- function definitions, described earlier (not allowed in property modules),

- axiom items of the form: **axm** <list of variable declarations><list of formulas>, where the formulas may only have free occurrences of the declared variables, (not allowed in class modules), and

- lemma items headed by the keyword **lma**, and can otherwise of the same format as axiom items. The contents of a lemma item can also be an entire module item (other than lemma or axiom item).

In addition any type module shall have exactly one **genbas** statement and at most one **obsbas** statement (possibly inherited). Procedure declarations, as well as function declarations in imperative style, are allowed in class modules.

A module is said to be the *owner* of the module items listed in its module body, if any. In addition it *inherits* those owned by the prefixing module instance, if any, and is thereby made an owner of these items too. For that reason the new module is sometimes said to be an *extension* of the prefix module. The owner relationship is of particular importance for functions, represented by their profiles and semantic specifications, since it gives rise to possibilities for a controlled kind of function overloading, see below. A function owned by a module M is also said to be *associated with* M, and to be a M-function. The set of functions owned by a module must have distinct names, thus no redefinition of inherited functions is allowed, with the single exception of function redefinition in subtypes and subclasses, essentially retaining the original semantics on the reduced domain.

Any non-property module, say $M\{T_1, T_2 \ldots\}$, can introduce requirements on its formal type parameters by an *assumption clause* in its left hand side. The clause lists one or more property module expressions, each with one or more formal M-parameters as actual parameters. The requirements expressed by a property expression, say $P\{T_1, T_2\}$, are that one of the actual parameters for T_1 and T_2 of any M-instance, say $M\{U_1, U_2, \ldots\}$, must own functions with profiles *greater than* or equal to those that would be owned by the property instance $P\{U_1, U_2\}$. A profile $f : D \longrightarrow C$ is greater than or equal to a second one $f' : D' \longrightarrow C'$ if and only if $f = f'$ (syntactically), $D' \preceq D$, and $C' \preceq C$.

In addition the associated functions must satisfy the axioms of $P\{U_1, U_2\}$. Thus, there is in general a proof obligation associated with any instantiation of M.

Any module can, by an *inclusion clause* listing one or more function module expressions, cause these module instances to be *included*, i.e. they (or more precisely their contents) are made *available* to the module under definition. At the same time those available to the former are also included. Type modules need no explicit inclusion clause in order to become available; an occurrence of a type expression anywhere in the right hand side, or as an actual parameter of a module expression in an assumption or inclusion clause, causes the inclusion of the corresponding type module. The same is true for class modules.

A module M under definition is only allowed to refer to modules previously defined. (Exception: no type module may refer to any class module, directly or indirectly.) Thereby a *definition hierarchy* (a partial order) is defined for the set of modules (not module instances) consisting of M and those which have instances available to M, where M is the single maximal element (and *Bool* is the single minimal one).

Ownership of functions is not altered by assumptions or inclusions. That makes it possible to avoid name conflicts between functions associated with different modules. It is considered practical to permit function overloading in the sense that the number and types of arguments of a function application can influence the binding of the applied function, with priority for binding to locally owned functions.

Assuming that most functions are owned by type modules, then, in the majority of cases of no local match, it is sufficient to search for a matching profile in modules which are *maximal elements* in the definition hierarchy, among those which occur in the argument types. In practical cases at most one match will be found in these modules (which in general depends on the actual parameters of the occurring module instances as well). If none is found, the function may be defined in a function module, or it may be a relative constant (i.e. the owning type module does not occur in the function domain). In these cases a wider search is required with a correspondingly greater danger of ambiguity especially for non-local constants. If several functions redefined in semantic subtypes can match, the one with the smallest domain which does not require argument coercion, is to be chosen.

As a means to resolve ambiguities, and to override the given overloading rules, ABEL provides notations for identifying the intended owner. (Usually the module name is sufficient, but there exist cases where the actual instance would have to be specified.) An owner M may be specified either by using the notation M' as a prefix or the construct at M as a suffix. For ordinary functional notation the prefix notation, $M'f(\ldots)$, reads well, but for mixfix notations ending with an operator symbol the at -construct is usually better, as in the examples of section 5.3. For operators and other mixfix notations starting and ending with operands good constructs are difficult to find; in ABEL one can e.g. choose between $M'(\ldots \mathrm{op} \ldots)$, $(\ldots \mathrm{op} \ldots)$ at M, and $M'\hat{\ }\mathrm{op}\hat{\ }(\ldots, \ldots)$ for specifying the owner of an infix operator.

The advantage of function overloading is illustrated by the fact that any type T, even a formal one, owns the following predefined module items:

> **func** $\hat{\ } = \hat{\ } : T \times T \longrightarrow Bool$
> **func** $\hat{\ } \neq \hat{\ } : T \times T \longrightarrow Bool$
> **def** $x \neq y == \neg x = y$
> **func** if $\hat{\ }$ th $\hat{\ }$ el $\hat{\ }$ fi : $Bool \times T \times T \longrightarrow T$
> **def** if x th y el z fi == case x of $\mathrm{t} \to y \mid \mathrm{f} \to z$ fo

It is required that any actual type module specifies the semantics of the equality relation either by a **def** item or by an **obsbas** statement.

It follows from the above rules for allowed contents of different kinds of modules that classes are necessarily fully constructive, whereas property modules are non-constructive since they do not contain **def** items. Type and function modules are primarily intended to be constructive, but semantics through **axm** items are not forbidden. The intention is, however, that the consistency of modules shall be established through later module extension by constructive function definitions satisfying the stated axioms. Thus, there is in general a proof obligation associated with module extension to prove any inherited axiom referring to defined functions only. The axiom is thereby redefined as a **lma** item. For any property module P consistency is established through proofs required in connection with instantiation of modules assuming P.

As an example of a type module we define the sequence type and a few non-generator functions which are used in the sequel.

> **type** $Seq\{T\}$ ==
> **module**
>   **func** $\varepsilon : \longrightarrow Seq$
>   **func** $\hat{\ } \vdash \hat{\ } : Seq \times T \longrightarrow Seq$ — right append
>   **1–1 genbas** ε, $\hat{\ } \vdash \hat{\ }$
>   **func** $\hat{\ } \dashv \hat{\ } : T \times Seq \longrightarrow Seq$ — left append
>   **def** $t \dashv q ==$ case q of $\varepsilon \to \varepsilon \vdash t \mid q' \vdash t' \to (t \dashv q') \vdash t'$ fo
>   **func** $\hat{\ } \vdash\!\!\vdash \hat{\ } : Seq \times Seq \longrightarrow Seq$ — concatenate
>   **def** $q \vdash\!\!\vdash q' ==$ case q' of $\varepsilon \to q \mid q'' \vdash t \to (q \vdash\!\!\vdash q'') \vdash t$ fo

endmodule

Notice that the parameter part is omitted for occurrences of the type under definition. This is in order to prevent a certain class of meaningless type definitions.

Parameterized type modules may be seen as higher order functions, giving new types when applied to type arguments. As such they are *monotonic* with respect to the subtype relation: $T_1 \preceq T_1' \wedge \ldots \wedge T_n \preceq T_n' \Rightarrow U\{T_1, \ldots, T_n\} \preceq U\{T_1', \ldots, T_n'\}$.

5.1 Syntactic Subtypes

We consider the problem of finding a one-to-one generator basis for the type *Int* of integers. In example 3 of section 3.1 a basis consisting of zero, successor, and negation functions was proposed. It is many-to-one, however, since $-0 = 0$ and $--x = x$ for $x : Int$. An alternative way to span the negative integers is to replace the unary minus by a predecessor function $S\hat{}$, but now $PSx = SPx$ for $x : Int$. A third possibility is to define the integers as pairs of sign and absolute value:

type *Int* $==$ *sgn* : $\{pos, neg\} \times abs : Nat$

where the right hand side contains some useful special notations. An *enumeration type*, say $\{a, b, \ldots, c\}$, is defined in the obvious way, by a one-to-one generator basis consisting of the listed constants. A *labelled Cartesian type product*, $a_1 : T_1 \times a_2 : T_2 \times \ldots \times a_n : T_n$, $n \geq 0$, is shorthand for a type, *Prodn*, defined as follows:

type $Prodn\{T_1, T_2, \ldots, T_n\}$ $==$
module
    func $(\hat{}, \hat{}, \ldots, \hat{}) : T_1 \times T_2 \times \ldots \times T_n \longrightarrow Prodn$
    1–1 genbas $(\hat{}, \hat{}, \ldots, \hat{})$
    func $\hat{}.a_i : Prodn \longrightarrow T_i$ for $i = 1, 2, \ldots, n$ — component selectors
    def $(x_1, x_2, \ldots, x_n).a_i == x_i$ for $i = 1, 2, \ldots, n$
endmodule

where the **def** item is short for a definition by a **case** with a single branch. (Notice that the case $n = 0$ is useful; *Prod0* is a kind of null type whose only abstract value is the empty tuple.)

However, the one-to-one property of the above labelled product is not quite right, since $(pos, 0)$ and $(neg, 0)$ should be considered equal. In order to arrive at a definition of the *Int* type by conventional means we may use another stndard construct, a *disjoint union*:

type *Int* $==$ *zro* : $() + pos : Nat1 + neg : Nat1$

where *Nat1* is the type of non-zero natural numbers, and the "labels" in this case represent generators, sometimes called "injector functions":

func *zro* : $\longrightarrow Int$
func *pos* : $Nat1 \longrightarrow Int$
func *neg* : $Nat1 \longrightarrow Int$

A one-to-one generator basis for *Int* may consist of these three functions.

We may notice in passing that the constructs of type products and labelled disjoint unions are type forming mechanisms of an expressiveness directly comparable to that of type modules with one-to-one generator bases (and without syntactic subtypes). In particular, a recursive type definition corresponds to a generator basis containing generators other than relative constants. Notice that at least one generator must be a relative constant for a basis to be meaningful. Similarly, at least one component of a disjoint union must be non-recursive.

The above generator basis for integers, although correct, is not very practical, considering the need for explicit injector functions. Thus, if x is a *Nat1* then the corresponding integer must be written $pos(x)$. A better idea is to define the *Int* type as the head of a family of *syntactic subtypes*, all defined simultaneously. The types *Zero*, *Nat1* and *Neg1* shall be the minimal or *basic* subtypes, where $V_{Zero} = \{0\}$, $V_{Nat1} = \{1, 2, \ldots\}$, and $V_{Neg1} = \{-1, -2, \ldots\}$. By taking the generator domains as suitable subtypes we may obtain a one-to-one basis. Their codomains should be basic types, which are thereby pairwise disjoint by definition: $Zero \sqcap Nat1 = \ldots = \emptyset$. Intermediate subtypes may be user defined as indicated. (If some are left out they will be added behind the scenes in order to make the family into a lattice with *Int* as the maximal element and $\emptyset$ as the minimal one.)

> **type** *Int* **by** *Zero*, *Nat1*, *Neg1*
>   **and** $Nat = Zero \sqcup Nat$,
> $Neg = Zero \sqcup Neg1$,
> $Nzo = Nat1 \sqcup Neg1$ ==

> **module**
>   **func** $0 : \longrightarrow Zero$
>   **func** $S\hat{} : Nat \longrightarrow Nat1$ — basic successor
>   **func** $N\hat{} : Nat1 \longrightarrow Neg1$ — basic negation
>   **1–1 genbas** 0, $S\hat{}$, $N\hat{}$
>   **func** $succ : Int \longrightarrow Int$ — successor
>   **def** $succ(x) ==$ **case** x **of** $neg(x') \rightarrow -pred(x') \mid$ **others** $\rightarrow Sx$ **fo**
>   **func** $pred : Int \longrightarrow Int$ — predecessor
>   **def** $pred(x) ==$ **case** x **of** $0 \rightarrow NS0 \mid Sx' \rightarrow x' \mid N(x') \rightarrow NSx'$ **fo**
>   **func** $-\hat{} : Int \longrightarrow Int$ — negation
>   **def** $-x ==$ **case** x **of** $0 \rightarrow 0 \mid Nx' \rightarrow x' \mid$ **others** $\rightarrow Nx$ **fo**
>   ... ...
> **endmodule**

5.2 Semantic subtypes

Computers work with numbers of limited size, which can be identified as a semantic subtype of the corresponding unrestricted type. Thus, the following subtype of natural numbers would be appropriate for ten-bit number representation:

> **type** *TenBitNat* $==$ $n : Nat$ **where** $n \leq 1023$
> **module**
>   **func** $S\hat{} : TenBitNat \longrightarrow TenBitNat$

$$\textbf{def}\quad Sn == (Nat'Sn)\text{ as } TenBitNat$$

... ...

    endmodule

In redefining an inherited function it is permitted to modify the profile by replacing any occurrence of the prefix type (or any supertype of it) by the subtype under definition. The redefined function must behave as the inherited one, except possibly for a possible error caused by a final coercion.

    In order to give a more substantial example we define a fragment of a type module of binary trees of nodes containing values of some type T, to be subsequently restricted to the subtype of "search trees".

    type $BinTree\{T\}$ ==
    module
        func $nil : \longrightarrow BinTree$ — empty tree
        func $tree : Bintree \times T \times Bintree \longrightarrow Bintree$ — non-empty tree
        1–1 **genbas** $nil, tree$
        func $infix : Bintree \longrightarrow Seq\ T$
        def $infix(b) == $ **case** b **of** $nil \rightarrow \varepsilon \mid tree(l,t,r) \rightarrow infix(l) \vdash v \dashv infix(r)$ **fo**
    endmodule

The *infix* function computes the sequence of node values taken in infix order. Search trees are binary trees whose infix sequences are *sorted*. In order to define that notion we first have to introduce a suitable concept of *ordering relation*.

    property $SortOrd\{T\}$ ==
    module
        func $\hat{}<\hat{}\ : T \times T \longrightarrow Bool$
        axm $x, y, z : T \bullet$
            $\text{d}\ x < y,$
            $x < y < z \Rightarrow x < z,$
            $x < y \Rightarrow x < z \lor z < y$
        lma $x, y, v, w : T \bullet$
            $x < w < y \land \neg v < w \land \neg w < v \Rightarrow x < v < y$
    endmodule

where the first axiom specifies $\hat{}<\hat{}$ to be a total function.

    When defining a general concept of sortedness of sequences an ordering relation must be assumed for the element type, and for maximum generality the assumption should be as weak as possible. The property module *SortOrd* expresses the weakest notion of order which permits a concept of sorted sequences, such that sortedness is maintained by element removal and correct insertion. As indicated by the notation, a "strong" ordering relation is intended, like $\hat{}<\hat{}$ on integers. It may be noticed, however, that $\hat{}\leq\hat{}$, $\hat{}>\hat{}$, and many other binary relations over different types satisfy the same axioms. This indicates that a mechanism for function identifier substitution will be useful when instantiating modules. In ABEL a notation exemplified as follows is used: $SortOrd\{U\}$ **with** $\hat{}\leq\hat{}$ **for** $\hat{}<\hat{}$.

    funcs $SeqSort\{T\}$ **assuming** $SortOrd\{T\}$ ==

module

    func $\not{<}\hat{}$: seq $T \longrightarrow Bool$ — sorted wrt. $<$

    def $\not{<} q ==$ **case** q **of** $\varepsilon \to t \mid q' \vdash x \to$

            case q' **of** $\varepsilon \to t \mid q'' \vdash y \to \not{<} q' \wedge y < x$ **fo fo**

    lma $q_1, q_2, q_3 : Seq\,T$, $x : T \bullet$

        $\not{<}(q_1 \dashv q_2 \dashv q_3) \Rightarrow \not{<} q_2,$

        $\not{<}(q_1 \vdash x) \wedge \not{<}(x \dashv q_2) \Rightarrow \not{<}(q_1 \vdash x \dashv q_2)$

endmodule

The fact that *SortOrd* is assumed entails the following consistency requirements for any actual parameter U for T: that the function profile $\hat{}<\hat{}$: $U \times U \longrightarrow Bool$ (or a greater one) occurs in the module instance U (or is assumed for U if U is in turn a formal parameter, as in the exmple below), and that this function satisfies the axioms of that property module.

    We are now in a position to define the concept of search trees as a semantic subtype of binary trees, using the two auxiliary modules above.

    type *SearchTree{T}* **assuming** *SortOrd{T}*

               including *SeqSort{T}* $==$

               $b : Bintree\{T\}$ **where** $\not{<} infix(b)$ **convex**

module

    func lkp : $SearchTree \times T \longrightarrow T$ — look up

    def $lkp(s,t) ==$ **case** s **of** $nil \to \bot \mid tree(l,t',r) \to$

            if $t < t'$ **th** $lkp(l,t)$ **el**

            if $t' < t$ **th** $lkp(r,t)$ **el** t' **fi fi fo**

    func add : $SearchTree \times T \longrightarrow SearchTree$ — add or replace

    def $add(s,t) ==$ **case** s **of** $nil \to tree(nil,t,nil) \mid tree(l,t',r) \to$

            if $t < t'$ **th** $tree(add(l,t),t',r)$ **el**

            if $t' < t$ **th** $tree(l,t',add(r,t))$

            el $tree(l,t,r)$ **fi fi fo qua** *SearchTree*

endmodule

The consistency requirements on the included *SeqSort* instance are validated syntactically by the assumption in its environment. Notice that the function value of the look-up function may contain non-redundant information, since $\neg t < t \wedge \neg t' < t$ does not imply $t = t'$ for the weak ordering relation assumed. For the search tree property to be maintained by *add* the node value t' must in that case be replaced by t.

    The keyword **convex** asserts an important property of the defined subtype: that any subtree of a search tree is itself a search tree. In general the formulas which must be proved in order to establish the convexity property are determined mechanically by the generator basis and the restricting predicate. In this case there is an obligation to prove: $\not{<} infix(init)$, and $\not{<} infix(tree(l,w,r)) \Rightarrow \not{<} infix(l) \wedge \not{<} infix(r)$. The proofs follow using the definition of the *infix* function in module *BinTree* and lemma 1 of module *SeqSort*.

    The convexity has the syntactic consequence that the variables l and r introduced in discriminators on search trees are of type *SearchTree* (not *BinTree*), thereby avoiding coercions of arguments to *lkp* and *add* in the recursive definitions of these functions. An important semantic consequence is that induction hypotheses are justified for subtrees in proofs by generator induction over search trees.

The notation qua *SearchTree* in the *add* definition serves to avoid coercion of the function body which is syntactically of the type *BinTree*. There is an associated obligation to prove that the function value is in fact a search tree. That can be achieved by proving

$$\slash\!\!<(q_1 \vdash infix(s) \vdash q_2) \wedge \slash\!\!<(q_1 \vdash v \dashv q_2) \Rightarrow \slash\!\!<(q_1 \vdash infix(add(s,t)) \vdash q_2)$$

by generator induction on $s: SearchTree$ for arbitrary node value sequences q_1 and q_2. In the non-trivial case that s is of the form $tree(l, t', r)$ the proof goes through using induction hypotheses for l and r, as well as lemma 2 of the *SeqSort* module and the lemma of module *SortOrd*. Then, by taking $q_1 = q_2 = \varepsilon$ we obtain the desired result: $\slash\!\!< infix(s) \Rightarrow \slash\!\!< infix(add(s,v))$. (Notice that the restricting predicate may be assumed for any search tree.)

5.3 Many-to-one generator bases

We define a type of abstract finite maps from a "domain type" X to a "codomain type" Y. A map may be compared to a partial function from X to Y, which is defined for at most a finite number of arguments.

```
type Map{X,Y}  ==
module
    func init :  ⟶ Map                           — empty map
    func ^[^↦^]: Map × X × Y ⟶ Map               — update map
    genbas init, ^[^↦^]
    func ^[^] :  Map × X ⟶ Y                     — apply map
    def   m[x] == case m of init → ⊥ | m'[x'↦y] →
                    if x = x' th y el m'[x] fi fo
    obsbas  ^[^]
endmodule
```

The **obsbas** statement defines the equality relation on maps as the strict restriction of:

$$(m_1 = m_2) == \forall x : X \bullet (m_1[x] == m_2[x])$$

which may be useful for proof purposes, but is not a constructive definition. The definedness predicate d^[^] of the map application function may be derived as explained in section 4. The result is the following TGI definition:

$$\textbf{def } \text{d } m[x] == \delta_x \text{ and case } m \text{ of } init \to \textbf{f} \mid \text{d } m'[x'] \to$$
$$x = x' \vee \text{d } m'[x] \text{ fi fo}$$

By means of the definedness predicate equality on maps may be defined without the use of strong equality in the right hand side:

$$(m_1 = m_2) == \forall x : T \bullet \text{d } m_1[x] = \text{d } m_2[x] \wedge (\text{d } m_1[x] \Rightarrow m_1[x] = m_2[x])$$

The equality definition still is not constructive, due to the quantifier in the right hand side. It is possible, however, to give a definition of the *Map* type entirely within the TGI framework in terms of a semantic subtype. The idea is to restrict the generator universe to a set of *canonic forms*, one for each equivalence class. Then, redefining the generators so that they generate canonic maps, the subtype is made to appear to have a one-to-one generator basis. This in turn makes it possible to give a simple TGI redefinition of the equality relation. Assuming that there is a *total order* $\hat{}<\hat{}$ on the "argument" type X of *Map*, we can identify canonic representatives of the form:

$$init[x_1 \mapsto y_1][x_2 \mapsto y_2]\ldots[x_n \mapsto y_n], \quad \text{for} \quad x_1 < x_2 < \ldots < x_n \quad \text{and} \quad n \geq 0.$$

The notion of total order may be expressed as follows:

> **property** *TotOrd*$\{X\}$ == *SortOrd*$\{X\}$
> **module**
> >   **func** $\hat{}<\hat{}$: $X \times X \longrightarrow Bool$
> >   **axm** $x, y : X \bullet$
> > > $\neg(x<y \wedge y<x)$,
> > > $x<y \vee x=y \vee y<x$
>
> **endmodule**

Since *TotOrd* is defined as a extension of *SortOrd*, it inherits the contents of the latter. Seeing a property as the conjunction of its axioms, the inheritance implies that the extended property is *stronger*. Thus *TotOrd*$\{T\} \Rightarrow$ *SortOrd*$\{T\}$ holds for arbitrary type T, and the implication is established syntactically.

Assuming this property for the type X we can express formally the concept of map canonicity:

> **funcs** *MapCan*$\{X,Y\}$ **assuming** *TotOrd*$\{X\}$ ==
> **module**
> >   **func** *canonic* : *Map*$\{X,Y\} \longrightarrow Bool$
> >   **def** *canonic*(m) == **case** m **of** *init* $\rightarrow$ t | $m_1[x_1 \mapsto y_1] \rightarrow$
> > >   **case** m_1 **of** *init* $\rightarrow$ t | $m_2[x_2 \mapsto y_2] \rightarrow$
> > > $x_2 < x_1 \wedge$ *canonic*(m_1) **fo fo**
>
> **endmodule**

Finally we may define a convex subtype of *canonic maps*:

> **type** *CanMap*$\{X,Y\}$ **assuming** *TotOrd*$\{X\}$
> >   **including** *MapCan*$\{X,Y\}$ ==
> > m : *Map*$\{X,Y\}$ **where** *canonic*(m) **convex**
>
> **module**
> >   **func** *init* : $\longrightarrow$ *CanMap*
> >   **func** $\hat{}[\hat{}\mapsto\hat{}]$: *CanMap* $\times X \times Y \longrightarrow$ *CanMap*
> >   **def** $m[x \mapsto y]$ == **case** m **of** *init* $\rightarrow m[x \mapsto y]$ **at** *Map* | $m_1[x_1 \mapsto y_1] \rightarrow$
> > >   **if** $x_1 < x$ **th** $m[x \mapsto y]$*Map* **el**
> > >   **if** $x < x_1$ **th** $m_1[x \mapsto y][x_1 \mapsto y_1]$ **at** *Map*
> > >   **el** $m_1[x \mapsto y]$ **at** *Map* **fi fi fo qua** *CanMap*
> >   **func** $\hat{}=\hat{}$: *CanMap* $\times$ *CanMap* $\longrightarrow Bool$
> >   **def** $m_1 = m_2$ == **case** (m_1, m_2) **of** $(init, init) \rightarrow$ t
> > > | $(m_1[x_1 \mapsto y_1], m_2[x_2 \mapsto y_2]) \rightarrow m_1 = m_2 \wedge x_1 = x_2 \wedge y_1 = y_2$
> > > | **others** $\rightarrow$ f **fo**
>
> >   **func** *crep* : *Map* $\longrightarrow$ *CanMap*   — canonic repr.
> >   **def** *crep*(m) == **case** m **of** *init* $\rightarrow m$ | $m'[x \mapsto y] \rightarrow$ *crep*(m')$[x \mapsto y]$ **fo**
> **endmodule**

In order to establish the convexity there is a obligation to prove: $canonic(init)$ and $canonic(m[x \mapsto y]) \Rightarrow canonic(m)$, which is easy. In the semantic redefinition of the generator $\hat{}[\hat{}\mapsto\hat{}]$ there is a need to refer to the original generator. Therefore the standard rule of function overloading must be overruled. It is practical to use the at-construct in this case because the mixfix notation of the function begins with an operand and ends with an operator symbol. Notice that the innermost (i.e. leftmost) generator application of $m_1[x \mapsto y][x_1 \mapsto y_1]$ at Map refers to the redefined one (since the variable m_1 is of type $CanMap$).

The qua-construct introduces an obligation to prove that the redefined function generates canonic maps: $canonic(m[x \mapsto y])$ for $m : CanMap$. The latter proof goes through by generator induction on m, using the lemma $canonic(m[x' \mapsto y']$ at $Map) \wedge x < x' \Rightarrow canonic(m[x \mapsto y][x' \mapsto y']$ at $Map)$, for $m : CanMap$, also provable by induction on m.

Both redefined functions must behave as the original ones on the restricted domains. So one has to prove in addition:

$$\forall x : X \bullet m[x' \mapsto y][x] == m[x' \mapsto y] \text{ at } Map[x] \quad \text{and}$$
$$m = m' \Leftrightarrow \forall x : X \bullet (m[x] == m'[x]), \qquad \text{for } m, m' : CanMap.$$

The proofs, which are by generator induction on m and m', are easy. The redefined equality relation corresponds to that of a one-to-one generator basis. This implies that consistency can not be violated through the definition of functions by means of generator induction over $CanMap$.

The function $crep$ computes the canonic representative of an arbitrary map, and can thus be seen as a mechanism of "unfailing" coercion to the subtype. Notice that function overloading implies that the generator applied to $crep(m')$ in the $crep$ definition is the one redefined in $CanMap$. Also the type (codomain) of $init$ has been redefined locally. Therefore type analysis shows that the body of $crep$ is of type $CanMap$, which implies that the function value is indeed a canonic map. It is fairly easy to see that it is idempotent, and that $crep(m) = m$ for $m : CanMap$, and thus for $m : Map$ and Map equality.

It may be noticed that the predicate $canonic$ and the corresponding redefined generator $\hat{}[\hat{}\mapsto\hat{}]$ are the only non-trivial parts of the construct $CanMap$. In particular the redefined equality relation and the $crep$ function could be specified automatically, given a syntactic indication of the purpose of the subtype. Also all the proof obligations may be identified mechanically. The proof concerning the redefined equality will in general only go through if the canonic forms described by the restricting predicate are in fact in a one-to-one correspondence with the abstract values defined for the supertype.

The $CanMap$ type invites function specifications that exploit of the properties of canonic representations in order to improve the efficiency of expression evaluation, seeing TGI specifications as applicative programs. This, however, is likely to make the function definitions look more like algorithmic implementations than abstract mathematical specifications, which is not always an advantage for logical reasoning and easy understanding. For instance, let the composition operator $\hat{}\oplus\hat{}$: $Map \times Map \longrightarrow Map$ denote the "union" of two maps, where components of the right argument override corresponding components of the left argument. The following semantic definition is easy to understand:

$$\textbf{def } m \oplus m' == \textbf{case } m' \textbf{ of } init \rightarrow m \mid m_1[x \mapsto y] \rightarrow (m \oplus m_1)[x \mapsto y] \textbf{ fo}$$

A more execution efficient version can be made for canonic maps, using an algorithm similar to that of merging two sorted sequences:

$$\textbf{def}\ m \oplus m' == \textbf{case}\ m\ \textbf{of}\ init \to m' \mid m_1[x_1 \mapsto y_1] \to$$
$$\textbf{case}\ m'\ \textbf{of}\ init \to m \mid m_2[x_2 \mapsto y_2] \to$$
$$\textbf{if}\ x_1 < x_2\ \textbf{th}\ (m \oplus m_2)[x_2 \mapsto y_2]\ \textbf{at}\ Map\ \textbf{el}$$
$$\textbf{if}\ x_2 < x_1\ \textbf{th}\ (m_1 \oplus m')[x_1 \mapsto y_1]\ \textbf{at}\ Map$$
$$\textbf{el}\ (m_1 \oplus m_2)[x_2 \mapsto y_2]\ \textbf{at}\ Map\ \textbf{fi}\ \textbf{fi}\ \textbf{qua}\ CanMap\ \textbf{fo}\ \textbf{fo}$$

This indicates that specifications optimized with respect to ease of reasoning and understanding naturally belong to the *Map* module, (although there is no consistency guarantee for functions defined by generator induction over the *Map* type), whereas a redefinition with better execution efficiency may be given in *CanMap*. As usual, one would be obliged to prove the strong equality of the two definitions as applied to canonic maps.

The following stronger result also proves the consistency of the definition of $\hat{\ } \oplus \hat{\ }$ in *Map*: $(crep(m) \oplus crep(m'))[x] == (m \oplus m')[x]$, for $m, m' : Map$, $x : X$, where the *crep* function computes the canonic representative of an arbitrary map, and the definition of equality on *Map* through the observation basis has been used. Notice that the redefined $\hat{\ } \oplus \hat{\ }$ operator is applied in the left hand side. If the operator is not redefined then proof of $(m \oplus crep(m'))[x] == (m \oplus m')[x]$ is sufficient to show consistency of the definition in *Map*, because generator induction is only applied to the second argument. Again, these proof obligations may be identified mechanically. Notice that they are formulas at the TGI level since the universal quantifier occurring in the equality definition could be made implicit. That is not the case for a proof obligation in the form of a congruence axiom.

Also the map application function $\hat{\ }[\hat{\ }]$ could be redefined with better efficiency for canonic maps, however, we leave it to the reader to provide a more execution efficient version, and to prove it correct.

5.4 Type simulation

The fact that types easy to reason about are often impractical for computational purposes implies a dilemma as far as program development is concerned; one may have to choose between easy reasoning and computational efficiency. Fortunately, however, there is a way of achieving both ends: we may reason and program in terms of an easy type T and compute in terms of an efficient type T', provided that T' *simulates* T in a certain formal sense. We shall explain the concept of type simulation using an example.

More efficient versions of several functions on (canonic) maps may be obtained (on the average) by representing maps as search trees. We can make use of the type *Search Tree* defined above by first introducing a type of *nodes* consisting of a *key* part and a *data* part:

type $Node\{Key, Data\}$ **assuming** $SortOrd\{Key\} == key : Key \times data : Data$
module
    func $\hat{\ } < \hat{\ } : Node \times Node \longrightarrow Bool$
    def $x < y == x.key < y.key$
endmodule satisfying $SortOrd\{Node\}$

A proof that the *Node* type satisfies the *SortOrd* property consists in proving that the *SortOrd* axioms, $\neg(x < y \land y < x)$ and $x < y \lor x = y \lor y < x$, hold for $x, y : Node$. This is trivial on the assumption that they are satisfied for *Key* values. Given these proofs it is established that $SortOrd\{X\}$ implies $SortOrd\{Node\{X, Y\}\}$ for arbitrary types X and Y.

The type $Search\,Tree\{Node\{X,Y\}\}$ *simulates*, in the sense defined below, the type $CanMap\{X,Y\}$, for arbitrary types X,Y which satisfy the assumption of $CanMap$. (This assumption, $TotOrd\{X\}$, implies $SortOrd\{X\}$, which in turn implies the property assumed by the $Search\,Tree$ module for its actual parameter, $SortOrd\{Node\{X,Y\}\}$. We may thus conclude, without additional proof obligations, that the actual parameter of the $Search\,Tree$ module satisfies the property assumed for the formal parameter.)

1. There is a total function, often called an "abstraction function", transforming "concrete" search trees to "abstract" canonic maps:

   func $A : Search\,Tree\{Node\{X,Y\}\} \longrightarrow CanMap\{X,Y\}$
   def $A(t) == A'(infix(t))$, where
   func $A' : \{q : Seq\ Node\{X,Y\}$ where $\!<\!q\}\longrightarrow CanMap\{X,Y\}$
   def $A'(q) ==$ **case** q **of** $\varepsilon \to init \mid q' \vdash n \to A'(q')[n.key \mapsto n.data]$ **fo**

   (The fact that the argument q is a sorted sequence shows that it would be sufficient to use the simple version of the generator $\hat{}[\hat{}\mapsto\hat{}].$)

2. Let $m = A(t)$ and $m' = A(t')$. Then the functions of $Search\,Tree$ simulate those of $CanMap$ as follows:

$$m = m' == infix(t) = infix(t'),$$
$$init == A(nil),$$
$$m[x \mapsto y] == A(add(t,(x,y)), \text{ and}$$
$$m[x] == lkp(t,(x,\hat{})).data,$$

   where the second component of the second argument to add is redundant.

The simulation relationship can be established by proving the criteria 2 as they stand, for the given abstraction function. An alternative, which is somewhat simpler, is to prove the "abstract" axioms of the $CanMap$ module, case-free versions, translated in terms of $Search\,Tree$ functions:

1. $infix(init) = infix(init)$ $== t$
2. $infix(add(t,(x,y)) = infix(init)$ $== f$
3. $infix(init) = infix(add(t,(x,y))$ $== f$
4. $infix(add(t_1,(x_1,y_1)) = infix(add(t_2,(x_2,y_2)) == t_1 = t_2 \wedge x_1 = x_2 \wedge y_1 = y_2)$
5. $infix(add(nil,(x,y)))$ $== infix(add(nil,(x,y)))$
6. $infix(add(add(t,(x_1,y_1)),(x,y))) == infix(\text{if } x_1 < x \text{ th } add(add(t,(x_1,y_1)),(x,y))$
                                     el if $x < x_1$ th $add(add(t,(x,y)),(x_1,y_1))$
                                     el $add(t,(x,y))$ fi fi)
7. $lkp(init,(x,\hat{}))$ $== \perp$
8. $lkp(add(t,(x_1,y_1)),(x,\hat{}))$ $==$ if $x = x_1$ th y el $lkp(t,(x,\hat{}))$ fi

The formulas 1-4 are the translations of equality axioms, 5 and 6 correspond to the redefined generator axioms, and the last two are the translations of the inherited axioms for map application. Proofs of no. 4 and no. 8 follow from the observation that the add applications occurring in the left hand sides are translations of canonic maps and therefore left linear search trees. No. 6 requires a proof of the lemma $infix(add(add(t,(x_1,y_1)),(x,y)) ==\blacksquare$ $infix(add(add(t,(x,y)),(x_1,y_1)))$. The remaining proofs are entirely trivial. It can be shown that the truth of 1-8 implies the existence of a total abstraction function satisfying the criteria 2 above.

According to the definition of the simulation relation the type $CanMap\{X,Y\}$ simulates its supertype $Map\{X,Y\}$, where the abstraction function is the identity, and the redefined functions in $CanMap$ directly simulate those of Map. Since the simulation is a transitive relation on types, it follows that $SearchTree\{Node\{X,Y\}\}$ also simulates $Map\{X,Y\}$.

A semantic subtype whose abstract value space is a proper subset of that of the supertype is said to simulate latter *partially* if the generators and other functions are redefined. In that case redefined producer functions, and at least one generator, may be less defined on the sudomain than the original function. For instance the type *TenBitNat* defined at the beginning of section 5.2 is a partial simulation of *Nat*.

5.5 Classes

A typed value, like the number 3, is a mathematical object represented by an immutable data structure in a running program. The same is true for values representing large volumes of data, like long sequence values or trees with many nodes. In an applicative environment there is no such thing as making changes to existing data structures, so, instead one has to create new values, may be from scratch, even for high volume structures equal to existing ones except for small changes. There are cases where one can not afford the luxury to ignore inefficiencies like that, but has to use an imperative approach in order to assume more direct responsibility for the use of storage space and computing time. In particular, it may be necessary to manipulate high volume data structures by incremental updating.

This motivates the introduction of *classes*, which are similar to types, except for the following differences:

1. Whereas the generator functions of type modules give rise to immutable *values*, those of a class give rise to *objects* whose contents or state may be subsequently changed.

2. Imperative style procedure declarations are allowed as module items of a class, with the syntax:

   proc <name> (**var** <varpar>, **val** <valpar>) ==<body>

   where <varpar> is a list of typed formal *variable parameters* (or in/out-parameters) and <valpar> is a typed list of formal *value parameters* (or in-parameters). The latter is the default parameter kind. <body> is a list of imperative style statements, which may include assignment operations, procedure invocations, alternatives by if- or case-constructs, and loop constructs.

3. assignment operations as well as parameter (argument) transmission is by *pointer copying* for class objects in order to avoid unnecessary copying of high volume structures, whereas these mechanisms conceptually are by value copying for typed values.

A procedure invocation is a statement of the form **call** <name> (v, e), where v is a list of variables, the actual variable parameters, and e is a list of expressions, the actual value parameters. The net effect of this call will be a simultaneous assignment to the actual variable parameters, $v := f_{\text{name}}(v, e)$, where f_{name} is called the *effect function* of the procedure. Its function value is a tuple whose components correspond to the individual variable parameters.

The state space of an object of a given class C is equal to the value space of a corresponding type T_C. The latter may be obtained by modifying the class module definition as follows:

1. The initial keyword **class** is replaced by the keyword **type**.

2. All references to classes in the definition are replaced by references to the corresponding types.

3. Procedure declarations are replaced by the introduction and definition of corresponding effect functions.

A class C is said to (partially) simulate a type T if its associated type T_C is a (partial) simulation of T. In that case T can be taken as a (partial) specification of C, i.e. an abstract interface.

ABEL provides a mechanism for the internal updating of objects by defining the variables introduced by discriminators to be *assignable* whenever the discriminand of the **case**-construct is a class object (other than a formal value parameter). The combination of pointer copying and internal object updates may result in a quite complicated program logic, unless the use of object expressions and assignments to object variables are restricted. The problem is that confluent accessible pointers are object aliases which may result in difficult side effects in updating operations. There do exist restrictions, syntactic except for the use of subscripted variables, which are sufficient to prevent aliasing by pointers, and still allow efficient programs up to a point, see [3].

Freedom from pointer alias implies that program semantics are exactly as if classes are replaced by their corresponding types (provided that internal updates are interpreted as wholesale object assignments).

As an example we first define a concept of "lists" of T-elements in the form of a type (which is nothing but our old sequence concept in disguise):

```
type List{T} ==
module
      func nil : ⟶ List
      func extend : List × T ⟶ List
      1–1 genbas nil, extend
      func append : T × List ⟶ List
      def append(t, l) ==
      case l of nil → extend(l, t) | extend(l′, t′) → extend(append(l′, t), t′) fo
endmodule
```

Notice that the *append* operator extends a list at the "wrong" end, and for that reason a whole new list value must be created by the repeated use of the *extend* generator.

As a contrast, let us define the list concept as a class. Then the append operation can be defined in the form of a more efficient procedure, which generates only one new *extend*-object:

```
class LIST{T}  ==
module
      func nil : ⟶ LIST
      func extend : LIST × T ⟶ LIST
      1–1 genbas nil, extend
      proc Append(val t : T, var l : LIST) ==
      case l of nil → l := extend(l, t) | extend(l', t') → call Append(l', t) fo
endmodule
```

The type associated with this class is exactly the type *List*; in particular the *append* function is the effect function of the *Append* procedure. That can be proved using standard Hoare Logic on the body of the latter.

Although the *Append* procedure need not regenerate the old list, it does have to search for the far end of it. For maximum efficiency to be obtained a pointer to the last list element would have to be stored as part of the data structure, for instance as follows:

```
class FIFOLIST{T}  == (first, last : LIST{T}) where
                       last = case first of nil → nil | others → end(first) fo
      module
            proc .APPEND(val t : T) == const new := extend(nil, t);
                                       case last of nil → first, last := new, new
                                       | extend(l, t') → l, last := new, new fo
      endmodule
```

where *end* is a function locating the last element of a non-empty list. Whenever a class is a subclass of a labelled product, we use the ad-hoc notation of a dot to the left of a local function or procedure name to indicate an implied parameter of the class under definition. And since a product has only one generator, we omit the case construct as usual and let the implied argument be a tuple whose components are named as indicated by the labels. Thus *.APPEND* stands for $(first, last).APPEND$ in the procedure declaration. The implied parameter of a procedure is by definition a var parameter; thus by this syntactic trick the labels of the class prefix are made to behave as assignable variables, but only inside the class body. The dot notation is used in procedure calls as well. Thus, for $FL : FIFOLIST$ the statement call $FL.APPEND(a)$ would append the T-value a at the far end of the list FL.

In this way subclasses of labelled type or class products are made to resemble classes as in SIMULA 67.

Unfortunately the pointer *last* causes an alias on the end element of a nonempty list. Consequently the verification of this last class can not be made using ordinary Hoare Logic. Notice, however, that any user of any instance of the class *FIFOLIST* is protected from the difficulties caused by the internal alias, provided that the "representation variables" *first* and *last* are unassignable from outside the class, by disallowing case-constructs on objects of classes of this kind.

6   A Case Study

The following requirements to a lift control system with n lifts in a building with m floors are formulated by Neil Davis of STL, England:

1. Each lift has a set of buttons, one button for each floor. These illuminate when pressed and cause the lift to visit the corresponding floor. The illumination is canceled when the corresponding floor is visited (i.e. stopped at) by the lift.

2. Each floor has two buttons (except low and high), one to request an up-lift and one to request a down-lift. These buttons illuminate when pressed. The buttons are canceled when a lift visits the floor and is either traveling in the desired direction, or visiting the floor with no requests outstanding. In the latter case if both floor requests are illuminated, only one should be canceled. The algorithm used to decide which to serve should minimize the waiting time for both requests.

3. When a lift has no requests to service, it should remain at its final destination with its doors closed and await further requests (or model a "holding" floor).

4. All requests for lifts from floors must be serviced eventually, with all floors given equal priority (can this be proved or demonstrated)?

5. All requests for floors within lifts must be serviced eventually, with floors being serviced sequentially in the order of travel (can this be proved or demonstrated)?

This informal description may be understood in many ways, perhaps even in conflicting ways. It is difficult to check whether the lift system is over- or under-specified. For instance, the following two requirements are not expressed above, but seem quite obvious:

- A lift should not make unrequested stops.

- A lift should not pass a floor if there is a request on that floor for a lift in the direction of travel.

This motivates the need for a formal treatment.

We shall present an abstract specification of the lift control system described above. All requirements will be formalized, except that our specification will not be concerned with priorities or minimization of waiting time. In order to demonstrate object oriented programming with the ABEL class concept, we present an imperative implementation of the lift system with class objects corresponding to the hardware components of a real lift system, such as doors and buttons with associated signals. The implementation may be improved by adding emergency buttons. Other aspects of real lifts like "fullness" may also be added.

6.1 Abstract Specification

In order to formalize these requirements, we shall use (time) sequences of events, considering events caused by a user of the lift system (InEvents) and observable events caused by the lift system (OutEvents). An execution may be seen as a possibly infinite sequence of events. In order to avoid infinite sequences, our specification will be expressed by means of finite, initial parts of these sequences, called *histories*, in the style of [1]. Safety is expressed by specifying that each possible history r satisfies some predicate on r. It is not obvious how to specify liveness by means of finite sequences, and neither how to give a complete specification of the lift system.

However, it is possible to give an abstract specification of the lift system by its *ready set*, i.e. the set of events which the system is ready to accept next (at a given point in an execution) [12]. The ready set is formalized as a function, *lift*, of the event history. In order to avoid non-determinism in the specification we consider a fixed but arbitrary execution (i.e., there is an implicit outermost universal quantifier on the execution).

Safety properties are expressed by specifying non-readiness; in particular P is an *execution invariant* if $P(\varepsilon)$ holds and if $P(r) \wedge e \in lift(r) \Rightarrow P(r \vdash e)$. (When rewritten as $P(r) \wedge \neg P(r \vdash e) \Rightarrow \neg e \in lift(r)$, the non-readiness becomes evident.) For instance, the predicate **hist** defined by:

$$\text{def hist } r == \text{ case } r \text{ of } \varepsilon \to t \mid r' \vdash e \to \text{ hist } r' \wedge e \in lift(r') \text{ fo}$$

is an execution invariant, identifying the possible lift system histories.

Formulas of the form $Q(r, e) \Rightarrow e \in lift(r)$ express basic (one-step) liveness properties. For instance, $e \in InEvent \Rightarrow e \in lift(r)$ expresses that the lift system is always ready to accept an input event. Similarly, we may express that if there are unserved requests, there will be at least one out-event in the ready set. Other liveness properties may be proved by wellfounded induction. For instance, in the case where there is one lift, we may prove the liveness properties of requirement 4 and 5 as follows:

Let $m(r, z)$ be a (worst case) measure of how many moves the lift, at a point r in an execution, may need to serve a particular request z, such that $m(r, z)$ is always nonnegative, and $m(r, z) = 0$ implies that the request is served. By means of the ready-set, we may prove that any request eventually will be served as follows:

$$m(r, z) = N > 0 \Rightarrow (\forall e : OutEvent \bullet e \in lift(r) \Rightarrow m(r \vdash e, z) < N) \wedge$$
$$(\forall e : InEvent \bullet e \in lift(r) \Rightarrow m(r \vdash e, z) \leq N) \wedge$$
$$(\neg \exists e : OutEvent \bullet e \in lift(r)) \Rightarrow m(r, z) = 0$$

assuming underlying fairness. This may be generalized to the case of several lifts.

We shall below give a specification of the ready set and define a measure which may be used to prove requirements 4 and 5. The safety requirements stated in requirements 1 to 3 are proved by an execution invariant (OK).

6.1.1 Description of Events

It seems reasonable to consider the following input events for the lift system (caused by the users):

- $bl(x, y)$ — push the button for floor y in lift x.

- $bf(y, d)$ — push the button for direction d on floor y, where d is one of $\uparrow$, $\downarrow$.

A $bf(y, d)$-event will satisfy $y = lo \Rightarrow d = \uparrow$ and $y = hi \Rightarrow d = \downarrow$ where lo and hi are two integer constants identifying the low and high floor, respectively. We assume that $hi - lo = m - 1 > 0$.

As an immediate effect of pushing a button, the button should be lit (unless already lit). This should take no abstract time. We can express this by defining a button-push as an output event as well. (A bl or bf output event has no effect when the button is already lit. We could omit such output events in the output history, as discussed later.) A consequence is that an output history will define the full timing between input- and output-events.

It then seems reasonable to consider the following output events for the lift system:

- $bl(x, y)$ — light the button for floor y in lift x (unless already lit).

- $bf(y, d)$ — light the button for direction d on floor y. (unless already lit).

- $v(x, y, d, o)$ — lift x "visits" floor y and indicates (by appropriate lamps) that it will move in direction d. Here, d may have the value $\updownarrow$, which means that the lift is free (to move up or down). The doors are open (or opening) if o is true, otherwise they are closed (or closing).

The doors will be open(ed) if either button $bl(x, y)$ or $bf(y, d)$ is lit, and the two buttons will be turned off (if lit). (It will become clear that the lift cannot be free when a button on floor y was lit.)

¿From the given informal specification, it is not clear whether a visiting lift should indicate its planned direction. Without any indication, it is not always possible to determine if a visiting lift is an up-lift or a down-lift, and a person entering will not know whether the lift will continue in his direction. We have therefore chosen to include a parameter for the direction in v-events.

It may be argued whether passing a floor without stopping and opening doors should be an abstractly visible event. However, such an event is observable if there are lamps, either inside lifts or outside lifts, indicating the floor position of each lift. It seems useful that each lift indicates the current floor position so that a person pushing a button requesting a stop at a certain floor knows whether that floor is passed already. The chosen event language is rich enough to fully express the abstract behavior of such lift systems.

To illustrate how sequences of events can describe lift behavior, we point out some essential ideas. It will become clear that a $v(x, y, d, o)$-event can follow another $v(x, y', d', o')$-event provided y is the next floor after y' in direction d', or y equals y' and o is true. (When d is $\updownarrow$, y must equal y'.) For instance the output history

$$bf(5, \downarrow), ..., v(x, 5, \downarrow, true), v(x, 5, \updownarrow, true)$$

indicates that the person pushing the down-button on floor 5 had left when lift x stopped. Since no request appears inside the lift, it waits with open doors. It is here assumed that the $bf(5, \uparrow)$-button is not alight. Otherwise, the output history

$$bf(5, \downarrow), ..., bf(5, \uparrow), ..., v(x, 5, \downarrow, true), v(x, 5, \updownarrow, true), bl(x, 8), v(x, 5, \uparrow, false)$$

indicates that the person waiting for an up-lift was served after no one took advantage of the down-lift.

6.1.2 The Specification

In order to specify the lift system, we define some helpful functions and predicates which may be thought of as high level observations of the state of the lift system after a given history r. These functions are defined constructively below, except the nd-function, which is characterized by axioms expressing minimal requirements corresponding to the informal requirements.

```
type Lift      == 1..n
type Floor     == lo..hi
type Dir       == {↓, ↕, ↑}
  module
  func dir : Floor × Floor ⟶ Dir          — the direction from one floor to another
  def  dir(y1, y2) == if y1 < y2 th ↑ el if y1 > y2 th ↓ el ↕ fi
  endmodule
type LPos      ==(f : Floor × d : Dir) where          — Lift Positions
                     ¬(f = lo ∧ d = ↓ ∨ f = hi ∧ d = ↑)
type BF        == LPos where d ≠ ↕          — Floor Button positions
type BL        == (l : Lift × f : Floor)          — Lift Button positions
type V         == (l : Lift × f : Floor × d : Dir × o : Bool)          — V-event
type InEvent == bl : BL + bf : BF
type Event    == bl : BL + bf : BF + v : V


type ESeq      == Seq{Event}
  module
  func ˆ@ˆ : ESeq × Lift ⟶ V          — the last v-event involving the lift
  def  r@x         == case r of ε → (x, startfloor, ↕, true) | r ⊢ e → case e of
                         | v(z) → if x = z.l th z el r@x fi
                         | others  → r@x fo fo
  func nd: ESeq × Lift ⟶ Dir          — the next direction of the lift
  func nf: ESeq × Lift ⟶ Floor          — the next floor the lift will be at
  def  nf(r, x)     == (r@x).f + if (r@x).o th 0
                         el if (r@x).d = ↑ th 1  el if (r@x).d = ↓ th −1 el 0 fi fi fi
  func A: ESeq × Lift × Floor ⟶ Bool          — is the lift approaching the floor?
  def  A(r, x, y)   == ((r@x).d = dir((r@x).f, y) ≠ ↕)
  func Rbl: ESeq × Lift × Floor ⟶ Bool
                     — Rbl(r, x, y) tests if there is an outstanding bl(x, y)-request
  def  Rbl(r, x, y) == case r of ε → false | r ⊢ e → case e of
                         | v(l, f, d, o) → if x = l ∧ y = f th false el Rbl(r, x, y) fi
                         | bl(l, f) → if x = l ∧ y = f th true el Rbl(r, x, y) fi
                         | others → Rbl(r, x, y) fo fo
  func Rbf: ESeq × Floor × Dir ⟶ Bool
                     — Rbf(r, y, d) tests if there is an outstanding bf(y, d)-request
  def  Rbf(r, y, d) == case r of ε → false | r ⊢ e → case e of
                         | v(l, f, dd, o) → if y = f ∧ d = dd th false el Rbf(r, y, d) fi
                         | bf(f, dd) → if y = f ∧ d = dd th true el Rbl(r, x, y) fi
                         | others → Rbf(r, y, d) fo fo
  func R: ESeq × Lift × Floor × Dir ⟶ Bool
   — R(r, x, y, d) tests if the event v(x, y, d, true) will serve any outstanding requests
  def  R(r, x, y, d) == (Rbl(r, x, y) ∨ Rbf(r, y, d)) ∧ ¬r@x = (x, y, d, true)
  func OK: ESeq ⟶ Bool          — all safety requirements
  def  OK(r) == case r of ε → true | r ⊢ e → OK(r) ∧ case e of
                         | v(x, y, d, o) → y = nf(r, x) ∧ d = nd(r, x) ∧ o = R(r, x, y, d)
                         | others → true fo fo
```

axm

$\qquad$ **if** $\exists y : Floor \bullet A(r,x,y) \wedge Rbl(r,x,y)$ **th** $nd(r,x) = (r@x).d$ **el**

$\qquad$ **if** $nd(r,x) = \updownarrow$ **th** $\forall y \neq (r@x).f \bullet \neg Rbl(r,x,y)$

$\qquad$ **el** $Rbf(r,(r@x).f, nd(r,x)) \vee \exists y, d \bullet nd(r,x) = dir((r@x).f, y) \wedge R(r,x,y,d)$ **fi fi**

lma

$$OK(r) \Rightarrow (nf(r,x), nd(r,x)) \in LPos$$

endmodule

where the constant *startfloor* defines the starting floor of the lifts. Typing of variables in axioms and lemmas is omitted when already (uniquely) introduced in the module body. As the lemma expresses, OK ensures that no physically incorrect move may occur.

The *ESeq* module is non-constructive because nd is non-constructive. Internal consistency of the module is easy to show since all other functions are constructively defined, for instance it suffices to define a constructive lift strategy as follows:

type *LiftStrategy* $==$ *ESeq*

$\qquad$ **module**

$\qquad$ **def** $nd(r,x) ==$ <keep a non-$\updownarrow$ direction when useful (wrt. internal or external requests),

$\qquad\qquad\qquad$ otherwise take a useful direction, if any, and $\updownarrow$ if none.>

$\qquad$ **endmodule**

(Such a strategy will be formalized in the implementation.) As a proof obligation one must prove that the redefined nd-function satisfies the axioms in *ESeq*.

Finally we specify the ready set of the lift system:

type *LiftHistory* $== r : ESeq$ **where** $OK(r)$

$\qquad$ **module**

$\qquad$ **func** *lift* : *LiftHistory* $\longrightarrow$ *Set{Event}* $\qquad\qquad\qquad\qquad$ — ready set

$\qquad$ **axm** $e : Event, r : ESeq \bullet$

$\qquad\qquad e \in lift(r) \Rightarrow OK(r \vdash e),$ $\qquad\qquad\qquad\qquad\qquad$ — safety

$\qquad\qquad e \in InEvent \Rightarrow e \in lift(r),$ $\qquad\qquad$ — always ready to take input

$\qquad\qquad R(r,x,y,d) \Rightarrow \exists e : OutEvent \bullet e \in lift(r),$ $\qquad$ — general liveness

$\qquad\qquad Rbl(r,x,y) \Rightarrow \exists e : OutEvent \bullet e \in lift(r) \wedge e.l = x$ $\qquad$ — internal liveness

$\qquad$ **endmodule**

The last axiom expresses that *v*-events will re-occur as long as there are outstanding requests. ¿From this one-step liveness one may prove that any request eventually will be served, by the inductive technique explained above. One may use the following measure for a *bl*-request:

func $m : LiftHistory \times BL \longrightarrow Nat$

def $m(r,(x,y)) ==$ **case** $r@x$ **of** $(x,f,d,o) \rightarrow nat(f = y \wedge o) * 2 * (abs(f - y) +$

$\qquad\qquad\qquad 2 * nat(dir(f,y) = d) * $ **if** $d = \uparrow$ **th** $hi - f$ **el** $f - lo$ **fi**$) - nat(o)$ **fo**

using the following function from *Bool* to *Nat*: **def** $nat(b) ==$ **case** b **of** $t \rightarrow 0 \mid f \rightarrow 1$ **fo**

A similar measure can be given for external requests.

$\qquad$ Observe that the functions $\hat{\,}@\hat{\,}$, *Rbl*, and *Rbf* depend on the history r; the other functions depend on the history only through these. Thus in an implementation consisting of the current position and openness of each lift, *Rbl*, and *Rbf* as (array) variables, the history variable may be eliminated. (*Rbf* is always false outside *BF*, thus this part need not be stored.) Even though such an implementation gives a reasonable data structure, it is too high level in the sense that it does not produce output which is related to the hardware of a real lift system, and it does not describe how to operate the lifts in parallel.

6.2   Implementation Outline

According to object oriented principles, we model the lifts as objects, each with its own activity. Each lift should have a door, internal buttons (one for each floor), and a "lift control unit" which gives signals to the lift engine and takes care of displaying the position (floor and direction) of the lift by appropriate indicators located inside and outside the lift. In addition, the lifts share a "floor control object", controlling the external up- and down-buttons.

This structure can be modeled straightforward in ABEL. We first give a sketch of the ABEL implementation: The classes and procedures are motivated by the hardware components indicated above, and the (observing) functions correspond to what is directly visible for persons using the lift system. Module prefixes are not shown in order to focus on module interfaces rather than their insides.

We next show how ABEL classes may be used to describe the hardware components, and then build an imperative implementation of the lift system on top of these classes.

```
class Button ==
  module
  proc .on                              — available for users
  proc .off                             — turns off the light
  func .ison : Bool                     — is the button illuminated?
  endmodule

class Door ==
  module
  proc .open
  proc .close
  func .isopen : Bool
  endmodule

class LiftCtrl ==
  module
  proc .newdir(d : Dir)                 — involves displaying the new direction
  proc .move                            — involves moving the lift
  func .f : Floor
  func .d : Dir                         — (.f, .d) is the indicated position,
  endmodule                             — it must always be a legal LPos.

class FloorCtrl == IMap{BF, Button}

class Lift == (d : Door, i : LiftCtrl, B : IMap{{lo..hi}, Button})
```

```
module
  func init(startfloor : Floor) : Lift;
  proc .start(var c : FloorCtrl)
endmodule
```

We may now program the whole lift system:

```
class LiftSystem == (c : FloorCtrl, L : array Lift)
  module
  func init(n : Nat1) : LiftSystem == (init(off), init(lo)↑n)
  proc .start == < for each i, simultaneously do call L[i].start(c) >
  proc .bf(p : BF)
  proc .bl(p : BL)
endmodule
```

The ABEL language mechanisms for parallel computation is not yet fully decided. However, objects are naturally turned into concurrent processes by having a means to start them simultaneously. (For instance by a cobegin-construct.) Interaction is done by calling procedures and functions local to other (non-active) objects.

It is understood that the body of a procedure local to an object has an implicit critical region locking the object. In the lift example, the shared c object has no internal activity and acts like a monitor, in the sense of Hoare. When there is more than one lift, the lift system has non-trivial aliasing to c, and global reasoning about the value of c can not be done by simple Hoare logic.

The users of the lift system could be modeled as user-objects calling the bl- and bf-procedures. Such calls correspond to abstract bl- and bf-events. The protection rules prohibit objects using the lift system to interfere with its internal components. Thus, the given interface of the lift system allows natural usage and prohibits misuse.

6.2.1 Hardware Specification

A very simple piece of hardware is a flip-flop (a finite state machine which two states: light-on and light-off), with a flip operation changing the state. By extending this class with $turn\_on$ and $turn\_off$ operations, both idempotent, we obtain a more high level concept, a switch. We may see a button as a switch, letting the turn on and -off operations be software operations and letting the flip-operation correspond to hardware signals. (Alternatively, with somewhat more advanced hardware, the turn on and -off operations could correspond directly to hardware signals.)

```
class FlipFlop == {off, on}
  module
  func init : FlipFlop ==off
  proc x.flip == x := case x of on →off | off→ on fo
  func x.ison : Bool == (x = on)
endmodule
```

```
class Switch == FlipFlop
  module
  proc .turn_off == if .ison th call .flip fi
```

proc .*turn_on* == if ¬.*ison* th call .*flip* fi
endmodule

class *Button* == *Switch* with *on* for *turn_on*, *off* for *turn_off*
class *Door* == *Switch* with *open* for *turn_on*, *close* for *turn_off*, *isopen* for *ison*

A door may also be described as a switch, letting *isopen* corresponds to *ison*, *close* to *turn_off*, *open* to *turn_on*, provided its operations are taken as signals to the door mechanism.

The lift control may be modeled as a subclass of *LPos* (thus implementing f and d) letting *newdir* and *move* update the f- and d-components appropriately.

6.2.2 Implementation

The following structure is an expanded version of that above, defining all remaining procedures and functions.

type *Dir* == $\{\downarrow, \updownarrow, \uparrow\}$
  module
  func ˆ + ˆ : $Dir \times Dir \to Dir$
  def $d1 + d2$ == if $d1 = \updownarrow$ th $d2$ el $d1$ fi
  func −ˆ : $Dir \to Dir$
  def $-d$ == case d of $\updownarrow \to \updownarrow \mid \uparrow \to \downarrow \mid \downarrow \to \uparrow$ fo
  endmodule

type *LPos* == $(f : Floor \times d : Dir)$ where $\neg(f = lo \wedge d = \downarrow \vee f = hi \wedge d = \uparrow)$
  module
  func *nextfloor* : $LPos \to Floor$
  def *nextfloor*$((f,d))$ == $f +$ case d of $\updownarrow \to 0 \mid \uparrow \to 1 \mid \downarrow \to -1$ fo
  func *pos* : $Floor \times Dir \to LPos$
  def $pos(nf, nd)$ == if $(nf, nd) \in LPos$ th (nf, nd) el $(nf, \updownarrow)$ fi
  endmodule

class *LiftCtrl* == $i : LPos$
  module
  func *init*$(f : Floor)$: $LiftCtrl$ == $(f, \updownarrow)$
  proc .*newdir*$(nd : Dir)$ == $i := pos(f, nd)$; < *display* >
  proc .*move* == if $d \neq \updownarrow$ th
      < *move one floor* > ; $i := pos(nextfloor(i), d)$; < *display* > fi
  endmodule

class *FloorCtrl* == $M : IMap\{BF, Button\}$
  module
  func .*nextdir*$(p : LPos)$: Dir;
  func .*ison*$(p : LPos)$: $Bool$ == if $p.d \neq \updownarrow$ th $M[p].ison$ el *false* fi
  proc .*off*$(p : LPos)$ == if $p.d \neq \updownarrow$ th $M[p].off$ fi
  axm
      if $M.nextdir(p) = \updownarrow$ th $m = init(false)$ el

$\exists p' : BF \cdot M.nextdir(p) = dir(d.f, p'.f) \wedge M[p'].ison$ **fi**
  proc $.on(p : BF) ==$ **call** $M[].on$
 endmodule

class $Lift == (d : Door \times i : LiftCtrl \times B : IMap\{\{lo..hi\}, Button\})$
 module
 func $init(startfloor : Floor) : Lift == (false, init(startfloor), init(off))$

 func $.useful(p : LPos) : Bool ==$ **if** $p.d = \updownarrow$ **th** $false$
   el $B[nextfloor(p)].ison$ **or** $.useful(pos(nextfloor(p), p.d))$ **fi**

 func $.search(d : Dir) : Dir ==$ **if** $.useful(pos(i.f, d))$ **th** d **el** $\updownarrow$ **fi**

 func $.nextdir(c : FloorCtrl) : Dir == search(i.d) + c.nextdir(i)+$
   if $i.d = \updownarrow$ **th** $search(\uparrow) + search(\downarrow)$ **el** $search(-i.d)$ **fi**

 proc $.serve(\mathbf{var}\ c : FloorCtrl) ==$ **if** $B[i.f].ison$ **or** $c.ison(i)$ **th**
  call $d.open$; **call** $B[i.f].off$; **call** $c.off(i)$; $< wait >$ **fi**
  — the waiting (some amount of time) is needed to let people enter or exit the lift
 proc $.start(\mathbf{var}\ c : FloorCtrl) ==$ **loop**
  if $i.d \neq \updownarrow$ **th** **call** $d.close$; **call** $i.move$ **fi**;
  call $.serve(c)$;
  if $\neg.useful(i)$ **th**
   call $i.newdir(c.nextdir(i))$; **call** $.serve(c)$;
   call $i.newdir(.nextdir(c))$ **fi** **endloop**

  proc $.on(y : Floor) ==$ **call** $B[y].on$
 endmodule

Finally, the bl- and bf-procedures of the lift system is implemented as follows:
  proc $.bf(p : BF) ==$ **call** $c.on(p)$
  proc $.bl((x, y) : BL) ==$ **call** $L[x].on(y)$

 Notice that the ABEL protection rules do not allow assignment to the components of a class object outside the class, thus the only way to update the floor component of a lift control object is by calling the move procedure. If correctly initialized, the lift control will therefore always indicate the position where the lift actually is.

 The most serious hardware errors which are possible in a real lift system are: the door-operations open and close, and the move operation. These may be seen as partially implemented by the hardware, for instance if the lift engine stops working the real move operation aborts. This will cause the lift (calling the move) to abort; however the floor control will not abort and the rest of the lifts will continue as a $n - 1$ lift system (provided the $nextdir$-function of the floor control is fair).

 A particular lift strategy may be given as in the following extension of the floor control class:

class $SimpleFloorCtrl == FloorCtrl$
 module

func $.isonfloor(f : Floor) : Bool == .ison(pos(f, \uparrow))$ or $.ison(pos(f, \uparrow))$

func $.useful(p : LPos) : Bool ==$ if $p.d = \updownarrow$ th *false*
      el $.isonfloor[nextfloor(p)]$ or $.useful(pos(nextfloor(p), p.d))$ fi

func $.search(p : LPos) : Dir ==$ if $.useful(p)$ th $p.d$ el $\updownarrow$ fi

func $.nextdir(p : LPos) : Dir ==$ if $.useful(p)$
    th $search(pos(p.f, \downarrow)) + search(pos(p.f, \uparrow))$
    el $search(p) + search(pos(p.f, -p.d))$ fi
endmodule

Correctness

The abstract v-events are not directly visible in the implementation, because the components of a v-event are computed one by one. Naturally the o-component is computed last. At a call on *serve* or on *close*, inside the *start*-procedure, all the information in a v-event is present. More precisely, those *serve*- and *close*-calls which cause the state of the lift to change, since the previous *serve*- or *close*-call, correspond to abstract v-calls.

We may add mythical statements (enclosed by { and }) computing the abstract v-events as follows: Immediately after the *serve*-calls and the *close*-call inside the *start* procedure insert:

$$\{call\ c.add(x, i.f, i.d, d.isopen)\}$$

where x identifies the lift, as explained below, and *add* is a mythical procedure of the floor control class. (A mythical procedure may only update mythical components.)

Assumimg r is added as a mythical component of the floor control data structure, we define the *add*-procedure as follows:

$$proc\ .add(e : V) ==\ if\ r@(e.l) \neq e\ th\ r := r \vdash e\ fi$$

The parameter x must be given as a mythical parameter to the *start*-procedure, since it is not known inside the lift class. The *start* call inside the list system class must then have the form: call $L[i].start(c, i)$. Similarly, the bl- and bf-procedures are decorated with mythical statements extending r with the appropriate bl-and bf-events.

The safety part of the abstract specification is proved by partial correctness (using Hoare logic) showing that the state assertion $OK(r)$ holds immediately after each mythical *add*-call. In order to prove this, we may use $OK(r)$ as loop invariant, and

$$\forall y : Floor, d : Dir \bullet Rbf(r, y, d) = M[(y, d)]$$

as representation invariant of the floor control, and

$$\forall y : Floor, i : Lift \bullet Rbl(c.r, i, y) = L[i].B[y]$$

as representation invariant of the lift system.

The proof of the liveness part of the abstract specification requires total correctness reasoning: To prove that for a given lift there is a v-event in the ready set, when its B is not all off, it suffices to prove that each mythical *add*-call will lead to a mythical *add*-call extending r (assuming B is not all off). Since it is obvious that no lift can lock the floor control, we may use its representation invariant, and assume that it always is ready.

The input events correspond to *on*-calls on the buttons. Such a call can always be performed expediently, since all button-operations are quick. In particular, no lift object may cause a button to deadlock. Thus, the system is always ready to accept input-events.

References

[1] O.-J. Dahl: " Can Program Proving be Made Practica?" In *Les Foundements de la Programmation*, M. Amirchahy and D. Néel, Ed., INRIA, 1977

[2] O.-J. Dahl: "Object Oriented Specification." In *Research Directions in Object-Oriented Programming*, B. Shriver and P. Wegner, Ed., MIT Press, 1987.

[3] O.-J. Dahl: *Verifiable Programming.* To appear in The Hoare Series, Prentice Hall.

[4] O.-J. Dahl, D.F. Langmyhr, O. Owe: "Preliminary Report on the Specification and Programming Language ABEL." Research Report 106, Dept. of Informatics, University of Oslo, Norway, 1986.

[5] K. Futasugi, J.A. Goguen, J.-P. Jouannaud, J. Meseguer: "Principles of OBJ2." In *Proceedings, 1985 Symposium on Principles of Programming Languages and Programming*, Association for Computing Machinery, 1985, pp. 52-66. W. Brauer, Ed., Springer-Verlag, 1985. Lecture Notes in Computer Science, Volume 194.

[6] J.V. Guttag: "The Specification and Application to Programming of Abstract Data Types." Ph. D. Thesis, Computer Science Department, University of Toronto, 1975.

[7] J.V. Guttag, J.J. Horning, J.M. Wing: "Larch in Five Easy Pieces." Digital Systems Research Center, Palo Alto, California, July 1985.

[8] O. Lysne, O. Owe: "Error Recognition and Strictness in Guttag Definitions." Research Report, Dept. of Informatics, University of Oslo, Norway, 1991.

[9] O. Owe, O.-J. Dahl: "Generator Induction in Order Sorted Algebras." Formal Aspects of Computing, 3:2-20, 1991

[10] O. Owe: "Partial Logics Reconsidered: A Conservative Approach." Research Report 155, Dept. of Informatics, University of Oslo, Norway, 1991.

[11] D. Prawitz: *Natural Deduction.* Almquist & Wiksell, Stockholm, 1965.

[12] N. Soundararajan: Personal communication.

The PROSPECTRA Methodology and System: Uniform Transformational (Meta-) Development

Bernd Krieg-Brückner[1], Einar W. Karlsen[2], Junbo Liu[1], Owen Traynor[3, 1]

In the methodology of PROgram development by SPECification and TRAnsformation, algebraic specifications are the basis for constructing *correct* and efficient programs by gradual transformation. The combination of algebraic specification and functionals increases abstraction, reduces development effort, and allows reasoning about correctness and direct optimisations. The uniformity of the approach to program and meta-program development (for transformation, proof and development tactics, command language, even library access and system configuration) is stressed and related to the generic structure of the PROSPECTRA system.

1. Introduction

The project PROSPECTRA ("PROgram development by SPECification and TRAnsformation") aims to provide a rigorous methodology for developing *correct* software and a comprehensive support system. from 1985 to 1990, it was sponsored by the Commission of the European Communities in the ESPRIT Programme, ref. #390 and #835, as a cooperative project between Universität Bremen (Prime Contractor), Universität Dortmund, Universität Passau, Universität des Saarlandes (all D), University of Strathclyde (GB), SYSECA Logiciel (F), Computer Resources International (DK), Alcatel Standard Eléctrica S.A. (E), and Universitat Politécnica de Catalunya (E) (cf. [Krieg-Brückner 88b, 89a, b, 90], [Krieg-Brückner, Hoffmann 91],[Hoffmann, Shi 91]). Presently, related work at Universität Bremen is funded by the Bundesministerium für Forschung und Technologie in the national project KORSO („Korrekte Software").

The Methodology of Program Development by Transformation (based on the CIP approach of TU München, see e.g. [Bauer et al. 85-89]) integrates program construction and verification during the development process. User and implementor start with a formal specification, the interface or "contract". This initial specification is then gradually transformed into an optimised machine-oriented executable program. The final version is obtained by stepwise application of transformation rules. These are applied by the system, with interactive guidance by the implementor, or automatically by compact transformation scripts. Transformations form the nucleus of an extendible knowledge base.

Overall, PROSPECTRA provides a powerful specification *and* transformation *language* with well-defined semantics that reflects the state-of-the-art in algebraic specification combined with functionals, and a comprehensive *methodology* covering the complete life-cycle (including re-development after revisions), integrating verification in a realistic way, supporting the development process as a computer-aided activity, and giving hope for a comprehensive formalisation of programming knowledge. A *prototype system* is operational, with a uniform user interface and library management including version and configuration control, that gives complete support and control of language and methodology to ensure correctness.

This paper gives an introduction to the methodology of PROgram development by SPECification and TRAnsformation in § 2, with an example of transformational development (as it is supported by the system) in § 3, and focusses on algebraic specifications with functionals in § 4. In § 5 and § 6, it is shown, how the approach can also be applied to the development of *meta-programs*, i.e. the development of efficient transformations and the formalisation of Transformational Program Development; the effect of the uniform approach to the generic development of system components is finally described in § 7 to § 9.

[1]Universität Bremen (D), [2]CRI (DK), [3]University of Missouri St-Louis (USA)

2. PROgram development by SPECification and TRAnsformation

2.1. Objectives

Current software developments are characterised by ad-hoc techniques, chronic failure to meet deadlines because of inability to manage complexity, and unreliability of software products. The major objective of the PROSPECTRA project is to provide a technological basis for developing *correct* programs. This is achieved by a methodology that starts from a formal specification and integrates verification into the development process.

The initial *formal requirement specification* is the starting point of the methodology. It is sufficiently rigorous, on a solid formal basis, to allow verification of correctness during the complete development process thereafter. The methodology is deemed to be more realistic than the conventional style of *a posteriori* verification: the construction process and the verification process are broken down into managable steps; both are coordinated and integrated into an implementation process by *stepwise transformation* that guarantees *a priori* correctness with respect to the original specification. Programs need no further debugging; they are correct by construction. Testing is performed as early as possible by *validation* of the formal specification against the informal requirements (e.g. using a prototyping tool).

Complexity is managed by abstraction, modularisation and stepwise transformation. Efficiency considerations and machine-oriented implementation detail come in by conscious design decisions from the implementor when applying pre-conceived transformation rules. A long-term research aim is the incorporation of goal orientation into the development process. In particular, the crucial selection in large libraries of rules has to reflect the reasoning process in the development.

The support of correct and efficient transformations is seen as a major advance in programming environment technology. The central concept of system activity is the application of transformations to trees. Generator components are employed to construct transformers for individual transformation rules and to incorporate the hierarchical approach of PA^{nn}dA (PROSPECTRA Anna/Ada), TrafoLa (the language of transformation descriptions), and ControLa (the command language); in fact, these turn out to be all sublanguages of the same language, for user program, transformation, proof, and system development. This integration and uniformity is seen as one of the major results of the PROSPECTRA project (cf. § 5-9, [Krieg-Brückner 88a-90], [Krieg-Brückner, Hoffmann 91], [Karlsen, Krieg-Brückner, Traynor 91]). Generators, in particular the Synthesizer Generator (cf. [Reps, Teitelbaum 88]), increase flexibility and avoid duplication of efforts; thus the overall system complexity is significantly reduced.

2.2. The Development Model

Consider a simple model of the major development activities in the life of a program in (2-1). The *informal requirements analysis* phase precedes the phases of the *development* proper, at the level of formal specifications and by transformation into and at the level(s) of a conventional programming language such as Ada. After the program has been installed at the client, no maintenance in the sense of conventional testing needs to be done; "testing" is perfomed *before* a program is constructed, at the very early stages, by validation of the formal requirement specification against the informal requirements.

The *evolution* of a program system over its lifetime, however, is likely to economically outweigh the original development by an order of magnitude. Changes in the informal requirements lead to re-development, starting with changes in the requirement specification. This requires re-design, possibly by *replay* of the original development (which has been archived by the system) and adaptation of previous designs or re-consideration of previously discarded design variants.

Requirements Analysis

- **Informal** Problem Analysis

- **Informal** Requirement Specification

Development   ⇑ *Validation*

- **Formal**   Requirement Specification   ⇑ *Verification*

- **Formal**   Design Specification   ⇑ *Verification*

- **Formal**   Construction *by Transformation*

Evolution

-          Changes in Requirements ⇒ **Re-Development** ⇑

(2-1) The PROSPECTRA Development Model

2.3. Specification

A requirement specification defines *what* a program should do, a design specification *how* it does it. The motivations and reasons for design decisions, the *why's*, are recorded along with the developments.

Requirement specifications are, in general, non-constructive; there may be no clue for an algorithmic solution of the problem or for a mapping of abstract to concrete (i.e. predefined) data types. It is essential that the requirement specification should not define more than the *necessary* properties of a program to leave room for design decisions. It is intentionally vague or *loose* in areas where the further specification of detail is irrelevant or impossible, i.e. it denotes a set of models (cf. [Krieg-Brückner 90] or Part I in [Krieg-Brückner, Hoffmann 91]). In this sense, loose specification replaces non-determinacy, for example to specify an unreliable transmission medium in a concurrent, distributed situation [Broy 87b, 89].

Design specifications denote abstract implementations. They are constructive, both in terms of more basic specifications and in the algorithmic sense. For a loose requirement specification, the design specification will usually restrict the set of models, eventually to one.

As an example take the specification of Booleans in (2-1), as it might appear for the standard Ada type. Some axioms (such as associativity, commutativity, distributivity) specify important properties of Booleans, but they are non-operational, whereas other equations can be interpreted as operational rewrite rules, see also (5-3) below. Several axioms here are redundant and can be derived from others.

Note that BOOLEAN is an algebraically specified Abstract Data Type (as the others below) such that its values can be manipulated in user-defined functions, etc., whereas axioms in the specifications are of a built-in type LOGICAL that denotes two-valued logic (without undefined). For better readability, the LOGICAL operators are written in the usual mathematical notation, e.g. ∨ instead of **or**.

In the example for natural numbers in (2-1), some general, non-operational properties are given first (more are needed to characterise the natural numbers completely). Then two alternative sets of rewrite rules are given (corresponding to the two boxes side by side; only a few rules are shown as an example): one for a linear presentation based on zero and succ as constructors, the other for a binary presentation based on zero, dble and dble1 as constructors. They play an important role for (automatic) simplification during transformation below. Each set represents a different design decision. Using the Conditional Equational Completion subsystem (cf. [Ganzinger 87]), each set of rewrite rules has been made terminating and confluent. The general properties are the basis for derivation of the more technical rewrite rules: cf. e.g. sqr x = x * x and the sets of corresponding rewrite rules for sqr.

(2-1) Specification: Booleans and Natural Numbers)

```
package BOOLS Is
   type BOOLEAN Is private;
   false, true:     BOOLEAN;
   "not":           BOOLEAN —> BOOLEAN;
   "and", "or":     BOOLEAN × BOOLEAN —> BOOLEAN;
axiom for all x, y, z: BOOLEAN =>
   true ≠ false,        not false = true,      not true = false,      not not x = x,
   x and false = false,  x or true = true,      x and true = x,        x or false = x,
   x and (y and z) = (x and y) and z,    x and y = y and x, x and x = x,
   x or (y or z) = (x or y) or z,        x or y = y or x,   x or x = x,
   x and (y or z) = (x and y) or (x and z),    x or (y and z) = (x or y) and (x or z),
   x or not x = true,  x and not x = false,
   x or y = not (not x and not y),       x and y = not (not x or not y);
end BOOLS;
```

```
package NATS Is
   type NAT Is private;
   zero:   NAT;
   succ:   NAT —> NAT;                        dble, dble1:   NAT —> NAT;    - - *2, *2+1

   one:    NAT;
   "+", "*":  NAT × NAT —> NAT;
   "<=":     NAT × NAT —> BOOLEAN;
   "–":      (x: NAT) × (y: NAT:: y <= x) —> NAT;
   sqr,div2: NAT —> NAT;
axiom for all x, y, z: NAT =>
   x + (y + z) = (x + y) + z,    x + y = y + x,    x + zero = x,    x * one = x,    ...
   (x + y) – x = y,              x <= y → x + (y – x) = y,
   dble x = x + x,    dble1 x = (dble x) + one,    (x + one) + x = dble1 x,
   div2 (dble x) = x,    div2 (dble1 x) = x,
   sqr x = x * x,    sqr (x + y) = sqr x + dble (x * y) + sqr y,    (sqr x) – (sqr y) = (x + y) * (x – y),  ...
```

one = succ zero,	one = dble1 zero,
x + zero = x, zero + y = y, (succ x) + y = succ (x + y), x + (succ y) = succ (x + y),	x + zero = x, zero + y = y, dble(x) + dble(y) = dble(x + y), dble(x) + dble1(y) = dble1(x + y), dble1(x) + dble(y) = dble1(x + y), dble1(x) + dble1(y) = dble((one + x) + y),
(succ x) + (succ y) = succ (succ (x + y)), - - *derivable*	
sqr zero = zero, sqr (succ x) = (sqr x) + succ (x + x), ...	sqr(zero) = zero, sqr(dble(x)) = dble(dble (sqr x)), sqr(dble1(x)) = dble1(dble((sqr x) + x)), ... ;

```
end NATS;
```

An example of a non-operational requirement specification is that of a *concept* to be used in other specifications, breaking down, generalising and re-using specifications, cf. (2-2).

(2-2) Parameterised Specification: Concept of a Monoid

```
generic
   type M Is private;
package IS_MONOID Is
   predicate isMonoid:  M —> (M × M —> M);
   axiom for all n: M; "⊕": M × M —> M =>
      isMonoid n "⊕" <–> for all x, y, z: M =>  x ⊕ n = x,  n ⊕ x = x,  (x ⊕ y) ⊕ z = x ⊕ (y ⊕ z);
end IS_MONOID;
```

As another example of a specification consider lists in (2-3). Note that we may have two views of lists: either constructed by empty and cons or by empty, "&" and single (one of the views is, of course, enough as a requirement specification). Depending on the view, lists have different algebraic properties; in the second case those of a monoid (associativity and neutral element empty). Such strong properties become important for reasoning about optimisations, as we will see below. The definition of the selectors head and tail ensures uniqueness of models up to isomorphism. They are partial functions, i.e. only defined if the pre-condition on the parameter holds. Similarly, a pre-condition on cons could be introduced, stating, for example, that the length should be less than some number MAX_SIZE. cons becomes a *partial constructor function*, LISTS defines bounded lists (cf. [Krieg-Brückner 88b]); corresponding definedness premisses must then also be included in the equations.

(2-3) Requirement Specification: Lists

```
with IS_MONOID;
generic
   type ITEM Is private;
package LISTS Is
   type LIST Is private;
   empty:  LIST;
   cons:   ITEM —> LIST —> LIST;
   "&":    LIST × LIST —>   LIST;
   single: ITEM —>   LIST;
   package LIST_IS_MONOID Is new IS_MONOID (LIST);
axiom    IsMonoid empty "&";
   isEmpty: LIST —>                    BOOLEAN;
   head:   (x: LIST :: ¬ IsEmpty x) —> ITEM;
   tail:   (x: LIST :: ¬ IsEmpty x) —> LIST;
axiom for all e: ITEM; l: LIST =>
   isEmpty empty = true,     isEmpty (cons e l) = false,
   head (cons e l) = e,      tail (cons e l) = l,       (single e) & l = cons e l;
end LISTS;
```

Implementation: What remains for abstract specifications is a mapping onto some suitable specification at a lower level of the system hierarchy, i.e. a standard one or one that has already been implemented. Certain abstract types (schemata) that correspond to predefined Ada types (constructors, selectors, other auxiliary functions and their algebraic specification), for example record, or the usual recursive variant (or union) types (free term constructions for lists, trees etc.) are standard in $PA^{nn}dA$ (see [Kahrs 86]). They are turned into an Ada text automatically as an alternative (standard Ada) notation for the package defining the abstract type. We assume that a standard Ada implementation using access types (pointers) and allocators is still considered to be "applicative" at this level of abstraction and that side-effects of allocation will be eliminated during the development process by explicit storage allocation if required.

2.4. Transformational Program Development

Each transition from one program version to another can be regarded as a transformation in an abstract sense. It has a more technical meaning here: a transformation is a development step producing a new program version by application of an individual transformation rule, a compact transformation script, or, more generally, a transformation method invoking these. Before we come to the latter two, the basic approach will be described in terms of the transformation rule concept.

A transformation rule (e.g. (2-4)) is a schema for an atomic development step that has been pre-conceived and is universally trusted (modulo some applicability conditions), analogously to a theorem in mathematics. It embodies a grain of expertise that can be transferred to a new development. Its application realises this transfer and formalises the development process.

Transformations preserve correctness and therefore maintain a tighter and more formalised relationship to prior versions. Their classical application is the construction of optimised implementations by transformation of an initial design that has been proved correct against the formal requirement specification. Further design activity then consists in the selection of an appropriate rule, oriented by development goals, for example machine-oriented optimisation criteria.

Language Levels: We can distinguish various language levels at which the program is developed or into which versions are transformed, corresponding to phases of the development:

- formal requirement specification: loose equational or predicative specifications
- formal design specification: specification of abstract implementation
- applicative implementation: recursive functions
- imperative implementation: variables, procedures, iteration by loops

All these language levels are covered by PAnndA, cf. [Krieg-Brückner, Hoffmann 91].

(2-4) Transformation Rule: Linear Recursion with Associative Operation to Tail Recursion

	$\cong$	
$f: S \longrightarrow M;$ axiom for all $x: S \Rightarrow$ $\quad B x \rightarrow \quad f x = T x,$ $\neg\, B x \rightarrow \quad f x = f(H x) \oplus K x;$ such that $\quad f$ does not occur in B, T, H, K $\quad n: M;$ $\quad$ axiom for all $x, y, z: M \Rightarrow$ $\qquad (x \oplus y) \oplus z = x \oplus (y \oplus z), \quad x \oplus n = x;$		$f:\ S \longrightarrow M;$ $g:\ S \longrightarrow M \longrightarrow M;$ axiom for all $x: S; y: M \Rightarrow$ $\qquad\qquad f x = g\, x\, n,$ $\quad B x \rightarrow \quad g\, x\, y = (T x) \oplus y,$ $\neg\, B x \rightarrow \quad g\, x\, y = g\, (H x)\, ((K x) \oplus y);$

(2-5) Transformation: Linear Recursion to Tail Recursion: length

length:\ LIST $\longrightarrow$ \ INTEGER; axiom for all $x:$ LIST $\Rightarrow$ $\quad$ IsEmpty $x \rightarrow \quad$ length $x = 0,$ $\neg\,$ IsEmpty $x \rightarrow \quad$ length $x =$ length (tail x) $+ 1;$	length:\ LIST $\longrightarrow$ INTEGER; len:\ \ \ \ LIST $\longrightarrow$ INTEGER $\longrightarrow$ INTEGER; axiom for all $x:$ LIST ; $r:$ INTEGER $\Rightarrow$ $\qquad\qquad$ length $x =$ len $x\ 0,$ $\quad$ IsEmpty $x \rightarrow \quad$ len $x\ r = 0 + r,$ $\neg\,$ IsEmpty $x \rightarrow \quad$ len $x\ r =$ len (tail x) $(1 + r);$

Matches: $\qquad\qquad\quad \oplus \quad \approx\ +\ \text{-- on INTEGER}$
$B x\ \approx\ $ IsEmpty $x, \qquad T x\ \approx\ 0,$
$H x\ \approx\ $ tail $x, \qquad\quad K x\ \approx\ 1$

Parameters: $\qquad\qquad\quad n\ \ \approx\ 0$

(2-6) Ada Program: Applicative and Imperative Body of length (with Unfold of len)

```
function LENGTH (X: LIST) return INTEGER is
begin
   if IS_EMPTY (X) then
      return 0;
   else
      return LENGTH (TAIL (X)) + 1;
   end if;
end LENGTH;
```

```
function LENGTH (X: LIST) return INTEGER is
   V: LIST:= X; R: INTEGER := 0;
begin
   while not IS_EMPTY(V) loop
      V := TAIL(V);   R := 1+R;
   end loop;
   return R;
end LENGTH;
```

Many developments at lower levels can also be expressed at the specification level, for example "recursion removal" methods transforming into tail-recursive functions [Huet, Lang 78], [Bauer, Wössner 82], [Krieg-Brückner 87a]. As an example, consider the special case that $\oplus$ and n form a Monoid, where $\oplus$ is an arbitrary associative operation, expressed here at the specification level. The rule in (2-4) could be generalised and adapted further to apply to equations with constructors on the left instead of selectors on the right-hand sides. Assume that we want to derive a body for length (see 2-5). It is not in tail-recursive form: the addition of 1 still has to be made upon return from the recursion. By applying the transformation rule in (2-4), however, we can embed it into a function len that is tail-recursive, see (2-5). len can thus be transformed into a local loop, see (2-6).

In general, the applicability condition, namely that ⊕ is an associative operation with neutral element 0, has to be proved with the aid of the Proof Subsystem (cf. § 8.5). However, the system keeps track of user-defined axioms and conditions that are valid in a particular context in a special attribute, the so-called local theory (cf. § 8.5). This attribute is available in the Proof Subsystem; it is also available during transformation such that an automatic search for a required property can be made and no interaction from the user is required when it is successful. This would, for example, be the case when the monoid property is stated on a parameter of a function as in § 4.2.

3. An Example of Transformational Development

3.1. From Requirement to Design Specification: Split of Postcondition

Let us have a look at a more comprehensive example illustrating the transformational approach, as supported by the PROSPECTRA system. The example is rather academic due to space limitations, but several design decisions yielding non-trivial solutions can already be exhibited.

First consider a transformation rule that is representative for the class of *"program synthesis"* or *"problem solving"* transformations. The transformation is applicable to a whole class of problems that can be solved by iteration in the classical style of predicative programming promoted by [Hoare 69], [Dijkstra 76], [Gries 81] and others. If the characteristic predicate ("postcondition") specifying the result of a function can be split into a conjunct of an invariant and a terminating condition B, and if a starting value E and a termination function H are provided as parameters to the transformation, then a recursive function can be generated, and the precise conditions for its correctness can be stated. These conditions are given as applicability conditions on the rule in (3-1); they are instantiated automatically and need to be proved before the rule is applied (with the aid of the Proof Editor), or delayed and proved during replay.

(3-1) Split of Postcondition

f: $(x: S) \longrightarrow (z: R :: \mathbf{Inv}(x,z) \wedge \mathbf{B}(x,z))$;	$\cong$	f: $(x: S) \longrightarrow (z: R :: \mathbf{Inv}(x,z) \wedge \mathbf{B}(x,z))$;
~~such that~~		g: $S \times R \longrightarrow R$;
$\mathbf{Inv}(x, E(x))$,		axiom for all $x: S$; $y: R$ =>
$\mathbf{Inv}(x,y) \wedge \neg B(x,y) \rightarrow \mathbf{Inv}(x,H(x,y))$,		$\quad\quad f(x) = g(x, E(x))$,
term $(x, E(x)) = $ True		$B(x, y) \rightarrow \quad g(x, y) = y$,
		$\neg B(x, y) \rightarrow \quad g(x, y) = g(x, H(x, y))$;
		term: $R \longrightarrow$ BOOLEAN;
		axiom for all $x: S$; $y: R$ =>
		$B(x,y) \rightarrow$ term $(x, y) = $ True,
		$\neg B(x,y) \rightarrow$ term $(x, y) = $ term $(x, H(x,y))$;

(3-2) shows the application to the square root of natural numbers. It is based on the specification in (2-1); a more mathematical presentation is used here, e.g. +1 instead of succ. We made a particular design decision here in the order of the conjuncts and in the choice (or "invention") of E and H. By reversing the order as in (3-3), the interpretation of invariant and terminating condition is interchanged; the "loop" corresponding to the tail-recursive function then runs "down" instead of "up". H can be chosen to decrement from n. We can even choose a better starting value n div 2; note that one has to be careful about 1 in the presence of integer division (by 2); this error was actually discovered using the system to do the proof of the invariant for the starting value. A non-trivial termination function H is given in version 2:

Newton's algorithm adapted to integer division. The invariant condition is harder to prove than it looks because of integer division here; it took several pages with the Proof Editor.

(3-2) Split of Postcondition: Integer Squareroot, version 1

sqrt: (n: NAT) —> (k: NAT:: $k^2 \leq n \wedge (k+1)^2 > n$);

Matches:

$Inv(n, k) \approx k^2 \leq n$,

$B(n, k) \approx (k+1)^2 > n$

Parameters:

$E(n) \approx 0$,

$H(n, k) \approx k+1$

Applicability Conditions:

$0^2 \leq n$,

$k^2 \leq n \wedge \neg (k+1)^2 > n \rightarrow (k+1)^2 \leq n$,

$sqrtTerm(n, 0) = true$,

sqrt: (n: NAT) —> (k: NAT :: $k^2 \leq n \wedge (k+1)^2 > n$);
sqrt1: NAT × NAT —> NAT;
axiom for all n: NAT; k: NAT =>
$$sqrt(n) = sqrt1(n, 0),$$
$(k+1)^2 > n \rightarrow \quad sqrt1(n, k) = k$,
$(k+1)^2 \leq n \rightarrow \quad sqrt1(n, k) = sqrt1(n, k+1)$;

sqrtTerm: NAT —> BOOLEAN;
axiom for all n: NAT; k: NAT=>
$(k+1)^2 > n \rightarrow sqrtTerm(n, k) = true$,
$(k+1)^2 \leq n \rightarrow sqrtTerm(n, k) = sqrtTerm(n, k+1)$;

(3-3) Split of Postcondition: Integer Squareroot, version 2

sqrt: (n: NAT) —> (k: NAT :: $(k+1)^2 > n \wedge k^2 \leq n$);

Matches:

$Inv(n, k) \approx (k+1)^2 > n$

$B(n, k) \approx k^2 \leq n$

Parameters:

$E(n) \approx max (n \ div \ 2, 1)$,

$H(n, k) \approx (k+(n \ div \ k)) \ div \ 2$

Applicability Conditions:

$(max (n \ div \ 2, 1) +1)^2 > n$,

$(k+1)^2 > n \wedge \neg k^2 \leq n \rightarrow ((k+(n \ div \ k)) \ div \ 2 +1)^2 > n$,

$sqrtTerm(n, max (n \ div \ 2, 1)) = true$

sqrt: (n: NAT) —> (k: NAT :: $(k+1)^2 > n \wedge k^2 \leq n$);
sqrt1: NAT × NAT —> NAT;
axiom for all n: NAT; k: NAT =>
$$sqrt(n) = sqrt1(n, max (n \ div \ 2, 1)),$$
$k^2 \leq n \rightarrow sqrt1(n, k) = k$,
$k^2 > n \rightarrow sqrt1(n, k) = sqrt1(n, (k+(n \ div \ k)) \ div \ 2)$;

sqrtTerm: NAT —> BOOLEAN;
axiom for all n: NAT; k: NAT=>
$k^2 \leq n \rightarrow sqrtTerm(n, k) = true$,
$k^2 > n \rightarrow sqrtTerm(n, k) =$
$$sqrtTerm(n, (k+(n \ div \ k)) \ div \ 2);$$

3.2. Optimisation by Transformation: Embedding and Finite Differencing

Embedding is a method that can very often be applied to improve efficiency: to embed into a more general function that can be (re-)used for other purposes, to avoid multiple computations ("common subexpression elimination"), to prepare for Finite Differencing ("strength reduction", see the next section), etc. We find a "costly" subexpression *E* and embed into a second function with an extra parameter.

(3-4) Embedding

f: S —> R;

axiom for all x: S =>

$B(x, E(x)) \rightarrow f(x) = H1(x, E(x))$,
$\neg B(x, E(x)) \rightarrow f(x) = H2(x, E(x), f(L(x, E(x))))$;

such that

$FreeVars(f(x)) \supseteq FreeVars(E(x))$,

$T = TypeNameOf(E(x))$,

$defined (E(x))$,

$y \notin FreeVars(H(x, E(x)))$,

$FreeVars(E(x)) \cap BoundVars(H(x, E(x))) = \emptyset$

≅

f: S —> R;
g: S × T —> R;
axiom for all x: S; y: T :: y = E(x) =>
$f(x) = g(x, E(x))$,
$B(x, y) \rightarrow g(x, y) = H1(x, y)$,
$\neg B(x, y) \rightarrow g(x, y) = H2(x, y, g(L(x, y), E(L(x, y))))$;

The version of rule (3-4) is special for recursion with one terminating case; it can be generalised. Note also that the property $y = E(x)$ is maintained as an invariant in this version. Most of the applicability conditions can be derived automatically from available static semantic attributes. It is applied to the example in (3-5). The choice of a "costly" subexpression E is implemented as a parameter to the transformation, thus it is an explicit design-decision; an automatic choice would require some notion of relative efficiency or complexity analysis.

(3-5) Embedding: Integer Squareroot

sqrt1:   NAT $\times$ NAT $\longrightarrow$ NAT;
axiom for all n, k: NAT =>
    $(k+1)^2 > n \rightarrow$ sqrt1(n, k) = k,
    $(k+1)^2 \leq n \rightarrow$ sqrt1(n, k) = sqrt1(n, k+1);

Parameter: $E(n, k)$ $\approx (k+1)^2$

Matches:
$B(n, k, E(n, k))$ $\approx E(n, k) > n$
$H1(n, k, E(n, k))$ $\approx k$
$H2(n, k, E(n, k), f(L(n,k,E(n, k)))) \approx f(L(n, k, E(n, k)))$
$L(n, k, E(n, k))$ $\approx (n, k+1)$
$E(L(n, k, y) \approx E(n, k+1)$ $\approx ((k+1) + 1)^2$

sqrt1:   NAT $\times$ NAT $\longrightarrow$ NAT;
sqrt2:   NAT $\times$ NAT $\times$ NAT $\longrightarrow$ NAT;
axiom for all n, k: NAT; sq: NAT:: sq = $(k+1)^2$ =>
       sqrt1(n, k) = sqrt2(n, k, $(k+1)^2$),
sq > n$\rightarrow$ sqrt2(n, k, sq) = k,
sq $\leq$ n$\rightarrow$ sqrt2(n, k, sq) =
            sqrt2(n, k+1, $((k+1) + 1)^2$);

Finite Differencing

Finite Differencing (cf. (3-6), after previous embedding) is representative for the class of *optimising* transformations. Application areas are: generalization of strength reduction, Early's "iterator inversion", algorithms on sets or graphs such as Schorr-Waite's garbage collection algorithm, Habermann's Banker's algorithm, Knapsack problems, or optimised completion techniques (see [Sharir 82], [Paige 82]). The idea is to avoid that the "costly" subexpression of the Embedding is computed over and over again in each recursion; instead, only the increment is computed each time. This increment is supposedly an expression that is less "costly" to compute, for example using multiplication or addition instead of squaring; this corresponds to "strength reduction" in compiler optimisations.

(3-6) Finite Differencing

| $E(x) \oplus \Delta E (x, y)$ |
| such that $y = E(x)$ |

$\equiv$

| $y \oplus \Delta E (x, y)$ |

After embedding, we need to find an arbitrary operation $\oplus$ (this could be a binary numeric operation, or set union, for example) and an increment ΔE such that

$E(L(x, y)) = E(x) \oplus \Delta E (x, y)$

This can be done interactively by using other transformations to bring the expression into this form ("conditioning" for the subsequent transformation), e. g. by applying equations available in the context as rewrite rules, cf. (3-7). We can then apply the finite differencing transformation rule of (3-6), see (3-8); the applicability condition holds since the property $y = E(x)$ (sq = $(k+1)^2$)was maintained as an invariant.

Goal-Oriented Transformation

(3-7) Goal-Oriented Transformation: Application of Equation as Rewrite Rules

| $((k+1) + 1)^2$ |

| $(k+1)^2 + 2*(k+1)*1 + 1^2$ |

-- *apply eq'n:* $(x+y)^2 = x^2 + 2*x*y + y^2$

(3-8) Finite Differencing: Integer Squareroot

sqrt2:   NAT × NAT × NAT —→ NAT;
axiom for all n, k: NAT; sq: NAT:: sq = $(k+1)^2$ =>
    sq > n—→ sqrt2(n, k, sq) = k,
    sq ≤ n—→ sqrt2(n, k, sq) =
        sqrt2(n, k+1, $(k+1)^2$ + 2*(k+1)*1 +1^2);

sqrt2:   NAT × NAT × NAT —→ NAT;
axiom for all n, k: NAT; sq: NAT:: sq = $(k+1)^2$ =>
    sq > n—→ sqrt2(n, k, sq) = k,
    sq ≤ n—→ sqrt2(n, k, sq) =
        sqrt2(n, k+1, sq + 2*(k+1)*1 +1^2);

Parameter: ⊕ ≈ +   - - *on NAT*

Matches:
$$E(x) \oplus \Delta E(x, y) ≈ (k+1)^2 + 2*(k+1)*1 +1^2$$

After this transformation, $\Delta E(x, y)$ should be simplified and is then expected to be "cheaper" than *E(L(x, y))*. The simplification uses a set of rewrite rules, provided as a parameter (note the more mathematical presentation in the example, e.g. +1 instead of succ).

Simplification

(3-9) Simplification using Equations as Rewrite Rules

2*(k+1)*1 +1^2

k+k +3

Parameter: (succ x) + (succ y) = succ (succ (x + y)),
    sqr (succ x) = (sqr x) + succ (x + x)

Towards Automated Development Methods: Finite Differencing with Inverse Operation

As a second strategy, finite differencing can be done automatically, if an inverse operation ⊖ exists such that *b* ⊕ *(a* ⊖ *b)* = *a* holds, see (3-10). Note that ⊕ and ⊖ may be abitrary operations of the type of *E*, for example union and set difference. The equation relating the operations is conditional on some predicate *P*; ⊖ (or ⊕) is often only partially defined, such as - on naturals numbers, cf. (3-11). For sets, *b* must be contained in *a*, for lists with concatenation and a (properly defined) list difference, *isHeadOf b a* must hold. This predicate must be proved for the instantiated expressions. Applied to the example in (3-11), the result is, of course, the same as in (3-8, 9) above.

(3-10) Finite Differencing with Inverse Operation

E(L(x, y))
such that
  y = E(x),
  T = TypeNameOf(E(x)),
  axiom for all a, b: T =>
    P (a, b) → b ⊕ (a ⊖ b) = a,
  P (E(L(x, y))) (E(x))
	y ⊕ (E(L(x, y)) ⊖ E(x))

As an example of a composition of two transformations into one (cf. also § 5), the implemented transformation combines finite differencing with automatic simplification (similarly, embedding and finite differencing could be combined into one compact transformation, a development method). For this purpose, a set of (conditional) equations is provided as an additional parameter; it is the user's risk, that this set of rewrite rules is terminating. The equation (succ x) + (succ y) = succ (succ (x + y)) can be derived from the other rewrite rules (cf. (2-1)) and is used for symbolic rewriting (terms with variables). We can provide equations for natural numbers based on 0 and succ or on the binary constructors 0 and dble, dble1 (i.e. *2, *2+1), achieving different results in (3-9), (3-11), and (3-12).

Applying this method of Finite Differencing (combined with Embedding) again (3-13), we achieve a progressively longer list of parameters that can be evaluated in parallel, with less and less complex operations.

(3-11) Finite Differencing with Inverse Operation: Integer Squareroot

```
sqrt2:    NAT × NAT × NAT ⟶ NAT;
axiom for all n, k: NAT; sq: NAT:: sq = (k+1)² =>
   sq > n⟶ sqrt2(n, k, sq) = k,
   sq ≤ n⟶ sqrt2(n, k, sq) =
                        sqrt2(n, k+1, ((k+1) + 1)²);
```

Parameters: ⊕ ≈ +   ⊖ ≈ −   - - *on NAT*
            E(n, k) ≈ (k+1)²
            P (a, b) ≈ a ≥ b
   rules: (x + y) − x = y,
            (succ x) + (succ y) = succ (succ (x + y)),
            sqr (succ x) = (sqr x) + succ (x + x)

```
sqrt2:    NAT × NAT × NAT ⟶ NAT;
axiom for all n, k: NAT; sq: NAT:: sq = (k+1)² =>
   sq > n⟶ sqrt2(n, k, sq) = k,
   sq ≤ n⟶ sqrt2(n, k, sq) =
                        sqrt2(n, k+1, sq + k+k +3);
```

Matches:
$E(L$(n, k, y))   ≈ E(n, k+1)   ≈ ((k+1) + 1)²
ΔE (x, y) = $E(L$(x, y)) ⊖ E(x)   ≈ ((k+1) + 1)² − (k+1)²

Applicability Condition:
for all x, y: NAT =>   x <= y → x +(y − x) = y,
P (E(L(x, y))) (E(x)) ≈ ((k+1) + 1)² ≥ (k+1)²

(3-12) Finite Differencing with Inverse Operation: Integer Squareroot, Binary Operations

```
sqrt2:    NAT × NAT × NAT ⟶ NAT;
axiom for all n, k: NAT; sq: NAT:: sq = (k+1)² =>
   sq > n⟶ sqrt2(n, k, sq) = k,
   sq ≤ n⟶ sqrt2(n, k, sq) =
                        sqrt2(n, k+1, ((k+1) + 1)²);
```

Parameters: ⊕ ≈ +   ⊖ ≈ −   - - *on NAT*
            E(n, k) ≈ (k+1)²
            P (a, b) ≈ a ≥ b
   rules: (x + y) − x = y,
            (sqr x) − (sqr y) = (x + y) * (x − y),
            x * one = x,   (x + one) + x = dble1 x,

```
sqrt2:    NAT × NAT × NAT ⟶ NAT;
axiom for all n, k: NAT; sq: NAT:: sq = (k+1)² =>
   sq > n⟶ sqrt2(n, k, sq) = k,
   sq ≤ n⟶ sqrt2(n, k, sq) =
                        sqrt2(n, k+1, sq + dble1 (k + 1));
```

Matches:
$E(L$(n, k, y))   ≈ E(n, k+1)   ≈ ((k+1) + 1)²
ΔE (x, y) = $E(L$(x, y)) ⊖ E(x)   ≈ ((k+1) + 1)² − (k+1)²

Applicability Condition:
for all x, y: NAT =>   x <= y → x +(y − x) = y,
P (E(L(x, y))) (E(x)) ≈ ((k+1) + 1)² ≥ (k+1)²

(3-13) Embedding and Finite Differencing: Integer Squareroot

```
sqrt2:    NAT × NAT × NAT ⟶ NAT;
axiom for all n, k: NAT; sq: NAT:: sq = (k+1)² =>
   sq > n⟶ sqrt2(n, k, sq) = k,
   sq ≤ n⟶ sqrt2(n, k, sq) =
                        sqrt2(n, k+1, sq + k+k +3);
```

Parameters: ⊕ ≈ +   ⊖ ≈ −   - - *on NAT*
costly expr: E(n, k)   ≈ k+k +3
               P (a, b) ≈ a ≥ b
   rules: (succ x) + (succ y) = succ (succ (x + y)),
            succ (succ x) − x = succ (succ zero)

```
sqrt2:    NAT × NAT × NAT ⟶ NAT;
sqrt3:    NAT × NAT × NAT × NAT ⟶ NAT;
axiom for all n, k: NAT; sq: NAT:: sq = (k+1)²;
          su: NAT :: su = k+k +3 =>
          sqrt2(n, k, sq) = sqrt3(n, k, sq, k+k +3),
   sq > n⟶ sqrt3(n, k, sq, su) = k,
   sq ≤ n⟶ sqrt3(n, k, sq, su) =
                        sqrt3(n, k+1, sq + su, su +2);
```

Applicability Condition:
for all x, y: NAT =>   x <= y → x +(y − x) = y,
P (E(L(x, y))) (E(x)) ≈ (k+1) + (k+1) + 3 ≥ k+k +3

Converting Depth to Breadth of Computation

Another possibility is an unfold of the recursive function on itself ("unrolling" the recursion, see 3-14)): the number of recursions is halved, but, at the end, some computations may have been superfluous. Such a transformation could be applied several times, bounded by pragmatic considerations; this would correspond to a cache in hardware, trading chip space for speed. One would also apply Finite Differencing to the thus newly created "costly" expressions, e.g. sq+su or even comparisons such as sq+su > n, thereby converting depth of recursion into cascades of conditionals, program length and complexity of computation within one recursion, and complexity of computation into breadth of parallel evaluation in the parameters (supposedly corresponding to one parallel "cycle" in hardware). Combining an efficient algorithm (by some complexity measure), such as version 2 in (3-3), and an efficient implementation of basic types, we could thus derive algorithms to be used for (semi-automatic) VLSI implementation. "Silicon compilers" only deliver a result that is (hopefully) as correct as their input; therefore the derivation of correct and efficient algorithms at the software level should be of prime importance. Note that the target of the development (i.e. the complexity or "machine" model of the underlying operational semantics and the basic types), such as binary arithmetic and parallel evaluation (of parameter tuples) significantly determine the design decisions.

(3-14) Unfold of Recursive Call: Integer Squareroot

```
sqrt3:    NAT × NAT × NAT × NAT ––→ NAT;
axiom for all n, k: NAT; sq: NAT:: sq = (k+1)²;
            su: NAT :: su = k+k +3  =>
sq > n→ sqrt3(n, k, sq, su) = k,
sq ≤ n→ sqrt3(n, k, sq, su) =
                    sqrt3(n, k+1, sq + su, su +2);
```

```
sqrt3:    NAT × NAT × NAT × NAT ––→ NAT;
axiom for all n, k: NAT; sq: NAT:: sq = (k+1)²;
            su: NAT :: su = k+k +3  =>
sq > n→ sqrt3(n, k, sq, su) = k,
sq ≤ n→ ( sq+su > n → sqrt3(n, k, sq, su) = k+1,
            sq+su ≤ n → sqrt3(n, k, sq, su) =
            sqrt3(n, (k+1)+1, (sq+su)+(su+2), (su+2)+2)  );
```

Parameter: sq > n→ sqrt3(n, k, sq, su) = k,
                sq ≤ n→ sqrt3(n, k, sq, su) =
                            sqrt3(n, k+1, sq + su, su +2)

Partial Evaluation

A collapse of the chain of embeddings can be achieved by *partial evaluation*, a combination of unfold and simplification, see (3-15).

(3-15) Partial Evaluation: Integer Squareroot

```
sqrt:    (n: NAT) —→ (k: NAT :: k² ≤ n ∧ (k+1)² > n);
sqrt1:   NAT × NAT ––→ NAT;
sqrt2:   NAT × NAT × NAT ––→ NAT;
sqrt3:   NAT × NAT × NAT × NAT ––→ NAT;
axiom for all n, k: NAT; sq: NAT:: sq = (k+1)²;
            su: NAT :: su = k+k +3  =>
            sqrt(n) = sqrt1(n, 0),
            sqrt1(n, k) = sqrt2(n, k, (k+1)²),
            sqrt2(n, k, sq) = sqrt3(n, k, sq, k+k +3),
sq > n→ sqrt3(n, k, sq, su) = k,
sq ≤ n→ sqrt3(n, k, sq, su) =
                    sqrt3(n, k+1, sq + su, su +2);
```

```
sqrt:    (n: NAT) —→ (k: NAT :: k² ≤ n ∧ (k+1)² > n);
sqrt3:   NAT × NAT × NAT × NAT ––→ NAT;
axiom for all n, k: NAT; sq: NAT:: sq = (k+1)²;
            su: NAT :: su = k+k +3  =>
            sqrt(n) = sqrt3(n, 0, 1, 3),
sq > n→ sqrt3(n, k, sq, su) = k,
sq ≤ n→ sqrt3(n, k, sq, su) =
                    sqrt3(n, k+1, sq + su, su +2);
```

C Program

Finally, an Ada or C program (see (3-16)) can be generated; actually, the C program contains the basic operations of the data type (cf. (2-1)) such as succ or (succ zero) instead of +1 or 1. A representation of NAT by the predefined integer type would eventually make this replacement by unfolding the basic operations by their implementation. This representation is still a crucial step since it implies a transition from unbounded natural numbers to bounded integers; the operations all become partial.

(3-16) C Program: Integer Squareroot

```
sqrt:    (n: NAT) —→ (k: NAT :: k² ≤ n ∧ (k+1)² > n);
sqrt3:   NAT × NAT × NAT × NAT ––→ NAT;
axiom for all n, k: NAT; sq: NAT:: sq = (k+1)²;
            su: NAT :: su = k+k +3  =>
            sqrt(n) = sqrt3(n, 0, 1, 3),
sq > n→ sqrt3(n, k, sq, su) = k,
sq ≤ n→ sqrt3(n, k, sq, su) =
                    sqrt3(n, k+1, sq + su, su +2);
```

```
NAT sqrt (n)
  NAT n;
{ return sqrt3 (n, 0, 1, 3); }
NAT sqrt3 (n, k, sq, su)
  NAT n; NAT k; NAT sq; NAT  su;
{ If (sq > n)    return k;
  If (!(sq > n))  return sqrt3 (n, k+1, sq + su, su +2);}
```

4. Functionals

This section describes the combined advantages of functional programming and algebraic specification: a considerably higher degree of abstraction, avoiding much repetitive development effort by the use of homomorphic extension functionals as "program generators". The importance of the *combination* of algebraic specification with higher order functions should be stressed. The ability to specify *partial* higher-order functions (i. e. with conditions on functional parameters) has been an important contribution of PROSPECTRA to the theory of algebraic specifications. The algebraic properties of functionals allow a high level of reasoning *about* functional programs, and permit general and powerful optimisations, supported by the PROSPECTRA approach. The combined advantages of algebraic specification and higher order functions apply to program and meta-program development in the same way, cf. § 5.

4.1. Methodological Advantages

Higher order functions (with functions as parameters and/or results, cf. e. g. [Bird, Wadler 88], [Bird 89], [Möller 87]), allow a substantial reduction of re-development effort, in the early specifications and all subsequent developments. This aspect of functional abstraction is analogous to parameterised data type specifications such as generics in Ada. (4-1) shows some examples. Note that the type parameters are still stated as generic parameters (corresponding to parameterised specifications). The need to instantiate these parameters explicitly (cf. **new** IS_MONOID (LIST) in (2-3)) is sometimes tedious; polymorphic functions would be a help here.

(4-1) Generic Functionals

```
generic
   type S is private;
   type T is private;
package UP is
   Up:         (T × T —> T) —> (S —> T) —> (S —> T) —>  S —>  T;
axiom for all "⊕" T × T —> T; f, g: S —> T; x: S =>
   Up "⊕" f g x = (f x) ⊕ (g x);
end UP;
```

```
generic
   type S is private;
   type T is private;
package PAIR is
   PairHom:    (T × T —> T) —> (S —> T) —>  S × S —>  T;
axiom for all "⊕" T × T —> T; f, g: S —> T; x, y: S =>
   PairHom "⊕" f (x, y) = (f x) "⊕" (f y);
end PAIR;
```

It is an interesting observation that many definitions of functionals have a restricted form: the functional argument is unchanged in recursive calls. A functional together with its (fixed) function parameters can then always be explicitly expanded by transformation. Thus the major advantage of functionals appears, at first glance, to be "merely" one of abbreviation. In contrast to generics, tedious explicit instantiation is avoided for functional parameters, in particular for partial parameterisation ("Curry'ing"). However, working with functionals quickly leads to a new style of programming (i. e. specification and development) at a considerably higher degree of abstraction. As we shall see below, much repetitive development can be reduced to the application of homomorphic extension functionals; these can be considered as a kind of "program generators".

It is this aspect, that many functions should have the property of being homomorphisms, that goes beyond the correctness properties expressible in standard functional programming (in Miranda, for example).

There, one tends to think only in terms of free term algebras (lists, trees etc.). Here, we have the whole power of algebraic specification available to state, for example, that the properties of a monoid hold and are preserved by a (homomorphic) function, indeed by a functional for a whole class of applications. Development (optimising transformations etc.) need be made only once for the functional. In fact, the recursion schema of homomorphic extension (see [von Henke 76], [Böhm, Berarducci 85]) provides a program development strategy ("divide and conquer", cf. [Smith 85]) and an induction schema for proofs.

In meta-programming, these homomorphic extension functionals are important for the concise definition of program development tactics (see § 5.4). The algebraic properties of functionals allow a high level of reasoning *about* functional programs (postulated in [Bird, Wadler 88], [Bird 89]) that is supported by the PROSPECTRA system.

4.2. Homomorphisms and Homomorphic Extension Functionals

The functionals Map, Filter, Reduce of [Bird, Wadler 88], [Bird 89] and others are special cases of a more general homomorphic extension functional, see (4-2). Hom corresponds to the Monoid view of list construction (cf. § 2.3 above) and thus to a program development strategy by (binary) partitioning. An analogous homomorphic extension functional corresponds to the linear view and thus to a linear "divide and conquer" strategy. Map can be defined as an automorphism (i. e. a homomorphism to the same structure); in fact it can be defined more generally to map between two lists of different component types.

Note the use of nested generics in (4-2), corresponding to a parameterised specification that can first be (partially) parameterised by the source (this could be a list but also, say, a stack or queue having the same (sub-) specification), and then sometime later by different target monoids as actual parameters for M. Again, at this stage only the target type is given, and at yet a later stage, a neutral element and a binary operation are supplied along with the other parameters of Hom.

As an example for the instantiation of a homomorphic extension functional, existential and universal quantification of a predicate over a list can be defined by homomorphic extension of the predicate over lists, using the algebraic properties of Booleans. Map and Filter are defined as automorphisms from LIST to LIST; this is a simplification of the general case, where lists of x's are mapped to lists of y's.

Note that Hom requires that the target algebraic structure has the properties of a monoid (the function composition operator • and the identity function Id are assumed to be universally defined in this paper). In this case we can transform Hom using the monoid properties of lists and employ the recursion removal transformation of (2-4) that is only applicable, if ⊕ and n form a monoid (cf. [Bauer 82], [Bird, Wadler 88], [Bird 89], [Krieg-Brückner 89a, b, 90], [Krieg-Brückner, Hoffmann 91]). With the aid of an auxiliary Function H2, a linear, tail-recursive version is obtained. In functional programming, such a global optimisation is not possible since we could not be sure that the binary operation is associative in general; there is no way to state such a requirement in a standard functional programming language. In conventional programming or algebraic specification without functionals we would have to separately prove the property and optimise for each case (each instance of the functional).

(4-2) Homomorphic Extension Functionals over Lists

```
with IS_MONOID;
generic
   type ITEM is private;
   type LIST is private;
   empty:  LIST;
   "&":    LIST × LIST —>  LIST;
   axiom for all x, y, z: LIST => x & empty = x,   empty & x = x,   (x & y) & z = x & (y & z);
   single: ITEM —>  LIST;
   isEmpty: LIST —>  BOOLEAN;
   head:   (x: LIST :: ¬ isEmpty x) —> ITEM;
   tail:   (x: LIST :: ¬ isEmpty x) —> LIST;
   axiom for all e: ITEM; l: LIST =>
      isEmpty empty = true,              head ((single e) & l) = e,
      isEmpty ((single e) & l) = false,  tail ((single e) & l) = l;
```

```
package LIST_HOMS is
   generic
      type M is private;
   package HOM_TO is
      package M_IS_MONOID is new IS_MONOID (M);
      Hom:  (n: M) —> ("⊕": M × M —> M:: isMonoid n "⊕") —> (ITEM —> M) —> LIST —> M;
      axiom for all n: M; "⊕": M × M —> M:: isMonoid n "⊕"; h: ITEM —> M; e: ITEM; x, y: LIST; r: M =>
         Hom n "⊕" h empty          = n,
         Hom n "⊕" h (x & y)        = (Hom n "⊕" h x) ⊕ (Hom n "⊕" h y),
         Hom n "⊕" h (single e)     = h e;
      H2:   (n: M) —> ("⊕": M × M —> M:: isMonoid n "⊕") —> (ITEM —> M) —> M —> LIST —> M;
      axiom for all n: M; "⊕": M × M —> M:: isMonoid n "⊕"; h: ITEM —> M; e: ITEM; x, y: LIST; r: M =>
         Hom n "⊕" h z              = H2 n "⊕" h n z,  - - embedding for tail-recursive definition
         H2  n "⊕" h r empty        = r,
         H2  n "⊕" h r (single e & y) = H2 n "⊕" h (r ⊕ (h e)) y;
   end HOM_TO;

   package AUTO is new HOM_TO (LIST);
   Map:    (ITEM —> ITEM) —>         LIST —>  LIST;
   Filter: (ITEM —> BOOLEAN) —> LIST —>  LIST;
   Filt:   (ITEM —> BOOLEAN) —> ITEM —>  LIST;
   axiom for all f: ITEM —> ITEM; p: ITEM —> BOOLEAN; x: ITEM =>
   Map f   = Hom empty "&" (single • f),
   Filter p = Hom empty "&" (Filt p),   p x → Filt p x = single x,   ¬ p x → Filt p x = empty;

   package toITEMS is new HOM_TO (ITEM);
   Reduce:   (n: ITEM) —> ("⊕": ITEM × ITEM —> ITEM:: isMonoid n "⊕") —> LIST —> ITEM;
   axiom for all n: ITEM; "⊕": ITEM × ITEM —> ITEM:: isMonoid n "⊕" =>
   Reduce n "⊕" = Hom n "⊕" id;

   package toBOOL is new HOM_TO (BOOLEAN);
   Exist, ForAll:  (ITEM —> BOOLEAN) —> LIST —>  BOOLEAN;
   axiom for all x: ITEM; a, b: LIST =>
   Exist = Hom false "or",        ForAll = Hom true "and";
end LIST_HOMS;
```

5. Formalisation of Program Transformation

The Meta-Development Methodology

The methodology for program development based on the concept of algebraic specification of data types, and program transformation can be applied to the development of transformation algorithms, i.e. for program-manipulating programs or *meta*-programs. Starting from small elementary transformation rules, we can apply the usual equational and inductive reasoning to derive complex rules. All the methodology and transformation technology for program development is carried over to meta-program development.

In Program Development by Transformation [Bauer, Wössner 82], [Bauer et al. 85-89], [Partsch, Steinbrüggen 83], an elementary development step is a *program transformation*: the application of a transformation rule that is generally applicable; a particular development is then a sequence of rule applications. The question is how to best formalise rules and application (or inference) strategies, in general how to develop program transformation programs or *meta*-programs.

The approach taken in PROSPECTRA is to regard transformation rules as equations in an algebra of programs, to derive basic transformation operations from these rules, to allow composition and functional abstraction, and to regard transformation scripts as (compositions of) such transformation operations. Using all the results from program development based on algebraic specifications and functionals we can then reason about the development of meta-programs, i. e. transformation programs or development scripts, in the same way as about programs: we can define requirement specifications (development goals) and implement them by various design strategies; in short, we can develop *correct*, efficient, complex transformation operations from elementary rules stated as algebraic equations. Homomorphic extension functionals are important for the concise definition of program development tactics.

5.1. The Syntactic Algebra of Programs

We can define the Abstract Syntax of a programming language such as PAⁿⁿdA by an algebraically specified Abstract Data Type: trees in the Abstract Syntax correspond to terms in this algebra of (PAⁿⁿdA) programs, non-terminals to sorts, tree constructor operations to constructor operations, etc., see (5-1). Most constructor operations are free, except for & corresponding to List concatenation.

(5-1) Abstract Syntax for Expressions and Expression Lists

```
with NAMES, LISTS;
package EXPS Is
  type EXP Is private;
  package EXP_LISTS Is new LISTS(EXP);   subtype EXP_LIST Is EXP_LISTS.LIST;
  mkName:   NAME ⟶    EXP;    - - concrete phrase: ⌈ n ⌋
  mkTuple:  EXP_LIST ⟶ EXP;   - - concrete phrase: ⌈ el ⌋   If empty or single, otherwise: ⌈ ( el ) ⌋
  mkCall:   EXP × EXP ⟶ EXP;  - - concrete phrase: ⌈ e₁ e₂ ⌋
  ... a definition of selectors and their axioms is omitted for brevity; for homomorphisms etc. see below
end EXPS;
```

(5-2) Concrete Syntax Phrase and Abstract Syntax Term

```
axiom for all x, y: EXP ⟹
  ⌈ not x and not y ⌋ =
  mkCall (mkName boolAnd) (mkTuple    (   (single (mkCall (mkName boolNot) x)) &
                                          (single (mkCall (mkName boolNot) y)) )  );
```

Although we are interested in the operations of the *abstract* syntactic algebra of programs, it is often more convenient to use a notation for *phrases* (program fragments with schema variables) of the *concrete syntax* corresponding to appropriate terms (with variables) in the algebra. Phrases provide a concise notation for large terms, cf. (5-2) for a small example (boolAnd, boolNot stand for further subterms denoting special names). The brackets ⌈ ⌋ are used whenever a (nested) phrase of the concrete syntax is introduced. In this paper, we are not concerned with notational issues at the concrete syntax level nor with the (non-trivial) translation of phrases from concrete to abstract syntax. Specifications of abstract types such as in (5-1), including selectors and other auxiliary operations, are automatically constructed from a given abstract syntax specification in the PROSPECTRA system.

5.2. Transformation Rules: Equations in the Semantic Algebra

In the approach of the algebraic definition of the semantics of a programming language (cf. [Broy et al. 87]), an evaluation function or interpretation function from syntactic to semantic domains is axiomatised. The equational axioms of such functions induce equivalence classes on (otherwise free) constructor terms. In other words, we can prove that two (syntactic) terms are *semantically equivalent*, in a context-free way or possibly subject to some syntactic or semantic pre-conditions. Such a proof can of course also be made with respect to some other style of semantic definition for the language. Thus we obtain a *semantic algebra* of programs in which transformation rules are equations as a quotient algebra of the *abstract syntactic algebra* in which only equations for & exist.

(5-3) shows examples of transformation rules for Boolean expressions, i.e. of type EXP, analogous to the algebraic properties of Booleans, i.e. of type BOOLEAN. These examples are, of course, very simple-minded; in general, one has large syntactic phrases and complex context conditions as applicability conditions.

(5-3) Transformation Rules (in the Semantic Algebra): Boolean expressions

```
axiom for all x, y: EXP =>
   ⌈ not x and not y ⌋ = ⌈ not (x or y) ⌋,      ⌈ not x or not y ⌋ = ⌈ not (x and y) ⌋;
```

The major kind of transformation rules we are interested in is the *bi-directional transformation rule*, a pair of semantically equivalent terms: an *equation* in the semantic algebra of programs that is provable by deductive or inductive reasoning against the semantics. All rules in this paper are of this kind. All considerations about interpreting equations as rewrite rules apply (confluence, termination, etc.).

A *uni-directional* transformation rule corresponds to a relation between semantic models such that each model in the range is a robustly correct implementation of some model in the domain; thus it corresponds to a semantic inclusion relation in a model-oriented sense. Again this notion is taken from the theory of algebraic specification (cf. [Broy, Wirsing 82] for the converse relation as the approximation relation ≤ on (transformation) functions in [Möller 87]). It formalises the notion of correctness with respect to some implementation decision that narrows implementation flexibility or chooses a particular implementation. These rules are of course not invertible (a decision cannot be reversed) and, interpreted as rewrite rules, are not confluent in general. In this paper, we restrict our attention to bi-directional rules although most considerations generalise.

We can apply all the power of the algebraic framework to transformation rules specified in this way, for example the deduction of new rules using equational or inductive reasoning, even completion techniques (cf. [Ganzinger 87]).

5.3. Basic Transformations: Operations in the Syntactic Algebra

From each transformation rule or set of related rules, i.e. equations in the semantic algebra, an elementary transformation operation can be constructed in a straightforward way as a partial function in the *abstract syntactic algebra*, see (5-4): it maps to a normal form in the quotient algebra corresponding to the equations. Each equation is considered as a rewrite rule from left to right (or from right to left), and, if the system of rewrite rules is confluent, yields a corresponding normal form. The function corresponds to an identity in the semantic algebra and achieves a kind of normalisation in the syntactic algebra.

(5-4) shows an example of a basic transformation function derived from a single transformation rule: deMorgan applies deMorgans laws in expressions. Similarly, a basic applicability predicate (5-5) can be derived from the transformation rule (possibly including contextual or semantic applicability conditions in addition to the syntactic ones). Note that the others can be expanded using simple syntactic predicates (to be defined jointly with the Abstract Syntax). Other basic transformation functions and predicates are defined analogously. More simplification rules could of course be used on Booleans, cf. [Krieg-Brückner 89a, b, 90b].

(5-4) Basic Transformation Function: deMorgan

```
deMorgan:      (e: EXP:: is_deMorgan e) —> EXP;
axiom for all x, y: EXP =>
  deMorgan ⌈ not x and not y ⌋ = ⌈ not (x or y) ⌋,   deMorgan ⌈ not x or not y ⌋ = ⌈ not (x and y) ⌋;
```

(5-5) Basic Applicability Predicate: is_deMorgan

```
is_deMorgan:  EXP —> BOOLEAN;
axiom for all x, y: EXP =>
  (is_deMorgan ⌈ not x and not y ⌋ = true,        is_deMorgan ⌈ not x or not y ⌋ = true,
   others → is_deMorgan x = false);
```

5.4. Transformation Functionals: Homomorphic Extensions and Tactics

In analogy to tacticals in [Gordon et al. 78], we might call some transformation functionals *transformals* since they embody application tactics or strategies for applying elementary transformations over a larger context. Consider for example (5-6): if some transformation function *f* and its applicability condition *p* are given, then *Try* provides a totalisation (extension to identity) if *p* does not hold.

(5-6) Functional: Try

```
Try:        (p: EXP —> BOOLEAN) —>  (f: (x: EXP:: p x) —> EXP) —>  EXP —>  EXP;
axiom for all p: EXP —> BOOLEAN; f: (x: EXP:: p x) —> EXP; x: EXP =>
  p x →  Try p f x = f x    ¬ p x →  Try p f x = x,
tdeMorgan:    EXP —> EXP;
axiom tdeMorgan = Try is_deMorgan deMorgan;
```

More important for application tactics are *homomorphic extension* functionals, in this case the structural extension of the effect of a (local) transformation or predicate over larger terms. This is an extension of the basic case for lists in § 4.2. In (5-7), Hom extends a function on names over expressions. This version is rather simple-minded (but general, as we shall see below in (5-10)), it does not apply the homomorphism recursively to the constituent parts of an expression automatically; one has to supply this recursion ("from the outside") in the call. For automorphisms, (5-8) shows such a version.

As an example for application tactics, consider (5-9): AtLeaves applies a basic function to all leaves of an expression (names in this case); Sweep applies the basic function f to every subexpression. SweepP is a similar (pseudo-)homomorphic extension functional for predicates, see (5-10). Analogous definitions can be made for more complex expressions, statements etc. (cf. [Krieg-Brückner 88a, 89a, b]). In fact, general definitions of homomorphic extension functionals could be constructed automatically for a given abstract syntax, in the same way as the construction of an algebraically specified type for an abstract syntax in the PROSPECTRA system.

(5-7) Basic Homomorphic Extension for Expressions and Expression Lists

```
generic
   type E Is private;
package EXP_HOM Is
   Hom:        (NAME —> E) —> (EXP_LIST —> E) —> (EXP × EXP —> E) —> EXP —> E;
   axiom for all fName: NAME —> E; fTuple: EXP_LIST —> E; fCall: EXP × EXP —> E;
                    n: NAME; e1, e2: EXP; el: EXP_LIST =>
     Hom fName fTuple fCall (mkName n)       = fName n,
     Hom fName fTuple fCall (mkTuple el)     = fTuple el,
     Hom fName fTuple fCall (mkCall (e1, e2)) = fCall (e1, e2);
   end EXP_HOM;
```

(5-8) Derived Homomorphic Extension (with recursive application)

```
   package EXP_LIST_HOMS Is new LIST_HOMS (EXP, EXP_LIST, empty, "&", single, isEmpty, head, tail);
   package AUTO Is new EXP_HOM (EXP);
   package EXP_PAIR_EXP Is new PAIR (EXP, EXP);
   RHom:  (NAME —> EXP) —> (EXP_LIST —> EXP) —> (EXP × EXP —> EXP) —> EXP —> EXP;
axiom for all fName: NAME —> EXP; fTuple: EXP_LIST —> EXP; fCall: EXP × EXP —> EXP =>
   RHom fName fTuple fCall = Hom fName (fTuple • Map (RHom fName fTuple fCall))
                                        (PairHom fCall (RHom fName fTuple fCall));
```

(5-9) Transformation Tactics for Expressions: AtLeaves *and* Sweep

```
   AtLeaves: (NAME —> EXP) —> EXP —> EXP;
axiom for all fn: NAME —> EXP =>
   AtLeaves fn   = RHom fn id id;
   Sweep:      (EXP —> EXP) —> EXP —> EXP;
axiom for all f: EXP —> EXP =>
   Sweep f      = RHom (f • mkName) f f;
```

```
   everydeMorgan:  EXP —> EXP;
axiom   everydeMorgan = Sweep tdeMorgan;
```

(5-10) Homomorphic Predicates for Expressions

```
   package toBOOL Is new EXP_HOM (BOOLEAN);
   package UP_EXP_LIST_BOOL Is new UP (EXP_LIST, BOOLEAN);
   package UP_EXP_PAIR_BOOL Is new UP (EXP × EXP, BOOLEAN);
   package EXP_PAIR_BOOL Is new PAIR (EXP, BOOLEAN);
```

```
   SweepP:  (n: BOOLEAN) —> ("⊕": BOOLEAN × BOOLEAN —> BOOLEAN:: isMonoid n "⊕") —>
                (EXP —> BOOLEAN) —> EXP —> BOOLEAN;
axiom for all n: BOOLEAN; "⊗": BOOLEAN × BOOLEAN —> BOOLEAN; p: EXP —> BOOLEAN =>
   SweepP n "⊗" p = Hom (p • mkName)
                         ((Up "⊗") (p • mkTuple, Hom n "⊗" (SweepP n "⊗" p))  - - Hom on lists
                         ((Up "⊗") (p • mkCall, PairHom "⊗" (SweepP n "⊗" p));
```

```
   Exist, ForAll:  (EXP —> BOOLEAN) —> EXP —> BOOLEAN;
axiom for all p: EXP —> BOOLEAN; e: EXP =>
   Exist p    = SweepP false "or" p,
   ForAll p   = SweepP true "and" p;
```

6. Formalisation of Transformational Program Development

Various authors have stressed the need for a formalisation of the software development process: the need for an automatically generated development "history" [Wile 86a]. Approaches to formalise development descriptions contain a kind of development program [Wile 86a], functional abstraction [Feijs et al. 87] and composition of logical inference rules [Sintzoff 87], [Jähnichen et al. 86].

The meta-program development paradigm of PROSPECTRA leads naturally to a *formalisation of the software development process* itself. A program development is a sequence (more generally: a term) of transformations. The system automatically generates a transcript of a development "history"; it allows replay upon re-development when requirements have changed, containing goals of the development, design decisions taken, and alternatives discarded but relevant for re-development.

6.1. Development Scripts: Composite Transformation Functions

In Program Development by Transformation, we can regard every elementary program development step as a transformation; we may conversely define a *development script* to be a composition of transformation operations (including application strategies for sets of elementary transformation operations). In this view we regard a development script as a *development transcript* (of some constant program term) to formalise a concrete development history, possibly to be re-played. A *development script* is, in general, a formal object that does not only represent a documentation of the past but is a plan for future developments (cf. also its use in the command language ControLa, see [Marcuzzi 91] and § 8.1). It can be used to abstract from a particular development to a class of similar developments, a *development method*, incorporating a certain strategy.

The abstraction from concrete developments to development methods, incorporating formalised development tactics and strategies, and the formalisation of programming knowledge as "transformation rules + development methods" will be a challenge for the future.

6.2. Development Goals: Requirement Specifications

A *development goal* is a requirement specification for a development script, i.e. a transformation function employing a certain transformation strategy, yet to be designed. It can be a characteristic predicate for the respective transformation function or the post-condition of the application of some set of transformation rules. For example, we can state the (converse of the) desired goal for normalisation of Boolean expressions as in (6-1); this would be generalised for several sets of rules.

(6-1) Development Goals: Normalisation of Expressions

```
  not_normExp:      EXP —>    BOOLEAN;
axiom for all x: EXP =>
  not_normExp = Exist is_deMorgan;
```

Often, the application of some set of rules requires the satisfaction of some pre-condition established by (previous exhaustive application of) some other set of rules, i. e. as the post-condition of this set of rules. Note that such intermediate conditions never need to be checked operationally as long as it can be shown that they are established by previous application of other rules. If these conditions can be defined structurally (or "syntactically"), as in our example, then they characterise certain normal forms. This leads to a substantial improvement in the modularisation of sets of rules and separation of concerns, consequently ease of verification. Transformation functions having structural normal forms as applicability conditions correspond to Wile's syntax directed experts [Wile 86b].

6.3. Development Tactics: Transformals

Exhaustive application of some set of rules can be expressed by suitable transformals. While can be used to apply a transformation function f as long as some condition p holds. Similarly, Iterate iterates a local transformation function f as long as some local condition p holds somewhere, see (6-2). These transformals correspond to a kind of "Markov algorithm" tactics when generalised to sets of rules.

(6-2) Development Tactics: While, Iterate

```
While, Every, Iterate: (EXP —> BOOLEAN) —> (EXP —> EXP) —> EXP —> EXP;
axiom for all p: EXP —> BOOLEAN; f: EXP —> EXP; x: EXP =>
  ¬p x → While p f x = x,              p x →    While p f x = While p f (f x),
  Every p f x = Sweep (Try p f) x,              Iterate p f x = While (Exist p) (Every p f) x;
```

(6-3) Application of Development Tactics: Iter_normExp

```
Iter_deMorgan:   EXP —> EXP;
axiom for all x: EXP =>
  Iter_deMorgan x = Iterate Is_deMorgan deMorgan x;
```

6.4. Development Rules: Equations over Tactics

We would like to improve the transformation tactics even further. As far as possible, we would like to achieve the same strategic effect (the same development goal) by different, increasingly more efficient, application tactics. A transformation from one tactic to another is possible by development rules, see (6-5). *Development rules*, i.e. equational properties of development scripts, allow us to express and to reason about design alternatives or *alternative development tactics*, and to *simplify developments* by considering them as algebraic terms in the usual way. (6-6) shows the development of a derived rule by equational reasoning. It may be used to simplify iterated application into a single bottom-up one-sweep application. This rule is used in (6-7) to simplify our example since we can prove the premise.

(6-5) Development Rule: Elimination of While

```
axiom for all p: EXP —> BOOLEAN; f: EXP —> EXP; x: EXP =>
  p x ∧¬p (f x) →  While p f x = f x
```

(6-6) Development Rule Derivation: Iterate ⇔ Every ⇔ Sweep

```
                                      Iterate p f x = While (Exist p) (Every p f) x,   -- definition of While
  Exist p x ∧¬ Exist p (Every p f x) →  Iterate p f x = Every p f x,                    -- elimination of While
  Exist p x ∧¬ Exist p (Every p f x) →  Iterate p f x = Sweep (Try p f) x;              -- definition of Every
```

(6-7) Derivation: Iter_normExp

```
axiom   Iter_deMorgan = Sweep (Try Is_deMorgan deMorgan);
```

Uniform Approach

The uniform approach to program, meta-program, proof and meta-proof development has had some major practical consequences. Since every manipulation in a program development system can be regarded as a transformation of some "program" (for example in the command language), the whole system interaction can be formalised this way and the approach leads to a uniform treatment of programming language, program manipulation and transformation language, proof and proof development language, and command language; the uniformity has also been exploited in the PROSPECTRA system yielding a significant reduction of parallel work, see § 7 - § 9.

7. The Generic Development System

The actual development system for the PROSPECTRA methodology is a rather large and complex set of inter-related tools. The various components are brought together, in a unified way, by structuring the system to reflect the methodology it supports. The methodology itself has also been employed to develop and structure many of the constituent system components.

The PROSPECTRA system structure is notable for a number of reasons:

(i) The orthogonality achieved by treating all system's activities as transformations

(ii) The uniform interface to all system components

(iii) The preservation of the ´simple´ transformation paradigm even in the Meta Development Systems

(iv) The uniform management of *all* system objects in the library (even parts of the system itself)

(v) The description of the interface to all system components in the specification language PAnndA-S

The sub-systems shown in (7-1) to (7-4) are instances of the generic development system. Generation of a particular system component requires some instantiation of the various generic components, in particular an *Editor* in the Front End and some *Translator* in the Back End. For almost all kinds of developments, the required instantiation or specialisation of specific components can be done within the system; exceptions are, of course, translators to the target languages. Note that the *PAnndA Transformer* is the same generic component, but instantiated with a possibly different set of transformations.

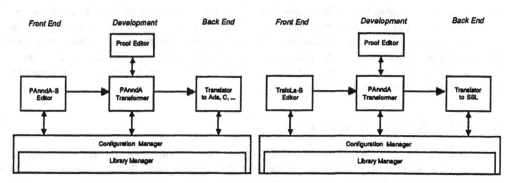

(7-1) The Program Development Subsystem   (7-2) The Meta Program Development Subsystem

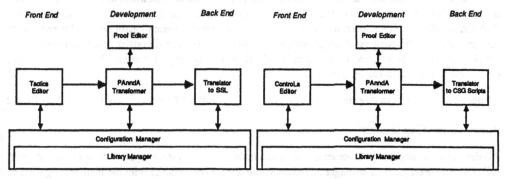

(7-3) The Proof Tactics Development Subsystem   (7-4) The System Development Subsystem

The relationship between the generic development system and the (generic) transformational development model is rather straight-forward. We start the development with an initial requirements specification (using an *Editor*). The specification is then passed to a *Transformer* for further development and refinement. Correctness conditions are ensured by the *Proof System*. Finally, a *Translator* will generate an executable version of the objects produced by the Transformer and configure some environment for compilation/execution of these objects. All activities are recorded and carried out under the supervision of a controller in the context of some library. The *Library and Configuration Managers* coordinate and organise the various objects passed between and processed by the other system components.

Activity	Component
Initial Formulation of Requirements	PAnndA-S Editor
Development to Constructive (and Optimised) Design	PAnndA Transformer
Verification of some Correctness Conditions	Proof Editor
Translation to Target Language (Ada, C or other)	Translator to Ada, C

(7-5) Activities and Components for Program Development

As an example take the instantiation of the generic development system to the components used for program development in (7-1). The table in (7-5) illustrates the activities and the different components employed. This example shows the manner in which development proceeds in a typical subsystem. Each of the individual steps described varies in complexity. Some are completely automatic while others require a high degree of user guidance. In this particular case, the translator to Ada only unfolds abstract type definitions (introduced by pre-defined type definiton schemata) into proper Ada text; in the case of C, for example, a little more work must be done.

All activities can be carried out within a single development framework since each of the objects manipulated by the various system components has been defined as a type in PAnndA-S. An activity in some system component can then be formulated as a PAnndA-S specification, denoting a transformation over this object type, as described in § 5 for meta programs. The specification of the activity can then be developed in a transformational manner and ultimately installed in the appropriate component as a transformation on the objects processed by that component.

8. The System Components

Associated with the generalised presentation of (7-1) to (7-4) are a number of actual (sub)systems. In reality, these do not exists as distinct components within the implementation. For each conceptual system, its implementation is realised in terms of a combination (or particular instantiation) of some generic system components. This approach enables the system structure to be presented (learned, used, and implemented) in a simplified way. In particular, the Front End components are instantiations (and extensions) of the PAnndA-S Editor. All development components are composed of a basic transformer shell together with task specific transformations. A proof component, for example, would consist of a transformer shell, transformations for proofs, and an additional mechanism for proof representation. The following, actual, development subsystems can be identified:

- Program   • Meta Program   • Proof   • Proof Tactics   • Command and Control

8.1. The Controller

All development steps and movements within and throughout the various system components are controlled by a general purpose manager called the *Controller*, in accordance with the methodology. It also provides a uniform interface to the user, as well as supplying a means of interfacing the various system components that must communicate. Each system command is formulated as a transformation in the Controller subsystem; the command language Controla is a sublanguage of the (meta) specification language PAnndA-S.

The Controller interprets actions upon the various objects stored in the library and starts up the appropriate component for manipulation of an object in a way consistent with the requested action. For example, a revision request on a PAnndA-S object causes the controller to retrieve the contents of the appropriate specification from the library and to start up the PAnndA-S Editor on this specification. Given that general commands are issued in the context of library objects, the controller determines the component and object combinations appropriate for the context and associated request.

Every system activity is viewed as a tranformation from an initial state to some final state of the system. The controller is based on the concept of a *local state* of a component, and regards a specific component as a function with the following signature:

Component: (User_Interaction × Library) —> Local_State —> Local_State

The local state contains the minimal set of information that a given component needs to carry out the associated transformation. The library manager, the configuration manager, the specification editor, the transformer, the proof system etc. all have associated local states. For example, the local state for a specification would consist of the specification itself together with the configuration of the library defining specific versions of modules used by that specification. Roughly speaking, a global state is a local state of some component embedded in a configuration of the library.

Each user interaction is then seen as a transformation from one (local) state to a new (local) state. When a development subsystem is invoked, the initial (local) state is constructed from the current content of the library that represents the global state of the system. The global state of the system can be changed in two ways: either by invoking simple library commands that do not require the facilities provided by other components, or by invoking a specific system component. Since all components are considered as functions on the local state, a component can be called from another in a *call-return relationship*, with an initial local state as a parameter. The component then returns either the changed local state resulting from the call of the component (confirmed development) or the initial local state (cancelled development). The change is then incorporated into the current library structure by turning the local into a global state.

The Controller is responsible for recording the actual development steps in the development history: a *log and replay script* (a step by step account of the activities carried out by the developer resulting in the refined/revised object) is stored and associated with the development. Scripts are written in the CSG script language that has been designed to express every possible action carried out using a system (this is a PRO-SPECTRA extension of the Synthesizer Generator, see [de Miguel 91]). The replay of actual developments is facilitated by the CSG script interpreter. The replay of a development script can either be fully automatic or involve the user in a step by step replay.

There exist several ways to generate a script for further (re)play. One is to record the development history of an object, another to specify it using the ControLa development subsystem. In general, the ControLa development subsystem allows to abstract from concrete developments (in the form of log scripts) to a representation on the level of the ControLa specification language, i.e. a subset of PAnndA-S. This means that developments themselves are formal objects that can be manipulated (cf. sections 2 and 5.2) and provide the basis for abstraction from particular developments to general methods that can be re-used.

8.2.   The Library and Configuration Managers

The current *Library Manager* is based on the prototype design and implementation described in [Houdier 91]. The Library Manager supports concurrency in the sense that several users can develop new objects simultaneously. Essentially it consist of two components: an underlying object base and a user interface.

The Object Base stores *all* the objects that are manipulated or referenced from within the system, together with all the relationships defined between the stored objects. The object base is incremental in the sense that nothing is deleted or changed during development; new versions are added as derivations of existing versions. Mechanisms to purge/delete objects are supplied for maintenance purposes (although these functions are not considered to be part of the development framework, but rather functions that would be used by a project/system administrator, in connection with archiving activities).

The *LibLa editor* constitutes the interface between the user and the object base and allows the user to display and modify the information contained in the underlying object base. The editor manipulates partial but consistent views of objects. Such views are defined in terms of so-called LibLa trees. LibLa is aimed at representing the hierarchical structure of libraries (such structure being used to reflect the development activities in PROSPECTRA). Version Management, as every other operation in the system, is understood as a set of transformations on a language, in this case LibLa. The LibLa transformers are particular in the sense that they have side effects on the underlying object base. The Library Manager adopts an object-oriented approach to object management since the various non-terminals of the LibLa language correspond to object types of the underlying object base.

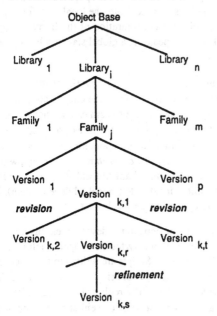

(8-1) Structure of the Library

The conceptual model of the object base, as it is embodied in the definition of the LibLa grammar, is as follows. Each *object base* consist of a set of libraries, and *libraries* in turn of a set of families. Each *family* contains a set of related versions of an object with a particular name (for example the name of a specification module in PAnndA-S), organised into a version tree showing the development relations among the versions. A *version* is either a refinement or a revision of an (initial) version, depending on whether the development was correctness preserving or not, respectively. Moreover, additional information such as the development history (represented as a CSG script), textual documentation, status information, and so on, is stored in the library with each object. In particular, the total development history of a version is the concatenation of the particular development histories of its ancestors along a path to the original root version. A schema for a LibLa structure is given in (8-1).

Besides development relations between versions within one family, the library also records the relations between versions of *different* families (as depicted by the with-clauses of a specification or program in PAnndA). Such with-relations form a directed acyclic graph. The versions belonging to such a graph are called a *configuration*. Configurations are defined and manipulated using the *Configuration Manager*. With-dependencies are generally handled by calling the Configuration Manager from one of the development components in a call-return relationship. The Configuration Manager may also be called directly from the LibLa Editor since configurations are first class objects: they can be created, revised and refined as any other object on the level of the library. This utility is vital when refining the definition of (PROSPECTRA) system configurations using the system itself, see § 9.3.

8.3. The Editors

The Specification Editor is a language based editor for PAnndA-S, the specification language of PROSPECTRA, and serves as a basis for all other (sub)language editors derived from it, such as for TrafoLa ([de la Cruz 91]), ControLa, etc. Its main purpose is to allow the user to enter requirement specifications and then check such specifications for syntactic and static semantic correctness. The Specification Editor(s) have been generated using the Synthesizer Generator [Reps and Teitelbaum 88], extended in the

PROSPECTRA project, and make heavy use of its facilities for attribute grammars and incremental attribute (re-)evaluation.

Knowledge of the language syntax and context conditions have been built into the editor. This knowledge is used to assess whether a specification contains errors and where such errors occur. The static analysis is performed interactively and incrementally during editing rather than by compilation. Two editing paradigms are supported: text editing and structure editing. In the text editing mode, phrases are entered on a character by character basis. Structure editing guarantees the syntactic correctness; specifications are created top-down by inserting new well-formed templates in the skeleton of previously entered templates.

Context errors are detected by the static semantic analyser, a function of the editor that may be enabled or disabled during an editing session as appropriate. The static semantics of the specification language has been inspired and partially derived from the static semantics of Ada, with all the inherent complications for the static semantic analyser in performing overload resolution of names and expressions, modelling scope and visibility rules and instantiating generic packages. Consequently, the static semantic editor incorporates the notion of separate development ("separate compilation") of modules as a means of improving the general performance of the editor. In addition, it is possible to change fragments of a specification in isolation from the rest of the specification and thus momentarily avoiding change propagation.

The specification editor for PAnndA-S has an associated utility that supports the definition of a limited set of (Ada) types. A type declaration is entered by the user in its conventional (Ada) syntactic form. The equivalent Abstract Data Type form (a signature of constructor, selector and other operations with appropriate algebraic axioms) is then generated by transformation upon user request. This facility is referred to as a (pre-defined) *type definition scheme*. Type definition schemes are currently provided for the Ada enumeration, (recursive variant) record types, etc., and for the definition of the abstract syntax of languages, i.e. for the definition of tree types. The type definition schemes form the basis for type development towards a particular target language, such as Ada, within the program development system. A translation to C is near completion; corresponding type schemes for other target languages are being incorporated. The type definition scheme for tree types provides a basis for generating the term algebra of an object language. This term algebra is later used in developing transformers within the meta development system. Translations to SSL and TrafoLa-H (see § 8.6) are available.

8.4. The Transformer Shell

The central component concerned with program development by transformation is the *PAnndA Transformer Shell*, a language based component (used to apply transformations) for the complete wide-spectrum language PAnndA. The Transformer Shell is invoked from the LibLa Editor in a call-return relationship and is used during all transformational development phases, instantiated to a particular Transformer.

There is one fundamental distinction between the Specification Editor and the Transformer Shell: the Specification Editor is used for developing revisions of specifications and allows non-correctness-preserving operations in the form of text and structure editing commands. In contrast, neither structure nor text editing is allowed within the Transformer Shell. Only the application of correctness preserving transformations is admissible to change or refine the object being developed.

The Transformer Shell displays the program being developed as well as the set of applicable transformations in a given context (for example the transformations applicable to a selected subexpression). The reduction of the list of applicable transformations to a minimum is an important consideration for the user interface. In the extension of the facilities of the Synthesizer Generator made during the PROSPECTRA project, applicability (and therefore suppression of in-applicable transformations) can also be checked w.r.t. static semantic conditions. The Transformer Shell is a shell (or frame) in the sense that the required set of transformations must be developed, using the PROSPECTRA system, and then included in the generation of a new and extended version of a PAnndA Transformer.

Context information, needed for checking applicability conditions of transformations, has been provided by means of various attributes. Attributes have been defined for static semantic analysis of PAnndA programs, for example, attributes for reasoning about the type of expressions, properties of named entities, and the scope and visibility of names. Additional attributes are provided for reasoning about the semantics of specifications in terms of functions and their defining axioms. These attributes, termed the *local theory* (cf. § 8.5), contain all signatures and axioms accessible from the current context. The local theory forms the basis for efficient proof development and for the checking of semantic applicability conditions, i.e. for context-sensitive transformations.

Parameterised transformations, another extension of the Synthesizer Generator, may require information from the user at application time. Such parameters can be supplied using the parameter editor, either following the copy/paste paradigm, in which a suitable fragment is copied from the program proper, or by providing the parameter by editing. In the latter case the fragment will be analysed for static semantic errors in the context of the application and the transformation for which it is a parameter.

One notable component of the Transformer Shell is the unparser. The built-in attributes for static semantic analysis are used by the unparser to perform visibility and scope analysis of names. An unambigous unparsing of the program is provided, on the basis of this analysis, by automatic insertion of expanded names and qualified expressions when needed. Transformation rules are generally relieved from taking into account most of the visibility rules of Ada since names are represented in a unique way in the Transformer Shell.

8.5. The Proof Subsystem

The Proof Subsystem is based on the Transformer Shell. The basic Shell is augmented with facilities for representing proof derivations. All refinements and developments in the Proof Subsystem are formulated as transformations of logical formulae, i.e. terms of the specification language. An instantaneous representation of developments is provided that allows interactive replay and re-development of proofs. The Proof Subsystem is fully integrated with the Transformation Subsystem. The transformation writer is provided with a set of functions defining the interface to the Proof Subsystem. The justification required for the correctness of a transformation rule, not normally known until the transformation is applied in some context, may be included, via these functions, in the definition of the transformation itself. When the transformation is then applied in some context, the Proof Subsystem will be called to justify the instantiated applicability conditions. Details and example proofs may be found in [Traynor 89a, b] . Proofs have associated theorems, these may be used directly in subsequent development (of both proofs and programs) by including a reference to the proof in the configuration of the development. A complete integration of the Proof Subsystem with the PAnndA Transformer Shell requires not only that the logical formulae (generated, for example, by a transformation and corresponding to some applicabilty condition) be passed from the Transformer to the Proof Subsystem, but also context information is required, in particular, the local theory.

The Local Theory

The local theory has been defined to serve two purposes: firstly, to allow context-sensitive transformations to perform developments using axioms and definitions visible in the current context, secondly, to aid in proving proof obligations resulting from applicablity conditions (and in deducing properties of specifications), by providing the definitions needed for such deductions.

Context-sensitive transformations are seen as a major advance in transformation technology: transformations can be more automated and need less interaction with the user. One way to do this is by using the static semantic information in the context, for example to check type or visibility information. In addition, however, axioms from the local theory can be used to try to derive semantic context conditions automatically (for example the property of associativity) or as rewrite rules to provide automatic simplification.

The local theory is a normalised representation of all axioms and definitions that are accessible from the current context. All specialised specification language constructs are removed from the normalised representation. This normalised representation is in the spirit of the kernel language used to define the formal semantics of the language, cf. [Breu et al. 91].

The normalisation, while flat, still retains structure. This is done by requiring that the local theory is accessed and filtered using the syntax of the original specification. For example, all objects relating to subtypes are represented with respect to their base types (plus appropriate restrictions). However, they may be accessed via a reference to their original subtype. Interface functions (available when defining transformations, tactics, and when browsing interactively) are also defined to allow filtered views of the local theory to be generated dependent upon context. Such mechanisms are necessary since, even for small specifications, the local theory is rather large.

In addition to the Proof Subsystem and the basic *Transformer Shell* described in § 8.4, there is another component in the system that can be used for proofs and as a transformer: the Conditional Equational Completion subsystem (see [Ganzinger 87], [Bertling et al. 91])

8.6. The Translators

The Translators at the back end of the system define projections from efficient PAnndA formulations of problem solutions to a target language for implementation and execution, cf. also the type definition schemes in § 8.3. The system currently supports a number of target languages (TrafoLa-H is a powerful, higher order language, with associated compiler and interpreter, for pattern matching and transformation, not discussed here; see [Heckmann, Sander 91], [Alt et al. 91]):

Language	Purpose
Ada, C	General program development
SSL	Definition of transformers to be incorporated into the Transformer Shell, and re-development of the system in itself
CSG Script	Formulation of executable development scripts and recording of histories
TrafoLa-H	Definition of transformers to be executed by a separate transformation engine

9. Meta Development and System Development

9.1. Meta Development in the System

Meta Program Development

Transformation development is done using the Meta Program Development Subsystem following the methodology for meta program development (cf. § 5, 6). Transformation rules are specified in TrafoLa-S, the transformation specification sublanguage of PAnndA-S. In addition to the PAnndA-S constructs, it contains some syntactic abbreviations for phrases (PAnndA program fragments in their concrete syntax form) and context-sensitive transformations to translate into canonical PAnndA-S.

Activity	Component
Specification of Transformations	TrafoLa-S Editor
Development of Meta Programs for Transformation	Transformer (General + TrafoLa)
Translating Transformations to SSL	Translator to SSL
Incorporation of Transformations into a Transformer	Configuration Manager, Synthesizer Generator

(9-1) Activities and Components for Meta Program Development

The subsystem for meta program development in (7-2) is another example for an instantiation of the generic development system; cf. also (9-1). The editor for TrafoLa-S is derived from that for PAnndA-S; the requirement specification is frozen; a PAnndA transformer with general transformations (and possibly special ones for meta development) is then applied to develop meta programs in the framework, and finally a particular kind of specification is compiled into an applicative tree manipulation program in SSL, the input language of the Synthesizer Generator. Note that in this case, objects produced by a particular target generator are subsequently incorporated into the system itself by the configuration manager. For example, a meta program for transformation may have been developed within the system; it is then compiled, integrated into a revision of the configuration of the transformer, and may then be executed with that version of the transformer in subsequent sessions.

Proof Tactics Development

The proof system also has an associated meta development component. Proof tactics development is carried out in exactly the same way as meta program development. The same components and languages are employed. The resulting transformations for proofs are then analogous to the tactics used in the LCF system [Gordon et al. 78]. An additional set of transformations is provided to allow the basic tactics for logical expressions to be developed into *true tactics*. Instead of merely transforming logical formulae, these *true tactics* generate proofs when applied to a logical formula (rather than just the result true or false). The proof trees correspond to the construction of a proof for a given logical formula. A typical scenario for meta proof development is given in (7-3), (9-2) .

Activity	Component
Specification of Tactics	Tactics (TrafoLa-S) Editor
Development of Transformations	Transformer (General Trafos)
Lifting Transformation (Expressions -> Proofs)	Transformer (Proof Generator Trafo)
Translating Tactics to SSL	Translator to SSL
Incorporation of Tactics into a Proof Editor	Configuration Manager, Synthesizer Generator

(9-2) Activities and Components for Proof Tactics Development

9.2. System Development

The System Development Subsystem (cf. (7-4), (9-3)) for the command language ControLa provides the facilities for enriching the development environment with new commands and scripts. Commands are formulated on the level of ControLa, an applicative subset of PAnndA-S. ControLa specifications are entered using the ControLa Editor, a restricted PAnndA-S editor, which checks that the specifications are within the ControLa subset of PAnndA-S. A translator is provided from ControLa specifications to executable implementations in terms of CSG scripts. In addition, a translation is provided from abstract CSG scripts (the form in which concrete developments are recorded, cf. § 8.1) to basic ControLa expressions. Concrete developments can therefore be manipulated and abstracted on the level of ControLa using the PROSPECTRA methodology; this provides the basis for abstraction from particular developments to general methods that can be re-used. Thus the ControLa subsystem is both a System Development and a "Development Development" Subsystem.

Activity	Component
Specification of (System) Developments	ControLa Editor
Development of Developments	Transformer (General Trafos)
Translating Developments to CSG Scripts	Translator to CSG Scripts

(9-3) Activities and Components for System Development

ControLa is restricted to the formulation of developments on pre-defined system objects. The system environment is specified in a pre-defined package that defines the types and the basic operations necessary to express system developments. It defines the basic notions of control such as (local) states, state transitions and composition of commands. The model of the system is in terms of state transitions and reflects the methodology by considering every activity as a transformation (cf. § 8.1).

Due to the unified approach to the system model and implementation, the user interacts by means of transformations on local states. The functions for formulating system development can be grouped into four categories: pure functions to compute values on predefined types such as integers, strings and booleans; constructor functions to manipulate abstract syntax trees (they are basically imported from the packages defining the abstract syntax trees of the various languages of the system), selection functions to extract information from a given state, and finally state transition functions that are the only ControLa functions capable of expressing side effects. User interactions have been modelled as non-strict (or lazy) state transition functions with user inputs defined in terms of non-strict parameters to functions.

9.3. Developing the System in Itself

All the various components of PROSPECTRA should, ultimately, be described as configurations of objects under the control of the library. Currrently, most of these objects have been written by hand in SSL, the specification language of the Synthesizer Generator. As the system evolves, such a representation of the system components then allows the re-development of these components within the sytem itself. Small pieces of a component can be replaced by an equivalent piece that has been completely developed within the PROSPECTRA system.

Re-generation of components should also be done from within the system. The transformations for re-generation of components take a revised configuration in the system part of the library for that component and generate commands that, when interpreted, result in a new version of the component being produced. If, for any reason, such a re-generation is not successful, then the old version of the component is obtained by backtracking in the development history for the component.

Such incremental re-development of the PROSPECTRA system, using the system and the PROSPECTRA methodology, imposes a number of restrictions upon the way in which the original system was developed. To re-develop the system in an incremental manner requires that sensible increments be defined. Also, these increments should have minimal couplings with other components within the current re-development. The original developer of the component has already chosen the, hopefully, cohesive increments for such re-development (defined by the structure of the source code and the inter-dependencies between source modules). This requires that the abstract and actual structure of the original component take into account the possibility of subsequent, transformational, re-development. The re-development of system components within the system may be seen as a kind on maintenance activity. Hopefully, components of the system have been structured in such a way so as not to hinder maintenance.

The re-development restriction arises from the nature of the re-development process; it is incremental. If the system was completely re-developed and re-implemented as a whole, such problems would not arise.

Re-development of Framework Components

The central constituents of the PROSPECTRA system, transformations, are already completely developed within the system as described above. However, the way in which re-development of one of the framework components, such as the proof subsystem, is undertaken, may illustrate how general system re-development is carried out.

Given a module, which has been developed within the system and is to be used to replace some existing system object, a configuration for the system component being developed must be identified. The configuration is then revised. The revision replaces the reference to the original, hand coded module with a reference to the new, transformationally developed module. For example, the propositional rules for the manipulation of sequents within the proof subsystem will be formulated in PA^{nn}dA-S and developed to an efficient implementation in SSL. The resultant SSL module replaces the existing module in the configuration of the proof subsystem.

From the configuration, a projection is defined that produces the dependency information required to generate a configuration control file. The configuration control file is subsequently used to control re-compilation of the component. A generate command is then issued that starts the re-generation process. The resultant component is finally added to the actual system configuration, a library object defining the structure of the whole PROSPECTRA development system.

10. Conclusion

Transformational Program Development

An overview of the PROSPECTRA methodology and its objectives has been given. The power of compact development methods using the transformational approach has been illustrated by an example in § 3.

Algebraic Specification and Functionals

The importance of the combination of algebraic specification with higher order functions has been stressed in § 4. The functional programming paradigm leads to a considerably higher degree of abstraction and avoids much repetitive development effort, in particular through the use of homomorphic extension functionals. Only the combination with algebraic specification allows reasoning about correctness. For example, the statement of properties for parameters of a functional (such as those of a monoid) are not possible in conventional functional programming languages. The (first order) algebraic properties of types with the (higher order) algebraic properties of functionals allow general and powerful optimisations.

Meta-Development and Formalisation of Program Development

An important aspect of the PROSPECTRA approach is its use for *meta-development* and formalisation of developments (§ 5, 6). The methodology and transformation technology for program development is carried over to the development of *transformation programs*. Moreover, an automatically generated transscript of a development "history" allows re-play upon re-development when requirements have changed, containing goals of the development, design decisions taken, and alternatives discarded but relevant for re-development. A *development script* is thus a formal object that does not only represent a documentation of the past but is also a plan for future developments. It can be used to abstract from a particular development to a class of similar developments, a *development method*, incorporating a certain strategy.

The approach of PROSPECTRA is to regard transformation rules as equations in an algebra of programs, to derive basic transformation operations from these rules, to allow composition and functional abstraction, and to regard development scripts as (compositions of) such transformation operations. Using all the results from program development based on algebraic specifications and functionals, we can then reason about the development of meta-programs, i. e. transformation programs or development scripts, in the same way as about programs: we can define requirement specifications (development goals) and implement them by various design strategies, and we can simplify development terms, re-play developments by interpretation, and abstract to development methods, incorporating formalised development tactics and strategies; in short, we can develop *correct*, efficient, complex transformation programs and development methods from elementary rules stated as algebraic equations. The abstraction from concrete developments to methods and the formalisation of programming knowledge as transformation rules + development methods will be a challenge for the future.

Uniformity of the Approach

Since any system interaction can be formalised as a transformation of some "program" (term), the PROSPECTRA approach leads to a uniform treatment of programming language, program manipulation and transformation language, proof and proof development language, also command language and even library access. This uniformity has been exploited in the PROSPECTRA system, see § 7 to § 9.

The specification language PAnndA-S is also used as the transformation specification language TrafoLa-S. In this case, an abstract type schema to define Abstract Syntax is predefined, and translation to the applicative tree manipulation language of the Synthesizer Generator [Reps, Teitelbaum 88] (used both as an Editor and as a Transformer Generator in the system) is automatic. ControLa, the command language of the system, is also a subset of PAnndA-S: development histories can be treated as formal objects, developed, translated to executable scripts, and (re-)played.

There is a close analogy to the development of efficient proof tactics for given proof or inference rules (transformation rules in the algebra of proofs). This is the basis for the development of the Proof Sub-system in PROSPECTRA, cf. § 8.3, § 8.5, [Traynor 89a, b].

Context-Sensitive Transformation, Filtering of Proof Obligations

Experience with the transformational approach and the implementation of non-trivial transformations has shown, that context-sensitivity of transformations is essential. Transformations need complex applicability conditions; thus the first requirement is that such conditions can be specified. As has been demonstrated in the examples, the combination of algebraic specification and restrictions on parameters (such as the monoid property) is quite powerful in this sense. Objects (and terms) can be "lifted" to meta-objects (and terms) and thus can become subject to manipulation during transformation and proof.

Furthermore, complex applicability conditions give rise to complex proof obligations. It is crucial to discard as many of them as possible automatically. The use of static semantic attributes, representing, for example, type information, allows the automatic check of static semantic conditions. A special context attribute, the "local theory"(cf. § 8.5), contains the set of all applicable axioms and theorems, accessible during proof. It also permits a search, during transformation, for some implicit parameters with certain restrictions (e.g. an associative operation and the corresponding neutral element), or some limited automatic theorem proving, leaving those conditions that need user interaction during proof as a residue. Thus a combination of compiler technology, theorem proving and a knowledge-based approach achieve the required filtering of proof obligations and need for interaction. This is one reason why the integration of construction and verification in the transformational approach of PROSPECTRA becomes practical.

Another use of attributes is the filtering of available transformations in the menue. It is quite important that those transformations that cannot be applied to a given term do not clutter the menue; they should be suppressed and not shown. Structural applicability is checked by the built-in pattern matching; (static) semantic applicability conditions can be defined to be checked automatically before the transformation is shown to be (potentially) applicable in the menue; others are only checked when the user has selected a transformation or are filtered out as residual proof obligations.

The Synthesizer Generator [Reps, Teitelbaum 88], one of the major tools to implement the system, provides trees with attributes and incremetal re-evaluation. However, parameters with interaction from the user, static applicability conditions, interaction with the Proof Editor, re-computation of the context when moving about in trees, recording of the development history etc. all had to be added to the Synthesizer Generator to adapt it to the needs of PROSPECTRA (cf. [de Miguel 91]).

Comparison with Other Approaches

From all the approaches and systems for transformational program development (cf. [Partsch, Steinbrüggen 83]), two should be mentioned here for comparison: CIP (cf. [Bauer et al. 85 - 87]) and KIDS (cf. [Smith, Lowry 90], [Smith 91]).Both support requirement specification and stepwise refinement with correctness-preserving transformations in a kind of wide-spectrum language. CIP is oriented towards a Pascal or Algol-like target language, KIDS towards REFINE. Neither system supports higher-order functions (but cf. [Möller 87]). Non-determinism as in CIP is not included in PROSPECTRA since it complicates the notion of equivalence of programs and therefore transformation; instead, it is replaced in PROSPECTRA (for most purposes) by a choice of model in a loose specification, even when specifying distributed systems with the aid of non-strict functions; this aspect is not treated here due to lack of space (cf. [Weber 91], [Broy 87-89]).

The KIDS system is mainly aimed at the algorithm design phase, from non-operational specifications. It is quite automatic but lacks a certain generality. The proof system is separate and not so smoothly integrated into the approach as in PROSPECTRA. Due to the use of the Synthesizer Generator, the PROSPECTRA system has a user-friendly interface (suppressing, e.g., non-applicable transformations from the menue) compared with CIP. The Library Manager in the PROSPECTRA system can save and retrieve development histories; this makes re-development possible.

The major difference in the approaches is the treatment of meta-development of compact transformations and methods. CIP allows composition of transformation rules etc. based on a notion of transformational expression; this is general and permits easy extension of transformation knowledge but does not allow the development of efficient transformation programs and compact abstract methods. KIDS has some powerful built-in design tactics, but no tactics definition facility is provided for the user.

Research Perspectives

Considerably more work is needed in the areas of automating the transformational process, development of efficient, compact context-sensitive transformations (using, e.g., incremental attribute evaluation), of a classification and categorisation of transformations in the system to allow specific sets of transformations to be used more effectively in a goal directed development situation, and of goal-orientation during transformation, driven by efficiency considerations and target systems, trying to assist the user in the choice of transformations and methods. The abstraction from concrete developments to development methods, incorporating formalised development tactics and strategies, and the formalisation of programming knowledge as transformation rules + development methods, will be a challenge for the future. Current research focusses on methods for the early stages of development to aid the finding of problem solutions and the synthesis of operational versions.

The experience of PROSPECTRA shows that more research is needed in specification language design, concerning, in particular, the structuring of specifications, programs, proofs and developments, i.e. development in-the-large. Structuring, e.g. by powerful mechanisms for abstraction and genericity, is crucial for the re-usability of specifications, programs, proofs and developments and thus a foundation for the development of libraries and standardisation of specifications etc. A starting point for the design of SPECTRAL ([Krieg-Brückner, Sannella 91]) was to combine the mutually complementary experiences of PROSPECTRA and Extended ML (for aspects of development in-the-large). SPECTRAL is very general and quite compact. It will be the basis for future work on a methodology and system, incorporating the aspects of uniformity described above.

Acknowledgements

We wish to thank the other members of the PROSPECTRA project, in particular Pedro de la Cruz, Bernd Gersdorf and Alain Marcuzzi, for their contributions, and Stefan Sokolowski for his suggestions.

References

[Alt et al. 91] Alt, M., Fecht, C., Ferdinand, C., Wilhelm, R.: TrafoLa-H Subsystem. *in* [Krieg-Brückner, Hoffmann 91], Part III.

[Bauer, Wössner 82] Bauer, F.L., Wössner, H.: *Algorithmic Language and Program Development.* Springer 1982.

[Bauer et al. 85] Bauer, F.L., Berghammer, R., Broy, M., Dosch, W., Gnatz, R., Geiselbrechtinger, F., Hangel, E., Hesse, W., Krieg.-Brückner, B., Laut, A., Matzner, T.A., Möller, B., Nickl, F., Partsch, H., Pepper, P., Samelson, K., Wirsing, M., Wössner, H.: *The Munich Project CIP, Part 1: The Wide Spectrum Language CIP-L. LNCS 183,* Springer 1985.

[Bauer et al. 87] Bauer, F.L., Ehler, H., Horsch, B., Möller, B., Partsch, H., Paukner, O., Pepper, P.,: *The Munich Project CIP, Part 2: The Transformation System CIP-S. LNCS 292,* Springer 1987.

[Bauer et al. 89] Bauer, F.L., Möller, B., Partsch, H., Pepper, P.: Formal Program Construction by Stepwise Transformations - Computer-Aided Intuition-Guided Programming.*IEEE Trans. on SW Eng. 15: 2* (1989) 165-180.

[Bertling et al. 91] Bertling, H., Ganzinger, H., Schäfers, R., Nieuwenhuis, R., Orejas, F.: Completion. and Completion Subsystem. *in* [Krieg-Brückner, Hoffmann 91], Part I and Part III.

[Bird 89] Bird, R.: Lectures on Constructive Functional Programming. *in*: Broy, M. (ed.): *Constructive Methods in Computing Science.* NATO ASI Series F55, Springer (1989) 151-218.

[Bird, Wadler 88] Bird, R., Wadler, Ph.: *Introduction to Functional Programming.* Prentice Hall, 1988.

[Böhm, Berarducci 85] Böhm, C., Berarducci, A.: Automatic Synthesis of Typed Lambda-Programs on Term Algebras. *Theoretical Computer Science 39* (1985) 135-154.

[Breu et al. 91] Breu, M., Broy, M., Grünler, T., Nickl, F.: Semantics of PAnndA-S. *in* [Krieg-Brückner, Hoffmann 91], Part II.

[Broy 87] Broy, M.: Predicative Specification for Functional Programs Describing Communicating Networks. *Information Processing Letters 25:2* (1987) 93-101.

[Broy 88] Broy, M.: An Example for the Design of Distributed Systems in a Formal Setting: The Lift Problem. Universität Passau, Tech. Rep. MIP 8802 (1988).

[Broy 89] Broy, M.: Towards a Design Methodology for Distributed Systems. *in:* Broy, M. (ed.): *Constructive Methods in Computing Science.* NATO ASI Series F55, Springer (1989) 311-364.

[Broy et al. 87] Broy, M., Pepper, P., Wirsing, M.: On the Algebraic Definition of Programming Languages. *ACM TOPLAS 9* (1987) 54-99.

[de la Cruz 91] de la Cruz, P., Mañas, J.L.: TrafoLa-S Reference Manual *and* TrafoLa-S Editor. *in* [Krieg-Brückner, Hoffmann 91], Part II and III.

[Feijs et al. 87] Feijs, L.M.G., Jonkers, H.B.M, Obbink, J.H., Koymans, P.P.J., Renardel de Lavalette, G.R., Rodenburg, P.M.: A Survey of the Design Language Cold. *in:* Proc. ESPRIT Conf. 86 (Results and Achievements). North Holland (1987) 631-644.

[Ganzinger 87] Ganzinger, H.: A Completion Procedure for Conditional Equations. Techn. Bericht No. 243, Fachbereich Informatik, Universität Dortmund, 1987 (also in *J. Symb. Comp.*)

[Gordon et al. 78] Gordon, M., Milner, R., Wadsworth, Ch.: Edinburgh LCF: A Mechanised Logic of Computation. *LNCS 78* .

[Heckmann, Sander 91] Heckmann, R., Sander, G.: TrafoLa-H Reference Manual. *in* [Krieg-Brückner, Hoffmann 91], Part II.

[Hoffmann, Shi 91] Hoffmann, B., Shi, H. (eds.): Annotated Bibliography of the PROSPECTRA Project. PROSPECTRA document P.M3-MM-17.10. Universität Bremen, 1991.

[Houdier 91] Houdier, D.: Library Manager. *in* [Krieg-Brückner, Hoffmann 91], Part III.

[Huet, Lang 78] Huet, G., Lang, B.: Proving and applying program transformations expressed as second order patterns. *Acta Informatica 11* (1978) 31-55.

[Jähnichen et al. 86] Jähnichen, S., Hussain, F.A., Weber, M.: Program Development Using a Design Calculus. *in:* Rogers, M. W. (ed.): *Results and Achievements,* Proc. ESPRIT Conf. '86 . North Holland (1987) 645-658.

[Karlsen, Krieg-Brückner, Traynor 91] Karlsen, E.W., Krieg-Brückner, B., Traynor, O.: The PROSPECTRA System: A Unified Development Framwork. In: Rus, T. (ed.): Proc. Second Conf. on Algebraic Methodology and Software Technology (AMAST), *LNCS* (1991) (to appear).

[Krieg-Brückner 87a] Krieg-Brückner, B.: Systematic Transformation of Interface Specifications. *in:* Meertens, L.G.T.L. (ed.): *Program Specification and Transformation,* Proc. IFIP TC2 Working Conf. (Tölz '86). North Holland (1987) 269-291.

397

[Krieg-Brückner 87b] Krieg-Brückner, B.: Integration of Program Construction and Verification: the PROSPECTRA Project. in: Habermann, N., Montanari, U. (eds.): Innovative Software Factories and Ada. Proc. CRAI Int'l Spring Conf. '86. *LNCS 275* (1987) 173-194.

[Krieg-Brückner 88a] Krieg-Brückner, B.: Algebraic Formalisation of Program Development by Transformation. *in:* Proc. European Symposium On Programming '88, *LNCS 300* (1988) 34-48.

[Krieg-Brückner 88b] Krieg-Brückner, B.: The PROSPECTRA Methodology of Program Development. *in:* Zalewski (ed.): Proc. IFIP/IFAC Working Conf. on HW and SW for Real Time Process Control (Warsaw). North Holland (1988) 257-271.

[Krieg-Brückner 89a] Krieg-Brückner, B.: Algebraic Specification and Functionals for Transformational Program and Meta-Program Development. *in:* Diaz, J., Orejas, F. (eds.): Proc. TAPSOFT '89 (Barcelona) Part 2. *LNCS 352* (1989) 36-59 (invited paper).

[Krieg-Brückner 89b] Krieg-Brückner, B.: Algebraic Specification with Functionals in Program Development by Transformation. *in:* Hünke, H. (ed.): *Proc. ESPRIT Conf. '89*, Kluver Academic Publishers (1989) 302-320.

[Krieg-Brückner 90] Krieg-Brückner, B.: PROgram development by SPECification and TRAnsformation. *Technique et Science Informatiques* Special Issue on *Software Engineering in ESPRIT* (1990) 136-149.

[Krieg-Brückner, Hoffmann 91] Krieg-Brückner, B., Hoffmann, B. (eds.): PROgram development by SPECification and TRAnsformation: Part I: Methodology, Part II: Language Family, Part III: System. PROSPECTRA Reports M.1.1.S3-R-55.2, -56.2, -57.2. Universität Bremen, 1990. (to appear in *LNCS* 1991).

[Krieg-Brückner, Sannella 91] Krieg-Brückner, B., Sannella, D.: Structuring Specifications in-the-Large and in-the-Small: Higher-Order Functions, Dependent Types and Inheritance in SPECTRAL. Proc TAPSOFT '91, *LNCS* (1991)

[Marcuzzi 91] Marcuzzi, A.: Controller *and* System Development. *in* [Krieg-Brückner, Hoffmann 91], Part III.

[de Miguel 91] de Miguel, J.A.: CSG Scripts Language *and* System Development Components. *in* [Krieg-Brückner, Hoffmann 91], Part II and III.

[Möller 87] Möller, B.: Algebraic Specification with Higher Order Operators. *in:* Meertens, L.G.T.L. (ed.): *Program Specification and Transformation*, Proc. IFIP TC2 Working Conf. (Tölz '86). North Holland (1987) 367-398.

[Partsch, Steinbrüggen 83] Partsch, H., Steinbrüggen, R.: Program Transformation Systems. *ACM Computing Surveys 15* (1983) 199-236.

[Reps, Teitelbaum 88] Reps., Teitelbaum: *The Synthesizer Generator and The Synthesizer Generator; Reference Manual.* Springer, 1988.

[Sintzoff 87] Sintzoff, M.: Expressing Program Developments in a Design Calculus. *in:* Broy, M. (ed.): *Logic of Programming and Calculi of Discrete Design.* NATO ASI Series, Part F36, Springer (1987) 343-365.

[Smith 85] Smith, D.R.: Top-Down Synthesis of Divide-and-Conquer Algorithms. *Artificial Intelligence 27:1* (1985) 43-95.

[Smith 91] Smith, D.R.: KIDS - a Knowledge-Based Software Development System. *Automating Software Design,:* AAAI Press (1991) (to appear).

[Smith, Lowry 90] Smith, D.R., Lowry, M.R.: Algorithm Theories and Design Tactics. *Science of Computer Programming 14:* (1990) 305-321.

[Traynor 89a] Traynor, O.: The Methodology of Verification in PROSPECTRA. PROSPECTRA Study Note S.3.4.-SN-19.0, University of Strathclyde, 1989. (in [Krieg-Brückner, Hoffmann 91], Part I)

[Traynor 89b] Traynor, O.: The PROSPECTRA Proof Editor. PROSPECTRA Study Note S.3.4.-SN-15.2, University of Strathclyde, 1989. (in [Krieg-Brückner, Hoffmann 91], Part III)

[von Henke 76] von Henke, F.W.: An Algebraic Approach to Data Types, Program Verification and Program Synthesis. *in:* Mazurkiewicz, A. (ed.): Mathematical Foundations of Computer Science 1976. *LNCS 45* (1976) 330-336.

[Weber 91] Weber, R.: Distributed Systems. *in* [Krieg-Brückner, Hoffmann 91], Part I.

[Wile 86a] Wile, D. S.: Program Developments: Formal Explanations of Implementations. *CACM 26:* 11 (1983) 902-911. *also in:* Agresti, W. A. (ed.): *New Paradigms for Software Development.* IEEE Computer Society Press / North Holland (1986) 239-248.

[Wile 86b] Wile, D. S.: Organizing Programming Knowledge into Syntax Directed Experts. Proc. Int'l Workshop on Advanced Programming Environments (Trondheim). *LNCS 244* (1986) 551-565.

The B-Method

J.-R. Abrial*   M. K. O. Lee   D. S. Neilson   P. N. Scharbach
I. H. Sørensen
Information Science and Engineering Branch
BP Research, Sunbury Research Centre
Sunbury-on-Thames, Middx TW16 7LN, UK

September 6, 1991

1   Introduction

Formal methods of software engineering offer a number of benefits. Firstly, they enable the production of reliable software systems for which all possible behaviours can be accurately predicted and verified to meet their functional specifications. Secondly, they have excellent potential for automation, which will reduce software production costs. Thirdly, they encourage accountability and reusability from specification through to coding, facilitating the task of software maintenance.

Existing applications of formal methods have failed to demonstrate these benefits convincingly. This can be traced to a lack of both a methodology and adequate tool support covering not only the application of formal methods to specification, but also to design through to coding.

The application of formal methods to real-life software is an impractical task (particularly for verification) without powerful tool support and the methodology must be geared up to the formal production of large software systems. The B technology (comprising three components - the B-method, the B-tool and the B Toolkit) is designed to scale up formal methods for practical application.

The B-method is a formal software development process for the production of highly reliable, portable and maintainable software which is verifiably correct with respect to its functional specification. The method uses the Abstract Machine Notation (AMN) as the language for specification, design and implementation within the process. AMN is a sugared and extended version of Dijkstra's guarded command notation [2], with built-in structuring mechanisms for the construction of large systems.

The method is supported over the entire spectrum of activities from specification to implementation by a set of computer-aided tools. The B Toolkit comprises automatic and

---

*Consultant to BP Research. Address: 26 rue des Plantes, Paris, France

interactive theorem-proving assistants and a set of software development tools: an AMN type checker, specification animator, proof obligation generator, and specification and code generators, integrated with the proof assistants into a window-based development environment. The development tools are all supported by a common platform: the B-tool. The latter is a program, based on a pattern-matching and rule-rewriting mechanism, for the introduction, manipulation and analysis of formal objects.

This paper discusses the B-method; for a description of the B-tool see [1]. Although the B Toolkit is not discussed in detail here, all elements of the B-method are fully supported.

2 The B-Method

We introduce first the notion of an Abstract Machine, and discuss some basic elements of AMN. This leads us to the Generalised Substitution Language (GSL), which provides the formal semantics for AMN. We then outline AMN concepts for structuring specifications. These are crucial for managing the sheer size of real-life specifications and their correctness proofs. Formal refinement within the B-method is then discussed. Finally, we turn our attention to the structuring of implementations within the method.

2.1 Abstract Machine Notation: Some Basic Concepts

In the B-method, specifications are organised and presented as Abstract Machines [3], formal state-based models immediately processible by the B Toolkit, which performs type checking, records dependencies and generates obligations for proving consistency. Clauses within the AMN declare a context of global constants, given abstract sets and their properties, to which reference may be made within the specification. Further Abstract Machine clauses provide a list of state variables, an invariant constraining and relating the state variables, and operations on the state variables, the latter having optional parameters and results. The operations provide the interface for the outside world to the state variables encapsulated within the Abstract Machine.

Abstract Machines may be parametrised (with possible parameter constraints) so that instances of machines can be reused in the incremental construction of more complex machines (see Section 2.3).

Proof of internal consistency of an Abstract Machine requires demonstration that within the context of the machine, each machine operation, when invoked within its stated precondition, maintains the invariant on the state variables, once the latter have been initialised to establish the invariant.

Thus if C is a predicate on the context of an Abstract Machine with parameter constraint predicate K, state invariant I and initialisation T, then for each operation S with precondition P, we have the proof obligations:

$$C \wedge K \Rightarrow \exists x.I$$

$$C \wedge K \Rightarrow [T]I$$

$$C \wedge K \wedge I \wedge P \Rightarrow [S]I$$

In the above, $[S]I$ is read as 'S establishes I'; the notation and interpretation are discussed further in section 2.2.

An element of the B Toolkit, the *Analyser*, automatically generates the specific proof obligations for an input Abstract Machine, reduced to set-theoretic lemmas on which the consistency proof depends. Proof of these lemmas may be undertaken using the B Toolkit proof assistants.

Operations are specified in a pre/post condition style: state variable changes are abstractly specified as substitutions of new values for old, under stated preconditions. Operations may be specified using a number of AMN constructs, which are a syntactic sugar for a basic set of generalised substitutions. The latter form the Generalised Substitution Language.

Another element of the B Toolkit, the *Animator*, allows symbolic execution of Abstract Machines, so that specifications can be tested against specific operational scenarios (usability testing).

2.2 The Generalised Substitution Language

The Generalised Substitution Language is used, in a sugared form, to specify Abstract Machine operations. GSL is a generalisation of Dijkstra's guarded command notation, enhanced with preconditioning and unbounded choice. Each generalised substitution S is defined as a predicate transformer (or function) which transforms a postcondition R into its weakest precondition $[S]R$. When the weakest precondition is satisfied, S is said to *establish* R. S may take any one of the following forms:

- $x := E$ (simple substitution):

  x is a variable and E is a set-theoretic expression. $[x := E]R \Leftrightarrow$ replacing all free occurrences of x in R by E.

- $x_1, .., x_n := E_1, .., E_n$ (multiple substitution):

  $x_1, .., x_n$ are distinct variables and $E_1, .., E_n$ are set-theoretic expressions. $[x_1, .., x_n := E_1, .., E_n]R \Leftrightarrow$ simultaneously replacing all free occurrences of $x_1, .., x_n$ in R by $E_1, .., E_n$ respectively.

- $x_1 := E_1 \parallel ... \parallel x_n := E_n$ (an alternative form for the above notation).

- *skip* (empty substitution or no-op):

  $[skip]R \Leftrightarrow R$.

- $P \mid S$ (preconditioning):

  P is a first order predicate, $[P \mid S]R \Leftrightarrow P \wedge [S]R$.

- $P \Longrightarrow S$ (guarding):

  P is a first order predicate, $[P \Longrightarrow S]R \Leftrightarrow P \Rightarrow [S]R$.

- $S1 \, [] \, S2$ (bounded choice):

  $[S1 \, [] \, S2]R \Leftrightarrow [S1]R \wedge [S2]R$.

- $@z \cdot S$ (unbounded choice):

  z is a distinct variable, $[@z \cdot S]R \Leftrightarrow \forall z \cdot [S]R$, where z is not free in R.

2.3 Structuring and Constructing Specifications

In order to manage the formal specification process it is essential that specifications can be constructed and verified in an incremental way, and that existing specifications can be reused to form new specifications. Whilst in the construction of programs we are concerned with separate compilation, in the construction of large specifications from component parts we are concerned with separate verification and proof.

The B-method achieves separate verification and proof by employing what we call the *semi-hiding principle*. Following this principle, a *variable* from one Abstract Machine can be used within other Abstract Machines but not modified from within a using machine. Hence, the invariants of a used machine do not add to the proof obligations of a using machine.

Within AMN, existing Machines with distinct variables can be *used* to form new specifications following the semi-hiding principle. Machine *parametrisation* and *renaming* mechanisms allow for particular instances of different machines, as well as distinct copies of the same machine, to be used within a single new machine.

The *variables* of a constructed machine include the collection of variables from each of the *used* machines; the *invariant* includes the conjunction of the invariants from each individual machine. New variables can be introduced and new invariant conditions (a 'glueing invariant') can be imposed. The initialisations from the used machines are inherited.

An *operation* from a used machine may be *promoted*, in which case it becomes an operation of the new machine. Also, new operations can be constructed from existing operations. The theory of Abstract Machines (together with the semi-hiding principle) guarantees that all existing invariants are re-established by the newly constructed operation without the need for further proof. Hence, it is sufficient to prove that the new operations re-establish the new invariants. Furthermore, certain common subsequent modifications to the used machines (e.g. strengthening of the invariant) do not affect the using machine.

The theory of Generalised Substitutions includes laws which permit the *calculation* of their weakest preconditions.

In the construction of new operations an existing operation can be further constrained by adding a new precondition, the operation can be applied conditionally and, most importantly, operations from different machines can be put together to operate in parallel (using $\|$).

Given S from one machine and T, U from another, we have laws such as :

$S \, \| \, skip = S$

$S \, \| \, (P \, | \, T) = P \, | \, (S \, \| \, T)$

$$S \parallel (T [] U) = (S \parallel T) [] (S \parallel U)$$

$$S \parallel (P \Longrightarrow T) = P \Longrightarrow (S \parallel T) \text{ if } S \text{ 'terminates'.}$$

$$S \parallel @z \cdot T = @z \cdot (S \parallel T) \text{ if } z \text{ is not free in } S.$$

The construction of large specifications can be complex and machine support is essential to manage the process. The B Toolkit provides a set of tools for managing the files which make up a single software development. A *Configuration* tool automatically maintains and presents the dependencies between individual constructs. A *Status* tool records and presents the status of the development path, (including the proportion of proof obligations currently discharged at each stage). A *Checkpoint/Remake* tool allows for the restoration of proofs after selected modification.

2.4 Refinement of Abstract Machines

An Abstract Machine specification is not necessarily executable, and certainly the abstract model of the state of the machine as well as the formulation of the operations can not readily be translated into executable code (nondeterminism being an important aspect of abstraction). To facilitate translation into code, the Abstract Machines must be *refined*.

Within the B-method a *refinement* of an Abstract Machine allows us to *change* the model of the state in order to get closer to the data structures of the final implementation: this is called *data refinement*. This is achieved by means of a change of variables, and a set of new operations which refine each of those in the original machine. The new operations are simply those of the original machine with the change of variables performed.

Operations may also be reformulated without changing the state model, using an extension to the GSL of Section 2.2 which allows for the sequential composition as well as the iteration of substitutions. The reformulation is intended to be closer to the control structure of the final code. This is referred to as *algorithmic refinement*. The GSL laws for the sequencing and loop constructs are:

$$[S; T]R \Leftrightarrow [S][T]R$$

and

$$[T]Q \wedge$$
$$\forall d \cdot (Q \Rightarrow V \in NAT) \wedge$$
$$\forall d \cdot (Q \wedge G \Rightarrow [S]Q) \wedge$$
$$\forall d \cdot (Q \wedge G \Rightarrow [n := V][S](V < n)) \wedge$$
$$\forall d \cdot (Q \wedge \neg G \Rightarrow R)$$
$$\Rightarrow$$
$$[T; \textbf{while } G \textbf{ do } S \textbf{ invariant } Q \textbf{ variant } V \textbf{ end}]R$$

A series of refinements is typically carried out before a satisfactory formulation is achieved, each being a data or algorithmic refinement, or a combination of the two.

The refinement relation defined within the B-method possesses some fundamental properties which are of great practical importance in performing incremental development and proof. The refinement relation is *transitive*, which means that we can incrementally verify the final implementation by verifying each individual refinement step. The refinement relation is *monotonic* with respect to all the constructs of the Generalised Substitution Language, which means that the subcomponents of an operation refinement can be refined independently.

The refinement of an Abstract Machine incurs a number of proof obligations. We consider the most general case of simultaneous data and algorithmic refinement. Let y be the list of state variables of the machine to be refined, I the machine invariant, B the initialisation, P the precondition of an operation of the machine, and K the operation (generalised substitution), with optional results r. Further, let z be the list of state variables of the refinement, J a predicate relating the state variables of the Abstract Machine and its refinement, C the initialisation of the refinement, Q the precondition of the refined operation, and L the refined operation (generalised substitution). Then the proof obligations for the correctness of the refinement of the machine are:

$$\exists y \cdot I$$

$$[B]I$$

$$\forall y \cdot (I \wedge P \Rightarrow [K]I)$$

$$\exists y, z \cdot (I \wedge J)$$

$$[C]\neg[B]\neg J$$

$$\forall y, z \cdot (I \wedge J \wedge P \Rightarrow Q \wedge [L']\neg[K]\neg(J \wedge r = r'))$$

In the last proof obligation above, L' stands for the substitution L within which the variable r has been replaced by r'.

On submission of a proposed refinement to the *Analyser* tool, the corresponding abstraction is automatically identified and proof obligations are generated by comparing the refinement against the specification. The GSL laws above are used by the tool to reduce the proof obligations to a number of set-theoretic lemmas. Their proof may then be undertaken using the proving tools. This process requires no manual intervention by the user.

2.5   Structuring and Implementing Designs

In AMN an *implementation* of a specification or refinement is given by providing a concrete algorithm for each of the specified operations. These algorithms are written in AMPL (Abstract Machine Programming Language). Although the language resembles the notation used in refinements, non-executable constructs (e.g. unbounded choice, preconditioning, ||) are not allowed, whilst executable constructs such as sequential composition (;) and iteration (**while...**) are.

An implementation is still an Abstract Machine (variables with associated substitutions), and can therefore be checked against its specification using the rules for correctness for refinements. However, the formulation of an implementation now lends itself readily to translation into a 'safe' subset of an existing programming language, such as C, Pascal or Ada. This translation is carried out by coding assistants within the B Toolkit. The automatic translation into code gives rise to further proof obligations to be discharged.

An important aspect of design within the B-method is the use of existing Abstract Machines within an implementation. This allows us to construct designs - and large software systems - in the same way as we construct specifications. An Abstract Machine together with its operations can be *imported* into an *implementation*, making the imported variables (state) and the imported operations 'known' to the importing machine.

The special rules for importation (called *full hiding*) ensure that the correctness of an implementation depends only on the abstract specifications of the imported machines (i.e. independent of their refinements). The full hiding principle dictates that the imported variables cannot be modified or used within the algorithms of the implementation. This principle ensures that the importing *implementation* and the imported machines can be separately verified. It ensures also that the imported machines can be independently refined, implemented and modified so long as they meet their original specifications. This clearly has important benefits in the construction of a large software system.

The machine *parametrisation* and *renaming* mechanisms allow the importation of particular instances of different machines, as well as distinct copies of the same machine, into a single implementation.

The *variables* of an implementation consist of the collection of variables from each of the *imported* machines; the *invariant* includes the conjunction of the invariants from each individual machine. New invariant conditions ('glueing invariants') can be imposed. Note that none of the variables is used or modified directly by the importing implementation.

When constructing a design (*implementation*) using importation we must ensure that all the operations meet their specifications. The rules for operation implementation are identical to the rules for operation refinement. In addition, we must ensure that all imported operations are used within their preconditions.

The GSL can be used for the construction of new algorithms employing imported operations. The laws for the *calculation* of the weakest preconditions of these algorithms, which take the preconditions of used operations into account, allow us to fully verify such algorithms. All these laws are used by the B Toolkit verification condition generator (the *Analyser*).

The B Toolkit is being extended to cover all stages of the development process. The *Configuration, Status* and *Remake* tools control the dependencies between the files for specification, refinement and implementation as well as the files for their related proof obligations. However the tools have yet to be extended to administer the dependencies between these files and the final code modules.

3 Conclusion

The B-method is designed to provide a homogeneous language and a methodology for the formal specification, design and implementation of real-life software systems. Therefore, the features of incremental construction and proof have been guiding principles in its development. A full account of the B-method and its theoretical foundations is to appear shortly as a book by J.-R. Abrial. An environment, the B Toolkit, supports formal development activities from specification to coding. The toolkit itself is supported by a platform, the B-tool, which is now commercially available from Edinburgh Portable Compilers Ltd. The B Toolkit will soon be ready for alpha testing, and it is planned to make it commercially available in due course.

References

[1] *B-Tool User Manual* and *B-Tool Reference Manual*. Edinburgh Portable Compilers Ltd., 1991.

[2] Dijkstra, E.W. A Discipline of Programming. Prentice Hall, 1976.

[3] Abrial, J.-R. A Formal Approach to Large Software Construction, in *Mathematics of Program Construction* (ed. J. L. A. van de Snepscheut). Springer Verlag, 1989.

Mathematical Methods
for Digital Systems Development

Donald I. Good and William D. Young[*]

Computational Logic, Inc.
1717 West Sixth Street, Suite 290
Austin, Texas 78703-4776
good@cli.com, young@cli.com

1 Introduction

As the effects of electronic computing become increasingly pervasive, the potential for serious negative consequences caused by malfunctioning or incorrect computing systems also increases. Errors in digital systems usually result from the failure of the designers to accurately *predict* the behavior of their system under intended circumstances of use, or to *foresee* novel conditions of use for which the system was not originally intended.

The potential for failure of software, particularly, has increased in recent years as software has grown explosively in size and complexity. Commercial aircraft often have tens or hundreds of thousands of lines of operational code. Accounting and weapons systems routinely have code measured in millions of line. This explosion in software size has reached what some sceptics would consider absurd heights with the proposed Strategic Defense Initiative, certainly the most ambitious software project ever conceived. Its designers have envisioned fielding a system estimated to contain up to 40,000,000 lines of code. Merely coordinating such a vast endeavor and assuring that

[*]This work was supported in part at Computational Logic, Inc., by the Defense Advanced Research Projects Agency. The views and conclusions contained in this document are those of the author(s) and should not be interpreted as representing the official policies, either expressed or implied, of Computational Logic, Inc., the Defense Advanced Research Projects Agency or the U.S. Government.

the myriad pieces fit together smoothly is a monumental task, leading many to question whether such a project could ever succeed.

In addition to the complexity arising from the sheer size of the code, inherently more complex application domains are coming increasingly under automatic control. Modern concurrent, distributed, and real-time applications often involve subtle time-dependent and sequence-dependent interactions among multiple processors or interactions with an unpredictable physical environment. Such applications severely tax the analytic powers of the human charged with assuring the quality and "correctness" of the code. Humans are notoriously poor at managing the kinds of complexity found in these applications. When the stakes are raised with the addition of critical safety and security concerns, effectively eliminating any margin for error, the point is quickly reached where the types of informal analysis traditionally applied to achieve software quality becomes totally inadequate to gain acceptable levels of assurance.

This inability to gain adequate assurance in the quality of software contributes to the much-lamented "software crisis" described as follows in a U.S. congressional staff report.

> As the complexity of systems increases, Government managers find that the software they buy or develop does not achieve the capabilities contracted for, that it is not delivered at the time specified, and that the cost is significantly greater than anticipated. Indeed, many recent examples of cost overruns and degraded capability cited as examples of Government waste, fraud and abuse can be related to problems in the development of computer software.[10]

The standard approach to attaining assurance in the correctness of software is to test it. Testing is an *inductive* approach to predicting software behavior. Programs are tested on a selection of potential inputs; software modules that behave adequately for these inputs are deemed suitably reliable. Modules that misbehave on test cases are "patched" until adequate behavior is attained. Critics of this approach to enhancing software reliability often quote the famous aphorism of Edsger Dijkstra that testing "can be used to show the presence of bugs but never to show their absence." Of course, some small programs can be exhaustively tested. It is usually infeasible, however, to assure the absence of errors by testing because, except for the most trivial programs, the potential input space is simply too large for exhaustive testing. Hence, according to well-accepted industry figures, software produced by standard "good" software engineering practice typically contains around 1-3 errors per 1000 lines of code. At this rate, a software system of 1,000,000 lines of code could be expected to contain 1,000 to 3,000 errors. Though there is a large research community investigating ways to improve the efficacy of testing, testing alone is clearly limited.

The field that has come to be known loosely as *formal methods* attempts to achieve software reliability by applying mathematical modeling in the construction of digital systems. Using rigorous and mathematically-based techniques that model programs and computing systems as mathematical entities, practitioners of formal methods attempt to *prove* that program models meet their specifications for all potential inputs. This approach augments traditional testing-based software engineering practice with *deductive* approaches to predicting software behavior and offers promise for enhancing the quality of software, at least in selected applications.

Of course, actual computing systems–physical machines and the software that runs on them–are not mathematical abstractions. It is only *models* of these physical systems that are accessible to rigorous mathematical reasoning techniques. Care must be taken in validating that such models capture relevant aspects of our systems and in extrapolating the results of the mathematical analysis to the physical reality. But, carefully applied, these methods can significantly improve the predictability and reliability of computing systems.

In the remainder of this paper we explore the role of formal methods in digital systems engineering and illustrate one significant application of formal methods–the construction of a hierarchical verified systems. This system comprises a compiler for a simple high-level language, an assembler and link-loader for an assembly level language, and a microprocessor with its gate level realization. We also describe a verified multi-tasking operating system.

2   Mathematical Modeling in Engineering

The key concept underlying the application of formal methods is the notion of a mathematical *model* of a computing system. We will shortly discuss models of several moderately complex systems. But first, to understand the potential contribution of mathematical models to software engineering, consider the role of models in a more traditional engineering discipline such as civil engineering, as in the design and construction of a bridge.

The civil engineer brings to this task a wealth of knowledge cultivated through a long process of education, apprenticeship, and practice. He or she has a keen grasp of the principles of structural dynamics, stress analysis, properties of materials, and diverse other fields relevant to this discipline. Moreover, our engineer has available an extensive catalogue of sound principles of design, well-tested engineering techniques, and previously successful design examples. On the basis of this solid foundation of knowledge and experience, the engineer produces an initial design (model) that specifies the structure of the bridge, length of spans, the size and composition of supporting members, etc. The development of this design is a highly creative process guided by the overriding goal of a structurally sound, functionally suitable, and aesthetically pleasing end product.

With an initial model or design in hand, by the application of well-understood mathematical techniques the engineer can *calculate* whether a bridge built according to this design will perform its intended function and support the expected load. This process of verifying mathematically the properties of the design is essentially a partial "proof of correctness" of the design, i.e, rigorous evidence that the design meets its specifications. Often these calculations will show the engineer's initial design to be perfectly adequate. This is not too surprising since the design process itself was guided at every step by good engineering principles and accompanied by an ongoing process of mathematically verifying portions of the design before they were incorporated into the evolving whole. A design "proven" in this manner can guide the construction of the bridge with a high degree of confidence that the resulting structure will stand the load.

Certainly, structurally sound bridges were built before sophisticated analytic techniques were available. The *Pons Fabricus* of Rome is still in use almost twenty centuries after its construction. But its longevity is due largely to the fact that, from a modern standpoint, it was massively "overengineered" for its expected load of ancient carts and foot traffic. The Roman engineers did not have available the mathematical modeling techniques that allow their modern counterparts to calculate stresses in their designs and hence compute safety factors. The result was obviously quite durable, but also much more massive and costly to build than other structures that would have sufficed.

Using mathematical modeling in any engineering discipline is not infallible, of course. A memorable experience in many engineering students' educations is viewing the riveting 1940 film of the collapse of the Tacoma

Narrows bridge. This film is a spectacular reminder of the limitations of even good engineering practice. Moreover, it illustrates a fundamental limitation of modeling; by definition a model is an abstraction of reality. A model may abstract away or simply overlook factors that ultimately prove to be important. The results, as with the Tacoma Narrows bridge, can be catastrophic.

Still, no modern engineer would seriously suggest abandoning mathematical modeling in civil engineering. The use of mathematical techniques to investigate properties of a design *before* it is realized in steel and concrete yields too many significant benefits. These include the obvious benefits of cost reduction and enhanced assurance that the design is safe. Less obvious are the concomitant benefits including: more efficient use of materials; discovery and elimination of errors early in the design process; the ability to efficiently investigate multiple design options; the possibility of automated assistance in the design process; enhanced communication between the design and construction teams; and better documentation of design decisions. Moreover, a widely used common formal notation for expressing designs aids the development of a convenient and accessible archive of engineering successes that other designers can study and emulate; that is, designs become more readily reusable. Because of these benefits of mathematical modeling, a modern civil engineer would never adopt the approach to bridge design of "let's build it and see if it works." Yet amazingly this is a common approach to the construction of complex digital systems.

3 Applying Mathematical Modeling to Digital System Design

The field of formal methods attempts to gain the benefits of mathematical modeling in the design of digital systems in much the same way that modeling is used in design in more established engineering disciplines. Exactly what falls under the umbrella of "formal methods" is widely debated, but it includes at least:

- *specification*: the use of a standard notation to describe desired behavior or properties of a system;

- *verification*: the application of rigorous reasoning techniques to assure that a program satisfies its specification;

- *transformation*: use of (correct) semantics-preserving transitions to develop an implementation from a specification.

Notice from our previous discussion that each of these activities have analogues in traditional civil engineering practice.

Specification is merely the statement of desired properties of a design, whether that design is of a bridge or of a computing system. Those properties may be stated informally in English or some other natural language, or formally in the language of mathematical logic or another notation. Since a natural language like English is notoriously ambiguous, it is desirable for significant designs that the specification be captured in some standardized notation if possible. Of course, there are likely to be less readily quantifiable or formalizable aspects of the design as well, eg. involving aesthetic concerns and the degree to which the design harmonizes with its intended setting. This means that formal specifications are usually only partial specifications. For any realistic system, there are desirable properties that it is not possible or desirable to formalize.

Over the past few years a variety of specification languages have been devised; some of the most widely used being Z, VDM, Larch, Gypsy, and OBJ. Though some of them have been used for specifying systems other than computing systems, for our purposes we view the role of a specification language as providing a well-defined and unambiguous formalism for expressing desired properties of computing systems. Some of these languages take a *declarative* approach in which the desired properties of the system are stated without reference to the mechanisms by which these ends are attained. Other languages take a more *procedural* approach in which the properties are stated in terms of an "abstract implementation" of the system displaying one way in which the desired results can be obtained. Available formalisms range from the structured version of first-order logic and elementary set theory found in Z to the full-blown programming language including concurrency and data abstraction found in Gypsy.

Verification is the process of establishing rigorously that a design meets or satisfies (some of) its specifications. For a bridge design, "verification" may involve computation of the stress that the design will bear and determination whether the resulting safety factor is adequate for the intended traffic. For a program it means showing through rigorous analysis that every execution of the program will have the desired effect. Some of the desirable properties of a design may not be suitable for verification. The aesthetic properties of a bridge or the efficiency of a computing system may be left unspecified, and hence are "verified" only informally.

Finally, transformation involves the derivation of a more complete design from a less complete one or from a specification. In civil engineering, an earlier design may be adapted to meet a later need, or a chief engineer's design may be elaborated by his or her assistants according to accepted engineering principles and practice. In programming, it may mean the modification of a program via various semantics-preserving transformations to gain additional efficiency or functionality, or the instantiation of a program "schema" to gain an instance suitable for some programming task.

To allow either verification or transformation, there must be an underlying *logic* for reasoning about specifications and programs and proving appropriate relationships between them. That is, a specification language by itself is not very useful unless there are rules of inference by which the specification can be related to an implementation. The most crucial property of such a logic is *soundness*–it should be impossible to derive any false conclusion from true premises using the rules of inference of the logic. Lack of soundness in the logic may permit a program to be "proven" to meet its specifications when it actually does not do so.

Often, automated assistance is available for recognizing (parsing) specifications and programs, for processing and storing them, and for reasoning about them. These range from simple parsers for checking the syntactic adequacy of specifications to complete verification systems providing automated support for all phases of the verification process. For example, one of the most mature implementations of formal methods for software development, is the Gypsy Verification Environment[1]. This system provides automated support for interactively editing programs and specifications, parsing them, generating logical formulas sufficient to assure that a program satisfies its specifications, checking the proofs of those formulas, and interactively modifying a program and its specifications while maintaining an accurate view of the changing proof status of the program.

4   The Boyer-Moore Logic and Theorem Prover

A wide diversity of methods and automated systems that support their use are available. To illustrate the utility of formal methods, we concentrate in this paper on one approach used at Computational Logic, Inc. in developing a highly reliable *hierarchically verified* computing system. This is the logic devised by Robert S. Boyer and J Strother Moore and its supporting proof system[4, 5].

The Boyer-Moore logic is a simple quantifier-free, first-order logic resembling in syntax and semantics the Lisp programming language. Terms in the logic are written using a prefix syntax–we write (PLUS I J) where others might write PLUS(I,J) or I+J. The logic is formally defined as an extension of propositional calculus with variables, function symbols, and the equality relation. Axioms are added defining the following:

- the Boolean (logical) constants (TRUE) and (FALSE), abbreviated T and F;

- the if-then-else function, IF, with the property that (IF x y z) is z if x is F and y otherwise;

- the Boolean connectives AND, OR, NOT, and IMPLIES;

- the equality function EQUAL, with the property that (EQUAL x y) is T or F according to whether x is y;

- and inductively constructed objects including natural numbers, ordered pairs, and literal atoms.

In addition, there is the ability within the logic to add user-defined inductive data structures.

The logic also provides a principle of recursive definition under which new function symbols may be introduced. The following, for example, is a definition within the logic of a list concatenation function APPEND.

```
(APPEND X Y) = (IF (LISTP X)
                   (CONS (CAR X) (APPEND (CDR X) Y))
                   Y).
```

This equation submitted as a definition is accepted as a new axiom under certain conditions that guarantee that one and only one function satisfies the equation. One of these conditions is that certain derived formulas be theorems. Intuitively, these formulas insure that the recursion terminates by exhibiting a "measure" of the arguments that decreases, in a well-founded sense, in each recursive call of the function.

The rules of inference of the logic, in addition to those of propositional calculus and equality, include mathematical induction. The formulation of the induction principle is similar to that of the definitional principle. To justify an induction schema it is necessary to prove certain theorems that establish that, under a given measure, the inductive hypotheses are about "smaller" objects than the conclusion. Using induction it is possible to prove such theorems as the associativity of the APPEND function defined above; this can be stated as a theorem in the logic.

```
Theorem ASSOCIATIVITY-OF-APPEND
(EQUAL (APPEND (APPEND A B) C)
       (APPEND A (APPEND B C)))
```

Notice that this theorem provides a partial *specification* of the APPEND function. It is one of myriad properties of this function and its relation to others that can be defined and proved within the logic. Notice also that this theorem, once proven, becomes available for use in the proofs of subsequent theorems. In particular, we can use it as a *rewrite rule*–i.e., we can interpret it as sanctioning the replacement of any expression that matches the left hand side of the equality by the corresponding instance of the right hand side. Thus, for example, the expression

```
(APPEND (APPEND V (APPEND W X)) (APPEND Y Z))
```

can be readily shown to be equal to

```
(APPEND V (APPEND W (APPEND X (APPEND Y Z))))
```

by two applications of ASSOCIATIVITY-OF-APPEND interpreted as a rewrite rule. By defining and proving rewrite rules, it is possible to build up a powerful theory for proving interesting facts about a specific domain.

As we will illustrate shortly, the Boyer-Moore logic can be used to build mathematical models of even quite complex computing systems and to state interesting properties of them. Since the logic contains rules of inference, it is also possible to construct proofs of these properties as in any of the more familiar formal mathematical systems. However, as mathematical objects, models of large scale computing systems tend to be quite complex. Proofs of their properties are often highly repetitive, involving a large number of cases and sometimes tedious low-level reasoning. As noted earlier, humans are notoriously poor at managing this type of complexity. Automated proof assistance can help in managing complexity and in guaranteeing that cases are not overlooked. Much of the most tedious reasoning can be done mechanically.

A powerful mechanical theorem proving program has been written by Boyer and Moore for reasoning about expressions in their logic (and distributed free of charge via anonymous file transfer). The Boyer-Moore theorem prover is a computer program that takes as input a conjecture formalized as a term in the logic and attempts to prove it by repeatedly transforming and simplifying it. The theorem prover employs eight basic transformations:

- decision procedures for propositional calculus, equality, and linear arithmetic;

- rewriting based on axioms, definitions and previously proved lemmas;

- automatic application of user-supplied simplification procedures that have been proven correct;

- elimination of calls to certain functions in favor of others that are "better" from a proof perspective;

- heuristic use of equality hypotheses;

- generalization by the replacement of terms by variables;

- elimination of apparently irrelevant hypotheses; and

- mathematical induction.

The theorem prover contains many heuristics to control the orchestration of these basic techniques.

The system displays a script of the proof attempt allowing the user to follow the progress of the proof and take steps to abort misdirected proof attempts. From the script it is often apparent to the skilled user how to improve the prover's knowledge base so that a subsequent proof attempt will succeed. The script printed by the prover in discovering the proof of the lemma ASSOCIATIVITY-OF-APPEND is shown in Figure 1.

In a shallow sense, the prover is fully automatic; the system accepts no advice or directives from the user once a proof attempt has started. The only way the user can alter the behavior of the system during a proof attempt is to abort the attempt. However, in a deeper sense, the theorem prover is interactive; the system's behavior is influenced by the data base of lemmas that have already been formulated by the user and proved by the system. Each conjecture, once proved, is converted into one or more rules and stored in the prover's database to guide the theorem prover's actions in subsequent

```
(prove-lemma associativity-of-append (rewrite)
      (equal (append (append x y) z)
      (append x (append y z))))
```

Call the conjecture *1.

Perhaps we can prove it by induction. Three inductions are suggested by terms in the conjecture. They merge into two likely candidate inductions. However, only one is unflawed. We will induct according to the following scheme:

```
(AND (IMPLIES (AND (LISTP X) (p (CDR X) Y Z))
                   (p X Y Z))
     (IMPLIES (NOT (LISTP X)) (p X Y Z))).
```

Linear arithmetic and the lemma CDR-LESSP can be used to prove that the measure (COUNT X) decreases according to the well-founded relation LESSP in each induction step of the scheme. The above induction scheme leads to two new goals:

```
Case 2. (IMPLIES (AND (LISTP X)
                      (EQUAL (APPEND (APPEND (CDR X) Y) Z)
                             (APPEND (CDR X) (APPEND Y Z))))
                 (EQUAL (APPEND (APPEND X Y) Z)
                        (APPEND X (APPEND Y Z)))),
```

which simplifies, applying the lemmas CDR-CONS and CAR-CONS, and opening up the definition of APPEND, to:

    T.

```
Case 1. (IMPLIES (NOT (LISTP X))
                 (EQUAL (APPEND (APPEND X Y) Z)
                        (APPEND X (APPEND Y Z)))),
```

which simplifies, unfolding the function APPEND, to:

    T.

That finishes the proof of *1. Q.E.D.

Figure 1: Proof of the lemma ASSOCIATIVITY-OF-APPEND

proof attempts. Often these are rewrite rules, but there are other specialized types of rules as well.

A data base is thus more than a logical theory; it is a set of rules for proving theorems in the given theory. The user leads the theorem proved to difficult proofs by programming its rule base. Given a goal theorem, the user generally discovers a proof himself, identifies the key steps in the proof and then formulates them as lemmas, paying particular attention to their interpretation as rules. The key role of the user in the system is guiding the theorem prover to proofs by the strategic selection of the sequence of theorems to prove and the proper formulation of those theorems. Successful users of the system must know how to prove theorems in the logic and must understand how the theorem prover interprets them as rules.

Using this approach the Boyer-Moore prover has been used to check the proofs of some quite deep theorems.[1] For example, some theorems from traditional mathematics that have been mechanically checked using the system include proofs of: the existence and uniqueness of prime factorizations; Gauss' law of quadratic reciprocity; the Church-Rosser theorem for lambda calculus; the infinite Ramsey theorem for the exponent 2 case; and Goedel's incompleteness theorem. Somewhat outside the range of traditional mathematics, the theorem prover has been used to check: the recursive unsolvability of the halting problem for Pure Lisp; the proof of invertibility of a widely used public key encryption algorithm; the correctness of metatheoretic simplifiers for the logic; the correctness of a simple real-time control algorithm; the optimality of a transformation for introducing concurrency into sorting networks; and the correctness of an implementation of an algorithm for achieving agreement among concurrently executing processes in the presence of faults. When connected to a specialized front-end for Fortran, the system has also proved the correctness of Fortran implementations of a fast string searching algorithm and a linear time majority vote algorithm. Many other interesting theorems have been proven as well.

It is important to note that all of these proofs were checked by the same general purpose theorem prover, not a number of specialized routines optimized for specific problems. Still, despite its apparent versatility and mathematical acumen, the Boyer-Moore theorem prover does not have any deep mathematical insight. The proof of each of these quite difficult theorems was achieved through the clever automated heuristic application of

---

[1]Some of these proofs used the interactive enhancement to the Boyer-Moore prover developed by Matt Kaufmann[8].

some simple proof strategies and through the development of powerful theories under the guidance of a human mathematician. The theorem prover's contribution is in assuring the soundness and consistency of the result and in attending to many of the low-level proof chores and record keeping for which the human is ill-suited. This is not to say that mechanical provers could not make a genuine contribution to the more "creative" aspects of mathematics. For example, mechanical theorem provers developed by L. Wos and his colleagues at the Argonne National Laboratories have answered a number of previously open questions in mathematics[12]. For the foreseeable future, however, mechanical provers are likely to remain a useful tool of human mathematicians rather than a replacements for them.

In assuring the correctness of computing system, a powerful prover such as the Boyer-Moore prover can play several useful roles. Many of the theorems that arise in context of program verification are relatively uninteresting from a mathematical perspective yet may be quite tedious to prove, requiring the handling of numerous quite similar cases. One useful role for a mechanical prover is in assuring that all cases are covered and in handling much of the low-level proof effort. That is, the prover can be used as the "proof engine" in a system that processes specifications and programs, even if those specification and programs are not expressed directly within the Boyer-Moore logic. It need only be possible to translate conjectures into the Boyer-Moore logic for presentation to the theorem prover. An earlier version of the Boyer-Moore prover was used in this fashion in the Hierarchical Development Methodology[11] of Stanford Research Institute.

An alternative approach is to use the Boyer-Moore logic directly as a specification language. Within the logic it is possible to model interesting computing systems and to state desired properties of them. With the support of the theorem prover we can then develop proofs of these properties, i.e. verify the system with respect to its specification.

An approach that has been used successfully by the author and others has been to model computing system as abstract "machines" defined as function in the logic. Such an abstract machine is a mathematical model characterizing each possible operation in the system by its effect on a "state"; this model gives an *operational* characterization of the behavior of the machine.

5   Mathematical Modeling of Digital Systems

Consider modeling a typical computer at the assembly language level. At each step in the execution of a program, the machine retrieves an instruction from memory and executes it; this is the so-called "fetch-execute cycle" of the machine. To model the execution of the machine for N steps we define the function:

```
(MACHINE STATE N) = (IF (ZEROP N)
                        STATE
                        (MACHINE (STEP STATE) (SUB1 N))),
```

where STATE contains the abstract state of the machine including the memory, registers, error flags, program counter, etc. This function "runs" for N steps and then terminates returning the state which results. Termination is guaranteed since the (natural number valued) counter N is decremented in each recursive call until it reaches zero.

The function STEP defined as follows.

```
(STEP STATE) = (EXECUTE (FETCH STATE) STATE)
```

Notice that the functions MACHINE and STEP characterize a broad class of computing systems.

The details of fetching and executing particular instructions is buried within the functions FETCH and EXECUTE; Specific machines are defined by formalizing these functions. Typically, the EXECUTE function is merely a large IF expression that describes the effect of each of the legal types of instructions for the machine and the effect of each on the state of the machine. For example, it might take the form:

```
(EXECUTE INST STATE)
=
(IF (IS-HALT-INSTRUCTION INST)
    STATE
(IF (IS-ADD-INSTRUCTION INST)
    <perform add operation>
(IF (IS-MULT-INSTRUCTION INST)
    <perform multiplication operation>
    <other possible operations> )))
```

Models such as this have been used to formally characterize a number of hardware devices, including several microprocessors[6, 7].

In addition to the modeling of hardware devices, similar techniques can be used to define the semantics of programming languages. Here we think of the defining function as an "interpreter" for the language and the state of the machine as the memory or collection of data structures on which the program is operating.

For an assembly level language in which a program is merely a list of simple instructions, the form of the interpreter is very similar to the function MACHINE above. For a higher-level language in which various statement types contain other statements as subparts, the structure of the interpreter becomes more complicated. Consider a high-level programming language that contains, among others, the following constructs:

- skip: do nothing;

- stmt1; stmt2: execute stmt1 and then stmt2 in the resulting state;

- while b do stmt: as long as b remains true, repeatedly execute stmt;

- if b then stmt1 else stmt2: if b is true execute stmt1, otherwise execute stmt2.

Conceptually, the interpreter function for this language might take the form:

```
(INTERPRET PROGRAM STATE)
=
(IF PROGRAM is <skip>
    STATE
(IF PROGRAM is <stmt1; stmt2>
    (INTERPRET <stmt2> (INTERPRET <stmt> STATE))
(IF PROGRAM is <while b do stmt>
    (IF <b> evaluates to TRUE in STATE
        (INTERPRET <while b do stmt>
                   (INTERPRET <stmt> STATE))
        STATE)
(IF PROGRAM is <if b then stmt1 else stmt2>
    (IF <b> evaluates to TRUE in STATE
        (INTERPRET <stmt1> STATE)
        (INTERPRET <stmt2> STATE))
 <other constructs of the language> ))).
```

Such interpreter semantics or *operational semantics* have been written for programming languages for many years. As early as 1962, this approach was used by John McCarthy to describe the semantics of the Lisp programming language.

Given an accurate operational characterization of a machine or a programming language, we can precisely describe the effects of a program running on that machine or written in that language. Moveover, we can state and prove interesting properties of the language itself. For example, the following rather trivial theorem is easily provable of the language characterized by the INTERPRET function.

```
Theorem: EQUIVALENCE-OF-WHILE-AND-IF
(IMPLIES <b> evaluates to FALSE in STATE
         (EQUAL (INTERPRET <while b do stmt> STATE)
                (INTERPRET <skip> STATE))).
```

One use of this theorem is to sanction a compiler to replace any occurrence of a while statement by a skip, assuming the compiler can establish statically that the test of the while is false. Such ability to reason formally about the language, as opposed to reasoning about programs in the language, has been largely neglected.

Given a mathematical definition of a system–a language or a machine–we can also potentially verify that the system is correctly *implemented* on lower-level machines. Almost any system is constructed "on top of" another conceptually lower-level system. A high-level language, for example, is useful because it provides convenient computational abstractions that are not available directly on the hardware platform that supports it. The language is implemented by a compiler that translates high-level language programs to semantically equivalent assembly level language programs. That is, the abstractions of the high-level language are really provided in terms of the abstractions available at the assembly level (and possibly by the operating system of the machine). The abstractions of the assembly language are provided in turn by an assembler on top of the abstractions of the hardware. The abstractions of the hardware model are provided by some collection of hardware gates, wires, and registers.

Thus an applications programmer is typically relying upon a rather sizable collection of system software and hardware, including compilers, assemblers, operating systems, and the underlying machine hardware. The "correctness" of an applications program, then, ultimately depends upon the correctness of the underlying support software and hardware, over which the applications programmer has little control. This means that effort expending in applying even the best formal methods to guaranteeing the "correctness" of a program may be vitiated if the supporting layers are flawed.

One approach to dealing with this problem is to apply our methods to the analysis of the underlying support software and hardware and building applications on top of a "stack" of verified components. This is called *systems verification*[3]–the "layering" of verified components to construct highly reliable hierarchically-structured computing systems. Each "layer" (except the lowest) is proven to be correctly implemented on the next lower layer in the hierarchy.

Using abstract machine models we can characterize the semantics of the individual layers in our stack. To connect adjacent layers, we need to have a way of formally establishing that a lower level machine "implements" a higher level machine. Formally, let $Int_A : S_A \rightarrow S_A$ and $Int_C : S_C \rightarrow S_C$ be interpreter functions that define two machines M_A and M_C. (The subscripts A and C are chosen to suggest *abstract* and *concrete* machines, the higher and lower level machines, respectively.) Let $MapUp : S_C \rightarrow S_A$ be an abstraction function that maps a concrete state to an abstract state, and let $MapDown : S_A \rightarrow S_C$ map an abstract state to a concrete state. *MapDown* is the function that takes us from the higher level abstraction to the lower level. For our high-level language, this would be the compiler that translates a high-level state containing a program and its data structures into a low-level state containing a corresponding assembly language program with its data structures. The *MapUp* function in turn takes a low-level state and "reads out" the results in terms that are meaningful in the high-level context. An example of *MapUp* is the function that takes bit strings in a computer memory and prints them out as numbers or characters depending on the context.

We say that M_C *implements* M_A if the following theorem holds.

This theorem is a formalization of the "commuting diagram" depicted in figure 2. Intuitively, it asserts that there are two possible ways to obtain the results of an (abstract) computation:

1. run the abstract interpreter directly on the initial abstract state and view the results;

2. map the abstract state down to a corresponding concrete state, run the concrete interpreter, and map the results back up to the abstract world.

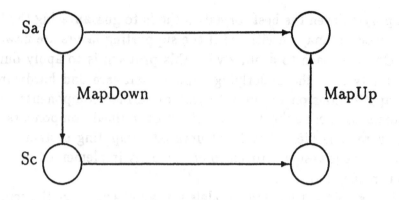

Figure 2: Equivalence of Machines

If these two approaches always yield the same result, then the abstract layer is correctly implemented in the concrete layer. With a little thought, it easy to see that this is a reasonable abstraction of what is usually mean by saying that a compiler is correct or that a piece of hardware is correctl implemented in some technology.

In the Boyer-Moore logic the correctness theorem is stated roughly a follows:

```
Theorem: IMPLEMENTS-RELATION
(IMPLIES (GOOD-STATE ASTATE)
         (EQUAL (MAPUP (INTERPRET-C (MAPDOWN ASTATE)))
                (INTERPRET-A ASTATE)))
```

The hypothesis (GOOD-STATE ASTATE) assures that the initial abstract stat is a legitimate state from which to begin. Obviously, specific layers are onl fully defined when we have completely defined the functions GOOD-STATE INTERPRET-C, INTERPRET-A, MAPUP, and MAPDOWN.

Suppose that we can prove two such theorems establishing the correc implementation of machine M1 on M2 and of machine M2 on M3. These the orems are represented by the commuting diagrams in figure 3-(a). Unde certain conditions, it is possible to compose the machine definitions to ob tain the theorem represented by the commuting diagram in figure 3-(b) To be able to compose the commuting diagrams in this fashion it must b the case that the two abstract machine definitions "in the middle" corre spond exactly. That is, the concrete-level machine for the upper diagran must match exactly the abstract-level machine for the lower diagram. Also $MapDown_1$ must always yield a state that satifies the GOOD-STATE predicat for machine M2. If these conditions are satisfied, we will have establishe that the high level machine M1 is correctly implemented on the machin

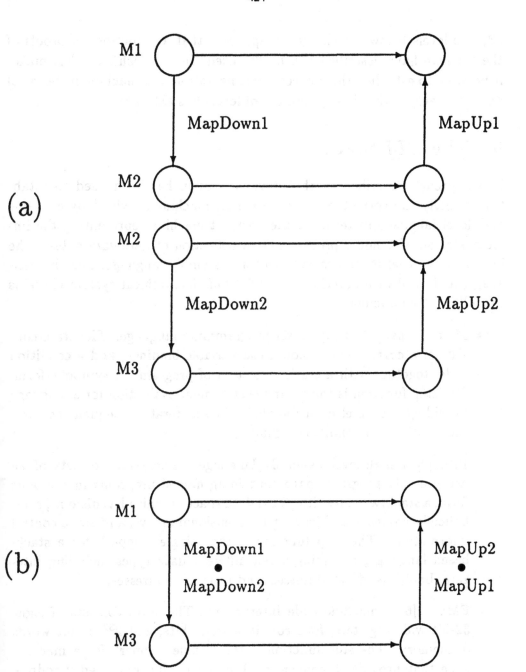

Figure 3: Composing Equivalence Theorems

M3, two levels below. It should be apparent that any number of proofs of the type we have described can be "stacked" in this fashion. This makes it possible to establish the correct implementation of a machine in terms of another machine that is any number of levels less abstract.

6 The CLI Stack

The approach described in the previous section has been used to establish formally the correctness of an abstract machine provided by a simple high-level language in terms of the abstract machine representing the implementation of a micro-processor by a collection of hardware gates. The intermediate level machines represent an assembly language, machine language, and hardware functional design. This hierarchical system contains the following components.

- Micro-Gypsy[13]–a high-level programming language. The state consists of a current expression, local variable bindings, and a condition code, together with a static collection of programs in symbolic form. The step function is the recursive statement evaluation for a language providing if-then-else, begin-when blocks, iteration, sequencing, procedure call, and condition signaling.

- Piton[9]–a high-level assembly language. The state consists of an execute-only program space containing named programs in symbolic form, a stack, a read-write global data space organized as disjoint, symbolically named variables and 1-dimensional arrays, and some control information. The step function is the "single stepper" for a stack-based language, providing seven different data types including integers, Booleans, data addresses, and program addresses.

- FM8502[6]–a machine code interpreter. The state consists of eight 32-bit wide registers, four condition code bits, and 2^{32} 32-bit words of memory. The step function is the "single stepper" for a machine code that provides a conventional, orthogonally organized 2-address instruction set. This machine is comparable to a PDP-11 in the complexity of the ALU and instruction set. However, the machine lacks interrupts, supervisor/user modes, and support for virtual memory management.

- Gates–a register-transfer model of a microcoded machine. The state is a collection of 32-bit wide registers and latches, various one bit flags and latches, an array of 2^{32} 32-bit wide words representing memory, and a ROM containing microcode instructions. The step function uses combinational logic to determine the new contents of the various state-holding devices as a function of the current values and signals arriving on various input lines such as the reset, the data acknowledgement and the data in lines.

Relating each pair of adjacent machines is an *implementation* or *MapDown* function, represented formally as a function in the logic, that maps a higher-level state into a lower-level state. The implementation function is known as a "compiler" for the step from Micro-Gypsy to Piton, but as a "link-assembler" for the step from Piton to FM8502. In addition, for each such pair of machines we define the *MapUp* function that is a partial inverse of the implementation. The *MapUp* function for the Piton implementation, for example, interprets bit strings in the FM8502 memory as elements of the various data types of Piton.

The correctness of each implementation is characterized by a theorem in the Boyer-Moore logic representing an appropriate commutative diagram as explained above. Each of the implementations has been proved correct:

- the correctness of a gate-level register-transfer model of a machine code machine,

- the correctness of a link-assembler from an assembly level language to binary machine code,

- the correctness of a compiler from Micro-Gypsy to assembly language, and

These proofs were all constructed by the Boyer-Moore theorem prover.

We have proved the additional results necessary to let us "stack" the three correctness results. For example, a legal Micro-Gypsy program that executes without high-level errors is compiled into a legal Piton program that executes without Piton-level errors, etc. We thus obtain a theorem that tells us that the error-free execution of a legal Micro-Gypsy program can equivalently be carried out by the microcode machine on the low level state obtained by compiling, link-assembling, loading, and resetting the gate-level machine. Furthermore, we constructively characterize the number of microcycles required. The current CLI short stack can be represented as the following collection of components:

```
Gates -> FM8502 -> Piton -> Micro-Gypsy -> Applications
```

We add applications to the "top" of the stack since each verified application written in Micro-Gypsy is really an extension to the stack and possibly provides additional abstractions above what is directly provided in that language.

The result of tying all these efforts together into a unified whole is that an applications programmer can devise a solution to his programming problem and reason rigorously about his efforts within the framework of the high-level language, confident in the knowledge that his program will be translated into a semantically equivalent representation running on hardware at a much, much lower-level of abstraction. He retains the conceptual benefits of the abstraction provided by a high-level language without the worry that the execution environment of his program is undermining those abstractions. We have built several simple application programs in Micro-Gypsy and used the verified stack to translate them to a semantically equivalent load image for the FM8502 microprocessor.

Using the same basic approach described above we have also implemented and proved correct a simple operating system, called *Kit*[2]. Kit is a small operating system kernel written for a uniprocessor von Neumann machine, and is proved to implement a fixed number of conceptually distributed communicating processes on this shared computer. In addition to implementing processes, Kit provides the following verified services: process scheduling, error handling, message passing, and an interface to asynchronous devices.

The proof of correctness involves showing that a certain block of about 3K 16-bit words when executed by the target machine implements a fixed number of isolated target machines capable of communicating only through shared I/O buffers. While Kit is not big enough to be considered a kernel for a general purpose operating system, it does confront some important operating system phenomena. It is adequate for a small special purpose system such as a communications processor.

The uniprocessor for Kit is very similar to the FM8502 microprocessor but was developed concurrently and more or less independently. A consequence of this is that Kit does not fit precisely into our verified stack. But because of the similarity of the two machines, we are confident that we could produce a verified stack with a multiprocessing operating system sitting between the machine code level and the Piton level.

We hope to be able to eventually incorporate Kit-like operating system capabilities into the verified stack between the machine code level and the Piton level. This will allow us to run several communicating parallel Piton processes. It may also permit Micro-Gypsy to be extended to include Gypsy concurrent processing capabilities and I/O.

The verified stack is far from a state-of-the-art software development environment. The components are special-purpose and limited in functionality. However, it serves as a convincing proof of principle. Formal methods can be used in the construction of highly reliable computing systems of at least moderate complexity. Verified components can be assembled into a system that is more than simply the sum of its parts, one that provides a level of assurance that any piece alone could not provide.

7 Conclusions

Formal methods are not a complete solution to the "software crisis." Even a hierarchically verified system is not guaranteed to be absolutely reliable. A number of things can go wrong.

- The specifications may have been wrong or incomplete.

- A verified system may be functionally entirely correct but intolerably inefficient; efficiency concerns are seldom addressed in formal specification.

- The verification process may be flawed or not carried out carefully enough.

- The tools supporting the verification process may not provide a correct implementation of the underlying logic.

- The verification may have been carried out to a certain level of abstraction but the system fail at some even lower level.

These and other important concerns must be addressed; important research issues are still to be faced.

The methods currently available certainly are not mature enough to make any substantial contribution to enhancing the level of assurance in, say, the Strategic Defense Initiative. However for smaller critical applications, they can make a real contribution of enhanced assurance. This potential contribution has long been recognized in specialized areas, notably secure computing and safety critical applications. The work on the verified stack has shown that by following a systematic mathematical approach supported by a powerful automated proof tool, highly reliable systems can be constructed. Additional applications of such methods will undoubtedly emerge.

References

[1] Robert L. Akers, Bret A. Hartman, Lawrence M. Smith, Millard C. Taylor, William D. Young, *Gypsy Verification Environment User's Manual.* Technical Report 61, Computational Logic, Inc., 1990.

[2] William R. Bevier, "Kit and the Short Stack," *Journal of Automated Reasoning*, 5(4), December, 1989.

[3] William R. Bevier, Warren A. Hunt, Jr., J Strother Moore, William D. Young, "An Approach to Systems Verification," *Journal of Automated Reasoning*, 5(4), December, 1989.

[4] R, S, Boyer and J S, Moore. *A Computational Logic*, Academic Press, New York, 1979,

[5] R, S, Boyer and J S, Moore, *A Computational Logic Handbook.* Academic Press, Boston, 1988.

[6] Warren A. Hunt, Jr., "Microprocessor Design Verification," *Journal of Automated Reasoning*, 5(4), December, 1989.

[7] Jeffery Joyce, Graham Birtwistle, and Mike Gordon, "Proving a Computer Correct in Higher Order Logic," University of Calgary, Department of Computer Science, August, 1985.

[8] Matt Kaufmann, "A User's Manual for an Interactive Enhancement to the Boyer-Moore Theorem Prover," Technical Report 19, Computational Logic, Inc., 1988.

[9] J Strother Moore, "A Mechanically Verified Language Implemenation," *Journal of Automated Reasoning*, 5(4), December, 1989.

[10]   James H. Paul, Gregory C. Simon, "Bugs in the Program, Problems in Federal Government Procurement Regulation," U. S. House of Representatives, September, 1989.

[11]   L. Robinson and K. Levitt, "Proof Techniques for Hierarchically Structured Programs," *CACM*, 20(4): April, 1977.

[12]   Larry Wos and William McCune, "Challenge Problems Focusing on Equality and Combinatory Logic: Evaluating Automated Theorem-Proving Programs," Springer-Verlag Lecture Notes in Computer Science 310, *Proceedings of the 9th International Conference on Automated Deduction*, May, 1988.

[13]   William D. Young, "A Mechanically Verified Code Generator," *Journal of Automated Reasoning*, 5(4), December, 1989.

Lecture Notes in Computer Science

For information about Vols. 1–461
please contact your bookseller or Springer-Verlag

Vol. 462: G. Gottlob, W. Nejdl (Eds.), Expert Systems in Engineering. Proceedings, 1990. IX, 260 pages. 1990. (Subseries LNAI).

Vol. 463: H. Kirchner, W. Wechler (Eds.), Algebraic and Logic Programming. Proceedings, 1990. VII, 386 pages. 1990.

Vol. 464: J. Dassow, J. Kelemen (Eds.), Aspects and Prospects of Theoretical Computer Science. Proceedings, 1990. VI, 298 pages. 1990.

Vol. 465: A. Fuhrmann, M. Morreau (Eds.), The Logic of Theory Change. Proceedings, 1989. X, 334 pages. 1991. (Subseries LNAI).

Vol. 466: A. Blaser (Ed.), Database Systems of the 90s. Proceedings, 1990. VIII, 334 pages. 1990.

Vol. 467: F. Long (Ed.), Software Engineering Environments. Proceedings, 1989. VI, 313 pages. 1990.

Vol. 468: S.G. Akl, F. Fiala, W.W. Koczkodaj (Eds.), Advances in Computing and Information – ICCI '90. Proceedings, 1990. VII, 529 pages. 1990.

Vol. 469: I. Guessarian (Ed.), Semantics of Systems of Concurrent Processes. Proceedings, 1990. V, 456 pages. 1990.

Vol. 470: S. Abiteboul, P.C. Kanellakis (Eds.), ICDT '90. Proceedings, 1990. VII, 528 pages. 1990.

Vol. 471: B.C. Ooi, Efficient Query Processing in Geographic Information Systems. VIII, 208 pages. 1990.

Vol. 472: K.V. Nori, C.E. Veni Madhavan (Eds.), Foundations of Software Technology and Theoretical Computer Science. Proceedings, 1990. X, 420 pages. 1990.

Vol. 473: I.B. Damgård (Ed.), Advances in Cryptology – EUROCRYPT '90. Proceedings, 1990. VIII, 500 pages. 1991.

Vol. 474: D. Karagiannis (Ed.), Information Systems and Artificial Intelligence: Integration Aspects. Proceedings, 1990. X, 293 pages. 1991. (Subseries LNAI).

Vol. 475: P. Schroeder-Heister (Ed.), Extensions of Logic Programming. Proceedings, 1989. VIII, 364 pages. 1991. (Subseries LNAI).

Vol. 476: M. Filgueiras, L. Damas, N. Moreira, A.P. Tomás (Eds.), Natural Language Processing. Proceedings, 1990. VII, 253 pages. 1991. (Subseries LNAI).

Vol. 477: D. Hammer (Ed.), Compiler Compilers. Proceedings, 1990. VI, 227 pages. 1991.

Vol. 478: J. van Eijck (Ed.), Logics in AI. Proceedings, 1990. IX, 562 pages. 1991. (Subseries in LNAI).

Vol. 479: H. Schmidt, Meta-Level Control for Deductive Database Systems. VI, 155 pages. 1991.

Vol. 480: C. Choffrut, M. Jantzen (Eds.), STACS 91. Proceedings, 1991. X, 549 pages. 1991.

Vol. 481: E. Lang, K.-U. Carstensen, G. Simmons, Modelling Spatial Knowledge on a Linguistic Basis. IX, 138 pages. 1991. (Subseries LNAI).

Vol. 482: Y. Kodratoff (Ed.), Machine Learning – EWSL-91. Proceedings, 1991. XI, 537 pages. 1991. (Subseries LNAI).

Vol. 483: G. Rozenberg (Ed.), Advances in Petri Nets 1990. VI, 515 pages. 1991.

Vol. 484: R. H. Möhring (Ed.), Graph-Theoretic Concepts in Computer Science. Proceedings, 1990. IX, 360 pages. 1991.

Vol. 485: K. Furukawa, H. Tanaka, T. Fuijsaki (Eds.), Logic Programming '89. Proceedings, 1989. IX, 183 pages. 1991. (Subseries LNAI).

Vol. 486: J. van Leeuwen, N. Santoro (Eds.), Distributed Algorithms. Proceedings, 1990. VI, 433 pages. 1991.

Vol. 487: A. Bode (Ed.), Distributed Memory Computing. Proceedings, 1991. XI, 506 pages. 1991.

Vol. 488: R. V. Book (Ed.), Rewriting Techniques and Applications. Proceedings, 1991. VII, 458 pages. 1991.

Vol. 489: J. W. de Bakker, W. P. de Roever, G. Rozenberg (Eds.), Foundations of Object-Oriented Languages. Proceedings, 1990. VIII, 442 pages. 1991.

Vol. 490: J. A. Bergstra, L. M. G. Feijs (Eds.), Algebraic Methods II: Theory, Tools and Applications. VI, 434 pages. 1991.

Vol. 491: A. Yonezawa, T. Ito (Eds.), Concurrency: Theory, Language, and Architecture. Proceedings, 1989. VIII, 339 pages. 1991.

Vol. 492: D. Sriram, R. Logcher, S. Fukuda (Eds.), Computer-Aided Cooperative Product Development. Proceedings, 1989 VII, 630 pages. 1991.

Vol. 493: S. Abramsky, T. S. E. Maibaum (Eds.), TAPSOFT '91. Volume 1. Proceedings, 1991. VIII, 455 pages. 1991.

Vol. 494: S. Abramsky, T. S. E. Maibaum (Eds.), TAPSOFT '91. Volume 2. Proceedings, 1991. VIII, 482 pages. 1991.

Vol. 495: 9. Thalheim, J. Demetrovics, H.-D. Gerhardt (Eds.), MFDBS '91. Proceedings, 1991. VI, 395 pages. 1991.

Vol. 496: H.-P. Schwefel, R. Männer (Eds.), Parallel Problem Solving from Nature. Proceedings, 1990. XI, 485 pages. 1991.

Vol. 497: F. Dehne, F. Fiala. W.W. Koczkodaj (Eds.), Advances in Computing and Information - ICCI '91. Proceedings, 1991. VIII, 745 pages. 1991.

Vol. 498: R. Andersen, J. A. Bubenko jr., A. Sølvberg (Eds.), Advanced Information Systems Engineering. Proceedings, 1991. VI, 579 pages. 1991.

Vol. 499: D. Christodoulakis (Ed.), Ada: The Choice for '92. Proceedings, 1991. VI, 411 pages. 1991.

Vol. 500: M. Held, On the Computational Geometry of Pocket Machining. XII, 179 pages. 1991.

Vol. 501: M. Bidoit, H.-J. Kreowski, P. Lescanne, F. Orejas, D. Sannella (Eds.), Algebraic System Specification and Development. VIII, 98 pages. 1991.

Vol. 502: J. Bărzdiņž, D. Bjørner (Eds.), Baltic Computer Science. X, 619 pages. 1991.

Vol. 503: P. America (Ed.), Parallel Database Systems. Proceedings, 1990. VIII, 433 pages. 1991.

Vol. 504: J. W. Schmidt, A. A. Stogny (Eds.), Next Generation Information System Technology. Proceedings, 1990. IX, 450 pages. 1991.

Vol. 505: E. H. L. Aarts, J. van Leeuwen, M. Rem (Eds.), PARLE '91. Parallel Architectures and Languages Europe, Volume I. Proceedings, 1991. XV, 423 pages. 1991.

Vol. 506: E. H. L. Aarts, J. van Leeuwen, M. Rem (Eds.), PARLE '91. Parallel Architectures and Languages Europe, Volume II. Proceedings, 1991. XV, 489 pages. 1991.

Vol. 507: N. A. Sherwani, E. de Doncker, J. A. Kapenga (Eds.), Computing in the 90's. Proceedings, 1989. XIII, 441 pages. 1991.

Vol. 508: S. Sakata (Ed.), Applied Algebra, Algebraic Algorithms and Error-Correcting Codes. Proceedings, 1990. IX, 390 pages. 1991.

Vol. 509: A. Endres, H. Weber (Eds.), Software Development Environments and CASE Technology. Proceedings, 1991. VIII, 286 pages. 1991.

Vol. 510: J. Leach Albert, B. Monien, M. Rodríguez (Eds.), Automata, Languages and Programming. Proceedings, 1991. XII, 763 pages. 1991.

Vol. 511: A. C. F. Colchester, D.J. Hawkes (Eds.), Information Processing in Medical Imaging. Proceedings, 1991. XI, 512 pages. 1991.

Vol. 512: P. America (Ed.), ECOOP '91. European Conference on Object-Oriented Programming. Proceedings, 1991. X, 396 pages. 1991.

Vol. 513: N. M. Mattos, An Approach to Knowledge Base Management. IX, 247 pages. 1991. (Subseries LNAI).

Vol. 514: G. Cohen, P. Charpin (Eds.), EUROCODE '90. Proceedings, 1990. XI, 392 pages. 1991.

Vol. 515: J. P. Martins, M. Reinfrank (Eds.), Truth Maintenance Systems. Proceedings, 1990. VII, 177 pages. 1991. (Subseries LNAI).

Vol. 516: S. Kaplan, M. Okada (Eds.), Conditional and Typed Rewriting Systems. Proceedings, 1990. IX, 461 pages. 1991.

Vol. 517: K. Nökel, Temporally Distributed Symptoms in Technical Diagnosis. IX, 164 pages. 1991. (Subseries LNAI).

Vol. 518: J. G. Williams, Instantiation Theory. VIII, 133 pages. 1991. (Subseries LNAI).

Vol. 519: F. Dehne, J.-R. Sack, N. Santoro (Eds.), Algorithms and Data Structures. Proceedings, 1991. X, 496 pages. 1991.

Vol. 520: A. Tarlecki (Ed.), Mathematical Foundations of Computer Science 1991. Proceedings, 1991. XI, 435 pages. 1991.

Vol. 521: B. Bouchon-Meunier, R. R. Yager, L. A. Zadek (Eds.), Uncertainty in Knowledge-Bases. Proceedings, 1990. X, 609 pages. 1991.

Vol. 522: J. Hertzberg (Ed.), European Workshop on Planning. Proceedings, 1991. VII, 121 pages. 1991. (Subseries LNAI).

Vol. 523: J. Hughes (Ed.), Functional Programming Languages and Computer Architecture. Proceedings, 1991. VIII, 666 pages. 1991.

Vol. 524: G. Rozenberg (Ed.), Advances in Petri Nets 1991. VIII, 572 pages. 1991.

Vol. 525: O. Günther, H.-J. Schek (Eds.), Advances in Spatial Databases. Proceedings, 1991. XI, 471 pages. 1991.

Vol. 526: T. Ito, A. R. Meyer (Eds.), Theoretical Aspects of Computer Software. Proceedings, 1991. X, 772 pages. 1991.

Vol. 527: J.C.M. Baeten, J. F. Groote (Eds.), CONCUR '91. Proceedings, 1991. VIII, 541 pages. 1991.

Vol. 528: J. Maluszynski, M. Wirsing (Eds.), Programming Language Implementation and Logic Programming. Proceedings, 1991. XI, 433 pages. 1991.

Vol. 529: L. Budach (Ed.), Fundamentals of Computation Theory. Proceedings, 1991. XII, 426 pages. 1991.

Vol. 530: D. H. Pitt, P.-L. Curien, S. Abramsky, A. M. Pitts, A. Poigné, D. E. Rydeheard (Eds.), Category Theory and Computer Science. Proceedings, 1991. VII, 301 pages. 1991.

Vol. 531: E. M. Clarke, R. P. Kurshan (Eds.), Computer-Aided Verification. Proceedings, 1990. XIII, 372 pages. 1991.

Vol. 532: H. Ehrig, H.-J. Kreowski, G. Rozenberg (Eds.), Graph Grammars and Their Application to Computer Science. Proceedings, 1990. X, 703 pages. 1991.

Vol. 533: E. Börger, H. Kleine Büning, M. M. Richter, W. Schönfeld (Eds.), Computer Science Logic. Proceedings, 1990. VIII, 399 pages. 1991.

Vol. 534: H. Ehrig, K. P. Jantke, F. Orejas, H. Reichel (Eds.), Recent Trends in Data Type Specification. Proceedings, 1990. VIII, 379 pages. 1991.

Vol. 535: P. Jorrand, J. Kelemen (Eds.), Fundamentals of Artificial Intelligence Research. Proceedings, 1991. VIII, 255 pages. 1991. (Subseries LNAI).

Vol. 536: J. E. Tomayko, Software Engineering Education. Proceedings, 1991. VIII, 296 pages. 1991.

Vol. 537: A. J. Menezes, S. A. Vanstone (Eds.), Advances in Cryptology – CRYPTO '90. Proceedings. XIII, 644 pages. 1991.

Vol. 538: M. Kojima, N. Megiddo, T. Noma, A. Yoshise, A Unified Approach to Interior Point Algorithms for Linear Complementarity Problems. VIII, 108 pages. 1991.

Vol. 539: H. F. Mattson, T. Mora, T. R. N. Rao (Eds.), Applied Algebra, Algebraic Algorithms and Error-Correcting Codes. Proceedings, 1991. XI, 489 pages. 1991.

Vol. 540: A. Prieto (Ed.), Artificial Neural Networks. Proceedings, 1991. XIII, 476 pages. 1991.

Vol. 541: P. Barahona, L. Moniz Pereira, A. Porto (Eds.), EPIA '91. Proceedings, 1991. VIII, 292 pages. 1991. (Subseries LNAI).

Vol. 543: J. Dix, K. P. Jantke, P. H. Schmitt (Eds.), Non-monotonic and Inductive Logic. Proceedings, 1990. X, 243 pages. 1991. (Subseries LNAI).

Vol. 544: M. Broy, M. Wirsing (Eds.), Methods of Programming. XII, 268 pages. 1991.

Vol. 545: H. Alblas, B. Melichar (Eds.), Attribute Grammars, Applications and Systems. Proceedings, 1991. IX, 513 pages. 1991.

Vol. 547: D. W. Davies (Ed.), Advances in Cryptology – EUROCRYPT '91. Proceedings, 1991. XII, 556 pages. 1991.

Vol. 548: R. Kruse, P. Siegel (Eds.), Symbolic and Quantitative Approaches to Uncertainty. Proceedings, 1991. XI, 362 pages. 1991.

Vol. 550: A. van Lamsweerde, A. Fugetta (Eds.), ESEC '91. Proceedings, 1991. XII, 515 pages. 1991.

Vol. 551:S. Prehn, W. J. Toetenel (Eds.), VDM '91. Formal Software Development Methods. Volume 1. Proceedings, 1991. XIII, 699 pages. 1991.

Vol. 552: S. Prehn, W. J. Toetenel (Eds.), VDM '91. Formal Software Development Methods. Volume 2. Proceedings, 1991. XIV, 430 pages. 1991.